THEM

THEM

Voices from the
Immigrant Community
in Contemporary Britain

JONATHON GREEN

SECKER & WARBURG
London

First published in Great Britain 1990
by Martin Secker & Warburg Limited
Michelin House, 81 Fulham Road, London SW3 6RB

Copyright © 1990 Jonathon Green

A CIP catalogue record for this book
is available from the British Library
ISBN 0 436 20005 8

Printed in England by Clays Ltd, St Ives plc

For my Mother,
and in memory of my Father

Contents

	Introduction	I
	Acknowledgements	11
1	Images of England	13
2	Forerunners	27
3	The Decision to Leave	38
4	Crossing the Line	73
5	The Moment of Arrival	85
6	The Shock of the New	101
7	Learning the Culture	109
8	England: Another Country	114
9	The English People	121
10	The Class System	144
11	Knowing Your Place	150
12	The Immigrant Life	157
13	A Roof Over Your Head	188
14	The Job Market	193
15	Teach Yourself English	228
16	The Problem of Identity	242
17	The Question of Assimilation	250
18	Feeling English	277
19	Xenophobia: The White Man's Burden	289
20	Racism: Keep Britain White	302
21	Politics: Taking a Stand	331
22	Black Self-images	342
23	Pictured by the Press	349
24	The Black Community	353
25	Staying On	356
26	Thatcher's Britain	380
27	The Generation Gap	386
28	Into the Future	396
29	A Multicultural Britain?	404
	A Note on Immigration Law	408
	Interviewees	410

Introduction

'If we went on as we are, then by the end of the century there would be four million people of the New Commonwealth or Pakistan here. Now that is an awful lot and I think it means that people are really rather afraid that this country might be swamped by people with a different culture. And you know, the British character has done so much for democracy, for law, and so much throughout the world, that if there is a fear that it might be swamped, people are going to react, and be rather hostile to those coming in.'

Margaret Thatcher, MP, 1978

'Cricket, cathedrals, "Land of Hope and Glory", [and] an enduring distrust of foreigners . . . classically define the best of England.'

Tony Marlow, MP, 1989

I

England has always been a hotchpotch of contrasting races and nationalities. Most obviously one can see this in the national language, a complex blend of infinite roots, and in the people themselves, the English, a mongrel mix drawn primarily from Europe, but increasingly spiced by a new infusion of less proximate populations. For all their vaunted 'national characteristics' the English, like most other nations, remain the product of wide-ranging variety. And that variety has rarely been as apparent as it is today.

The Norman Conquest of 1066 was itself the climax of a series of such invasions, as each of a succession of dominant European tribes or nations tried its hand at crossing the sea and imposing a new rule on the native British. Romans, Germanic tribes, Scandinavians had all appeared, subjugated, held power until gradually they found themselves absorbed and, eventually, supplanted. The last military invasion of the country was nine centuries ago, but a succession of other 'peaceful' invasions has followed. It was the relative stability that followed the Normans that made such new 'invasions' possible. No longer invaders, the newcomers were now immigrants.

Some, immigrants pure and simple, arrived voluntarily, choosing to quit the land of their birth and looking to a new one for fresh chances and a new home;

others, exiles, émigrés and refugees, arrived willy-nilly, driven from their own countries by prejudice or politics, and forced to seek refuge in more congenial surroundings. Whatever the cause, while never a self-proclaimed *pays d'exil* like France, England continued to offer sanctuary to some, fresh opportunities to others, and, within the inevitable constraints of legislation and bureaucracy, a home to all.

Immigration remains a constant factor in the development of English society. But if its style is very much as it has always been, its content, in other words the nature and origins of the immigrants themselves, has changed radically. Until the mid nineteenth century the influx of immigrants was relatively restrained, arrivals tending on the whole to be refugees. Small groups of economic immigrants – notably the influential and highly assimilated Jewish community, or the Irish, exchanging the privations of famine for hard labour on the railways – did exist, but on the whole people were leaving England, rather than arriving. Seekers after a new life looked not to England, but to further flung areas: the New Worlds of first America and then the Antipodes. A variety of events changed this situation. Political upheavals in Europe, continuing poverty in Ireland, intensified pogroms against the Jews in Russia (a very different breed to those of German or Spanish origin who preceded them) – all these events and more led to a substantial increase in the numbers of those seeking security in England. Immigration on a scale that had not been previously experienced became commonplace. It paled beside the massive surges of humanity that swept over America, but by the turn of the century, England had a notable immigrant community. The Huguenots, fleeing six-teenth-century France, had taken over a few streets in Spitalfields; the Jews, hounded from nineteenth-century Russia, seemed to be making a ghetto of the whole East End.

Jews, Irish and Italians: these were the main immigrant communities by World War I. There were the occasional curiosities – Greeks, a variety of middle Europeans, even the Chinese, providing a homegrown 'yellow peril', first (1885) in London's Limehouse, and later (1911) in Liverpool's Pitt Street – but they were relatively unimportant. World War II and its aftermath, which boosted the national mix with boatloads of Poles, Lithuanians and other escapees first from Hitler and then Stalin, underlined, but did not really alter the immigrant status quo. England remained essentially English, with nary a hint of today's 'multiculturalism', although the main immigrant groups, now firmly established, maintained something of their own identities, converted in British eyes to easily categorized stereotypes, discrete within the larger picture, but easily accessible. Like the rest of society, the immigrants knew their place. The Jews as tradesmen, Italians as entertainers-cum-caterers, and the Irish as labourers. Some rose and prospered, some declined and fell. They inspired affection and snobbery, welcome and rejection, and in the end, from all but a

2

die-hard minority, indifference. 'Yids', 'Wops', 'Paddies' and the rest, inevitably, if gradually, found themselves all absorbed more or less into the greater English society. The tide of Englishness washed away the overt differences, subsuming all in the general flow of the national identity. And why not? One thing made such assimilation a matter of course: whatever their origin, no matter in what debased patois they chattered, they were, after all, white.

The first black or brown men and women to appear in England were strictly curiosities. Often they would be seamen, passing through ports like Liverpool, Bristol or London. Simultaneously the early white explorers and colonizers might bring home, like one more raree show, a living souvenir of the world's distant lands, sometimes a king's son, often a personal servant, in either case paraded and offered for inspection, barely different from some new spice or exotic botanical specimen. During the nineteenth century the flow increased marginally, boosted by students and some professionals, as well as those who simply emigrated for the adventure of geographical change. By the end of World War I these pioneers had been succeeded by some slightly more settled communities, still mainly around the ports. But these were tiny groups, numbered in hundreds, not thousands. For example, as late as 1949, there were only one hundred Asians in Birmingham (although there was a substantial Jewish community).

All this changed after 1945. After the war successive governments began looking outside England for new workers to help the steadily improving economy of the 1950s which could no longer be serviced by the indigenous population. They began recruiting in the Commonwealth, notably in the islands of the West Indies, and found that the black populations were more than willing to make the journey. They barely needed the alluring government invitations. England was 'the mother country', many of them spoke its language, worshipped in the same church, experienced the same education. Home life was often hard and even the skilled and the middle class saw England as a land of opportunity. At home the population was increasing, and with it the levels of unemployment and poverty. Such jobs as were available were often low-paid. England beckoned and the boat-trains began arriving from Southampton, disgorging their passengers, many still in the summer clothes in which they had left home, on to the platforms of Victoria Station, where some, undoubtedly, would soon be at work.

The flow of West Indians was still restricted until 1953, but thereafter it increased dramatically, governed directly by Britain's labour needs, reaching its first peak in 1956, slowing slightly for the next three years, then taking off again from 1959. Some 10,000 people arrived in 1954, 24,000 a year later, and 26,000 in 1956. By 1959, 36,000 more had arrived. In 1961, a second peak, some 75,000 made the trip. Concentrated in London, they began carving out their own centres: north of the river around Notting Hill, Paddington and

3

North Kensington, south in Brixton and Stockwell. At the same time enclaves developed in all the major provincial cities. The government, keen to house this new labour force, created a new breed of landlord, usually white, whose substantial incomes depended directly on putting the often rickety roofs over the heads of these new ghetto-dwellers.

Whatever one's qualifications back home, much the same jobs were on offer. In fairness many immigrants were merely swapping one labouring job for another (at a higher rate), but those with higher aspirations fared no better: downgrading was a constant. Menial jobs, manual labour, some work in hospitals (as porters and orderlies), on London Transport and in the Post Office. Homegrown qualifications counted for little, the 'newcomers' joined the labour pool at its lowest level. The immigrants were predominantly male, although the flow of women and children slowly increased as more men became esablished and sent for their families. These women also worked in hospitals (but as nurses) as well as in catering and other service industries.

The earliest Asian immigrants (from pre-partition India, incorporating both today's Pakistan and Bangladesh) were as much of a curiosity as were the blacks. Some degree of Asian community has existed in Britain for at least two hundred years, but the earliest arrivals were more transient than immigrant. Indian seamen (known as Lascars) who had jumped ship might set themselves up as itinerant peddlers or as tea-shop proprietors. Others worked as entertainers, a tradition that can be traced to the seventeenth century. Often they stayed in England for no more than three or four years, but on returning home would send another member of their family to take up the business. This rotation became a regular system. Some Indians were also drawn to medicine, although their practices were generally limited to working-class areas, where the 'black doctor' presented an object of mixed fear and fascination.

Like the West Indians, the Asians were subject to the same sort of push (poverty, unemployment at home) and pull (a buoyant English economy offering money and jobs) factors in the acceleration of post-World War II immigration. They too had been conditioned by the 'mother country' myth. The slight difference was that while West Indians tended to migrate in response to known labour needs, the Asians moved come what may, whether or not jobs were available, although they too received a share of government advertising. On the whole, however, the similarities outweighed the differences. Economic migrants began to arrive regularly from 1955. Starting at around 10,000 a year, Asian immigration peaked in 1962 at 47,000 arrivals, declining to 26,000 in 1964. The majority of Asians went to London, with smaller centres building up in the West Midlands and the textile towns of South Yorkshire. They lived initially in lodging houses, where they rented accommodation, and tended to be given unskilled employment. For all the stories of Asian advancement, the bulk of these immigrants, and their families, remain poor.

A new type of Asian immigrant, coming not from the subcontinent but from East Africa, had begun arriving in England as the former colonies took on independent African governments during the 1960s. Between 1965–68, 35,000 left Kenya; under Milton Obote 24,000 left Uganda between 1968–71, and the rest of the population (some 28,600) were expelled by Idi Amin in August 1972. These East African Asians were not the generally unskilled immigrants of the 'fifties, but in many cases merchants and skilled craftsmen who had until recently provided the mercantile classes of their respective African countries, carving out their new lives after the primary immigration from India. Involuntary emigrants this time, they were in fact refugees, driven by political pressure, unlike their predecessors from the subcontinent, who came looking for a better life. Trading on the security of their British passports, the East African Asians looked first for sanctuary and only then for wealth.

Like the West Indians, whose impoverished backgrounds have often been transmuted into poorly paid occupations in England, the East African Asians have gravitated towards employment that reflects their earlier status. They have remained merchants, albeit in many cases on a substantially reduced scale, although a good number have become very successful. The ubiquitous corner shop, once the traditional purlieu of the 'nation of shopkeepers', has taken second place to the new mini-markets, where whole families keep the door open late at night, and provide a range of goods that have helped expand British taste far beyond its previous insularity. Where the West Indians might be seen as succeeding the Irish, the immigrant labourers of an earlier era, so have these East African Asians followed on from the mercantile Jews.

Such social niceties, of course, are less respected by the dominant white population, to whose less particular eyes, racist or otherwise, immigrants are simply immigrants. The government may have dignified the coloured population with the euphemism 'New Commonwealth' (as opposed to the 'old', white Commonwealth of Australia, New Zealand and Canada, and indeed of long seceded South Africa, whose immigrants are always welcome) but there are no bonds of kith and kin here. Like the Jews and Irish before them, no immigrant group, however successful or diligent, is uniformly popular. White immigrants may have managed, in time, to merge with the larger population, but they continue to arouse a degree, however publicly submerged, of racial hostility. But their whiteness undoubtedly protects them: a conspicuous nose or a touch of the brogue pale quite literally in the face of black skin when considered as a racial badge. Hostility towards black immigrants has been more conspicuous and more intense. Excepting the efforts of Oswald Mosley's British Union of Fascists (which duly turned its feeble if vicious attentions to the blacks in the 1959 election campaign, when it sought to capitalize on the Notting Dale riots) there have been no organized demonstrations against the Jews, let alone the Irish, in this century.

The first white versus black race riots occurred as early as 1919 in Cardiff, Liverpool and a number of other ports where there existed a noticeable black population. They were allegedly inspired by white working-class fears that immigrant blacks, recruited during World War I, were taking their jobs. New outbreaks followed the next war, notably in Birmingham, where in 1948 a crowd of two hundred and fifty whites stoned a lodging house in which some Indians were living, and in Liverpool where a mob attacked an Anglo-Indian café. A year later a thousand-strong mob attacked a black hostel in Deptford and in 1954 there were two days of racial warfare on the streets of Camden Town. Hostilities sputtered on through the 'fifties – for many immigrants their first experience was the landlady's defiant proclamation: 'No Blacks' – until August 1958, when riots in the Chase, the black centre of Nottingham, and across most of West London (notably the run-down Notting Dale area) made racial disturbance into a national preoccupation.

That preoccupation remains as central as ever to the national psyche. For those who cherish such fantasies, the decline of an Empire where 'natives' supposedly 'knew their place' has been made even more bitterly poignant by the arrival in England of those same natives, hellbent on equality. Tougher immigration controls appeared in 1962 and 1968, limiting the influx of foreign workers, but the mood of the 1960s was fundamentally liberal, offering a degree of new racial self-awareness to the coloured, and particularly the black community. England's blacks echoed their counterparts in America with calls for the raising of black consciousness and the setting up of indigenous black institutions. A new generation of blacks began to emerge: the children of the original 'newcomers'. Their parents had used a passport to assert their rights of entry; these children needed only their birth certificate. Despite, or perhaps because of the liberal climate, there were new outbreaks of prejudice: Enoch Powell's speech in April 1968 prophesying 'rivers of blood' fanned the flames and England's ever-dormant racism burst into ugly prominence. Less than a decade later a revived fascist party, the National Front, turned on the coloured community, this time targeting Asians, rather than West Indians. This fresh outburst evaporated too: the election of 1979 of a right-wing Tory government meant that NF extremists, alienated by Labour, now found a welcome in the mainstream and duly faded from prominence.

This has not meant, however, that these new immigrants have simply been absorbed into English society as have their white predecessors. The 'new' communities have certainly established a more settled place for themselves, but what is seen essentially as a 'problem' continues to intensify. The boom economy of the 1950s, which brought so many immigrants to England, has been replaced by a very different reality. The 'eighties too were allegedly buoyant, but that boom is perceived as dead today and in its legacy, the

6

slimmed-down industries, and the emphasis on service occupations (traditionally the preserve of women, often as part-timers), the black population has suffered conspicuously. Too often restricted – whether by under-qualification or institutional racism – from capitalizing on the 'Thatcher boom', they remain, when employed, at bottom of the labour market. A whole generation of black youth, with apparently many more to come, now seems destined to long-term unemployment. The frustrations this creates, cranked up by an often unsympathetic relationship with a mainly white police force, were seen most recently in the nationwide riots of 1981 and the regular flare-ups, notably a number of similar riots in 1985, that have persisted; they will doubtless be seen again. And while Asians are less emblematic of contemporary race-related problems as are West Indians to the leader-writers of Dockland, they are equally vulnerable to the strictures of 'Thatcher's Britain'. Asian 'success stories' are seized upon by government propagandists, but for most the corner shop remains what it always was, the preserve of hard work, long hours, and minimal profits.

Race has never retreated far from the front pages. Racism, that 'safe hatred' as Colin MacInnes put it, is an integral part of the nation's culture. Immigration as such is less of a worry. Tory legislation (notably the 1981 Nationality Act with its removal of the right of those born in Britain to automatic British nationality) has seen to that. Still, the idea of 'swamping' by some alien horde remains a potent stimulus to impressionable sensibilities. The Tory party's more rabid right-wingers are determined to foment hostility to the promised influx of Hong Kong Chinese in 1997, carefully selected though such refugees will be. Far more immediate is the role of those immigrants who are already here and the impact they are having, and are destined to have, on this country. The 'eighties began with the nationwide riots of 1981, blamed first and foremost on second-generation West Indians; they ended with the 'Rushdie affair', in which the Muslim community, still mainly first-generation immigrants, initiated their still-running campaign against the alleged blasphemies of Salman Rushdie's book, *The Satanic Verses*, and earned themselves instant condemnation as the Ayatollah Khomeini's Bradford-based fifth column. In both these cases, it was not the headline but the subtext that mattered: *Why* are black (and Asian) youngsters torching the inner city? *Why* do Muslims feel they must burn a book to maintain their cultural identity? Just what is the role of Britain's immigrant community? Kneejerk responses, whether impeccably liberal or determinedly racist, won't and can't offer answers.

Today, as rarely before, the immigrant population of Britain, whether first or subsequent generation, is playing a central role in the national discourse. In such contentious areas as education, employment and crime it seems impossible to divorce the general debate from a consideration of the unresolved specifics: the way these phenomena involve the black and brown populations. In their turn, these immigrants, no longer willing to stand on the margins, demand a real voice in a society of which they are so integral a part. The aim of this book has been to offer a small platform for some of those voices, as well as to their peers, whether Vietnamese 'boat people', political exiles from South America or refugees from a harsher era in Eastern Europe. Naturally what follows is filled with a wide variety of personal experiences, but the text does not focus exclusively on the discussion of immigrant life. As much as anything it is a view of England and the 'native' English through foreign eyes.

II

I interviewed one hundred and three people for the book, mostly during 1989. They are all first-generation immigrants, people who made the trip themselves. Given that the immigrant population is currently estimated (first and second generation) at around four million (two per cent of the national population), this is a tiny, infinitesimal fraction, barely eligible as a decent sample were I conducting an opinion poll. That being said I have attempted to get a reasonable cross-section of those considered immigrants, and readers should find that the proportion of one nationality or race to another roughly approximates the degree each impinges upon the national consciousness. In other words, echoing the preoccupations of the media, who in turn may be seen to reflect the consensus view, there are more West Indians and Asians here than, for instance, German-Uzbeckis or Iranians brought up in Bulgaria. There is also a fair sprinkling of Jews, Eastern Europeans and North and South Americans, as well as Vietnamese, South Africans, Australians and several other represent- ative individuals. There are no Welsh, Scots or Irish, all of whom too have the best reason for seeing themselves as immigrants to a thoroughly alien land, but whose long proximity to the English has, for my purposes, rendered them ineligible for inclusion.

All of which I trust is acceptable, but why, it might be asked, in a book which increasingly addresses the role of what can be bracketed as the 'black community', is the author white, middle class and by some standards privileged? Another white liberal voyeur battening guiltily on to the plight of others? This is not mere breast-beating. It was a question posed by a number of interviewees and underlined, I felt, by the silence of a number of black media figures who chose to ignore my requests for a conversation. Then again, there is the question asked particularly by non-black refugees: how could their stories, often quite horrifying, be mixed in with those of others? Their problems were unique, special, they needed a book for themselves. Indeed they do, virtually everyone does, and I constantly marvelled at the diversity even of those one-hundred-odd lives so much of which has had to be cut from the transcript. But biography was never my intention. What matters is the overall experience.

8

Thus certain individuals appear here under pseudonyms without, I hope, diminishing the overall effect: the individual, I would claim, is less important than the experience. I am grateful to everyone who has happily allowed their name to be used; I would not belittle those who preferred anonymity.

I began this book in the hope of establishing an appealing, but not, if I am honest, wholly believed theory: that the immigrant experience in itself transcends differences between race, colour and creed, and between wealth and poverty. As I wrote in the letters that accompanied my requests for an interview: 'The premise of the book is that there are certain experiences common to all immigrants, irrespective of the date of their arrival, the old life they abandoned and the new one that immigration set in motion. Obviously there are differences between the circumstances that led to each individual's journey to Britain, and those they encountered after arriving, but I believe there are also great similarities.' Carefully trimming, I added, 'I am, of course, open to contradiction' and as the following pages attest, contradiction was pretty much the norm of what I found. Britain, for all its much vaunted liberal democracy, is as racist, as insular and as self-protective as any other nation. That it still bears the scars of more than two centuries of Empire is hardly destined to ameliorate these problems. That its government currently seems consumed by 'Little England' ideology merely compounds them. Of course Britain is by no means unique. One can and does find racism, intolerance and insularity in every country, whether its population is primarily black, white or yellow, Christian, Muslim or Jewish. But my book is about Britain, more specifically England (and even more so its big towns and cities rather than its countryside), and it is upon the home team's record that I, and my interviewees, have concentrated.

The fact is that to be poor, and worse than that, black too, is to lay oneself open to the least enviable of contemporary fates. Even successful immigrants, while they decry the stereotyping of the black or brown communities as second-rate, and urge their contempories to achieve rather than acquiesce, are forced to acknowledge the ways in which they are placed at a disadvantage by this society. Racism, whether overt (and as such paradoxically easier to combat) or institutional (an almost ineradicable national trait), remains too powerful, too pervasive. The imperial hangover has yet completely to pass beyond the agonies of the morning after. Its relicts, deprived of a world map coloured predominantly pink, have been forced to recreate imperial attitudes at home. The multicultural society, a phenomenon much beloved by forecasters of every background, is still a demographic rather than a social concept. For the white immigrants, often politically rather than economically motivated, circumstances have been very different. They have no more uniformly succeeded than have blacks and browns uniformly failed, and in many cases their critique of the 'host country' is even more acute, but their path has been very different. Many coloured communities claim no desire for assimilation, but is the choice even theirs? 'I'm not a Jew, only Jew-ish,' said Jonathan Miller, neatly disclaiming his ethnicity. There is no such thing as 'black-ish'.

So why me? In the end the answer is simple: I wanted to do the book. More pertinent is the fact that I too am an immigrant, albeit second generation. My mother was born in Lithuania, and while my father came from Birmingham, his family too vanish into the mists of nineteenth-century central Europe. Despite a lifetime spent in England, an English education, partner and children, I feel only remotely English myself. In a country where the past has not yet wholly disappeared beneath the crass simplifications of the 'heritage culture', I have no roots. My history is not here, although thanks to Hitler and Stalin I doubt that as a Jew I could trace it in Europe either. If among other things books are a means of working out one's own life, then so certainly is this one. I trust that those to whom I have talked, and who have been so generous with their own reminiscences and attitudes, will forgive me this self-indulgence.

Acknowledgements

My tapes generated over half a million words. The finished product is somewhat nearer 200,000. My apologies to everyone who offered me time and now finds him- or herself under-represented or even absent. The cutting room floor remains the cruellest taskmaster. I can only say how grateful I am for every interview and how much I enjoyed them all.

Given quite literally millions of potential interviewees, I have depended almost without exception on word of mouth and personal recommendation for my choice. Thus, as well as the people who were kind enough to permit me to enter their lives, ask a succession of intimate questions and then vanish, a number of individuals (some of them interviewees themselves) helped me in compiling the book. They suggested possible interviewees, effected introductions, and sent me to see their friends. All of which proved invaluable, and I list them here, with sincere thanks, and in no order other than the alphabetical:

Gina Adamou, Muhammad Ali, Bodrul Alom, Simi Bedford, Frances Bentley, Rosie Boycott, Duncan Campbell, Jane Carr, Anna Clayden, Peter Dale, Kumal Daliwal, Justine Denys, Dan Franklin, Zerbanoo Gifford, Edward Gretton, Antony Harwood, Mike Hodges, David Jenkins, Hannah Kodicek, Dr Thi Phuong Ly, Sara Maitland, Sarah Martin, Colin McCabe, Caroline Merton, Simone Mondesir, Byron and Brigitte Newman, Heather Page, David Papineau, Jeremy Paxman, Teddy and Jill Peiro, Igor Pomerantsev, Ian Rich, Robina Rose, Gretel Salinger, Rachel Silver, Catherine Townshend, Nicholas Weaver, Rose Wild.

With the exception of the 1988 Act, all information on Immigration Law (see p. 408) is drawn from A. H. Halsey's *British Social Trends Since 1900* (1988).

Special thanks are due to Heather Laughton, herself a New Zealander, but long since resident here, whose transcription skills have dealt magnificently with a selection of polyglot tapes.

Finally, my thanks to my copy editor Lesley Bryce, and above all to my editor Dan Franklin, who while mercifully not faced with a manuscript the monstrous size of that which I offered up on our previous collaboration, has once again made his own invaluable contribution to my efforts.

Jonathon Green

1 Images of England

'Very green, very small, very jewel-like, very distant, rather
damp, but excessively interesting, where people spoke properly
and things were calmer than they were where one came from.'

PETER VO: I knew it was a place which had clouds, and the English people are
very quiet, calm and indifferent. There was a saying [in Vietnam] 'You are as
indifferent as an Englishman.'

FATIMA IGRAMHIM: England was a quaint, sweet little country where the
aristocracy was still functioning, not like Germany, and I always had the feeling
that England was a little backward, where everybody wore tweed jackets and
wellingtons. I'd heard of Churchill, who was seen as a good guy. The Nazis
had been bad, so Churchill was seen as a hero. England was good: people said
that England tries to be fair, it tries not to be the aggressor, it only steps in
after war has been declared by someone else. I saw the English as a class above
the Americans: it was this fairness, tolerance. We knew a little English history:
the Kings and Queens, and the legends: the knights of the Round Table,
Robin Hood. We read Dickens. They give you a very strange impression of a
very strange, very poor country. We knew that England had looked after Karl
Marx when he wrote most of his books, and we also read what he had written
about England. We knew that there had been children working in the mines
and that kind of thing.

MIGUEL ZAMBRANO: England for me was a small grey country. The English
were polite, a bit hypocritical but in a funny way. I used to like David Niven,
Dirk Bogarde – English gentlemen. I was aware of Diana Dors, Dickens, *Black
Beauty*. I thought the English were very cruel people. We [in Chile] didn't
discuss English-Spanish affairs, the Armada, etc., but for us most pirates were
English, although good sailors. But our navy was built like the Royal Navy, so
there was the myth of the gentleness, the correct dress of the English. To dress
in an English way was to be elegant and formal, Niven-like.

TEDDY PEIRO: We never came in contact with them. They only mixed with
the natives on certain occasions – mainly with the doctors, etc. That very
colonial attitude. In Buenos Aires was the English Club, you couldn't get in

13

there. We didn't understand why England was also called Great Britain and the United Kingdom – why three names? All I knew of England was what I read. I used to read Dickens. I was very fond of the famous detective, Derek Lawson, and his assistant Tinker. What I knew about England from reading was Croydon airport – Derek Lawson was always arriving there. I would think, 'Oh, if one day I could be at Croydon airport.'

MOSES SPITZ: We had a preconception about the British in Argentina. They were seen as the rich imperialist conquerors. They were just another power trying to make business there. We knew that the railways had been built by the British and very wrongly built too. The local people reacted against this and kept at a distance. There was not really any contact. The image we had of the British in Britain was of a very nice polite properly dressed people, with their bowler hats and umbrellas.

RAJAN UDDIN JALAL: I thought I was coming to a dream land. We were told that people are so nice and friendly that if you lose your direction, if you get lost on a journey, they will actually take their car and deliver you to your destination.

MARIA VOROSKOI: My father told me that when he was here anyone coming to England, of course you didn't need a passport. If you wanted to set up in a business, you just started off, then in a year or so someone would come and say, 'Well, how is your business doing? Have you made some profits, have you any tax due?' That was the atmosphere – very relaxed. When my father was staying in Oxford he went to Blackwells bookshop and wanted to buy some books. He selected what he wanted, but he had forgotten his wallet. He told the assistant and said he'd be back the next day. The assistant said, 'No, take them.' He said, 'I'm a foreigner, you don't know me, you trust me with all these expensive books?' They said, 'Sorry, we don't understand.' So he said, 'Is my English that bad?' 'We understand what you say, but we don't understand what you mean. If you need the books, obviously you are going to pay for them. So take them.'

We only knew one country where there was an absolute democracy, where there was a permanent system, and that was England. So I can't tell you how much admiration and love for England there was in our house. We didn't need to fantasize about England, we had factual information. I didn't actually think about going there. It was just wonderful that it existed. Later on, after World War II, I knew a painter in Paris who told me, 'If England ever disappears, then I would be frightened, because England is the only grown-up country in the world.'

14

BRIGITTE NEWMAN: One's vision of England, then and now, very much depends on social class. The groovy, the cool, the hip people, whatever they are called by the young in France today, still consider English music, English clothes, English punks, English drugs to be the *ne plus ultra*, the *crème de la crème*. The chi-chi people think that tweed, Shetland, cashmere, colour-coordinated things are the ultimate. Scotland, the moors, 'le English breakfast'.

MANDY MERCK: My view of England was very sub-*Country Life* with literary and historical fillips. My mother encouraged an interest in English culture, literature, history, which I as the eldest child got a lot of. I liked it, and wanted to go there. I thought it would be thatched cottages, stately homes, fantastically liberal and fantastically traditional at the same time. I wanted both those things. I identified liberality with the upper middle class in a Bloomsburyish way. My mother and grandmother read *Alice in Wonderland*, *Winnie-the-Pooh*, *Now We Are Six* to me. *The Child's Garden of Verses*, bits of Yeats, which I pronounced Yeets until I was fourteen. Bits of Shakespeare were decanted. My mother's the kind of person who watched the cycle of history plays, packaged by the RSC, and shown on PBS. She adored *Brideshead* and *Jewel in the Crown*. There was always the notion of Oxbridge being terribly interesting, although in an unspecified way.

MIKE PHILLIPS: What I knew about England was that it was cold. I had read a couple of books by Dickens and I had read a book by Conan Doyle and I had a slightly confused notion of what England was like. I thought it would be like Dickens: like *Pickwick Papers* and *Great Expectations*. I wasn't foolish enough to think it would be Victorian any more, but you do have this vague notion that was linked with what you read in books. There weren't any other books available.

RONALD HARWOOD: My mother had been born in London and when very young had come to South Africa. The picture of England handed on to me was of a golden land where London was mecca. The English system of justice was the finest in the world. English imperialism was a splendid thing and indeed, without it, I'd be speaking either Lithuanian or Polish and all the huge inheritance I have of English theatre and literature, which has made my life possible, would not be there. I was brought up on Henry Irving and Shakespeare; Browning, Shelley and Byron. I loved English cricket too. In 1947/8 they came to South Africa, these gods from another land.

MARCEL BERLINS: My school in South Africa was very much along the lines of an English public school, although it was run by the government. They taught us English Literature. We played rugby, had a pipe band and wore kilts. Somehow we were affiliated to the Black Watch, through the Transvaal Scottish. Many of our teachers were English born and educated. I got very interested in cricket, too. I read English newspapers and supported an English football team. (Being French, I couldn't pronounce Tottenham Hotspur, so I looked down the list and found As-ton Vil-la.) I felt positively about England because it had cricket and decent books.

RAMESH VALA: Our school in Kenya played cricket against St Mary's, the white public school. They were considered the strongest school cricket team in Nairobi. The first thing was that we had a kit inspection – if you had anything other than creams, proper whites, you were out. No matter how good you were you were out if you were playing an English team. Then when we went along there – they'd never played us, they had no idea what we were like – it came as a complete shock to them when we bowled them out for 67. So we batted and after a while we needed only two runs to win. I was at the bowler's end and backing up. So I was out of my crease and what the bowler should have done was touched the bails and warned me. He tried to do that, and my tutor, an English tutor who was umpiring, gave me out. I didn't argue – that was not allowed – but afterwards I asked what was going on. He said, 'I'm sorry, but we're not supposed to beat them at this game.'

ANNE-MARIE WOLPE: I finished school when I was sixteen and went to university. That was a period of extraordinary change in South Africa. The Nationalists came into power in 1948. There was a fervent vitality in the university of whites who had come back from the army. It was all extremely exciting. It was at that stage that England, which had made no impact on me when I was growing up, was the place one really wanted to go to. Because of the culture, *kultur* with a capital *K*. Culture where things happened – art and music and dancing were all there. I was part of a bohemian kind of group at university and Europe seemed something quite fantastic and exciting. France might have sounded wonderful, but I had no French, so that was out of the question. So England became a kind of ideal, tripping around in the back of one's mind.

CHRISTOPHER HOPE: I learned about England through books and pictures. I was a voracious reader, but what really got to me was Jeffrey Farnol, the *William* books, *The Wind in the Willows* – books which gave you a picture of a rural England, very green, very small, very jewel-like, very distant, rather damp, but excessively interesting, where people spoke properly and things were calmer than they were where one came from. So England was a kind of mental refuge. English speakers of my generation in Africa formed similar portraits – a distant

16

green settled island. What made it settled was that the class thing was settled. Certainly in the books there were those who talked properly, and those who worked for them. That was a kind of achievement to us, because the matter seemed relatively settled. And they were all white. It seemed far less complicated, and so it had a very deep attraction, particularly since Africa is in every respect other than that: awfully large, wonderfully mixed, very hot and totally unsettled in every aspect. Though England was never 'home' to me, particularly as my Irish grandfather was a vehement republican and our family perspective was that all the ill in the world had been caused by Cromwell and in a sense still was.

MARIA VOROSKOI: My father had visited England in 1896, when he was about twenty. He wanted to learn English and he also went as a representative for a business to help with his expenses. The two years he spent there really changed his life. For ever after he read *The Times* and we children were taught English from the age of five. If my father was cross he never raised his voice, but *The Times* would shake in his hands. We had an English nanny. We were brought up on Kipling and Oscar Wilde fairytales. Later on we read through English literature: by the time I was twelve I had read all of Wilde. Then Huxley, Somerset Maugham; we had a real knowledge of the subject. We subscribed to an English art magazine, *Studio*. We were always taught that England was the *only* civilized country in the world, and that Hungary was a backwater. I don't think at this stage this was arrogance – it was just unashamedly telling the truth.

STEPHEN VIZINCZEY: I grew up in Hungary during the war and it was a very rough experience. My father had been killed by the Nazis in 1935. At times I would dream that my father didn't really die – that some day someone would come from the British embassy. The same story as *Little Lord Fauntleroy*. So one of my very earliest images was of Little Lord Fauntleroy riding a pony in a big park. I would have liked that. Then, as I got older, I found that Shakespeare was the national poet and dramatist in Hungary. The greatest Hungarian poets translated him and many of his plays are almost as good in Hungarian as they are in English. There's no young intellectual in Hungary who doesn't grow up on Shakespeare. Indeed he probably had more influence on my childhood than he would on a child in England. Burns, Keats, the Renaissance poets were very important. I was also lucky because in the '50s I was in film and drama school – which meant free tickets. For five years I spent every evening in the theatre. My dream that was one day I might write a play for Olivier, although I wanted to write in Hungarian.

The first time I actually saw Englishmen was around '45, when they and the French and the Americans came into Salzburg. It struck me how much poorer they looked than the American soldiers.

* * *

VERNA WILKINS: In Grenadan schools we had history: the Tudors and Stuarts. I did biology: the flora and fauna of Great Britain. Literature: Shakespeare and the classics. Talk about irrelevant! We learnt poetry parrot-fashion. The temperature would be ninety degrees in the shade and there we were rattling on about 'St Agnes Eve, ah bitter chill it was, the owl for all its feathers was a-cold . . .' I had no idea what cold weather was. We had a sort of Dickensian view of England. It appeared that there were no working classes in England. We read nineteenth-century novels which were all very middle class and our view of England was very middle class. As a colony we saw a lot of middle-class white people. There were no package holidays, all we saw were the government people, the aristocrats and the pseudo-aristocrats.

RAMESH VALA: We would get up at five-thirty every morning at home and read the papers. The first thing we turned to were the sports pages, and we knew each and every thing about the First Division, we knew all seventeen counties that played cricket. You listened to the World Service on Saturdays for the news. We used to have a weekly general knowledge competition at school, and listening to that helped. So when I first arrived I could name every cricketing county, the football teams, and I knew a fair bit about England in general.

MICHAEL IGNATIEFF: I was born in Toronto in 1947. One half of me, my mother's side, is Scottish Presbyterian divines, school principals, Canadian intelligentsia of a highly self-improving and moralizing kind. So there is a family connection to these islands which goes back to the late nineteenth-century imperial past. My father's side is white Russian and begins its association with England in exile in 1919. So the minute I come out of the womb, as it were, I have very strong but rather complex ties to England. My earliest memories are of Prince Arthur Avenue, a leafy street of substantial three-storey houses inside which you find ticking clocks and carpets and a very imperial scene. Very British. One of my earliest memories was seeing a governor of the Bank of England, or so he was described to me, bestriding my grandmother's mantelpiece and pontificating to us colonials about what life was like. I grew up in a Toronto where we listened to the Queen's Speech at Christmas, we commented on it, opinions were asked. I don't think Christmas lunch could begin until we had heard the Queen. Everything paused. We stood up for the national anthem in the cinemas. Our school atlases had large bits of red and we had a very keen sense that the little red bit that was Canada was part of something bigger. The last imperial generation.

DON ATYEO: I was born in 1950 in Colac, Victoria, a small country town about a hundred miles away from Melbourne in probably the most boring part of

Australia, the Western District. My father was the local shopkeeper. I went at the age of eleven to a boarding school where I stayed for the next five years, during which time I suppose I was taught to become an Englishman. It was a fake public school, an extremely fake public school. English masters, Latin being taught in the middle of sheepville, someone's idea of what a English public school would be like *circa Tom Brown's Schooldays*. Houses, uniform, rules, bells, single sex, cold showers, lots of beatings, bounds, very few chances to get out. When the Christine Keeler affair broke, we were all called into the assembly hall where the headmaster gave us a lecture about what he presumed was on everyone's lips. 'Boys, you've obviously been talking about this girl Keeler and wondering what's been going on back in the mother country. Well, I'm here to tell you that it's just a lot of silly girls doing a lot of silly things. Dismissed.'

Everything in those days was still looking towards Britain. We read British literature; Australian literature was considered good and patriotic and you had to read it to show the flag, but in the end it was really second-rate. Mother England was where it was at. England, home and duty, mother of parliaments and all the rest, and I pretty much believed it – there wasn't anything else on offer. 'God Save the Queen' was the national anthem, and if you moved during the anthem when you went to the Regent Picture House in Colac you were thrown out; if you didn't stand up you were thrown out.

PETER TATCHELL: The Australian education system of the early 1960s gave me an unreconstructed imperial view of history. I was taught that Australia was an outpost of British civilization on the fringes of South-East Asia. The implicit message was that Australia was surrounded by alien and potentially hostile cultures, particularly 'Red China'. Maintaining and celebrating the link with Britain was therefore seen as important. In school, British history was given as much prominence as Australian history. I was taught about all the Kings and Queens of England. Britain was portrayed as the 'Mother Country' and the foundation of Australian civilization. To me, however, it seemed a rather old-fashioned society.

DON ATYEO: It was much more English than the English. My mother, who was a very conventional, very much a small town woman, would go down in the blazing hundred-degree heat in the middle of the summertime, down the main street to buy her groceries and she'd be dressed in a pair of long white kid gloves. No one thought this was in any way odd. All her friends dressed like that. She hated the Australian country. Her passion was collecting illustrated books of English roses. If she says 'country', she doesn't mean anywhere in Australia. 'Country' is the Cotswolds. But she was born there and I'm fourth generation.

19

SUSAN WILSON: We thought of ourselves as English. We called ourselves British. When we filled out forms to go to teacher's college and my boyfriend of the time described himself as 'New Zealander' we all thought he was a terrible radical. We were rather afraid of the consequences. We all wrote 'British', always. But there was a kind of hatred of England as well, it was a curious thing. My family background was one of dissent. I'm descended from a man who's mentioned by William Cobbett as being jailed for refusing to pay tithes. My father was terribly proud of this. We had this funny close contact with England; we were 'England's farm'. My mother would dress us in brown lace-up shoes and tweed coats, little woolly hats – we were terribly English-looking children.

CARMEN CALLIL: There's no English blood in our family at all. It's Irish and Lebanese. We were always told that Britain was poor and we had to look after it. I was terribly sorry for it. We sent parcels. But it was not the mother country. Some people may have been brought up to think of Britain as the centre of the universe, but I wasn't and nobody else I knew was. We thought the Pope was great. I read Australian history at university. It wasn't a popular subject but it was what I wanted to do. Otherwise we learnt English and European history. I loved English literature, and was surprised when I came here. I thought it would be a very small place with little figures popping around in it. I'd adored Austen and Dickens, Dickens mostly. Especially *Great Expectations*. I was aware that the convicts who had been sent to Australia had been sent wrongly, that it was all Britain's fault, that they had behaved disgustingly to their own people. Sending your own away would not be considered at all acceptable in my family – either on the Lebanese or the Irish side.

BRYAN GOULD: I was brought up in a very conventional family, which in its own way was very patriotic, reasonably royalist. My father had republican tinges, but I was quite royalist. It was just accepted that it was a good thing to be British. It was still very common to refer to England as 'home'. I didn't think of it so much as home, but I'd go to the pictures as we still called it, and see the Pathé newsreels from London, and there was Big Ben or whatever. I did look upon that somehow as I imagined a Roman citizen would look upon Rome, however far-flung he might be. To him Rome was the centre and for me it was the same thing with London. It was the centre of my cultural world.

* * *

MIKE PHILLIPS: Britain was the metropolis, we lived on the periphery. That's what it means to live in a colony. You don't think of England as the home of democracy, the mother of parliaments, that sort of thing. You don't experience those ideas in that way. When I became conscious World War II had just ended, and you thought you were on England's side. We had public holidays for the Queen's birthday, all the rest of it. Most of the people I knew belonged to the Scouts or the Wolf Cubs. I was a Wolf Cub, dyb dyb dyb.

MARY DENYS: In St Lucia I was a Brownie and later a Girl Guide and we'd sing 'Land of Hope and Glory' and 'God Save the Queen', standing there in the hot sun, singing about England, the land of the free and the motherland. Later on the exodus started, everyone began going to England, and we'd say in patois, 'You're going up the mountain.' That was coming up to England. We really thought that England was a place to which you could just come. You would come to work but it would be easier than at home. I thought that life in England would just be easier.

GINA ADAMOU: What we thought of was it would be Coke and hotdogs and chocolate, that kind of thing. The impression was that it was a big country. We really did feel that England was full of gold – all you had to do was come to England and get rich. The money's there for the picking. I'm sure that's what my parents thought. A big country and a rich country.

MIKE PHILLIPS: The thing about being brought up in a colony is that it's small. Geographically it may be big, but the world of the colony is small, however many people there are. You feel almost at a distance from the big world, the world where things happen and decisions are made. That's what England was, a place where people made decisions, a place where power was. So if you were ambitious, that's where you wanted to go.

VINCENT REID: I was really clued up. I'd learned about King Henry VIII. I knew how far it was from Glasgow to London, although I had no concept of what these places meant. The kind of education one received in Jamaica was basically an English education. The mother country, the empire. You learned about England, not about the West Indian islands. I didn't know there were any West Indian islands. When somebody was introduced as coming from Trinidad or Barbados, I wondered what it was. Maybe another town? We had no idea. Not because of any lack of interest on my part in these kinds of areas but just because they weren't made available. I think it was a deliberate policy, for us to be tied to the so-called 'mother country'. So coming here was in a sense like coming home. And then, being illegitimate myself, in so far as I thought about it at all, it was like meeting one's mother for the first time. Albeit an illegitimate child that she's slightly ashamed of, because of her past.

BHAJAN SINGH CHADHA: England meant the mother country to me. In those days, the '30s, the '40s, England was still a world power. I believed in England

– I had no alternative, I'd been brought up like that and Kenya was still very much a British colony. Our teachers, who were highly educated Indians, taught us English history. There was no Kenyan history as far as we were concerned, except what had happened since the British had arrived. My feeling was that I had been brought up British and that I would die British. I had a British passport, I respected the British authorities.

BERNIE GRANT: We knew everything about England. We had English history, we knew the English customs, Guyana had an English governor and the country was run by English Civil Servants, the whole system was orientated to England. The judges were English, white people controlled the banks and so on. So we were very well versed in the British, and particularly the English, way of life. I was never impressed with the 'mother of parliaments' myth and all that. On the contrary, I was aware of what the empire had been about, the way that Britain had colonized the world. It made me very angry. I was politically rebellious. I knew what was going on around the world, especially in Africa and in Cuba. I was still in Guyana during the Cuban revolution so Che Guevara and Fidel Castro were big heroes to us. So I was certainly not one of those people who saw Britain as the mother country and made that the reason for their coming. As far as I was concerned I came here to get some qualifications and go back home.

SIMI BEDFORD: We didn't see England as the mother country – rather it was seen as the place to go and acquire the skills to get rid of the mother country. It's a very different attitude than that found in the West Indies, from where people came to England which they very much saw as the mother country. It's a very different situation there: you're looking at a country where you've had slavery for four hundred years, whereas in Nigeria you'd only had colonialism for forty or fifty. Nigeria was only colonized around 1911–12 and the British left in 1960. Also they only penetrated a very short way into the interior. It wasn't like Zimbabwe or Kenya. This was the white man's grave. They didn't dash out to live for ever, they just wanted to exploit it and get out. There are people in the north or in the interior who probably had no idea of whether they'd been or gone or even who 'they' were.

MICHAEL IGNATIEFF: There was some sense of the need to visit England, not perhaps as an immigrant, but almost as a pilgrimage. This was fostered by a number of consumer durables: Tate and Lyle's Golden Syrup, the Austin A40 (which in 1956 was my idea of a sexy car), later the Mini. Meccano sets. Little steam locomotives. There was this feeling that 'Made in England' was synonymous with quality. All of which bred in an infant a very strong sense of Britain. Also the Coronation in 1953. We were in Washington DC at the time and we saw it and I felt tremendously close to it. Now it all seems like archaeology, belonging definitely to another age. These identifications are with quality goods, most of which are now out of business; with a monarchy which seems to me now quite risible, although there is a picture of me standing as a six-year-old boy open-mouthed with wonder when Princess Elizabeth visited Washington DC and there I am waving my little British flag, absolutely in the grip of a particularly royalist fantasy of a quite Canadian kind. Though my images of England were not wholly fantastical. Our encounters with England were cut across with reality in all its starkness. I'd heard about how dirty London was in the war, how bashed up it was. My mother was always very careful not to allow a romance of London in the Blitz to creep in, there was a very strong sense of this as a time of terror and fear and extreme fatigue and filth and unpleasantness as well as more positive images.

TESS WICKHAM: In Holland most kids learn a certain amount of English. I was helped to a degree because my father had been to school here and they had lived in England for quite a while. So whenever there was secret talk in the family he would always lapse into English. I had read a little English literature: Thomas Hardy, bits of *Hamlet*. My thrill with England originally was when we visited when I was about fifteen and walked down the King's Road and Mary Quant's first shop, Bazaar, was open and there was the Chelsea Antique Market, and people walking around from all over the world. I didn't realize what was really going on, but it seemed to me that they were all living alongside each other. It was a fascinating mixture of society. My image was of this open, cosmopolitan society, which England, ever since I have come here, has done its best to disprove. The main charm of London was that from Holland it provided very nearby exotica. All the exotic tribes – including the English – seemed to be wandering around the King's Road, and with them a very rich history. I was here to study anthropology and I treated England as a museum. The whole country was like a huge version of the Pitt-Rivers Museum. I saw my visit as some kind of extended fieldwork.

YASMIN ALIBHAI: Then came the '60s. It really hit us: suddenly these English people who were always coming out to Uganda were not proper as they usually were, now these degenerates were arriving. It really hit me, because this was the first time I had ever seen the English as weak, as vulnerable, as capable of making mistakes. Whatever we had thought of them before, the Englishman was the hero. They were invincible, they had power, they were god-like, completely, completely pure and untainted. Lots of hippies came to East Africa and suddenly I began to see this new type of English person. I couldn't believe it. They would talk to us, which was an unusual experience. Some of them joined our school as teachers and had very radical ideas and we all fell in love

23

with them. We would write love letters to them, we would do anything they asked us to do. It was such a contrast. The only English person you'd ever seen was male, wearing these immaculate clothes, woollens in the tropical heat, the Brylcreemed hair – which made them superhuman. Suddenly here were these unkempt white people, who you also assumed were powerful and clever and rich. But these loose-limbed, badly-spoken, completely aimless people who started talking to you were quite different. It was like opening a Pandora's Box, and parents began getting completely petrified, because a new mythology was set up: England was a bad place, it was full of drugs, don't send your children. So the generational conflicts began. England became more and more attractive to teenagers, but not for education, for very different reasons: pop music arrived in a big way. Elvis and Cliff had been safe, although the community had been a little edgy, but '6os music was different. So several things happened: we lost all respect for the British, and started seeing them for the political sharks that they really had been.

* * *

DON ATYEO: When I left it was as much because I was seduced by the idea of England, of swinging London (it was late swinging London but there was still the idea of cheesecloth and Carnaby Street and velvet trousers and the King's Road, as by being driven out of Australia. It was English rock bands who came over for these huge great tours. Paul Jones was bottom of the bill, just quit Manfred Mann, the Small Faces playing 'Itchycoo Park', their new record, the Who at the top of the bill singing 'I'm a Boy'. So you got that lot and you were pretty well hooked on rock'n'roll for ever. Boom-boom-boom. They were exotic, wonderful, skinny, weedy. The Small Faces were just amazing. Tiny. We were Australians, butch, meat-fed, corn-fed and milk-fed, and here were these people who would fit into one leg of your jeans. They were so exotic and so hip and you just devoured the rock papers and everything like that and it all seemed to emanate from Britain.

NAIM ATALLAH: Before I came here I thought that the British were terrible. The Mandate was in operation in Palestine and Jews were coming there, to form a Jewish state, which of course was something the Arabs fought. The British would turn up at 4 a.m., drag us out of our homes, and keep us all day in the sun in stadia, to punish us. As a child I was dragged by British soldiers over the butt of a gun. I thought, 'God, they're so uncivilized, the British, so barbaric in their treatment of people.'

GERTRUD HARTWIG: I had always found the idea of coming to England appealing. I knew some English, I worked in the import-export business. I knew that it was a reasonably tolerant country; we felt that things that had

24

happened in Germany would not easily happen in England. One was familiar with the English sense of humour, which I found attractive. I felt that they were a more balanced people than the Germans, that they wouldn't lose their heads so easily.

SHREERAM VIDYARTHI: Our textbooks in India used to have entries, essays, articles singing songs of praise for England and the honesty of the English people and the greatness of English inventors and that kind of thing. English history like that was stuffed down our throats. At that stage we had more eulogies about the United Kingdom in our heads than anything about India. What registered on my mind was the strength of character, the discipline, the punctuality, the honesty, these virtues made sense to me. Though just because the English had these things I didn't assume that the Indians didn't. I never felt that one culture was superior to the other. Never. It never occurred to me. But what we learnt through those essays, through those lessons was important; it was character-building.

MANDY MERCK: I was very well aware that I was lesbian in my teenage years and I knew England had already legalized homosexuality and abortion. I had this sense of a liberal culture in England. I remember reading an article by Mary McCarthy that said the English have always been cooler about sexual diversity. In English public schools, boys get up to all sorts of things with the other boys and nobody panics about it. I thought, 'Good, that's where I want to go.'

EVA JIRICNA: There are two ways that information gets to you if you are brought up in a socialist country like Czechoslovakia. First of all the education at school is something that is dictated by the government. You learn that everything was invented by Russian scientists – unfortunately nobody knew about it. Modern literature, modern architecture, were almost nonexistent. On the other hand you have your parents who remember the period before the war and what they used to learn when they were at school, and they make sure that their children get a little bit of perspective. So I knew quite a bit about England, where my mother had been for about a year to study English when she was young. She had lots of friends who she kept in touch with, at least up until 1948, because after that it became very difficult to communicate or keep in touch. She did talk a lot about England, she was very interested in it. She liked the lifestyle. She was very good at languages and she was good at English and English literature. She still speaks it very well. I don't know whether she tried consciously to imbue me with this interest, but she did talk about things she saw – doubledeckers, things like that – and for a child this created all sorts of images – which then prove to be right or wrong.

25

PETAR OBRATOVIC: In Yugoslavia, we all had certain preconceptions about England. We knew that all English television serials were done well, because they were about these historical things and they looked much better than our television. We knew about the Royal Family. The Queen is important, Churchill had been a very popular figure. English as allies in the war, English as not knowing whether to support the Chetniks or the partisans. Always English, not British. The difference between Welsh and English for instance doesn't exist. There was a difference between the English and the Scots – the Scots would be seen as stingy, in a very anecdotal, joking way. They would figure in jokes about England. 'A taxi crashed in Glasgow and eleven people died', that sort of thing. The Irish were seen as a separate nation and we knew all about Ireland's fight for independence. We read English books at school. Later there were films. Mainly American, but you would know English films too. Things like *Blow Up*, which were very important. But English culture mainly came through studying English at school. When we learnt English at school it was always English English. Proper English, BBC, Oxford English. Never American English.

KAREL KYNCL: My image of Britain was mixed. On the one hand, as a Czech, the role of Chamberlain and of Britain in 1938 was terribly negative of course, it was a stab in the back; on the other hand during the war London was, as it was traditionally, a place for political refugees. It was the seat of the provisional Czechoslovak government and so on. So we made a difference between Chamberlain's England and Churchill's. The difference between appeasement and the war that Britain fought. There were quite a number of Czechoslovaks taking part in the Battle of Britain. There were Czech military units fighting with the Allies. But Munich was such a trauma that it was very very hard to get rid of it.

JAROSLAV BRADAC: The idea of Munich and what the British did to Czechoslovakia was force-fed to me as something to never forget. As a kind of history lesson, and there is a deep resentment, a bitterness on that score. But like a lot of the history I learned, a lot of my education, this was to some degree biased. Because of my father's influence I learned to take everything with a pinch of salt. I didn't simply suck up everything that I was told. I was sceptical. Because it was a regime which had its own ways of manipulation and I had always been slightly suspicious of it. You develop a system where you over-compensate for what you get told. So if Britain is full of capitalists with the cigars and the big bellies and the top hats and all of that, just caricatures, you learn to believe almost the opposite.

HANNAH KODICEK: History at school was terribly coloured, it was so black and white. Here go the top-hatted capitalists, the Dickensian image of England, there was no mention of culture or anything, apart from the poverty and the capitalism. Imperialism, that was Britain. Bloodsuckers. You name it. It was so awful that we couldn't believe it could be so awful. So instead it became rather like those countries in fairytales where sausages grow on trees, there are butter mountains, that kind of thing. You lie back and roasted chickens fly into your mouth.

JAROSLAV BRADAC: Many people who visit me now, including my own sister, actually think everything in Britain is pink, everything is wonderful – because they are told that it's awful. The propaganda was often so stupid; they told you it was black, you thought it was wonderful, they told you it was wonderful, you thought the opposite. You did not follow the official line, instead you read between the lines. So when Mrs Thatcher tours in somewhere like Poland everyone loves her, because they don't even want to think that the propaganda may be even a little right.

The first time I went back to Prague, about six years ago, after fourteen years of being here, and we were talking about Cruise missiles, which was a hot subject then. I was asked what my views were. I was definitely *not* a Thatcherite, very suspicious of the whole thing, and when I said this I was being ridiculed. Put down as a liberal *Guardian*-reading pinko. By people in Prague! They actually thought that Mrs Thatcher is wonderful and if you don't vote for her you are not welcome in the house. It's a different ball-game now, but at that time she was tough with the Russians, and the Russians were never liked. My enemy's enemy is my friend.

2 Forerunners

'My father came to improve his standard of living, to earn some money, go back home, buy some land and give his children a good start in life. But he never did go back.'

GINA ADAMOU: The people who came to England were either from villages or from a poor background. They came for a better life. The better Greeks didn't come. The ones with money. They might come to shop, to have a holiday, then they'd go back. The ones who did come were the ones who had no money, from villages where they lived off their land. They wanted a better life. So many of them went into restaurants – they were uneducated, they hadn't much money and that's what they could do. People saved, and people helped out. My husband's parents gave him money for the journey. My own parents helped, my aunt who was here helped. Two of my aunts, my mother's sisters, were married to Englishmen. One was in the airforce, the other was in the army. So those links were there. The younger one used to write regularly and suggested to my parents to come over here, because it was a better life. Why don't you come over here with your girls, your five daughters – it's an easier life. My parents came a few months before us and borrowed money to bring us over. From a bank. My grandmother brought us over. We were all under-age. And she stayed, looking after the family while my parents went out to work. When my parents came it was definitely immigration. Goodbye to Cyprus for ever. They came to make a new life, full stop.

MIKE PHILLIPS: My father came here from Guyana in 1950–51. It was a kind of unofficial movement, coming to England, that people joined. He had been involved in a strike as a shop steward and the story was that after that he wouldn't get any work. By coincidence, my eldest sister was graduating from school. She wanted to study, but they couldn't afford the places that were available, so they came here. My grandmother and my auntie looked after me. That lasted for four or five years. A couple of years later my mother and my elder brother went to join him. What you did when you arrived was to walk up and down looking for somewhere to live and he had walked for days looking for somewhere to live and for a job. He got a room in a house in Islington where some other people from Guyana lived. He had a job as a railway porter. Leaving home wasn't an odd thing. People went away looking for work all the time. They went to the oilfields in Trinidad; in earlier years they had gone to places like Costa Rica, Panama, Cuba. There was this constant coming and going of able-bodied men. This was a culture in which families were left.

WILF WALKER: The only way out of the Caribbean was to emigrate. They'd been doing it since the '20s, leaving the Caribbean and going to America and Canada. Everyone was geared to getting away. My father came here in 1959. Before that he had jumped ship and lived in America for nearly seven years. So we had all thought we would be going to America. My grandmother's sister had gone to America in the '20s and initially he lived with her. She had a huge family there, they've done very well. In those days they lived in Brooklyn, New York. My father enjoyed the life, lots of smart clothes, lots of new friends, he'd send money home every month. He didn't feel pressured to get anything together – that would happen *eventually*, that was his trip. He had studied radio and TV engineering, but after seven years it wasn't happening, and he wasn't making any headway in terms of becoming a legitimate citizen. So in the end he went to the immigration people and gave himself up. They said, 'We're going to deport you, but if you pay your own fare and leave, then when you get home you can reapply for a visa and we'll let you in legally.' He needed a sponsor for that, but when he got back to Trinidad no one would do it. So there he was: he'd been abroad for a very long time, and now he was stuck back in the shack with the family.

MANZOOR BAHADUR: Our family traditionally were farmers, but my father broke away from that tradition before Partition. He worked on ships for five or six years, then decided in about 1953 to come to England. In fact he jumped ship, as indeed did a lot of immigrants from India or Pakistan in those days. Initially there were a lot of difficulties. The immigration laws in those days said that if you could avoid getting caught for two years from the date you jumped the ship, you could then openly go to the police and say, 'I've managed to escape from you for two years, now I want to make my stay official,' and you were entitled to a passport. My father came to Bradford to see a friend, another ex-seaman, who had already settled here. His friend just said, 'You'll stay now. I've settled here and I think you'll be all right. Forget about the ships.' It was hard to save money on the ships. Here there was an opportunity of working hard and really saving.

MUHAMMAD ALI: My father had come here in 1956, one of the first Pakistanis to come. He came to improve his standard of living, to earn some money and go back home. He came to live here at the most for five years. Make some money, go back home, buy some land or some property and just earn enough to live by so that he could give his children a good start in life. But he never did go back. It is in human nature that whatever you've made, you always want to make more. Like gambling. 'Let's stay for another year and make some more, and then with more money when we go back we'll be able to buy more land.' But the longer they stayed the more they became involved with the social life of this country. Then they brought over their families and that was really the turning point.

TONY ROBINSON: Why did we come? The heart of man is never satisfied. Someone will always tell you if you go across the road there, you can get £25 more. So therefore with that philosophy you always go, to see if you can get more. Wages in Jamaica were very low and here are people coming to England and earning £25, £30 a week, a lot of money. So you say, 'Well, if I emigrate and spend five or six years there, I can put together enough to come back, set up a business, get a nice home, whatever.' So you came to make some money and then to go home again. So you emigrate. What they didn't tell you was that you have to work night and day and suffer for it. You start to cry, you say, 'I'm sorry I left my homeland.' You come here and life is not a bed of roses. You cry. You say why did you leave your own shore. In those days things had been better. That's how it seems when you start to compare England with your home in Jamaica. But you have come and you say, 'OK, I will do five years.' But the five years turns into ten, and the ten into fifteen and the fifteen goes to twenty. Until you find that you're not going to go home, that you've reached a place when you can't move. You've got children. Your life is here.

MUHAMMAD AYYAZ: My father came here to Bradford and started working as a labourer in a textile mill. Up till around '66 people had all been singles, then their families started to join them. Which meant that they began changing their views: initially they thought that they were here to work until they were sent home, so they would do that for three or four years, earn as much as they could, save, and eventually go back. But they didn't go back. I suppose as much as anything it was because they were allowed to stay on. They didn't expect to be allowed to stay, but they were given indefinite stays and quite a number actually became British; my father became British in '67. So then they knew that they were not going to be sent back.

BODRUL ALOM: People from east Pakistan, now it's called Bangladesh, started arriving in this country in the mid-1950s. Some of them had worked on the big ships and they began realizing that immigrant labour forces were very much needed in this country. So they began coming to this country to fill that need. Prior to that there had been Bangladeshis involved with World War II, fighting as colonial troops. So, through coming here as merchant seamen or fighting for the British in the war and learning something about Britain, people decided to start coming to settle here. Initially most of them worked as sailors, then as labourers, then gradually they moved into the clothing trade. Some people did work in factories, in light industry. After that, in the '60s and early '70s, some people decided, since there was still work available, to bring over their relatives and associates and members of their family. They came in on work vouchers. From them the news spread, mainly by word of mouth, and people began applying to their appropriate High Commissions to come and settle in this country.

MUHAMMAD AYYAZ: In '60–61 there was a dam being built in the Naipur district and people were being moved by force off their land. Then the British government told them they had a shortage of labour, would you send us some people. People started coming. Some were seaman. They came illegally and simply jumped ship and stayed. When they went back to Pakistan they said if you compare the wages it's much better in Britain. It was very simple: you went along, got your Pakistani passport and were given entry clearance. No questions asked.

CASH BHOGAL: It was extremely difficult for my father when he arrived because there was very little employment on offer to the Asian community. He could speak and write English, because he had gone to university, and that made a very big difference. But there was a great deal of discrimination faced by the first generation of Asians, just as the West Indians had faced it before. You could only find jobs in factories or in other places where the English no longer felt that they were fit to work. People didn't complain, but then complaints wouldn't have filled your stomach. It was necessary for those early immigrants not only to maintain themselves in the United Kingdom, but they also had to support their families back home and pay off their debts. So they couldn't afford to be out of a job, or complain about a job or the conditions in which they were working.

BHAJAN SINGH CHADHA: By profession I was an accountant and book-keeper, but there was no chance of getting a job like that in England. In Kenya I had been in great demand, but I could see that the only coloured people who had any chance of getting a job were those who would do labouring jobs. Not even the buses at that stage. There were jobs in places like Bradford in the textile industry, but I came straight to London, to Southall. I looked in the papers and they were full of offers for jobs that I wanted – accountant, bookkeeper, things like that – but when I went to get one, oh God, there wasn't the first chance. It was something very new for most of the employers to have an Indian appear and try for a job. These days Indians are common in clerical jobs, but not then. I would turn up and ask for a clerical job, there I was in my turban and so on, and they were very surprised to see me. So I realized that the only job I could get too was a labouring job.

CASH BHOGAL: The assumption in India was that it would be so easy to get a job here. Which was true. In '50s and early '60s it was extremely easy to get a job [in Britain], you could change jobs overnight, there was such a shortage of labour and the country wanted to rebuild after the war. But there was discrimination and there still is discrimination. My father was advised by prospective employers that despite being a Sikh he should have his hair cut, which he did. This sort of removing of the things that made you stick out make it easier in those days to find employment in areas where it wasn't desirable to wear a turban, such as the bakery trade or in the foundries, where the furnaces generated a tremendous amount of heat.

BHAJAN SINGH CHADHA: There were three places for Indians in Southall to get work: the rubber factory, the concrete factory or in the catering department at Heathrow airport. The money was very good, of course, but that wasn't what I wanted. If you were very highly educated you might get a clerical job in central London, but nothing else. There were no middle-class jobs. So after a great struggle with my feelings I took off my turban, shaved my hair, and

31

applied for a job as a postman. It was not what I wanted to do, but I had come and it would have been very difficult just to give up and go back. It was a choice between the post office or labouring. Most of the Southall community worked at the rubber factory. The local whites wouldn't work there. The conditions were too dangerous for your health. I did get the offer of a job there and I had a look but I decided against it. The money was good, there was a lot of overtime, people used to come down from the Midlands to work there, but it was very unhealthy. The owners of the factory started off the Southall Asian community: they bought the first house in Southall that was occupied only by Indians – who were labourers at the factory. It stopped them having to come from east London where they had been living before. After that the trend started and more and more Indians started to live in Southall.

YASMIN ALIBHAI: My father was indolent and bright. Before he had arrived in Africa he had travelled to England at the age of fifteen. He was mad about England, and he had been completely besotted with the idea of settling there. He lived here until he was about thirty and then moved back to Uganda. He was already dreaming of taking his children to England, but there was never any money. In 1955 he made some money through some scheme and decided that he was going to pack us all off to England. We all had to quit school – I was six, my sister eleven, my brother twelve – and we were packed off here with my mother. We were given a bit of money, not very much, put on a ship, and we arrived here in the middle of the winter with instructions to go to Poole, in Dorset, because he knew some woman there who was going to take good care of us. It was just incredible. It was a complete nightmare for my mum, who didn't speak English, who had no idea why he had sent us over, no idea about schools or anything. We had four very bizarre months. The woman in Poole was very kind, she was a landlady of a bed and breakfast place, but the money ran out, my mother got very ill and in the end she sent him an ultimatum saying that she wanted to come back home. He had no money by then, but his brother sent us our fares. My brother and I went back with my mother but my sister refused. She'd told all her friends she was going, how could she go back so soon? So she stayed.

* * *

SIMI BEDFORD: The big excuse given by the colonial government for holding back Africans was claiming they hadn't sufficient skills to do the jobs. Nigerians are desperately keen on education for its own sake and they also wanted national independence. Before the war they had gone to England, usually at university level, to get the skills to become lawyers, become doctors or whatever, and gone back at the same level as the colonials. The next generation, after the war, thought, well why not go one better, because independence was that much nearer and Africans would actually be taking over, why not actually send their children to British schools and that way get exactly the same education from the start? It was a way of getting round the received wisdom of an administration that was, let's face it, deeply racist, that said Africans were not able to govern themselves. People of my parents' generation admired certain things about the British – their efficiency and their organization and the very fact of the way they'd got over there and grabbed half the world as an empire – and in the same way as one's relatives would send children to my grandfather's house to learn, so there was the same thing in sending children to England in order to get the skills and ability and tools that would enable you to run the place yourself. I get the feeling that my father was a bit of a trailblazer in this idea of sending children to British for their schooling. He had gained so many advantages by going to university, now we could get even greater advantages by going to school as well. We could really meet the English on their own terms.

VICTOR WILD: My uncle decided to emigrate. England was his ideal because at the turn of the century the world map was red, he had tremendous respect for that because he thought that Switzerland really was a piddling little country. And to Britain he came. He had done an apprenticeship as a baker-confectioner, he had been more or less allocated to that by his foster-father. This opened many doors to him, because he was very skilled. He found a job in France, then he heard about a job in Bradford, Yorkshire, because there was a big continental community there – the textile industry attracted a lot of Germans and Swiss, a lot of Poles. It was a very cultured society in Bradford in those days; they had more orchestras and art and civilized living in Bradford than in many other places. But he hadn't had the sense to learn any English at all. He had a hilarious journey across the Channel in a storm in the middle of the night, drinking with some English people he had met, and singing songs. He arrived at Victoria Station, knowing no English, carrying a large suitcase and started looking for a train to Bradford. He caught various wrong trains, and for a long time he asked people where the Bradford train was, which no doubt he pronounced in his Swiss accent. Most people treated him as though he was off his head but finally some kindly gentleman who could speak German directed him to a taxi and told him to go to King's Cross. And from there he managed somehow to get to Bradford. He joined this Swiss firm that was doing pretty well but he had ambitions to set up his own business. His big problem as a foreigner was that although he had the skill and he had the enthusiasm nobody would really lend him any money to set up in business. He wanted to set up his business in Harrogate. He'd gone to Harrogate as a consultant, he was an expert at making hand-made chocolates. Harrogate was then the number one spa town in Britain and he thought this is more like it, compared to Bradford, which was pretty dirty, a forest of tall chimney stacks. Nobody

33

would treat him very seriously, then of course the First World War broke out. And he had the misfortune of being called Fritz Bützer. Anyone with any kind of a name that smacked of Germany had rather a rough time. He wasn't interned, because the Swiss were neutral, but he had a few stones thrown at him and so on. This situation persuaded him to change his name to Frederick, which he thought was more suitable, and he called himself Belmont. He kept desperately looking for money. Then in one of the places he stayed he met an English girl, very vivacious, who took a fancy to him and he took a fancy to her and they got married. This girl had an aunt who was a fairly wealthy widow and in 1919 they persuaded her to lend him the vital £1,000 which he needed. He opened a nice shop with a little café above, in Harrogate. Tea-rooms. My aunt knew how to serve 'dainty teas' as they were called. The Princess Royal would visit, and various war heroes who lived nearby; they had quite a good influx of people like that. It was called Betty's.

SHREELA FLATHER: My father had been in England for sixteen years during the time he was growing up. The Great War intervened, which had made it a longer stay. He was very attached to England and he would go there [from India] every summer holiday. Sometimes my mother joined him. So it was expected that I would go too for my education. My brother had won a place at Cambridge, but the war started the day he was due to leave Bombay. I went to a school which was very nationalistic and we were quite strongly anti-British. So I was anti-British and anti-England too. I was embarrassed by my father, because he was so pro-English and keen on promoting the English way of life. He liked to speak English, he had all his clothes made in England, he liked the food. He ate his Indian food with a knife and fork, he spoke very good English, all that sort of thing. I grew up with two cultures right from the beginning. Two languages, two kinds of food. In the evening we always had the choice of an English meal or an Indian meal. There were two separate kitchens. In some ways he was typical of well-off, educated Indians, who had had some experience of England, but he did it to a greater degree than some. He was very Anglophile.

GRETEL SALINGER: I was here for three months in 1914. England was beautiful and I loved it. I had the most wonderful time here. My cousins were very, very well-to-do bankers here and they had a marvellous house in Avenue Road. With a butler and a chauffeur, things which I was not used to at all. I saw things that I had never seen before. I had never seen in my life lobster, I had never seen oysters. When we had them I had to watch out how they were eaten, I had to look out very carefully to make sure I didn't make any blunders. I was introduced to English Jewish society. That was marvellous: the Oppen-heimers, the Baers, all the rich Jewish families. I was fêted that summer from one ball to the next ball, I went to Ascot, I went to Epsom, the Derby, I went to everything. There wasn't anything my family didn't take me to. I went to the theatre, I went to concerts, I heard Chaliapin, I heard Caruso, everyone. I did the Season. I had a marvellous time and I got engaged but unfortunately that didn't take place. I enjoyed it immensely. But I had to go back because the war began. I would have married and certainly I would have come to live here then if there had been no war. He was one of the sons of a family of important bankers. We met again after the war and became friendly then. He's dead now.

MICHAEL IGNATIEFF: My father comes to Britain from Russia in 1919 at the age of seven. Goes to Colet Court preparatory school. Leaves in 1928 and moves to Canada, where he becomes the standard Canadian immigrant boy: he works on the railroads, works on a blasting crew in British Columbia, puts himself through high school and college and then in 1936, gets a Rhodes scholarship to Oxford. He then spends most of the war years in London. Which is also crucial: both my mother and my father spent the whole war in London, and that is constitutive of their identities as people. They both fell in love, although with other people; a very deep association with England was formed. So when I am growing up he feels absolute, passionate identification with Britain. He has this very corny, sentimental attitude. He gets on a bus in London and looks at the people, especial cockney 'characters', and whispers 'These are the people that won us the war.' England is this completely miraculous place that won us the war.

ALLA WEAVER: My father had decided that when I leave school I must study abroad. Paris was frivolous – I might be in moral danger – while England was stable, solid and highly moral. England meant *nothing* to me. All my culture was directed towards Europe. My mother spoke German fluently, I used to speak German most of the time – much to my father's distress – I spoke Russian, I spoke French, but I also spoke English perfectly well. Every afternoon somebody else came and gave me a lesson in French or whatever. So I had English lessons. My teacher was [Vladimir] Nabokov. He was writing already and he was kept alive by his Jewish wife who was a secretary and a most dedicated, most devoted wife. Vera. He seemed to have been a very devoted family man, and he was a very conscientious teacher, though he didn't like teaching ordinary little girls at all. For a term I went to stay in Paris and went to a French *lycée* to improve my French, when I was about thirteen or fourteen. It was *ghastly*, I hated it, because a French *lycée* is infinitely stricter than a Prussian girls' school. I insisted, and my parents agreed, that I must not come back to Germany having missed a whole term, especially of Latin which wasn't my best subject. So I had to be kept up. Somebody used to come and teach me Latin. Russians always employed Russians, fellow refugees, Jews or not. Our dentist was Russian, our doctor was Russian, they had to be Russian. So when I was in Paris I was taught Latin by somebody who turned out to be *the* biographer of Dostoyevsky: Matyuski.

LEENA DHINGRA: In 1947, when I was five I came here to Europe, to Paris. My father had studied in England and in France and in Germany, after the war he was anxious to know what had happened, who was alive, who was dead. So he took a sabbatical and got himself some assignments with different papers saying he would report on Europe after the war. He was a writer, a poet, and he taught English literature. While he was in Paris UNESCO was being set up and he was offered a job as press officer for three months. This was a precarious existence in any case. Then, while we were here Partition took place and suddenly there was nowhere to go back to.

SHREELA FLATHER: In late 1947 we spent six weeks in England. It was beginning to get cold, winter was approaching and it turned out to be a very famous winter, extremely cold. I was just devastated. I thought it was just about the worst place that anybody could be catapulted to from America, where we had been staying. America was the land of plenty, of lights, of wealth; while in England there were still great restrictions, austerity was still in place, there was nothing to eat. But my father had a friend who had a newsagent's shop and he was very kind to me. He would give me chocolates. Also every visitor got extra rations, so we did quite well on the chocolate front, but not much else. What really amazed me was that the people seemed to know nothing about India. Even at that age I felt these were the most incredibly silly things. Such as, 'I'd like to go to India, but you know, it's all these snakes . . .' I used to try to work this one out. But I couldn't. There were snakes, yes, but we didn't actually have them crawling all round the house. Or, 'Do you ever see tigers?' Well, unless you go to the zoo, you don't actually see that many tigers.

SHARI PEACOCK: My parents were always thinking about going home. There were those classic immigrants' dinners where everybody gets drunk and starts talking about Iran. You grew up dividing the world into us and them, and 'them' means the Bulgarians, where you live. Us is the small community of ex-pat Iranians. The ideal was to leave this god-awful country and go somewhere. Either back to Iran or go further west. Every ambitious Iranian, and eastern European, looks west. That very much included me. Tourists looked good and they drove cars and so on. Germans, British, you couldn't tell but they were blond people. They were glamorous, but for us in Bulgaria even Czechoslovaks were glamorous. In the hierarchy of east European countries they were better off. There were all the relatives who stopped off on their trips to Paris, London, New York, wherever. They were terribly glamorous, glamour personified. I had

36

this terrible feeling when I saw them. They carried big bottles of Biba perfume and wore shiny clothes and had records of the Beatles or Dylan – even if they were already three years out of date. But this was glamour. They were always suggesting we should return. They kept saying that we were wasting our time and it wasn't fair on me and my younger brother. So this meant you grew up with the feeling that sooner or later you would leave. I had a vague amorphous destination: west.

EVA JIRICNA: My first trip to the West came in 1965 when I won a prize while I was doing a post-graduate course at the Academy of Fine Arts. There was a student competition associated with the Congress of Architects, which was held in Paris. All the winners went to Paris. That was something I really hadn't experienced before. It was really like a dream. Later that year I came to London, with the Czech exhibition in the Design Centre. So I had a glimpse of London. It was all very frustrating. You could see the gap between what was happening in Czechoslovakia and what was happening in England. But I really didn't seriously consider the option of emigration at all. I'm definitely not full of nationalistic feelings and I'm definitely very objective when it comes to which country does what and what people are good at, but somehow you feel that it's your duty to stay where you were born. You have a relationship with everybody else who happens to be in the same trouble and you just feel it would be letting people down if you emigrate. All your friends and everyone else who hasn't got the same chance. There was a little migration: people would go on a business trip and would not return – that was the only 'official' way. Or you might have a visa to visit your relatives if you happened to be lucky enough to have someone in your family living abroad, and then you wouldn't come back. I had no relatives abroad.

PALOMA ZOZAYA: When I was about eighteen I went to see a tarot reader. She was amazing. Even before she had turned the cards over and looked at them, she said, 'You're going to go somewhere, a European country where they speak English.' And there's only one, after all. I thought she was mad. I said, 'I'm certainly not going to go to England, that's impossible.' I was toying with the idea of going to Europe, of course, but I was thinking of Paris. I had been to the French Lycée in Mexico City, so I spoke fluent French. Or maybe Spain or Italy, a Latin country. So I had never thought of England.

3 The Decision to Leave

'I saw no future for myself, my family or my children.'

GRETEL SALINGER: When the Nazis started to take over, by about 1934, my husband tried to find a buyer for our factory. In the first year, '33, we didn't want to think about it, we didn't want to know about it, but in 1934 we did know it. It had to be. As he was absolutely decided that he wouldn't sell the factory to any Nazi, we had very great trouble finding another buyer. The Nazis came nearer and nearer and pressed him and pressed him and pressed him and when he wouldn't sell finally that day they put him into a concentration camp, inside Germany, in the prison on Alexanderplatz in Berlin. But luckily we found somebody. We had already started negotiating with a very important member of the German artistocracy. He was not a Nazi. He bought the factory. He was half-Polish and he paid us some in zlotys which he sent to England, and the rest in German marks. The same night he paid us, the Nazis came and confiscated all of it. Then they freed my husband from the camp. He was there for four weeks. Fortunately we still had very good connections because of his work. We didn't have to pay anything, our friends helped us. But we didn't have a penny. We came to England with ten marks. But once we had paid the so-called duties which we had to pay for the pleasure of leaving Germany, we could escape. We left on 14 August 1938. That was very late. Luckily we still managed to get all our furniture out.

BIANCA GORDON: The conditions of life for Jewish people worsened in Nazi Germany, and it was difficult to escape the impact of the situation. My family was deeply religious and closely knit. My parents, particularly my father, maintained a remarkable sense of calm and confidence in the future. They believed that their Maker would protect us and our people. We were not to fear, yet I did – secretly – though I derived strength from their faith and belief. When Hitler ranted in his speeches, which loudspeakers relayed in the streets of Berlin and not even closed windows would eliminate, my father's conviction that the man had cancer of the throat gained strength. The man is mad, the man is sick, he would not last. In any case, my father always turned his eyes towards the *Ausland*, the free countries, beyond Germany. 'The *Ausland* will not allow it to happen, the *Ausland* will not tolerate such a regime. They will step in and come to our rescue.' I derived comfort from my parents' trust and hope, but at times had difficulty. We heard the storm-troopers marching through the streets of Berlin, marching and singing dreadful songs: 'When Jewish blood flows from the knife, things will be so much better . . . A vulgar, obscene song. Men in uniform marching through the streets outside our house, singing such songs in a vibrant city, a city of culture, of wonderful theatres, operas, concert halls – we had the choice of so much. And now, sitting in your room, you heard these songs. Singing at the top of their voices, and singing as if they meant it! I was frightened of these manifestations of hatred and incitement to murder. This wasn't done secretly. These songs weren't sung in the beer-cellars of Nuremberg, they were sung in the streets of Berlin. There were journalists, the foreign press, foreign diplomats. Did they not hear? This aspect of our experience has given me a lot of heartache, particularly after my arrival in this country. The world knew, yet the free world allowed it all to happen, and did not open their frontiers to our people.

Right up to the time my father was taken away, on October 28 1938, I held on to my parents' confidence in God and in the *Ausland*, who were as aware as we were of what was going on. They would step in and bring down this government. We were inside Germany and realized that in the event of intervention from outside we might go under, but that was preferred to the world remaining indifferent and doing nothing. My father, who had left Poland in 1911, actually liked the German people. As an orthodox Jew he felt more secure in Germany than he had felt in Poland. He did not believe that the Nazi regime would endure. I have often wondered whether my father was able to retain his faith after his deportation to Zbaszyn (the no man's land between Poland and Germany) and the subsequent two years in Buchenwald, where he perished in September 1941. I believe that he did, and that his deep faith, optimism and moral strength enabled him to endure two years of hell.

SIR CLAUS MOSER: It gradually got worse. More beatings, more windows broken, but that was still before the yellow stars were introduced. That didn't come until '37. Around '35 my father's private bank was taken over by the Deutsche Bank. He was allowed to carry on going into his office, but was no longer the true proprietor. There was no compensation, of course, not at that time. In 1936 my father was fifty-one. He was at the peak of his career: he owned a bank, he was on a lot of boards of directors, he was a respected figure, with a wide-ranging life, a happy family, many friends. He of course felt desperately strongly about Hitler to give all that up, but he realized, as clearly as anyone that the future for Jews in Germany was hopeless, even horrendous. In fact we got out relatively easily, with most of our furniture and other resources.

GRETEL SALINGER: There was one loophole when one left Germany. You were allowed at that time to book through Thomas Cook trips wherever you wanted to go. While we still had money we bought air tickets, dozens of tickets, everywhere. We thought if they're lost, they're lost, but if they're not, then we can cash them when we get to England. Then we booked a trip to Dutch East India and we looked for many friends of ours and we invited them to join us. There was a condition whereby you could take with you 50 marks per day for boarding expenses. But we told them all that nobody was going to spend any board money. They'd get enough to eat on board the ship. But they would take board money with them which we would give them, which they were allowed, and then they would give the money back to us. So we made £500 in board money. That was our fortune, with which we arrived in England. The trip took three months. Each day brought us in £50, which was shared between us and my parents whom we had taken with us. So we saved £50 per day. So we got my parents out with us and then left them in Holland before we went to England. That was in January 1939. And from Holland they, along with the rest of my family, were all deported to Auschwitz.

ALLA WEAVER: The intellectuals, the outstanding people, left; the well-to-do left, and if they left soon after the taking-over by Hitler they got away with quite a lot of their fortune. They didn't have to forfeit whatever the percentage was later. My father had this wonderful foreign passport and was sitting under the same roof as these very reputable lawyers; he became trustee to a number of extremely wealthy German Jews, who were his personal friends and who were anxious to leave and to leave their affairs with somebody absolutely trustworthy. They didn't expect to be back, absolutely not, and my father had to supervise the selling off of their assets.

SIR CLAUS MOSER: Then of course, things became quickly more difficult during 1937. It got harder and harder to get goods and money out. By 1938 it had become horribly tough: it was a case of escaping, not leaving. After that leaving was a question of survival for Jews, which it had not been for us. Some of our family on my mother's side stayed in Germany, and some ended up in concentration camps. We ourselves – my parents and my brother and I – left when my father's mother (who had been too ill to leave) died. We were indeed fortunate, and no day should pass without remembering the millions of Jews who ultimately perished.

GERTRUD HARTWIG: Finally we decided that at least we members of the younger generation should try to get out. This was 1938. I was married, we were living in Berlin, and we would sometimes visit my family in Hamburg. The last time we made the trip the danger had already grown very great from the Nazis. Looking Jewish, as I do, I kept away from my husband and sat at the other end of the train compartment, so as not to be identified with him. He didn't look Jewish. At that stage the Nazis would see someone they thought was Jewish and would just grab them, take them off trains, whatever. Perhaps we should have tried to leave earlier, but in those situations, one hangs on, one hangs on. Of course the situation was on one's mind to some extent, but we didn't actively think of leaving before '37. It was very difficult. You were restricted as to what you could take out. You had to make declarations about everything; there were long queues building up, filled with Jewish people getting their permits to leave; it was very difficult to get the various clearances one needed. They would say, 'Come back tomorrow, come back tomorrow' – they didn't make much effort to accelerate things. They weren't very co-operative, of course.

GRETEL SALINGER: We had to get our passports. This gave us very great trouble. We had to pay terrific amounts of money, this duty that you had to pay to get out of Germany. They called it *'Reichsfluchtsdole'*. Then we had to ask to be allowed to take things out of Germany. We were not allowed to pack unless there was a Nazi supervising our luggage as we packed it. It was known that if the man came at seven o'clock in the morning to supervise your packing and you offered him breakfast and he takes it, then you are safe, then he's not a bad Nazi. But if he doesn't accept even a glass of water, then be careful. One talked to other people who had experience and this is what they told us. So there we were. He came at seven o'clock and my husband said, 'Nice to meet you, would you like some breakfast?' 'I'd love some breakfast.' I sighed with relief. We knew that he wasn't a bad Nazi. Then at about ten o'clock he said to us, 'Where do you go?' So my husband told him that we were going to Holland where I had some family and he had to have a kidney operation. He said, 'That's very strange. I have got a brother-in-law in Holland because my sister married a Jew and he emigrated to Holland. Would you be kind enough to take some shirts for him?' You don't know what that meant to us! We knew then that he meant pack anything you want. He said, 'I have to go out for an hour and then I come and then we pack.' We had already learnt from other people's experience that it was still a risk, it could have been just a farce, he might just have been pretending, but we took the risk. We had 3,000 marks in cash and we put them in our suitcases, not knowing what was going to happen. If we were caught we would be sent to a concentration camp. He came back and said, 'Which of the cases do you want packed especially well?' We knew what he meant, and we said, cleverly, 'Oh, they are all the same.' And he packed them, and tied cords around them and whatever we didn't take, he took home with him. Next morning he rang to say, 'I only want you to know that your luggage has arrived safely in Holland.' We were very lucky. So we went to Holland and my husband had his operation – he was terribly ill.

ALLA WEAVER: In 1939, two days before the war, I was in Paris, having persuaded my parents not to stay in Berlin after the Soviet-German pact. I was about to be married to my husband and I damn well wasn't going to stay trapped in Germany. It's one of the very few times in my life when I was quite determined. My father was persuaded to leave Berlin by a Nazi lawyer who heard of the pact as soon as it happened and who insisted that he left. And I insisted and my father said, 'OK, we'll go to Italy and take a ticket via Paris.' So there we were in Paris, and my father was still dragging his feet about it all, saying, 'Well there's no need for you to go to London even if war breaks out, which is unlikely. Tony (my husband) is in the cavalry and he'll join up and the Channel will always be open and he'll come and collect you.' My husband will come and collect me! On a horse riding across the Channel! But my father still wanted to keep up the pretence that all was normal. I was in Paris and champing to go back to England. I was then at the Courtauld, working for an MA in a very desultory way. In the Champs-Elysées I saw my tutor, Anthony Blunt, with another chap. I was so excited. I left my mother and rushed up to Blunt, explained our position and asked whether he thought it was wise to wait until the war broke out, if that should happen, and then to join my fiancé. He said, 'You must leave now, because once war is declared your visa will not be valid.' So I dashed back to my mother who said, 'Who was that?' 'Anthony Blunt.' She looked him up and down and said, 'Now I know why your Tony looks like he does'. She felt that he was always so casually dressed. Not at all what my mother thought of as an English gentleman. And he was called Anthony yet he didn't look at all like Anthony Eden. He had strange manners and he didn't speak French and his Latin wasn't as good as my father's.

So my mother said, 'Aha, I see. Who's the other one?' 'I don't know, he's not a lecturer, I've never seen him. All I know is that he's an old Etonian.' 'How do you know?' 'Oh he had a dirty old Etonian tie on.' I now realize that it was Guy Burgess. People were coming back from holiday. I met one of the Courtauld lecturers on the boat. 'If you have any problems at customs I will help you.' But in fact I just sailed through.

MARY ROSE: One day in 1945 I was sitting in a café and in comes an enormous man, a civilian, I presumed he was an American. Not at all the type of man I liked: enormous, blond, too fat, squinted a bit. He came in and said in perfect German, with a north German accent, 'Would you mind if we sit at your table?' Now I was very haughty towards all the occupying people. So I just said, 'Yes, of course.' He was English, working as a translator. But the moment he sat down I knew, this is my lot. I am in love with him. We started off by having a long conversation about the principle of believing in personalities, Hitler, whatever – falling for personalities. A very serious conversation. Then he said 'Can I take you home?' So he took me home, and said, 'I'll come tomorrow and pick you up, we'll go for a walk.' I thought, I must be crazy. I was staying with a very nice family. I told them. They said, 'Oh he's English, not so bad.' But I felt terrible.

So next day he wasn't there but another translator turned up. 'Mister Rose isn't here yet, but he's sent me to make his excuses.' Eventually he turned up, but I didn't want to go out with him in his uniform. It was a very hot day. He had this pair of red swimming trunks, and I had made myself a swimsuit out of a shawl, and off we went, walking through the town in our swimsuits. Then we started living together.

Ten days later, most of the translators were sent home – they'd been spending most of their time making money out of the black market (although poor old Reggie didn't make anything – he spent all his time with me). But he had to go and he left me his address and I gave him three addresses where he could contact me. That was that. Meanwhile I went to Stuttgart and started working as a housemaid for an artist who had managed to survive the war despite being an anti-Nazi. I was waiting for Reggie. Three months later, in December, I was sitting with the family, making the wreaths you have at Christmas and there was this knock at the door. Somebody answers it, 'It's for you.' There was Reggie. So I moved to Frankfurt with him, still working as a housemaid.

One day Reggie asked me to marry him. He thought I would just say, 'Yes darling.' But what I said was, 'I'll have to think about it.' Because it meant going to England, and becoming English. Would I say yes because I wanted to marry Reggie, or did I just want to escape from Germany, where things were difficult? Basically I was very patriotic. I loved Germany. I didn't want to leave my country in the lurch. I didn't want to run away to what after all was an enemy country. But in many ways the British were like us – they had nothing. It was the Americans who had so much, and they did make me feel a bit sick. The British soldier who had only a little ration of chocolate and shared that with a child, has done more to convince people how we would all have to get on after the war than anything else.

I didn't come to England just because I wanted to come to England. I had to think: am I running away, what am I doing? In the end I decided to marry Reggie. I liked him, he had come back to find me, I really loved him. So we got married. People were nice, they were helpful, we managed to sidestep most of the paperwork. I wanted to see my family before I left, which meant going to East Germany, which was very difficult. Reggie of course couldn't come. I went to the East with this forged paper an aunt of mine in West Germany had given me: it gave me permission to come back to the West. I had to stay at this centre. Men slept here, women there, married couples there, and they had the most space. On the way I met this wounded officer. I helped carry his case and when we arrived we just decided to be 'married'. We didn't even know each other's name. So there we were, and in comes a Russian officer inspecting the place and we are shown off as 'a young German couple who have chosen to settle in East Germany and build the future'. So we made up this wonderful story, what else could we do – we didn't want to let him down.

MARIA VOROSKOI: My decision to leave Hungary was quite spontaneous. In 1947 I had to organize an art exhibition. So quite legally I flew to Italy and then to France, where I had very good friends. They said to me, 'You're mad, don't go back.' I stayed in Paris for two months, which I enjoyed very much, although there was a strike which cut off all the power supplies and I walked all over the city. Then when the first plane was available I came to England and started pursuing my career – photography – here. Then I met my husband and it was a sort of whirlwind: he proposed and I thought that he was silly, but after some time I thought he was right and I still think he was right. We were married, and in due course our son arrived. Getting married automatically made me a British citizen, though that was certainly not the primary motive. But I had not intended to stay in Britain. I had my return visa to France, where my friends had promised to find me jobs, but I had certainly left Hungary. I wasn't sure whether I would go back, but I did want to chance to work elsewhere. I still had a few friends in Hungary, whom I dearly loved. So it wasn't an escape.

ANNE-MARIE WOLPE: We left South Africa because of politics. The Rivonia arrests. It was 1963. Harold, my husband, was caught trying to leave the country; he was in fact grassed by the husband of a cousin of mine. We never proved it, but we believe it to be the case. He was picked up at the border. After a series of complicated manoeuvres I helped him escape. Four people escaped and I organized it.

It was quite a horrendous period. My youngest child was about ten weeks old. He had been desperately ill, close on death – it was heavy, heavy drama. The first torture cases had happened. My brother was arrested and became one of the Rivonia treason trial defendants. He was subsequently released. Harold's escape made world news. It was very dramatic – it was the first time anybody had beaten the Nationalist government. They escaped first in Johannesburg, then went across the border to Swaziland and then, dressed as priests, went to what was Bechuanaland. Then the problem was to get them out. The South Africans sent in people to get them but that was discovered. The first plane that came to get them was bombed. Finally they got away, though that plane nearly crashed, that kind of thing.

I had been in and out of jail myself – though only for a day – and then into hiding. I'd gone to pieces, I knew I couldn't cope any more, and I'd been warned that I would be charged with aiding the escape and I wanted to get out of the country. I had a valid passport. There was a conference. My lawyer went to the Special Branch and said that I wanted to leave. They conferred for a day and at five o'clock that evening they said, 'Yes, OK.' My lawyer said, 'Go.' I said it was a bit difficult. I had no money, three children aged from five months to six years. My father had died earlier that year, my brother was in jail, my sister in Natal and my mother couldn't cope with emergencies. So things were difficult. Then somebody gave me £100 and I packed a bag and left the next day. I had to leave the children with my maid and the nurse. The youngest was still ill, under 24-hour-a-day care. I got on a plane for London. By that stage Harold was in Nairobi. He came to London two days after I did. Our arrival here was not planned. It was simply a question of freedom for me – I didn't want to spend a few years in jail. I told the customs I had come as a tourist and they accepted that.

I felt no regrets at leaving. Not at all. Just a tremendous relief of pressure. It is very difficult, very frightening, living with the threat of imprisonment. They frightened me; they were very angry with me. This was a brutal system, they had been torturing people and they got close to torturing me but I was very lucky. They hadn't yet touched white women, but within six months they started.

CHRISTOPHER HOPE: I began writing satirical verse at school, highly politicized, highly disrespectful. I realized that it either made people laugh or made them angry. I had no idea of leaving South Africa then. As I became politically active, I realized that it would be difficult to write and to express myself politically against the South African regime, and that I'd have to choose. So I chose quite deliberately to leave. There was a certain amount of political pressure, because my work was stopped from being broadcast on local radio, and it was made plain to me that if I wrote anything of any length I would find it difficult to get it published. So I left in 1974. I came to Europe because that was the one place I imagined that I knew. I've always intended to go back, but at that stage I just had to get away. If I was to write anything of any substance I'd have to do it somewhere else, and Britain was the logical place to head for.

MARCEL BERLINS: I did two years of my doctorate in Paris, then got tired of it. I got interested in Chinese life, language, calligraphy, and was accepted at the School of Oriental Languages, doing Chinese. So I gave up law and applied for my exemption (from French national service) and they said, 'Sorry, you're not getting one.' 'Why?' 'Because next year you'll switch again. So you're going to do National Service.' I said, 'OK,' because a lot of my friends had done their two years and been sent all over the colonies doing interesting things. But they said, 'No.' I had to do square-bashing in Clermont-Ferrand. 'Why can't I go abroad?' 'Because that's only for graduates.' 'But I am a graduate.' 'Not a French graduate.' We argued this back and forth, and eventually they lost patience. They said, 'Normally we'd put you in prison, but because of your past history, we'll give you seven days to leave the country, and you must understand you can never come back, and you'll be stripped of all your rights.' I thought about it. I didn't really want to join a bunch of seventeen-year-olds doing eighteen months of running round the yard. I was so pissed off with the authorities. When they said, 'You can never come back', I didn't really think of the consequences.

PETER TATCHELL: From the late 1960s, I was involved in the mass campaigns against conscription and the Australian intervention in the Vietnam War. I helped organize the huge 'Stop Work To Stop The War' demonstrations which blockaded the centre of Melbourne with 100,000 people (ten per cent of the city's population). I was also active in clandestine work, encouraging and aiding young men who were refusing to do national service and fight in Vietnam. The idea was to undermine the war effort by encouraging thousands of young men to refuse conscription. It was hoped that this mass defiance would make the draft unworkable and force the government to change its policy. I was, myself, determined not to be conscripted for what I regarded as an unjust and immoral war. Faced with the prospect of two years' imprisonment, I decided to go abroad until the war was over. I planned to travel around Europe and chose Britain as my first stop, largely because it had a familiar language and culture and because I knew I could easily get work in London.

*   *   *

VU DUY TU: My wife has a sister who came to the UK in 1962. She studied here and married an Englishman. She was working for the British Refugee Council and after the takeover [of South Vietnam] in 1975 she made contact with my wife and applied for us to come to England. We knew nothing about it. Then, perhaps two years after she first applied, my family were granted a visa, but not me. My wife received all the documents and the visa from my sister, but she didn't want to go. If she went, then everyone should go, including me. So she left it in a drawer. When I was released from the re-education camp my wife wrote to her sister to say that I was home. Her sister sent another application form for me, asking for a family reunion. I didn't know about this either. I had never dreamed about escaping to the UK. Not even when I left the camp did I think, I must leave Vietnam. Never, never. But luckily just a month after coming home, one day, one very beautiful morning I received a telegram from the UK embassy in Hanoi to tell me that the UK government accepted me as a refugee. Whenever I could get an exit visa from Vietnam, I should let them know and the embassy would arrange for the family to go to England. So I am very happy to receive that telegram. But I am very suspicious. I suspect everything. I trust nothing and nobody. There's no way I'll get an exit visa. So I just leave it. For two months I didn't even touch the letter. But one of my brothers encouraged me, he said, 'Just try. Just try. Don't be silly.' So I said, 'OK, I'll try,' but I dare not go to the police station. I was frightened of the secret police. But we did apply for an exit visa and it took eighteen months to come through.

PETER VO: After my release from the camp I tried to get permission to move around the country but that was turned down. I didn't dare ask to leave Vietnam altogether. But something happened that made the area officer change his mind about me. I had a friend, my wife's godmother, and she organized escapes from Vietnam to a free country. She had been captured by the police, then she had escaped but was being pursued. She arrived at my house and asked for refuge. I could not refuse. We let her to stay with us for some days.

Now, maybe thirty years before, when the French government had sentenced a Communist prisoner to death, that prisoner escaped, and a lady had helped him. Thirty years later that prisoner turned up, now a colonel in the army, and found that same lady, who was now over eighty years old, who had helped him. He knew some people wanted to leave the country and said, 'You helped me to escape all those years ago, now I can help you in return.' She thanked him for the offer, but she said, 'No. I am too old now. But my daughter is in hiding and she wants to leave this country.' That daughter was my wife's godmother. So he said, 'OK, whatever, I don't mind.' I knew nothing about this meeting.

One day he arrived at my home, with some policemen, and one rang the bell of my house. I was so scared. I thought that this was someone coming to take me away. I thought they were coming to recapture me because of my past in the camps and the fact that now I was harbouring someone who was working against the state. But that gentleman said to me, 'Don't be afraid.' He told me the name of my wife's godmother, and that he knew she was staying in my house. I couldn't speak. But the godmother heard him and she appeared. So he came in my house and didn't arrest me, and when the local police chief heard this, he believed that I had important contacts high up in the army and after that he stopped paying attention to me. I was able to move around without asking permission. It was a great relief. So then I was able to prepare for leaving Vietnam.

VU DUY TU: After my release I spent two years before I was able to go to the UK. I didn't work, I wasn't allowed to. I just stayed at home. During the first year I was still considered as under a form of house arrest. I wasn't allowed to leave Saigon. I could go shopping but that was it. Every Monday I had to report to the police: where did I go, who had I seen, who I have talked to and what had we talked about? The local policeman, responsible for my area, could visit me any time he wanted, day or night. He didn't need an invitation. He would just open the door, go directly to my bedroom, directly to my kitchen –

anywhere he wanted. He wouldn't say hello. If I said hello, he'd just say, 'Yeess?' and I'd say, 'What is it, what do you need from me?' 'It doesn't matter. I just want to visit.' He would look round my house, everywhere. I'd offer him a drink, he'd say, 'Never mind.' Sometimes he just came in, sat down and kept quiet for hours. I didn't dare open my mouth to ask what he wanted. I just sat and waited for him. He looked at me. Sometimes just a couple of minutes, sometimes hours. He wanted to show me, 'I am here. All the time. Be careful.' Sometimes he'd read my newspaper, sometimes he'd just smoke. Then suddenly he'd say, 'OK, goodbye.' And he'd go. It could happen at midnight, two o'clock, three o'clock. There'd be a knock at the door and he'd be there, with a gun, a machine-gun, four or five others. 'Open the door, quick! This is the police!' So we all wake up. 'Where is your family? Go to the lounge. All of you sit in there.' So I had to wake up my wife and children and we all go to sit in the lounge. 'Is there anyone else here, any strangers?' 'No, please check.' So they go and check. Then they check my name, my wife's name, my children's names. Then, 'OK, thank you, go back to sleep.' It's very frightening.

NGUYEN DUC PHUONG: By 1980 I saw no future for myself, my family or my children. We knew that the children of families like mine could not get educated beyond secondary school. I saw no future and I began to think about escape. Somebody came to see me. Through a friend of my wife they knew that I could drive a boat after being a naval officer and spending a lot of time at sea. The first boat people had started escaping two years earlier so this was something that had become quite common. So they asked me if I can drive a boat. Of course I agreed. Then they planned secretly. They gave me a map and I calculated a route. There were three ways of escaping. You could go north to Hong Kong, out to the sea-lanes and then to Malaysia, Singapore or the Philippines, or round the coast to Thailand. The coastal route is easier, especially since the boats didn't have proper navigational instruments and you could always see the coast, and it's shorter, but you get pirates waiting near Cambodia, and you have the government security forces patrolling the coast. The Hong Kong route is longest and most hazardous. The weather can be very bad. The route to the sea-lanes is long, but if you avoid the winter months, when the weather is bad, then the winds will help you. We went in June so even if we had broken down, the winds would have blown us where we wanted to go. So I planned that route. The planning took about two weeks. They had bought the boat before. It wasn't a sea-going boat, it had been used to transport cargo up and down the river, but they had modified it a little. That was difficult but they paid something to the security forces to look the other way. In Vietnam you can pay for everything. Some money went to the government, but the lower ranking officers, who you actually paid, kept a lot of it. I was introduced to the other people involved, also officers and NCOs of the previous government. I didn't trust them immediately. There were many types in the old navy and I had to see who will be useful for the trip – we had to limit the numbers. I heard that many of the passengers paid for the trip, though my family and I paid nothing.

* * *

STEPHEN VIZINCZEY: I had fought in the [Hungarian] revolution in '56, got involved in smashing Stalin's statue, and then I had to go. I heard rumours about myself: I had been arrested and was on my way to Siberia, but I had managed throw a piece of paper out of a train before passing the border into Russia. It was only a rumour, but these rumours had a tendency to come true and I didn't want to wait to find out. It wasn't easy to get out. I came with my first wife. We found someone who said they would guide us across the border into Austria, in return for our watches. So we gave him our watches, but when we got into the forest the guy got scared and left us. It was a dark night and we were wandering about in this forest and we didn't know whether we were in Hungary or Austria. In fact we crossed back and forth across the border several times – but we ended up on the right side.

EVA JIRICNA: In 1968 I came to England with the intention of working for six months for the GLC. I really wanted to work abroad, because I wanted to experience new working conditions and new ways of design. I was constantly being offered jobs in Germany and America and everywhere else but the government wouldn't let me go. In 1967 there was a Congress of Architects and there I met someone who was a deputy architect of the GLC and he invited me over to London. He managed to get a work permit for me, and so I came over on 1 August 1968.

The Russian invasion took place on 20 August. I had thought that things were improving. I could never possibly believe in my naïvety that there would be an invasion. The situation changes so drastically when you get out of the country and you suddenly start reading proper newspapers, and you can get some kind of dialogue on information. Which is not the case at home. Though in 1968 it was becoming more and more possible to speak freely. Therefore though we all knew that the situation was not at all one hundred per cent safe as far as the Dubček government was concerned, but I could never, ever, imagine that the Russians would actually invade the country. But my uncle, who had been in prison, came to see me to say goodbye, and he said, 'Well if you can leave,' – I was supposed to be leaving by the end of the week – 'if you can leave tomorrow I would speed it up and go.' He was absolutely adamant that the Russians would not give in and that they would invade. We were all laughing at him. I thought that in 1968 in the middle of Europe something like a physical invasion was practically impossible. It's naïve, but maybe it's some kind of self preservation, not wanting things like that to happen. I was about twenty-nine and one is not really experienced enough to make a proper judgement on the situation. So when I came out and I started reading all the articles I *still* couldn't believe it.

JAROSLAV BRADAC: After the Russians arrived I decided I wanted to get away for six months. I wasn't thinking that I would leave for ever, I just wanted to get out for six months. I was deeply dissatisfied with what was going on. I had got my diploma, but I had realized that even the college was not as it used to be – I had made a slightly political comment in one of my pictures and I began to hear that I shouldn't have done so. I did a series of etchings called 'Faith, Hope and Charity' and for Faith I had a five-pointed Soviet star and the blind leading the blind; implying that everyone followed the dogma Lenin had worked out in 1917 and it simply didn't work. On top of that I wasn't keen to go into the army, which was the next thing I was facing. So I got a passport which at that time was still very easy. I went to Italy, Paris, and on 17 October 1969 I came here for just ten days. It was part of my holiday, I was still going to return. I had my rail ticket, my swimming trunks in my suitcase and I was going to spend ten days in England and go via Amsterdam and Hamburg back to Prague. But this was when the border was closed and I happened to be here. I got a letter from my parents – 'Hang about, we don't know what's happening. Just wait where you are.' So that's what I did. Originally I was just waiting.

HANNAH KODICEK: It was a great relief to leave. I just wanted to find somewhere where I felt there would be order. I didn't like the system, but more than that I disliked the chaos, which meant that you could never trust anybody. You would sometimes be not quite sure whether you could talk to your best friend. This fundamental lack of anything to lean on, this lack of safety nets. There were no walls, there was no floor. Just this sense of uncertainty. You can't even get it by hanging on to the Party. You have a number of choices: either you join the Party which means that materially and jobwise you are OK. You have a career ladder and all that. But as far as your friends are concerned you are an outcast – nobody trusts you. You can't get friends within the Party, either, because you can't trust them. So you choose between the career and no friends or trust, or at the other extreme to be a dissident, work against the regime, which means you may end up in prison or in the mines, your children will never be educated and you are actually jeopardizing your whole family existence. Or you may be in the middle, just trying to hang on somehow, which is what most of my friends' families were doing. Trying to compromise, trying not to betray the family and friends. But that is a very precarious path to tread. The people who are in charge of a system like that know jolly well. It's the best way to manipulate people. There's

50

nothing to hold on to and any carrot, any sardine, that's dangled in front of you is alluring.

IVAN KYNCL: I was taking pictures for Charter 77. Between 1977 and 1980 they confiscated my films ten times but they never found anything, because every time I was able to change them for blank films. I was arrested a few times. One time was at the funeral of Patocka, one of the first spokesmen for Charter 77, who was killed during his interrogation. That was in March 1977, just after my back operation. So I had this plaster, 8.5 kilos, all over my body, and I took my camera to the funeral. I shot everything that I saw and I was just on my last film when I was arrested. As usual they confiscated the film, but I swapped the exposed stuff for blank films and put the used rolls under my plaster. But they knew that I was very much involved with the dissidents. So in 1979 they arrested me again; this time they accused me of plotting to kill President Husák. Of course that was nonsense, they just wanted to arrest fifteen people who they knew supported Charter 77. So they arrived at my studio. They found my archives. I had two sets: one official and one unofficial. The first was just normal people, everyday material, maybe 20,000 negatives. The unofficial material was spread around my friends, they never found it. I would develop the films and get them out of the house immediately. But they confiscated my archives. In 1980 they returned them, but they had destroyed them all with chemicals. So they arrested me and beat me in the cell because I refused to co-operate and give them fingerprints and so on. I was recovering from a broken back and they still beat me with truncheons. I was only imprisoned for a few days, but they didn't close the case. Over the next four months I had thirty-five interrogations. Every one lasted around five hours. At the same time I had my own secret policemen who followed me everywhere I went, day and night. It didn't stop me taking pictures. I would give them the slip: I would visit a friend, they would post themselves at the front door of the building and I would slip out of the back door, take some pictures and a few hours later leave at the front and they would start following me again.

KAREL KYNCL: When I returned from prison I went back to my job as an archivist in a hospital. In January 1977 I was fifty. I was given 1,000 crowns (£200) as a reward for my excellent work in the archives. A few days afterwards it so happened that my signature appeared on Charter 77 which had just appeared. The most unbelievable hysteria was launched by the media against all the signatories. So the hospital, which had just given me my award, was forced to throw me out. After that it was quite impossible to find another job. I applied to be a parking lot watchman – I was totally qualified, I had been in jail (which they usually had been), I was not exactly healthy at the time, I was a partial invalid, but the employer consulted the Central Committee of the

51

Communist Party of Czechoslovakia to see whether this parking lot watchman should be hired. They told him: No. It was a public job, out in the open, and what would happen if a western journalist took a photo of me? That would harm the interests of the republic abroad. So I was banned from the job. I applied to be stoker in the National Museum in Prague. I had seen an advertisement in the papers. I went, they were delighted: thank God somebody is willing to take on the work. Then they looked at me, 'Aren't you . . .' I said, 'Yes, I am.' They said, 'Then it's impossible – you're forbidden to work in the field of culture.' I asked, 'Is stoking the boiler part of culture?' They said, 'No, but the National Museum is.' I tried for many many other jobs. It was a Kafkaesque, Orwellian situation. I could not watch a parking lot, but when I applied to run an ice-cream stand in the park, they did not call the Central Committee and I was accepted. This lasted for three months, in full view of the public, but in the end the secret police had me thrown out again. But we survived. My wife did some jobs, people were very kind to us. It was also possible to publish translations under another person's name, a front-man who was all right with the authorities and who would give you a part or even all of the money he was paid. I put out about twenty-five books like this, under other names. Then at the end of '77 I was finally given a paper that stated that as a partial invalid I was able to work in a special establishment for partial invalids.

IVAN KYNCL: In August 1980, after many interrogations, they told me that I had two options: one was go to prison, because they claimed that they knew what I did. That wasn't true because if they had really known about the films I was taking and smuggling out I would have been imprisoned long before. The other was to leave Czechoslovakia. They confiscated my nationality and gave me a paper which stated that I was former Czech national and must leave within three months. So I was stateless, and I still am. I hadn't wanted to leave. I felt that the work I was doing was very important, that it was important to show both the people at home and those in the West what was going on. So I felt what I did mattered. But after a few years I felt I was just doing the same pictures of the same people and the same secret policemen in the same situations over and over again. It became very frustrating. I also realized that if I didn't leave now, then I would go to prison. So when I was deciding where to go I wanted to choose somewhere which had a language that I could use all over the world. That was English. Also I had smuggled my material to London. So I took my paper to the English embassy to apply for a visa. I had already been there to see if it would be possible. There was a feeling in England that Charter 77 should be helped so it was very easy for me and for my family to get refugee status even before I arrived here.

KAREL KYNCL: In 1981 I was arrested again and spent the next year in prison in Prague before I was released without trial. Nobody had expected that I would be released, but it happened. When I came home I realized that I faced two possibilities – both very unacceptable, both stupidities. Either to stay and to risk spending the rest of my life behind bars, which was a very, very concrete danger. Or to apply for emigration and to go into exile. And of the two stupidities this second one seemed more acceptable. So we decided to apply for permission to emigrate. Twelve or thirteen years earlier a secret police interrogator had told me, 'If you don't like the country' – and this is how they interpret your attitude – 'there is a car in front of this building and we can deliver you to the border tomorrow if that's what you would like.' They knew very well that I didn't want to emigrate. When I really did apply their attitude was very different. They did everything to prevent us from leaving the country.

During my life as a journalist I had come to know English diplomacy quite well. It was stone-faced, detached, very, very rigid. To my amazement, during my second imprisonment, a member of the embassy went officially to see my wife and handed her a letter offering asylum, and then repeated his visits every week, asking after me. This continued after I had been released. Every official visitor from Britain was instructed to ask his Czech counterpart: when will they release me, when will they let me leave? They collected answers – which were of course contradictory. After about ten months the British ambassador told me, in a wonderful example of English understatement, 'I can't say that the Foreign Minister has lied to me, but he was certainly not telling the truth.' I don't really know why they had chosen to help me. I had been a listed by Amnesty International as a prisoner of conscience twice. Maybe they knew that after years of refusing to leave, I had begun to change my mind. A month later, I was told by the authorities that I had to leave the country within two weeks. To their amazement I refused. I told them, 'We have been trying in vain to get out for almost a year. Now you would like us to leave in two weeks. No. We need at least a month to get ready.' They left the room, then after fifteen minutes came back and said, 'All right – a month.' A month later, in mid-February 1983, we left Czechoslovakia and came here.

WITOLD STARECKI: From 1974, or even earlier, till 1982 I was always both considered and felt myself to be a semi-dissident. I wasn't in the underground, I wasn't writing samizdat, but I was working from within to fight the system to the best of my ability. When martial law was declared in 1981 I was working in Polish television, running a school for graduates of film school. I was making my second drama and there was at the time a general policy amongst Solidarity that people with established names were not to do films, because that would imply that they supported the system, but that the less-known people, like me, should carry on working. So martial law is declared. I am already in production, and there is a question of whether or not I stop my film. I went to see the Polish Film Society, the union of Polish film-makers and very anti-government,

53

to find out what their policy was on my film. They told me that the policy was to help people like me, but to have the big names withhold their work. So I kept on shooting. But Solidarity disagreed. They wanted nobody to work. Suddenly I found my name published on Solidarity's list of collaborators. I couldn't believe it. I went back to the Film Society and said, 'What is this? I'm working according to your policy, you know my track record, what am I doing on this list?' So they told me that Solidarity didn't accept their policy, even though the bulk of the Society was in Solidarity too. There were private enmities, jealousies, but really I couldn't make sense of this. All my life I had been working for this movement, why was it turning against me now? So they said, 'Well, Solidarity feel that you will be a good example. If you are on the list, everyone else will be scared.' I said, 'I don't believe this, and I can't go along with it.' That was the moment that I decided that there was no longer any place for me in Poland. The only reason that I had stayed, not making money, not having my films shown, but still struggling on, was the belief that I was doing it for some purpose. Although what was amazing and nice was that ninety-nine per cent of my friends just laughed at the list and ignored it.

* * *

NELLY SALAS: I was involved in politics myself, of course. People who think can't just watch, they must do something. If something wrong happens, you have to stand up and say no. Which in Argentina becomes a problem. I was working with various community groups. I met my ex-husband in the mid-'70s. He came from Uruguay and he had already been jailed there for three years, on political grounds. The same things were happening there as in Argentina. He had left Uruguay without permission. He had been released from jail and he was supposed to report every two weeks to a local military base. But instead he escaped to Argentina and they couldn't find him. But the military who ran Argentina, Chile and Uruguay all worked together. So the Uruguay police asked the Argentinian police to search for him. We weren't exactly underground, but we lived among the poor people and they protected us. People told me that my husband was in danger, that people were looking for him.

MIGUEL ZAMBRANO: My wife had been saying for months, 'We have to leave the country, something's going to happen and it's going to be very nasty.' I said 'No, I can't.' Then came the army coup against Allende, Tuesday 11 September 1973. Once I knew it was a success, our only chance of survival was to hide. The military had control of the whole country. My wife and kids went into hiding outside Santiago. We saw things I'll never forget. They had killed the president, there were bodies in the river, summary executions everywhere, they sent tanks and planes against resistance workers in factories. People were full of fear and hate. If you dressed as a labourer and happened to be in the

54

wrong place, you would get shot. The only people they trusted were well-dressed people living in good residential areas.

NELLY SALAS: The UN had an office in Buenos Aires which operated under the Geneva Convention where you could apply for political asylum. What made it very difficult was that the authorities, the police and the army, knew everyone who was going there. Not just Argentinians, but refugees who had arrived from other countries. People who had fled Chile after Allende was murdered. People like that. Even making the application was dangerous: the army knew the UN had their office and what they did there. They couldn't go in – the UN had diplomatic immunity – but they could wait nearby and grab people when they arrived. So going to the office had to be done quite secretly. When the people who worked for the UN began to realize what was going on, that people weren't turning up for appointments because they'd been snatched by the police two hundred yards from the door as they stepped off a bus, they started to let people stay in the office for two or three days. They had safe houses where they put people, or they would put them in hotels under false names, and they would wait there until they could leave. It was too dangerous for my husband to go, and I had to make the application. I remember a woman, perhaps from Bolivia, with three children, and her husband had been taken out of his house, and she was desperate. They told her to come back in a few days and then, perhaps, there would be news. She was begging them, crying, saying, 'I can't go away, if I leave here they will arrest me!' So they had to hide her until she could leave the country. It was like being a Jew under Hitler. Exactly the same. People disappeared, they were tortured, you dig in a garden now and you find bodies from those days. They killed whole families. It was just terror. You could be walking along and a car would stop and just snatch you away. And if your relations did manage to track down the car and make a complaint to the police, the police would just say the car was stolen and that they didn't know anything.

MIGUEL ZAMBRANO: They came to search the house where we were staying – Cubans were supposed to be hiding there. I showed them my ID, and because I was dressed all right, middle class, etc., it was OK. But then they became more selective, and so the circle began closing in. They arrested me for things that somebody else did. When they interrogated me, they asked the wrong questions. I was left-wing, I was politically involved. By their standards, they had enough against me – I was an active Party member, so were my friends – but I think though they were looking for the person who'd been in my position before me. They threatened to kill me, there and then, but they tortured and interrogated me instead. Where were the machine-guns, all that. They kept asking the wrong questions for eighteen months.

55

MOSES SPITZ: There are no clear-cut situations if one is in the position we were in Argentina. There are just moments when one knows that the best one can do is flee the country. It becomes clear in one's mind that that is the best one can do ... I came May 1st, 1975, fifteen years ago. The reign of terror had just started. People were beginning to disappear, a good friend disappeared, another friend was found dead.

I was a professor at the University of La Plata, in the Faculty of Science. With a political manoeuvre they managed to exclude a very large number of professors and appointed those selected to teach according to their plans. There was no formal dismissal or expulsion neither was there a responsible authority to whom one could address one's queries. There was just something like a blacklist and my name was amongst those belonging to the opposition, 'the internal enemy' as they called the people who dared criticize. As the process advanced and the 'dirty war' continued, nearly every section of society was seen as an enemy in one way or another.

LYDIA SPITZ: The first thing that happened to us was that my husband was dismissed along with a lot of other professors. Nobody could tell him why. There was no authority you could go to and ask what was going on. I myself was having my own problems. I was a psychiatrist in a large psychiatric hospital. I also had a number of private clients. We, the psychiatrists, started to be bothered by the police who came to ask us to give them the names of our patients and information about them. They were looking for people who might have joined the Montoneros or any other subversive group who were beginning to go clandestine. And because so many of them were treated by psychiatrists as they all had their conflicts and all sorts of mental problems, the police wanted to check up on them. I knew that, and I could not give out their names, not a single name, because that would have compromised their lives. Other colleagues were in the same situation, we had meetings at the hospital where we all worked and decided not to give out names. But the police insisted, and the pressure was building up. People began to be killed, to disappear – the first person to be killed in La Plata was one of my patients. This first victim was found riddled with bullets. His son, a boy of fifteen, had to go with his mother to identify the body – he went crazy after that. He kept asking, 'Why was his whole body perforated with bullet wounds when only one bullet should have been more than enough to kill him?' It was horrible! The world was turned upside-down. It was nothing to do with us as people, it was not the people's choice. Clearly, it was not our war. We were not subversives. We were not Montoneros. There were 30/50,000 people on their lists. I thought my husband would be on one of those lists too. He thought that I would be on one. More people were disappearing. It happened every day. In the midst of this turmoil my husband made up his mind: 'All right,' he said 'if they are looking for me they won't find me empty-handed.' He got hold of two pistols. He got them loaded and stood there waiting for them to come. He was crazy! I was terribly frightened. We had a little boy and our girl and they were terrified too. It was then that we decided that we could not stay. It was impossible! Neither my husband nor I were able to work or to do anything. The children were overwhelmed by the daily events.

MOSES SPITZ: I knew I was crazy. I could never make up my mind whether I would really use them or not if the situation arose. That does not make sense. If I had started to resist them they would just have blown up the whole house. There was no way I could have defeated them or saved myself. It was a sign of desperation more than anything else.

LYDIA SPITZ: This situation lasted for twelve weeks. Moses learned about his dismissal from the University when we had come back from holiday. That was February 1975. I argued with myself: 'What are we doing here?' He can't stay here. He was not sleeping. Every night I would open my eyes and I would see him standing at the window looking outside, waiting for them to come . . .

MOSES SPITZ: There were definite mechanisms of self-protection. Every morning when we woke up we would look in our newspaper and the first thing was to see how many people have been killed today, and how they were killed, and so on. Almost naturally we were inclined to think, 'Well, he may have been involved. Surely, this chap . . . he may have been involved in something.' It was not a matter of maybe them – 'the death squad' – being right. No. It was, if he was involved and I was not, I know I am not, then they won't come for me. This was the way we wished to reason, the way we tried to comfort ourselves in order to survive. When we discussed things with our friends, we would find that all of us were more or less thinking along the same lines. But I knew very well that they would come. Of course, they would come.

LYDIA SPITZ: We began to think about emigrating. Where to? We started to have meetings with a few other Jewish couples with the idea of going to Israel. There were six families. We wanted to leave together and settle, as a community, in Israel.

The discussions went backwards and forwards but we could not all agree. We all had different feelings. Some people did not want to give up their houses, their jobs . . . their material things. That did not matter that much to us, although we had this newly-built house, a beautiful house which had been designed and furnished specifically for us. We had good jobs, everything was going well. This was the first time in our life we had a decent house. Later on the Israelis offered my husband a research post to work on virology but he was

57

working on cancer. He did not want to change direction, but was prepared to do it as a last resort. That was in the south of the country. I was offered a post in a hospital in the north. So we gave up our plans for Israel. But in 1974, before any of this had started, my husband had invited a number of scientists from different countries, to a conference he organized in his Department at the University. It was the contacts that he had made there that made him decide a year later to try to go to England.

NELLY SALAS: We applied to go either to France, England, or Australia. The first country to offer us a visa was England, three or four months after we had applied. It was a shock. They sent us a telegram which said we had two weeks to leave. We had to pack up and go, just like that. I felt it was as if one was a plant which one day was just uprooted and taken off to another town. Terrible.

MIGUEL ZAMBRANO: England was the only country that offered shelter for the whole family. The others said, 'You come, then your family can follow.' I said to myself, 'England!' I had offers to go to Biarritz, and Holland. Holland is a miserable place. England is paradise in comparison. Biarritz is quite similar to Cartagena, almost a copy. I wanted to go there, but they wanted me without my family. On 21 March 1975 I was released, but conditionally, so every fortnight I had to check into military HQ. Then I was arrested again on 29 June. Another man came, saying things against me. My wife said to me, 'You're stupid. I said before the coup that we should go. We have visas, tickets, everything, what are you waiting for?' The British government had given us visas, and the tickets came from the Committee for European Immigration. But I was so happy to be released, I just started working again. Anyway they didn't want me to leave the country. They said very clearly to my wife, 'You can leave, but he's not going.' They knew I was a journalist – dangerous for them. They said, 'We suspect you of being a top man, that you've been training other people.' When Angelica showed them our tickets, they said, 'This is international Communism, we know how powerful they are.' Finally Angelica said, 'Let's go now.' Members of my Party also said, 'Go now. They're going to kill you eventually. They haven't proved anything in a court of law, now they'll shoot you.' I still said no. I kept on working, business was going well – I was quite prosperous. Then they arrested me a second time. One of the prosecutors told my lawyer, 'The military are going to kill Zambrano.' And the Secretary of the Court said, 'Go now, they're looking for you.' We found out that our old flat had been searched at 4 a.m., everybody pushed outside with guns at their heads. They were looking for me. Even then I was reluctant to leave, but we decided to go. It was winter, the border with Argentina was closed. Heavy snowstorms. I had no passport.

MOSES SPITZ: We did not want to go to America, it did not seem to have the sort of lifestyle we liked. We preferred Europe. I knew people from England who I had met in my job. My best possibility of finding work was in London and Cambridge where we had a very good friend. Also in Stockholm, Paris, Basle or Israel. So I bought a round-trip ticket that would take in the lot. It was still quite easy to leave. I got my passport. I got my ticket. It was not that they wanted us to leave, but they were not that efficiently organized. One department had one bit of information, another would have something different. There were nine independent intelligence services, each with its own department, each with its own way of doing things. They did not talk to each other. Even in 1976, when the worst of the killing was going on, they did not try to co-ordinate. The Navy had their list, they killed their people. The Army had their list. The Air Force had theirs. The police had theirs, even within the police there were different departments. They were even killing members of each other's squads.

LYDIA SPITZ: In the end we had to push my husband very hard because he did not want to leave. He wanted just to go into the country. He had the feeling that this situation was going to be short, that it was going to blow over and that then things would go back to normal. But it did not. In fact it got worse. So he got this ticket, three months' round-trip. We went to say goodbye to a colleague, another professor, the food was excellent but our friend was not happy to see us go. He believed that we had to stay on and help to normalize the country. 'How?' we asked. A year later we received his letter from Venezuela where he emigrated with his family. Another good friend, also a professor, came to say goodbye. He could not understand what we were doing. We pleaded with him to leave. I do not think he was exactly naïve, but he said, 'I have nothing to fear. My thoughts, feelings and beliefs are absolutely clear and open. I say what I think I should. I do what I do. There is nothing wrong with it.' A few months later he disappeared and two days later he was killed and his body, riddled with bullets, was found somewhere in a lonely street.

* * *

VICTOR WILD: In the 1930s even Switzerland felt the draught of the Depression. It was all very unsettling, talk of revolutions and goodness knows what. It was then, in 1936, that my uncle, who had no children, wrote to my mother and said, 'How about sending your lad to me? I'll look after him and I'll educate him and give him the opportunity of going into the business.' She was a very loving mother and it must have been quite a thing for her. But she agreed that if I wanted to go she would agree. I find it extraordinary today how strongly, at the age of thirteen, I felt, yes, I want to go. I was very happy at home; we hadn't much money but I wasn't made to feel the absence of money.

I didn't suffer from it, even if I couldn't do what some of my friends did. But there was something about this England that attracted me as an adventure.

DON ATYEO: There was an assumption that sooner or later you would leave. If you had any intellectual pretensions, or cultural pretensions – and they were very much pretensions at the age of eighteen – you looked towards England. Australia was a very ill-mannered and illiterate country. It was very repressive – they were still tearing the centre pages out of *Playboy*. I read *Portnoy's Complaint* in a xeroxed copy which was circulated round my university. It was an extremely provincial country and the authorities were determined to keep it that way. So by the age of eighteen I was determined to leave. Anyone who was looking towards a career in the arts felt that way. If you wanted to be an accountant or a lawyer, then you stayed, but otherwise – writing, journalism, art – your first move was to get out. It had been like that for years. Immediately before me were the Clive Jameses, Germaine Greers and so on, but before that there had been people like my uncle who left in the '30s, when there was a huge wave of people hopping on the boat. He was an artist and an architect and he had left at about the same age as I did, around twenty, and for exactly the same reasons: stifled by the puritanism and provincialism of Australia. So it wasn't that I was special, it was just a thing that you did. Leaving wasn't something, however, that you did for good. It was a long way away, and you were very conscious that it was a long way away, so you thought when you left that you were just going for a while.

SUSAN WILSON: My own coming to England from New Zealand is a nice contradiction. Mine was a family who had definitely wanted to leave England. I didn't come here deliberately. I had a very chequered career. I got expelled from teachers' college for being involved in radical politics. I had been considered an unsuitable influence on the class and probably a Communist. I was very left-wing and my boyfriend at the time was Maoist. I trained as a nurse after I'd been expelled – nurses didn't mind what my politics were. After I qualified I worked in the head injury unit in the neuro-surgical department. Then I got totally fed up and felt I was going to be stuck there forever. So in 1976 I decided to go to South America with a boyfriend. Everyone thought I was crazy, particularly my left-wing friends. They were very paranoid about the CIA and they said, 'You'll be jailed, you'll be in trouble. Why don't you go to China?' But I went to Peru. This old neuro-surgeon told me, 'Why don't you go for God's sake? It'll be a great experience. Just wear old army clothes and carry an old bag and you'll be fine.' And it *was* a wonderful experience. But I had a ticket all the way to Paris – that was the cheapest way to get to South America – so I used it. I got sick in South America and what happened was I came on to London. I spoke the language, and I went into hospital. I had

60

amoebic dysentery. Nothing very dramatic but just enough to make me really quite ill.

DAVILIA DAVID: The way to get into theatre in those days was to come to England, to RADA – which was the only drama school we'd heard of in Australia. Then you'd come back and get all the leading parts. Also, if you came from a small town, England was very much the mother country and to go to England was to return to one's roots. Most people 'did' Europe for a couple of years before coming home to settle down. So my sister and I, once we'd decided to go, booked the boat eighteen months ahead and started saving for the fare; it was £146.

RONALD HARWOOD: All my childhood, coming to England had been my goal. At the time it was because England seemed so glamorous, so romantic. Now, at fifty-four, I think it was probably due to psychological problems I might have had about wanting to escape the family background. My parents were terribly unhappy, although I seemed to cope and was never disturbed by it. But I do think that part of this passionate urge to get away was due perhaps to that. I had wanted to be an actor from an early age. My father was a Lithuanian and not much interested in it, but my mother, who had come from England with Polish parents, thought all art, and especially the theatre, was one's salvation. When I was a child the film that had most affect on me was Olivier's *Hamlet*. I saw it six times and my sister gave me 78 rpm records of it. I played it endlessly. So in 1951 I came to England to study acting.

JOHN LAHR: One of my problems was that in New York I was working as a critic and I was being touted as and was indeed offered the job of theatre critic on *Time* and on the *New York Post*. That was in the early '70s. All my theatre friends wanted me to do it – they could see good reviews for the rest of their lives. But it was nowhere for me, a dead end. So in a sense coming to England was a way of changing my act, in every way. The literary way, the metaphysical personal way, and growing up. The great thing of my adult life has been raising my son. I have just loved every minute of being a father. My father, because of the hand fate dealt him, and his own monumental self-involvement, was not 'there'. He said to my mother, 'You had 'em, you raise 'em.' He was present at the conception and that was about it. Had we lived in Manhattan we probably wouldn't have had a child, because it was too unhappy a scene, too frenetic and fraught. Also I would have been drawn by all the input of New York, the excitement, the job offers, the things that happened.

FERDIE ERASMUS: I was in South Africa, just gone through a nasty divorce. I was thirty-five, chief quantity surveyor for a company with 20,000 employees, director, general manager of an area the size of England, had a Mercedes, a BMW, a couple of houses. I'd always had a driving ambition to do well, but never knew quite how I was going to do it. I'd always had a tremendous affinity with England and I knew if I left, it would be to go to England. I came over in 1986 on a business trip – well, just to have a look round really. I was mesmerized by Heseltine, the Westland affair. I thought, 'By God, these people don't half rabbit on about things. In South Africa, it would be finished – end of story.' Anyway, I came across, and met a girl on the train. We became friends and I decided, 'Sod it, meeting her is an extra incentive to come across.' It was either stay in Jo'burg, become managing director, have a nice house in the country, or go to England and start at the bottom, and it was really at the bottom. I came over with £300, whereas I'd been earning a six-figure salary in South Africa.

MICHAEL IGNATIEFF: In winter 1978 I accepted a fellowship to teach at King's, Cambridge, starting the next academic year, 1979. By that time I had met and married my English wife. There is in every Canadian boy that sense that is so well captured in Judy Garland's song: 'For years I've had it preached to me and drummed into my head / Unless you've played the Palace, you might as well be dead.' And for all Canadian boys the Palace is not in Canada. It is England, or the States, or 'anywhere but here' as the Canadian motto runs. How I fell for that I now look at in wonderment. I think you can have a very central and interesting and important life in Canada if you want to. Though temperamentally I was more European than Canadian. So coming to England was coming back to Europe. It wasn't coming home, because what I came to was something that made much fewer claims on me than the word 'home'.

* * *

BHAJAN SINGH CHADHA: After '57–58 our financial position was not too good. The Africans were getting trained and were starting to operate in direct competition to the Indian community in Kenya. They were taking over more and more of the minor jobs. On the other hand British power was decreasing all the time and it was generally becoming accepted that one day the British would leave. All of which meant that our lives were not as secure as they had been. Our family business was not doing very well. So everybody was starting to look towards England as somewhere where we might find a second chance. It was still easy to enter England. If you were a Kenyan citizen and had a British passport, there was no problem. All I had to do was go and get my passport stamped. I wasn't thinking of coming permanently. I wanted to come and make some money, really I was following a trend. I was married and had two little daughters, but I couldn't get a very good job so I thought I'd go and see what England had to offer.

62

GULZAR KHAN: I came to England from Pakistan in 1962. At that time there was a trend coming through – people were starting to go to England. They would tell you, 'There's a lot of money.' People would go there and come back rich after four or five years. The idea of making more money made a lot of difference – my pay was 200 or 300 rupees, about £20, a month.

The Kashmiri people who have come here are mostly from the Mirpur district, though I am from the Ponch district, from where very few people have come – there may not be more than 1,000 in the whole of England. The Mirpuri people had started coming in the early '50s – some worked on the ships. They came here, saw the opportunities, brought over their friends, then their families and so on. They knew much more about England than we did. So while I was in Karachi there were lots of people selling everything – their family gold, their family land – to pay for air tickets to England. The fare was around 1,300 rupees. Everybody was trying to come to England. The idea was not to stay, it was to come, to make money and to go home. A five-year plan. To be honest, I wasn't that interested in coming. But I had a friend. He was from Mirpur and he was very interested in coming to England. We had a mutual friend who was the president of Kashmir at that time. My friend told me that if one had a prominent figure who would vouch for you and give you references, it was easier to get a passport. But I wasn't interested. I had a pretty good job, I was a Customs inspector, I had a couple of people working for me, I was fine. I had a wife, a family. So leaving was not my goal. But when my friend suggested I get references from the president I thought, well, I'd try. So I saw him and he said, 'What can I do for you?' I told him that I wanted to return to Kashmir and I wanted a good job. He said, 'If you come back and if I give you a job, it will be a political job, and after two years or whatever I shall be off and then the next person will sack you. Is there anything else you want?' So I said, 'I want to go to England.' He said, 'Go and bring the forms.' I brought them, he signed at once and gave them to me. Then I filled them in, and added a photograph. He signed that too. So I got my passport, it was 1958. I didn't leave till '62 – my enthusiasm was still not that great. I had the passport in my pocket, but still I wasn't interested. I was transferred from Karachi to Lahore, then to the north-west frontier. Then another friend of mine wanted to come to England and he said, 'Let's go together.' This time I was persuaded. I thought, 'OK, I'll go for four or five years.' I had nothing to go to, no job. But we knew that the immigration laws were changing, that from 1 June 1962 there would be restrictions on visas. Before that there were no problems. So I applied. I borrowed some money, bought my ticket and flew to England in April.

SHREERAM VIDYARTHI: I was working as a journalist on the *Times of India* when I heard from a few friends from my earlier days who had already emigrated to England on labour vouchers. Up to 1962 there was a system where overseas Commonwealth citizens could apply for labour vouchers and come to England in search of work. You didn't have to have a job, what you needed was the voucher. Jobs were plentiful in England in those days. They had worked on building sites and in tea-packing factories and Wimpey bars. They made £6 a week which, when you converted it into rupees, seemed like riches. These friends had last seen me in Bombay, in abject poverty, and hadn't kept up with what had happened since. In fact as a journalist I was making good money – between my salary and my freelance work I was making around 2,000 rupees a month, which was very good pay – but my friends still assumed that I was a poor sod scribbling through the nights for nothing. And they thought, 'Let's get him over to England and help him grow rich.' So they engineered some kind of a scholarship through a college in Sussex. They obtained a document which claimed that I had been given a scholarship that would take care of me and my wife. I would pay my fare and I could come to England and study. The prospect of going abroad for further study and enhancing my brilliant career didn't enter my mind: a career I already had, but the idea of opening up my mind, of brightening my image, of increasing my learning, that did fascinate me. I thought I'd go, I'd study and I'd make a new career. It wasn't England that appealed, but broadening my mind certainly did. So instead of sensibly taking leave without pay, securing my career in case I needed to come back, I promptly resigned, sold all my belongings, bought two plane tickets and landed in England. I wasn't leaving India, but on the other hand I wasn't worried whether or not I came back. It wasn't an act of emigration, it was just moving in order to further my aims, to expand my abilities.

RAJINDER SINGH: I didn't really know much about England when I was growing up, but later, when I was in the Navy, I did start to wonder whether we could go there or not. My elder brother did emigrate there, but up to then we did not know we had the right of abode in this country because our mother was illiterate, and she knew nothing of such things. In 1955, when my brother arrived, he wrote to us to say that we had British nationality and that we could come over here. But even then we didn't bother to come. In 1962 my youngest brother applied for admission as part of the voucher system quota. And on that basis he was allowed to settle in England in 1963. But we still did not utilize our right. Then in 1972, when my eldest brother retired from the military in India, he went to the British High Commission and asked for permission to emigrate. But they refused him admission, because we had lost our parents' passports – my father had a British passport, my mother had an Indian one – and we had no proof of our being born in Tanganyika. They asked us to prove that we were really our father's sons. They wanted to get proof in writing from

64

people who had lived in our village. Luckily another brother, who had been in Lahore during Partition, had got both the passports and explained to the British that this brother was the oldest, and while he had had both the passports, during Partition he had been forced to flee and leave everything there. So they agreed. We had our birth certificates and on that basis he did give us entry. Even then I didn't bother. But after he had settled he pressed me to come over because now most of my family was here. In 1975 he came to India and brought my mother to England. So after all that I decided that I should go. But when I applied for entry it took me nine years to get it. I had a son, who at that time was sixteen years old. When they ask you to fill in the forms, they ask, 'Who will follow you to England later on?' I had only my wife and my son to follow me. So I gave their particulars on the form. He was sixteen. If he had been over eighteen, he would not have had the right to come – he would no longer be dependent on me. They told me that there was a big queue for admissions and that it might take some time until my name came up. They gave me a statement in writing that said that they would consider my son's age to be that which it was when I made my first application. Moreover they will consider his case right up to the twenty-fifth year of his life, provided he is wholly dependent on me. But what happened was this: in 1984 my son became twenty-five. Two weeks after his birthday they wrote to me accepting my application, but not his. They cheated me. I fought the case over here but they dismissed it. My wife came over here for a while, but she was ill here and she has gone back. My son is still in India. So I had to come by myself. It was a very difficult decision: my family is split up and I am not satisfied over here.

NISSIM ELIJAH: One of my wife's cousins, Ben Samson, was First Admiral of India, Lieutenant-General. He was sent to Israel for specialized training. But after independence word got round, 'We don't want foreigners,' so slowly they started getting rid of us. Close friends suddenly cut me dead. Officers started shouting at me, and eventually I resigned. I had been demoted to Superintendent. I should have been very much higher up. I was not the only one. Jews were considered as foreigners, as were the Anglo-Indians. Finally, I decided it was no place for me or my children, there was no future there. That was in 1962. After Partition we had hoped it would get better, but it got worse. Active anti-Semitism emerged. There was an underground movement to throw all foreigners out. Some of us were actually told, 'We don't want you here, why do you stay?' We sent a deputation to Indira Gandhi. She said, 'Oh, I don't know anything about it.' So we started to clear off – some to Israel, others to America, Canada, England, Australia. I opted for England because I'd worked with English officers, and I'd studied a lot of English, as well as French.

RAMESH VALA: After primary education [in Kenya] I went to secondary school, the Duke of Gloucester School. This was an Asian equivalent of a British public school. I wanted to be a lawyer, I'd wanted to be a lawyer when I was eight. I can't explain it. We had an English teacher from Warwickshire and he told me that if I wanted to do law, there was only one place: the London School of Economics. I was brash enough to think I would get in, and luckily I did. In 1963 the idea was that if you were British and if you held on to your passport you had the right to come to Britain. That stopped in 1968, after which you had to apply for a visa, to get a voucher rather than just come. In 1968 those who reckoned there would be a better life in Britain came over; the very rich had already moved most of their money out, but they didn't want to leave, they had a terrific life in Kenya. It wasn't as dramatic an exodus as what happened in Uganda. This was a matter of 3,000 people rushing out in a week, because of what the Labour government in London was doing on immigration. In Uganda you had 30,000 who were driven out by Amin. But there were all these people working out the best way to get into England: if you came via Dublin you weren't stopped – they assumed you were coming from Europe – whereas if you came in direct you were likely to be stopped, you were likely to spend some time in a detention centre. But we did not leave. I came in October 1973. In 1963, with the children being the age they were, and my mother having just died, my father had come under intense pressure to become a Kenyan citizen. People said, 'If you go to England, you're not educated, your children are very young, what will you do there?' So he handed in his British passport and took Kenyan citizenship. But we children retained the British passports we had been given prior to independence. So I was permitted to enter to pursue my studies, but I still needed a voucher if I wanted to settle here.

PO-YEE WONG: I was born in the Republic of China, of a middle-class family. My father was a poet. My initial education was Chinese, then I went to Hong Kong and had some English education. I wanted to become a doctor – either western or oriental. One uncle had a Chinese herbal shop in Hong Kong, and one is a Chinese physician. I was involved heavily in Chinese medicine. But there's no Chinese medical school in Hong Kong, only western medical education is recognized. Without a certificate you could only work in the black market, and I didn't want that. I tried to get into the School of Nursing, but didn't realize how difficult it would be. Before then, England was never in my mind. I had no connection in family terms with the British in Hong Kong, my environment was Chinese. Anyway, it didn't seem I could get a medical career there, and a friend suggested I try England. To get in, I needed a combined student and work permit, to come here to study nursing. It was too easy to get here. I got addresses out of *Nursing Mirror*, wrote to some hospitals, and one was very keen and they arranged the paperwork for me. When I got the permit, I realized for the first time that I would be leaving Hong Kong. I arrived around 1970, three months too early. I wanted to make sure my English was good before I started work.

NIEN-LUN YEH: I came here by sheer chance. I was teaching in a post-graduate school. Indeed, if I had stayed on, maybe I would have a better career than I do here. I could at least be an associate professor. But I was very keen to see the world. And at that time (1980) China had just opened the doors to the outside world. The government encouraged people to study in the West through all possible channels. Private, official, whatever. They couldn't afford to send so many official students but they encouraged individuals to go abroad to study if they could. My wife (Cui Qu) and I had been married for one year, but we had to part. Like mine, her father is also a famous writer and our families had known each other for many years. Though we had always worked and studied in different places. I came first to York University. I had applied to various universities but they accepted me. They didn't know of my father and I knew nobody here.

CUI QU: I was a paediatrician in China, I'd been working at a large children's hospital for six years. My husband came here first. I didn't especially want to come here but I knew that my husband had always wanted to go abroad. I had a very good job and at that time I didn't want to go anywhere. But my husband wanted to go, the door was open and I couldn't stop him. At first I was worried, very, very sad: if my husband went abroad and I could not go to join him what will happen to me? But he said, 'I go first. Either I come back after my year of study or you come to England and join me.' I thought, 'All right. I'll take a trip to England, stay there for a short time and then make him come back to China with me.' I wanted to see the world too, but I didn't want to leave China for good. I felt that starting a new life in a strange new country would be very hard work. Also I loved my job, I cared about the children, it was my profession and if I left to visit England, then I would have to go back.

* * *

VINCENT REID: It was 1948. I was thirteen. My old man had read in the *Gleaner* about the wonderful opportunities that were being offered to us, to black people. You could come to England and you could get work and so on. It was just work. The ads for the buses and the hospitals came later, and they were largely aimed at Barbadans and the like. The first recruitment was simply to get a labour force into this country. Certain kinds of laws had been passed in this country, the Education Act (of 1944) was a very important one, which meant that you could now have education up to the age of fifteen. Therefore you need a kind of holding labour force, some people that could fill the gap. Also of course the expectations of English people were such that these kinds of

67

brutal work, working unsocial hours, doing the kind of jobs that we finally did, the English didn't want to do, because their expectations had been raised. None of that was spelt out. What was spelt out was that coming here would offer you a great opportunity for continuous labour.

MIKE PHILLIPS: I was fourteen when we left, 1955, coming up to 1956. My grandmother told me we were going and things began to arrive, like warm clothes. Sweaters. We got on a boat, a Dutch boat, and it took twenty-one days. It left Guyana and went to Surinam and then to Southampton. I remember driving to the boat along Shell Road where we lived, in an old rickety car, which belonged to a man who as I recall was called Mr Nightingale, who used to drive people back and forth, and all the kids, all these kids that I grew up with, we were born the same year and we'd been together every day of our lives, and they were all lined up, shouting and waving . . . I've never seen them again. It makes me cry now. We went on this boat and in Surinam we picked up a company of Dutch soldiers who were going to Holland.

MICHAEL DE SOUZA: My father had left Trinidad in about 1956. There was no work and no money and at that time the British government were really trying to encourage people to emigrate, saying that England is your country and there's opportunities and we want you. I don't think they actually advertised, but that was the mood. A short time later he sent for my mum, then my brother, then myself. That was 1960, I was six. The whole experience was very strange. I didn't know where I was going, I didn't know I was going abroad, that I was leaving my family. It was very traumatic. I was living with my great-aunt and my cousins, I couldn't really recall my mum living in Trinidad. So when it came time for me to go to England they didn't even tell me what was happening. They did it in such a horrible way. One day they dressed me up in my little shorts and whatnot and said, 'Right, we're going to get our photo taken.' So we went to this place, posed up, stiff, not smiling, got to be like a surfboard. Maybe it was for a passport, maybe it was a memento for my great-aunt. Anyway, that was the first stage. The next stage was, 'Come on, we're going.' And I'm saying, 'Where?' I don't know where I'm going. That was it. Someone held my hand, took me to this boat and that was that.

DESMOND GITTENS: My ambition was to follow my family heritage and join the British merchant navy. But I never achieved it, not the British merchant navy. Instead I joined a Norwegian ship. That was because of a simple stupid incident in Trinidad after I left school. I belonged to a steel band, and a steel band at that time was also a gang. It wasn't just a musical gang, it was the gang of the area that you lived in. I came from what you might call an underprivi-leged, bad area. If you went outside that area you would be picked up by the police. I was picked up by the police in September 1957 and was charged with riotous assembly and all sorts of silly things. I was actually doing nothing. Just walking around. But I was out of my area and I was asked where I lived and I gave the address and as soon as they realized the area that was that. So I thought it best – 'Desmond, get out of this, get out of here.' I went down to the Norwegian Consulate and I was fixed up on board a ship that used to go up the Mongo River in Surinam to bring back aluminium. That job lasted eighteen months, two years.

TONY GIRARD: I was in my late teens, and I was more or less on my own. My elder brother was in Barbados. The rest of my family were working, but I couldn't get a job. Everybody was leaving for England. People would ask me, did I want to go to England? I'd say, 'No, England's too far.' I had no intention of coming up here. People saw me as mummy's boy, but England was too far. What would happen if I got bored, got lonely? I couldn't just run back home. After a while I decided to join my brother Harry in Barbados. I stayed there for thirteen months. When I returned home my other brothers, Peter and Dennis, had both gone to England and by now most of my friends, if not all, had already left for England. They were leaving for survival. As simple as that. There was no work at all, or hardly any. We all had British passports and there were ships dropping in on their way to Britain virtually every week. Every week you'd see so many hundred people leaving for England. It became an exodus. I'd go and see them off. They'd go, then later they'd send for their families. Then their friends would go and so on. My mum wasn't keen. I was the last of the children. I didn't want to leave her but people told me, 'If you've got to go, go.' The day I left she came up. 'What's the matter? You going and you're not saying goodbye.' I said, 'No. I'm just going to tell a few friends goodbye. I'll be back.' She says, 'Oh, you'd better kiss me now.' She knew what I was doing. She did not want me to go, but she knew that I was off. I couldn't bear seeing her waving on the wharf. It was 1960.

WILK WALKER: My father had left Trinidad in 1958. The family say that I'm the one who suggested England. I don't remember. My father had a friend who was already here, working for BCC, which is now RACAL. They had studied electronics together. He was working in the American bases, repairing BCC telecommunications equipment. So there were jobs and my father came over by himself and got one. He came on a very posh cruise liner called the *Southern Cross* which occasionally took normal passengers. It wasn't a usual immigrant boat. My father came here, worked for a year, then sent for my mother. The plan was that they would send for the two eldest sisters. I was the eldest child, but it was best to get the girls away as soon as possible. But because what was happening to me was so grim, because I was so unhappy in

69

Trinidad, I wrote to my parents and said I felt really wretched and that they had to send for me first. So they sent me the money and I bought my own ticket. When I went to get a passport I was told to get a birth certificate; when I went to get my birth certificate I was told that my birth had not been registered. I was fourteen and I didn't officially exist. Fortunately I did have a baptismal certificate and I was able to use that. So I bought my ticket and I left. I didn't tell anyone. I figured that anything would be better than what I was going through in Trinidad. I had no real friends, no real life, I was feeling very very wretched and inferior and I thought anything would be better than that. My father had felt exactly the same thing when he left. The wretchedness of being poor and black in that island.

VINCENT REID: The expectation was that West Indians wouldn't settle. In a way I don't think that the black people who came here were ever seen as immigrants. They were seen as temporary labourers, almost as the *Gastarbeiter* are in Germany today. The expectation was that in a couple of years or so, if that long, we would return home. There were two reasons why I was brought, aged thirteen. One was that I had got a scholarship to St George's College, the best school in Jamaica. But clearly my family couldn't afford to send me there. The scholarship covered all the fees, but in the holidays there would be nobody to look after me. Secondly they thought, well, coming to England would give me the opportunity to acquire an education and to progress. They had no idea of what England was like, therefore they had no idea of education there or of anything else. Just this kind of optimism.

BENNY BUNSEE: I always had an intellectual curiosity, a desire to understand the world in which I lived. I left home after my mother died. There were three deaths in my family within six months – my two brothers died and then my mum. So I left home. I began to travel, all over South Africa. I was footloose, a feckless writer. My mother died of poverty really. One of my brothers had just come out of prison; he was my mother's favourite. A week after he came out of prison he was run over by a bus. I went around looking for him, all the police stations, the hospitals, I couldn't find him. I heard there had been a bus accident – I never thought it could be him. Two months later my other brother died, which was too much for my mum and she died also. So after that I left home. That was the end of all roots. The struggle in South Africa, what had happened in my family, my own intellectual crisis over my identity, the state of our people all combined. And I wanted to get out altogether, I wanted to leave South Africa and try to begin life somewhere else. So I left. I went to Zambia, I went to Tanzania. This was 1960. And when I was in Tanzania I began thinking about coming to England, to settle here, to enjoy the freedoms here, to educate myself even more. To gain more knowledge, to get that easy access to books and literature which was impossible in South Africa. I would see the

70

New Statesman or *The Observer* and see all these books being advertised and think, 'Oh my God, if I could just get all these books . . .'

* * *

BRYAN GOULD: The assumption that at some stage one would come to Britain is common now but it was less so then. There was never really a moment of decision. I had done very well at school, always winning this, that and the other. I won a national scholarship to go to university when I was fifteen, that sort of thing. In my last year at secondary school, when I'd won this scholarship, a boy some years ahead of me had won a Rhodes scholarship to Oxford. He was a great hero in the school. So that created in me the idea that to get a Rhodes scholarship was a very good thing, a feeling in which my parents, who actually knew very little about it but were very ambitious, backed me up. So when I went to university and began to realize I was doing very well it began to occur to me that I might actually win a Rhodes scholarship. And I did win one. I was intensely interested in British politics. Heaven knows why, being that far away. So part of the attraction was that winning the scholarship would bring me to Britain.

MANDY MERCK: The first thing was that I went from the Midwest to Smith, a women's college in Massachusetts, no small step, in fact a vast culture shock. The culture shock in going to Smith was vastly more than moving from Smith to Oxford. For the first time I was in an extremely rich, class-stratified environment where people were actively anti-Semitic, anti-Irish. One Boston girl referred to the 'pig shit Irish' in front of an Irish room-mate. In a sense, Smith sent me to England though it was rather a wrong turn to go to Oxford, academically. It was a disaster. Vocationally it led me up the primrose path for a very long time. But I didn't want to be an American graduate student in a Midwestern campus with Chianti bottles on the wall, and furtive memories of once being in Europe for a fortnight. I wanted to do it, to be it. Then I'd loftily snub it. I was in the grip of Europhilia, which even then I thought was a bit naff. I wanted to climb to the top and look down the hill. The best way seemed to be to go and live there for a while. I assumed I would return to the States, but I didn't.

BERNIE GRANT: I was very lively kid and I passed all my exams when I was very young but I think I got a very raw deal from the Jesuits who ran my school: they wouldn't put me into the sixth form because they felt that I had a discipline problem. They thought I was a bit of a radical. So they put me in a form called 5th Remove, which was rather like a purgatory where you had to spend a year before you were allowed into a sixth form and did A levels. The point was that

71

everyone in the sixth form was a prefect, and they couldn't face having me as a prefect. So I got fed up with this and I left and I worked as an analyst in the laboratory of an aluminium company for the next couple of years. I came to England to complete my education. I was working in the bauxite industry and now I wanted to be a mining engineer. My mother had already left Guyana and was living in Britain, so I came to join her. She had come over in 1960 to work and for her health. She had high blood pressure and she needed a more temperate climate. She was teaching. I arrived in 1963, I was nineteen.

SHARI PEACOCK: I left Bulgaria in 1975. What happened was that an uncle of mine who as an architect, who was always travelling around, had given a few lectures at the Architectural Association in London; also he had a friend who taught there full time. Meanwhile I had just started studying architecture in Bulgaria. So he said, leave it and we'll take you to London. He deposited enough money in a bank for me and my mother to come and stay as my chaperone for a year. But after a year they got rather fed up with paying for us, and said they would arrange for me to get a grant. I managed to get a grant from the Iranian government.

CINDY BLAKE: I came to England in 1977. I had been working for Jimmy Carter and then in a bar and the combination of the two were crazy-making. I needed to get away. I wanted to go to Vienna, but I stopped off in London on my way to Vienna. I decided on the trip because I'd seen a Perry Como Christmas special about Vienna and I thought that would be a good idea. But I stopped off here and that's when I met Bill, my future husband. I did get to Vienna eventually, but I decided that I'd confused Vienna with Venice and that's where I really wanted to go, although Perry Como had sung in Vienna. Vienna was horrible, but Venice was nice. I travelled around, but then I came back because Bill wanted to marry me. I didn't actually realize that I'd be living here for the rest of my life. It didn't quite sink in.

MIRANDA LOVETT: I was working as the sort of girl Friday to a Chinaman who lived in the penthouse of an apartment building in New York, which he shared with an Englishman, whose name was Byron Lovett, my future husband. They both worked out of the apartment. He worked for a company that represented artists, illustrators and designers. I saw this name on the door and this name was so completely foreign. It wasn't like Bob Smith or whatever. He smacked a little bit of the '60s. He wore crushed velvet ties, Deborah and Clare shirts, very fitted velvet jackets and those Stirling Cooper trousers with the codpiece. That look which was so different from the chinos and Lacoste shirts which people I knew were wearing. It was new and kind of cool. I slowly started doing work for Byron and we started going out about a month later, then I stopped working for them and I got another job which I kept for three years and I started living with Byron. What finally brought me to London was that in September 1973 he moved back here. We had never talked about marriage, we had never talked about spending the rest of our lives together or anything like that. It was just wait and see. But I came here and I think that he had decided that he did want to marry me and he wanted to see how I got along with England and how England got along with me. So about six months later he asked me to marry him. A lot of people have suggested that it must have been a huge decision for me, coming to England, but that wasn't the decision – the decision was whether I married him, it had nothing to do with whether I lived here or whether I could live here or would be happy living here: it was just if you love someone and you're going to marry them, that's it.

4 Crossing the Line

'You get on board and off you go. It wasn't planned. It was never a deliberate act of immigration, just an adventure.'

VICTOR WILD: There were no dramas on the journey from Switzerland. By the time I made the trip there were airplanes and we flew to Croydon. It took three hours. My uncle came down to meet me. The journey was perfectly smooth although airplanes in those days flew pretty low and you were carefully forbidden to have any cameras in case you photographed the Maginot Line, which was the big thing. You were very carefully watched as you flew over France that you didn't produce a camera out of your rucksack. Tensions were growing in Europe, a lot of paranoia about spies.

BIANCA GORDON: Being selected for a *Kindertransport* was not due to merit, but simply luck. Those of us whom came were not selected because we were more deserving, more gifted – nothing of the kind. It was sheer luck. This is important to stress because people have the impression that many who came on the *Kindertransport* must have been carefully selected. They appear reasonable, have, by and large, settled down and proceeded to build up their life constructively. Those chosen must therefore have been considered special. This was not the case. Sheer luck enabled the 9,732 of us to get out. Over a million children were killed in the Holocaust. Our awareness of this has caused many of us great anguish.

Following *Kristallnacht* we had one week to prepare for our departure. We were allowed hand luggage – a rucksack or a small case. At some unearthly hour of the morning, on a very cold winter day, December 13, 1938, we gathered in darkness at the Anhalter Bahnhof in Berlin. The timing was deliberate: planned in this way, so that the German people should not see what was happening. We gathered in the large station waiting hall when suddenly we were told to proceed to the platform. Hurriedly, we had to move on without our mothers, and without being able to say goodbye. This was a further shattering demonstration of Nazi cruelty. There were, I believe, six hundred of us crowding into the train. The platform was empty. For us it was a heartbreaking farewell. No one there, to comfort, or to be comforted. As we crossed Germany, more children were picked up, but invariably empty platforms, children without parents, and no farewells.

We were accompanied by Jewish welfare workers or teachers, the majority of whom had to go back again. Before we reached the Dutch border, the social worker in charge of our transport came into our compartment and asked to inspect our luggage. This was to ensure that no delays would occur at the frontier. I opened my case, and he noticed a bundle of letters, letters from dear friends who had emigrated. They were precious belongings to which I clung. He advised that they must be torn up before we reached Holland. He was afraid the Gestapo or the SS might delay our departure to check 'secret documents'. I was very sad, and wept. I sat by the window, and tore up the letters which had meant so much to me. The tears may have been a delayed reaction to the cruel farewell scene at the Anhalter Bahnhof.

At the Dutch frontier the scene changed. A marvellously warm-hearted welcome was extended to us on every station in Holland. Women and children were boarding the platform with hot drinks – it was a very cold winter – and chocolate, cakes and sweets. It was hard to trust our eyes. We had come out of an inferno into a civilized world, where there were people – strangers – with kind faces, smiling at us and greeting us warmly.

MARIA VOROSKOI: In 1947 it was still reasonably easy for me to travel, although it was not so for everyone. It was terribly difficult to get a passport. Since my brother had been in the resistance he had been asked to join the Hungarian police force. The people who recruited him were later executed as traitors to the great Communist cause. One day my brother told his boss, 'I'm finished. I'm leaving.' They offered him anything he wanted but he rejected everything. What he really wanted was to see the restoration of the old monarchy. He got a small motorboat and set himself up as a motor taxi driver on the Danube. It suited him much more than being a policeman. Then someone tipped him off that because he had left the police he was now on a blacklist. He tried to get permission to leave, but they kept saying, 'No passport.' Then his best friend, whose father was a leader of the monarchist movement, was one day just spirited away and never heard of again. Someone said to my brother, 'Look out, you might be next.' So my brother escaped, in the most daring way as he always did everything. He just put on his riding boots and went down to the frontier. It was harvest time and the peasants were in the fields. He went up to some of them and said, 'I always enjoy harvesting, let me join in.' They told him, 'Sir, if you're mad, be mad,' and they gave him a scythe. So he started working, and as he worked he watched the way the guards patrolled the border and started timing them. He knew the fence was electrified during the night, though it was turned off during the day, so he had to go during the day. So he waited until the guard was as far away as possible, then leapt the fence into Austria. There were Austrian peasants, also harvesting, and he told them the same story, and started harvesting with them. The guard saw him as he marched back and gave him a look as if to say, 'Didn't I see that tall guy on the other side?' Then a woman arrived on a bicycle with food for her husband. My brother persuaded her to let him ride the bike, with her on the crossbar, to the nearest railway station and from there he went to Vienna. Eventually he went to Australia, where he died in 1987.

* * *

VINCENT REID: To get on the *Empire Windrush* you had to cough up £28 10s as an adult, then £14 for me, half-price. For somebody who was poor this was quite a sacrifice. Just for the privilege of coming to the mother country to do their brute labour. But the money was paid and we got to the *Windrush*. That trip was the point at which I woke up to . . . the word 'racism' wasn't used in those days: it was called 'the colour bar' or 'racial discrimination'. We landed in Bermuda, about three days into the voyage, and we all came ashore and went to a cinema. For the first time in my life I experienced a racially segregated audience. You paid your money but you had to sit in a certain place based on the colour of your skin. As far as I personally was concerned it didn't strike me as being anything absurd, but the other people on this boat, returning servicemen and so on, resented it and there were fights. I suspect that we helped desegregate Bermuda. They wanted to refund our money, but some of the men said, 'No way, we want to see the film and we're going to see it.' And we did.

MARY DENYS: It was one of these Italian boats, the *Bianca C.* The sea and I do not get along, and I was so seasick. It wasn't only me. You could see the sick going this way and that, up and down along the floor of the cabin. I was so sick. They had to give me injections. It took about fifteen days. Every time you passed the dining-room you'd hear someone else throwing up, and the smell . . . It was terrible. There were a couple of hundred of us. Loads of people. Some people got divorced on that boat, some people got married. What happened was that there's a man over here. He sees a picture of a girl back home, he sends for her to come and get married. But she meets another man on the boat and instead of going with the guy in England she turns up with somebody else. There I am in my cabin, being sick all the time, and at the same time the girl who's sharing it is having a bit in the other bunk. I was too sick for any of that. We went to Tenerife first, then docked at Genoa. The rest of the journey was overland by train. What a surprise it was arriving at Genoa, to see these men with guns, the Italian policemen. I was frightened; we'd never seen anything like it. We had to lug our things from the boat to the train and after the train onto the ferry across the Channel from Calais to Dover and then by train to Victoria.

MICHAEL DE SOUZA: The boat trip was a terrible experience in its way, though I managed to cope with it. I could play around – it was a big space for me to play. But I had the responsibility of looking after my aunt. She couldn't travel and she was sick. There was cold salt water to shower. It was some Italian ship, the SS *Ascania* of the Grimaldi line. Literally a banana boat. My dad was paying, he sent us money. There were at least a hundred people, probably more. Certainly it took long enough to embark, and there was a lot of people, a lot of queuing. People were agitated, because it was a two-week trip and it was rough for a lot of the journey. My aunt stayed in bed for nine of the fourteen days. The food was real crap; none of the crew tried to make you feel comfortable in any way. I went all over the place, in the boiler room, in the hold. There were a whole lot of sacks of flour, things like that, but it wasn't for the passengers, it was what they were shipping.

VINCENT REID: The food was excretable rubbish. You had to go really hungry to eat it. Even then you didn't want to. I think it was the government who were running it. Clearly, even under those wretched conditions there had to be a subsidy of some sort. The government was involved in the recruitment so presumably they were involved with the boat. There were about four hundred people, not including the returning servicemen. I was the only boy. It was strange. I had my first homosexual encounter. I was roaming about the ship, I think I was the only person allowed to roam about the ship; this guy was the cook. I was lured into the kitchen and promised all kinds of goodies – butter and cheese and so on – and obviously I wasn't going to say no to that. When the conditions of getting this stuff were laid down that was something else. I didn't run away. I was quite a big boy, nearly 5'8", I could have looked after myself.

DESMOND GITTENS: In 1960 I stowed away on the *Southern Cross*; it used to go to Australia, taking migrants from Britain to Australia. The £10 assisted passages. It had a ten-day passage to Southampton. A couple of my close friends were on their way to Britain to study. That's crucial – they're the ones that actually feed you if you're a stowaway. The liner was so huge that I believe the colour thing played a big part. The people who were in charge of the ship couldn't recognize the difference between the paying black passengers and somebody who had stowed away. I didn't see it as a criminal activity: it was definitely an adventure. I was a young man, I was accustomed to ships, I had family in Britain and I was thinking anything would better than staying and waiting on another ship, so you get on board and off you go. It was literally a decision taken in two days. The day that my friend said that he'd bought the ticket and ship was leaving on such and such a date and the day I got on board. Two days. But it wasn't planned. It was never a deliberate act of immigration, just an adventure.

MICHAEL DE SOUZA: Gradually I found out what was going on and where I was going. I knew I was going to meet my parents. So I was thinking about that and wondering what it was going to be like. I just couldn't remember them. Especially my dad. It was terrible. I believe it was most traumatic thing that could have happened, I don't think you could get anything worse. I was only six.

* * *

IVAN KYNCL: I came to England via Vienna, where I had some negatives that I had smuggled out earlier. I had thought that I would go on from Vienna by car through Germany. But when I reached the border between Austria and Germany, my paper was no longer valid. It had only lasted until I left Czechoslovakia. I couldn't go back to Austria, because I only had permission to travel through, not to stay. So I was in the border post for sixteen hours while they discussed where I could go. The Germans didn't want me – my paper was not valid – the Austrians wouldn't have me back for the same reason. But after sixteen hours they sent me back to Vienna, and said that I had to fly directly to London from there. So I borrowed some money and flew from Vienna to London.

KAREL KYNCL: Our son had already left. He was a sort of unofficial photographer for Charter 77. He had wanted to study photography at the school of art in Prague but because his name was not exactly good he went through a series of interrogations, of being shadowed and so on. He applied for emigration in 1980 and left the country shortly before I was arrested. So he was in England already. Our daughter, who is older and still lives in Czechoslovakia, drove us to the border in her car. We drove to a checkpoint about six kilometres from the border and she was told that she had no permission to go any further. All our luggage was on the car, so what now? A soldier asked me if I drive. 'Of course, but I have no driver's licence any more.' 'No matter. Please drive yourself to the border, unload your luggage, then

77

bring the empty car back. Then I will arrange for someone to drive you back to the border.' So my wife said goodbye to our daughter, I sat behind the wheel, drove to the border, left the luggage there and came back with the empty car, my last journey inside the country. I said goodbye to my daughter, and then some unsuspecting West German tourists were stopped and asked to take me to the border. They were horrified – they didn't know who I was and I couldn't explain. But they drove me back and we crossed the border. Ten steps across the border was our son, taking pictures of our crossing. It was the first time we saw each other for almost three years. He took us to a very posh car, a second-hand BMW, painted gold, and said, 'This is my present.'

MIGUEL ZAMBRANO: The Chilean government gave me this safe conduct: the Colombian government could escort me to the airport. I stayed very close to the ambassador: one yard away and they could have grabbed me. I saw the hate in the policemen's faces. They were pointing their guns at me. But one sergeant came up and said, 'I hope your stay away from the country will not be for long, but while you're away, educate yourself, and one day you will be able to use that in the service or your country. I hope you come back soon.' He at least didn't hate me.

* * *

PETER VO: I found someone who organized escapes, and I paid him to help us. I paid four ounces of gold per head. I had still some money saved up. He used the money to buy a boat, to bribe various officials, all sorts of things like that. I trusted him, he was already a friend. That was the most important part of escaping, finding someone one could completely trust. He arranged everything. Getting enough food and drink, a boat, hiring a navigator. All I had to do was get the money and hand it over. He told us what to do, where to go and what time to be there. Otherwise we would miss the boat. We could take nothing with us. Each person could take one suitcase only. Plus any money or jewellery we had. But we lost it all on the way, stolen by pirates.

NGUYEN DUC PHUONG: On the night we left we were taken by a small sampan out to a bigger boat which was waiting on the Mekong River. There were a couple of hundred people on the boat. People came from many directions, coming on small boats at night. We took nothing with us except for one change of clothes. We set out on a day near a holiday – we thought that there would be lots of people moving around and that would make it easier. That night we reached the bigger boat. There was another man there who knew the river. He guided the boat to the mouth of the Mekong where it joined the South China Sea. Then I took charge. I had planned to sail towards the international sea-lanes. I knew them from the days when I was in the navy. My plan was that if we couldn't get picked up by some international ship along the sea-lanes, I would go to Malaysia. Because there had been many boats of refugees over the past two years, many ships passed us without stopping even though I knew from my days in the navy how to fly the signals that let other ships know that you were in trouble and that they had to stop. As we went up the river we were chased by the Communist navy. But because it was night they had to communicate with lights and we ex-navy people knew the Morse code, we could read their communications. We could see how they were planning to catch us and we avoided them. There is a island off the coast, along our route, which used to be a big prison camp. The Communists had stationed some boats there. Before I went to sleep I had told the officer who was steering, 'When you get near this island be careful and change the route.' But he was a mechanic, not a navigator, and he forgot. So the Communists picked us up on their radar screen. So in the middle of my sleep I was woken up by my colleague, 'There's a Communist ship!' I woke up. It was a terrible experience. It was quite cold but I was sweating. I ordered full speed although the mechanic warned me that we might break down. We were using salt water to cool the engines and at full speed that could destroy the engines. This was not a boat designed for the sea: it was trembling. I knew about stability of ships' structures and watching that made me worry a lot. But after a while my colleague who was watching the Communists said that one of them had disappeared. After ten or fifteen minutes he told me that we'd lost the other one too. So I said, 'OK, we can reduce speed.' I think what happened was that the weather was so bad that the Communists couldn't follow us very far. We couldn't go back, but they had to and if they followed us too far they wouldn't have been able to reach their base. So then we were able to reach the sea-lanes.

PETER VO: After the first day's sailing our engine broke down. All we could do was sit in the boat and wait. There were two hundred people on a small boat, about eighteen metres long, and nearly four metres wide. And of course there wasn't enough food and water. So we were just drifting with the wind and the current. So the pirates attacked. Five times. They took everything. By then I had been chosen as leader, and I told the people, when the pirates arrive, don't do anything to annoy them, don't do anything stupid. If we tried to fight back against them they would kill us. I explained that what the pirates wanted was money, jewellery, clothing, whatever. So please satisfy them. If they were going to harm us, then we had to fight back, but otherwise, just go along with what they want. I told them that if we didn't get in their way, and gave them what they wanted, then they weren't going to harm us. In that way we saved our lives. We accepted losing our possessions, but the one thing left, the precious thing, was our lives. We didn't tell them what we had, but they searched the boat for what they wanted. So they see a watch, and they say, 'I like this watch' and you say, 'OK, have it.' We didn't offer anything, so there would be something left over for the next lot. They didn't harm us, which was very lucky. When we arrived in Thailand the first question was whether anyone had been killed or raped and we said no, and they were very surprised. It took eight days of drifting before we were discovered by a US navy aircraft. We signalled to them, an SOS, and they informed a British cargo ship, who changed course to rescue us. So being picked up by the British meant that we were entitled to go to England.

NGUYEN DUC PHUONG: On the third day we were picked up by the British cargo ship which brought us to Singapore. At first it stopped, to see what we were doing out there. We tried to come alongside but they set off again. We followed and after ten minutes they stopped again and shouted to us that just one person could come aboard. I was the only one who could speak English, though I'd forgotten most of it after two years in jail, and I climbed onto the ship. I told the captain that we had lost a lot of water and fuel. We had been chased by Communists and we had been supposed to meet up with a small boat with extra water and fuel but because we were running away from the Communists we didn't have the time to wait for it. The weather was very bad and the boat had got lost. We had to catch the tide and we couldn't wait and search for it. After a discussion with his crew the captain said that they could only allow the women and children to come on board. But when I went back to our ship and told the people what the captain had said, they all just said, 'No, we'll all just climb on board. You can't just take the women and children. What about their relatives?' So everybody climbed up on to the British ship. The captain ordered me to count everyone and calm them down. He gave them food, fresh water. I went back to our boat with another officer and we confirmed that nobody was left on board. They tied our boat to theirs and towed it behind them. He told us that we were going to Singapore, where there was a refugee reception centre and that was where we could disembark. There was plenty of room on the ship – and after you'd survived, it didn't matter where you slept. It had taken two and a half days for us to get picked up, which was quick, but if that British ship had acted like all the others then after another half day the children would have started to die. We had finished our fresh water. We had enough fuel, although we had lost a lot, but the fresh water was nearly finished. The civilians, who had never been to sea, used too much water too quickly. I couldn't stop them, because I had to use all my time driving the boat.

* * *

PETER TATCHELL: I had always wanted to travel and see different countries and cultures. So leaving Australia wasn't an incredible emotional wrench.

80

Because I had been involved in inciting young men to refuse the draft, and helping draft resisters on the run from the police, there was a possibility that the authorities might have tried to stop me leaving the country. I therefore chose to leave Australia via the least obvious route. I booked on a ship sailing from Melbourne to Sydney, but stayed on for its next destination, New Zealand. From there, I sailed to Britain on the *Fairsky*. It had the cheapest fare available: A$439 for a cabin on E Deck. It was below the waterline, right at the bow of the ship. The voyage to London took seven weeks via Fiji, Tahiti, Panama, Curacao, Lisbon, and Rotterdam.

SUSAN WILSON: I knew very little about Europe, except what I'd seen on films or on television, or what I'd read about. We flew Avianca, Colombian airlines, it was a frightful trip, absolutely frightful. At every stop the air hostesses just went off arm in arm with the Captain. They went off drinking, I think, and then got back on the plane. I was really scared and it was awful. We touched down at Madrid and there were all these security men with white gloves and grey uniforms, formal, polite and peculiar. Then the next stop was Paris where we landed at Charles de Gaulle, which was still new with all the glass tubes, terribly glamorous Air France hostesses, who looked as if they were out of a Buñuel film. We were completely dazed, wearing these strange South American clothes. They probably thought we were terribly silly but we quite fell in love with the place. I'd never seen anything quite so big and so modern, so futuristic. It was dazzling. I thought this is *Europe*, this is wonderful. Then we flew to London.

DON ATYEO: It took me about two years to get here. Most people had taken the boat, but I got very much sucked into the hippie trail, whch was just beginning. You were starting to meet people almost on your doorstep – places like Bali, where there'd be whole enclaves of people, French, English, Scots, whatever – and for the first time the world was coming towards you as much as you were going to the world. Before that, when you hopped on a boat from Sydney, all you had for company was Australians. Even if you hopped off in Aden or Bombay or whatever you didn't have the time to get involved with the population – there were still very few travellers. So you stuck with your friends. You arrived in London and maybe picked up a Qantas hostie and stayed in Earls Court and you either made it or you buggered off back again. But you had to be here to discover the world – on an easy basis with nice English-speaking foreigners. But with the hippies England was for the first time moving in the opposite direction – as was Europe and America. So in that new situation it took me two years to get here. 1970–71. I did the hippie trail, but in reverse: Indonesia, Bali, Malaysia, Thailand, Laos, Cambodia, India, Pakistan, Nepal,

Afghanistan, Iran. Buses, trains, a lot of hitch-hiking. Most of the places had never seen hippies; in the wilder bits they hadn't actually seen white people, or not in the kind of close contact that the hippies brought. But the hippies were the first to be invited to their houses, meet the family, hang out, fuck their daughters.

NGUYEN DUC PHUONG: We stayed three months in Singapore at the refugee reception centre in a camp in the remote part of the island, in the north. There were more than a thousand refugees there. I had no choice about coming to England. The Americans had promised that all former officers of the South Vietnamese forces would be automatically allowed entry to the US if they could escape, but it didn't happen. An officer who had been with me on the ship tried to persuade the Americans to take him but they sent him a letter saying life in America was the best but that compared with life in Vietnam, life in Britain was at least better than that. I think they wanted to unload their refugee burden. So I didn't want to try the Americans and then get the same sort of letter. The Americans did interview me, because I was a former officer, but they said that because I had been picked up by the British ship, I had better go to England. It didn't matter. What I wanted was freedom. I liked the Americans but I liked the British too. Like most Vietnamese, if we receive help from someone, we remember. To us all foreigners were the same. It wasn't a matter of like or dislike, what mattered was the help. After three months in Singapore I was told that my family would be flown to England. Life in the camp wasn't good – too many people and not enough space, but it was still better than prison in Vietnam. We went to England automatically. If you had been picked up by a British ship and you hadn't already found a sponsor in another country then you could go straight to England. That was the same for every country – if their ship picked you up, you could go there.

SHREERAM VIDYARTHI: After a year and a half in India my wife came back to England in search of me. We had not communicated. She did not know that I had been in Europe. What could I have told her? What was there to say? She believed that I had gone back to England and was having a good time, perhaps. She wanted to find me. She found a job working in Littlewoods as a shop assistant. One day, in Germany, I heard from a third party that she had had an accident at her work and that she had left my son in the care of a nanny – which was unheard of in my family – and I decided to come to England. But the consul in Stuttgart would not issue me an entry certificate. To him I was a wanderer, I had no money, no resources. He insisted that I should have a return ticket. I bought one back to Stuttgart. He said, 'No, you must have one to India.' In the end he told me that I would never be granted an entry certificate. So I took back my ticket, told him that he had no business telling me to which country I had to buy the ticket, and walked out. Half of Europe was open to Indians without a visa. It was only England that was fussy. So later on I came to Holland and I met a Dutch boy I had already befriended in Yugoslavia. I told him what had happened in Germany. He said, 'Come on, let's find a cure for the malady.' He told me that if I wanted to enter illegally, he could arrange it, but I rejected that completely. I wanted to go legally and with my head held high: 'I'm going to walk in, not crawl in.' So he said, 'OK, let's find another way.' And he looked at me and said, 'My God, you've got whiskers, you've got an army trenchcoat on, you've got torn trousers, you don't even have a sleeping bag to sleep in, you definitely don't have a bowler hat on your head – you don't qualify as a human being as far as the English are concerned, let alone a potential immigrant.' That evening he made the rounds of all his ex-girlfriends and at every door he knocked he asked for something respectable for me to wear. Somebody gave me some trousers, somebody gave me a jacket and somebody gave me an overcoat and somebody gave me a hat and somebody gave me a tie and that evening I shaved my beard. The next morning I looked like a proper city gentleman, including the umbrella and bowler hat. Then he printed up a decent-looking visiting card in the name of a bookshop in India. With all this I went to Rotterdam, saw the consul and received my entry certificate in less then ten minutes. The consul was even good enough to look after my baggage while I looked around Rotterdam while waiting for the ferry. But I boarded the ferry two hours early, because I didn't want anyone to change their mind. I came into Harwich, boarded the train, came into Liverpool Street, took the tube to Marble Arch and nobody stopped me.

SHARI PEACOCK: When you arrive in another country you never think, 'I'm going to stay here for the rest of my life.' As long as I could prolong my visa for another six months, another year, that was fine and that was as far as I could think. To do this you would go to a place in Croydon called the Home Office. That was another horror. The sort of parochial, provincial, narrow people I had shared my first flat with, that type of person worked there. You had a huge room full of Third World people, with the occasional sprinkling of Americans or whatever, and it was just so demoralizing. You sat there for hours and hours until they finally called you. Then they questioned you and wanted to know if you had money in the bank, if you had full-time enrolment in college, and if you satisfied them they would give you the visa and write in their fussy bureaucratic handwriting: 'Do not think this entitles you to stay in this country, you are only here for the next six months.' That would be every six months. So marriage was very much a matter of legitimizing my stay, although it so happened that we were in love as well.

83

CINDY BLAKE: It wasn't a snap coming into this country, even married. When I first came here I had been going out with Bill for a couple of months. I went back to America, I came back and I was given three months on my passport – the first time you get six months, the second time three. So I had come back to live with Bill and I was given three months. After two months – I've only known the guy for what is it, five months? – I went to Croydon to get an extension on my residence permit. There was a woman behind the counter and she said, 'Why are you staying?' I had produced all this money, all these travellers' cheques, something that you could live on for a year, no problem, and I said, 'I'm staying because I'm in the middle of a romance and I want to see if it works out.' I pulled out wads of money, loads of money, but they were not interested. They wanted me out. She gave me three weeks and said, 'If you do not have a printed announcement in a newspaper of your engagement by three weeks' time you're out of here.' I said, 'Look, take pity on me, what do I do, go to this guy and say, "Three weeks, you've got to marry me or else"? That's not right, it's not fair.' She just said, 'Tough luck. This is it.' I had this feeling that she was angry that yet another American woman had stolen an eligible Brit.

Eventually it worked out because I went to America within that three weeks and he followed me and proposed and that was fine. But after we'd gotten married, about a month and a half later, I got a knock on the door one afternoon: a plainclothes policeman shows his badge and says, 'I want to see your husband's clothes and your clothes in the same closet; wedding pictures, marriage licence obviously, passport . . .' you name it. So I had to take him upstairs, show him all this stuff. And he said, 'We're not really chasing you, we're chasing the Arabs, but we have to be fair.' I showed him everything, though I didn't know whether this was legal or not. But I got the impression that they did not want me. They just didn't like me. Now I always go through the British immigration line when I've been abroad. They say I'm not allowed to, but I always do.

JAROSLAV BRADAC: There were stiff exchange controls at the time and when the Customs official on the train to Calais asked whether I had any money I genuinely said, 'Yes.' I had sold a few etchings, part of my diploma work, when I was in Paris. It was the first time I had ever really had any money of my own. I was so proud of it. Usually you didn't have any and they didn't like students with no money and so on. Especially from the East. But this time I had 800 francs and I'd borrowed another 200 and I was so proud to tell him. And he promptly confiscated 700 of them because I was only allowed to take 300 out of the country. I got them back later on, but at that stage he took it away. I was so proud, I just wanted to say, 'Here's my money, now for once leave me alone,' but he took it away! It was very funny.

84

IVAN KYNCL: A few months after I arrived I went to Germany by car. And all the time I assumed that the West would think not that I was a hero, but that I had struggled with the system and I had brought things to the West which were good. How wrong I was. I was crossing from Germany to France and they stopped the car and found the pictures I had taken of Czech prisons. 'What is this?' they asked. I told them that I had taken these pictures illegally. I expected them to say, 'Oh good, well done.' Instead they looked and said, 'Really?' I spent the night in a border post. They brought in special people who asked questions which I wouldn't answer. I discovered that night that all secret policemen, MI5 or people of that sort, it doesn't matter where you are, the West or the East, they will always treat you the same. They think, 'If he could do it to them, he can do it to us.' They're all colleagues, with more in common together than with people like me.

HANNAH KODICEK: The British were absolutely amazing. They were wonderful. The Customs couldn't say anything much because as far as they were concerned we had come for a month's holiday. Obviously they knew what was going on, but they accepted what we said. I'm sure someone had told them to let people like us in. And it wasn't just the Customs. The whole of Britain was terribly welcoming to the Czechs. The first place we stayed was upstairs in this very big house in Blackheath with a family. They had heard on the radio an appeal: 'Give a room to a Czech refugee.' So that's how we came in. Everybody was absolutely overwhelmingly helpful. Maybe some of them did feel guilty about Munich, but I think that most of them were just genuinely moved by what was happening at the time. We had one suitcase, our baby, and thirty quid.

5 The Moment of Arrival

'When you arrive in another country you never think, "I'm going to stay for the rest of my life."'

SHARI PEACOCK: Journeys on the train, stopping off briefly with relatives in Paris, back on the train, clattering along, through the rain and there it was, exactly as I had imagined it: England. Everyone very polite and very reserved, just what I expected. The moment I arrived I just loved it. I thought this was it. The sheer amount of colour, you could not believe it. It was close to a religious ecstasy to walk up and down Knightsbridge or Oxford Street. I was still very gawky and uncouth and I didn't have many friends yet and I'd just walk up and down Oxford Street in a daze. I just loved the colours and people and food. Everything. Things like going to pop concerts, getting drunk, being on my own – this was all unbelievable. I had a little English, and when I arrived I spent the first month at a language school improving it. It has to be said that I learned the basics in that month. It was very very intense, watching television all day long. If I was on my own there'd be the TV on really loud, trying to concentrate on what it was saying and just eat the words because I wanted so much to speak this language.

DON ATYEO: When I got here London was very very disappointing. It wasn't exotic. I'd been through serious exotica by then and London didn't really match up to Teheran or Bangkok. You could deal with that level of letdown. But from being something special as a traveller, as a white traveller in foreign lands, as an interested traveller who had been made to feel special because you were dealing with the ordinary people of these countries, who had never had contact with foreigners, here you were not special at all, and you were painfully not special. You were just another Australian rattling around Earls Court.

My first night I slept on the Embankment. It was very cold, but it wasn't all that bad – everyone was doing it then. I was kicked awake by the cops at 3 or 4 a.m., these bully boys who didn't like hippies. I had this sleeping bag which my mother had made from a space blanket, which was brilliant and I'd carried it for two years. But I realized suddenly that I'd been lying in human shit all night. If I'd been in another country I would have washed it off, but it was indicative of the way I thought I'd made it, that I'd arrived at the end of the journey, that I just threw it away. So there we all were, these hippies, and you just followed the leaders who walked off to stand outside the Circle Line station until it opened then you went round the Circle Line for a while, sleeping and dozing till daybreak. My first night in England. 1972.

SUSAN WILSON: We landed quite early in the morning and we got a bus from Heathrow to town. We went to Earls Court. It was a joke really, but we had a friend who lived in Earls Court. He wasn't there. We got on a bus, but the conductor threw us off. It was the time of a lot of bomb scares and we had big packs so she threw us off. We got a cab. We had this list of people we could go and stay with, the idea was to sleep on their floors, but we really didn't know what we were doing at all. As the afternoon and evening wore on our list got less and less. No one was at home, things were looking worse and worse. But we found a friend who said that her friend – we didn't know him – would let us sleep on his floor in Bayswater. So off we went to this very fashionable little flat inhabited by this gay couple. It sounds silly but I knew nothing about gay life. These two men shared this bed and made each other tea in the morning and chatted away together and I was quite shocked.

86

The first night I slept there I woke up with a great start about four in the morning thinking I'd left the lights on, but it was dawn! The dawn never takes place at four in New Zealand. I couldn't get used to that. We'd arrived on Spring Bank Holiday and there was a pub down in Earls Court full of people who were wearing fifties clothing, all these girls with huge dresses, high pony tails, and Teds in drape jackets. It was fabulous. I thought, 'Gosh, the people still dress like that now. How exciting!'

RONALD HARWOOD: I arrived on 21 December 1951 – the only date I ever remember other than my birthday – and I dropped to my knees and kissed the quay at Southampton. As I stood up I said, 'This is the greatest day of my life.' And someone I had travelled over with said, 'Yes. Until the next one.' It poisoned the moment and I've never really forgiven him.

PALOMA ZOZAYA: I arrived in England in 1980. There were a couple of friends here already and I was able to stay with them for a couple of weeks. One of them had been here for two years, and had married an Englishman. They had their life very nicely organized and they had no desire to have it disturbed by some Mexican arriving and settling into their flat. They made it very clear that I could stay for two weeks, and then I would have to find somewhere else. So I went to the Mexican embassy, who weren't very helpful in certain areas: notably when a Mexican walks in and says, 'I don't have any accommodation. Can you help?' But the secretaries were very friendly and told me about hostels and things. I ended up in a hostel in Victoria. I lived there for about six months while I was having interviews with various schools – RADA, Central, LAMDA and so on.

DAVILIA DAVID: We arrived on 30 December 1960. It was very cold. We looked for snow, but there wasn't any. My plan was to go to RADA, then go home as a star, but I was wrong. I couldn't afford the RADA fees and nobody had told me that there were scholarships for foreigners. Instead I went to all sorts of classes, night school and so on. I stayed in Earls Court to begin with. It was still terribly Australian and I was shocked by the sort of Australians I met: real Barry McKenzie prototypes. The men would come over in groups, swill beer, knock off everything in sight. Then I started a job in the City. It was at a very old-fashioned insurance company in Chancery Lane. On my first day I turned up in hat and gloves, just as my mother had told me to do.

CARMEN CALLIL: On the way over I got off the ship at Naples – I couldn't stand the ship a second longer – and waltzed round Europe with two girlfriends, and fell in love with sailors from the American fleet. Then came to London. It was terribly cold. I didn't have the right clothes. I didn't have any money. I was just a bum. There were hundreds of us. I worked for Australia House for a while, selling honey and mutton, in my little blue uniform with Australia on my breast. That was a disaster. Then I worked in Derry and Toms, Pontings.

SIMI BEDFORD: I wasn't really looking forward to going to England, but everyone made it seem so exciting. I was a confident sort of child and I assumed that it would be pretty much the same as it was in Nigeria. Little did I know. So I came over to England with my step-grandmother. She had a brother who lived in Neasden. We came over on the boat and arrived at Liverpool and went to Neasden. Liverpool was very grim, all bombed-out. I was absolutely struck by how minute the houses were. I was also struck by the fact that there were no servants. The first morning I went out to look for them in the garden. The house was obviously too small for them, so I assumed that there must be some kind of servants' quarters in the garden. I whizzed out but of course there weren't any. We were staying with my step-grandmother's sister, Auntie Ethel, and her husband Uncle Claud, who was a bus conductor. I didn't think to ask why their lives were so different to ours in Nigeria. I noticed that they had rather a small house, but I just assumed that this was how other people lived.

CASH BHOGAL: My father started off working in Birmingham. We joined him in 1962. We couldn't come before that because we didn't have the money for the fare. I was about six. It was certainly quite a shock. Heathrow wasn't the place it is today, much more of a little shed. My father met us, there was my mother, four brothers and one sister, and he had hired a taxi to take us all the way to Birmingham.

GULZAR KHAN: I went straight to Birmingham. Three of us who had come together stayed there for four weeks with some people who had already come from our district. They were very helpful: they fed us, took us around, showed us the social security office, helped us fill out forms and so on. At that time there were no families. Just houses with rooms and three or four beds in each room. People would use the same bed in shifts. I didn't see the community as poor, because the living standards in England were so different to Pakistan. The buildings were different, the houses were different – lots of things. I wasn't consciously comparing anything, but it was just a very different society.

* * *

BENNY BUNSEE: I was in Tanzania for about a year, but I had no roots there. I didn't belong. I worked as journalist and with the money I saved I was able to come here. I had left South Africa without a passport, but the Indian government had given me a passport since my parents had been born there. Immigration to England was still not so tough. It was just beginning to change,

88

but at that stage I was able to come to England without any difficulties. They didn't ask me any questions at all. I came by plane. A friend paid my fare. I was very happy when I arrived. It was a nice bright sunny day in September. It was very beautiful and I thought what a wonderful place this is, and I liked London very much. I started off living in Bayswater. But there were problems. I needed a haircut, and it took me two weeks before I went into a white barber-shop – I couldn't believe the person would cut my hair.

VINCENT REID: We got off the boat at Tilbury and caught this train to Victoria, and what struck me as really weird was to actually see that the train driver was white. I expected him to be black. I also expected all the porters and so on to be black – because that's how it was in Jamaica. I'd never seen a white person work in my life, until I actually came to England. That stuck in my mind. When I looked at the people, comparing them to the passengers that were coming off the boat – we had all kinds of floral dresses, bright clothes – the English people seemed drab and shabby. Of course I didn't know anything about rationing and things of that sort, but still . . . I thought, 'Hell.'

WILF WALKER: When we arrived at Southampton it was nearly dark: it was late afternoon, wintertime. I didn't understand it. You get shuffled along with everyone else: you don't really know what's happening, you're in this tunnel, you can't see. The next thing I was on a train to London, and I got off and there were my parents. That was when I started to notice things, before that it was really just a blur. My father put his coat round me and then we drove and drove, it seemed like forever, and we got to this room in Shepherd's Bush where the three of us lived. There were still trams, factory chimneys, everything was black and dirty. There were no bathrooms in the houses, we had a single room for the three of us.

MICHAEL DE SOUZA: The boat arrived at Southampton. We took a train up to Waterloo where we met my mum. I didn't know who she was. My dad was there. Big hello, but I didn't know who he was. I didn't know what was going on. Then we took a cab to Ladbroke Grove, to Southam Street.

When we were travelling in the taxi the first thing I remember was saying, 'Oh no, them houses are real horrible.' There was no blue and no green. Everything was brown, black or very, very dark bottle green. It was terrible. I started to feel awful, I was really upset. Even though the trip had been two weeks, when I landed it just seemed like a day since I'd left Trinidad and I thought, well I could just go back. Back home I was really independent and free. Over here I came to strange people, it was cold, and I was wearing silly little shorts and a short-sleeved shirt. That's all I had, no luggage. Then we came to the house. They had two rooms, top of this house. My mum, dad and brother lived in one room, and my uncle (my mum's brother) in the other.

PETER TATCHELL: I arrived at Southampton docks in late August 1971. Travelling into London by train, my first impression was how green and luxuriant England was by comparison with the dryness and barrenness of much of Australia. Approaching Waterloo, I felt a sense of horror at the sight of thousands of grey slate roofs for as far as the eye could see. It was just like those old films of Charles Dickens's novels. I thought, 'How could people live like this? In these houses all squashed together? With tiny little gardens and hardly any trees?'

MICHAEL IGNATIEFF: My first sight of England is in 1954. I am seven. I have the sharpest and most pleasurable memories of coming up on the boat train from Southampton in sepulchral gloom at four o'clock on a November evening. Fog closing in. All the English spaces being different: the railway carriages being narrow, different smells, Woodbines in the air, the pervasive dampness, fog and chill everywhere, characters in cloth caps with white scarves, incredibly gnarled old gents carting your luggage to the train. I really felt that I had come from surburban North America, where everything is bigger, expansive, kind of tanned and genial, to this kind of cramped, struggling, grimy, dirty old world. I was quite entranced by it. I felt it was very magical, very exciting, very dense. It seemed a very adult world. This is possibly retrospective projection, but I felt that I had left the world of genial suburban childhood to encounter the one where history actually happened.

BERNIE GRANT: The first thing that struck me was how cold it was. Everything you touched was cold – the food was cold, the furniture was cold, the table was cold. I couldn't understand it, I couldn't believe it. I couldn't believe the way the houses were built – all joined together, they looked like dolls' houses to me. They were so small. I also noticed that here were white people who seemed very poor. Everything was very colourless, grey. Just the one colour. Everyone had grey overcoats, there were no bright colours or anything like that. For the first few months I was pretty miserable. There was no great culture shock, but when I saw the conditions that the black community was living under I wanted to go back home.

MIKE PHILLIPS: We arrived on 3 January 1956, in the afternoon, around three o'clock. The boat didn't dock at Southampton, but my mother and father came out on a tug and took us to the dock. It was a very curious business to be coming to England, it was like going to the moon. The strangest thing was the climate. It was so cold. It was January, you breathed and smoke came out of

90

your mouth – this was *weird*! By the time we got to London it was dark. It was foggy. Not a thick fog, but just smoky and you could see these circles around the street lights. I had never seen or imagined anything like it. My impression of the houses was of these brick things. I had never seen brick houses, ours were all wooden; and I had never seen terraces, houses all joined together. It was like brick cliffs. All terribly gloomy. Grey, gloomy, lowering, threatening.

NELLY SALAS: My family had been Indians and I loved the land, the plants, the animals, all the natural things. I have no religion. If you ask me if I believe in God, I tell you, no; I didn't see him and I don't think he has ever seen me. But nature is different. For my ancestors God was in the moon and the sun and for me the sun is like my father. In Argentina you are in a country where the sun is hot, it burns you; then I came here as a refugee in 1977, and thirty hours later it was cold, dark, I felt as if I had gone down into a very deep hole, all black, cold. It was terrible. We left Heathrow in the train and it was dark, about four o'clock on a winter afternoon, and suddenly I thought, in this country I can never be happy. It is impossible: everything is too dark, too cold, and the people are different.

MIKE PHILLIPS: Balls Pond Road, where we lived, wasn't really a black area, that sort of thing didn't really exist in 1956. Rationing had ended not long before and I was amazed at the number of places that were still just piles of bricks and people would say, 'That's a bomb site.' I remember the rag-and-bone man, the coalman and the milkman with their horses, the shouting they did when they came down the street. There was a blacksmith's forge in Balls Pond Road. It was all very interesting. It was the year of rock 'n' roll, of James Dean, Suez, Hungary. In a peculiar way it was very exciting.

MICHAEL IGNATIEFF: We lived a year in London in an apartment in Prince's Gate, Kensington. So my formative memories are of this winter spent in this absolutely freezing apartment. I went to a local private school. Because I came from genial surburban North America I could barely read or write or converse in any known language and so the British regarded my reading and writing as quite appalling. I hated it. I hated all these little grey woolly socks, the little grey Marks and Sparks uniform. That aspect of England made me miserable, but I couldn't shake the feeling of being in a very great city. The thundering noise of London and these huge red buses looming out of the fog with their lights all smeared by the fog. It was very exciting. It wasn't what I had imagined. But instead of finding it a great comedown from some illusion of what it would be like, it was a comedown, but it was something else again. It had nothing to do with the gold coach and the Coronation and royalty, it had to do with the intense griminess and dirtiness and strain of London, and to this day I have the same mixed feelings. I have a sense that London is like no other place in the world. It's bloody awful half the time, but I can't quite get it out of my system.

DESMOND GITTENS: Of course it was all entirely different. I had been out of the country, out of my country before. I had been to a metropolis and I'd seen the developed world. It was not an entire shock to see huge buildings, fast cars, lots and lots of white people. But white people at that time tended to look all the same, particularly in Britain where you had people dressing so much alike. Everyone was like bowler hats or, up in the north, big old grey coats. They seemed to me to be all the same. That was part of my culture shock. And I knew nothing about any difference between the North and South, as far as I was concerned it was all England. I knew the names of the cities but I didn't know which one was where. I didn't know that Manchester, where I was, was in the North. I'd heard of Manchester and I'd heard of Liverpool, South-ampton, London and Edinburgh, but where they were in relation to each other I hadn't got a clue. But having the buffer of family to take you around in the early days helped. Take you around, sign on with the NHS, sign on with the employment exchange, look for a job, that cushioned it quite a lot for me. Also I had done a bit of music, I had belonged to a steel band and the steel band was very very popular in the North. We played in the evenings in these clubs around Manchester – Didsbury, Cheetham, Hulme, Stretford, places like that.

ZERBANOO GIFFORD: It was a wonderful arrival: I was coming home, to see my parents, to see Father Christmas, to see television. I remember wearing my uncle's gloves and coming through London airport with sheer excitement. I just thought I was coming to paradise. It was cold and everything else but it was just so wonderful. The sheer excitement of arriving at the hotel my parents ran and going into our rooms. There was no feeling that I was coming to somewhere miserable or drizzly. A lot of people felt depressed and miserable when they arrived but not me. My parents were here and they'd set up home, and that was what mattered to me. It was this excitement: I just loved going to Southend, and I loved having thin club-sized sandwiches, I still remember watching *Bill and Ben* and everything. Black-and-white television. The greatest excitement for me was going up the down escalators. I couldn't understand what an escalator was because in Urdu and Hindustani there's no such word – it's just a stair – so I couldn't understand how a stair moved. I went up and down escalators and lifts. We had ice factories in India but it was so exciting to come here and see real ice, not just ice in blocks. The whole terminology was different, it was new and exciting. Growing up in a hotel is wonderful. You meet so many people. Everybody from India stayed with us. It's great fun, much better than being in some little surburban box. I met everybody.

* * *

NGUYEN DUC PHUONG: We flew to London, to Heathrow, and then we went in coaches to the centre on Thorney Island in Hampshire. My first impression was that it was cold. Also the towns and villages seemed to be isolated. As we drove down the roads I saw very few people. Back in my country you would see a lot of people on the road. The place we stayed on Thorney Island was also very isolated from its surroundings. Where you went to live in England depended on your personal circumstances and whether the local council could accommodate you. I had an uncle who had arrived a year before me and he lived in Bath. So I wanted to live near him. At that stage I just knew Britain by one geography lesson at school. The thing I remember was that my teacher pronounced Portsmouth as Ports-*mouth*. I knew there were Kings and Queens but that was it. But I didn't care what the place was like – I wanted a country where I could settle. I knew English and in Britain they spoke English. So after three months they told me that there was a place to live in a small town near Bath called Bradford-on-Avon. I accepted it. I didn't care where I lived, because what we were getting was freedom. So I settled my family there in this small town. Other people, who only wanted to live in big cities, waited longer, sometimes a year. My rent was paid by the DHSS.

SIR CLAUS MOSER: The four of us came out of Germany in April 1936. My brother and I were settled in a boarding house in Sussex, and then my brother went to Dulwich College and I went to Frensham Heights in Surrey. My parents then went back for some months – to clear up their affairs – which illustrates how easy it still was.

Frensham Heights was rather a progressive coeducational boarding school, where the arts were dominant. My parents returned to England in the autumn of '36 and settled in Putney, where they lived until their deaths many years later. It was quite a change for them, from being well-off in Germany to living fairly modestly in England. My father never worked again, largely for health reasons. He was able to buy the house in Putney but relatively speaking they were living a much more modest life than in Germany, determined above all to ensure a good education for my brother and myself.

I was tremendously homesick during the first few months in Sussex, conscious of having escaped. Because of our English governess we spoke quite a lot of English. I was fortunate that there were a lot of other refugees at Frensham Heights. It was a very liberal school and there were lots of Jews, and I was received with open arms. Even so I was homesick for the first couple of terms, governed by the fear of what might be happening to my parents. My brother perhaps had a slightly more difficult time at Dulwich, a much more traditional school.

TEDDY SCHWARZ: I went to Cambridge first, stayed there two–three weeks. There was a refugee committee of the International Students Service. I still remember Miss Bunbury in Belsize Avenue, who took me in, gave me a room. Miss Bunbury was strange. She got it into her head that the Nazis hated the *New Statesman* more than anything, so one night she burned all the copies she had, in case of invasion. A good liberal woman. Officially there were no refugees. The government ignored the situation. I was retrained – I'm a fully trained chiropodist. In Dartford I did it for a bit, but I didn't like it. It was a three-year course, by the way. I had a loan to set up this clinic. I didn't have a choice, there was nothing else on offer. They pressured me: this is the coming thing.

BIANCA GORDON: I came to this country on the second *Kindertransport* on December 13, 1938. We started our life here at a reception camp, a holiday camp in Dovercourt, not far from Harwich, where we had landed. The BBC and the newspapers had appealed to the public to offer us homes, and people responded in a remarkable way. I was very fortunate in having been offered a home by a vicar and his wife in Norwich. They had responded to the appeal, because they considered it the Christian thing to do, to offer a home to a Jewish child. They were wonderful people, who showed remarkable under-standing and warmth. They did their utmost to help me adjust to life here. I was very fortunate, and feel a deep sense of gratitude to the Revd and Mrs Robbins. I was of an age when I could have been used as a domestic help. Revd and Mrs Robbins sent me to school, because they considered that my parents would have wished me to continue my education. They were anxious for me to have a religious education and suggested that I should either go to church or to synagogue. They preferred me to go to synagogue, because again they imagined that my parents would wish me to do so. Unfortunately, life with the Robbins came to an end when, exactly a year after my arrival, the vicar died suddenly of a massive heart attack. A vicarage is a 'tied cottage', and Mrs Robbins had to vacate it, and I became homeless. There were generous offers, by the Society of Friends, of other homes in Norwich, but I was reluctant to move to another family. War had broken out, and fears for the safety of my parents left behind mounted. I was very worried, as many of us were, that the Germans might invade England. I decided to join the Zionist youth group, of which I had been a member in Berlin. A number of my friends had managed to get out of Germany just before the doors closed. They had come on agricultural permits with the intention of moving on to Palestine. After the fall of France, I joined a *kibbutz* on the land, first in Wiltshire, then in other places – Staffordshire, Shropshire, and Redhill, Surrey. It was good to be together to work, to study and to share our anxieties about events. We feared that an invasion was imminent. We were much more worried than the majority of those British people with whom we had contact. They were very confident, but we lived in fear: we had seen evidence of German military might.

GRETEL SALINGER: Once we arrived in England we had to report to the police station. In the meantime we had been deprived of our nationality by the Nazis. We were 'dis-naturalized'. The authorities found out that we had taken money out of the country and they announced our names in a book that appeared every week in Germany. It had our names down as 'personally dis-naturalized'. In their mind it was a great shame, but for us it did a lot of good. That was the end of our German citizenship. The passport we had had to pay so much for was no use any more. So when we arrived in England we were stateless. So we were no longer Germans, we were neutrals. Eric, my husband, was interned. We got him out very quickly, but he took it very badly. There was a collection of old medals to help the war effort and he sent his Iron Cross as his contribution. It was all over England, on the radio, in the papers. We didn't get our English naturalization until after the war, 1947.

* * *

TEDDY SCHWARZ: Internment was two-tiered. There was a protected zone, and London was separate. I just happened to be in London, heard about this on the wireless, so I went back to Dartford, went to the police station and they took me to Rochester – no, Maidstone. We were separated from the army proper by barbed wire. We were finally transported to Huyton, a bigger camp, and from there to the Isle of Man, and then later to Canada. The camps were full of intellectuals, so we had classes. There were a great number of scientists there. In Canada I was interned with Klaus Fuchs, a very, very nice person. We didn't complain: what can you expect from the English – you make allowances.

ENNIO CAMISA: In 1940 war broke out and I got interned, me and my brother. That was lovely. I call it lovely now. When you were interned you didn't like to be interned but when I come to think about it, it was lovely. I was in the Isle of Man, in a camp. It wasn't an ordinary camp: we were in a hotel. I stayed there for four years. After four years I come out. I always wanted to keep myself fit, so when someone comes out and says, 'Do you want to go work on a farm?' I did. I worked on the farm. I used to go out at nine o'clock in the morning. It was a very big farm and the food we had was more than in an hotel. We'd leave the camp at half-past eight or eight o'clock, and arrive at the farm by nine. Half-past ten they used to come around with a pot of tea and bread and butter. Not just a cup of tea, a pot of tea, you could have as much as you like. One o'clock, between twelve and one, there'd come a meal, lunch. Three-course lunch. It was very good. The farmer gave us this. Then we'd start work at half-past one, till five. Before we left the farm we'd have another pot of tea, and bread and butter. It was all right. I'd never worked in a farm. The first day my back was terrible, but when I saw the meal, the good food like that, I keep on.

95

The rations weren't very big in the camp: slice of bread in the morning, slice of bread at lunchtime and in the evening. If you weren't doing anything that food was enough for you, but if you were working you need more. The farmer had crops and cattle: 44 milking cows, 80 ordinary cows, 450 acres. A very big farm. I used to do everything. Cutting turnips, hay, there's always something to do. Cleaning the stables, always something. I work at that farm for eleven months. It's an airport now. From there we changed the camp. From Douglas we went to Ramsay. Ramsay I work on another farm. This was the same. Good food, good meals and when you get used to working on the farm, you get used to the exercise. We weren't like prisoners of war, it was like a family.

BIANCA GORDON: Some of our people were interned. This was a testing, and for some a traumatic experience. Having been segregated by German and Austrian society, and then offered shelter by the UK, the country which had rescued them, it was hard for them to face tribunals as Germans or Austrian 'enemy aliens'. This was a bitter pill to swallow, adding insult to injury, when interned with Germans and Nazis, and sent off to the Isle of Man, to Canada and Australia. As a friendly alien – my parents were of Polish descent – I escaped that fate.

TEDDY SCHWARZ: It was only the Jewish refugees who resented it. They had the great hope they'd be freed. This was very disagreeable for the political refugees. The Jews were not willing to join in communal action to make things comfortable. It was a complete split. We even had a gun-runner there. Even in Canada we had divisions between Jews and Aryans – Aryans was the term the Canadians used. The political refugees tried to sabotage this separation of Jews and Aryans. Our Jewish contingent were so convinced they'd go to America. We just shrugged and said, 'Our judgement is that you will never be free to go there. But if you think so, we won't stand in your way. But anybody who wishes to come with us, declare yourself as an Aryan.' And a number of them did. Particularly Mr Reeder, this gun-runner. I said, 'What do you think about this?' He said, 'I've heard this before, this separating Jews and Aryans, I come with you.' A realist. We had a number of fifteen–sixteen-year-olds interned with us and Reeder took charge of them, and taught them English and French. Highly educated guy. Don't know what happened to him. He'd run arms to Spain.

SIR CLAUS MOSER: The internment camps were a regrettable episode. We refugees felt we had become increasingly integrated into society. So it was a great shock for all of us in 1940 when we were interned. But for me, at seventeen, it also was a bit of an adventure and only lasted three months. My brother was less lucky. He was interned for a year and got to the Isle of Man; I only got as far as Huyton. But for the older generation, like my father, the shock was much worse. After all, they had given up a great deal to emigrate, and were Hitler's greatest enemies. So it was almost beyond understanding now to be behind barbed wire here. My father was shaken to the core. There were suicides. Of course it was due to panic by the government which believed that there were a number of spies in the country, and their reaction was to go for wholesale internment of anybody of German, Austrian and Italian origin. I remember one group who had settled here around the turn of the century, from Poland, and they still couldn't speak a word of English. They didn't know what had hit them.

ENNIO CAMISA: I didn't feel annoyed that I was being interned. They didn't say 'You've got to come inside.' They didn't say they wanted to intern you because you're not safe. They just said, 'Well, there's a war, we've got to intern you.' They didn't force us, anything like that. They said, 'Pick up all you've got to pick up.' The only thing was we had to close the shop. We lost the shop, the one in Old Compton Street. They closed it and let the shop to somebody else. When I got back four years later to the shop, there's somebody else and I can't get it back.

SIR CLAUS MOSER: I myself had quite an interesting time. At Huyton everyone sought a role or a job. There was a camp university, with Nobel prize-winners amongst the teachers. There was sport. There was a bank, and camp currency, although there was nothing to buy. I remember queuing up at the bank for money – although heaven knows what I did with it behind barbed wire. There was a café on a corner of a housing estate where we assembled for cream cakes and coffee. That was at the height of the Battle of Britain, 1940. No one knew where the coffee and cakes came from. The British officers who were our guards would sit with us for afternoon tea, and some of us refugees got up a gypsy band. A chap called Landau, a mathematician, set up a camp statistics office to keep records of camp numbers and so on and he asked me if I'd like to be his assistant. I so enjoyed it that when I got out I went to LSE to study statistics and that's how my career began.

* * *

NELLY SALAS: All my life I had believed that I would never leave Argentina – my country was my house. I would never leave. So the whole situation was terrible. I didn't think about what leaving meant, and I didn't want to think. We arrived at Heathrow on 8 December 1977 and we were taken to a hotel in west London, just near Portobello Road. I spoke no English, maybe one word. Nor did my husband. We spent only twelve days there, because we didn't want to be in London. I never liked big cities, even though I had lived in Buenos

97

Aires for many years. We were in a state of shock. The only good thing was that everyone else at the hotel was Latin American, all in the same situation. Most of them had children as well and they were worse than us and you looked at them and thought, 'Well, maybe it isn't that bad for us.' Our plan was to live outside London, maybe to rent a small piece of land on which we could work, produce things, sell produce – eggs, potatoes, whatever. That was what we thought. But we were wrong: not in England. So there was this family in Coventry, Chilean refugees, and they offered us a room in their house. We took the opportunity.

MIGUEL ZAMBRANO: The group who should have been at Heathrow to help us, weren't there. I'd got the impression that I was going to be welcomed by somebody important. There was nobody. I had no passport, nothing. A senior immigration officer said, 'Who are you? Another lot of communists coming over here?' He was shouting, 'Why do you come to this country?' Very aggressive. He said, 'You must have a passport, you're not allowed in without a passport.' I said, 'We are refugees, here's the letter that allows us to come in.' They insulted us, abused us. I started panicking. They said, 'We're sending you back on the next plane.' This went on for fifteen–twenty minutes. Finally this woman appeared saying, 'Give us your money, give part of it for the cause of fighting against repression.' This was a very left-wing organization. We were all in a state of shock. She told us, 'You will be taken to a reception centre. Afterwards we'll relocate you and your family will join you.' She was a Trotskyist, I wasn't. I was a refugee. She said, 'You will be in a true socialist organization, you will join our party here.' I said, 'All I want is for my family to join me and for us to start a new life and do what I can to support my people.' Here's this little English lady who's never been to Chile telling me what to do, in very poor Spanish. She was also very dirty. We ended up in a hotel in Shepherd's Bush. It was summer, and we'd come from winter, wearing winter clothes, so we were very hot. But before leaving the airport I saw a seagull. They are the most beautiful birds, I used to carve them all the time. Seeing that made me decide that this was the country for me.

* * *

MARY ROSE: I had to start my life here on my own. My husband had to leave almost at once: he had bought a boat which had to be picked up in Scandinavia. We lived first in a hotel off the Bayswater Road, off Queensway. We didn't have much money. I started working, doing sewing for an Austrian woman and earning my keep. Nobody spoke German, so I learnt to speak English. I made some friends in the hotel. One day Reggie phoned – the boat had been stolen, he was being delayed – and asked, 'Can I speak to Mrs Rose?' I said, 'Reggie, I'm talking to you.' He couldn't grasp how well I'd picked up English. Then I was fed up with the hotel and I found a furnished room and by the time he returned I had settled in. I think this was all very good for me. To experience the country on my own footing. I found people extremely friendly and helpful. There was a Jewish friend of Reggie – a little bit of a fly-by-night, an abortionist, a real back-street boy – and he brought some black market butter to send to my parents in East Germany, which I felt was a sign that he didn't mind me being German. That was the most moving thing. This is how people were to me. I changed my name. Ilse Rose didn't sound right, so I took one of my other names, Mary, and used that.

NAIM ATALLAH: When I came, it was just after the war, and everything was still rationed. No chocolates. We ate mostly rabbit, very little other meat. And the weather. In Haifa it was sunny all the time. Here it was gloomy, and there were separate seasons. But I loved it. At that tender age I was very impressionable and living in this new and different atmosphere affected my life completely.

VICTOR WILD: I arrived in Harrogate and looked around. It's supposed to be rather hilly though to me it looked quite flat. I arrived into an extraordinary household: my uncle and aunt had no children; they had a resident maid. I arrived really knowing no English at all, so only my uncle could talk to me, nobody else. That was rather hard. There were no young people around at all. It was very strange for me. Uncle and aunt were always rushing off to business and maybe they took me along a bit but they'd always tell me, 'Wait here,' and I'd be sitting for hours on a chair waiting for them to finish. It wasn't too happy an experience initially and I looked forward to going to boarding school because there there would be young people.

GINA ADAMOU: I should have gone to school for a while – I was still under-age. But they decided that they weren't going to register me. They wanted me to stay home and look after my younger sister. They kept me at home for a whole year, looking after my younger sister and my grandmother. I became the little housewife. Cooking, cleaning, looking after the baby who was only three or four. That went on for a year. They had a Greek who taught at the English school to come in once a week and give me private lessons. I used to love the English language anyway. I had learnt it from uncles back in Cyprus, so carried on from there when I got here. And this went on for a year. Then when eventually my grandmother got better, by that time I couldn't go to school. You left school at fifteen in those days – so I couldn't start after that. No one came knocking on the door – I don't think they knew I existed. They should have, really.

MANDY MERCK: I got off the plane at Heathrow and into a train for Didcot, Reading, then Oxford. I was very surprised and dismayed. The Thames Valley did nothing for me. I saw all these pubs that said 'Courage', and thought, what a picturesque name for a pub. Then getting to St Hugh's, which is not a pretty place, and thinking, 'This isn't so great.' Trying to have lunch in the buttery, 'This is really not so great.' I quite liked salad cream. I'd never had anything that déclassé. I didn't adjust very well to St Hugh's, to say the least. I'd really prepped for Oxford as myth. Read *Brideshead* seventeen times. I knew my Bloomsburys. That was a great way of affiliating as a lesbian in the late '60s, to know about Virginia Woolf and what she'd been up to, to know a little bit about Vita Sackville-West, etc. Oxford wasn't as classy as I'd expected. St Hugh's was a very petit-bourgeois college with a lot of plump Welsh girls reading French and wanting to make good marriages. The food was unspeakable, the tuition was lousy, the place didn't look very nice.

JAROSLAV BRADAC: The summer previously I happened to have met someone in Prague who was part of a British delegation of designers and typographers who said, 'When you are in London, give me a call.' I thought, 'That's not something you can count on,' but he was surprisingly kind, the first true English eccentric I had met. I did ring up and to my astonishment he actually waited for me at Victoria Station, though I missed him. He had a tiny little cubbyhole office off Leicester Square. He was a publisher/designer. The second day I was in London, after I had found a youth hostel to stay in, he took me to the East India and Sports Club in St James's Square, the ultimate contrast with my youth hostel. He also helped me to write a letter so that I could have my ten-day visa extended for a year. There was no problem from the British Customs. Czechoslovakia was news. The British were very sympathetic and although I arrived a year after the invasion, I sailed on the tail-end of that sympathy. If they had given me trouble I would have gone. I was not in a fighting mood. I was happy to be here, I decided to wait and they made it easy for me. They gave me a work permit straight away . . . everything was easy.

HANNAH KODICEK: I arrived in London on 20 September 1968, a month after the invasion. A lot of dramatic stories happened. Ours wasn't dramatic but I did have a dramatic version that I sometimes told at dinner parties. I just got so bored with all these people saying, 'And how did you get out?' When I told them the truth and said, 'Quite easily actually' I could see that they were visibly disappointed. So I worked up this story about minefields and us carrying a basket with the baby and shooting from the big watchtowers and dogs. All nonsense, of course, but it entertained a lot of people. Even if you tell them afterwards that it's not true, they're pleased to have heard it that way. But it really was so easy. It was still very much a period of flux, a lot of toing and froing. The wall really came down about six months to a year later.

EVA JIRICNA: I was only going to leave for six months; I felt I would be back either for Christmas or certainly for the next summer holiday. My brother who was only seventeen, came over. Then it all changed. On 14 September 1969 the Czech embassy issued a warning that whoever was still outside Czechoslovakia and was not intending to return by that date was going to be treated as an illegal immigrant. If we didn't go back straight away we would lose our citizenship. I had realized that the situation was getting pretty serious but I still thought it couldn't go back to the way it was before the invasion. I couldn't believe they would take things back to the absolute control of the '50s or early '60s. Then two things happened. My brother, who was supposed to go to university, received a letter from my sister. It was a copy of one from the university and said that due to the fact that I was now an illegal immigrant – which I wasn't because at that point I still had a valid Czech visa – he was not going to be allowed to take up his place and instead he was to start his armed service.

At that point I realized it was serious. I realized that somebody already wanted to get rid of me. There were people with whom the regime was uncomfortable and there were quite a number of my friends who were told they were not wanted and could they please get out of the country. I felt that after this letter I was included. So if I had gone back I would have lost my job and would have really been in trouble. I knew that if my brother went back he would never be able to study because I remembered from when I was young I had plenty of friends who were not allowed to attend university just for political reasons. Also I was splitting up with my husband. So personal reasons combined with political ones and I decided not to go back.

6 The Shock of the New

'I really didn't realize how different it was over here.'

CHRISTOPHER HOPE: Given my prior impressions of England I decided that Plato was quite right to kick poets and writers out of his republic – they tell the most dreadful lies. My very sharp images of that settled, civilized, 'other place' had only a minute tinge of truth in them. Britain was a deeply foreign country, populated by the most unruly natives. A very strange and turbulent place. The only thing one had in common with the natives here was the English language. That was the only connection. The British made it quite clear that we were foreign. It was more complicated for them because unlike other people from elsewhere, we were also white. So we *seemed* like them, but the moment you opened your mouth, and the way you reacted to what you found around you, distinguished you immediately. Particularly in places outside London. Eerie it is. The echoing emptiness of the countryside. I found it remote, strange, still and deeply foreign. Your exoticism was a wonderful thing to behold in the eyes of your neighbours. But it wasn't their recognition of *our* foreignness that struck me, rather it was the other way round: to me *their* foreignness was so profound and disturbing and was made all the worse by the fact that I spoke the language. I had felt that I was at least a little bit English, and I discovered painfully, over a period, that I wasn't.

PETER TATCHELL: By comparison to the wide open spaces and modernity of Australia, it seemed as if London hadn't changed much from what I'd been taught in school about nineteenth-century Britain. The city was dirty. People were poor. Their clothes, houses, cars and faces looked run-down and old-fashioned. Nevertheless, I was fascinated by the sense of history in London; that there were buildings and places which dated back to the Romans and beyond. As a gay person, I was also enthused by the existence in London of a radical movement for lesbian and gay equality. After the repressive homophobic atmosphere of Australia, that was tremendously exciting and liberating.

DON ATYEO: The English were totally different to what you thought. The English were involved in their own lives, in the first place. We were there in Australia seeing these boatloads of ten-quid immigrants coming over and saying 'Give us a job, guvnor', and we were the great Australians, the bronzed men of the soil helping out this mix of remittance men and refugees from Birmingham and you knew they were all second-rate and you walked among them like gods. But you came here and, man, they didn't give a shit about you. You were an Australian and it didn't matter. Maybe you'd been to a boarding school in Australia but so what. You'd never be a hooray Henry and you knew that very very quickly. You knew you'd never make it into the upper classes. You had come to somewhere where you expected to be embraced and what happened was that not only were you ignored, but at that time you were actually a figure of fun. There was 'Barry McKenzie' which had been running for years, and there was *Oz* magazine, which people like Auberon Waugh put down as some kind of scrubby provincial rag. That was it.

ALLA WEAVER: London was deeply depressing, dirty, cold and ugly, and my general feeling was: this is not what I want, this is terrible. I was booked in a club, a girl's hostel which was called a club, which was in Earls Court. Earls Court I hated. Earls Court was dreary beyond words, long streets of colonnaded, badly-painted houses. The people who lived there were the middle classes on small incomes. Mainly in boarding houses. One or two houses were a little bit better, divided into maisonettes, but I don't think that anybody inhabited the house as it was intended with maids in the basement and so on. The hostel was not for students, as far as I could make out. Some were middle-class girls who studied (to my surprise) hairdressing. The place was deserted over the weekend, most of them had parents in the country. The food was very poor. The rooms were cold. I was called to the secretary a few weeks after arrival and talked to like an idiot. She didn't realize that I spoke English, I had this strange surname, Periplatnik, and she enunciated each word and said something about coins: foreign coins had been found in the cigarette machine. Did I know anything about it? I said, 'Show me the coins. Whoever put them in doesn't know the value. These are Dutch guilders and they are worth about twice your English shilling.' And while she continued to talk to me in these slow sentences, I added, 'And I do not smoke and never have smoked.' I took that very badly. I took that as an anti-foreign interview.

MIGUEL ZAMBRANO: We were in this shanty town hostel in Shepherd's Bush. Women smoking, kids crying, men in despair, all of them refugees. They talked in slogans all the time. It was all very surrealistic. Next morning at 7 a.m. someone knocked on our door and started abusing us, 'Why aren't you awake? People are waiting for you!' It was the landlord, a Chilean. He said, 'You're supposed to be preparing breakfast for everybody!' I was in despair. How could I bring my family to this – was this democracy, freedom? The first day a friend arrived about 11 a.m. I had $60 in my pocket. We thought dollars would buy anything. We didn't have any English money. We embraced and I said to him, 'I need a drink.' He said, 'There's nowhere you can get a drink now.' I said, 'Look, I need that drink.' We went for a walk to Shepherd's Bush Green. I saw all the rings off Coca-Cola cans and couldn't believe it – I thought they were rings off gas grenades, the ones the Chilean police use. That was my first day in London.

DON ATYEO: I had believed that I would find a culture that I could just slot into without any trouble, and everything was alien: the beer was different, their pubs were different, all their habits were different. You couldn't even get into it. You were disbarred from this society on so many levels. I was quite open about being confronted by alien cultures and adapting to them, but here you couldn't. You were an Australian and that worked against you – you were a joke. Whenever you opened your mouth it was all kangaroos and so on. The British were a pretty insular race. They hadn't travelled. You expected it to be much more glamorous. You expected to look out of your window and there would be Mick Jagger walking down the street. Maybe he was, but not on my street. You expected to wander out there, 'Hi, Mick, liked the last album.' 'Thanks Don'. But that never happened.

KATHY ACKER: I really didn't realize how different it was over here. I really thought it was no more than moving to another city, another urban centre, where, all right, some things would be different, but on the whole I would continue to negotiate back and forth. I'd work in both places, I'd keep moving, and so on. I didn't realize how different it really was. It wasn't for six or eight months that it hit me that I was in a very foreign culture in every respect. At one point I began to believe that I really didn't understand what anybody meant any more. I started asking my friends, 'Do you like me?' It was as if you had lost your language but you don't have the new one yet. So you're really lost. Little things. I didn't know that when you bought an appliance you had to put this stupid plug on. Appliances in New York come with plugs. So I would call people and ask how do you put the plug on. They'd say, 'Kathy, this is ridiculous!' The cultural ideas of society and identity are totally different, almost black and white really. Very, very different. For instance, if you're at a dinner party here, what matters is that you keep the conversation going, it's like a dance. You're thinking of everybody else and you're thinking, 'Well, I should say this thing at this time and that will keep things going, or make things more interesting,' whatever. 'This person isn't talking, I'll say this so they can.' Or it's a game of wit. But either way you're always thinking of the other people and how the conversation will go. In America on the other hand people don't talk about a subject – the theatre, books, whatever – they talk to each other and they talk about themselves. It's still bad manners here to say, 'Hi, I'm getting really famous' or 'Hi, my career is going in this manner . . .' It isn't done.

ESTHER IZUNDU: At home if somebody falls down, you say 'Sorry' as you help them up. Once when a lady fell, I did this. She kept saying, 'It's not your fault, there's nothing to be sorry for.' Another shock, I got a job in a Kentucky Fried Chicken shop in Sauchiehall Street [Glasgow], working at night, so my husband would be home to look after our baby daughter. There was a woman working there, aged about fifty-eight, and everyone called her Theresa. I had never called an elderly person by their Christian name. A woman who is relatively older than you, you call 'sister' or 'big sister'; if she's as old as your mother, you call her mama; an older man is uncle, big brother or papa. So I find it difficult to call this woman Theresa. I was only twenty-three. But there were girls there younger than me and the way they talked to this older woman horrified me. They were very rude, 'You go and do this. Sit there, do this.' I wouldn't dare treat her that way. After ten years I can now call people 'Mrs', but still not by their Christian names.

GULZAR KHAN: My friends had said that I was going to a very forward, advanced country, a very honest country. When you go into a newspaper shop you put down your money, then take your change and pick up your newspaper.

Nobody is watching you. There are no thieves, no pickpockets. They leave the milk on your doorstep, you leave the money and they'll leave your change. Nobody will steal it. My goodness! I arrived here and I looked around and saw that wasn't happening. I asked myself, 'Where is that?' I saw there were thieves, there were pickpockets, you only had to read the papers.

* * *

BHAJAN SINGH CHADHA: The England I had expected was what I had seen in the pictures, but what I found was not so bad. I used to watch Charlie Chaplin films and there would be very, very rich people and very, very poor people in the East End. I had concluded that things in the East End would be very bad. People were as poor as the poorest parts of India. But when I came here it seemed quite prosperous in comparison to India. My first stop was in Barking, which was the East End, and I was surprised to find how well-off the people were. They came to work in cars, that was very surprising.

DON ATYEO: What you wanted was pea-soupers and London buses and rock'n'roll. A bit of Dickens and a bit of Carnaby Street. I had the most extraordinary perceptions. There was the West End at one end of a road and there was an East End at the other – just like that. Some kind of huge great Champs-Elysées linking the two. The glittering West End and the East End, which was like little Jack the Ripper streets and you would walk from one to the other because it was all there on display. Piccadilly Circus, Oxford Circus ... they sounded so exotic: what did they have? Carousels, lights, streamers, balloons?

CUI QU: I was very secure in China. If I had no money I could have asked my parents, they would buy me clothes, everything like that. Even though I worked. But when we first came here we had to live very differently. Our home in China was much much better than the place we lived in here, which had to be a very cheap place. We had hot water, television and so on, but we had all that in China. I thought, 'Oh my God.' I was shocked. I went to Oxford Street and I couldn't believe it. There were so many beautiful things, but look at the price. Oh no. I can't afford anything.

RAMESH VALA: I went to Oxford Street and I'd never seen such masses of people, all out shopping on a Saturday. Then there were the tubes, the idea that you had thirty seconds to jump on or you'd miss it. I started getting rather depressed when I realized that at four in the afternoon, this was winter, that it got dark. I couldn't cope and I couldn't understand what I was doing in central London living in this hall of residence next to the Post Office Tower. It was cold. I went to my first law lecture and only two of us had proper trousers, a tie, a blazer. Yet I had been told that I had to dress up for lectures. I went home, took off the jacket, the trousers, the tie and put them away and didn't wear them again after that. It was jeans from then on. I felt terribly lonely. Your first inclination as an immigrant is to look for your own people and make friends there. I ended up making friends with a few Welsh people, none of whom had ever seen an Asian before.

GULZAR KHAN: Living standards in England were so different. The buildings were different, the houses were different – lots of things. The biggest difference was in the relations between males and females. You would go out and everyone was sitting in the streets together, and it was strange what was happening: why is it happening in public places? We spent four weeks in Cardiff. Near the castle is a big park. The girls were lying on top of their boyfriends and they were kissing and we were shocked. We looked at each other: 'What is happening here?'

VERNA WILKINS: The fact that there were white people digging the roads or doing menial jobs in England didn't bother me: it was their country and they should do their own digging. I was very surprised though to find illiterates.

FIRDOS ALI: I had studied British history to O-level standard, because it used to be part of the curriculum. It painted a funny picture, a nice picture of England: a fair-minded people, the British sense of justice, all that. You read Eliot, Browning, Marlowe; you read Macaulay: England was the oldest democracy in the world. One good shelf of European books would outdo all the literature of the East. I was brought up on Shakespeare, things like that, though when I came over here I found that people didn't know as much as I did. I was sitting with a group of people – Asian and British – and I started reciting this sonnet by Elizabeth Barrett Browning – 'How do I love thee, let me count the ways . . .' – and these white people started looking at me. They said, 'Do you think in English when you speak in English?' I said, 'No. I think in Kashmiri, then I translate it into English, then I speak to you. I have a computer up here.' It was a stupid question, embarrassing. You think in your own language. What I didn't know was that I wasn't talking to some fucking intellectual. I'd expected the British not only to be democratic and just, I also assumed they would be literate. Ridiculous, but that was the brainwashing I had picked up reading English history.

MICHAEL DE SOUZA: I had never seen so many white people, I had never seen a big city. There was one guy I knew back in Trinidad who was Indian, and because he wasn't black I thought he was white. So the first weekend in London came and my brother and all his friends were off school. So he wanted

106

me to meet them. I had this real little Trinidad accent. So I went downstairs onto the front steps and he introduced me around. All I could recall were these accents which I couldn't understand at all. ''Ere, Ken, this your bruvva?' I just started to swear. I told my brother, 'I don't like these people at all, at all, at all.' I ran upstairs. I couldn't understand *what* they were talking about. These were white kids, there weren't really any black kids yet.

PALOMA ZOZAYA: I was very lonely. I started to wonder, 'Where can I go to meet people who have the same interests that I have?' I decided to go to the film festival at the South Bank. So there I was one day, sitting next to a man who laughed all the way through the film at the same things I laughed at. We seemed to enjoy the film very much, and found the same bits amusing. So I thought, 'Well, quite likely we could have a coffee.' It wasn't a matter of flirting, anything like that, it was just a matter of wanting to make friends and meet someone who might have the same kind of mentality that I did. The film finished, and the lights came on, and we both got up and just went our own ways. No contact. It really hit me, the way people wouldn't make any contact in a situation like this. I find this extreme discretion here very surprising. I find it even with my English husband. I'm terribly nosy and I get terribly angry with him sometimes. I tell him, 'Did you see that man . . . did you notice that couple . . . did you . . . ?' and he doesn't. It seems as if people just go from A to B and whatever happens between A and B has no relevance. Which is certainly not the case in Mexico. If you go out somewhere you might stop to talk to people, or you might look at people, or whatever. But here there's no street culture. People live indoors. No café culture, no promenading up and down. And then there's the eating habits. The English diet is remarkably lacking in fresh vegetables, salads and fruit. I can understand that you have to eat lots of fried foods to put up with the cold weather, but to me that diet is still absolutely shocking.

It was hard to make friends. Men don't look at you in the street, so you start wondering, is there something wrong with me? As soon as you get out of England, men start turning round to look at you again, and that's very reassuring. Feminists might not agree here, but it is very reassuring. You don't smile at people here, you get into the underground trains and immediately hide your face behind a newspaper.

DON ATYEO: I got very disillusioned with England at first. Because I was a nothing. Not only was I an Australian, and on those grounds alone an intrinsically interesting person, but I had also been along the hippie trail, and had been to far more countries than most English hippies. I thought my knowledge would be looked upon, if not as a guru – I didn't have that level of pretension – but at least as a man of wisdom, and at least someone to lay. They should have been lining up in Hyde Park. Hyde Park was another thing. My ideas of what it would be like arriving here obviously had been modified on my travels, but I did think that I'd be walking around, long blond hair, flowing robes, dressed like Gandalf or someone out of *The Hobbit*, and the English women would be queuing up to hear my words of wisdom and suck my dick; of course they didn't want to know.

YASMIN ALIBHAI: I had a lot of mixed emotions when I finally came. Those childhood longings were still there: I did want to see what it was like. I also felt odd: the central theme throughout my life was that I had never felt that I belonged to any group or to any country. This used to depress me. I loved East Africa but I never felt that I belonged there, and I thought that England was where I'd belong. The mother country image was quite strong for a while. These people whom I had met, these children of the '60s who did treat you with respect, I had warmed to and I expected that most of England would be like them. In many ways, since I was in Oxford, my hopes were fulfilled. But it was also an immensely snobbish place. Socially I was very happy and made a lot of friends, and people were very good, but institutionally they were very hard and very snobbish. It wasn't just because the work was hard or they criticized my work, they were actually deeply racist. The idea that I, an Asian woman, could dare to think that I could do an M. Phil. in English. Dons would say, 'Why don't you go to Leeds and specialize on V. S. Naipaul?' They had great fun at my expense and I used to be completely daunted by those remarks. As I was by the typical Oxford student who made you feel that he or she knew everything and that basically you were vermin. It took me a long time to understand that that was just a pose and that if you analysed what they were saying, it often came to nothing, but they said it in a way that impressed. I swore then that any child of mine was going to acquire that facility, because it's the basis of the whole of English society and it was something that I lacked. Oxford was mixed feelings. It took the sting out of me, I became a less politically angry person immediately. I was mesmerized by the apple trees and the tea on the lawns and all that. I had fantasized about it in Uganda, and it was all there.

7 Learning the Culture

'A tourist cannot imagine that the natives might be stupid, because you don't speak their language.'

WITOLD STARECKI: Nobody who hasn't spent at least five years here knows the British at all. I am starting to understand a bit. It's a very hard culture to learn.

HANNAH KODICEK: Our experiences on arrival were influenced by that naïvety of youth, lack of English language, and a complete ignorance of the class system. The people we were staying with were very relaxed and very beautiful people but a lot of their friends and relations were much more rigid. We used to be invited to massive parties, all the time. We didn't realize that we were dragged along as a sort of novelty, the token Czech. People used to stare you earnestly in the eye and say, '*Do* tell me about this, *do* tell me about that, how *frightfully* fascinating . . .' and of course they weren't fascinated at all, but we didn't know all the little nuances that we know now.

KATHY ACKER: All my friends joke with me about being an American. They all say, 'Oh I hate Americans.' So I respond. I think when I first came over here I didn't always recognize it, and it was there, though mainly from journalists. When my first book came out here I didn't know what to make of the journalists because I didn't understand the rules. They were very hostile, although at first I thought they were being nice. Because when they are hostile here, journalists appear to be acting extremely nice to you. Whereas when they like you they'll start taking the piss out of you a little, asking you real questions – it's not so nicey-nicey. This thing in English etiquette whereby you are exquisitely polite to the people you dislike most. That's not the way in the States. If a journalist dislikes you in the States the attack will be very up-front. The codes here of indicating what you mean are the most devious I have ever come across in the western world. You just don't say what you mean. The methods with which you go about saying what you mean – it's a second language I had to learn. I had to learn what intention corresponded to what manner of speech. The code is absolutely not direct. It is wit, it is irony. It's like learning a dance. One day you feel proud: gee, I can do it now. Which makes you much less American by doing that; Americans can't handle it at all. I go over to America these days and I can twist my friends just like that, which I never could before. Look at Americans who go on the Jonathan Ross show. Virtually none of them can handle him – he just takes the piss out of them and

Americans don't take the piss. It took me almost four years before I felt I had cracked the code.

DON ATYEO: Once you'd scratched the surface the English did become familiar as people. Occasionally you would tell some other Australian, 'The English, they're a funny race' or whatever, but actually they're not. In fact they're very close to what I was brought up as. Still, the English are a very very hard people to approach and it is a hard culture to learn. Even if you're white, employed in the media, all that. When I had just arrived, I'd see those Holland Park youth hostels filled with flags of all nations, living together cheek by jowl, and a lot of them were terrified to go out. They would go on little forays to see something – maybe the Tate, whatever – then rush back and sit back in their multicultural exile community. I presume this still happens. The English expect you to come to them, to work with them: their way of doing things is right and you have very little to offer. They don't want to hear too much about your experiences.

BRIGITTE NEWMAN: It is a marvellous exciting renewal of one's life to have to discover lots of funny little things at an age where one can take life for granted beause one is through one's education, one's manners and everything else have been put in, and if one stays in the same place there is nothing left to discover apart maybe from black magic or Buddhism. But if one moved to another country one discovered crumpets, jumble sales, when to say 'love', 'dear' and 'one' and one gets it right sometimes and wrong sometimes and it's very challenging and very amusing.

MIGUEL ZAMBRANO: We played around on the zebra crossings, stopping the cars, feeling important. In those days they did stop – they don't now. Then we went for a drink and the barmaid called us 'Love'. I thought, 'My God, she's calling me "love" straight away, this is going to be easy.' Another day we were in Oxford Circus, and my friend said, 'We'll insult all these people in the queue. You see? They don't understand, don't react.' Then one girl said: 'What a foul mouth you have.' My friend wanted to die. This girl was Spanish, you see.

PO-YEE WONG: I found the language different from what I had read in books – so much slang, and not used as precisely. One day I was crossing a road and a man was coming the other way. He meant to be friendly, but he said, 'Hello, love.' What a shock! In Chinese 'love' and 'like' have such precise meanings.

PETAR OBRATOVIC: I was never aware how troublesome it was to change countries. I was alone, I had no professional or social identity. There was the lack of known things, things that I based part of my safety on, social clues that we pick up, or knowledge of the streets or whatever. For my first year in London I had a great need to learn the actual geography. Just to get an inner representation of the way the town is laid out. I did know the language, which did help, though what I knew didn't go much beyond the level of an English person with a low IQ. To extract what was actually going on in my mind and put it into English was practically impossible. People found it hard to understand me. I was very displeased by how little I could express all these thoughts.

MIRANDA LOVETT: For a very very long time I assumed that because England and America speak the same language we would be similar. To me that is the greatest mistake that I made and it was the hardest thing for me to understand. It took me ten years to learn British culture and a lot of the reason it took so long was that the stumbling blocks I came across made me so angry. The politics annoyed me, the social structure annoyed me, the little cultural differences made me angry. I was like a bull in a china shop. I learned to live alongside the English and to accept them as they are and not to fight them and not to try to turn them into something that suited me and not to try and turn myself into something that suited them. There's no doubt that to live in England you have to come to them, but I really don't feel that I have compromised and yet I find that I have a completely different relationship with the English now than I did when I arrived.

* * *

PETAR OBRATOVIC: It was all right while I was still a student and was thinking of going back, but once I had decided not to go back . . . where was I? where did I fit? what was I going to do? I suddenly realized how complex British society is and I realized that I don't fit anywhere. I had no class, but that was just a part of it. I was completely displaced. There were certain segmented parts of my experience through which I knew here I did fit, for instance I was attached to St George's medical school, so I knew I fitted there, but in general I felt that I fit only into the category of 'foreign', which is outside the major system. I really needed to fit somewhere. I became a member of the tennis club – that was all right, whatever language I spoke. That was a little island of full experience that I could have. Though at the club they thought that maybe I was a spy.

BRIGITTE NEWMAN: Fitting in is interesting. Having lived for two years on my territory with my husband, I now had to take on his past, his life, his friends, his flat – where he had lived for fifteen years. Learning the country came after learning the relationship. What I discovered about my English husband through moving into his territory. The first culture shock was those abysmal calor-gas things, with the bottles. There was no central heating in this flat. No central heating in France is unheard of, apart perhaps from four French eccentrics who live in little *hameaus* in the countryside. Central heating is just something one has, central heating is never turned off in France. It comes on on 1 October and stays on for the winter, whatever the temperature. But this is very much the attitude of the English middle and upper classes to pleasure. There's the same thing with food and drink. It goes through everything, and I think that one of the few pleasures an English man allows himself is his morning crap. This attitude leads to things like the Engllish pub, though it leads to some very great qualities also. Let's face it, there is a very positive aspect to negating one's pleasure, which is that one is tough and hard and one can cope with an awful lot of things and one is not self-pitying and self-indulging, both of which are very, very frowned upon in England. Wars, I'm sure, are great things to the English.

RAMESH VALA: I was coming to terms with life in England: changing weather, things like that. The whole process of learning in England was so different to what I had experienced in East Africa. There you were spoonfed; there was no question of disagreeing with a tutor – that could lead to problems. Here it was different: people discussed topics, they disagreed with the tutor, you could express your own views. I didn't have that much time to assess the English, but those I met I found extremely reserved. Unless one talked about football, things like that, it was very difficult to break ground. Getting accepted meant hanging around the bar, talking about football, playing darts. I had two or three friends from my old school and we were learning England together.

PETAR OBRATOVIC: I learnt certain differences. Not that I learned the subtleties, but I knew the main differences. I learnt about the differences between different parts of England. I learnt a lot about differences between classes, I learnt about how far apart are the parts of this society, which I never realized. I had met the English when I worked in Algeria and we really got on well. They all came from different classes and they all mixed. But they told me, they might mix in Algeria, where they were expatriate workers, but they would never talk to each other in England. I started learning about the ins and outs of British politics. I started buying newspapers – even if I still turn to the foreign news before the home news – and I learnt about the differences between the tabloids and the others, the dailies and the Sundays. I learnt how distinct interests are. I began working with the mentally handicapped right away and I began visiting their families so I had to learn about language. In the first year or two I really learnt a lot about how the British function. I was quite amazed about how different to Yugoslavia it is.

FATIMA IGRAMHIM: You have to make a conscious effort to learn the English culture; I don't think I've done so well. Sometimes if the two or three friends I really like are not around, I think of all the people I've met and wonder who I could really call if I wanted to talk to somebody. Then I feel I haven't done well. If my friends are around, then I feel that I've done quite well.

In the end I have not learned the English yet. I kind of understand them, but I can't respect them for the way they are. I know what their likes and their dislikes are, but I don't work on that level. But I have changed: I'm less spontaneous, I keep my opinions more to myself, I try to be less loud or strong as a woman, because that is looked down upon. You should be more charming and more feminine – all these stupid things. I've been lectured about not being properly English. I was in a restaurant and the food was very bad and I said that we should send it back. Then this man said, 'You can't do this here, don't make such a fuss, this is very Germanic, you can't be such a perfectionist. Can't you just grin and bear it?' As a foreigner you're not meant to make trouble.

PETER VO: In the Thorney Island camp they taught us a lot about British life in terms of the festivals that come up during the year – Christmas, Easter, Valentine's Day, bank holidays. We were given the opportunity to have a look at England: London, Brighton, the seaside, the countryside. We learned to be British. We met an English family, ate with them, talked with them and listened to them. We tried to learn so we could infiltrate into this new society. We had to accept that now England was our home, there was no hope of returning to Vietnam, this was our new home. It was a second home but it was still home. Permanently. So it was important to learn how to act like the British people. I learned a lot.

VICTOR WILD: As an immigrant you gradually change. I found one of the big differences was in humour. Swiss humorous magazines now seemed very clumsy compared, say, to *Punch*. Heavy-handed. I began to realize that I wasn't Swiss any more really.

SHARI PEACOCK: After the first six months, after which my mother went back to Bulgaria, I began sharing a flat with some English people. Two other girls and two men in a flat in West Kensington. I found them in an ad in the *Evening Standard. That* was when the trouble started. This was where I saw Englishness at its worst, its unglamorous side. These were provincial girls who had come from out of London, small towns. Two were secretaries. There was one man who was studying to be an accountant, and the other didn't seem to do anything and eventually went off to India and got caught with drugs. It was this really grim house, I had never been used to living with other people. If you took a bath and forgot to wash the bathroom properly they'd come and nag you. There were a lot of notes left around: 'Please use only one quarter of the milk', things like that. I wasn't a very good flatmate, I'd been spoilt by living with my parents, but I learnt fast. Here were the blond people, the same as those I had seen at the seaside in Bulgaria, and in the context of their own country they were very dreary. A foreigner, a tourist, cannot imagine that the natives might be stupid, because you don't speak their language. In that state everybody else is more intelligent than you are. But when you live somewhere you gradually see that people may be quite dull or even stupid. We just didn't get on. It wasn't that I was foreign, it was just that I was a bad flatmate.

BRYAN GOULD: In many ways I already knew the British culture, and in some ways I found it very congenial. I think a lot of people are still puzzled by me for that very reason. Here I was, an immigrant, I had the option of all sorts of different lifestyles, yet I had chosen this. People would say, 'You're supposedly a radical in politics, why have you become – as they see it – a stereotyped Oxbridge graduate dark-suited Englishman?' To which I answer, I just happen to like a lot of the things that those sort of people do. I share their interests in some ways and I can't see any point in deliberately setting myself up against the establishment on things that don't particularly matter to me. You don't need to wear jeans to the office in order to demonstrate your radicalism.

8 England: Another Country

'The English want the world to be as they expect, the way that is comfortable; they don't like the challenge, quite simply, they don't like the challenge.'

CARMEN CALLIL: I love living in England, I wouldn't live anywhere else, and I've been terribly lucky. I'm not a typical Australian in that I was raised to believe that Britain was the centre of the universe – so I've never felt inferior here, never had a chip on my shoulder, never worried about my accent or my foreign name. Though people here would constantly ask about my name, where did it come from. My grandfather took his given name, Halil, and anglicized it to Callil. We were a prominent Melbourne Catholic family and nobody there had ever questioned it. I don't have a persecution complex about living in Britain, although I don't think my personality is very suited to the country. I should have stayed at home. Most people tell me how awful I am. I probably am, but it does become wearing. I love the culture here. I love London, I love

North Kensington, my house, my friends, going to movies, the newspapers, the argument, the television, the food, the roast beef and two veg. and I don't mind the weather. At home I wouldn't have had such stimulating companionship. I would have had a much narrower life. I love being near to Europe, though I loathe travel. Most of all I like the variety of friends I've made here, which I would never have made in Australia. I love the stories of my friends' lives. Though if I'd have been born here I would have left.

KATHY ACKER: England is far more sexist than America. The boys hold hands here like nowhere I've ever seen. For a woman to have a career here, just a plain old career – not a job, not factory work – is still unusual, it's something that is not accepted. That kind of thing is still new. I heard someone on radio, saying how proud they were because they'd decided to work for a living. Well, a lot of people do. No one would ever comment on it in America because everyone works for a living. Most women there, if they can, have careers. It's not a radical thing. I think that it was the women who were harder to adjust to for me than the men when I came here. It's a basic difference in the expectations one has about how one lives one's life. It's this matter of career and your relation to work and to success and to identity. To my mind the English feminist movement was still interiorizing a lot of role models that to me seemed to centre a bit around the Virgin Mary. Models that don't exist so much any more in the United States. This business about separatism. It is not of importance theoretically any more. Whereas here it still is. That dichotomy, where you have to choose either/or, is indicative of a very early part of the movement. Basically they don't have power.

BENNY BUNSEE: There are lots of things about British and western culture that I genuinely don't like. Obviously the racism, but there is also the breakdown of the general social relationships, even the love relationships, the way feminism has become an abiding force in western society, although I accept that the liberation of women is vital. It seems that this society is leaving things like compassion and love behind it and becoming totally individualistic. Modern western society seems simply to be duplicating the ego-values of male individualism. The child sexual abuse here definitely upsets me. It may happen throughout the world, but it takes place on an extensive level here and that really upsets me. It's one of the things that is driving me out of this society. The barrenness of the white youth – punks and so on – they seem so nihilistic, so alienated. They have no politics, no sense of direction. The whole phenomenon of Thatcherism, the way it has stifled everything in this country.

MIGUEL ZAMBRANO: We've only been in our house about fifteen months. It's beautiful, but we're surrounded by these dirty animals – well, it's an offence to animals to call them that. These people destroy everything. Londoners – the worst of the lot. They're ignorant, arrogant, no manners. You have the best and the worst of everything in this country. The best scientists, the worst labourers – they're lazy and unimaginative. You have the best cars in the world – Bentley, Rolls-Royces – then just rubbish, nothing in the middle. The best TV in the world, the worst radio – except for Radio 2, 4 and LBC – the rest is rubbish. The best press, the *Financial Times* – but the rest is rubbish. I read the *Telegraph* (it's very informed) and the *Mail*. You have the best people and the worst people – you don't have average people.

MARIA VOROSKOI: England is still the only grown-up country in the world. It does have maturity. By which I mean the background that has been built up slowly, well, and which has roots. And it means that there are a group of people who still carry on with those achievements. I don't find it in France, I don't find it in Italy. Only the best is good enough in England, but when you find it, the best is better than anywhere else. England stands here like a tower, with two giant children: America and Russia. England remains a marvellous place, filled with so many marvels; if only people don't clutter it up with rubbish. Maybe what has happened is that the essence of England has become watered down by the vast number of people. The countryside is changing because more and more houses are needed, more and more roads are needed.

TESS WICKHAM: The things I like about England are the classical beautiful things. Designed English parkland. Designed landscaping, which is beautiful. I love Scotland, which is not England. The thing about the English is that they are people of the word, and I don't need to be that close to them. The major contribution of the British is that of language. That's what I appreciate most about them, though I don't think I need to stay in England to gain the benefit of it.

They're visually illiterate and that offends me daily. It's also a gross exaggeration, there are exceptions to the rule, but until quite recently there was no sense of design. Even now I am sceptical of the supposed design consciousness. High street design awareness is a total con, someone's just got it across that design pays. It's not understanding more about the importance of form and design. That's why they all love Prince Charles, why they all want to retire behind a classical façade. It's more predictable, more comfortable, nothing confronting and demanding of the mind. They want what always was, even if what they get is a completely crappy version of what always was, they still prefer the pastiche, the complete crap version of what they're used to, to something that is visually demanding, that you have to respond to. The visual side of the mind is not treated as one of the senses that is part of human development. The visual world is simply something that is there, you have to

116

live with it, though you'd prefer to live surrounded by trees. They want trees everywhere, pot plants everywhere, mud everywhere, mud, mud, glorious mud. This total disrespect for the visual world, which is not really treated as part of our senses. It's frivolous, like food or drink, the physical world is not particularly of any importance.

The English want the world to be as they expect, the way that is comfortable; they don't like the challenge, quite simply they don't like the challenge. It's a means of softening the edges, bringing the country into the city, and not respecting individual worlds. All this neo-classicism is complete hypocrisy anyway: behind the façade is the usual computerized office. In some ways the English are cerebral, although they're not intellectual; and they're not sensual in any respect. It's down to respect for words and the way in which words, not physical phenomena, manipulate the environment.

SHARI PEACOCK: The quality of food once you get out of London is just incredibly awful. In a country like Iran the poorest peasant would eat better food. Aesthetically and sensually this country is very disappointing. It's very good cerebrally but otherwise . . . Leaving London, those little provincial towns, the ugliness, the awful architecture, I still find that very depressing. Bulgaria isn't exactly an aesthetic paradise, but it has places that have more character.

PETAR OBRATOVIC: I love the way that the English can express different opinions and still stay friends, or at least stay on a civilized level. In Yugoslavia if you had the sort of confrontational opinions as you see on television here, you would have to take your guns out or something, or you would be ashamed. There would really be a lot of shame: you are fighting for yourself, not just for a view-point. Here you can have different opinions, and be proved wrong and still not be ashamed. So I like that sense of possibility. I also enjoy the way society works. I can travel, I can afford more things, even though I'm actually worse off financially. I can be less worried about things I would have been worried about in Yugoslavia. I like the countryside. I like the sights, I like stupid things. Though I miss the sun, the smells, the taste of tobacco . . . I love the cosmopolitan sense of Britain. I like the fact that people can come here – there are so many other nations who are interested in coming, so they come, whatever the British think about them.

MICHAEL DE SOUZA: I believe that this country gives you the opportunity to free up yourself. In the West Indies you can't. You've got to go with the norm or you're an outcast. The one thing I know about England is that it's very tolerant. So if you're in a tolerant society you can use that opportunity to do what you want to do. You're given time. They're so tolerant that they don't even realize that you're building up your arms. This is why I find I'm in a strong position. I'm no great success, but the one thing that really does satisfy me is that I haven't been pushed into any bracket.

CHRISTOPHER HOPE: Yes, you are permitted to say what you like, until it affects somebody directly and then you'll be stopped. Either by laws, or by well-marshalled groups whose job it is to make sure that people are not touched too deeply. If they are, blood flows, and one can't have that. I was here during some of the worst outbreaks in Ulster, and it became apparent to me immediately that when the blood starts to flow for real everybody – governments, the rest of society – moves to stop it. Look at the censorship during the Falklands War. We did not see a corpse, either British or Argentinian, throughout that entire war. Why not? Because it was *our* people out there, it was *our* war. One could hardly show the mothers, relatives, the people next door such pictures. People understand what is expected of them. In extreme situations they'll accept restrictions on their liberty of a sort that would make a commissar weep. That was deeply instructive. All talk about freedom of expression goes out of the window and without any comment from those who are at other times very quick to point out diminution of liberties. Maybe that's the way with a homogenous people, and why immigrants remain not part of the whole.

* * *

MICHAEL IGNATIEFF: What I liked about coming here was coming to a post-imperial clapped-out, self-doubting, run-down old country, which is what Britain definitely was at the end of the '70s. The country seemed run-down, crummy, fatalistic. Yet in a curious way I rather liked that. I liked it as an expatriate because those kinds of cultures leave you lots of room. You can be what you want to be in a country that's very absorbed in its own decline. They leave you alone more. The ceiling may be lower for the natives, but I never felt that I was one of the natives. The rules didn't apply to me, and that is a big expatriate theme. I didn't need to know my bloody place and I felt that as soon as I arrived. For instance there was all this stuff in Cambridge about being a 'college man'. That I couldn't manage. It required this unbelievable kind of dowdiness. These people with stalk necks and tight little collars and Hush Puppies on their feet and frightful corduroys and awful misshapen hacking jackets. The ill-shapenness of English academics is kind of charming; in the end they're almost lovable beause they are so unbelievably out of it.

BENTHE NORHEIM: I think this sort of genteel decay is very appealing and it is very English. Since I've been here I've travelled around the country quite a bit, especially by the seaside, and in these seaside towns I could see images that exaggerated and emphasized the picture I already had of London. There's something romantic and sad about them. Rotten, smelly almost, but at the same time it has a very strong beauty. And I have always seen the beauty in things that are decaying.

MICHAEL IGNATIEFF: Cambridge showed a certain English virtue in action. England is unbelievably unequal and hierarchical, but with the hierarchical it is a career open to the talents. Example: if you were elected as a fellow at King's you could then be part of a college meeting of 110–115 fellows and basically help run the place. Your success or failure in those enterprises, it appeared to me, depended entirely on your personality and your persuasiveness. You could stand up in front of Lord Kaldor or Edmund Leach or Bernard Williams, any of the giants, and give as good as you got. There was a curious kind of democracy among this élite which I responded to tremendously favourably, because I had come from Harvard which operates on the kind of samurai warrior system: there were slaves and then there were samurai. The Cambridge experience was just in every way more humane and more demo-cratic. It was also a wonderful place for expatriates, which is another aspect of the British university system at its most open. Often it seemed as if the English were in a minority. That permeability of that academic élite to the outside was one of the things that made Cambridge interesting.

I appreciate that in certain cases this may be a very closed world, that for Indians and Pakistanis who come here, for instance, it can be a world in which lots of doors are closed but my experience was that these places, at the top, were actually quite permeable. Whether it's only permeable to whites is an objection to which I would not have much of a reply. There weren't all that many black or Asian faces at King's College, Cambridge between '79 and '84.

PETER TATCHELL: Britain seemed trapped in a time-warp of ossified traditions; a world where social class and ancient rites weighed heavily upon people's consciousness and everyday life. The class divisions were much more pronounced than in Australia, from the way people spoke to the socially distinct districts where people lived. However, it was also a more liberal society compared with Australia where, in the early 1970s, there was still censorship and capital punishment; where homosexuality and abortion remained totally illegal, and where there was no national health service or adequate system of social welfare. In these senses, Britain did seem a more enlightened society. The existence of the NHS was one of the things that I found particularly attractive. My mother suffered from severe asthma which, in the absence of socialized medicine in Australia, resulted in huge medical bills and caused us immense financial hardship. I can remember thinking, from a very early age, how unfair it was that we had to suffer constant impoverishment because my mother was ill. So the British NHS was something I greatly admired, and still do.

KAREL KYNCL: The Swiss and British governments both offered me and my family political asylum on humanitarian grounds and I had this question mark: which one to choose? Switzerland is a beautiful, tidy, wonderful country, it may have been that my financial situation, my standard of living might be better there, but I was sure that after six months I would be bored to death. I left my wife to decide, but privately I prayed that she would decide on England. I'm sure that after a while I could understand the basic psychology, the way things work in any continental country. But I am sure that I will die of old age in this country not understanding the basic psychology. You are really very, very different. This is a complicated, messy country, but one thing that matters a lot to me is that I can't ever be bored to death here.

MICHAEL IGNATIEFF: There is a live and let live about English society, but with very abrupt and sharp moments where that stops. Very sharp. For me the best example of that moment was the miners' strike. I wrote a piece which turned out to be a watershed in my own relations to England. It was a long piece on the strike in which I basically said that this thing is a fucking disaster from almost any way you look at it. It's everything about this country that I can't stand. I wrote this piece saying a plague on all your houses and one of the things I said was that there was lots about the miners' case that I couldn't see. What their case came down to was that other members of the community, other taxpayers, were being asked to subsidize the production of coal. That cost me all of my friends on the Left. A lot of people just read me out, and that was one of those moments was when I realized that I was and remain an American-style liberal. I don't have any basic primordial allegiance to the political tribes here. I have an enormous intellectual respect for those labour traditions, but it's not an organic relationship, it's a learned respect. I detest the kind of canting Home Counties bullshit that comes out of Mrs Thatcher's mouth with real, deep loathing. I've voted in every election since 1970 and I always vote Labour. That was the moment when I felt I don't belong to the tribes. I never will. Which leads to the bigger thought that I will never feel a true citizen. What it conjured up to me was analogous to being an adopted uncle in some happy but contentious family and living in that family, the friendly unmarried uncle who's invited to Sunday lunch, always showing up week after week after week and then suddenly there's some absolutely god-awful fight in the family and suddenly you're sitting there and this place is tearing itself apart and you just get up from the table and just want to walk out the front door. It's not in your blood, it's not in your bones, it's not your fight, it's phoney to claim that it

120

is and you hate everything that comes out of both sides of their mouths. It's too late to stand up and ponce around, the liberal decent guy in the middle, saying you're both wrong, and it was much too late to say that, although I'm glad I wrote the piece, in the strike. In fact I thought the Left were being canting hypocrites.

9 The English People

'The English family is a house covered by snow.'

CHRISTOPHER HOPE: The English are a fractious, belligerent and turbulent people who like fighting. Their history is threaded through with the love of action, particularly if it occurs elsewhere. You went off to fight people 'over there' and were rather good at it, and you brought home your trophies, hung your colours in cathedrals, remembered your battles and fallen and were jolly pleased about it, very proud of it, and it was held to be a remarkable thing. An astonishingly warlike lot.

FATIMA IGRAMHIM: The English are bound by so many things that don't bind other countries. They are bound by the class system, they are bound by a very, very bad school system, which makes them into cripples. In Germany we have mostly state schools and only if you're very bad in school, then your parents have to pay for a private school. Only those who are very bad and who can't go to our very good state schools go to private schools. So private education is looked down on. Class and education is linked here and it's very bad. It's bad for almost everybody. It's very unfair on a lot of people that they can't afford the best schools. The second sad thing is that class makes people full of prejudices and they don't seem able to free themselves from them. As a foreigner you don't really have a class – although people do try to find things out about you so that they can place you. Class means that if you're part of the aristocracy then you can do whatever you like and everyone will laugh, but if you're not, then you can't. In Germany education is the class system, and you can use it to transcend where you came from socially and nobody looks down on you because your father was a butcher or whatever. We don't have this things with accents, U and non-U and the rest of it. In general English manners are worse than German manners. The third sad thing is that people are bound by their houses. I find this a very difficult thing for me to like or to understand. In America and Germany and any other country I've lived in people don't own their own houses. Most people are not crippled by such an incredible mortgage as they are here. Outside England a house is not this important thing. People here, I find, are often very mean-spirited in the way that they don't spend money. They're always thinking, 'Oh, if I am going out to dinner, I owe this, I owe that, one quarter of my money has to pay the mortgage . . .' they're always putting up reasons for not spending.

CINDY BLAKE: There is no soul-searching like everybody does in America, nobody cared about all these crucial questions, which I felt was great. For a while. At that point in my life I felt that was wonderful, that English upper-class exclusion of emotion. Thank God I don't have to talk about myself; thank God people don't walk in the room and say, 'Are you suffering . . . ?' Now I'd give my eye teeth for that. Nobody asked any personal questions. You'd sit beside these people at dinner and nobody would ask you anything. Who you were, where you came from, nothing. It was great, I loved it. I don't know where they're taught to be like that but they're just a world apart, it's like a different species. I couldn't believe that it still existed to this extent.

FIRDOS ALI: People hold beliefs, they feel things, but they won't fight for them. Here, in England, they can raise interest rates, people will accept it without argument; they can raise the tax on cigarettes and booze and people will just take it lying down; fares on public transport go up, nobody argues; they completely fuck up the service and nobody complains. In Calcutta in 1961 the tram and bus fares were increased by what in English money would have been one fourth of a farthing and there was a general strike, four buses were burnt out, trams were derailed, and the government had to withdraw.

MARY ROSE: There's this kind of politeness that doesn't really mean anything. There is this story of a couple who have this American officer to stay. The morning he arrives they had the news that their son has been killed. But nobody talks about it: they don't want to spoil his holiday.

WITOLD STARECKI: The other side of what is called English hypocrisy is an attitude that does not wish to invade someone else's privacy. People are gentler to each other. It can reach a ridiculous state: you get a couple who are foreigners to each other because they don't want to intervene in someone else's fears. This Polish actress gave me the simplest definition of the difference: if a Pole doesn't ask you a personal question it means that he doesn't care about you; if an Englishman is asked a personal question he thinks you are rude. One of the reasons that many Polish immigrants do not make it here is that we don't operate in a straightforward manner, because of all the history and other circumstances. As as Pole I have a well-developed sense of metaphor, allegory, association and so on. My Polish audience automatically picks up on those things. Here people just get lost. They say, 'Give me a simple answer to a simple question,' but that is something that doesn't exist in Poland and it will take years for it to develop.

ANWAR BATI: On the whole I do like the English, but I don't like their hypocrisy, I don't like their cowardliness, I don't like their laziness. This is, anyway, a certain type of public-school upper-class Englishman who doesn't have the courage of his convictions, who will think one thing and say another in order to avoid embarrassment, in order to avoid a difficult time.

SHARI PEACOCK: Any foreigner has got a major problem with English people in terms of relationships. They're different bodies. The way they express themselves. These differences really go as deep as that. The way the body deals with stress, anything. The blood of the English, cliché though this is, just runs more slowly, and it's paler, it's blue, it's got to be. I used to think this was just men, because it's with lovers that you most notice these things, and I'd be thinking, 'God, how do these English women deal with these men?' and now I realize the women are the *same*. But it took so long to understand. The women are stiff-upper-lipped too, they don't talk either. They're constipated and everything else as well.

MIRANDA LOVETT: When I look at the English women whom I meet and I wonder what the difference between us is, the only word that comes to mind, it's not very nice but it's the only one I can think of, is that they are shallow. I think that the English are quite shallow. I think that shallowness sometimes produces greater needs in people in surrounding themselves with things – material, social or whatever, it doesn't matter – that will make them feel more secure. They say they're reserved but actually they're not. They're often very open and direct. A couple of weeks we had the granddaughter of a good friend of ours to stay. She's at Yale, twenty-two, and she's working over here for a while. We were talking about an evening she had spent with an English guy of her age. He's very funny, very immature, very boisterous. She was amazed at the coarseness of the conversation at dinner. I understood exactly what she meant. The English can be so proper and reserved and then you'll be in a situation like that where they're so basic, so coarse, and it's again a little bit of this thing where I feel they can dish it out but they can't take it. It's as if they like to see how far they can go in a situation. In a funny sort of way Americans of that age are much more sophisticated.

I've always had this theory that the English miss out on a part of their childhood that the Americans have. Americans go through a sort of rebellious period between the ages of fifteen and twenty and the English don't. They're always grown-up. As a result you find English people in their early twenties being very immature, because they haven't gone through that process of rebellion.

SHREERAM VIDYARTHI: When the English call themselves 'very reserved people, we don't like interfering, we don't like imposing' it is merely a way of covering up utter self-centredness and utter selfishness. More than a hundred families in Sittingbourne have dined at my table, some more than once. Some even uninvited – they came, we happened to be eating, we sat them at the table and we fed them. Not one of them in the eighteen years of my living there has invited me back. Maybe they're scared of spending five pennies on a cup of tea? I tell them to their face: they say, 'Well, you might have a point there . . .'

WITOLD STARECKI: While I was editing my second film for the BBC I received a call from a colleague: 'Witek, we are signing a petition against the government's banning of the film *At the Edge of the Union*. Would you like to join us? I told them that I sympathized, that this was exactly why I had come to England myself and I don't want to see censorship anyway. But on the other hand I feel bad about making any comments against somebody who invited me here and allows me to stay. So it's awkward. Give me time and I'll tell you in a couple of hours. I broke off for two hours and had a long talk with my editor. It was really hard: on the one side my sympathy was with the film-makers, on the other I felt bad about criticizing somebody – the BBC – who had invited me. So I called up Roger Mills, my mentor, and discussed it with him. He said, 'Look, if putting your signature here will jeopardize your stay in Britain, don't do it. If you feel that it doesn't, and you are sympathetic to the petition, do sign. We are not asking where you came from, just as a fellow director.' So I said I would sign. I rang back and said, Put my name on the list. The next day I bought *The Times*, but my name wasn't there. I rang Roger: 'What's the whole fucking fuss about? I've lost two hours of editing, I took this very seriously, and after all that where's my name?' He said, 'Don't worry. Count the names, are there twelve?' I counted, sure, there were twelve. I told him. 'There you are,' he said, 'they never publish more than twelve.' That I thought was extremely British.

JOHN LAHR: The hardest thing to get used to is the English reserve. Americans let it all hang out, say what they feel. In the nature of intimacy there may be something to be said for a little reticence. Though I find with a lot of English people I long for a more tactile response. Literally the space the English inhabit towards their fellow man, they stand apart from people more than Americans do. Americans really come right up on your chin.

It takes so much longer to get to know the English, but when you *do* get to know them, you get deep, deep in. In America people will place you with about five questions. You just roll your credits: I'll roll mine, you roll yours, just talk about work. The refreshing thing I found when I came here is that they don't talk about work. They force social intercourse to be in a generalized or neutral area, which I think is very good. One does have more of an exchange of ideas, you're drawn out of yourself, out of your self-involvement. The general quality of discussion, of talk, the value of self-expression is higher here.

* * *

WITOLD STARECKI: Bertrand Russell was asked by John Freeman what would be the one piece of advice he would offer? Russell said, 'Stick to facts, to reality.' That epitomizes the very Britishness of his thinking, whereas Descartes or Hegel would have said, 'Invent a system.' The British way is not attractive, but it's very practical, it's very healthy. People in England used to be brought up to run the world. Now they must face a world in constant crisis. This flexibility of adopting to a current situation is quite different to the Polish situation. I was brought up with a certain set of rules and you would die for them; you wouldn't change. That makes for great heroes, for colour, for romance. But not for common sense. People in England don't challenge the system. They are told something and they accept it.

PETAR OBRATOVIC: I quite enjoy the British self-control, the fact that the more you hate each other the more polite you are. Though sometimes I hate it: when something happens and my blood starts to boil and I become very rude and I have to think, 'My goodness me, how can I be so rude?' In the end I have to accept the way the British are, I have to accept their limitations because I came here and I have to take it as a package.

WITOLD STARECKI: On the one hand you have here incredible individualists, individuality is very highly developed; on the other you have people queuing without comment, following instructions without any challenge. It makes a very intriguing mixture – how do you manage to do both? There are so many contradictions in the British character that make it such a rich, unpredictable mixture. Sometimes it is really surprising. The fascination with crime – Jack the Ripper became a national hero. The English may kill their wives, but they put flowers on the grave. There is this ability to laugh at oneself, to distance oneself from one's own actions; like being a ghost talking about oneself. I get stability from the British, but I don't get the tension, the excitement that I get from east Europeans.

SHARI PEACOCK: The British take no pleasure in celebration. They make life drab. Lunches and dinners are not an event for the English. You just sit there.

125

I see these couples in restaurants, and the idea is simply that you're filling yourself. Food is fuel, not pleasure. Enjoying the sensual, enjoying food and drink is not considered especially praiseworthy, but what does life consist of but these pleasures? What is the beauty of life but in things like that? I can't come to terms with that. Any dinner in my family, in my community in Bulgaria, the whole family would gather together, there would be drinks beforehand, and chat, and there is this basic pleasure in communal conversation, of eating and drinking together. You can see it all round the Mediterranean, people chatting. There's just none of that here. I'm told it's all something to do with Protestantism.

BRIGITTE NEWMAN: The negation of pleasure is much deeper than just food and drink – after all the British are very knowledgable about wine, they owned Bordeaux for three centuries – and goes to the suppression of feelings. There is a great difference between a relationship between an English person and a non-English person. Little boys don't have feelings, little boys don't cry, little boys are men. When I met my husband he had never kissed his father. For a French woman that was abysmal. The Latins may not go as far as the Turks, they don't walk hand in hand, but if you have not seen your father for a while, then you will embrace him when you meet. I am delighted that I have accomplished that for my husband and his father, and they were both extremely pleased about it. This suppression of feelings as well as the negation of pleasure is present in everyday life and in every moment of a relationship.

TESS WICKHAM: What is important to the British? Not what they would call frivolity, not the quality of life, of food and drink, of socializing. It's chasing foxes on horseback, of putting your hands in the mud, of having a plot of land. That's something I have never been able to sympathize with. The English like their little houses, their little back garden, they like putting their hands in the mud. They like grit behind their nails, I don't know why. All the classes – that's the one thing that binds them together: gardening. There's nothing they love more than flowerbeds, a bit of black earth that has to be weeded. What about the beautiful green grass? Wonderful, calm green grass and all they want to do is create mud, more bloody mud. I hate it.

You can see it in the way that the garden suburb is extending in every direction: trickling into the countryside proper, trickling into London. This whole world of *Country Living*, magazines like that. Rustic kitchens, the Prince of Wales, the lot. It's all about softening the edges between the two, there's no concept of proper design in a city, of proper urban living, of accepting the one alongside the other. This mollification which ends in nothing. Urban life is quite different to country life and they should be able to exist in parallel. What's happening means that very soon we won't have much of either.

126

Essentially the English don't like urban life. London isn't really a city, it's a cosmopolitan agglomeration of many villages. Look at the London map: people living in their own little villages and they love them.

FATIMA IGRAMHIM: Living with Londoners is difficult. I am a very extroverted person. I have already taken on a very English characteristic, which is deprecating myself. I never used to have that, but I've had to change my personality living here. I used to be a much more exuberant and strong person. Louder, happier, more spontaneous. If I felt happy I'd shout it. I said immediately what I felt, I was very open. That's quite German and American too. In Germany we believe in talking about what bothers us, stuff like that, whether inside the family, with our lover, or even with our friends. People there talk to each other on the telephone for hours, discuss their problems – with their job, their children, their boyfriends – there's always a lot of discussion going on; a lot of talk, talk, talk. I regret the lack of that sort of intimacy. They don't want to talk about bad things, fears or problems. They just want to talk in general. They try to keep problems away from them and they don't tell you their problems either. The English might call this a virtue, but I do not find it a virtue. It makes everything false. Who can you turn to? Do you have to deal with all these things by yourself? In England everything is pushed under the carpet. Either people don't want to bother you with their real problems or with their feelings or their fears. In Germany people are always talking about their 'fears', what they fear about what happens in their lives. Not only women, men too. Everyone tries to work on themselves, they try to be aware, that's the big thing: to be aware of what you really want and what your inner workings are. Maybe Germany is a more psychological, more analytical country. There's nowhere in the world outside America where there are so many people in therapy of one sort or another. In England that's totally a no-no. Therapy to the English is slightly shameful. When I told a friend of mine that I used to go to therapy she said, 'What for, what for?' They have very big defences. Either you are mad or you're not. No in between.

MARY ROSE: I remember going on a course in Germany when I was in the Hitler Youth. The leader told me, we have to learn from the English: they are always right, and we have to adopt this attitude. But this eternally being right makes you completely blind.

FERDIE ERASMUS: The Englishman loves his habits. He's a carpenter, say, and every year he goes to Room 26 in Road 4 in Morecombe, and does that for twenty-five years. It's the same for those on the dole. I can't get people to work for me, even with all this unemployment. And the ones I get are terrible. You have to motivate them. At the Whitgift Centre, I went in one morning and

127

said: 'That's it, the canteen's closed. If you just want to eat all day, bugger off home.' The unions were on my back in twenty-four hours. I said, 'Let them work till midnight then, to make up the hours they haven't worked.' In the end I got them on my side. My attitude is: we're a team, let's get this going together. And then this Christmas party I threw. All these rough burly labourers turned up in their suits, all togged up and they had a great time. That's what it's all about, the rewards of hard work. I got a lot out of my staff – even when I wasn't there they worked twenty-four hours.

* * *

GERTRUD HARTWIG: The English accept you for what you are though the way we think is sometimes different – which doesn't do any harm. They may have some reservations, it is difficult to establish close relationships with the English, but once they accept you, they accept you. I am accepted in the office where I work absolutely as what I am. The English have a great sense of their past, and as a refugee I have no English past, but that's simply something one has to live with. They are more broadminded towards other races, other religions and so on. So long, that is, as they know their place and do not attempt to move too far into English society. I don't pretend to feel English, not at all, and it isn't my aim to do so. What I feel is that I am accepted as what I am, perhaps sometimes as rather a strange animal, but still accepted.

SIMI BEDFORD: What I like about the English is that although they have this idea about being totally superior, they do keep it mainly in their head, and they will accept you, in as far as they will ever accept you, for yourself. You may be an African and they may have problems with that but if they do take you on, if they do like you, you can be yourself. You'll never be as good as them but provided that you don't care about that – which I don't, because it's their problem not mine – then it's fine. The ones that like you like you come what may. Whereas the French consider themselves to be so intellectual that they really do despise African culture. Only one or two Africans – Fanon for instance – have ever got to the Ecole Normale Superiore or the Polytechnique. They'll accept you completely whether you're black or whatever, but you have to be French. Once you're completely French they'll accept you, but not until. But you have to abandon everything of your own, become completely deracinated.

BENNY BUNSEE: The British can deal with the most vicious level of differences in a very tidy kind of way. They take the steam out of it. It's part of how they colonized people and dealt with people, always dealing with this sort of contradiction. They were conquerors but they were a small nation and they didn't have the army to control the people and instead they developed what is called British diplomacy, a way of manipulating people to do what they wanted. So they could be nice about the most vicious arguments. The British, the English in particular, have committed the greatest crimes against people. They talk about the Germans, but their crimes are concentrated in the Nazi period, while British colonial history covers a huge period of time. They've caused enormous sufferings for millions of people, and they've got away with it. Nobody has come out and said, 'You are the original colonizers, you are the original white racists.' While the Germans remain outcasts, because of that Hitler period. The British are very good at adapting themselves. They know when they are defeated, or when they are weak, and they know how to adapt that situation. Even with those countries that they once colonized they still have a good relationship. The Vietnam war would never have happened if the British, not the Americans, were involved. They would have got out neatly.

CHRISTOPHER HOPE: There's a patronizing quality about the English, probably because they were a small island, able to go out almost at will and settle, work or conquer or do business or simply holiday around the world and were entirely free to do this, and almost regarded it as a kind of duty. They did it both eagerly and easily, almost naturally. What they seemed incapable of dealing with was when the colonial chickens came home to roost. That disturbed them when it faced them with mirror images of themselves: white Europeans speaking a mother tongue who yet remained rather strange.

FIRDOS ALI: The English suffer from what Fanon calls narcissism: the excessive fondness of oneself. Because actually they're a fucked-up race. Look at it. Who launched their bigotry on the rest of the world? A selected few. The working classes didn't think that way but they were brainwashed. The British colonialists were better psychoanalysts than Freud. Give them 'King and Country', 'Her Majesty the Queen'. The Lord of the Manor used to fuck the virgins before they got married and the masses watched and did nothing. But they're so damn stupid that even if they get a bit of education they still learn nothing. You can't say, 'Oh well they're an island race,' any more. Because the world is too small, the distance between places is too short. If they cannot reconcile themselves to that fact it makes them the most backward, the most underdeveloped people in the world. For me, Europeans in general, and especially the Americans, are the most underdeveloped people in the world: with all their psychic disorders, their drug problems, their Mafia mentality, their CIA and FBI mentality, afraid of new ideas, afraid of other people's ideas, I think they are a most backward people. To me the most advanced ages ever in the world were the Middle Ages, when Europe was *dark*.

BENNY BUNSEE: The English are colonizers within the context of British history, they've colonized the Welsh, the Irish and the Scots. They're not a self-critical people, they don't look at themselves and criticize themselves. So they can't look at their history and ask questions about what they have done. Even when they do get involved in things, they do it on a very superficial level. They can join the anti-apartheid movement, but they don't remind themselves that their own country is involved in the same oppression and ask what that means to them.

SHREELA FLATHER: At university I learned that certain things didn't go down well. I found it was best not to talk about my life outside England, because everyone assumed you were showing off. This was odd to me because it was just part of my life. I had a little more money than other people and it was best not to mention that either. The first term was hard, everyone was extremely polite. But what I found, and I have found this time and again in England, is that given the passage of enough time, then people do come to accept you. Even if no events happen during that time, just the fact that you've lived next door to somebody for two years or the fact that you met them a year ago and have since met them three times, the overall passage of time is so important. To an Indian it's not important. If you like somebody the fact that you met them yesterday is not important. With the English you have to have some passing of time. They have to get used to the idea of you. I find that if you do make the effort then people are very delighted – the English find it extremely difficult to make the effort, to make the first move, even if they want to. They find it difficult to do that with each other, it's not only with people who come from elsewhere. There's no two ways about it – they are not sociable; they think too much about socializing. If they want to invite somebody they think about the whole structure of this invitation, whereas if an Indian says come and see me, they won't think about it: if you come at dinnertime they'll offer you dinner, whatever. They're not going to worry about it. My husband is English, and if I say, well, let's do this or that, he worries about it. I don't. For us it just happens, but the English are more careful, more structured. They do respond when you make the effort, but they still don't feel at ease with you until some time has passed and they have met you a number of times. If I met somebody at a party, say, and I liked them, I would want to organize our next meeting straight away. They don't like that. You have to meet them at least twice by chance before you actually organize a meeting. I think it's some kind of anxiety.

WITOLD STARECKI: Some British characteristics are incredibly valuable and appealing to me. Take attitudes to friendship. In Poland you get very close, emotional ties, which can also break with a furore. So on the level of excitement and depth it's incredibly strong, like a love affair. As an emotional experience it's something that stays with you forever, and because of the circumstances of Polish life, you need more of that level of relationship in order to survive. Here you don't get the same thing, but, and there is a but, while it takes time to build a relationship here, once it has been built, once you have been approved, checked, sometimes for years, I believe you have a relationship that is much more solid than it would be in Poland. I like the lack of ostentation, the British reserve. If you don't know people well here they may seem cold, but they aren't. It takes time.

* * *

KATHY ACKER: It's hard to make friends here, hard to meet new people. You don't hang out here, people don't introduce you to other people here. The process of getting to know people is very slow. That's very frustrating, but when you do get to know them you're much closer than in New York. A friend of mine puts it this way: he says that when you meet an English person you meet a huge mountain and you have to get over the mountain and once you've gotten over that mountain then you're friends. When you meet an American you come to a beautiful landscape and you think, Oh this is wonderful and you go through the beautiful landscape or whatever – and then you get to the mountain.

PETER VO: The English family is a house covered by snow. When we look at the house covered by snow during the winter it could seem so cold, but if you go near to the house and knock at the door, and if once is not enough, then knock twice and if twice is not enough then knock three times, until the door opens. And when the door opens, you get inside and it is warm.

FIRDOS ALI: If a person drops dead in the street here no one gives two fucks. I don't know what happens in the countryside, where people still care about each other. But in the big city you get the 'I'm all right Jack, the hell with you' attitude. I was walking in Ealing, an old man carrying a shopping bag falls down. People walk around him, they don't even look down. I had to pick him up, his shopping and everything, and asked him, 'Sir, where do you live?' He told me. I took him home. I got him into his house, gave him a cup of tea. I thought, here's this old guy, he's in his eighties, doesn't anyone give a fuck? You learn more every day, every day you learn something new about the English. The most beautiful thing I have found in this country is the wrestling matches. Who watches them? Old ladies, seventy, eighty years old. Some really weird people. Getting up from their seats, screaming out their support so violently. I'm thinking, 'Hang on. What is this?'

FATIMA IGRAMHIM: I do like the fact that people are not so involved in your daily life. Not my friends, but the people in the streets. In Germany people look at you, they check you out, they give you their opinions right away, by their face, how you look, how you dress, stuff like that. People in the shops are much more brusque than here. I like the certain easiness about English. In many ways I like the same things that sometimes I hate. That people are more relaxed about their jobs, that they don't take everything about work so seriously, they aren't so intensely materialistic as the Germans.

PALOMA ZOZAYA: This coldness, this not getting involved, of preserving privacy too much, still shocks me. People don't look after each other. For instance if I go with a group of friends from school and we leave the pub and I have to go one way and all them have to go the other way, and over there this is a group of guys who are being a bit drunk, a bit obnoxious. If there was a woman in Mexico who had to do a journey on her own, someone would always say, 'We'll walk you,' or at least, 'Will you be all right?' But the English seem totally to dissociate from that. You finish your drink, everybody goes and if you have to make this journey on your own – that's up to you. It's not exactly uncaring, and they are much more reliable than my Latin friends. What's in fact a bit disappointing is the fact that most of my close friends are now Anglo-Saxon. You'd like to be able to say, 'We Latins stick together and my Latin American friends are the people I can really rely on', or even that if I ask people to dinner they are the ones that will turn up. But it's not that way at all.

VU DUY TU: In Vietnam we always talked about the phlegmatic English. They are very cool, reflective. But it's not true. They're very concerned about other people. They are a caring people. There are so many charities. We are very pleased to be here. At the beginning we had a little regret that we hadn't gone to America. We believed that maybe I should have gone to America, because I had been trained there. Also we have a lot of family living there. Maybe it might have been better in many ways, but after two years of living in the UK we travelled to America to visit our relatives. At first we were all very pleased but gradually we started to find out that life in America had completely changed in comparison with life in 1956 and 1970 when I was there for training. American society changed too fast. Everyone rushes all the time, like crazy, like robots, no time to talk, no time to share sentiments. I don't like it. You have to work hard here too but anyway I feel it's better.

* * *

JASWINDER AMAR: People do get jealous. When I moved into my house a colleague said, 'You people really work hard, don't you. I'm still in a council flat.' She doesn't come out with jealousy as such, but it's there. If you refuse to notice it, you can be happy, but if you do notice . . . I've given up worrying. I just won't acknowledge it. I'm very sensitive. Someone says something and I start thinking about it very much, but that is no help. All you can do is ignore

132

it. The English are lazy, they don't want to work. In America ninety-five per cent of the shop owners are Asian these days. I think that in England most of the grocery shops – which open at five a.m. and shut at twelve at night – are also run by Asians. English people can't work those long hours. Compare my English colleagues with me. Someone who works with me, has worked for twenty years for the same company, who earns more money than I do, but he doesn't have a house, she doesn't have a house. The way they are brought up, the way they go out every night, spend their money in the pub, we don't do that. From work I come straight home, from home I go to work. All my money goes into my savings. So in the end we are a culture who will stay and a culture that will survive.

NISSIM ELIJAH: A friend said to me, 'The trouble with us – foreigners and Jews – is that we work too bloody hard. The English don't like that. The normal Britisher likes to have his fun, his drink, his gambling, etc. Foreigners work too hard – no Englishman will work the same way. But we steal a march over them and they don't like it.' It happened to me – I worked hard, was good at it, so it was, 'Let's keep that bugger here, be less trouble for all of us.'

DON ATYEO: Compared to Australians the English are endemically lazy and they do recognize the qualities Australians have. We knuckle down and do a lot of work: you had an Australian secretary you were OK, you got an Australian dish-washer you were fine. Australians wake up at sparrow's fart, they're on the road at seven-thirty and the doors open at eight. Here the joint doesn't get going until ten. So it was very easy to look industrious. Australia doesn't have lunches the way they do here. I answered this ad in the *UK Press Gazette* and went to work for *Municipal Engineering* magazine, which sold sewage systems to local councils and so on. This was the first real job I had here. Suit and tie, nine to five. What threw me was the first day I went in I was taken out to the pub for lunch and there were four or five pints of beer, which I'd never really tackled before, and I was totally pissed. I couldn't work. It was anathema to an Australian. You got rat-arsed after work, but that was after work, the six o'clock swill. You raced in and drank yourself to death in fifteen minutes. But here, the idea of having these huge great lunches, where the pubs opened especially for it and closed afterwards, was just extraordinary.

RAMESH VALA: The idea that you have to have a bit of leisure, so it's off to the pub for a few drinks, the idea that weekends are sacrosanct, that you need two holidays every year, all that is changing. I don't really subscribe to the belief that the English are lazy. Though I do think that the years of empire, of running half the world, did work against the British. It took them a long time to get rid of the old machinery and realize that they too have to compete in the world. I think if you look at any successful civilization, it's been successful because there has been time for leisure, time to think. If you feel free, then you can do things. The English have a different attitude to life, which is nothing to do with being lazy. But Mrs Thatcher has created this regeneration amongst the English, which you see in the City where they all work from seven in the morning, and this is going to create a challenge to the Asians and the Jews: this generation is going to compete.

CARMEN CALLIL: I don't think the British are lazy. Though they do put up with too much and don't object enough. Britain is not an intellectual country at all. Writers are certainly not honoured in the way that they should be, nothing like that. It makes it very hard to sell books. It amazes me how little the British spend on educating their children, in the state system that is.

JOHN LAHR: The thing the British do better than anybody else is play. They hack around, they're amateurs, they love to potter. Middle Europeans see the artist as the moral ombudsman of a culture, and in that sense I would agree with them. In America, if you're a published writer, you're somebody weird and wonderful, you have magic. I think that's ridiculous. You're just a worker – OK, in a very visible way – but this artistic role tends to inflate and trivialize you. It's not seen as ordinary work, not the nine to five. Somehow you're a star. But here, in England, it's part of the culture, it's nothing special. I think that's better. I don't think you should be set apart: every person in every sphere makes his or her contribution. But if people say, 'Why be an artist when you could be a stockbroker' – I don't know anybody who wouldn't rather write plays or books than go to work from nine to five.

* * *

JAROSLAV BRADAC: To be an artist here is very strange. To say, 'I am an artist,' in Prague is to say it with pride. To say it here is considered a bit iffy, a bit strange. It's always associated with poverty, only strange people would go for it willingly. How could anyone who didn't actually have to do this, *choose* to do so? If you have anything between your ears, you'd *choose* to be an artist, a freelance . . . you would want to do that? It's still considered something really strange, something weird. To go willingly into a profession which does not guarantee you a Porsche or a mobile telephone . . .

JOHN LAHR: I can't accept that the artist is only a salon amusement over here. Tell me another country where plays get discussed in editorials, where the closing of an Alan Bennett play is a front page lead, where points of order are raised about the theatre in Parliament?

MICHAEL IGNATIEFF: The English are always being lambasted for being so anti-intellectual, but I've always thought that the idea of the English as philistines is a fatuous line, a continental misunderstanding of the culture that runs very deep. It's a very English kind of thing: you talk down your own learning, you talk down your own sophistication, and you actually get on and produce stuff that's regarded around the world as great poetry. You just don't show it off. There's no other European country which has quite so good a periodical press, daily quality press, television and radio combined. The quality of that cultural achievement is actually unrivalled anywhere in the world. That's sustained not only by us scribblers, but by a consuming audience who are very subtle and discriminating and demanding.

WITOLD STARECKI: The role of the artist in eastern Europe or South America has grown out of proportion. It happened due to particular circumstances that the artists were voicing the opinions of a nation in struggle, that's why they became so important. France is different. They have always been snobs about their culture – which I treat as a positive sign. The Italians as well. They both regard the artist as important. Here the artist is marginalized. Here you have 'common sense'. What matters is how you make a living, how you operate diplomatically, that's what counts, this is the solid ground on which a nation can function. With that basis, then you can have art as well, if you need it. Of course it's very flattering when an artist speaks for the nation, but I think it is better when a professional politician who is prepared and has the right tools does it, than when an intellectual simply speculates.

MICHAEL IGNATIEFF: All this stuff about the English being philistines is quite false. What there is is about a million people in the country who are the university-educated, professional middle classes, plus a very important class of self-educated working-class people. Then there is a rather small percentage of quite aristocratic people. Higher up, of course, it's all huntin' and shootin' and fuckin'. The culture of any society is sustained by these same fractions. It may be small, but the question of whether or not a country is philistine turns not on numbers but on how strong are the cultural institutions that that audience is prepared to support without subsidy. That's another thing. When people give me all this stuff about how wonderfully cultured France is, what they're looking at is a system of state cultural subsidy in which cultural goods are regarded as prestige instruments in the power struggle. I don't like the excessive English self-deprecation about their cultural seriousness and I don't like the way in which expatriates, particularly middle-Europeans, are always saying, 'It's a desert, these Anglo-Saxons are so . . .' It isn't true. And a lot of what passes for English culture is in the custody of the Anglican church, places where eastern European intellectuals don't go: in the hymns, in Bunyan, church fêtes, people listening to Radio 3 and 4, all that very unfashionable side of English gentility. Very middle class, very county, very away from London. These are the people who write me letters: 'Jolly interesting show you did the other night. Very puzzling . . .' They may ramble on in a completely alien vernacular to my own but it's a vernacular to be respected. The authentic voice of the English county middle classes – and God bless them.

SHARI PEACOCK: All the immigrants I know are incredibly ambitious. They all work harder than the British, but then *everybody* works harder than the British. The English don't work, they don't even know what the word means. This is something that never ceases to delight me. You were told back in Bulgaria all these sort of Iranian folk stories about the empire and how they're still used to it, and how they're so arrogant and they don't have to work and sure enough when I came here, like all clichés it was true. OK, this is my circle, I can't talk about bankers and businessmen, but I'm talking about painters, writers, illustrators, journalists, they in no way work nearly as hard as I do. Not that I am more successful than them, but perhaps as an immigrant I am more thorough. I don't know. And being outside the society an immigrant has definitely to work harder to get to the same place. Definitely. There is also that tradition of the gentleman amateur, working very hard but never letting anyone know.

MICHAEL IGNATIEFF: That stuff about gentlemanly amateurishness I found rather attractive. I liked the way in which brash, aggressive American types like myself were told to tone down and slow down. I took to that and I liked understatement. Some of those clichés are true: I like the wonderfully subtle strategies of English misdirection. I really enjoy it. I can't do them myself but they're fun.

TESS WICKHAM: Living here for the past twenty-five years has made me a cautious person. It's to do with the language. English is a beautiful language but it is also a very clever, devious language. It's like the English common law, which exists only as precedent. Other than statute, which deals with regulations, it's not simply written down. Everything is open to interpretation, it all depends on nuance. Which can be fine in the right context, but it can be used very deviously and dangerously and very often I feel totally locked out, shut out, totally by virtue of the use of language. I can hear what's being said, I can even interpret and understand the subtleties, but I know that what is said is designed to a degree. This sounds paranoiac. I think this is the reason why England became so powerful. English language is so clever. Always manipulating, never committing, always open to interpretation, all of which adds up to a very clever way of ruling. I don't think I've ever completely got to grips with it. Even with

136

my husband I can feel that what he's saying, and what is actually happening, is completely the result of something that is so ingrained, this linguistic manipulation that is so ingrained from schooldays onwards. I'm fairly streetwise, but when it comes to dealing with members of society who are influential you really come across a degree of manipulative use of language that I can't properly handle.

MARCEL BERLINS: In the Lord Chancellor's department I met a lot of ex-colonials – I'd never encountered people like that before. I didn't know my way round what was on, what wasn't. My private life was that of a student, and that was easy, because student life is the same almost anywhere. So during the day I was wearing a pin-striped suit and working with these establishment figures, and by night I was moving in student circles. The Civil Servants must have thought me strange – I didn't have their background, and I didn't catch a lot of the references. I'd read about these people and thought them caricatures, and here they were and they weren't caricatures. I met a chap who used public school slang as I'd read it in novels, and never heard people actually say before – 'By jove, I say old chap', etc.

SHARI PEACOCK: This takes us into the vast field of clichés, but the English are not frank and they are not open. It's not really hypocrisy, but there is some kind of severing between the feelings and the thoughts and the language. The language is dealing with words that are very much picked up from the surface of your emotions and the very, very deep things that go on the language doesn't tap, although often it might describe them circuitously, and this is what irony is all about. You allude to these feelings in other ways, but you never actually directly fish it out and say, 'That's what it is.'

NIEN-LUN YEH: Compared with the Chinese they are frank. I would say that compared with the Chinese not just the English but all western people are much more frank and honest. The reason, if I understand it properly, is that their life, although they have many problems, is much simpler, much easier than life in China or the Orient in general. Third World living standards are so much poorer and if you want to be better-off it doesn't just depend on your own hard work, but on so many other factors. A situation which forces people to think in very complicated ways. While here people are very straightforward. Though compared with Denmark, say, English psychology is infinitely more complicated – because, I think, of their empire and their links with the Orient, which has changed the way people think here. There is a big influence.

TESS WICKHAM: English is so good at hiding true meaning: you can interpret a sentence in so many ways. It can sound perfectly all right but you know it

137

isn't. What is known as 'British hypocrisy' is simply one exemplification of it. Double standards are hidden in the way the language is used. The snake is always in the grass but it's never overt, even if it's always there and you can always feel it to be there. I don't think the Dutch or the French or the Spanish or the Italians are any morally better, but their language doesn't cloud the issue in the same way. They may well do lots of bad things behind the scenes, but they don't have this clever, manipulative language. French has one meaning, it's as clear as it comes, there's no way you can alter that meaning. If something has to be done secretly, then it has literally to be done behind the scenes and someone has to be bribed. If England doesn't have that degree of corruption it's because there is no need for it. So however much one may think one has mastered the language, it can still shut you out, helped by the education that has created the language and the way in which the language has created the system. People can be so amazingly rude: someone will say something, and if you write it down and said So-and-so said such-and-such on the face of it there would be nothing rude about what was said, but when it was said it really was *so* rude.

* * *

FIRDOS ALI: The English character is strange, I can't understand it. When the English cricket team was selected to travel to South Africa in 1968 they included Basil D'Olivera. Vorster said no, the tour was cancelled. The English didn't argue. Later, when the black power salute was given in Mexico these same people would say 'Why bring politics into sport?' The fuckers! Why have you got these double standards? Either your mind isn't working properly, or what you're saying is that it's all right for Afrikaaners to bring politics into sport, but it is not all right for a black person to assert his dignity. The English will not countenance any violence in their own streets but they will encourage violence in the streets of other nations. Look how violent they became during the Falklands. 'Down with the Argies!' all that.

CINDY BLAKE: The English are really jealous, incredibly jealous. They're amazingly jealous. What bugs me is they're so hypocritical as well. I'll talk to some artist who tells me, 'I can't stand the American view of art, they have no taste, no culture,' but where does this guy sell his paintings? In LA. That's where he gets his money. Writers are saying, 'How can all these publishing houses be taken over?' but all these same guys are going to get much bigger advances. That's my feeling: we saved your asses and you're just jealous and pissed off. You're really pissed off because you can't get it together.

BENNY BUNSEE: The English are so closed. You can know an English person and you'll never learn his surname for ten years. You meet us, we'll tell you
138

our whole history in one day – my father's history, my grandfather's history. You never get that from English people, who are very reserved, very closed in. Everyone says this about them, even other Europeans.

NIEN-LUN YEH: If you compare them with Latin peoples, the English are definitely colder. I got the feeling that the real English, if they found that an immigrant doesn't speak the language as well as they do, then it is very difficult to make friends with them. They will be very polite, very friendly, but you can never make real friends with them, to talk deeply.

PALOMA ZOZAYA: It's a myth that the English are cold. I don't think that they lack feeling, they just have a totally different way of approaching things. A few months ago a friend of ours died in Paris. The partner was French and he was English. We had to deal with both sides of the family, and I was so much better off staying with my friend's English family, because there was so much less hysteria. The French were climbing up the walls and the English were grieving quietly – it was so much nicer to be with the English. That didn't mean that anyone was grieving any the less, there was just not that extreme emotion. I go back to Mexico now and they tell me that I've become a bit British, because I no longer get easily excited, but if you ask my mother-in-law she'll tell you that I am very excitable and very highly strung. I agree, but going back to Mexico I do sometimes feel a bit odd, because I have acquired to an extent that English capacity of sitting back and just letting things happen. This tendency of not getting emotionally involved straight away, while we Latins jump into getting emotionally involved as soon as there is an opportunity. The English certainly are reserved, but that's really a way of avoiding what might be boiling away underneath. My husband is a perfect example: he seems a very calm person, but sometimes he can erupt. The sort of crime there is in England, you don't find in Latin countries. People in Mexico City will shoot each other dead because of a parking space, but those murders which feature children buried under the floorboards of an old house don't really tend to happen in Mexico. The English keep things in, until they emerge in a very refined, very sophisticated way; Mexicans are more explosive. For daily life the English way is much better.

MICHAEL IGNATIEFF: I've worked in France and that is just so much more closed a society than England. One of the good effects of having had an empire is that the English are used to all these lesser breeds. They're used to having all these Canadians and Australians and so on underfoot. So this bred not internationalism, but a certain kind of benign indifference to people. Whereas French culture is much more set in the hexagon against the outside. It talks a lot of crap about being the *pays d'exil* and how welcoming it is. I never bought

139

that. Consequently I've never regarded England as being more closed than any other European society, or more difficult. The defining characteristic of this society is a slightly benign, slightly vague indifference towards newcomers, a generalized willingness to let them 'get on with it' (a great English phrase).

TESS WICKHAM: I don't like the artificial eccentricity you see in certain areas of middle-class society. I don't really understand what English eccentricity is, anyway. To me it's a fabrication. Playing at being a down-and-out aristo, whatever. I don't go for it. I don't think the English quite know how to be proper Bohemians, that's not in their character. It's a much more southern thing. They're far too hypocritical to be a proper Bohemian – even if they're eccentric they tend to have a home here and another home there. They're far too insecure to be Bohemians, to drift. I certainly don't know any myself. True Bohemianism is essentially continental, it requires a very different lifestyle, café life, a different climate, all these things that don't fit in here.

DAVILIA DAVID: What I like here is that I can be anonymous. I can do my own thing, I'm not accountable to anybody. It's more civilized here, more worldly. There's a tolerance for oddity, for Bohemian attitudes. At home you have to wear your Bohemian attitudes like a badge, then push them down people's throats. I don't have to do that here, I can dress how I want, I can do my own thing.

CINDY BLAKE: All this English eccentricity is just another way people have found to be boring. I'd seen these people, I'd met them, but it had been at my parents' dinner parties. Not my age group. Suddenly I was with these people who *gave* dinner parties. Which was news to me. People I knew in America did it as a joke. This was serious, and you had the right silver and you had the right table-cloth and people used to tell me how to do up the house and measurements for curtains . . . they were serious about their houses and their gardens and their receipes and they were in their twenties. These were things I'd seen when I looked over the banister at night. This was not me. What I was not prepared for when I came over was that people my age, and I'm still not prepared for it even at age thirty-six, to be so grown up, and to have their lives organized to such an extent. Very few people drop in on each other here. Friends do not call you every day and you'd feel funny if you called an English girlfriend every day, where it would be typical in America. You'd feel strange. You call them every other week, maybe. Maybe see them once a month for lunch and that's it. It's very tightly controlled. Very formal. I just think it's odd.

* * *

MIRANDA LOVETT: An old schoolfriend of my husband's arrived in New York with his new bride of a couple of months. We had dinner with them a couple

140

of times and I got along with his wife very well and he rang me up at work one day and said, 'My wife really likes you, dah dah dah dah, and could you show her around and take her out to lunch and so on?' So that's what I did. Now I'm used to talking to my friends every day. It's spontaneous, because of the way I am, the way I grew up, so when I came to live in London later I assumed that was what I could do. But I found that if I rang this girl up or if I dropped by it was a disaster. It really upset me. I was twenty-two years old and I didn't understand the etiquette of the relationship you have with someone here. And that is something that has taken me a long time. When I started living here we went to a dinner party at their house, I was maybe twenty-two and it was sort of a grown-up dinner party, the table was laid all nicely and there were four couples, they lived in the Cadogan Square area. These girls were pretty scary to tell the truth, just pretty scary. And after dinner I was chatting away to some gentleman I was sitting next to and after about ten minutes I felt someone kicking me under the table and I thought what the hell's going on. And he whispered to me, 'You know you're meant to be next door with the women.' I was twenty-two years old and I couldn't believe it. The last thing I wanted to do was to go sit with a bunch of girls that I didn't know, who scared me.

FATIMA IGRAMHIM: Talking about yourself is another thing you're not meant to do. Or your job or anything else you're really interested in. It has to be more about movies, books you've read, stuff like that. At dinner parties nobody talks about the real important things in life. No one wants to talk about serious things, their problems, but instead they all try to keep up a good façade and nobody tries to get into anything more deeply. Everything has to be made fun of and dealt with in a very light way.

PALOMA ZOZAYA: There is a reluctance to talk about serious things. I find that a lot. Everything has to have comedy in it, has to be entertaining, has to be light. Even the messages have to be disguised in comedy. People don't want to see the dark side of things – which I find fascinating, but maybe that comes from being a Mexican, we like death, artists like Posada, the English don't. Yet death is so interesting an aspect of life. I can't cope with comedy, I can't relate to comedy at all. I compensate for this by working in Latin theatre and we do deal with those themes. It's not that England lacks passion – no country that has a national writer like Shakespeare is passionless. But it's just this determination to live on the light side, the frivolous side only. The dark side is unacceptable. You feel this when an English person says, 'Hello, how are you, did you have a nice weekend?' and you are expected to say, 'Yes.' But you're not meant to say, 'No,' or even go into detail. People don't expect the whole story, they don't want it – it's just a simple social formula. Another way of putting it is that the English just make much less fuss.

141

CINDY BLAKE: I had thought the English would talk about concepts and what I've run up against for ten years is a series of anecdotes. The English are the most anecdotal people I've ever met – and they don't care if they repeat themselves. That's why at a dinner party a man will sit there and talk for an hour about himself and not care whether he's asked you a question. He'll tell the same story five times and not care. I guess there's something I do admire about that absolute refusal to accept that there's anybody else in the world. It does take a lot of guts.

CHRISTOPHER HOPE: There's no question that the British fail to take advantage of their immigrants. Immigrants are rather like women – they have to be twice as good to be taken half as seriously. There's a certain Anglican tolerance – we should do our bit for the Vietnamese and so on, we were obliged to take in the Ugandan Asians. But it isn't done with any great enthusiasm. And tolerance is often a mask for indifference. And indolence, and possibly also a more inward-turning quality native to the people. Too deep for me to understand, but it threads through the national characteristics of this island. The national character is strange and remote, yet oddly exotic. The British like laughing at others, but find it difficult when others laugh at them. It remains a fiercely island people, wedded to very old traditions, and distinctly odd. But a good place of refuge. If you are to be marooned, let at least the natives be interesting.

LYDIA SPITZ: The English see us a foreign. Our language is not a common language and even if we speak English correctly, it still is not the same – it is standard English, which is not the same as your mother tongue. I still do not speak English naturally. So communication requires a degree of effort, on both sides. I believe that the effort they have to make is a bit bigger than ours. They have to tolerate a lot of things when they deal with us. Also, the British have a very organized life in general; they do not like to be disturbed, unless they have planned it so. If you are invited, it is done in advance, you do not just drop in. If there is a children's party from four to six, you know that at six o'clock you have to be there to collect your child . . . This kind of rigidity means that you do not have spontaneous social contacts, you have conveniently organized contacts, which are highly unnatural forms of communication.

CHRISTOPHER HOPE: Much of the exoticism resides in the language, not one of words but of nuance and of the movement of many bodies in a small space. There is an avoidance of conflict and collision, unconscious but judged with wonderful delicacy and which must come from a long stream of history. It is also an island, and so much of the island is often forgotten by those who inhabit it, which is not surprising since they've spent hundreds of years pretending not

142

being an island, rather a platform from which they have launched themselves into the world at large – their real place.

SHREELA FLATHER: Certainly the British do have this feeling of superiority. One of the major difficulties arises out of this feeling of superiority to everyone else. I don't know why they feel that way. They're an island, they've never been invaded since 1066. So with this lovely moat around them it does make a difference. The empire was fantastic in its day, and they have always managed to defeat everyone else in Europe. Whether the attitude was positively dinned into them, or whether it was just one of the assumptions that came with empire I don't know. But it certainly was one of the most racist empires, no doubt about it. When you compare it to the Portuguese or even the French, who are racist but they will accept individuals – they don't accept groups, but they will accept individuals. The English don't accept either. If you become a black French person, with style and elegance and the French language and so on, they will accept you as that individual, although they might not accept all the black people. I meet Indians or blacks in France in an entirely different social environment to the one I am used to here, where one is always first and foremost an Indian. It doesn't matter what kind of individual you are. Of course people will always say, 'Ah, but you are different,' but that is so sickening. It's more than just patronizing.

BENNY BUNSEE: You never know what the English are really thinking, what's really going on in their minds, and the way they can change. If they have a particular personal interest, and they have to change to accommodate that interest, then they will change, without blinking an eyelid. The other thing is that they always like to be on the winning side. If the blacks start to become a powerful force in this country, they'll join them. That's what being a good loser really means – compromising with the winners. But in the end I don't know them as a people. I never know how the Englishman thinks. I never understand his psychology. I can understand other races, but the English, you never get to know them as a people.

MIGUEL ZAMBRANO: People here are racist, zenophobic, ignorant. I have experienced horrible things in this country. Once I was taking pictures outside Buckingham Palace and a mounted policeman charged at me. I swore at him and he nicked me. I called the NUJ from the police station, and they said: 'Oh, what a pity, we can't do anything for you. You've only been paying £37 a quarter, instead of £40.' I said, 'Nobody told me about that. I'm stuck here in a police station, under arrest. What sort of a union are you?' They wouldn't do anything for me, so I quit the NUJ.

143

TEDDY PEIRO: I like the British and in many ways I feel British. I have become more polite and attentive, specially since I married Gillian. She was horrified that I addressed my mother as *vieta*, the old one. Now if someone passes me the salt, I say, 'Thank you.' I like the way of life here, the way the people are. They do look down on blacks and Asians, etc., and I would like to eradicate that, but it's part of daily life in nearly every country in the world. And it's not as bad here as elsewhere. But you still find a great deal of gracious living here, more than in other places. I mean we can sit here on this patio, have a nice conversation, exchange views. I can go anywhere and I can say I don't like Mrs Thatcher, and nobody's going to kill me for saying it. I have no vote here though.

PALOMA ZOZAYA: I've learned to appreciate England. Living in England, the day-to-day life is incredibly comfortable. They're very clever, the English, and they've made life for themselves in their country very easy. Just the fact that you can pay your bills through the post, or through the bank: in Mexico you have to queue for a whole morning to pay your gas bill. In France you cannot make theatre bookings over the phone ... little details that make everyday life that much more pleasant. Also you learn to see how the English express affection, and emotion, which is in a very calm way, which is calming and soothing. That generation who went through the last war, they developed such an incredible inner strength, and they are very affectionate and they are also very open.

---

10 The Class System

'He cannot have strange manners, he's an old Etonian.'

TONY ROBINSON: The trouble in England is class distinction. From olden days the one class has always looked down on those beneath them. The English can never see anyone else as their equals. They sit up there and they look down on you and they spit at you down here.

KATHY ACKER: I have two friends who are sending their child to the most expensive public school in the country and to put it in an English way, they are not of that class. They're very much of the '60s. So the kid has a very schizoid life. Here are all these freaks coming round and he's off to this school. So I actually said something on the lines of their going beyond their class, and I immediately thought, 'My God, what have I said?' Other people said, 'Yes, that's the problem.' I have a feeling that Americans here are in a class of their own.

DAVILIA DAVID: I had these cousins in Surrey. They were fascinating – like visiting a museum. I still find that when I visit Glyndebourne or Henley it's back to observing the Pommies at play. The old fashioned upper-class Poms, museum pieces, arrogantly superior. Most of the bigotry came from people with entrenched attitudes, people had a chip on their shoulder. I worked at Bucks Club at the time of the Profumo scandal, I was a lunchtime waitress. All that school food was terribly popular – steak and kidney pie, bubble and squeak and so on. In Australia everything you eat is fresh – no old cheese or hung meat. I used to watch the bugs jumping out of the Stilton at Bucks. It was interesting working there, though, being a servant which meant you didn't exist, not as a person. That was a new experience for me. This attitude of 'them' and 'us' is so debilitating, depressing and negative.

ANNIE-MARIE WOLPE: I made the most amazing *faux pas*. Our immediate neighbour in Kent was an admiral, working in Whitehall. His wife was like this frightened little hen, who couldn't really talk, and he invited us for morning drinks. I didn't know this meant you dressed up. I think I got out of one pair of jeans into the next. I talked to men, but that wasn't done. I didn't know. The women were talking together about Winchester where some of their sons were at school. I didn't know Winchester, I knew Eton and Harrow but that was all. This woman was talking about her kids at Winchester and I said that I didn't think boarding schools were very good. And I talked proper, but not quite – you could still hear the South African accent, and Harold's accent was stronger. The admiral couldn't understand why Harold had to be at the LSE, which he said was 'a bit pink' and Harold said, 'I am.' They knew that he had been a lawyer and they knew that he had left, but they didn't know the circumstances. It was dire, absolutely dire.

SIMI BEDFORD: I was staying with an uncle, a sort of bank clerk, and his wife, who was white, in Croydon. They had this south London accent. Though I had no idea of this – coming from abroad it takes time to understand accents. But gradually I learnt, and when I would come back from the holidays to Madame Dulac who said 'peeaarno', 'plaarstic', all those long a's, and I'd be talking sarf Lunnon. She would say, 'Simi, *where* have you been?' I got very evasive and more and more snobby. The very worst thing in my life was when we used to come into Victoria Station on the school train. All these yahoos all over the place and looking forward to the holidays, while I knew I was going back to Croydon which I hated, not because it was poor, but they were just joyless. This enormous corsetted woman who flowed out over the top like a genie trapped in a barrel. She'd be standing on the station, highly intimidated by all these children and their hooray parents, very uncomfortable, and I'd be standing there trying to hold back so she couldn't see me. To my shame. It was terrible snobbery. She'd finally come waltzing up, ''Ello Simi!' and I'd go, 'Oh, hullo Aunty Bobbie.' 'Aren't you gonna give me a kiss then?' and stick out her chin and off we'd go to catch the train to Clapham Junction.

MIRANDA LOVETT: My mother said something once which seems so true. We were talking about someone who has a sort of uniform for work – a white shirt, a suit, braces – and my mother said, 'I always think that people who can only wear white shirts are desperately insecure.' There's a lot of truth in that. You can expand on that enormously: people who worry about 'them' and 'us' do have a chip on their shoulder, they do have this basic insecurity.

BRIGITTE NEWMAN: Coming to England and mingling with the aristocracy has been a total novelty and very entertaining. The class system in France is very different. The French aristocracy was annihilated in 1789; those who weren't killed were dispossessed of all their belongings. There is not as a rule much mingling between what remains of the aristocracy – which is as a rule very impoverished, and hanging on to very little – and the middle classes. There the middle classes are simply tradesmen, here they can be good fun. Snobbery in England is very different to snobbery in France. In France it is about status symbols – the right watch, the right shoes, whatever. The English are interested in upbringing, in family. Although there is a fair amount of mingling and I'm lucky enough to benefit from it. I may be a foreigner, but I am married to an Englishman, and as such take on his class. There is this instant social classification and I am labelled by my job, my husband, my address.

ANWAR BATI: I do move in reasonably smart circles, but I don't see myself as an intruder. I was there from the start and these circles have simply grown up through having the friends one does. Class has been the main determinant in my life in England, just as it is in the society as a whole. Years ago I was invited by Craig Brown to the birthday party of his then girlfriend. It was in Putney. The father of the girlfriend refused entry to some black chap – a Ghanaian, a Nigerian – basically on the basis that he was black. Until it was revealed that he had been at Eton with Craig, after which in he came. I felt contempt for the father and rather sorry for him.

ALLA WEAVER: I went to lunch with these people who lived in a little house near Buckingham Palace and gently it was conveyed to me that this was very smart. I couldn't understand why a little blackish box in a narrow street, a brick box, should be elegant. I thought it was nothing but snobbishness: what was elegant about it? I went in and there was a maid in a starched cap who announced me and there was this tiny drawing-room and a sofa and a young man lounging on it, reading the paper. And after a bit he left. And my contemporary, this Russian girl, said, 'What do you think of my Uncle Robert?' I said, 'I think he has strange manners.' 'He cannot have strange manners,' she said, 'he's an old Etonian.'

MIRANDA LOVETT: My husband had been to Eton. I didn't even know what Eton was. He happened to choose probably the only girl in New York who wasn't impressed by the fact that he had been to Eton. I had a chip on my shoulder about Eton. When he went to put our son down for Eton the man who would be the future house-master said, 'I notice your wife is American. How does she feel about this?' To which my husband replied, 'My wife thinks that most of the Etonians she's met feel that the world owes them a living.' I'd met a lot of people who went to Eton who in my opinion were complete assholes. Though one thing is true, if you take away the insecurities which is what really lies at the bottom of their problem, they are actually probably very very nice people and very worthwhile people.

FERDIE ERASMUS: Rhodesia is virtually classless. I like everyone calling me by my first name, but I've had to learn in England that you don't go to Sir Archibald somebody and say, 'Hey, Arch, how you doing?' You're out, mate, you don't get invited back to that club again. That's how they are. And if you go into a pub, everyone sits and looks straight in front of them. It's not, 'Hi, mate, how you doing? it's, 'Who is this guy? What does he want?' It's very much, 'Well, we're English, and we'll keep to ourselves, if you don't mind, old chap.' I respect that. I'll have my English passport in a few year's time and I'll be proud to be English.

NAIM ATALLAH: I've heard about the invisible barriers that foreigners come up against. The Jews, are there areas where they can't go? Maybe some of these exclusive clubs, and if they were blackballed, I would be too. But Jews are prominent in Thatcher's Cabinet, you see them in industry, on TV, in Covent Garden. So I don't really know which areas have these barriers. I haven't come up against them myself. I've always believed that if I was clever enough, proficient enough, I could get anywhere within the law. There's always someone who doesn't like someone else. I can't say that had I been British I would have been more successful. Would I? Maybe a little bit at the beginning, perhaps more doors would have opened more quickly had I been at Oxford and so on. Perhaps. When I first came into publishing I was considered a cowboy. They weren't very happy to welcome me. But having said that, there was nothing they could do about it. I won on their turf.

MIRANDA LOVETT: In a lot of ways it was more difficult for me at first than it would have been had my husband been American and he worked for Chase Manhattan and we had been sent here to the London office for three years. Then the English love you because they know you're leaving. But because I was married to an Englishman I had to be accepted first by his family, which took a very long time. They loved me, I was his wife, but I was still a difficult American. I looked around me and I saw a club and I realized that you just cannot penetrate the club. It infuriated me, and it brought out the reverse snobbism, the anti-establishment feelings. I remember my husband referring to our neighbours, who were extremely nice, an upper-middle-class couple, he was an accountant, and he referred to them as 'common' one day. I said, 'Who the fuck do you think you are calling them common?' It infuriated me, I hated that sort of talk. But he didn't really have an answer, they were just middle class.

CINDY BLAKE: I was amazed that I would be sitting at a dinner party and someone would refer to somebody as 'that doctor's daughter' in a tone that meant that there's something absolutely horrible and déclassé about being a doctor's daughter. Then I'd get my back up and I'd get angry and I'd trick them. I'd say, 'You know there are words that you can't say in Boston that mean that you're not upper class.' And they couldn't believe this. I'd say, 'If you say, "carpet", not "rug", for example, you're in bad trouble,' and their eyes would widen and they couldn't believe it. I'd say I went to boarding school and they couldn't believe *that*. They just assume that Americans are ill-educated (although most of us are).

* * *

MARY ROSE: What you have here is the complete separation between those who do the work and those who are only administrators. You work on completely different lines. This comes back to class. There is class in Germany but the educational system, whereby everyone starts off in the same schools, breaks it down. What keeps you together is your interests and of course your income group. One day I took some neighbour's children out – the mother was getting remarried – and we went to a pantomime and we had a bit of time before we came back. The children's father lives nearby, in a little house opposite these enormous council flats. So we went round to see if the father was at home. He was out, but this little girl looked at the council block and whispered to me, 'That is where the bad people live.' I asked her, 'Who told you that?' She said, 'Mummy and daddy.' I just said, 'I think you must have misunderstood them. I tell you who lives here: the people who make your life comfortable. The car menders, the shoe menders, the electricians . . .' 'Oh,' she said.

MIRANDA LOVETT: A few months after we were married we lived in a little house in Fulham and we didn't have a dining-room, but there was basement in the house with a sort of coal cellar and we decided to dig it out and make it into a dining-room. We had some workmen doing it who were hysterical. This little group of guys – there were three of them – I loved them more than anybody and I could relate to them better than anybody. I went through a reverse snobbism for a long time. Thinking that the upper-class English were the pits and here were these working-class guys who came into the house every day and were so funny and made me laugh: they were the people I looked forward to seeing.

BRYAN GOULD: Class exists in New Zealand, it exists in all societies but it's nowhere near as entrenched, as important, as finely gradated as it is here. It matters enormously here and I really did find it unpleasant. Experiencing the class system here marked me politically very strongly. There is an enormous difference between a New World country and an Old World country. In a New World country there is a freedom, a sense that everything is possible. When a person encounters a problem, it is to be resolved. How far you get depends on your own energy and ability, nothing else stops you. In other circumstances I would have been a revolutionary, so intolerant am I of being put down by people. I'm a very mild-mannered person but I will not be put down by anybody. I found that very irritating. Class seemed to me to be a means by which people were held back and told that they couldn't do things, and they were then reconciled to that fate by the class system. They were told that not only could they not do these things, but that was the natural order of things, that you should not be allowed to do them. All of which I found very very oppressive.

CHRISTOPHER HOPE: It's curious that there have been so few revolutions here. The times were ripe for it in both the eighteenth and nineteenth centuries. It may be because people could go out and assert themselves elsewhere. And all the armies sent out were working-class armies. That gets around those revolting working classes making mischief at home. Today's football hooliganism has its roots here – to go over the water and beat up foreigners and then call it war makes it respectable. Perhaps because it's a tiny island with a volatile people they've realized that any large explosion would have the most profound repercussions here.

HANNAH KODICEK: You can't get away from the class system, however hard the Communists try to erase it. But what was different in Czechoslovakia (apart from it being based on culture rather than money) is that everybody, but everybody, goes to the theatre, listens to music, probably plays some instrument, reads books and discusses politics and culture. You can walk into a café or a pub and you will meet groups of students and groups of professionals and groups of workers all discussing perhaps the same kind of things. Maybe not on the same level, but nevertheless aware and in some way participating in culture. There may be a few who just like to get drunk, but generally speaking there was much more of a levelling culturally and educationally. The first thing I noticed once I started speaking English a bit and trying to express myself is that what happens here is that there is a class who are far more educated than the Czechs generally, really, really wonderfully, that kind of mind that is so brilliant and so aware and so penetrating that you just sit back and gasp in admiration. Then there is a level of people who are generally very very highly cultured, aware, blah, blah, blah and then there is this abyss. Nothing. The culture doesn't seem to percolate downwards. There is this abyss, this desert, a vast nothing.

SHREELA FLATHER: The English don't realize that Asians have a class system too; a more convoluted class system than they would ever imagine. So it is rather sad that they do not understand that various groups of Asians are as different from each other as they are themselves.

---

11 Knowing Your Place

'The thing about England is that nobody has a god-given right
to succeed.'

MIRANDA LOVETT: England is governed by this idea of knowing your place. I don't think it's a nice way of putting it, but the gist of it is probably right. It's something the British are comfortable with. It's the way they want it, which is the way it came about in the first place. I don't know why, I think you have to go back hundreds of years to find the answer to that.

LEENA DHINGRA: What makes you acceptable to the English is a little like the way in which they ruled. You have to be integrated. You don't stick out too much, you must sort of disappear politely into the backcloth. You have to learn that very special brand of British understatement and slight hypocrisy, that's very important. You have to know how it works. To be an acceptable Jew you have to go around not being too Jewish.

SHREELA FLATHER: The British do have very strong stereotypes and they do resent it if you don't fall neatly into your stereotype. For instance the Asians are all law-abiding, quiet, good people, shopkeepers. The Afro-Caribbeans are not allowed to be middle class; the English don't really like meeting an educated middle-class Afro-Caribbean, because that spoils the stereotype.

MIKE PHILLIPS: One of the frustrating things and at the same time one of the things that makes English society constantly amusing is the difficulty people have with coping with anyone who doesn't know their place. Even now, I find that just being where I am and doing what I do, which is teaching media studies, causes people problems. I'll be sat in my office and somebody will come and knock on the door and open it and see me and ask, 'Is he in?' Because they don't expect me to be me. 'Is Mr Phillips around?' they say. They assume I must be a student. I'm a middle-aged man, sat in an office, clearly doing some work. They don't expect it. English people tended to have a place ready for you and they made it clear what they thought your place was. I came from a family and a culture which was thrusting, competitive. We came here to get on. We didn't come here to sweep the streets, we came to get on.

SHREELA FLATHER: The Jews are more confusing. They have learned how to camouflage themselves. I am amazed at hearing people talking about Jews in derogatory terms. There is no reason for anti-Semitism, but there is this really strong prejudice. The suspicion that someone might be Jewish, although no one is really sure – it goes around as some kind of whisper: 'So and so is *really* Jewish.'

LEENA DHINGRA: You have to trim off the rougher edges of your own culture to fit into the English culture. Those rougher edges, very often, are the things that make people see you in a prejudiced way. To fit into England you have to deny large chunks of yourself. You're not accepted. You might be liked and you'll certainly be tolerated. People won't stress the differences too much, because that's not really polite. So at the same time as they are being polite they're also denying you. You might say something and they'll think that's very 'quaint'. You cook something: 'What do you eat. Do you eat curries, what do you eat?' I say I don't cook very much. Salad and grilled fish. The word 'curry' doesn't exist for us. We don't call anything a curry. We don't sit there and say, 'What shall I make, shall I make a curry?' We don't have such a thing as a curry. So you have to deny. That is a very important part of the whole thing. To fit in you have to be less than you are. Less whatever it is. And if you do stick to certain things they are regarded either as being barbaric, or they are romanticized.

MIKE PHILLIPS: The first generation of black immigrants had no sense of identity with the English working class. Not because they were white, but because of what they were. They always appeared extremely idle, extremely lackadaisical, and the most irritating thing was that they accepted their place, they didn't want to get on. They thought we were odd: my father worked sixteen hours a day, all the overtime he could, and he never went on holiday; he saved up and bought a house. The people he was working with, first in the railways, later the Post Office, couldn't understand how he could arrive in this country and five years later buy a house. The point was that he never spent any money. What he wanted was the security, the stability his own house meant. In fact, for a lot of immigrants, when they felt that had gone as far as they could here, they moved to the States. My parents left in 1966 and went to New York. My father then went to evening classes and became a proper book-keeper and got a job at Columbia University. The next time I saw him, in 1973, he was ensconced in an office at the University as the treasurer of an academic foundation, spending weekends at Averill Harriman's house, they were on first-name terms. He had got on, but England wouldn't permit that.

DESMOND GITTENS: I wouldn't go so far as to say that I dislike the English. It would be crazy to walk around living in a place and dislike the people who live there. But there are a number of attitudes that I abhor. I dislike the fact that the English have never allowed me to feel patriotic towards this country. The class system, including racism, the way that you have to compete so terribly hard to get where you want to get. Really compete, because without being really clever and really good at it you hardly stand a chance if you are black. I tend to be very upset about what is happening to young black people. To see them being so alienated. We, being the first generation, would have thought that by now there would be a lot of assimilation. There is some: you have footballers, singers, so on, but that's knowing your place. Fulfilling traditional black roles. They haven't opened up things like the judiciary. They've allowed a few people to come in and play games with them, but they haven't really opened up the place. Those are the things that upset me. I don't carry around hate in me, though a lot of black people do. They have been so frustrated over the years that they're like walking timebombs.

MICHAEL IGNATIEFF: Class in England is fatal, and in some ways decisive and I felt it very early on. I married a woman whose family is entirely working class in origin. I met her in '76 and we were married in '78 and she comes from a family of carpenters and exhibition painters, the craftsmen and artisan end of decoration. She grew up in a council house in Shepherd's Bush, family of five, mother left when she was ten and a half, father was a foreman in a carpentry works, raised the children at home, she was the first girl in her comprehensive to go to university, to Warwick. That was my opening into another world. And what I have seen in that family is not abject subjugation or forelock tugging, or even terribly great social resentment, but, especially in the father, the deepest well of fatalism I have ever seen in another human being, which seemed to me profoundly social in character, because he's a man of tremendous skill and confidence. That's where I see something in England that strikes me as being just ghastly. Is this English? Would it be possible to find exactly the same person in another society? I don't know. Enormous sweetness of disposition, enormous gentleness, an enormous skill, married to a sense that life is for other people. That aspect of England fills me with enduring anger. I just don't think it's necessary. I see here that the stuffing was knocked out of a guy so long ago that you can't figure out how it happened. But the stuffing *was* knocked out – and that shouldn't happen.

PETER TATCHELL: I was amazed at how orderly and tranquil political demonstrations in this country were. The British tradition of radical protest seemed to have been forgotten. There was very little of the civil disobedience that I had been used to in Australia. Political demonstrations in Britain tended to merely consist of a leisurely Sunday afternoon stroll from Hyde Park to Trafalgar Square. They were very restrained events, lacking in political imagination. I put this down to the more traditional and deferential British culture. In this country, there are established ways of doing things. Just as the ruling classes have their own set of social manners, so too does the modern Labour Movement.

* * *

VICTOR WILD: I knew my place in England. Within the circles in which I moved I was accepted quite happily. My uncle and aunt were by this time quite prosperous. They had their bridge friends and their golfing friends. There was the middle-class society of Harrogate, though I think my uncle would have liked me to marry into the aristocracy. This would have pleased him enormously. I remember him saying, 'You know one day, laddie, you might be the Mayor of Harrogate!' I said, 'The Mayor of Harrogate – I don't want to be the Mayor of Harrogate.'

DON ATYEO: The thing about England is that nobody has a god-given right to succeed – which everyone has in America. If you are successful here you will be allowed to be successful, but that doesn't mean you get to join the upper classes. You have to know your place.

CINDY BLAKE: The lower class here seems so low in comparison with the American lower classes. There's not so much of a feeling that there is a chance. Even if you're in the South Bronx you'll think, 'Well, maybe I could score enough cocaine and sell it and make my way up the ladder.' There is no English dream. There's an American dream but there's no Canadian dream, no English dream, no French dream . . . no European dream of making it, of being Michael Dukakis with the Greek grandparents or whatever who came over on the boat. That doesn't exist here. There's not enough pie here for everybody to get a slice of it, so there are these just *desperate* people. Go down Oxford Street, you've never seen so many unattractive, desperate people in your life. There are people like that in New York, but there's life there and there's anger. Here the only time the anger seems to come out is at the soccer games. I miss that potential for anger. The Brixton riots . . . at least they were saying, 'This shits, this is lousy, let's do something.' Now it's all quietened down and nothing has been done. I can't believe they're not angrier. They've given up.

MICHAEL IGNATIEFF: A lot of the impatience I have with England is to do with having been brought up in a young society where kids are taught that anything is possible. My feeling about England still is that it is a tremendous relief to come upon people in this society who do think that anything is possible, that they can do as they please, because almost every English person I meet has this very strong sense that they should do what they ought to do, they should do what they are expected to do, they should do what they are told. They deal with those prohibitions with a variety of strategies: some of them are rage, some of them are fury, some of them are grudging compliance, some of them extremely comical acceptance. A lot of British humour is based on making a joke out of this absolutely insane system of social and personal moral constraints that this society works under. It's much deeper than class. It's much more European. The ceiling is just lower, spaces are slightly more cramped, there are just more people per acre.

YASMIN ALIBHAI: We come into this country and we say that we want to be equal. And you are saying this in a country which bases its entire culture and its history on the notion that inequality is a fact of life, and that if you challenge it you destabilize it and that in spite of that inequality England remains, relatively speaking, the best place in the world. Democratic, best press, best Parliament, better electoral system, the Royal Family – all those myths which form a little fence around most English people's heads. Then here we come as black Asians or Afro-Caribbeans and we talk about equality. It doesn't make any sense to the British. I'm not surprised that people will still tell you there is no racism here. That the English are a fair-minded tolerant race and all these problems have just been created by 'black trouble-makers' because they've nothing better to do. West Indians who give blues parties and smoke dope. The English, they say, are actually incapable of racism.

DESMOND GITTENS: I've been told many, many times, 'Oh, you're acting above your station, Desmond.' That sort of thing. So in a lot of areas you underachieve. Sometimes you're sitting in a meeting and you want to contribute but if you're there with people who think that if you do contribute you'll be acting above your station, you don't say anything. And if you do say something, first you get put down for saying it, then two weeks from now you might see your idea written in a report somewhere, ripped off and penned by somebody else. That creates underachievers. I don't want to think this is discrimination, I don't want my colour to stop me from doing anything, so I would always put this down to politics, bureaucracy. But things are so insidious in this country that sometimes you don't know what a person is using to discriminate this time. Class, colour, race, creed, you're not sure. There are so many choices for him to pull out of his pocket. Because of the prevalence of discrimination you tend to not be able to ignore it. Why do certain things happen – is it race or what? The idea that it might be racial is always there.

KAREL KYNCL: Sometimes I have a strange feeling that I could, by meeting people in the street, judge what strata of society they belong to, simply from their appearance. I live in Peckham and I have a feeling that the people there are a very special segment of the lower classes, who are more or less satisfied with their social status. I do feel that there is not enough drive in them to push them from one stratum into another one. I don't know whether this comes from lack of will, or from lack of possibilities. Whatever the reason, for a foreigner this is very visible. One would imagine that bad things you encounter in your life, whether big or small, would be accepted in a regimented country like Czechoslovakia with the attitude: nothing can be done, all right, with resignation. But you would expect that in a country like Britain, people would force them to be improved. In fact the opposite is true: in Czechoslovakia the people are much more pronounced in their criticisms and in their actions, at least on a local level, against something bad; and in this country – which is something I cannot understand – people accept these things without complaining.

BENTHE NORHEIM: Socially I found England very backward. Norway is a very democratic country and things have evened out very much. You don't see the differences between people the way you have here with the class system. I didn't know if I should laugh or cry sometimes, looking at the way people relate to each other, the way they play their roles so well in that class structure. This idea of knowing your place is something that I had never experienced in Norway, ever.

DON ATYEO: It took a long time before I knew what my place was. I was just as Australian. I wasn't attached here which meant you could be treated either way. Which gave you a lot of entrées. You weren't in a box. But the older you get and the longer you remain here the more you're conscious of the box and the harder you find it to deal with the class system. The accent's not so pronounced now and you're there not as an Australian any more but just one more of the rude mechanicals. You get dumped into the box very smartly and you can feel them doing it. Which is something I've never felt before. Before, when I was unattached, you could just float through it all. Your position is defined by your job, not who you are or where you came from. How far do you have to go to join the upper class? How far does Rupert Murdoch have to go? Murdoch actually rules America, he *is* Mr America. Murdoch, Donald Trump, a couple of others. Here, he might own *The Times*, he might own satellite TV, but he's just a vulgar Australian. He still needs a few token lords on his boards for credibility in those circles. I loathe the Royal Family. They're one of the great weaknesses of Britain. The heart of the class system. Unlike Australia, unlike France, unlike most other places you pick up your newspaper and you realize that you are actually second-class as a human because there is the Queen staring out at you. It is very debilitating, this feeling that you can never reach the top, which makes for a big ceiling on ambition.

MIRANDA LOVETT: The English are not tolerant, absolutely not. They're tolerant on a superficial level, because they're able to accept things on a superficial level, because they can always go back to knowing what their place is and knowing where they're comfortable, and feeling, 'Well, we're the way we are and we're not going to change.'

YASMIN ALIBHAI: I do think that there is a kind of respect you can win here if you can prove that you have fought through, and that you don't accept any nonsense. Though you still have to know your place and you have to remember it. In the end you are an immigrant and that hurts. It's funny how they make you feel that you don't belong. I was on a panel discussion with Asian women and I said that Mrs Thatcher was possibly the only woman in the world who made me feel ashamed to be a woman. I had three death threats. All from white men. One actually came to my house. They all said the same thing: 'You foreigner, how dare you come here, how dare you criticize our prime minister?'

12 The Immigrant Life

'When you're an immigrant you have a kind of a drive. People tell themselves every day that they came for a purpose. They didn't just come to live.'

MIKE PHILLIPS: To be an immigrant is to be a special sort of person: if you had taken the trouble to leave your country, to come thousands and thousands of miles it was like going to the moon. You didn't know if you'd ever get back home, you didn't know what you'd find. It was like dying. People always meant to go back: the old people were always saying, 'I don't want to die in this country. I won't leave my bones in this country.' Almost all of them have.

MICHAEL IGNATIEFF: One of the liberations of being an émigré or an expatriate is that it all comes down to you. You are a much more radical individualist than you are in your home culture. In your home culture you can call on your knowledge of the game, you call on being a member of the right religion or the right class or whatever, when you start life in your home country you call in all those debts. In my comfortable, middle-class, Canadian milieu I was definitely my father's son. I'm no one's son in this society. Everything that has happened since I have come here has been the result of my own efforts. In the new country you arrive, you don't owe anyone anything, you don't know anybody, so you have to make it on your own terms. I feel a great sense of attachment to England precisely because it has allowed me to get out there and with generalized indifference has neither aided me nor impeded me but just let me get on with it. So what has happened to me here is my own responsibility. Now none of this would be true if I were black, if I were Asian, and if I didn't have my education. None of it would have happened. I don't believe for a second that this is an open society. The extent to which talent is wasted in this society is sickening, but I won't subscribe to the fatuous fallacy that this is a closed, clapped-out society that is perishing precisely because it won't allow talent to rise. It's inconceivably more open than it was, though it's nowhere near as open as the 'career open to talents' view of the Tory ideologists.

NAIM ATALLAH: I liked coming to England. I had lived in a troubled part of the world – it had been an unsettled area for all of my life. I came here and there were no problems and I made a lot of friends and I loved the life. Part of it was I suddenly discovered freedom. At home, because I was the only son, I was virtually a prisoner – a prisoner of love, if you like – they still wouldn't let me buy a bike there in case I got run over by a car. So the first thing I did here

157

was to buy a bike – that was the biggest joy ever. There was no Arab community here. I didn't know anybody. All the students at the college were English. So I was thrown into this alien atmosphere, but I liked what I saw and I wanted to stay.

JOHN LAHR: Being Bert Lahr's son broke down a lot of barriers. Though my future mother-in-law still tried to get an injunction to stop me marrying her daughter, because I was an actor's son and Jewish to boot – my father's name meant nothing to her. That was good for me – I existed here as myself, without any shadow. When you are the son of a famous person, especially one who is loved, it throws a long shadow, and however whole you are as a person, it's still there. Here I was cut off and had to swim on my own personality. It helped me define myself for myself, being outside the culture, outside my father's influence. I could see myself more clearly, and saw America in a different way, and that's what interested me most.

IVAN KYNCL: My experience here has changed my life. In Czechoslovakia I started off as just my father's son. After that I was a dissident. Which gave me my first identity. I was a part of the group, we believed the same things, they liked me perhaps because what I did was daring, dangerous. But here I have done all sorts of things in a different world and I really have made a new life since 1983. I still want to know what is going on in Czechoslovakia, and I still want to help people there. But it was funny: in 1981 I met Milan Kundera in Paris. There was a demonstration about people in Czech prisons and I asked him if he would go to the demonstration. He said, 'Maybe.' But he didn't come. And what he said to me was, 'The first thing you must get is a horseshoe, and after that you can kick.' In other words, if you are nobody, nobody will hear you. This wasn't completely fair, because my father was already in prison and I couldn't wait to get a horseshoe before I started helping him. But he was right: up till now I haven't seen myself as anyone.

MICHAEL DE SOUZA: When you look at what we came to, not just black but all immigrants, I think we've come a long way. When I came racism was dread, it was so dread that you just felt no identity whatsoever, none. Coming from an environment where everything was so free and easy and nice and open you became more aware when things were not that way. You just felt no pride. You just had to emulate white people, that's all there was to do. You knew nothing about any black issue whatsoever. You knew nothing and you certainly get taught it. It was the same in Trinidad. I knew about Christopher Columbus before I even knew where San Fernando was, which was where I was born. I knew about lots of different things before I knew anything about being black. So you really don't have any role models. The men that I could see were just after women all the time, they'd dominate their children. They'd all been having a great time by themselves and then wifey arrives.

MARY DENYS: My children's father was waiting for me at Victoria. We got in a taxi and came to Maida Vale, W9. I still live there. I was quite disillusioned. I had had two bedrooms, a sitting-room and a kitchen in St Lucia; now I was living in a single room. It was very cold. The accommodation where I lived was bad, very bad. In one house you would have four or five families. But people were more friendly then. We used to sleep in the same room with the gas cooker. On Sunday or Saturday we'd go out. People would buy wine and we'd have a drink, we'd entertain. Nowadays everybody has living-rooms, sitting-rooms, they lock their doors. My mother had the children, they were still in St Lucia. The first thing I did was to send her some money. I wrote to her to say that we had believed that London was paved with gold, and it wasn't like that at all. We have to work so hard. But my mother wrote back to say that she didn't care whether it was paved with gold or not – I had to send money for the children. After a while I sent for the two of them. They were quite young, they were at primary school. After three months here I was pregnant again. I was working at Askeys, a wafer firm in Kensal Road. I left to have the child, then I started a new job at another factory in Kensal Road, where my husband worked. After I was made redundant there I worked in Beethoven Street stuffing teddy bears. After doing that I stayed looking after the children for a while, quite a while. Then I separated from my husband, I couldn't stand living with him any more. I went to live round the corner. I joined the Westminster Community Relations Council. I was vice-chairman there for a while. Alfred Dubs was involved. I was introduced by a fellow called Mango, he's dead now. Paul Boateng was chairman, I proposed him, so I suppose I started him off in politics. In those days I used to drink a lot. There was a man round the corner who made white rum and he would come round and sell it to me. I used to have parties, I'd invite all the CRC. They'd bring their wives, I'd cook, make punches, we'd all drink the white rum, they used to call it 'Mrs Denys' potion'. After two years I resigned. I found that they were doing nothing at all for the people. It was just talk. You'd go in with something you wanted and all that happened was that you'd get referred to somewhere else. They were doing nothing. So I lost interest.

DESMOND GITTENS: Most of my contemporaries who had travelled to England were either bus conductors or worked in restaurants or Lyons Corner House or wherever. I was a serviceman and I was paid and I was stationed in Regent's Park Barracks in Albany Street so I had a lot of privileges. I would go out at night, go to the clubs in the West End and not have to worry about rent or who washed the clothes or anything. All I had to do was get to reveille the following morning and appear on parade and that was enough. That was my introduction to London. It was also the first time I'd seen a large black community in Britain. Notting Hill, Brixton, Balham, mainly south London. People from the eastern Caribbean settled in Notting Hill, Shepherd's Bush, and that; people from further north, Jamaicans, settled in places like Brixton. Coming from Trinidad, I found myself more in and around Notting Hill, Harrow Road, places like that. Parties going on.

MICHAEL DE SOUZA: Every weekend we'd have a party. They say, 'Oh, bloody West Indian parties,' but it wasn't like that. It was just my family. My mum, my aunt, my cousins, really no men around as such. Cook our food, play our music, laugh and joke and it was real nice.

VINCENT REID: In 1958, I set up in business in Notting Hill. I had a restaurant called the Fiesta in Westbourne Park Road. Stephen Ward came down there, those kind of people. I knew the underground people. I read my poetry at the ICA in 1966, with Ted Joans, wrote three pieces for *IT*. I knew Colin MacInnes. He lived in St Stephen's Gardens. I went there, drank with him, I didn't regard him as really important at all, I thought he was a jerk. There was the Rio, run by a guy called Billy, in Talbot Road, though the name kept changing. It was also referred to as the Blues.

BERNIE GRANT: We used to go to clubs and so on. The Flamingo in Wardour Street, we'd see Georgie Fame, people like that; the Mangrove restaurant in Notting Hill occasionally. But the people I tended to mix with were the middle-class blacks, there weren't a lot of working-class black people that I knew at that time. They might not have been seen as middle class in Britain, but they certainly would have been back home. My friends' fathers were a dentist, a doctor, so on. They couldn't practise here, so they'd had to get jobs in factories and so on, but their values were still middle class.

VINCENT REID: Notting Hill was fun, it was exciting. There was a lot of caring. If you had a couple of quid in your pocket and you met a brother, you'd give him something: 'Go and eat.' You don't get that now. You give people money and they'd think you were a mug, so you don't do it. In those days . . . you never knew – a guy might be on his uppers today, but be all right tomorrow. Anything was possible then. There was a great deal of optimism. Of course the fact was that you had to find ways of translating the optimism into a way of living.

MANDY MERCK: Four days after arriving, I went down to London for the first time. It was really hot for October in England. The fashion was changing to maxis, but I was wearing a very short mini skirt. I remember walking through Kensington Gardens on a Saturday afternoon thinking: this is what I came for – the mists rising gently off the park; beautiful women with exquisite large dogs walking around Peter Pan's statue. Now I know where I am, this is what I want. I came down to London a lot for my social life. The first time I was in London, a Ghanaian guy picked me up in the park: 'I work in a club, would you like to come? I'll pick you up later.' I said 'OK.' I'd hardly dated at all at Smith. Socializing meant heavy weekends with Dartmouth boys if you were unlucky, Princeton boys if you were luckier. If you had affairs you didn't talk about it much. I was very naïve, Smith had prolonged my adolescence, and here I was suddenly in a culture where men in the street asked you out. I thought this was nice, and I wasn't scared. I should have been. He took me to a gambling club in South Kensington in a basement – Blaze's. The guy wasn't very heavy duty. I think he just wanted to have a girl standing next to him in the club.

LEENA DHINGRA: We lived first in Barnes which was really not the right place for us. It was a very suburban little area with these nice little houses. It wasn't really for the likes of us. We just felt very awkward. We were very different. Our whole lifestyle was very different. Partly it was just the eccentricity of our particular family. We planted these rose bushes, but we didn't know you had to prune them – they were climbing up all over the place. People would visit and we'd say, 'It's the house of the roses.' It was quiet most of the time until suddenly every holiday all the cousins and the friends who were studying here would descend. Suddenly there'd be this invasion of six or seven young men. Somebody was in Loughborough, somebody in Cambridge, somebody in Oxford. Then all their friends would come. Then it would revert to being quiet again. There was never any comment from the neighbours. But we didn't quite fit in. So we moved to a flat in St John's Wood. Then we moved to Swiss Cottage; then we moved here, to Hampstead, and then we didn't move any more.

* * *

CINDY BLAKE: I'm amazed that the English can keep all these people in their little ghettos. I went to play basketball in the YWCA in Brixton and it was like Harlem, but Harlem spills over. You see black people on subways anywhere you go in New York – you do not see black people in the West End. So by and large in large areas of London you do not see black faces and you react if you do. I miss black people. London is a very white town, and in the country . . . But how do they manage to keep people so segregated? I went to a party in Clapham where this yuppie couple were complaining that they had to live next to some black people, and I thought, 'What *is* this?' You'd be jumping up and down in the street in New York just to live next to someone who wasn't a murderer or a dope dealer or hadn't raped somebody. The idea that these people were sweating over the fact that they were living next door to someone who was black . . . this is antediluvian.

GINA ADAMOU: We started off living in Islington, near the market. That was where most Cypriot people went. We had two rooms and a small kitchen. My parents in the one room and the rest of us, five girls and my grandmother, in the other. A couple of double beds and a single bed. A small television in the corner. They worked very hard. They had five kids, and the grandmother. Had to feed them, pay the rent. My dad went back to his original job as a carpenter; my mother was a machinist. She was a good machinist – she had no problem finding jobs. Anything you can imagine she can make. She worked in a factory making ladies' coats. Owned by Cypriot people. To them this was very important, because they couldn't speak the language. They worked with Cypriot people, they shopped with Cypriot people, in fact in many ways they had very little to do with English society. It was really a ghetto.

BRYAN GOULD: For me assimilation is easy. In many ways I am deliberately and voluntarily returning to my English roots and one of the things I love about this country is that sort of atavistic sense of one's ancestors. If you're a Bradford Muslim, a Pakistani, the situation is just incredibly different. You don't have the options that I have. If you seek refuge in a community of your own kind which insulates you against the rest of English society, there's a very good reason. You would feel more comfortable there.

RAJAN UDDIN JALAL: People talk about ghettoization, but I call it sticking together, which is what the black and Asian communities must do. Otherwise we won't be getting any political power or anything else. There are drawbacks to that, I accept, but the situation has emerged as much because people don't feel sufficiently secure to move away from the ghetto areas as much as from any other reason. But gradually people from the East End are moving out, just like the Jews before them. They are moving on, buying their own houses. I estimate at least a thousand Bengali families have left Tower Hamlets. But that is also affected by today's economics. When the Jews moved out there was still an expanding housing market. That market no longer exists, which means one is not going to get that sort of movement again.

MIKE PHILLIPS: We were very isolated. Socially and racially. There weren't a lot of kids and most of them were older than me. My parents used to make great efforts to meet other Guyanese people with children. You'd hear about a new family coming and you'd go to see them. It was an all-black house, there were three families in our house. One of them had a daughter, but she was seventeen, a big girl, an experienced woman. I was fourteen and she went out with big men, of at least nineteen. I used to go to school and come back. I'd listen to the radio a lot, and that was nice. There was a bus stop just outside our window and I'd sit and look out of the window at the bus stop all afternoon until 'The Archers' would come on, and 'The Clitheroe Kid', all that stuff.

GULZAR KHAN: In 1962 our people kept themselves to themselves. Those who had jobs didn't have the time to go out. They worked twelve hours a day and when they came home they were too tired to do anything but eat and sleep. Those who had stayed at home were too busy going shopping, cooking for them, whatever, to go out. There weren't that many shops anyway. We were still a very small minority. Nobody had come with their family. That happened later. What happened was that people found that they were trapped, they couldn't make enough money to go home, so what happened was that they borrowed more money and sent for their families to come here. The difficulty was that when they were working they were spending money on themselves and only sending a little home. Moreover their minds were not working properly over here, because they were always thinking of their homes and families.

GINA ADAMOU: My parents didn't really try to become part of mainstream English society. Like most of the Cypriots who came in the early '60s they stayed very much among their own. Their children began to mingle in but they didn't. They did well, they employed all sorts of people in their factory, but otherwise they stayed very much inside the Cypriot community. They shopped there, went to a Greek doctor, dentist, optician ... Everyone helping each other in business. That kind of support is good, but in some ways it's bad. English society does have some good things to offer, it's silly to reject them all. They looked at English society with suspicion and they felt alienated. They led a parallel life and that still goes on today. They want to get on and be good citizens but not get involved, not make a fuss. What is sad is that they have passed some of that on to their kids. Their kids don't do the sort of things that younger people do. It is still a very closed community. As closed as the Muslims up in Bradford. Maybe it's the same with everyone who comes from a small, agricultural country. People who lived in villages.

MUHAMMAD AYYAZ: It looked strange to come from a village in Pakistan to this city. Bradford was a completely different city in those days. All the buildings were really black, where we lived was completely different. I was fifteen. I was sad to leave Pakistan, but it was my father's decision to bring me here. As far as he was concerned it was quite normal. We were mainly singles.

So they had these places where they used to go regularly, in the evenings, at weekends, and a male member would cook something and they would sit for hours and hours talking. It was very nice actually, I miss that. Or at weekends we used to go to the Pakistani cinemas. There were five when I came; there isn't a single one left now. I enjoyed that very much. Now it's all videos.

MANZOOR BAHADUR: I didn't enjoy being different to the other kids. I had my own religion, Islam, and my own culture. When the other kids went home from the school, they were out on the streets playing; I was sent off to the mosque to learn my religion. That's where I learned Urdu, in the evenings and at weekends. This continued for six years right up until I left school. It was like a different world going to school. You become a different person. When you come home and you speak to your father in your own language, in Punjabi, and the only place I heard it outside was when we went to visit one of my father's friends, otherwise it was always English. It was a close-knit world. There were shops, a Muslim halal butcher's, and one or two local Asian shops. For meat we had to travel across town a couple of miles, although you could get flour and other food items nearer home. People who lived in Halifax or Keighley used to have to buy chickens from a farm and kill them themselves; other meat needed a special trip to Bradford.

GULZAR KHAN: The particular difficulty and disadvantage was about the meat. You had to find out where the Muslim shop was which sold halal meat. There was one grocer, everyone would go, coming from two, three, four miles around. There were some deliveries. A family would leave a notebook with their order, their name and address, and that evening the grocer would bring their goods. What there was not was mixing or integration of any sort. No discussion between us and the white community.

MUHAMMAD ALI: My father lived in a very enclosed all-Asian environment. He did his work, maybe twelve hours a day, and then came back home. I didn't break out of the Asian community much myself. We lived in the inner city and all the community around was Asian. In the street where I lived, when I came in '69, there were three Asian families and all the rest were white. Within three years there were three white families and all the rest were Asian. It's still the case: two or three Asian people buy houses in a white street and the whites immediately start selling up. It's sad, but that's how it is. The white people show by their moving that they are simply not accepting the Asian or black community.

BHAJAN SINGH CHADHA: We saw that we were resented. Say if we went to a pub and we went into the saloon bar, we wouldn't be served until we moved to the public bar, which the landlord would very quickly tell us to do. It was very difficult to do things like buy motor insurance. They would make up some reason to reject you; they'd demand five years' driving experience in England, which of course nobody would have. Small things, but they build up. So we retreated in on ourselves and we preferred to live in our own communities.

MANZOOR BAHADUR: In some ways I would prefer to stay in an all-Asian community area. I do feel a bit safer here. It goes back to the time when I first came to this country. When we first came here white people said our food stinks, wogs stink. Funnily enough there's more white people eat our food now than they eat their own so we have broken that myth. Then it was a case of 'all blacks like to stick together, they live in the same area' but that wasn't through choice. In the early '60s my father tried to buy a house in what were mainly white areas and deal after deal fell through. People just didn't want to sell to Asians. The reason you got all-Asian areas was that as soon as we moved in, the white families moved out.

CASH BHOGAL: I think some parts of the Asian community are ghettoized. Partly because the community would like to reside in areas where there are other Asians or other black people and not be isolated in somewhere like Kent where you won't find many Asian shops or Asian people. They would rather live in areas where they have relatives, they don't want to move too far away and in that sense you can say that the ghetto is self-imposed. But at the outset it was perhaps because of the conditions of the housing available in certain parts of the United Kingdom. It was impossible to buy places outside the Asian areas, among the white community.

BHAJAN SINGH CHADHA: Buying a house was very profitable. All you had to do was raise, say, £1,000, even £700. Then you raised a mortgage. There were so many people who needed accommodation, it was easy to rent them out. When I arrived – by myself, I had left my family in Kenya – I rented a bed in a house in Southall. It wasn't very comfortable. There was a small room with five people in it, paying £1 2s. 6d. a week each. But there was no chance of getting anything better, although gradually, as more people set themselves up as landlords, the situation improved. We didn't mix with the white community. There were only very few Indian shops, maybe just the one. Indian stuff was very hard to find. We could never have imagined that the Southall of those days would become the Southall of today.

LEENA DHINGRA: I don't really belong to the Indian community here. It's very sad, in a way. I said to my mother once, 'Why didn't we go to Southall? Why didn't we go to look for a place in a place like Southall?' She said, 'Well, what would we have found in common with a place like that?' But it's Punjabi and we are Punjabi. But it's to do with the fact that we come from a slightly different . . . class. Though my family aren't snobby. It's more a cultural thing. My father spoke English, French, German, Arabic, Persian, Urdu. If he read Goethe he read Goethe in German. He was like a nineteenth-century intellectual. Anyway Southall wasn't yet the place it is now and to be honest it was much too far away for us, miles away. One needed to be central. We also are used to open spaces and you looked for a place that was near somewhere you could go for a morning walk, because that is part of the Hindu religion. Also we were not part of a wave of immigration which would have thrust us into a community. We weren't people who didn't know the language. My mother went to university, she taught in university . . . that's the difference. But in a way we are even more uprooted than everybody else.

CASH BHOGAL: The Indian community tended to stay together. There were enormous barriers, not just for me but for my mother and my brothers. The language was the main thing, but on top of this we generally didn't know where we could go even if we had wanted to. There were also the barriers of prejudice. Even at school, because you couldn't understand the language, you didn't know the customs or share the sense of humour, often you felt left out. It goes without saying that you were called names, etc. First you wondered why this was happening, then you grew much quicker for your age than you would have done otherwise because of this prejudice. In the end the only thing you could do was be aggressive. It's only recently that people have really recognized Asian youth as fighting back, but even in those days I can remember things happening. We weren't used to the climate, and the winter of '62–63 was one of the worst winters ever. Coming from our warm climate this was very shocking. So there we were in the playground, us few Asians and West Indians standing around, and some English boys and they started pushing us about. The only response was to form some kind of a group to protect ourselves. You weren't only being verbally abused, but you were also being physically assaulted.

MICHAEL DE SOUZA: My problems came as much from finding it hard to get into the culture as actually being attacked. Nobody made any real effort to help. I just tried to get on. If people had problems with me being black, then I tried to explain it to them if I could and tried to explain the differences between my mum and me. And there's a big difference between her and me and there's a certain difference between me and a little English boy. I could go to a little English boy's house and his mum would give us a plate of toast. She wouldn't get to know me too great, but it's all right. But I couldn't do that for my friends. Ask my mum to give us some toast, she'd ask us if I were totally mad, beat me, embarrass me and send me straight to bed. This is common: you just cannot

166

take it on your own head to invite people home as a child. You can't do it. There's no such thing as respecting your friends. They have to wait on the doorstep and all that. It's a funny, funny culture.

* * *

JAROSLAV BRADAC: The natural thing for any immigrant is to stick to one's own kind. First of all the language is a bit alien, so you can't always get your point across and all that. Therefore you often stick to people with whom you have a common language. But I always rejected any kind of a ghetto mentality. I was always aware what I did *not* want to be. If I had come to live in England, then I did not want to be a part of an émigré group, nostalgically thinking about what we don't have any more, how it was in the old days. It gets distorted. You start wallowing in the past. What you are missing is not the country of your origin – you're missing your youth. It isn't that the sun shone all the time and that things were better then, but actually something you just don't have any more. I went to the Czech club in my early days, a couple of times, and I found it *bizarre*. I saw people, in their forties I suppose, the émigrés of '48, and they were sitting playing popular card games which I remember but I had never mastered, for sixpences, and arguing whether tram number 16 turned right on a particular crossroads in Prague or left, or whether it went straight on! But for them, and they must be in their sixties now, the club is probably their second home, and they are probably still arguing over the same point. That mentality seems to have prevailed amongst the Czechs who went to Germany too. I stayed with various Czechs there for a while and they had Czech dentists, the person who came to repair the leaking tap was Czech, something went wrong with the car, the mechanic was Czech – it was a kind of mafia, only your own kind.

ANWAR BATI: I don't like clannishness. Though one does benefit from clannishness in England. One was quite soon aware that this country was a series of clubs and the more clubs you were a member of the better off you were. I always thought the ideal thing would be an Etonian, Oxonian Jew. That would be the best you could put together. All the perfect connections. I don't associate with the Pakistani community at all really. I don't like this thing where someone who is Pakistani hints to me: 'Well, we're both Pakistanis so that's all right then . . .' I don't like that. Equally I despise that feeling in other groups too. I don't like it among Jews, Greeks, whatever. This idea that we'll do this deal, it'll all be OK because we're the same. Well, we're not the same.

ENNIO CAMISA: I wasn't involved in the Clerkenwell community. There was an Italian club in Greek Street. It doesn't exist any more. I never went there,

167

because if I went there, I always met the people who would come into the shop. When they'd come into the shop, they didn't want to know how much is that, how much is that, they'd spend a lot of money. But if you'd meet them in the club, then they'd come in the shop and expect all this stuff for nothing. Or otherwise they hadn't got any money and they wanted things on credit. And if they had things on credit you didn't see any more of them. Lost the credit and lose the customer. It was very friendly, they'd come in the shop, 'Good morning ... good afternoon', I used to walk in the park, I'd meet them there, but I never went to the club. From Greek Street they moved to Charing Cross Road. At that time the club was all Fascist. I never liked it. I wanted to keep out of politics, no politics. I wasn't antifascist. I wasn't anything. I had left Italy before Mussolini took over.

WITOLD STARECKI: I didn't mix with the Polish community on principle. I wanted to learn this country, I had a bad taste in my mouth after my experiences in Poland, besides this the Polish community in Britain are not together because that is what they want – it is because they have no other choice. If you can't mix with someone you want to mix with – your neighbour who you think is nice but who you cannot really meet – and you still want to go out at the weekend, whether you like it or not you go to your fellow Pole. If you are in a small community the gossip comes, the bad blood comes, all the problems that come out of a small community.

JAROSLAV BRADAC: This clannishness is terribly unhealthy. I think the Poles are much more consciously clannish than the Czechs. It's also to do with numbers. There are many more of them, and there was a far larger Polish emigration after the war. I have angered a number of Czechs who ring me and assume because they are Czechs and just turn up they must be my friends. On what ground? Because we come from the same country? But that's not good enough.

EVA JIRICNA: I am not part of the émigré Czech community. I don't even know anybody. My brother is the only Czech person I really know. And he's married to an English girl and they live in Switzerland. His wife and children don't speak any Czech so even if I go over to stay with them we all speak English. I'm told there is a Czech community here and I know of people who spend evenings in some club off Ladbroke Grove but I've never really tried it. I find it really depressing somehow. You meet people who you otherwise wouldn't meet for no reason other than you come from the same country. You might sing national songs or what, I don't know. I guess that's what people do. But I have been successful and I have to accept that there are some people who haven't been as lucky as I have. They have had very hard lives. People who are doing very boring jobs and who really need somebody they can spend their life with outside working hours. Or people who couldn't find a job. People who feel very sentimental and very happy with people like themselves with whom they can talk about home. Some people haven't learnt English properly so they cannot communicate. The same thing applies to a lot of Poles. Sometimes the wife simply doesn't speak English. So they are very dependent on their Polish friends and they meet all the time and their children go to Polish schools and they have a completely different outlook to mine. I'm not criticizing people who do choose to spend their lives sitting eating Czech dumplings and drinking Czech beer, I don't want to be supercilious about it at all, but I've never felt the necessity.

WITOLD STARECKI: With age I have discovered that I am deeply Polish. There is no denying that. There are certain characteristics: the mentality, the attitude to certain sets of values, a confrontational nature, all these sorts of things. But I was never fanatically Polish. I never subscribed to the sort of village system where you're locked in a ghetto and you don't know the world. So I was never an extreme Pole. I wasn't hooked completely on Polish manias. The Polish community here would like to mix into the larger society, but I don't think that they have so many opportunities. In a way they are sentenced to be together. What is different between my case and that of most of the Poles who stayed here is that I did mix rather well into English society because of my profession. Artistic circles are much more flexible than others. If I were a lawyer or a doctor or a clerk there is no way that I would mix with the British. These classical, closed jobs don't mix. I have a lot of Polish friends within these professions and they don't have British friends. They may be very successful, they may deal with the British on a professional level or a drink at lunchtime, but nothing more. Being Polish is incurable, it's a lifetime inheritance, a disease.

DON ATYEO: All around me I saw, especially in Earls Court, Australians who were totally thrown by England. Coming over, thinking that the English were just like your big brothers, your mother or whatever, and they were totally bewildered by the reality. Here was Earls Court full of these Australians who were terrified of leaving each other and they went into Australian pubs, drank Australian booze and went to the Walkabout Club and reminisced about the price of things back home and talked to each other and they never fucking got out of Earls Court. Barry McKenzie was no fiction. The place was a real ghetto and the Australians were terrified to get out because everywhere else was so alien. You'd meet Australians and you'd have discussions and the first question was always, 'How long have you been away for?' and you'd say, 'Three years.' 'Wow . . .' and they'd only been away six months and there was this very much

169

'hipper than thou' syndrome. Then you could go into all these hokey pieces of shit about Vegamite or whatever, when of course you didn't want Vegamite at all. You never liked it when you were there, but you did all this cod-nationalistic stuff.

PETER TATCHELL: During my childhood, our family moved house seven times. So I got quite used to change and soon learnt to adapt to new situations and make the best of them. That served me well on my arrival in England. I quickly made many friends and settled into life here. Though I continued to campaign against the Australian intervention in the Vietnam War, I didn't fall into the life of an exile or restrict myself to an Australian milieu. I never found the exile mentality very helpful or productive. Indeed, I soon realized that I could do relatively little to influence events in Australia. In contrast, there were lots of interesting things happening in London and lots of things I could do to affect the situation here. It seems to me that if you've settled in a new country, there's no point always looking over your shoulder, back at the past where you came from. It's far more rewarding to look forward to the future where you are.

JASWINDER AMAR: The problem with protecting yourself by staying within your own culture is that if you do that you never learn anything about the rest of the world. You can't be happy doing that; you have to deal with English life too. So you have to fight, you have to be strong. If you don't fight for your rights you don't get anything. You just sit at home and think about all the things that people do to you. That's totally wrong, it's rubbish. You go and fight for a thing and you'll get it.

MARY DENYS: On the whole I stay in the black community. I walk down the street and if anybody says hello to me I'll say hello back. But if I say hello to you and you don't answer, I won't say it a second time. I look at a person and weigh them up, I wouldn't go into any white person's house if they don't invite me first. So I haven't actually had the chance of being rebuffed on race grounds in anybody's home. On the buses, yes. I have been attacked, and I've given as much as I got.

GINA ADAMOU: I loved education. I wanted to have it, but there wasn't a chance in our situation because, coming from a working-class background, they didn't believe in it. Girls would come out of school as soon as possible and go into some kind of trade. What mattered was that they should go off and learn a trade and contribute to the family. They never even *thought* of higher education. They thought it was something not for them or for the likes of us, or whatever. What I would have liked to have done was write. I loved writing,

170

literature. I would have loved to carry on with it. In Cyprus, at school, I wrote poems, short stories, you name it. When I first came here I was still doing it, and one of the Greek papers offered to publish my stuff – they loved it so much they want to publish something every week. My father wouldn't allow it. I was very upset. I never wrote since. My father put his foot down: 'No daughter of mine will do that.' If I did it I'd get too big-headed and he wouldn't be able to control us. That wasn't why he didn't let me go to school – it was more practical. If he had let me be published, if he had encouraged me, I would have done much more writing. Now I go to evening classes in English: I'm doing English GCSE.

*　*　*

MUHAMMAD AYYAZ: People see that through education there is a barrier building up between the younger generation and the older generation. They want their children to be educated and get a good job, but if the children tend to behave in a way which the English may see as liberal – to start saying, 'It's my life, it's my business,' and starting to live elsewhere, separately from the community – that's where resentment starts to grow. People feel that English education is seducing them away from the community. Sometimes this all happens just for two or three years, when the children are in their teens, then they settle back and that's it. Sometimes it goes on longer and that's when people are afraid. Sometimes it's a genuine fear, sometimes it is unfounded. People tend to fear that their children will grow up and stop behaving in the way that they behaved. Mainly it's to do with religion, that they grow up and leave the religion. They may do well in education, and go beyond school to university, but their religious education will be very very limited. The fear is that they will simply ignore that side of life, and think only of work and what have you.

GINA ADAMOU: We were very much controlled. My parents were very young, very young parents. They married very young. They came to England and they were really scared. Other Cypriot people would say things to them – this is a bad society, English society has loose morals, you have five girls – this scared them, really scared them. So we weren't allowed to do anything, not the most simple things. But they were simply scared, scared of what might happen to their girls. So they held on to us, imprisoned us in many ways. You couldn't do it. The only thing I was really interested in was pop music. I adored music. I used to save my pennies to buy the records. Occasional trips to the pictures. This was general among the Cypriot community. And it still exists to a certain extent today. They will keep their daughters in and arrange their marriages. My aunts were able to marry Englishmen but only because one of them was a divorcée. She would go out with her younger sister and they met these two

Englishmen. There were a lot of relationships like that, a lot of marriages like that.

*   *   *

ANWAR BATI: I had a profoundly embarrassing moment when in 1977 I went back to Pakistan with my mother, who then tried to arrange a marriage for me. I opted out of that and came back pretty swiftly after a fortnight, in order not to cause any further embarrassment, nor to be embarrassed any further. But if I did get married that's what my mother would want. An arranged marriage, preferably with some sort of distant relation.

JASWINDER AMAR: In 1983, while I was at college in India, I got engaged to a guy who lived in Leamington Spa, in England. In 1984 he came back to India, got married to me and brought me here. It was an arranged marriage. I had been at a boarding college then I came home and all of a sudden I was told that there was this guy. I didn't even see him. I was happy, but he and his family were not happy. They wanted to continue with the dowry system. What happens in an Indian marriage back home is that the parents have a responsibility to give their daughter all the things she needs in setting up a home. Because I was going to live in England, I didn't ask my parents for anything. I told them, 'Don't bother, you've spent so much money on my studies, why should you suffer to give me lots of money now?' But when I arrived here, my husband's family started asking me questions: 'Where is your bank book, what is in the account?' and so on. So I told them, 'I don't have anything.' They asked why. 'Go back to India and get it.' I refused. I said I wasn't going to get it. They locked me up and wouldn't let me out of the house for ten months. It was like being in a deep freeze. I was screaming to get out but there was no help – this situation was going to go on for ever unless I agreed to go back to India and get the money. 200,000 rupees. I didn't want to stay here, it wasn't making me happy, but I wanted to put up a fight, to challenge him, to show him that I could be something. I had no close family here, except my uncle by marriage. After ten months I realized that I was just wasting my time and I had to contact social workers or someone to help me. Though I had to get a neighbour to do that, because I was always locked in. I couldn't go out, I couldn't phone anywhere. I couldn't speak a word of English. I had only come here to get married. I was twenty, the youngest in my family, I knew nothing about England, I didn't know anything that was going on outside. But I managed, through my neighbours, to contact a girl who had come from the same village as me. She managed to visit me, and wrote to my parents explaining the state I was in and that I was kept locked up. She came to visit me, but my father-in-law told her to bugger off: 'Who are you to get involved in our family affairs?' But my father was very unhappy without me, he used to

172

sit down and cry all day thinking about my life here. She wrote again to my parents to get a letter from them demanding that she was to be allowed to visit me whenever she wanted. They sent her a telegram saying that. She also informed the police and the social services. So after ten months I was able to escape, and came down to London with her.

GINA ADAMOU: My husband and I have an arranged marriage. It turned out all right but it was an arranged marriage. My dad used to work with his cousin. The cousin came home and we knew him. And he was telling my dad all about this young man who was single and blah blah blah. So they brought him home to see me.

PETER ADAMOU: This was the sixth or seventh girl I went to see. They used to scare me. I had about five or six relations here and everyone would say, come and see me, I have a girl for you to see. They just took me around all over the place. Come on, we've got a nice girl for you to meet. So I'd go along, fat girls, thin girls, whatever. I'd say no, no I don't like her . . .

GINA ADAMOU: It was a cattle market. It was like trying to buy a settee or something. The man had a certain amount of choice but the girl didn't have as much. I was such a shy girl, a very shy girl. At that time I was very unhappy at home and I think they sensed it and felt that they had to do something about it before I ran away. I wasn't a wild person but I wanted some freedom, some things to do. I wasn't allowed to have friends, wasn't allowed to go out, wasn't allowed to go to the cinema. I would be timed, when did I get home. If you miss your bus they look at you suspiciously as if you'd done something wrong. If I came home late they would nag me to death. I couldn't have friends. Even my Cypriot friends were criticized – they weren't good enough. They didn't feel welcome in our home; we weren't allowed to go out ourselves, so we couldn't go to their homes. My parents would try to talk to me about getting engaged and I would say, 'No, no, no!'

One day my husband-to-be arrived with this cousin. My parents said, 'Go in there, there's a young man for you to see.' I refused to go. It took a long time to persuade me. I went in the room, I saw two young men sitting there and I didn't even know which was which. I ran out as quickly as I could. My dad came in the kitchen and said, 'Why will you not sit with him? Go and have another look.' I refused to go. So he left and came back and said, 'Do you like him?' I said, 'I don't know.' He said, 'Put it this way. Suppose you had to walk down the street with him, would you walk down the street with this young man?' Even as young and naïve as I was I said, 'Sure, why should I be ashamed to walk on the street with a young man? Or with anybody?' I couldn't understand his question. But he took this to mean I liked him. The next thing I knew everyone's congratulating me – 'My darling, you're engaged!' – and they sit down and start drinking and eating and so on. I was stunned. I said to myself, 'What on earth is happening here?' Then I thought, 'Wait a minute, wait a minute. Ha! Maybe this is your chance of getting out. Shut up.'

* * *

JASWINDER AMAR: I've become more English, more materialistic. These days I'm engaged to a guy who lives in Southall. But our tradition doesn't want me to see him; my uncle believes this very much. But I have already become torn apart from my culture by coming here and I want to be more independent. I'm not saying I want to run off with him, I'll wait until I'm married before I start living with him, but at least I want to see him. But my uncle, who lives in my house, won't allow me. And I do what my uncle tells me, I listen to him all the time. Parents and children are so close. And my uncle is worried that when I get married he will be so lonely. Then I think he may go back to India. But I want him to stay here after I get married, in my house, for at least a couple of years.

LEENA DHINGRA: In a way you're judged as to how integrated you are, or what your identity is. It is almost as if to feel a part of this community you've got to push aside and laugh at or dismiss certain aspects of your own culture. This notion of arranged marriages. The idea that it is awful, that somehow it is something very barbaric, and very low and very bad. That's not true. But people will ask me, 'Did you have an arranged marriage?' and I will say, 'No.' And that somehow makes my parents enlightened and whatever, but it's not necessarily the case *at all*. Probably had we been in a given situation and my parents had been able to semi-arrange my marriage – I don't come from a system where they are fully arranged, they're always semi-semi-arranged, you spread the word around and look for eligible people and your parents might say, 'I've met somebody really nice' – then probably I might still be married. In fact I married a Belgian. What happens is that you have things which are areas of culture and things which are areas of choice. Individual choice. And marriage ain't one of those for us. Marriage is regarded as an area of much too much a responsibility to be left to the kind of whim of passion, of romantic love. So for some people choice itself becomes a problem. Even for those for whom it isn't a problem you still like to feel that people are marrying within their community. People understand things better in the same community. You're marrying because you're going to have a family, responsibilities, children . . .

RAJINDER SINGH: I am not so rigid. I allow my niece to let the guy come over here. In our culture, so long as the couple are not married, we think that their meetings should be limited. I am not saying that she should not talk to this boy, that she should not visit him, but I don't want them to act as in the way Europe culture does: that they go out together every day, whatever. I brought them together, but I do not want them to act like westerners. If they meet all the time, they might get involved in something and that would be very bad. They are grown up, they know each other and everything, but at the same time you cannot control your emotions when you are together and you are young. So that is how I feel, it might be wrong, it might right.

SIMI BEDFORD: I met my husband-to-be. He was white. I rang my mother the very next day and I said, 'I've met the person I'm going to marry.' She just said, 'Oh yes.' There were no problems. The terrible problems came with the fathers. His and mine. His father would not have me in the house. It was pure racism. He died before the marriage. His mother and I got off to something of a bad start on account of this, but now, twenty-five years later, even though we're divorced, we get on very well. We can now appreciate each other's qualities and transcend those initial suspicions. In my father's case – and he died ten years ago – it wasn't so much that he was racist, but he was desperately disappointed that I wasn't going to go back to Nigeria. He also felt that an artist wasn't a suitable mate. Had my husband been a diplomat's son or whatever it might not have been quite so bad.

MIRANDA LOVETT: My husband wasn't allowed at my family's house because they didn't approve of our relationship. My father had a terrible chip on his shoulder about the English. For reasons I never found out he didn't particularly like England or the English. I think it was arrogance. There was nothing specific, but it was a sort of non-specific dislike. We never discussed it. We were Catholic. I had three younger brothers and sisters and they did not like the idea we were living together and they basically gave me a choice: either him or us. Being the way I was I said, 'For the moment it's him.' This wasn't a Henry James situation, I wasn't the nice American girl seduced by decadent Europe. It was him.

SIMI BEDFORD: Of a whole group of us who came from Nigeria about five married Englishmen. One had become very independent-minded and although you felt politically that you were very aware of racism, nevertheless we no longer really thought as African women. Therefore it was very difficult, because Nigerian men expected it to be very much a man's world, the way it had been in Nigeria. But in the middle of the whole '60s ferment, which I was experiencing in Durham, plus the fact that there was this amazing art department and my husband-to-be was an artist, I couldn't accept that. Here were people who weren't confined by ideas of race and class, and it seemed a much bigger, wider world. I didn't reject marrying a Nigerian because they were black, but because of the kind of the people they were. If I'd met black artists then it might have been different, but what I met were government ministers, people like that who I felt were really boring. The people whose values I could relate to happened to be white.

ZERBANOO GIFFORD: I had a party for my twenty-first birthday, which was where I met my husband. It was love at first sight. My parents weren't overjoyed that he was English. I think it's much easier for anybody to marry into their own race, their own class, their own everything. Because all the customs are all the same, it's just easier. You have been brought up with that. But having said that I can't think of anything more boring. It just seemed totally natural at the time. It seemed to me that I had known him in many lives before and he was the person for me. There was no doubt in my mind, no doubt that he wasn't the perfect person. Maybe the best thing I ever did was marry him. That was sixteen years ago. His parents were very good, very nice. His father's family go back to the Conquest. I tell them that they came over as marauders – at least we came peacefully.

VERNA WILKINS: I had been in the States, came back and went to live in Acton, where my sister was living. I was very unsettled, I couldn't stay put, not even in the same room, and I was all set to take off again. I was going to head back to the tropics. I couldn't cope with England. Then I met Paul, who was very much a '6os student, long hair, wayward, completely. He was studying psychology and the social sciences and meeting him was a tremendous breath of fresh air. He made me laugh again. After a couple of years we decided to get married and we've been married now for twenty-one years. My family didn't like it at all, although now he's the favourite. They were worried about me, I had just been widowed in my teens and they thought I'd suffered enough and that I should give myself some breathing space and not just jump into a relationship which was obviously going to be fraught. I was on his territory. They were worried for me. His mother was and is like a mother to me, a fantastic woman. When we met we liked each other, we got on very well, never mind the connection with her son, and we still do. She liked me as a person and she still does.

DESMOND GITTENS: I got married to a Jewish lady called Madeleine Solly. Her dad was an MP, the MP for Thurrock in the first Labour government after the war. When I met her she had a problem with drugs and it was me who actually brought her off drugs. It was a huge newspaper story back then in 1964. I had to run, back to the Caribbean. My first son was actually born in Trinidad. Her dad couldn't cope with it. But he died a couple of years after we got married. With her mother it was the usual mother-in-law thing. They'd expected her to get married to a nice Jewish boy – a doctor, perhaps a lawyer – and here she comes up with a Trinidad sailor.

SHARI PEACOCK: I met my husband at the Architectural Association, he was a student there too. We started going out, that was a year after I had arrived, and after two years we decided to get married. It was the only option – otherwise they wouldn't let me stay. So I got married. We stayed married for five years, so it wasn't completely for convenience. His family were very very English. What often happens in this sort of situation is that the family find you endearingly eccentric and they kind of adopt you. They were very kind, it must be said. But when we split up her mother told him, 'You do need somebody English to look after you.' So there was this vague feeling that maybe a foreigner might mean a bit of trouble. But I can't fault them. I still see them and I'm still very good friends with my husband.

ALLA WEAVER: The day I moved into the flat I met her cousin. I knew that she was going to have a cousin who will come occasionally. I was rather afraid of meeting this cousin: I knew what he was going to be like, an English officer, tall and fair, very stiff with a moustache. Well it turned out that he wasn't like that and that's my husband. Very, very unlike that, and very eccentric – otherwise he wouldn't have married me. So I met him in January '39 and he introduced me to his sister and took me down to meet his parents who were very conventional, highly conventional. His father was a barrister like mine, though he didn't much practise. His mother wasn't intellectual, but there were lots of books in the house, the father was a great reader. We decided to get married and by then it was nearly wartime. He went to Berlin to see my parents.

PALOMA ZOZAYA: I was very unhappy in England and I wanted to go home to Mexico. Then I met my husband, Julian, who is an antiquarian bookseller. I met him in this restaurant where I used to work two nights a week, in Camden Lock. I was the salad girl. I met him, and I hadn't really seen a man for about six months – I'd only seen these young boys at the school. I thought it was wonderful. We started having a very good time, we moved in together, we rented a studio in Belsize Park; I stayed on at the school after all, and did the last year and when it was time for me to finish school and come back to Mexico we decided to get married.

I find relationships here much calmer. One Easter he said, 'Come and visit my parents.' I said, 'You're mad. You don't see your mother for months, you're going back, you'll have so much to talk about together.' He said, '*You're* mad. We don't talk.' And they didn't. His mother was very calm, a very nice woman;

everybody got together, ate an awful lot, endlessly – chocolates, sweets, sandwiches, cakes, cream cake and more cream cake, tons of tea. It's a large family – six children, three of whom are adopted – and very warm and loving, but not like my family in Mexico.

ALLA WEAVER: I arrived back here from seeing my parents in Paris. My idea was to travel from Paris to Victoria, take a room in this hotel and wait for news from my fiancé. But when I arrived – nothing from Tony. He hadn't received any of my letters, but his parents had received one and sent me a telegram of welcome: they were delighted to hear that we were engaged and would I come at once to stay with them. That was a marvellous welcome, and very unlike what one or two of my fellow Russians had experienced with their in-laws. But I decided that I would jolly well wait for Tony. He turned up and we went down to his parents where we heard Chamberlain's speech saying that war had begun and his father decided that we ought to get married as soon as possible because otherwise I would be interned. So by special licence we were married.

The English family behaved all through my marriage with incredible kindness and forbearance for my un-English manner. If anything didn't suit them they didn't show it. My mother-in-law once said something about my red fingernails. Which were not approved of – fast. On the whole extraordinary kindness, extraordinary generosity. They asked Tony, 'Has she got any money of her own?' 'No.' 'That's very bad. A woman must have money independent of her husband. We will give her an allowance.' But I wasn't having an allowance, 'They can give you money and you can give it to me if you like.'

JASWINDER AMAR: Sometimes I sit down and I think, 'Jas, what is happening? You are torn apart from your culture, you want to be independent, but you're not allowed to.' Sometimes I think, 'Well, why don't I just get married and go to him?' but in the end I think that would be too quick. I got engaged to him a month ago and we haven't spoken since. I think that it is so good in our culture that families offer each other so much love. Look at me: I was alone here, and if I didn't have my uncle I would be so miserable, so lonely. If my uncle is doing his night work then I get so lonely, I just miss my parents. But I wouldn't start going out all the time with my English friends. They invite me but I say no. I go out occasionally to someone's party, with a very close friend, but I'm not out at discos till the early hours, going out with the boys, I don't do that. Before I became engaged this time all the people in the office were always asking me, 'Why can't you pick up anybody? You're outgoing, outspoken, you speak English well, what's the matter?' I just tell them to mind their own business. In the end one lives two lives. When I go out with English friends I try to adjust to their culture, but when I am at home I am in the Indian culture. You have to be two sorts of people, one in the office and one at home.

178

GINA ADAMOU: I was so shy, I was so scared of doing the wrong thing. I refused to go out until my second sister, Artemis, who is two years younger than me, came out with me. Otherwise I refused. Then gradually I felt more comfortable. The younger girls had an easier time. They had friends, they could go out. They still had to kick up a bit of a fuss, but at least they were allowed to go. And of course I started to pick up things from the other girls in the shop. Greek girls, English girls, the customers. They used to go out in the evenings and talk about their boyfriends, of course. You knew what was going on but you couldn't take part. You couldn't say very much either, because what can you say? They would say let's go out and I'd have to say I can't, and find some excuse. You couldn't say my parents don't allow me. The English girls, they probably thought that Greek girls were snobbish. How little they knew. We weren't snobs, we were *dying* to do it but we couldn't.

LEENA DHINGRA: One of the things that worried my father about me being in the West was that he saw this as a very rootless society, a very rootless culture. But at the same time because he was a Hindu, all he could do was not to say, 'This is what you must do, this is what you must not do,' but only to reply if I asked a question. Until I said, 'Papa, what do I do?' he wouldn't tell me. This of course made life very difficult for me. Because he also believed in this thing that is a part of the Hindu faith, that each person, each individual – is born with a certain makeup, certain contradictions, and you have to become more self-aware, have great self-knowledge, so that you can balance your way through. These are difficult things.

YASMIN ALIBHAI: My husband and I were divorced last year and I find what has happened to my life and my son's life completely incomprehensible. About eighteen months ago my husband announced that he was leaving, that he had been having an affair with one his students, an English girl much younger than him, and he had to go and live with her. To this day I actually cannot understand what he has done. I shock myself when I say it, and I spend a long time sitting, thinking through why he did it. It must be part of the western culture. The way he described it to me – it would make *him* happy, *he* needed to do it – I just can't understand it. It feels like a foreign language when he talks to me. I was struck by how different I am from mainstream life. When I told my mother she said, 'That's how I feel when people talk to me in the shops and they're talking too fast and I can't understand them.' So my value systems remain extremely eastern. He gets terribly frustrated by my inability to understand. Above all it's showed me just how eastern I am, and when I talk to my English friends they say, 'Oh well, it's happened now, surely you can be friends?' but that doesn't mean anything to me either. It's been very interesting to discover that you're deeply fundamentalist, if only about marriage.

179

LEENA DHINGRA: The closeness, the close-knittedness, the respect and courtesy to the elders that are there in the Indian family structure, that's part of being Hindu. I don't necessarily think that these traditions are a bad thing. I think that you do have family responsibilities. There are certain things I accept within the western culture: I agree that you do have a personal journey but that journey has to be one of personal growth, not just of licence. Freedom is related to your development, to your growth, to your becoming more human. Not just the freedom to fart around and do your own thing and irritate the rest of society. Along with freedom comes responsibility. I certainly wouldn't accept the encroachment upon that part of my freedom by my elders. But within that I also believe that one is respectful and looks after them and is courteous and I think that is a very nice and important part of the whole human relationship. You give them respect but you demand also respect from them, that they don't kick you about. The difficulty is negotiating it. My English friends totally accept the fact that when their parents come to a certain age they will go into an old people's home where they will be supported by the proceeds from selling the family house. Their parents would like it that way, to keep their independence. Indian parents would not expect that nor accept that. And there clashes can come.

RAJINDER SINGH: England is entirely different to India. Our social system is entirely different. When I came over here I found that I was just ignored. Nobody has the time to talk to you, everybody runs after his job, his work. When people from Britain would visit India, we would take leave from our jobs to look after them. But here it is very different. My opinion about Britain is that there is no social life at all. Nobody bothers about you; everyone thinks about materialistic things only, everybody is after money. Nobody wants to lose a day from work. Though now I may be the same – I have to do my job.

PO-YEE WONG: Immigrants should tread a middle path, retaining some of their own culture, but also mixing in the host country, absorbing its culture. Of course there are times when you want to be among your own kind. It would be fine if one's roots became less and less important, but you can't do that.

CUI QU: Mainland Chinese, when they come here, don't have the same sort of tight community that Hong Kong Chinese do. After the Cultural Revolution people stopped trusting each other. They stopped talking openly. You don't want to confide, to tell your plans for the future. That has carried on over here. We don't see many Chinese. My feeling is that we are in England now, why do I have to make friends with you just because you came from Peking too? We love China but we don't want to stay in a Chinese world. There isn't that expatriate community that the English create when they go abroad.

NIEN-LUN YEH: The Chinese community is very funny. On the whole they present no threat to any other nations, but they do threaten each other. They fight among themselves. On the other hand they also stick to each other. Every western city to which they have emigrated has its Chinatown. The Chinese community in Britain is subdivided into many small communities. The main one is Hong Kong Chinese. During recent years there have been an increasing number coming from mainland China. They are very well educated, at least university graduates, most are post-graduates. Then there are communities from Taiwan and from Singapore. They are different. Plus some from Vietnam. Most of the boat people are actually Vietnamese Chinese. The Hong Kong people don't like them at all.

* * *

RAJAN UDDIN JALAL: After leaving school in 1974 I didn't know what to do or where I was going. I spent five or six months in Bangladesh. My father came back with me and he decided to stay. I came back on my own. I saw Bangladesh and I realized that I didn't belong there either. So I came back to London, wondering what to do. I started working in the clothing industry, but what is important is that at the same time I started attending evening classes. There was a group of young people who would meet in the Asian studies centre at the Tower Hamlets Adult Education Institute. People who had spent all day working in the clothing industry – which was very busy in those days – and they would turn up at the AEI and discuss incidents, racial attacks, or Bangladesh. A group was gradually building up and this gave us increasing confidence. One teacher, he's practising law in Bangladesh now, was politically motivated and he was getting us to go to public meetings. Though it was very hard to mobilize our people, they were not attuned to society and politics here.

GULZAR KHAN: Early on we started to form our own immigrant organizations and discussion groups – political ones and social ones. We would help people filling out forms, with visits to the solicitors, the social security, the passport office. You were speaking to the officials, going everywhere with these people and interpreting for them. It was simply a matter of helping people survive. These days it's different – all those older people have educated children who can go with them and interpret and there is no problem. So just being able to speak English made one into a figure within the community, like it or not. Then we began to realize what was happening, that our community was way behind in England, and we began to wonder how we could help our people, who were not getting what they should be getting. So we knew that we ought to have our rights, but we still didn't know exactly what rights these were. And certainly nobody was telling us, they didn't want to disseminate that sort of knowledge to us. Because knowledge is power.

NELLY SALAS: I was desperate. When you don't speak the language, listening to English was like putting your head into a cave full of bees, all buzzing around. I was ill with the stress, the tension. Everything was very easy for my husband. Women liked him, things happened, he wanted to be free. Things were so bad for me that the Communist party there called me in and offered me a return ticket to Argentina. I knew that I couldn't go back: I didn't want to go back to my family in the situation that I was, and because I would have been in danger – my husband might have left me but they knew I had been his wife. Finally it was because I am very stubborn. I sat down and said, 'What do you think I am? I can do things and I will and I shall never go back, never.' For a while I settled down with my husband again but that was terrible. For years we didn't live together properly; he would go off for two and three months at a time. They had tortured him during his prison sentence and he had become quite mad, schizophrenic. It was terrifying. He treated me very badly, very badly. So during the time I lived in Leamington Spa I had to go into therapy too. I would go to Southampton where there was a doctor who spoke Spanish. But in some ways I say thank you to my ex-husband, because what he did forced me to start doing things for myself. I left him. I slept on the floor, I had no kitchen but I wouldn't go back. I said, 'I don't need you.' That made him furious. He knew I had nothing and he couldn't understand how I could manage alone. He told me that one day I would need him and one day I would come to knock on his door and beg him to take me in because I would never speak English and never get a job and I would depend on him for ever. I didn't say anything. He left and I cried for a long time. I had been doing English lessons before this, but I had learned very little – I thought that if I learned the language I would lose everything: my soul, my whole being, my identity. That day I thought, 'Who told you that I'm not going to learn English?' I went out, I phoned up my social worker and asked for a full-time English course. I spent six months there. I tried but I was in a very bad emotional state and the teacher spoke only in English and it was terrible for me. Some of the other refugees helped but I would be there at two or three in the morning trying to understand what had been said in the classes.

BALRAJ KHANNA: I used to cry in my little room at night; I used to say to myself, 'Why the hell did I come here? Why don't I go back?' I decided to, I even booked a passage. But as the day approached I said, 'I am not going to go back. I have come here to do something, I have come here with a purpose. I was going to go to university. Now I've decided that I have come here to paint and now I am going to stick to my guns.' There is this pride: you won't go home, you can't go home. I have to prove myself to myself. If I had gone back I would have been welcomed with open arms, but I would never have got away again. It would have been a moral defeat.

GULZAR KHAN: People began to realize that the five-year plan in which you came, made money and went back, was not realistic. The money wasn't there. So they had to think about staying longer. It would have been shameful to have come so far, to have sold up everything they had, to have burned their boats and then go back. They couldn't do that. How could they go back and face the people they had left? Apart from anything else they had borrowed a lot of money to get their tickets. They would have to pay that back. To go back as a failure was too difficult. So what people did was revise their plans; they got jobs, they started working more and more.

MIKE PHILLIPS: What happens when you're an economic immigrant, in fact an economic refugee, is that you discover that you can do things, that you have talent and ability, which couldn't be expressed in the situation in which you were born and brought up. You discover a huge wide world that you didn't know about, because you come from this small place, which is limited and pressed down by poverty, and in a curious way that was my father's experience. In Guyana he was just one step up from a dock worker, because he could make marks in a book; he knew how to keep books and that was what he did.

SUSAN WILSON: I was living in my Bayswater room and I felt like a fly perched on a ledge. I had a bicycle worth £15 and that was it. I had no winter coat. People thought I was quite rich, because I was always planning to go away. I was always managing to save a little bit of money from here or there and go off on some kind of trip. I was incredibly determined. When I went to art school I knew what I wanted to do and I went off and did it. I sold one of my first-year paintings and that was £500 which was a lot of money. I just felt very very determined. You've got to. Otherwise you're going to go under. There's nothing to fall back on. Nothing at all when you're an immigrant. So you've really got to pull out the stops.

IVAN KYNCL: You can look at my life here and read it like a fairytale: he grows up in Czechoslovakia, he becomes a dissident, he comes to England, works as a window cleaner, now he's quite successful. It's true, but then it isn't. I don't feel successful. For me success is for people to meet you and accept you for what you are, irrespective of your past. What I have been is lucky. I came at the right time to the right place and people saw my work and liked what I did and I have built on that. What I don't like about this society is the lack of chance to move. If you are born into a working-class family it is very difficult to rise. What is good about being a foreigner is that maybe they say 'bloody foreigner', that's all they can say. They can't put you into any other pigeonhole. I can meet the very, very rich or the very, very poor and it makes no difference.

CUI QU: We are quite proud of ourselves. Things have been hard here. We arrived and we went through very bad times, but things have worked out. We feel OK. We are not rich but we have a flat, we can take holidays each year. We are thinking about our future. We didn't decide to stay on at once. In the first year my father-in-law was here. He stayed for three weeks. He saw this room we were renting; it was awful. He was so angry: 'Why do you stay here? Please go back home. You must go. There is no future for you here. You must go back.' I said, 'All right.' We just wanted to make him happy, so we agreed. We said that we would go back after a few months. But soon my husband found a new job and we had a regular income, and I found a job teaching at SOAS. So we both have jobs and we can make money and we can go travelling. Then three years ago we bought our flat. I was so excited when we first moved into this flat. It's an awful flat but we had made a home here. If we work harder, we can make things better. Our son was born here, he's almost three. I want the best possible for him. I don't mind working hard. I have no real future in my own career and I must do everything for my little boy.

JOHN LAHR: I've grown up here. If I'd stayed in America, because of the nature of privilege and celebrity, I would have stayed in perpetual adolescence, as most American men do. They never face up to their responsibilities as parents, they never enter into their community. They spend their life in the pursuit of their career, the fantasy of their achievement. I found that was here for me. That I could work as hard as I wanted, but that I could live. Life would come in and I could enjoy it. There was just my family, the work, and living. I needed to slow down. I could make enough money to get by. We didn't have big expenses. We lived in a very nice flat, with nice neighbours. Life was fine.

VICTOR WILD: I believe in adapting yourself to your particular situation. I have no ambitions to go upward, although perhaps if one did one would be made to feel unwelcome. Whether it's a Swiss characteristic or whether its an immigrant characteristic, we adapt. I think the Swiss are quite used to being surrounded by all sorts of extraordinary nationalities and they are not a totally convincing nationality themselves – until there's a war when they all blend marvellously. I'm quite happy having a life in which I don't feel dependent on other people, a full life without having to knock on doors which might be opened rather reluctantly.

PO-YEE WONG: The tough experiences I had at the beginning gave me fighting spirit. I liked my first job, but it was so hard for me to advance, with people trying to keep me down. I hadn't come here to make a life, but because I wanted to better myself. I would have done well if I'd stayed at home, as I've done here, because I'm that sort of person. After I got my qualifications here, I felt there were still things I wanted to learn, to achieve, so I stayed. I learned English law, took an Open University course in social psychology, satisfying my enquiring mind. I don't use any of that professionally. My profession is medicine, and I will spend my life doing that.

CUI QU: It's not easy here but you feel freer than in China. Here you can get on with things by yourself, you are not constantly responsible to someone else in your work unit. You don't have to give reports on yourself to the party secretary, you don't have to go through self-criticism, to debate whether or not you are good enough for promotion. I enjoy my job, but if I decide to give it up, I can do something else, I can do acupuncture or whatever if I like.

VICTOR WILD: I've had a very enjoyable career. I married an English girl, a Yorkshire girl. I took over the business as managing director in 1950 when my uncle died. He was sixty-six. My aunt was in charge, since my uncle had finally become more interested in golf than in the business. We had big traumas with death duties, the business nearly had to be sold. He had just started to accept the fact that one day he might possbily die and he'd begun to talk to his solicitor about it, but he had a heart attack. He was a cigar-smoker, had a second-hand Rolls-Royce, liked to go to race meetings . . . a marvellous man but in some ways he wasn't very realistic. The estate duty office in those days insisted on cash on the nail, and we hadn't any cash on the nail. We had a very good business but we couldn't sell bits of it or the whole thing would collapse. But from then I found life even more enjoyable because now I really could decide where to apply my energies.

* * *

IVAN KYNCL: One thing I had promised myself before I left Czechoslovakia: that I did not want to be a political refugee. I was a human being, I live where I live, I don't want to spend my life as an émigré, a professional political refugee. But because my father and a number of my friends had been arrested shortly after I arrived here, I discovered that it's not that simple. I felt that I must help as best I can. I had helped when I was in Czechoslovakia and now I wanted to continue helping from London. Even though that meant being a professional political émigré. So I spent the next two years in Europe working to publicize events in Czechoslovakia. The problem was that I wasn't that comfortable doing this because it really put a stop to my own life. I had left Czechoslovakia, but I was still doing exactly the same thing. And I had started meeting people who wanted to give me work and I couldn't take up their offers because of being involved in politics. I had almost stopped being a photographer. I also wasn't sure whether I'd get the same feeling of freedom that I had had there. When you live in a black-and-white world you are either for or against the situation, it's very simple. But here, where life is full of grey tones, things are much more difficult. I remember seeing some demonstration, about what seemed a small thing to me, and I felt they were naïve, that they didn't know what real repression was, but later I discovered that those small demonstrations are just as important as larger ones, because otherwise the people here will one day wake up and they won't be able even to do that, naïve or otherwise.

KAREL KYNCL: As a refugee, as an émigré, you are in a sort of schizophrenic situation. You still regard yourself as taking part in the lives of your friends at home in the old country; and at the same time taking part in the lives of friends who are now spread all over Europe. Also you take part in the life of your new country. Which makes a very complicated life. But basically what is true is that you are much closer to what is going on in your old country than to your new one. There are quite a few Czech refugees in London but unlike the Polish refugees, who are much closer, the Czech community is not so close. I think that one of the most wonderful things that has happened to me is that I don't have to depend on that community. The one nice thing that the activity of the secret police does is to make the community of people who are critical of the system very close to each other. They disagree with each other strongly but still are able to talk to each other as friends. But if this police pressure disappears and you start to have the opportunity for free expression, for free thinking, then individualistic tendencies come to the surface, sometimes in a very disagreeable way. The life of a refugee is not a normal life, and that abnormality prevails even in areas where you would not expect to find it; the basic abnormality has its bearing on everything you do. It is a strange world, the world of refugees. I wouldn't avoid the émigré community, but I don't wish to be dependent on it.

ANNE-MARIE WOLPE: My time was taken up with sheer survival and getting to know things and coping with cold weather and kids and clothes and no money. That was quite a problem. But I found the relief of not waiting for a police raid, of not worrying about the phone being tapped, and not worrying about imminent arrest, was fantastic. That had been wearing, to put it mildly. That freedom was wonderful, but the British way of life was extremely difficult and I was depressed probably quite a lot of the time. We lived on charity for a year. It was incredibly difficult. There was a community of exiles, but it wasn't anything like as well organized as it is now. The majority were in Hampstead, people who'd been leaving from the '50s on. Mainly white. It was an enormous struggle for us. We moved at least seven times that year, going from place to place with children and no money. Extremely difficult. It's worse when you've had a privileged background and you don't know how to clean the bloody floor. Cooking with no money, finding very cheap cuts, that kind of thing. It's

186

awkward, to put it mildly, when you're unskilled at ordinary, everyday living. So our life was extremely difficult and very trying for a number of years. We moved and moved and moved.

PETER TATCHELL: In Australia, in the early 1970s, homosexuality was still punishable by imprisonment and forced psychiatric treatment. So, as a gay man, I felt a great sense of freedom coming to Britain. Most of the anti-homosexual laws had been repealed. There were gay clubs and magazines, and organizations which openly campaigned for lesbian and gay rights. We had none of these things in Australia and the fact that they existed in Britain made it an appealing country for me to live. Today, however, the atmosphere seems much more homophobic in the wake of the AIDS hysteria and Section 28.

GRETEL SALINGER: England was paradise, although we were not free to do everything; we were stateless, but after Germany, England was absolutely incredible. We were *free*! Here you didn't have to tremble when you saw a policeman. The policeman was nice to you; we didn't know policemen could be kind to you. In Germany they came to intern you, to arrest you. Here you could leave the doors open, you didn't have to lock them all the time. Everything was *wonderful* and we were like in heaven, although we had very, very little money. It was not that much different from the England I had seen in 1914. Of course things were different for me: I was very poor and sometimes hungry, but I still thought that England was still a wonderful country. The English were terribly kind.

After the war they made my husband a freeman of the city. In Germany he had invented a special method to be used in iron foundries. When we left, at risk of a death sentence, he smuggled the formula out and gave it to the English government. It was used throughout the industry and he became quite famous here through that. That was later. At first when people in the industry heard that he was in England and had no money they gave him some consulting work. Though the English workmen were not so nice. They thought he was a German and they wouldn't allow him to come into the factories. He had to work during the night when the workers were not there. The owners didn't mind, they knew the truth.

TEDDY SCHWARZ: The first thing that matters for a refugee is a bed and something to eat. I worked in the black economy — if someone wanted a room painted or an extra electricity wire, I would do it. Then I drifted around Soho, around the various cafés, the Black Horse, etc., and Dylan Thomas, John Barker were there. Then I worked for the Free German League of Culture. It was the greatest refugee organization abroad ever. We had a house in Upper Park Road, given by the Church of England — rent free. We had a theatre

187

there, over a hundred seats; a canteen or restaurant; lots of office space. We published different things. I also published on the Isle of Man when I came back from Canada. The FGLC had a monthly paper, and other wartime things.

ANNE-MARIE WOLPE: Our year in Kent had already been absolutely suffocating. To keep me sane I would put Nicholas, who was then about two, into the car and just drive round the back lanes. I knew Kent inside out, but I was desperately lonely and bored there. People didn't talk to one. They simply didn't. They're Brits. Kent is a most peculiar part of the world where people moved for status or for the name. The wives toddled off to the station and dropped their husbands and later the husbands came home and the wives fetched them and the lights were out – no lights at the front of the house unless there were visitors – the tom cats were castrated, the dogs didn't bark: it was like a living bloody death. It was *unbearable*. The first day I was there my neighbour turned up: 'My name is Betty' or whatever, there she was bearing a tray with tea on it. 'Do you like gardening?' I said, 'Yes.' I didn't know. We had rented this house, it was quite grotty really. Somebody's investment that he'd come to after retirement. She wanted me to garden because my weeds went into her garden. She lived there because of the name of the place. It was *unspeakable*.

---

13 A Roof Over Your Head

'I knocked on a few doors, asked the neighbours what it was like round here. They said, "It's not as bad as it looks." So I accepted it.'

ALLA WEAVER: I didn't terribly like my digs and my father kept saying, 'If you don't like the digs there must be somebody at the Courtauld who has a list of addresses suitable for students.' I said, 'I don't know. It's such an amateur set-up over there. The registrar's some stuck-up old Etonian, he won't know . . .' 'Do as I tell you.' 'Yes, daddy,' and I went to the Registrar and he said, 'Oh no, we haven't got anything like that at all. No, I do think I've got something in this drawer. Oh, yes . . . Would you care to look at this, it might be something?' I looked at it and there was an enthusiastic letter from an ex-student, whom I knew, saying Mrs Ackworth's boarding house, absolutely wonderful. So off I went to Mrs Ackworth's boarding house and indeed it was wonderful. She was a strange Irish lady who'd done a diploma at the Courtauld. She had lots of not very serious people there and she was a passionate collector, of anything.
188

Ephemera, old furniture, whatever. She had collected three houses in Ladbroke Grove which she filled with only the kind of people who she liked. And when she heard 'Courtauld' she gave me a sherry and said, 'Oh yes of course I've got a room.' I thought, 'Landladies who give you sherry . . .' I didn't think for a moment I could afford it. 'Can you pay £2 per week?' and I said that I could.

GERTRUD HARTWIG: The first place we lived was for a couple of weeks in a very miserable hotel. Then we found a boarding house – two rooms, reasonably good food – opposite Regent's Park. This second place was rather pleasant. But after a while it occurred to our son that some of the women who lived there seemed to have more than one husband. We said, 'What do you mean?' He told us, 'Well, every time I see them they are going into their rooms with somebody else.' We didn't take much notice. Then, a couple of months after we had lived there there was a terrific quarrel between the two proprietors. The police had to interfere and sure enough it turned out to be a brothel. There was another lady there, she was a funny type. She had a cousin who was a very well-known international lawyer, and whenever she talked to us she would mention this professor. She was very proud of him. She was always being invited out to meals and she would tell us, 'All this socializing is so exhausting, my dear.' She didn't realize that we had other worries than socializing. After that we arranged to move into a basement in Lancaster Gate. We were given a key to the flat and went there to have a look. The door wouldn't open. It had been bolted from the inside. We had to arrange with the landlord to have it opened, but he wouldn't hand over the proper key until we paid him key money. It was a terrible place: water was running down the walls, there was an outside toilet, it was all very unhealthy.

NISSIM ELIJAH: I arrived in 1962 and lived in the East End, in a Jewish shelter near Toynbee Street. It wasn't at all nice in the East End. I had brought money with me, that kept us going for some time. We boarded with an Indian woman in the East End, then I paid some key money to an Ashkenazi Jew and at least we were on our own, though still in the East End. We couldn't afford anywhere else. At that time, there was an anti-Semitic, anti-Indian backlash here. I thought the best place to lose ourselves was London. I would have preferred to be in the country, but we would have been so identifiable.

PETER TATCHELL: When I first arrived in London, I lived in a succession of bed-sits and shared flats in Chiswick, Dollis Hill and Shepherd's Bush. In 1978, I was offered a GLC hard-to-let flat at Elephant and Castle. When I first saw this huge sprawling 1930s housing estate, it brought back memories of the squalid housing I saw on my first train ride from Southampton. I felt very uncertain about taking the flat. I knocked on a few doors and asked a neighbour what the estate was like as a place to live. She said, 'Oh, it's not as bad as it looks.' So I accepted the flat and I'm still living in it now, despite all the attacks by fascist gangs which still continue periodically, even to this day, seven years after the Bermondsey byelection.

MIGUEL ZAMBRANO: They gave us our first place to live, the Trotskyists. A disgusting place, in Deptford. There were other extreme left-wing people living there. The chairman of the tenants association was from the National Front, but the majority of the tenants were black. A crazy Irish woman had a pony there, on the green during the day, and every night she brought it into her flat. So it was from one madness to another. I was so depressed. The first night it was pouring with rain, and the house flooded. It was by the railway, and there were lots of rats. We had to teach the children, 'These are not bad rats, they're good rats, but don't get close to them.' Surveyors said the whole house would collapse. These Trotskyists, they were so eager to get on and achieve things, and all they'd done was paint the house so it looked good. They brought other families there, with more children, more children. We agreed with the other families that we would share in repairing the house. But then still more people came, and they stole our bedclothes, everything. We covered ourselves with coats at night.

PETER VO: At the reception centre we were offered different homes in different areas. I was advised by English people don't go to London, because London is something terrible. Go to the seaside, go to the countryside, go anywhere except London. But I did not know of anywhere apart from London. So I believed it could be good, whatever people said. When I was interviewed I said I wanted to go to London, and people stared and said, 'Why?' But I said that to me London, a city, would be more familiar. I came from Saigon, which is also a big city and that's what I like. At the beginning I was very frightened of living in this flat. At first the estate was very run down, we had to do a great deal of work to make it fit to live in. But now things are improving around here. The estate had a very bad name when we came here, robberies and so on, but it's continuing to improve. Things are really becoming better and better. One day I might buy this flat.

BODRUL ALOM: When I was working in housing advice, white councillors would tell me that my people were too choosy. They said there were specific areas into which they would like to move. I would say, 'Why is that?' 'They tend to gather together, to shelter themselves against attacks.' There would be a problem, a white family would be attacking a black one. But the ones who get rehoused are the black family, the victims, not the whites who have started the trouble. If you really want to combat racism, it's the perpetrator, the racists,

190

who should be removed, not the innocent victims. But since most of the local estates are predominantly white, it is the minority families who get rehoused.

BENNY BUNSEE: When I began to look for a room, this was 1962, I found there were signs saying, 'For whites only.' I was surprised. But there was no Race Relations Act yet and you could say that. Those signs, which were all over London, were very alarming.

TONY GIRARD: At first I lived in Peckham with my brother. I was among friends. But it was different to home. I had grown up with my own room, now I was sharing a room with my brother. A single bed, a small wardrobe in the corner, a chest of drawers. That was all it could take. Two of us were forced to share that for ten months. I tried to find somewhere else virtually every day. It took me ten months of searching. Some were polite and said, 'It's gone, sorry.' Some as soon as they opened the door they'd slam it in your face. But I didn't give in – I needed a place. I'd ring up a number. There was one woman, she spoke very nicely, we made an appointment, told me about the deposit and so on, and that was fine. My brother had warned me, 'Whatever you do, save yourself an awful lot of hassles later on, mention to them that you're coloured.' So after everything was said, I told her, 'One more thing.' She says, 'What?' 'By the way I'm coloured.' 'Oh. Then you can't have the flat.' I said, 'Why not?' She told me, 'That's how it goes. We do not want blacks.' I said, 'We're quite respectable people.' 'Respectable or not, you're not having my flat,' and boom! down goes the phone. I can laugh now, but I felt it then. My brother was right – if I had gone round to see her, it would have been awful. Just over the phone it wasn't so bad.

BHAJAN SINGH CHADHA: The main resentment from the white community was the way we were buying up houses. Houses were changing hands very fast and that was definitely resented. They were going up in value. It was very difficult for a single English person to raise the deposit of £1,000, but what happened was that a group of Indians would get together and between them raise the deposit. The owners didn't mind selling to us, especially the old people who would sell up, get their money and leave. Though not everywhere: in some places in Southall there were committees formed by white people who promised not to sell their house to an Indian. That didn't last. Sooner or later they'd be offered enough money and they'd go.

LEENA DHINGRA: My mother bought this house in 1964. In those days people didn't particularly think of buying houses. But my mother had lost everything after Partition and she wanted to get a house. The house in Lahore was hers.

She had done the one thing people don't do, she had sold all her wedding jewellery to build this house. It was apparently absolutely wonderful.

BODRUL ALOM: Whenever we are accused of being under-achievers in education, no one I have ever seen mentions the effect of second-rate housing. The housing environment is directly related to children's intellect, intelligence, growth, and so on. Poor housing conditions have a bad effect on all these things. Yet no one has yet raised that issue in our community. Environment is critically important. I have seen eight or nine people living in a one-bedroom flat. We are not responsible for that. It is the authorities who create that situation. When we complain they just tell us that there is a shortage of appropriate housing. So most Bangladeshis are dumped into sub-standard housing, housing that is less popular among white people. They're falling down, damp, generally second-rate. Yet no one ever mentions the effect of this kind of housing on our young people.

In 1986 Tower Hamlets presented a report on the Bangladeshi community to a Home Office select committee, pointing out the problems we face. The committee then produced a report, but nothing has ever been done to act on that report. Why is that? Who is to be blamed for that? No institution is willing to take the blame for any of these problems, although in many cases they are the result of institutional failure. In the past grants have been returned to central government without making even half the use of them. Yet it could have been used effectively within the community, where it was definitely wanted. They could have consulted the community and found out what was needed, and where best to use the money but they don't do that.

NELLY SALAS: During the Malvinas war I was living in south London. I was terrified there, I didn't want my ex-husband to find me and try to get me back with him. I didn't know where he was, and I didn't want to know. So eventually I told my friend that I had to leave. He took me to the Joint Council for Refugees in Victoria. There I was helped a great deal. First of all I was found a room in a hotel in Bayswater. During the war I didn't speak to anyone. I didn't want to. It was a big hotel, full of prostitutes. But I thought, 'OK, if I don't bother anyone else, they won't bother me.' I would go down for breakfast, say good morning, everyone would answer. The owner of the hotel, the manager, a Filipino I think, I didn't like him at all. Once he asked me where I was from. I told, Argentina. That day I was going in and he was going out and he took my arm and said, 'Let's go to the park'. I said, 'No, don't touch me. What do you think you are doing?' I went to my room. The next day when I went down to breakfast I said good morning as usual but nobody replied. And a big man, an English man, said, 'I don't want to eat in the same room as an Argentine person.' Because the manager had told them who I was, just because

I didn't want to go to the park with him. So I bought something to cook snacks – I was so fed up with eating kebabs every day. In the end I phoned the Refugee Council, please find a place for me, but they couldn't. One night I made a rice pudding. I ate some, and left a little, half a cup for the next morning. Now sometimes I feel special things, these animal feelings. So when I went back to the room after work the next morning, I was sure that something had been going on. But I shut the door and told myself, 'No. Who would come in here?' I did my own cleaning, all that. Then I noticed some roasted peanuts, which I didn't eat, on the floor. I was hungry, and I thought I would eat my rice pudding. I was sure that there was something wrong, but there was no smell, no taste. I ate it. Half an hour later the room was spinning. For two hours I was vomiting, getting attacks of diarrhoea. I was sure someone had put something there but I was determined not to show that I had eaten it. But I was frightened to go out. After three or four hours I just said, 'Nelly, you haven't eaten it. You are all right. Just show them that you are all right.' I went out and phoned my friend and he said he would go to the Refugee Council and they would come round to the hotel. I said, 'No. They are going to kill me. Don't.' So I phoned up the Housing Association who I had been trying to get a house from. Before this I had contacted them and explained to them what was going on with my husband and they said they were sympathetic but they didn't want him to come round and break up their property. So I said that now he had a wife and a baby was on the way. So I was really free. It was the best thing I ever did. Three days later I had a letter offering me the flat I have lived in for the last seven years.

14 The Job Market

'On the phone they'd describe you as "frankly, tanned".'

WILF WALKER: I was unemployed and unemployable. I had stayed on at school but I was terrible at exams; it was just so that I didn't have to be exposed to the street. I didn't leave until I was eighteen, in 1963. When I left I had no job, no prospects. The careers officer sent me to loads of places, but nobody would give me a job. I got blanked right across the board. Even the labour exchange didn't know what to do. I had a part-time job, cleaning offices in Notting Hill; I had started doing that while I was still at school. Then my father got me a job in the BCC factory, where they assembled the equipment. That was on the Wembley estate; it meant I was leaving home at 6.45 in the morning. I did that for a year. Then I took an exam to work in the Post Office as a temporary clerical officer. They kept me on as a temporary for the next four years. My boss was a woman who smelt of stale pee. I'll never forget that. She had power over me, yet she smelt like stale piss, every day. I lived in fear of these people.

JASWINDER AMAR: I was doing a course as part of my British Telecom training. I had a colleague and he asked me what I was doing. He already had an Indian boss. When I told him he said, 'My God, you bloody Indian. You'll end up being my boss, and I've already got one already.' I said, 'What difference does that make?' and he started going on about the poor people in India, the starvation and so on. I said, 'Look, I'm not going to take that rubbish from you. We work hard. I am studying, right. You might not have even managed O levels, you were doing a labouring job when I was highly qualified in India. And I want to improve my skills, which I am doing. What has it got to do with you?' He went quiet. A year later I was working with various English guys and they started swearing at me. I had to leave the job, they were too racist for me.

BERNIE GRANT: I went for a job at the Post Office. You had to do this test to become a counter clerk. They gave me this test, a silly little test, elementary child's stuff, a bit of English and a bit of maths. Then I took it back to the desk, I'd finished miles before anybody else, and the guy seemed very angry. He starts asking me all sorts of questions. 'What's this? What's that?' I knew about Britain, so I knew the answers. Then he asked me, 'What's a tanner?' [six old pence], but I thought he'd said 'a tenner'. So I said, 'A ten-pound note.' So his eyes lit up and he said, 'Ah!' and it was as if he was saying, 'Got you at last!' He said, 'Well, if you don't know what a tanner is, I can't give you the job.' So I said, 'What's the problem?' He told me, 'You wouldn't be able to understand the people and they wouldn't understand you and there you are.' I thought, 'Bloody hell, that's a bit rich,' but that was it. I took it in my stride and eventually I got a job with British Rail, as a clerk in the civil engineer's department. It wasn't what I had set out to do, but I felt that you had to do something, you had to get some sort of job somewhere.

RAJINDER SINGH: Before the West Indians came in the '50s the white people wouldn't work in these jobs, they didn't like the unsocial hours. In those days they advertised in the West Indies, they gave people jobs before they had even arrived here. Now because of unemployment they want those jobs back and they have to find ways of getting rid of us. On Sundays and Saturdays the white people call up – 'I'm sorry, I am sick, I cannot work today' – but Asian and Afro-Caribbean people never go sick, they always work. So we say that they are discriminating against us, although they never agree.

RAMESH VALA: Asians still say that their success is based on British laziness, but I take the view that this was the colonial mentality: we don't want to clean the airports, run the buses, whatever – someone has to do it, so let it be someone different. What happened is that Britain imported people like the Afro-Caribbeans and the Asians and they did these jobs – and in many cases still do. I find it offensive that when one lands at Heathrow there are Asians running all the services – wiping the floors, cleaning the lavatories. For somebody in transit there is this impression that that is all Asians do in Britain. Who is going to give them better jobs? But gradually things are changing, Asians are learning from their white colleagues. They don't want to do the dirty work any more. Women are coming out their houses, giving up their lowly cleaning jobs. They want respect. The days when Asians just accepted the worst jobs are ending.

BHAJAN SINGH CHADHA: The more Indians joined the Post Office, the more we were resented there. We were not accepted by them; they wouldn't invite us to the pub, they wouldn't sit with us in the canteen; silly jokes were made against us. We tried to make friends with them but they did not want to know. Very slowly there were better jobs available to Indians but although I tried, I couldn't find a clerical job. I stayed in the Post Office till '66. Then a promotion was coming up and I applied for it, but it went to a European, a continental. He wasn't English, but being white he was given the job. I took that very seriously and I resented it very badly. This was my chance to get ahead and only because of my colour I wasn't given that chance. I left.

MANZOOR BAHADUR: There were two main areas where you got work in Bradford: textiles, and in some factories the whole shop floor would be Asian with one white foreman – the chief had to be white of course – and the other was the buses. People who could read and write, even if it wasn't too well, and who could speak a little bit of English, used somehow to manage to get onto the buses. When I left school at sixteen my father said to me, 'I will not let you work in textiles.' I said. 'What's wrong with textiles?' He said, 'There's no future for us, especially for my son.' He had three ideas for me: to be a doctor, a solicitor or an engineer. He went to my school and told the teachers what he expected from me. They told him that this was unrealistic, due to my very late start in education. But he got his wish because I did get some CSEs, which were sufficient for me to get an apprenticeship in engineering.

NAIM ATALLAH: I came here from Palestine in 1949, as a student, not an immigrant. I was doing science at Battersea Polytechnic. I wanted to be a journalist, but my father wouldn't have it. He said, 'You are good at maths, you must become an engineer. If you're a journalist in our part of the world, someone will kill you.' When the Israelis stopped all foreign exchange because they needed the money my father could no longer send me funds. I had no permission to work, so I had to return to Palestine. And return to what? There weren't opportunities for a Palestinian like me, they were bound to look after their own people first. I had no friends there. So I decided to stay. That was very difficult. [Sir David] Maxwell-Fyfe was the Home Secretary. He had been a judge at Nuremberg, he was very tough and he wanted to deport me. Some MPs took issue with him over the decision and eventually the Home Office relented – but on one condition: that somebody gave me a job. The job had to be manual and it had to help with the rebuilding of the country. I found a man who had been a member of the Palestine police, who was then working in quite a high-up job with English Electric in Stafford. I told him about my plight and he said, 'I'll employ you.' So I was employed as an unskilled labourer, tightening nuts and bolts on huge transformers. I did that for three years. It was a marvellous experience and taught me a great deal about human nature. I was the only Arab working there and the other workers would yell, 'Hey, you dirty Arab, where's your camel, then?' I had a rough time. But one day I rebelled, I think I hit someone with a spanner – after that we became great friends. I was one of the boys after that. When I left English Electric there were tears. But I had got bored working on the shop floor. I was London-orientated. I loved London, I loved big cities. Stafford was too small for me and I applied for an outside job and ended up as a steeplejack. That gave me nightmares, thinking about how next day I was bound to fall off, but it was a very important job – I got danger money. My pay packet was good. But I'm not a hoarder and I'd spend it all. I gave it up after six months, it was too much. After that I worked for six months as a porter at the Elizabeth Garrett Anderson Hospital in London. Despite being pushed into manual work, I loved it. I wasn't used to physical things, coming from my pampered background. Suddenly I was thrown into it and I realized that I wasn't a weakling. I was very strong. I loved it and I learnt so much from it.

DESMOND GITTENS: My cousin was in the coal business, delivering coal, and he got me a job as a coal miner, my first job in Britain. I didn't stay very long. There wasn't another black miner. So coming up from the mines going into the bath there'd be, 'Why bother to wash, you're not going to change colour, sambo.' These were friends. It was really harmless – these were friends, these were the same guys who would invite me for a drink at the pub and buy me drinks, invite me home on a Sunday afternoon or if there was a cricket match, 'Come along and see the match'. It wasn't malicious racism, it was just subconscious. You were put in a category and you were part of that. I was just the one, and unlike somewhere where there was a big black community, I wasn't a threat.

RAJINDER SINGH: We don't really experience racism from the white workers. Only a few people hate you. Though when I started my job for London

Underground my instructor and my chief clerk and even my area manager were so racist. The manager told me to my face, 'If I had any say in this department, you would not get a job – I do not like seeing people like you at my window.' But I passed the test and he couldn't do anything. I told the central manager, who was in charge of training when this happened. I said I didn't want the job, I wanted to go home. He asked me why. I told him what had been said to me, but the manager said, 'If you get through the test you're as good a booking clerk as anyone else.'

* * *

VINCENT REID: Black people have fought and died in two World Wars on the side of this country, fighting for democracy and so on, what this country believes in. I'm entitled to criticize English people, given the contribution we've made and given that we've not received any of the benefits. We've been excluded. We've not got democracy. I have no confidence that when I apply for a job I'm even going to be short-listed, let alone get it. Not because I have no confidence in my ability to do the job, but simply because I have no confidence in those who draw up the criteria to take the opportunity to find out whether I can do it.

SIMI BEDFORD: At university I wanted, like everyone else, to get a holiday job. I applied to Waterman's Pen and Ink factory. When I turned up to start work the personnel officer intercepted me and said, 'I'm terribly sorry, you're such a nice person, but I'm afraid we can't have you working here after all.' So I asked, 'Why not?' He said, 'The other girls have given me a petition: we can only take you on if we can provide a separate lavatory for you.' This was pretty stunning. It was my first experience of this sort of thing and I was too stunned to fight it. I just said, 'Fine.' So I went off to Selfridges and tried again. I applied to be a filing clerk. I was sitting there with this rather dowdy girl, greasy hair and bitten fingernails. No competition, I thought, but to my astonishment she got the job. So I asked the personnel person, 'Why?' 'Well,' she said, 'it's nothing to do with Selfridges, nor is it anything to do with you, but the girls in the typing pool . . . well, it just wouldn't be on.' So I said, 'Oh, OK.' But she said, 'We can offer you a job. Either in the soda fountain downstairs, or upstairs in the Jungle Restaurant. Not in the restaurant, you understand, the customers wouldn't like it, but working in the kitchen and washing up.' So I asked what the soda fountain job meant. I was allowed to work behind the counter there but I had to wear a flowery pinny and a great big purple bow. I rejected that, but I took the job behind the Jungle Restaurant. It was incredibly hot. And going into this kitchen it was like Alice going through the looking glass. Everybody outside, the customers, the shopgirls, were white. And everybody in this inner world, behind the scenes, was black. I could not believe it. I walked

197

in and there were all these black faces. I thought this is quite jolly, and we got on like a house on fire.

I immediately became a sort of unofficial shop steward. I was that bit more articulate. And the white woman who ran the place had the same problems with me as the people at school had. She could not accept that I spoke English better than she did. Because of the heat you just wore the regulation green overall and your underwear. She issued these and she made sure she gave me something that was designed for Two-Ton Tessie. You got paid a tiny amount. Lots of the girls were pregnant, standing all day, just the most awful job. There was tremendous antagonism between us and the waitresses. Sometimes you'd work at dishing up the food, which, considering the white customers supposedly couldn't have us serving them because we were so dirty and filthy – well, the waitresses never handled the food, it was us, the blacks, who served it up. If it fell on the ground, tough. The stuff we did to that food was nobody's business. If you leant on anything you got burned, you stank of cabbage. I'd take three showers every night and it made no difference. But the West Indians were fabulous and I began to realize that we had enormous amounts in common. All sorts of things. It was then I realized that race was much more binding than class.

GINA ADAMOU: I didn't experience any racism at first while I was in the house. It came later when I started working. One job I went for I was simply told by the manageress, I'm sorry, I like you very much and I would love to take you on, but my girls don't want to work with a Greek girl. I was shocked. That was my first experience of racism. I love London, I love English society and I couldn't understand why I wasn't wanted. Having English uncles and cousins I felt even more that I belonged. I never asked my uncles. I couldn't hurt them that way. Nor did I mention it to my parents. Though I did tell one of my aunts who was very close to me. In fact she used to go around with me to job interviews. So I spoke to her but to nobody else. And she said she was sorry but sometimes that sort of thing happened, even to her who was married to an Englishman and had an English surname and everything. She was very fair, she didn't look foreign, but she had an accent and that was enough.

MICHAEL DE SOUZA: I was about to leave school and I didn't know what I was going to do. My brother was working, he was a tool-setter. So when they asked what I wanted to do, I just said an engineer. That was it. At that time, 1970, there was lots of work. The careers officer didn't do anything for me, but I went and secured my own job. One day during my exams, when we didn't have to go to school, I went to Marsden's in the Harrow Road, they sell weighing machines, and I asked if they had any work and they said, 'Yeah,' and

I said, 'I'm leaving school soon, blah, blah, blah, and I'd like a job.' So they said, 'Fine, you've got a job,' and after I'd left school I started.

VINCENT REID: When I left school I wanted to be a tailor. It seemed to me to be the only possibility left for me. I went to the careers advice and the guy laughed like a drain. So I ended up in the Post Office as a telegram boy. This was 1950. I only did two years of school then I left when I was fifteen. Then when I was sixteen I went in the Air Force. I joined as a boy entrant. I didn't want to be a postman, it was a dead end, it wasn't a career, it was rubbish as far as I was concerned.

* * *

DESMOND GITTENS: I stayed in the mines about six or seven months, then joined the Army. This again came about because I was born just before the war and there was so much military influence. My mother was in the ATS, my dad was in the merchant navy during the war so there were always stories of torpedoes and U-boats and that sort of thing. There was a garrison near to where I lived in Trinidad. So it was you join the Army as well, get a soldier's cap and get a picture and send it home to mum and say, 'Mum, I'm in the Army.' National Service had just ended, I had just missed it but I volunteered. I joined the RASC, which is now called the Royal Corps of Transport. I worked as a clerk, a clerical officer, a private really. I stayed in the Army for two years and then bought myself out. It cost £90. I had been involved in a few deals while I was in the Army and I used that money to buy myself out.

VINCENT REID: I bought myself out of the Air Force in 1956. I was a corporal. I bought myself out because I wouldn't accept the racist rubbish that was going on. It cost £250 which was an awful lot of money in 1956. I have a letter from [Lord] Soames who was then Air Minister, or at least he was responsible for the Air Force. That's how far my case went.

BENNY BUNSEE: I had been a journalist in Tanzania and I started working at the BBC as a scriptwriter for *African Focus*. That really was an experience: they wanted you to write scripts which were heavily doctored. Things that were overtly left-wing, overtly political would be struck out. I was like a firebrand in those days: I just walked out. I started looking for another job as a journalist: impossible. Then I started trying to get a job as a senior clerk: I couldn't get that. I looked for a job as a junior clerk: I couldn't get that. I went to all the employment agencies. It was very funny. They'd be on the phone and they'd described you as 'frankly, tanned'. I didn't understand, and I asked one person, 'What is this frankly tanned?' They said, 'Well, it means coloured. Like you are.' Two or three told me very bluntly, 'You won't get a job in this country,' and they told me why: 'You're a coloured person' (they wouldn't call you black in those days) 'and it's difficult for you to get a job.'

MIKE PHILLIPS: I've been rejected for jobs because I was black and someone equally or even less qualified was white. But what you do if that happens is to piss off somewhere else. Don't get mad, get even. One of the things about the black population here is the extent to which people have come up through it, got their qualifications and gone somewhere else. It's the qualified people who leave. People don't notice, but what happens to the British black community is the number of people who do get qualified, and then they're off back to the Caribbean, to the United States, to Africa.

GULZAR KHAN: It was my third day in Nottingham. I went to British Rail and in the office they asked, 'What do you want?' I said I wanted a job. 'What's your name?' 'My name is Khan.' 'Mr Rogers is on his lunchbreak, can you come back later?' I said, 'All right.' What I didn't know was that there was another person named Khan who was also after a job. But I went back and met Mr Rogers who offered me a job and asked when I could start. I said, 'Straight away.' He said, 'All right. Come back tomorrow, bring your papers and you can start.' I went off but I was worried: how had I got the job? The next morning I turned up at the station. I was taken to the siding, handed over to the foreman in charge of cleaning and I started. There were quite a few Pakistanis there, about eighty per cent of the workers, and the rest were Poles and Ukrainians. Maybe four out of forty were English. When they saw me they said, 'Maybe Mr Rogers made a mistake.' What had happened was that Rogers had promised this job to another Khan, who was related to one of the men already working there. The relative went to Rogers and told him what had happened. But I stayed and I spent the next eighteen months with British Rail. Then I went to British Celanese as a colour mixer. That was where I stopped. I knew I wasn't going to get any better jobs. I had seen qualified people – BA, MA, LLB, people who had been teachers, barristers – and none of them got proper work. They were labourers, bus conductors, railway cleaners and so on. The jobs we got were always the worst, even if we were educated people who could read and write much better than the people who were in charge. They knew I had been an inspector of Customs, but that didn't matter. It's only in the last few years that people are getting promotions – inspectors on the buses and so on. But none of them get managerial posts.

BENNY BUNSEE: The only job I could get was working as a bus conductor. It was interesting in its own kind of way, travelling all over London, but in the end that was the level of work I was allowed. But I said, 'I'm not going to be a bus conductor all my life. This was not what I came here to do – I have to get out of this situation.' So I got a clerical job in the Civil Service in an area which was employing a lot of blacks, because they couldn't get anyone else. Sorting things out, filling in forms, these people there were zombies, half-dead already, and I could see myself becoming like them.

MANZOOR BAHADUR: People say that one of the problems we have is that the less educated you are in this country, the more content you seem to be. You sit there, you think, 'I'm unemployed, this country gives me the chance to sign on the dole, get my giro through the door.' This attitude makes these people think negatively about employment. Those who spend some time getting some qualifications want the 'equality of opportunity' that everbody's bandying about. But they don't seem to find it. Equal opportunity in their opinion is a myth. There isn't such a thing. You look at two people going for a job, black and white, with the same qualifications, maybe the black person even has better experience, but if there's any doubt the decision is given in favour of the white person. Many people in the black community feel that they are not given a fair chance in the employment field. I personally have no complaints about my own achievements.

RAJINDER SINGH: I had proper teaching qualifications, but I couldn't get a good job over here. My Indian degrees were genuine but the British department of education no longer recognized them. I tried to get extra qualifications, but the classes would have cost £3,000 and I couldn't afford that – so I dropped the idea. Instead I got a cleaning job for the first three months. One of my colleagues was told that there were some vacancies in London Transport as a bus conductor. Was I interested? I was. I filled in the forms and got a job. But after one year the route on which I worked changed to one-man operation. They offered me redundancy money or the option of choosing another job in London Transport. I became a booking clerk for London Underground. I have had that since 1987.

JASWINDER AMAR: The qualifications you get in India are never accepted here. I was an MA, but they didn't want to know when I arrived in England. Unless you had studied here, they don't want to know anything about your background. Maybe your degree is not quite as advanced as it would be in England, but they don't even want to let you use what you know.

BHAJAN SINGH CHADHA: I worked as a postman, delivering mail. I was one of the very few Indians to get that job. Some of my colleagues resented it, that I had managed to get a job that was better than labouring. After me a number of very well-educated Indians, mainly teachers, started to come and work at the Post Office. There were soon five or six of us and they would all be talking about their qualifications – 'I've got a degree in this, I've got a degree in that' – and all of us were postmen. I was the only one without a degree. Their degrees were useless here, their careers were ruined – they couldn't follow them up.

* * *

NGUYEN DUC PHUONG: When I came the government gave me a lot of money. I've studied for eight years, and now they aren't using me properly. My skills have been wasted, and I am not getting jobs that match my qualifications. If I waste my time like that, then the government who gave me the grant have wasted their money. In the end we have to be grateful. You get a good job, you might one day want a better salary for less hours. So if you can limit your wishes you will be happier. I was interviewed for one job and the engineer said that he was worried about my English. Would I be able to explain what I wanted to other people? So finally I had to say that if I had been able to write a thesis, then I could certainly write a report. But there are so many English people who have spent all their lives here and they still can't get a job. So how can I? My English is not perfect, sometimes I go to interviews and feel I have given a good impression and still I fail. I understand. If I am interviewed, a foreigner, and someone else English is interviewed with the same qualifications, you can guess who will get the job. I think I do suffer from that. But I will struggle on. My country still struggles on and so shall I.

NISSIM ELIJAH: I joined the Customs, starting on the lowest rank, as a clerical assistant, despite all my qualifications. In India I had had five hundred people under me, I had a chauffeur-driven car. Here I was just a messenger. But having been brought up to listen and obey, it never occurred to me to fight for myself. I thought your work would speak for you. It doesn't work that way. Then I took the Civil Service exam and came out pretty high. They offered me a job abroad, but my wife was sick by then. So I stayed here, but was discriminated against. I was twice put up to the Board, but to my disgust they asked me questions even higher-up officers couldn't answer. But I was afraid to change jobs. I'd come from an area in India where unemployment was endemic, where you stuck to the job you had. I learned before retiring that one of the Board members had said, 'This chap is good, let's keep him where he is.' You know the Civil Service: if they can't kick you out, they kick you up, otherwise you stay where you are. I should have retired with a comfortable pension, but today I'm neither here nor there. I don't qualify for benefits, and don't have enough to live comfortably. There is racism in Customs & Excise, and they don't like foreigners there. There was a Polish Jew there, and he didn't get the promotion he should have got either.

PO-YEE WONG: When it comes to things that matter, you feel the discrimination. For example, when they realized how ambitious I was, they weren't very

202

encouraging. They seem to want you to stay at a lower level. After I qualified as a nurse, I asked for further training, and they found excuses not to give it to me, but gave it to an English girl. I tried other hospitals, but I think my references did matter. They may have been unfavourable. But eventually I found a hospital that would accept me, as long as I didn't ask for further advancement. That second hospital was very friendly, I was happy there, and since I've been happy in other hospitals too. I stayed in the NHS for six years, then got married and had my family. I've been doing independent acupuncture and herbal medicine for more than four years. It is easier for a foreigner to work on their own, outside the system.

SUSAN WILSON: I got a job very easily, at St Thomas's Hospital. I thought that it would be really marvellous, much better than nursing in New Zealand. This was all part of the funny mishmash of preconceptions and prejudices that one has when you come from another country which has been a colony. I thought there would be great opportunities, it would be tremendous – instead I discovered that the pay was *lousy* and the conditions were *frightful* and we were never ever asked for our opinion on anything. I used to offer it and the houseman would say, 'Oh *really* . . .' or 'Well, I don't *think* we actually want to hear your point of view.' That was a shock. It's so important to ask the nurse, the nurse is there all the time. And I would certainly have been asked my opinion in New Zealand. And I was asked how to manage things. But not here. And if you did offer your opinion, even if it was proved right, they really told you off. The hierarchy at Thomas's was staggering.

CUI QU: I certainly have qualifications from China, for being a paediatrician, that I can't use here. All I can use here is my skills in acupuncture. I have been trained in Chinese and English medicine. I feel so annoyed. I have taken my baby to the hospital and I know that I can do what they do. But they say, 'Ah, where do you come from?' 'China.' 'Ah, China. We don't do those kinds of things here.' I was seeing patients, maybe sixty children every day, with every kind of disease. Here they just look down on you. I can't practise as a paediatrician here. No way. So we have to start at the bottom, we must work and build a new life. I try to help my husband by working here when I can. We can't rely on our families any more. I teach Chinese, things like that.

SHREERAM VIDYARTHI: My wife had taken a job in a tobacconist's. Prior to that she had worked in a laundry, then in a waste-paper sorting warehouse where she swallowed more dust than she had swallowed on the plains of India all her life. We were newly married and that is a time when women are very very delicate and very, very tender. At home she would cry – tears of blood perhaps – but outside she was not willing to let me suffer any kind of humiliation. She wanted me to be an upstanding, proud man out there, and be a good husband to her. It was her job that kept us in clothing and food for the next year.

GINA ADAMOU: After we got married we went to rented accommodation. We left home. I was at the hairdresser, he was working at his uncle's steak house. Washing up, then cleaning vegetables, and so on. Very difficult times for us. We were short of money, we didn't own anything, not as much as a radio. I was very, very lonely. I was a young married woman and my husband was working every night and I would go home and sit in this room without a TV or a radio or anything and slowly I got into the habit of going home to my parents. So my husband noticed this and he started looking for a daytime job and became a pastry chef during during the day. Not only this, but I had a baby a year after we were married. July '64, my daughter Christina. So it was very, very difficult times moneywise. I had three children within four years. My mother taught me how to become a dressmaker, so I could earn a little bit of extra money to help along. Our chance came when a friend of my father's had a fish shop and my husband and I rented it. There I was in my early twenties working six days a week in the fish shop. It was in Crouch End. Still there. We spent four years there in the '70s.

CASH BHOGAL: I practised at the bar for six and a half years before coming to work at Southall Rights. Race is certainly a bar at the bar. But I shall carry on. I don't see what else I can do. Having taken five or six years to qualify, then seven or eight practising, I can't see what other profession I could take up. There is certainly discrimination when you are trying to find chambers. You have in the bar itself a number of 'ghetto chambers', black chambers, and it is extremely difficult to get a tenancy, or even a pupillage in a white set of chambers. I was fortunate myself in that I was introduced to Mota Singh, the first black circuit judge in England, and he was kind enough to introduce me to a barrister in his chambers who took me on as a pupil for the first six months. After that it was slightly easier. I practised in a mixed set: some English, one Jew, two or three Asians and one African and one West Indian. I think black barristers have been condemned, as it were, to defence. There is very little civil work for them, largely due to the solicitors' instructions. A lot of people prefer civil to criminal work, cross-examining the police all the time, saying the same old things. So because you are always on the defence judges see you as being a problem. Defence barristers have to be more antagonistic; most judges were prosecutors, so they tend to suspect the defence.

MARY DENYS: When I left my husband and started living with another guy some kind person informed the DHSS that we were cohabiting. They came
204

and took my social security book away, with all their threats. I started doing cleaning. I was doing four cleaning jobs at one time. I go out at five-thirty in the morning and come in about ten-thirty. Then I go out at three in the afternoon and come back in the evening. I lost one of my jobs, working for Rentokil. I got the sack, without being given any reason at all. I was offered a teaching job, teaching reading at a local secondary school, but I declined, because in those days I used to drink too much, I just couldn't do it. I couldn't concentrate. I couldn't cope with the behaviour of the children.

ANNE-MARIE WOLPE: I got a job in academia by chance. I got a job as a sociologist in the unit of Yugoslav studies. Though I knew fuck all about it, absolutely nothing. The sociology that was done in the '60s hadn't been written by the time I had left university. That was nightmarish because I had to be one step ahead of everyone, while never knowing what I was doing. I had to learn Serbo-Croat out of a book, which was quite difficult. It was in that period – '65–66 – I became a feminist, which altered everything. I was one of the original British feminists. I then fell out with the head of my department. The children had all started school by then; Harold was well ensconced in his department, and I was offered a job in London. So Harold gave up Bradford and we packed up and went down to London. He took a job teaching sociology at the North London Polytechnic.

* * *

YASMIN ALIBHAI: Towards the end of my Oxford course I began to feel very uneasy. I felt that it was the most useless thing in the world to be doing what I was doing and that I owed it myself and to other people not to spend the rest of my life getting paid for reading novels. I had been living this luxury life for six years and I felt terribly guilty. So I never applied for a single university job. I wanted to do something more real. Initially I started teaching English. We had no money and I taught the refugees and immigrants who were around Oxford at the time. When you're teaching those groups it's not just learning a language, it's putting over ways in which you can resist the things which happen to you on a very low level, on a very pervasive level. There was the problem of being an immigrant, the problem of schools, how their kids were being treated, how they were treated by the bureaucracy, the DHSS. So if you had any political awareness you weren't just teaching a language or even a culture, you were teaching very very frightened people ways of survival, ways of challenging the system, of fighting what was happening to them.

SHREELA FLATHER: I started teaching in London, teaching a variety of very poor children in Battersea. Some of them were very poor, they needed to be washed when they arrived at school, they never saw books . . . But these were mainly white children. And they were very culturally separate. One talks about immigrants being different, but these were children who were culturally absolutely different from other white children. It wasn't simply class, but these were seriously deprived. People who had fallen through every net. I was terribly shocked by that: England was rich, this meant that the wealth was obviously very unevenly divided. So having heard that it wasn't that much of a shock to find that there were still people who hadn't been given their fair share of the resources.

MANZOOR BAHADUR: Racism in the engineering industry was overt. I will give you some examples that I personally experienced. There was a tool-setter, white, he'd been setting engineering machines for many years in this department. My job at the time was quality control inspector. This guy had just set a machine up and when I checked the component I noticed that this component was not the first sample produced on the machine. In fact, he had produced about fifty components. The rule was that batch production could not commence until the first sample had been passed as OK. Although the setter had broken the rules, I still decided to carry out the quality control function and found that the components were not to specifications. I brought the anomaly to the setter's attention and it was the normal practice that you'd submit a report to your own inspection department and one to the setter's supervisor outlining the faults. When this report was issued this setter really got angry. 'I've been doing this job for seventeen years. This report has landed me in a lot of trouble.' Only he was much more rude, calling me a black so-and-so and whatever. The setter was reprimanded for faulty workmanship but no action was taken about his racist behaviour. Another example that comes to mind is when I was a management service officer and had been requested to carry out a work measurement exercise in this particular department. When I got to the department the shop steward turned round and said 'Eff off you black so-and-so, we're not having some black person doing a time study on us. Go and send somebody else.' But management did back me on this issue by insisting that I carry out the work measurement exercise. But once again no action was taken against the shop steward for his racist remarks. I could go on to give many other such examples of direct racism during my employment in the engineering industry.

BENNY BUNSEE: I've led two major black workers' strikes in England. I made them and I led them. Black workers in Britain are *terribly* exploited. While I was at Nottingham University a group of Pakistani clothing workers came to us for assistance. They had just come out on strike and they took us to their factory where for the first time I saw the conditions in which black workers worked in this country. They worked seven days a week, they had half an hour for lunch, no tea break, no toilets, they worked overtime every day but they got no overtime pay, they didn't know properly what rates they were paid, they were abused by their foreman. They would be injured by the machines, but there was no compensation, they had no holidays. I couldn't believe these conditions. This was white bosses employing black workers. It would never, never have happened to white workers. So we won that strike. Immediately after that another strike broke out in another factory: similar situation, similar conditions. I began to investigate these conditions, these factories and I found things to be the same all over the Midlands. Through that I became involved in leading strikes where Asian workers had been discriminated against, were given low-paid jobs and so on. So I became heavily involved in this whole situation, either in strikes or as an activist, propagandizing for black workers. I organized the first ever trade union conference on racism. I travelled throughout Europe looking at the conditions of black workers and I found the same situation everywhere – they are atrociously treated in every country.

BERNIE GRANT: We had our own scene at international telephones. Because you needed a foreign language – French, whatever – there were people from all over the world: Africans, people from the Caribbean, everywhere – it was like a mini United Nations. So there were no problems there, but there were certainly problems in the postal side where the National Front were very strong. But our section of the Post Office was already multiracial so there weren't those sort of problems. What we did have to do was go and support those people who did have to fight the National Front so we did get involved. We also got involved with the South Africa situation. This was a period before international direct dialling and we had a policy in our branch of not connecting calls to South Africa. This created a lot of problems. Someone would ring up and ask to be connected to Durban and we simply said, 'Sorry, we're not connecting calls to South Africa.' They'd go mad and demand to speak to the supervisor and stuff and we would just disconnect them. We did a lot of sabotaging of those calls. If someone had managed to book a call, the ticket would go missing, all sorts of things. It still happens.

FIRDOS ALI: In 1971 I was working in a factory making electric accessories, and the majority of my fellow-workers happened to be West Indians. There was a West Indian shop steward who was not a very outspoken person, because he was feathering his own nest at the expense of the majority. So one evening there was a coup, he was sacked and I was nominated as his replacement. My very first act was to take the whole goddam place on strike. Obviously this didn't endear myself to the management. People were talking about me – wog, things like that – but the workforce liked me. They were working a fifty-two-hour week for £30 odd. No clothing allowances, nothing like that. I got them all these things, their earnings trebled. I was sacked myself after three or four years; it didn't matter because I had a new job lined up already: arts director of a voluntary organization, the National Association for Asian Youth.

MICHAEL DE SOUZA: I've been a youth worker, set up youth clubs, done work with unemployed kids in Peckham, done quite a lot of youth-related work. I also teach football and swimming. I did an MSC programme as a community sport worker and within a couple of months I was promoted to the supervisor of this team of fourteen people. I'm not working in a specifically black way. When I want my black culture I come home and I've got my music and got my posters and I smoke my herbs and that's fine, but when I'm out there that's not the image. I'm just me operating as a professional. Not as a black person. I teach football to this youth club. There's three full-time workers, white and black. In my dealings with all of them I try to use my common sense to figure out their jobs. I know my job. And that puts me in a strong position. I do my job well and I point out to them when they're not doing theirs well. The problem with a lot of black people is that they feel they can't stick their neck out, they can't work as an equal.

WILF WALKER: Working as a black businessman would be good if only more black people would realize that there are black businessmen who can deliver. In my business – rock promotion – there is lots and lots of black product and they're selling millions, but I'm not getting any of it. The business is run by whites, yes, but these black artists are in charge of their own destinies, they can motivate their agents and their management to employ black businesses. They mouth all these words about how they want to see black people make progress, but they'll still do their business with the white man. It's one thing going for a white lawyer, when you've got a white judge and jury, but in my business the colour of the audience doesn't matter. There's no colour thing at all. The audiences are ninety per cent white, but that's not the problem: the problem is in black people's heads in terms of working with each other on the highest level. I work with a lot of black acts at the beginning of their career, then at the point where they break and get big, they're all looking for white people to work with. There's this belief that your own people can't take you to this fantasy place, the imaginary world of real success. Which is absolute bullshit. They say that they're heavy politically committed bands, but they don't understand what the struggle is about, which is black people getting the means of production. It's not a question of cutting out white people. The artist can tell his manager, 'I want to see more black people involved in my work.' So the manager has to go to his mate the agent and tell him that, 'Yes, you may have your white mates, but if you want my boy . . .' Just look at some offers from black promoters.

208

That's all those motherfuckers have got to do and they are not doing it. I'm not begging for favours. I'm just saying: allow me to do business.

BERNIE GRANT: The impression is given, especially through the media, that all these blacks are good for is – maybe they're good at sports but that's it. There's nothing wrong with sport, you can get a good living out of it, but whatever you think you're good at you should be allowed to develop it. The brainy ones should be channelled towards the places that suit them, and the sports people go in the right direction for them. It's all part of the same thing.

TONY GIRARD: I met a chap once, he was a coach at Chelsea FC. He was looking for black kids. This was the late '60s. He had seen how talented black kids were in other countries and he'd been all over England looking for them and he couldn't find any. I told him, 'Don't worry. I know a lot of black people who were brilliant at sport back home, but then we came here and we had to fight for a roof over our head, we had to fight for a job, fight for everything and we had no time for sport. So don't worry about us, wait for the next generation.' Now of course black kids are all over football.

MICHAEL DE SOUZA: I played for Queen's Park Rangers when I was seventeen, in the youth side. There was a lot of prejudice: black players were weak, we were scared to go into the tackle – of course you're scared to go into the tackle if every time you go into a tackle ten white men go for you. And they will. This is what people didn't realize. Four or five will just commit themselves to doing something to you. You had no support from your own team. Your team-mates didn't like you, the opposition didn't like you and that's trouble. It's a lot easier now to play as a black person, but only if you play in a certain way. You have to be very, very conventional, not like in Holland or Italy where you can free up yourself. You can't do that here. They do control you. I don't regret not playing, because I still play a very important part in football. My job now, and the brief I have from the FA, is to educate children to a standard of football which they enjoy but is also a very high standard. Football being the way it is, I may not have had the same chance to influence the game that I would had I just played.

* * *

NIEN-LUN YEH: I was ready for the hard life we would have to lead at the start. But there are basic differences which affect the individual coming to live here. There is far more freedom in England, far more choices. Everywhere has office politics, but the difference is that if you don't like your job here, you can resign. Which I did. You can always start your own business, although that is very, very hard. That is what I have done. I have set up a sort of translation agency for technical work. Also a trade consultancy for the Far East and China. This was impossible in China, where everything is under the strict control of the unit for which you are working. You are told which job you will do – you have no choice. The legal system here is also more complete than the one in China. Your boss doesn't control everything. In China there is a simple rule: those with power control everything. You have privileges and you can override the law. The law exists, but top men are stronger. Their decisions decide everything. Not that this country is absolutely democratic, absolutely free. Class matters.

BHAJAN SINGH CHADHA: For members of any immigrant community the best way to succeed is to set up on your own. You arrive in a new country, you're not let into the mainstream, and you have to look after yourself. I left the Post Office in '66, but all the experience I had had in Kenya was still no use to me. I still couldn't find any clerical work. I decided to start a business on my own. I've been running my own shop ever since.

MUHAMMAD AYYAZ: Managers are afraid that if they appoint an Asian in a supervisory position then the white staff will not work. Whether it is true or not we don't know – very few Asians have ever been given the chance to find out. But the next generation, who have been born here, educated here, are not going to be satisfied with this situation. If they don't get a job they resent it very much. But the exclusion from the mainstream is in some ways lucky for us – quite a lot of people have started their own businesses, quite a lot of which are run as family businesses which employ quite a lot of our youngsters. Mainly groceries, butchers, clothing stores. There is this feeling in the community that if he can do well, I can do well. They tend to do the same thing. So you get these stereotypes. Many many Asians are involved in property. Now there are some solicitors coming along, some chemists, estate agents. If you're educated yet you don't get a good job you tend to think, 'OK, I'll do it myself.'

RAMESH VALA: I think the East Africa Asian community is on the move. Mr Patel who used to have a corner shop is moving into property now, or cash-and-carry. It's a bit like the Jewish community: at the end of the day you do want to own your own little business.

GULZAR KHAN: In 1967 I gave up working, and started working as a self-employed person. I became more and more involved in the community. I have a business too: I started with a grocery, then I improved on that, then I had a supermarket, then I sold that and bought some houses and now I have property. My eldest son is in business too, and the younger ones are in college. It has always been my opinion – although other people may feel differently – that I could not live on the state. Other than the twelve weeks before I started work with British Rail I have never claimed any benefits from the state. From August 1962 till today. Not a single penny.

SHREERAM VIDYARTHI: Before I arrived I had met a guy called Mr Sharma who wanted me to come to England one day and join hands with him in setting up a company to import books from India. He left me with a ton of catalogues and a ton of cards on which I was supposed to note them all down and I was ferrying them around in my rucksack. When I arrived here he had set up the company and one of the ways of helping legitimize my position was to become a director of the company. But he wouldn't take me on as a partner, he wouldn't register me as a director, he wouldn't give me the time of day. He expected me to work for him, but for free. He knew that if he didn't take me on, then after a while I would be thrown out and I would be out of his hair. As in all immigrant communities he was using a fellow-immigrant and exploiting him. After about six months I told him to stuff it. I worked at the BBC and started selling Indian clothes outside Hyde Park every Sunday. It was a good living.

BENNY BUNSEE: The vast majority of Asians in this country are really poor. The small commercial retailers that you do have are really working-class people trying to make it in a very difficult world. Nothing more than that. People who can't get the kind of employment that they want, because the conditions under which they work – starting at 6 a.m. to 10 at night, involving their whole families – it's a dog's life. It's a very oppressive situation. And you don't make very much money, quite frankly, for all that hard work. It's just not worth it. The Asian entrepreneurial class, which is very small, is really reacting and fighting against the kind of situation that they face here – the lack of opportunities and employment. Which is what drives a lot of black people into small businesses.

GULZAR KHAN: This myth of Asians doing well, making money – perhaps there are less than one per cent of the whole community who are doing well in that way. You hear Prince Charles saying it: 'Asians are doing so well.' When they do do well, it is because they work very hard, as I did in my grocery, from seven in the morning to ten at night. With the whole family working. Doing enough work for six people and taking only two people's wages. Yes, those corner shopkeepers have cash in their pocket, but it goes straight back to the wholesalers. I built my business up like that, working sixteen hours every day. When I started I turned over £150 a week and when I sold up it was turning over £2,500 a week. I tried to have everything people wanted; you came into my shop and I couldn't sell you what you wanted, I would make a note and the next time it would be there. But the youngsters who are meant to take over from us, they are saying, 'Why should we open sixteen hours a day?' They want a social life.

* * *

ANWAR BATI: In 1980 I applied to join LWT after seeing a newspaper ad. I got short-listed down to the last two. I was rung up the next day by the producer who said, 'Very sorry, you didn't get the job, but you were very close. So we'd like you to work here anyway. Tomorrow you'll be offered another job.' I thought, 'Wonderful,' having been trying to get into television for some time. The next day the phone goes, a chap I'd never met said to me, 'Sorry you didn't get the job, but would you like to work on *Skin*.' this was their ethnic programme. I said, 'No. You're offering me that job because my name is Indian. You've never met me in your life. That is hardly a good reason for me to take the job or for you to offer it to me. Plus I've never been to Southall in my life, plus I don't think it's a very good programme.' This conversation soon ended. I put the phone down and immediately thought, 'You idiot. You've been trying for two years to get into television, you could always move once you got in, why be so haughty.' Anyway, two hours later the head of LWT current affairs personally rang me, said, 'Sorry to insult you, would you like another job?' I said, 'Yes, sure.' So I went for another job and when the woman who was then head of minority programming asked why I hadn't taken the job on *Skin*, I asked, 'Why don't you take a job on a woman's programme?'

SIMI BEDFORD: I was at LWT for six years. This is liberal, media LWT, in 1980. I thought, these people are educated, they'll be enlightened and liberal, but in actual fact I have never, anywhere, met the kind of racism I met there. Never. The kind of prejudice and the kind of things people said. On my first day I got stuck in the corridor, quite lost. Someone came up, said, 'Hello,' and asked if I was looking for the dressing-room. So I said, 'No.' I wasn't a performer. So they said, 'Well, the canteens are that way.' The assumption was that if I wasn't performing I must be washing up or cooking. The racism wasn't admitted, but it was one hundred per cent present. Of course they'd deny it, and indeed most of it isn't provable – which is why it's so insidious. Of course, saying that you don't get jobs because of race is the easy way out and it's very easy to fall into that trap, but many white people do make these references completely unconsciously. They would deny that your blackness has any bearing on what they say. But even if they aren't conscious of what they say, it does make a difference. However liberal they are, when they see me coming for a job it isn't the same as when they see a white person, and they're lying if they say anything else.

212

MARCEL BERLINS: In '71 out of the blue I got a phone call from *The Times* Law Reports: 'Do you want to be a legal correspondent for *The Times*?' I didn't know what a legal correspondent was, and I wasn't a reader of *The Times*, and the *Guardian* didn't have such a thing. I'd never been a journalist even for a school magazine, never touched a typewriter, never typed a word in my life, didn't know shorthand. Anyway *The Times* interviewed me – that morning I read *The Times* from cover to cover – and got the job. I learnt later they'd been trying for months to get a legal journalist and hadn't been able to, and this was scraping well below the bottom of the barrel. This seemed to me a nice thing to do. I had no idea how newspapers worked. I didn't even know terms like 'copy'. The fact I couldn't type amazed them. I felt terrified, but it was just something to do. When I looked back a year or so later, to have your first job in journalism as a specialist on *The Times* was quite a strange thing to have achieved. But at the time it was just, 'Oh, this is quite fun.' *The Times* then was just trying to update itself. I fitted into it quite easily, although I hadn't the faintest idea how people operated there. I was never treated as an outsider, even though I felt one.

RONALD HARWOOD: My talent as an actor was not considerable. My vitality as a person was enormous. I was energetic, ambitious, single-minded. The brash colonial. Abrasive. I thought Olivier would retire when I came to England; I'd arrived, so he'd better give up. Anyway, in 1952 my mother said that she couldn't afford the fees at RADA. I was being taught by Joseph O'Connor, an actor who was working in the West End. He mentioned that Donald Wolfit would be doing a Shakespeare season at Hammersmith in '53, Coronation year. After class one day I asked if I could write to Wolfit, using his name. He was rather taken aback. He said I could say that he'd mentioned a season, but he didn't want to recommend me. I wrote and got a card back: the company was full. The first rejection I'd ever had for anything. But Lionel Bowman was homosexual and lived with Raymond Marriott, then drama critic of *The Stage*. We were having dinner that night and Raymond, who's still a close friend, said, 'Wolfit's a friend of mine.' So he wrote on my behalf and I got a letter: 'Mr Wolfit will see you at the Waldorf Hotel.' It was a year to the day since I'd set sail from South Africa, the day of the last great pea-souper. I walked from Marble Arch to the Aldwych. Wearing my audition suit, with holes in my shoes. I was waiting to go up, terribly nervous, and a young, dark-haired, handsome man came bounding down the stairs: 'I've got it! I've got it!' It was Harold Pinter. We've been friends ever since. John Osborne was seen that day too, but he didn't get in. I went up, saw Wolfit, and he said, 'I can pull you into the crowd.' My first job turned out to be leading on Sir Lewis Casson. I was so excited to be with a Great Name. Then Ronald Fraser, who'd been with me at RADA, and was Wolfit's dresser, was leaving because he'd won a prize, so I was made the dresser, but I kept going to RADA and going to the theatre at night – strictly against RADA rules. Then Sir Kenneth Barnes, founder and principal of RADA called me: 'Make a choice. Wolfit or us.' I chose Wolfit.

*   *   *

WITOLD STARECKI: In 1983 I won a British Council scholarship to come to London for a month to study musicals. While I was here I met Roger Mills of the BBC who commissioned me to make a film I had planned on the mentally ill in Poland. I had to go home – I had no money – and he gave me a letter of intent to show the authorities. Then he came to Poland and eventually we made the film and I moved to England. I've stayed here ever since.

HANNAH KODICEK: What I really wanted to do was study at the London film school, to become a film director. But without English, with a baby, with no connections, how could I do that? Forget it. Teach the piano. Then I met up with some people from the Black Theatre of Prague whom I had known before and worked with before I left. They had also left Czechoslovakia. We formed the Black Theatre Group of Prague, the remnants of the Black Theatre of Prague. We worked quite a lot, but in English culture, anything like animation or puppets, objects, magic, imagination is relegated to the children's sphere, or to cabaret or something. Whereas in Czechoslovakia it's seen on a par with poetry and rated higher than straight acting. So we could only do children's television or cabaret. We worked in some amazing places – semi-naughty cabarets in Monte Carlo, things like that, very interesting, it opened a door into part of a society that otherwise one wouldn't have normally encountered. We also did 'show biz' – things like Mike Yarwood, Paul Daniels. One wouldn't choose to do it, but that was the only way to get work. Then I went into children's television and did a lot of that. Meanwhile Michael Lindsay-Hogg found me. He needed a lady for Tom Stoppard's play *Professional Foul*. So I did that, I played the wife of a Czech dissident. I didn't have any lines in English and I only had three or four scenes but it was so beautifully written and so beautifully directed and the other performances were so good that it was a very memorable play. It meant that everybody was going 'Wow, *what* a performance, darling . . .' Suddenly casting people had me down as intellectual or dissident and for the next three or four years I kept playing those parts. Actually I'm much more into comedy and silliness and zany and writ large, but I haven't had a chance with that. There's the accent – I should have got rid of it. After the twentieth dissident or spy I got fed up.

WITOLD STARECKI: People who come here from eastern Europe and have been trained in the arts world, are doing quite well. They have had to work

214

under such harsh conditions that when they arrive here they find it much easier to operate. The obstacles that appear difficult for a British person are nothing for me. There's no comparison. We don't have that tradition of leaving shut doors alone. If a door is shut, we open it, rather than go away. We are great improvisers. If things don't go according to plan, we work out something else. Things never go according to plan in Poland, we're used to it. If I have too rigid a schedule I actually feel very bad – there's no room for manoeuvres. There is too much of what I would call 'chip thinking': you are a chip which goes with another chip to construct a bigger chip. In Poland we don't have that, we never developed chips.

IVAN KYNCL: I wanted to specialize in theatre photography and I started by taking pictures of Lyubimov at the Almeida Theatre for a drama magazine. I also promised them pictures from the performance. They said that would be impossible because the photo call was already long over. I said if I could take pictures of prisons in Czechoslovakia I could take pictures in an English theatre. So I bought tickets, I hid the cameras, and we went in. During the production I took pictures. After the second half the manager came up. He told me he was going to fetch a policeman, I said that would be nice because I had never had experience of the English police. He wanted to confiscate the film. Now my background came in useful: they had confiscated my films ten times in Czechoslovakia and every time I slipped them empty films. So this time as we were talking I swapped the films and handed them over. They promised to give them back after the weekend. When I asked if they would give me back my films, they said, 'What films?' and made as if they knew nothing about it. I was surprised and upset but I left, and told the magazine that they couldn't use the pictures because of what had happened.

In 1984, when we were really very poor, my wife suggested I should get some more theatre work. So I went to the RSC – I had nothing to lose – and they said they liked my work, but they could only take on a new photographer every couple of years. I was disappointed but a week later Terry Hands asked me to bring in my portfolio and from that time I have worked all round the theatre.

EVA JIRICNA: I was working at the GLC earning £80 a month and supporting my brother and myself. Designing primary and secondary schools. I was bored to death. I used to work extremely hard and the GLC was running out of work and no one was really doing anything and people were taking leaves ever so often and there was never anyone available when you wanted them and the section leader didn't seem to be interested in anything other than the musical education of his two daughters ... it was just a load of people sitting there waiting for their retirement like in any organization full of Civil Servants. I was

215

really in need of something that would make me busy and wouldn't leave me too much time to think. So I started looking for a new job and I joined a firm called Louis de Soissons who were the architects of Brighton Marina. I became an associate there and the job architect on this enormous project. De Soissons himself had been the architect of Welwyn Garden City and he had died in 1961. I spent ten years working on Brighton Marina, until 1978 when the project came to an end and then I did a competition for Westminster Pier with the engineers and contractors from the Marina project. We won it. Then my senior partner said, 'If you want to start your own practice I'll join you.' So we started this practice in 1978 and of course Westminster Pier never happened. In 1979 the project was cancelled and here I was doing nothing and my partner wanted to retire, so I started looking for *anything* I could do, anything. And I met somebody called Joseph [Ettedgui], who had a shop in Sloane Street and he asked me to do something in his flat, which I made a mess of, then he asked me to do a shop in South Moulton Street which was published and I did his flat again and that was widely published and I never looked back.

SHARI PEACOCK: I finished five years at the Architectural Association. Then you're supposed to start work. I had also been going to St Martin's to study drawing. The Architectural Association was just a doss really – it was great fun but you didn't do that much work. At the end you'd spend three weeks of not sleeping and doing your drawings and that's how you pass. But when I went to St Martin's I was very keen. Of course you couldn't get a grant to do drawing or painting from the Iranian government – that was far too luxurious and unnecessary a thing to do. But I just went on drawing and when I left I submitted some drawings to *Vogue*, the Cecil Beaton Award; the first time I tried I came second and the next time I won it. I had worked for about six months in an architectural office, which I found horrible – not the people but the work – but when I won the *Vogue* thing I started working freelance as an illustrator. I've made a living out of it. If you put your mind to it you can make a lot of money.

JAROSLAV BRADAC: For my first weeks I had a little money, plus the price of my ticket back to Czechoslovakia which I cashed in. This fellow who was helping me, had connections. He was sending me around various design studios and that's how I met someone who was doing the front covers and the design for *Encounter* magazine. I became the first illustrator they had ever used. It was so new to them they didn't even know what to pay me. I was drawing and the phone rang and they said, 'We'd like to employ you monthly to do an illustration of an article.' So I said, 'What sort of money are we talking about?' They said, 'Fifty,' and I said 'Thank you very much, that's wonderful,' and I put the phone down. Then I thought perhaps I misunderstood. Perhaps it was

216

fifteen – fifty was a hell of a lot of money then. So I had to ring them back. 'Is it five-oh or one-five.' They said, 'Five-oh,' and I went off to celebrate. I didn't have to wash dishes, I didn't have to look for that kind of work. Instead I had the opportunity to make a living doing what I was trained to do.

BALRAJ KHANNA: The question of succeeding here as an artist was a dubious one. In one respect I had no illusions about it. I had known from the start that it would be a struggle, there would be no grand overnight success. So I had prepared myself for this struggle, and struggle it was too. Not an enjoyable struggle either. There was a definite unpleasantness: you were constantly made aware of who you were. You had to spell out your name wherever you went, eyebrows were raised. It was because of the colour of your skin. There were quite a few Indian artists, and we were all having this commonly shared experience, of being kept out of the mainstream. There was no possibility of changing that. If you could paint tigers or fisherwomen on the coast of Bombay or little miniatures, then you could be regarded as an artist. But if you dared to venture into the realm of modernism, of mainstream art, you were not accepted, rather you were told, 'How dare you want to be one of us?' We Indian artists were the outcasts, the untouchables. At least in India the position of the untouchable is straightforward: there is the untouchable, you know it and he knows it. Here it all went on under the veneer of politeness, of apparent decency and charm and social grace. And given this veneer, there were sinister undertones. We had no possibility of ever being able to make it. There were a couple of Indian artists who started to do well, and they were very quickly put in their own compartment, but the mainstream was an area which was reserved for whites. By some divine decree it was by right theirs, and theirs alone. We were not supposed to have the temerity to wish to enter into that domain. Later on, by the early '70s, I became angry. I said, 'Dammit. They're not going to destroy me with all this – I am going to go on.'

* * *

FIRDOS ALI: I was interested in painting and writing. Obviously you couldn't get into painting and writing straight away – so I started working in a Wimpey Bar in the Strand, diagonally opposite the Savoy. I was a waiter, a good waiter, earning a lot of money, tips and everything. I had a nice growth of hair, people called me a young Omar Sharif. Then I became a manager at a Golden Egg, they owned Wimpey.

DON ATYEO: I'd been working on the Melbourne *Age* and I still had my letters of introduction to various Fleet Street people, very creased, very faded, but they were still there. But I didn't intend to work as a journalist again – I'd seen through the lies of the capitalist press, that sort of thing. I chose instead to get a job as a washer-up in a hamburger place. I was also really quite poor. Though I didn't feel at all worried: England would provide, England was the mother country. If you went broke in India or Afghanistan you were fucked, I'd seen it happen often enough, terrible things, but this was England. It was unthinkable to me that one might fall through the net, that one might be left without a house. So daft. But you didn't worry. You went and you blew your money on your 50p a night boarding house. Next thing you walked up the road and got a job. On the Earls Court Road, which was where Australians were. I started walking up the street and saying, 'Have you got a job?' and at the fifth or sixth restaurant they said, 'Yes, come and be a dishwasher for £22 a week.' Six days a week, 10 a.m. till 2 p.m. Slave labour. But I met a guy there and we hired a bedsit together, which cost us £5 a week, two beds, Baby Belling fell out of the closet, all that. So there you were. Life was fairly catered for.

NELLY SALAS: Rackhams, a big department store in Leamington Spa needed a person to work in the kitchen. I was worried about my English, but I took the job. The first two or three weeks were terrible: the English I had learned in class had nothing to do with the way people spoke in everyday life. But I was a good cook and I did the work and gradually I learned the language. I stayed for nearly two years, working very very hard. They exploited me, of course. Then I came to London where I met more Latin American people and after that I had the opportunity to join the Latin American children's project. I have been an organizer of the Latin American nursery – Mafalda.

ENNIO CAMISA: When I started you used to go down to Smithfield market and buy chickens, and sell them. Dead chickens. When I was about twenty-four I started making sausages, our own sausages. I used to like that very much. Before that I was just a boy around the shop. I didn't deliver; people came and collected things themselves. They didn't buy so much as they do now. The restaurants used to come, but they also went to Smithfield to buy wholesale. And people would buy a case of spaghetti, a piece of parmesan, some salami. They'd come themselves. In those days, when a customer spent two or three pounds, that was a big customer. We used to sell salami at 2/- a pound, now it's £4.20. Parmesan was 2/- a pound; one gallon of olive oil was 7/6. Case of spaghetti was 7/-, £28 now. I earned 36/- a week. But with that you could go very far. You could go to the cinema, 2/6, 2/4 was a good seat, 3/6 was the top seat. Then there were cheap cinemas. There were four cinemas in Tottenham Court Road. The expensive one was 1/6; the cheap one was 9d. We had an employee, an Irishman who we paid 32/- a week. He had a family, and he'd say. 'I'm very happy; I can do all right.' He'd pay 7/- for lodging and that left 25/-. He was very happy. We had the rooms over our shop.

218

VICTOR WILD: My schooldays came to an end in 1943. I went to London where my uncle had got me a job as a trainee at Claridge's Hotel. In the kitchens. He decided that catering not chocolate making was where the big future would be. He was very autocratic, he didn't discuss this, just said, 'Right, this is what you're doing.' Though he did give me the option of not going into the business at one point. He bought all my clothes and all my equipment and got me this job and then said, 'Right, do you actually want to do this or not?' What could I do. I wasn't exactly falling over myself to take it up as a career but I had no other strong preferences for a career. I spent a year at Claridge's while the flying bomb raids were still going on. Where we were struggling to feed the royalty from abroad who were all living there. The King of Greece lived there and the chef would announce, 'Deux côtes d'agneau pour le roi!' and we had some Communist chefs who used to be less than impressed. So the poor King of Greece didn't always get the very best of everything. At the end of the war I went back to Switzerland to do some training and then came back to England after that.

HANNAH KODICEK: We felt it doesn't matter what we do, it doesn't matter how we live, as long as we are in a democratic country. So we did those jobs that don't go on the CV later. Walking greyounds on the Catford stadium, being a barmaid, babysitting. My husband was a hospital porter and so on. We were also studying at the same time – we had scholarships to Trinity College of Music. We were both pianists. But the scholarship only covered tuition, not living expenses, so we had to find other work.

KAREL KYNCL: I was prepared to do whatever was necessary. By a stroke of luck I was invited to join the magazine *Index* where I still work. I also work as a freelance journalist and I am very, very proud that I am still making my living in the profession I love, and the only profession that perhaps I know a little about.

NAIM ATALLAH: Every year I had to go back to the Home Office to get my work and residence permits renewed. Finally they cancelled all the restrictions and said I could apply for British citizenship. I registered with the Ministry of Labour and said that I was available to be a journalist, but there were no jobs on offer. It was very difficult and I had to draw the dole. Then, after three months, I was called in to the Labour Exchange. They told me there was a job available at a bank. I had to take it. They weren't going to allow me to draw dole any longer. I said, 'I don't want to go into banking, I hate it.' They said, 'Well, that's your choice.' I had to go there and be interviewed. I thought, it's very easy to fail an interview. If I do that, they'll have to put me back on the dole. So I told the interviewer, 'I don't know a debit from a credit. It's all boring.' He asked me why I was applying for the job then. 'The Ministry of Labour sent me, I was forced to come.' 'Wonderful,' he said, 'you're just the guy we want.' 'Why?' 'You have no preconceived ideas. We can train you from scratch.' So he gave me the job and I became a bank clerk in the foreign exchange room at 62 Bishopsgate, recording the dealing transactions. One day a dealer got sick and the manager asked me, 'Can you deal?' I said, 'Certainly.' I'd never dealt in my life, but I'd watched and learned and that was how my life started in the business world.

GRETEL SALINGER: I didn't get a job but immediately I started working for charity. We had a furnished flat in Bayswater, next to Hilda Schlesinger who was a very famous Jewish lady. In Queens Court, Queensway. Immediately she hauled me into doing voluntary service for war work. The WRVS. I enrolled there and I worked like mad, day and night. I was collecting for the national war savings movement and Miss Schlesinger put me in charge of our block, collecting for war savings. So every Monday evening I went from flat to flat, and there were hundreds of flats, to collect war savings stamps or loans. I was very lucky because in this block of flats were hundreds of Greek shipowners who came to England, gave their fleets to England for transporting ammunition and so on in the Atlantic convoys. And these people did not go to the bank, because they did not trust banks. So they had cash, a lot of cash, in their pockets. Either they were paid very well for the trips to America and back, if the ship survived, and if they were sunk, the shipowner got compensation. It took me some time, but eventually I got their confidence and they banked with me. So I got masses and masses of money for the war collection.

PETER VO: When I arrived in 1981 I went to Bognor Regis college to study teacher training for one year. After that I came to London and spent another year's study in Thames Polytechnic. Then I got a job in the British Library. I left there because the pay was not very good and the job itself was not very interesting. I said to my superior one day that I had a degree and that I was qualified to do something more skilled. I wanted to use my brain. Please give me the chance. But I waited and waited and the chance did not come. So I left to take an enterprise course. Then I was unemployed for a few months until I got a job as a community worker, which is what I still do. Now I am working for the Department of Education as an administrative officer. I am also the founder of the local Vietnam community organization. I set up this community and was elected for three consecutive years as the chairman of the group. During that period I had a lot of contact with MPs, local councillors and so on.

VU DUY TU: I had a plan, a long-term plan for my family. My wife and I had to learn English. My children had to attend school. My wife and I wanted to spend at least two years in school, learning English as a second language. And then to learn some skills and then find a job. At that time we were living on supplementary benefit. That lasted only for fourteen months. After that I got a part-time job. Meanwhile I finished a training course at South East London College in maintaining refrigerators. I got a City and Guilds certificate. I spent a couple of months at that. Then my second job was community worker for the Social Services Department in Lewisham. That lasted for nearly a year. I took over from someone who was on maternity leave. That was four years ago. Now I work for the Vietnamese community in Hackney. Our committee purchased these premises two years ago, when it was a church hall. Now it's a community centre for refugees from Vietnam, Laos and Cambodia. There are about 20,000 Vietnamese in England, 400 Laotians and 400 Cambodians.

* * *

MUHAMMAD AYYAZ: These days there are two ways you can get a job. One is a clerical job, if you have a reasonable education, which will pay maybe £4,000. But if you move to a higher level, say £9,000, then it has to be a Section 11 job. Section 11 jobs were introduced by the central government about ten or twelve years ago, possibly even earlier. Nobody from the Asian community was getting a job within the local authorities anywhere in England, so they came up with this scheme for positive discrimination. They provided seventy-five per cent of the salary and the local authority provided the rest. So now local authorities are willing, quite eager, to appoint people. They were mainly social worker jobs, welfare jobs, and dealing only with Asian families. The idea was that this would help with the language barrier and the culture barrier. So Section 11 was created to get local authorities to employ Asians, which to some extent they have done – although it's a sort of apartheid – except that there are in fact more English people in Section 11 jobs than Asians. Often they're supply teachers, teaching EFL. Very rarely will you get a mainstream job in a local authority.

MUHAMMAD ALI: You're made to feel inferior here even when you have a job. In subtle ways. I don't have a Section 11 job, but working for Fullemploy means I am working for an organization which is committed to equality of opportunity and working towards that and trying to enable black people to have a better chance and to play a better role in the economic life of the UK. So I too am not really in a mainstream job. I do feel that I could have done better in a mainstream job. I've done a degree in chemistry, I've got a good honours degree, I've got an MBA. But I've applied for jobs and still I haven't been able to get them. The standard letters of rejection are very similar. 'I regret to inform you . . . we're keeping your records on file . . .' I know them by heart. I've had this job for three years and before that I had a Section 11 job. It's not impossible for an Asian to get a mainstream job but self-employment is certainly the best way of setting oneself up. A lot of studies have proved that black people with the same background and qualifications are twice as likely to be unemployed as white people. The disadvantage actually grows with your qualifications – the more education you have, the less likely you are to get a job. So qualified black people are maybe three times more likely to be unemployed.

MICHAEL DE SOUZA: I went for this job at the British Bath Company. Enamelling baths. He said, 'You're far too small, you couldn't carry a big heavy bath.' I said, 'Do these men carry baths on their own?' 'Well, they may do. If asked to they may.' So I just said, 'Thank you, sir' and I went. They just didn't want me. I could have been too small, but how big do you have to be to hold a ladle of enamel?

MUHAMMAD AYYAZ: There is a racist bias built into English society, the system, the laws all work against you. I have sat in on interviews, and I have had job interviews myself, and the things that go on – it's impossible for us to get the sort of job that we believe ourselves to be capable of doing. We'll get a job if, say, it is a Section 11 job, one that is only for Asians. We discuss this issue and there seems to be no way we can break through that barrier. When I didn't have a job this situation made me very frustrated, very bitter. Then I was lucky enough to get a job and since then I have stayed in work, although that is still a Section 11 job and sometimes I feel, why a Section 11 job, why not a mainstream job? It isn't the pay, which is reasonable, but it is this segregation. In the end it's a cosmetic exercise. These are special jobs, simple as that. Otherwise there would be no jobs for Asians in local authorities.

MANZOOR BAHADUR: I left engineering and became more and more interested in community work. I felt I could help the community a lot more in that sort of a job than just getting personal satisfaction from engineering. There I was going to get both. As a youngster coming here at the age of ten I had been filling in people's sick notes and writing letters for them as soon as I could read and write English. People used to come to our house and I'd be going to solicitors' offices at weekends and down to the DHSS during school holidays. So I had been involved with that level of community work at a very early stage through necessity. Not many Asians in the older generation could read and write in English. As I got older I thought, why not have a go at community work. So I got this job as the manager of the local multi-cultural community centre. It meant a drop in salary, but it gave me a lot more satisfaction. We've developed the centre to the stage where we have maybe seven hundred people every week using it for a wide variety of activities. After that I went into social work, an unqualified social worker to work initially with the Asian community. This was a Section 11 post. Basically, these posts were a form of affirmative action. Though, they did have a positive side because they gave black people jobs in a very specialized area of work. These posts gave an opportunity to gain a Certificate of Qualification in Social Work (CQSW). Some of my friends said that the problem with the CQSW was that there was very little input about black cultures. The way you solved a social work problem was based on the white situation.

BODRUL ALOM: The problem with Section 11 jobs is that the contracts are for three years. The idea was to create jobs which would help the community. It's a part of the Local Government Act of 1966. But because the contracts are short, they are not always able to appoint the best people for the job. People work for a year or so and then begin to lose their interest. To be honest there is no career in a Section 11 job. With a mainstream job you can enhance your career, but with Section 11 you have no choice, you are dumped in a place, and there is nowhere you can go from that place. The way I define my job is to try to bring some ego-satisfaction to the community. But these are things that should come from the mainstream. We Bangladeshis are rate-payers, we have the right to better treatment. We pay tax. Yet we are still treated as second-class citizens, but why should that happen? What are we not doing that the white community does? It wasn't our particular pleasure to come here, we were invited.

DESMOND GITTENS: In my job we run a hotel and catering course and place young people in hotels and restaurants around the borough of Kensington & Chelsea. We had a case where a placement officer, who was white, went into a hotel and she was told, 'Look, we don't mind having young people coming to work for us but we don't want any blacks because the clientele wouldn't feel happy with black people up front. They can work in the kitchen or as porters, but not up front.' So this problem came up in a staff meeting. She said, 'They don't want black people, so I'm not going to send any.' So I said, 'Here we are, two colleagues and you're saying you're not going to send any black people there because they say so. But surely if you do that we are not a team. It's illegal and my response would be to take this to the hilt. These people are discriminating and I shall go to whatever lengths I have to to make sure that they are stopped. Whether its the Commission for Racial Equality or the Hotel & Catering Board, whoever.' This discussion went on for a couple of weeks before my colleague realized what I was trying to say: that we are supposed to be a team and it doesn't matter what colour the young person is. We bring them in the centre, we train them, and it should be the same when we try to place them in a job. Of course discrimination exists, but when we find it we should do something about it. She was saying, 'Well I'm not inclined to get involved, that's a new trip for me, I'm not inclined to get involved in anti-discriminatory activities. I'm here to train youngsters to cook.'

SHREELA FLATHER: I spent six years at the Commission for Racial Equality (CRE). I think it is a body filled by people who do an enormous amount of good work. Though there are also those who don't. It is a terrible mixture, with people who think that if you are working in race relations you don't have to conform to any normal standards. The CRE in a way is all we've got. We're never going to get a British civil rights movement. People may say we should have one, but 'should have' is not the way things come about. It may emerge from the grass roots, but you can't expect the government to set it up. Because there is such a diversity among the migrant communities you can't put together enough like-minded people. There is a story from Trinidad, about the crabs in a tin. You put some crabs in a tin and every time one tries to crawl out, another one drags it back down.

I would like to see a stronger version of the CRE, more involved in law enforcement, in the Race Relations Act, and less involved in so many other areas. The CRE should be pushing forward employment cases, discrimination cases, race relations cases. In that way the CRE could be genuinely influential. I'd like to see class actions: so that when one person gets a ruling, it applies not just to that individual, but to everybody in a similar position. The problem is that we don't have the resources. You can't get legal aid in these complaints. There should be much stronger penalties for victimization against a person who loses their job when they go to a race relations tribunal. You can't get your job back, only compensation. However, I still believe that we have made more progress under the CRE complaints system than in any other way.

MIKE PHILLIPS: Positive discrimination is probably the only way of dealing with things, if it works properly and if it is what it says it is. Most of the time in this country – I think it works differently in the States – it seems that wherever you get anything that approaches positive discrimination the way that it works is not to do with people's ability. You just line up ten random black people and they're going to positively discriminate and put one or two of them in a job. But they're actually not looking, ever, ever, for the person who can do that job best. What they are looking for is the person who will be the best token representative, who will get the firm or the department the best publicity, or who will, in their minds, get people off their backs by appointing them. Once they've decided to employ a black person they are looking for a black person who won't be too black, or difficult to control, or isn't too full of themselves, too *arrogant* – any black person who has a modicum of self-confidence is *arrogant*. Anyone who rejects external notions of what they are is seen as
224

arrogant. So positive discrimination is not a way of getting good posts for good people, but instead tends to be a way for the system to inject a little bit of colour without actually disturbing the situation. In this country for positive discrimination read tokenism.

MANZOOR BAHADUR: I was the first qualified Asian quality control inspector at International Harvesters. It was quite an achievement for a black person, but I was ambitious and I felt this sense of levelling off, of not being allowed to go much further. Not necessarily through lack of capabilities, but because the amount of racism meant that my position was a sort of tokenism: that's as far as we're going to let a black person go. I certainly felt a token. I think when I got my first promotion, to inspection, it was because they felt it would look good for public relations, or employee relations if they had a black person at that level. I knew this, but I also knew that it opened the doors for other black people to get into those jobs. So people could see then that a black person could stand up to being called all sorts of names and stand the pressure. This was a job that generated hostility anyway, whether you're black or white. You were always saying, 'This isn't good enough.' When they offered me the promotion the management asked me, 'What happens if the shop floor go out on strike because you've rejected something or you've done something they don't like because of your colour?' I told them, 'I don't know why you're asking me that question, it's one you should be addressing yourself. If you're not willing to back me when I am right, then you might as well not give me the job, because I expect one hundred per cent backing whether the shop floor likes it or not.'

VERNA WILKINS: Affirmative action in jobs is necessary. Simply because of what has gone before. You do need it. The problem is that it can be counter-productive. You do get a lot of black people in positions that they've been given as part of affirmative action and they turn out to be ineffective and that launches a whole cycle. Able blacks should just come forward and be seen doing things well.

BERNIE GRANT: I see my job as helping find the jobs for all the kids. Our caucus is developing its own inner-city initiative. The Tory government claims to be colour-blind and says that everyone is equal and all that nonsense. Our plans will be geared to the black community. Affirmative action is a part of it. What we have to do is provide those young people with the resources to do their own thing. What I want to do is get the young people as skilled as possible; the second thing is to make sure that there is affirmative action taken so that they get a share of the jobs. I don't think that there is another way. Although the one alternative is to stop depending on Britain to provide the

225

jobs. That does two things: you instill a confidence in the young people, and you also make the power brokers here appreciate that they aren't so all-powerful and that the black community has an alternative to depending on them for jobs, begging them for houses and so on. There are plenty of other countries. Namibia will need skilled people, South Africa will be liberated some time and they'll need skilled black people. We get the skills and the experience here, then we can broaden out into the world. The parents have been immigrants, and maybe the children should be emigrants.

MICHAEL DE SOUZA: If you have realistic goals here, then with correct application I do believe that those goals can be realized. If you say, 'Oh the white man won't let me do this . . . I ain't working for the white man,' I say, 'Which white man?' Is there this big white man sitting up there somewhere saying, 'Right, you're all working for me.' They have this colonial attitude to white people and I don't. If I want to learn about colonialism I read about it and find out what it can do, the damage it has done and what it will take to undo it. Anyway, you don't work for the white man, you're working for the white woman: you look at your pound. Whose face is on it? If they want to say I'm working for the white woman, then fair enough. And apart from the Queen you've got Maggie Thatcher.

* * *

GRETEL SALINGER: When the war was over, in 1945, everybody in England who did especially notable war work was invited to Buckingham Palace. Out of each borough of London two people were chosen and I was one of the ones from Paddington. I had collected hundreds and thousands of pounds. I went off to Buckingham Palace for this garden party. The King and Queen, now the Queen Mother, and the two princesses went around talking to people at random. Maybe five thousand people there. I said to myself, 'I'm not here not to be talked to. That's out of the question.' So I followed the King. But he spoke only to men, so that was no use to me. And I didn't want to speak to the princesses, I wanted to speak to the Queen. So she went this way, I went that way, round the garden to meet her. I set my heart and mind on meeting her. I said to myself, 'You have to talk to me, you have to talk to me!' And she stopped. She turned to me and said, 'Where have you come from?' I ought to have said, 'From Paddington,' but what did I say? I said, 'I come from Germany.' She looked at me and said, 'And you are invited here to this party?' Very strict with me, I said, 'Yes, Your Majesty. I worked very hard during the war and I have collected millions of pounds for the war effort.' 'Oh,' she said, 'you mean you are a refugee from Germany.' 'Of course, Your Majesty.' 'That's different, my dear child. I'm glad you have escaped and made your way here.' Where I took my courage from I still cannot say, but I said, 'Yes, Your

226

Majesty, but may I tell you what happened to my family?' She said, 'Yes.' 'All my family have been killed in Auschwitz.' She made a gesture, like shielding herself. She said, 'If only I hadn't asked you.' I said, 'On the contrary, Your Majesty, this is my *kaddish*, the prayer we Jews have for the dead, that I could tell their fate to my queen.' She took both my hands and she pressed them and said, 'My darling child, I hope nothing else bad will happen to you and that you will enjoy your life and God bless you.' I stood there crying, crying, crying. Everybody asked me, 'What did the Queen talk to you about for so long?' If I would have just said what I ought to have said, that I came from Paddington, she would have just said, 'Paddington has done wonderfully,' or something. Finished. But through my silly nonsense I had this very long talk.

But that was not the end of the story. Exactly forty years after I spoke to her, in 1985, I was invited to join a friend of mine who was going to Buckingham Palace as part of a group of people who won VCs and GCs in the war. They meet every two years and the Queen Mother is their patron. This time my friend said, 'We are allowed to bring one friend with us, would you like to come?' I said, 'Would I like to come! I'd *love* to come and see the Queen Mother again.' So we had a wonderful service at St Martin's in the Fields, then we were taken in buses to St James's Palace and seated at lovely tables. I was seated between a lady and a gentleman whom I didn't know, but we got talking and I told her my story and said how much I still loved her. At five o'clock the Queen Mother went from table to table, talking to the VCs and GCs and then she came to our table and said, 'I hear there is a lady here at this table who has spoken to me once forty years ago. Who is that lady?' I nearly fainted. 'It's me your Majesty.' 'Come and talk to me. Where have we met?' So I told her the whole story all over and she remembered. She asked me how I did in the meantime. So I said that I did well, but I'd lost my husband and I was now ninety-two. So she said, 'Well, I can't catch up with you, I'm five years younger.' 'I know, your Majesty, and I love your Majesty.' She said, 'My darling, I am so pleased that I met you again and I wish you all the best.'

15 Teach Yourself English

'The worst thing that has happened to the black kids in this country is to be educated here.'

YASMIN ALIBHAI: The immigrant love of education is something to do not just with learning but with the social power it brings. There is a real and admirable belief that it gives you something more permanent and durable than money. Once you've got education within your soul, and you've got this style or arrogance or confidence, then nothing can take it away from you. And communities like the Asians, the Jews, the Vietnamese, do feel deeply vulnerable.

GINA ADAMOU: I'm obsessed with education, maybe too much, I don't know. My family think I'm mad sometimes. I don't know if they realize how important it is, but they haven't experienced the things I have experienced. One wants to become a teacher. She remembers her own experience at school and she feels that children from ethnic minorities are not always treated properly. If they have some kind of difficulty they are automatically put down. When she met the career officer when she was fifteen he simply told her she was wasting her time wanting to do A levels. He told her not to waste her parents' money or time; she should get a job. I went mad when I heard that. She feels that she was treated in that way throughout her school life. She wants to become a teacher to change that. I'm very proud.

NGUYEN DUC PHUONG: When I was in the refugee camp a group arrived from the county department of education and told me about opportunities for studying further. Then, when I had settled, someone from the local education authority came over and asked me what I wanted to do. I said that I wanted to study further. They said that I needed to improve my English. I said, 'Yes, of course' – at that time I spoke American English, not British English, and I had forgotten a lot of that in prison. They sent me to technical college to study engineering. But unfortunately the standards at the technical college were quite low. It was like secondary school again and I had done it all. So I approached the local education authority again. They said, 'Leave your name and address and we will contact you.' I waited several months. Then they wrote and said that while I already had a BSc and wanted a higher degree, they only dealt with undergraduates. The people I needed to approach were SERC (Science & Engineering Research Council) in Swindon. They sent me a form and I filled it in with the help of an English teacher. He gave me a letter saying I had enough English. But they said, 'You can't get a grant, you'll have to find the money yourself.' I asked my teacher, 'Why won't they give me a grant?' He didn't know. I approached Bristol University. 'Could I study further?' A doctor there arranged to see me for an interview. He asked me first about my English, then about what I had learnt. Finally he said that I knew enough to study for the higher degree. So I asked him for a letter to give to the grant authority. He asked why, and said, 'What did I need a letter for? You can study whenever you like – provided you have the funds.' I explained the problem and asked him to write the letter. He said, 'No problem.' Then I contacted the British Refugee Council. They sent me a letter asking whether I had enough English to study for the higher degree. I sent him a copy of the letter that said that I had no difficulty mastering it. Then they sent me another letter: 'Do you think you have enough knowledge to study in a British university?' This time I sent them the letter from the teacher in Bristol. Then they replied again: this was OK, but could I approach the university or the SERC for a grant. So I tried the university again, I saw the same doctor who had interviewed me. But he said, 'No, no. We do not deal with financial problems, this is your responsibility.' So I contacted the Refugee Council again. They said I should go back to the university, that they did have grants. Then I told them that I had been trying for a year without success. I asked them to contact the university themselves and explain my case. Then at last the Refugee Council said, 'Yes, we will provide a grant and you can go to Bristol and study.' It all took a year! But I thought about my two years in prison, so it was OK. But when I started, the doctor there told me that I could study, but if I commuted, which I had to do, I could not get a degree. I said, 'OK, you allow me to study, I will commute and I will get a degree.' He said, 'OK, you try, but I don't think so.' After two years I pass the examination and I get a master's degree. In Vietnam we knew that if you wanted to get a higher degree in engineering you had to come overseas. So in a strange way I had fulfilled my dream.

VICTOR WILD: Imagine the complications for a schoolchild faced with the English system. Feet and inches, gallons and pints, pounds shillings and pence, when you've never done it and nobody can really explain what it is. Academically I was really in trouble. I couldn't understand the lessons at all. Absolutely not.

MUHAMMAD ALI: I came to Bradford when I was fourteen. First of all I went to an immigrant centre where I learned English. Then I went to a secondary school where I did O levels and A levels. In a way I was lucky because I had to struggle a lot at the beginning, in terms of coping with all the changes, the new lifestyle, having to learn a new language and cope with the school life – all of which was very different. I was lucky to get a good report from the immigrant centre, which meant that I was put in the top stream in my comprehensive. That meant going at a fair pace. We had literature, which I could not comprehend at first, so it was a bit of a struggle initially. But I picked it up fairly quickly.

VICTOR WILD: The headmaster took me off. He couldn't even tell me where he was taking me but he took me up a country lane and in a little stone cottage there was an old lady. She opened the door and talked to me in what I later discovered was German, though I couldn't immediately recognize it as such. She was a Dr Skeat who had once been a schoolteacher but had now retired.

229

She was a very learned lady but her teaching aids were a little out of date. She had these ancient, musty volumes of nursery rhymes which creaked as you opened them. I was made to learn all about Little Boy Blue and Little Miss Muffet and Little Jack Horner and I really couldn't understand what this was all about. She had some difficulty in explaining to me what all these people were actually doing. It was my first encounter with English literature. This lasted two weeks and I had pretty intensive lessons and when you have no alternative you do learn a language pretty fast and very soon I was able to join the other boys in complaining about the food and all that.

RAJAN UDDIN JALAL: I couldn't speak English, which is a strange situation to find yourself, especially if, like me, you're about thirteen. You haven't been through primary education, you join your school half-way through the second-ary period. You can't adapt, and the whole thing is strange for you. You can't integrate wholly into the classroom, and I was attending language classes and I was attending normal classes – and I wasn't coping. I stayed on till I was fifteen and then I left. I couldn't adapt and I couldn't cope.

MUHAMMAD AYYAZ: There was one person in the community who was known to everybody – he taught everyone who had come from abroad – so naturally I was sent to him. All he said was, 'Go to college, Bradford College.' I went to Manningham where they had a small building and took a test. There were eight of us. They said, 'Write your name.' I was the only one of the eight who could write my name without looking at my passport. The others were sent away, but they asked me to stay on for another test. It was a mathematics test, which was very easy for me. Then I went over to the main building where I found myself in a class with the others again and they started teaching us ABCD, which to me was something ridiculous. I stayed in that class for one day and then I was moved. There were four classes and I was put in the third one. I stayed there two months, and then went up to the top class where I stayed two and a half years, which meant I kept repeating the same work, and I lost interest in it.

CASH BHOGAL: We got sent to the local infant school. There wasn't much of an Indian community in Birmingham, but it was growing. There were about three Asians and two West Indians in our school. The first disadvantage for me was that I couldn't speak English at all. Yet you were put into this classroom with a teacher that had no training as to how to deal with the needs of those people whose native language was not English. So the only way of learning was to pick it up as you went along. Later on, about two years later, they did try and make some arrangements, because by then there was a bigger influx of
230

Indians and they began to appreciate that they would need some assistance with English.

ANWAR BATI: I was never bullied except by one maths master in my second year. He was an old Indian army colonel, very right wing. I had always come top at maths, until that year. He always used to make fun of my name, and make fun of me and as a result I became bottom in maths and bottom in practically every subject thanks to that bullying. He wouldn't bother to explain things, but just trot out the basic definition. Basically he wasn't a very good teacher. I just shut up and lost confidence in myself. I didn't say anything at home. I put up with it. I went from the top of the A stream down to the bottom because of that experience.

*　*　*

SIMI BEDFORD: After about four days I found myself, after a detour via Harrods to buy my school uniform, taken to deepest Sussex, near Haywards Heath to this school, where everyone presumed the term had already started. I was the only black girl. I think someone at home had recommended it to my father. It was absolutely horrific. It was one of those rarified schools where, although a lot of snobbery and class barriers were breaking down after the war, the old system carried on. It was assumed that we would not work in any sort of career. What we would do was go to finishing school. So we had no lessons in the afternoon, it was all games. Plus a million different 'extras'. The food was just ghastly. I was made to sit in front of the food quite a lot. On the second or third day there I would still be sitting in front of sago pudding from two days before.

VICTOR WILD: My problems didn't really start until they sent me to boarding school. I was supposed to be going to Sedbergh, a public school up in the Yorkshire Dales but because I knew no Latin and no French they wouldn't accept me. I knew no English either. So I went first to a prep school that was connected to Sedbergh. One of these prep schools you read about: very small, only about thirty boys, and nobody could speak German there either. To add to my misery I was delivered two days too early – they had mistaken the date. So I landed in this extraordinary old house, with the headmaster and his wife. She was a tall, rather frigid figure who used to like wearing big hats, even indoors. They couldn't speak to me.

SIMI BEDFORD: On that very first day I was put in a room all by myself at the top of the house, in complete darkness, though they knew I had only been in England for four days and I was only six or seven. It was horrid. But I lived there every day for a week, because in fact there had been a terrible miscalculation and term hadn't started yet. I was taken up to this room, taken to the bathroom and then Matron appeared and said, 'Goodnight,' and went off. I screamed and screamed and screamed and screamed and screamed and nobody came. That happened every day for a week. Then all the other girls came back and then nobody would come near me because one of them told the others that if they touched me all the black would come off. I didn't tell anyone until the French mistress found me crying and asked what the matter was. So I told her and she put it right. That made me very good at French.

ZERBANOO GIFFORD: At age eight I was packed off to a boarding school in the English manner. Godstowe, a prep school in Brighton. I ran away, then went back and decided I'd better buckle down. I was an only child, I'd spent my whole life surrounded by lots of people and I just ran away by instinct. Suddenly to have all these rules and regulations. After Godstowe I went to Roedean. I did enjoy it, I made great, lifelong friends and learnt a great deal about certain aspects of British life. The way the Establishment works. I learnt discipline which I had never had, and to value friendship, which was very important because at the end of the day that was all that really mattered. It was what kept you going. It was a very spartan life. I felt completely different to the other girls, but then I was different. I had a different religion, which I continued to practise. That was something I learnt about the British: they were very tolerant. I started off going to chapel and all the rest and then I got fed up and told them that I was Zoroastrian and they said, 'We understand.'

BRIGITTE NEWMAN: The system the British middle classes and upper classes take on board at their public schools is hysterical. The segregation of the sexes, the toughening, the spartan element, the clan feeling, the idea that you belong to the school, you sing the school song, you learn the school verse, you stand on your head in a paper bag with your knickers down doing so, the bullying, the initiation ceremonies that the young boys go through, the rituals that leave you totally classified and coded, the fact that there are twenty-eight ways of wearing one's jacket depending on one's year, the buttons, the lapels, whether one may wear this or that waistcoat or socks, the fact that indeed one will get beaten if one has the wrong button of one's jacket done up, the beatings themselves . . . I am amazed that after all that one ends up with a charming husband with reasonably normal bed manners. It's fascinating, and I wonder how they get there, how they jump the bridge from school to life. Because it's all very extraordinary to a foreigner. It's a pretty extreme education, which has as its consequence the denial of pleasure, the learning of one's place. It's Army stuff. When you join the Army you have to learn to obey, to obey orders blindly. At the same time you are made to feel that you are ready to die for the group you belong to. Public schools are very similar. You can only take all that humiliation because at the same time you are given the uniform. Uniform is *not* something that just makes everybody look the same and therefore is modest. It is something that puts you aside from the others and makes you special, and I am convinced that that is how it is understood in public schools. So when English people tell me the uniform is good because it breaks down social barriers and makes everyone equal, they are wrong. There are no social barriers to break down in a public school: the uniform makes you part of a group and makes you proud of it.

MIRANDA LOVETT: It was very difficult for me to decide whether our kids should go down that road – private schools, Eton – but one of the things I have realized – and I may be completely wrong – is that if you come out of these establishments an asshole, it's because you went in an asshole and you're going to be an asshole for your whole life. What goes on at home is far more important than what goes on at school. I know there's a paradox, I know they're at boarding school, but they're our children. I go to their prep school and I see them and I'm going, 'Come on boys, give me a kiss!' and they back off. They said to me once, 'Not here, please!' I'm like a Jewish momma when I get there. All the other mothers go (English accent), 'Oh, hello Harry, how are you. Jolly good term you've had this time.' I'm not like that. I've made sure they remain very aware of their American side. And for the first forty-eight hours of a holiday there's definitely a deprogramming.

LYDIA SPITZ: In a way our home life worked to neutralize the effect of English schooling. We had a very different attitude to bringing up children. When our son started secondary school he was scared stiff by the stories students already attending the same school told him. Corporal punishment was administered according to the seriousness of the 'crime'. It worried us too as we knew that fear would not help our son to settle down and perform well at school. We were advised that if we were against corporal punishment, which we were, we should write to the headmaster and explain our views on this. So we did, we explained that our child was never punished in any way, that we were against corporal punishment on principle and could never accept it as a method of correcting misbehaviour. The headmaster promptly replied that they had virtually no corporal punishment anyway, but if the child behaved in such a way as he deserved it, he would be dealt with in the same way as they did with any other child. We felt hopelessly sad and expected to have trouble but luckily enough we never did.

MICHAEL IGNATIEFF: School is decisive in English society. Single-sex education does something very odd to English men. I'm much less troubled by the overt educational elitism of these places than I am by the single-sex thing.

I should add I'm the product of those schools myself and maybe that's why I am hyper-sensitive to that system.

LYDIA SPITZ: When I learned about corporal punishment I could not believe it. It was like a regression to the Dark Ages, particularly when I related it to what we were trying to achieve as teachers in our developing country. Finding out that this country, to whose ideals we looked up, had so many deficiencies, so many gaps in its 'educational system'. It is not that I dislike the level of acquisition children reach, it is just the concepts behind it. The tendency perceived – in the kind of training – to suppress personal development and individual initiative, to mould children's personality into a final product which must fit in exactly with society's requirements.

Quite familiar with the proverb 'you can lead a horse to water, but you can't make him drink', and having come to realize that it is possible to teach until doomsday, but this does not necessarily result in learning, it appeared to me that new approaches to education were imperative.

ENNIO CAMISA: I went to school for two or three months. At that time school finished at fourteen, you can't go after fourteen, they send you out. If you pass, if you don't, it doesn't make any difference. At fourteen you've got to go out. The school was in Chelsea, the Italian school, Dom Bosco College. It doesn't exist any more. I got the 19 bus. And at fourteen they said, 'You've got to go.'

* * *

MICHAEL DE SOUZA: I went to Warnington Infants' School. My mum took me and it was tears, deep worries. I didn't stay long. It wasn't too bad. There were two guys who really looked after me. The teacher was quite good, very friendly, and made me feel relaxed. I left there and the next episode of crap came about. My mum didn't have much contact with the school and when I had to leave the infants' she wasn't even aware of it. So I turned up at infants' school one day and the teacher said, 'You're not here. You've left. You're at Bevington.' I said, 'What?' I don't even know where it is, but I had to deal with it, and I ended up going to my first primary school on my own. That was tears and frightening. Fortunately one of my friends from Warnington was there and again he looked after me.

MANZOOR BAHADUR: I was the only Asian boy at my school. The treatment I got from the teachers was absolutely great. I don't think any other child could get that sort of attention in today's schools. I couldn't speak English when I arrived, not a word. In fact I hadn't even been to school in Pakistan to read Urdu, let alone English. To the credit of my teachers when there were English lessons I would be taken out of the classroom and given lessons to myself.

'That's a finger, that's a hand, that's a leg,' and so on. So that's where my formal education started. Even at that very early age I felt it was a challenge. Whether it was because I had missed out on education in Pakistan, but I thought, 'I've been missing something here. There's nothing wrong with school life, it's quite good. Perhaps I've got a bit of catching up to do.' So I set my sights on doing well and I enjoyed it. But because there weren't many Asian kids around we used to get picked on. It was natural enough – kids always pick on a scapegoat, and I was something different. The number of times I'd go home and either someone had given me a good hiding or I'd given someone a good hiding. My father just said, 'Don't ever get scared. If they find out that you're scared, then life really will become a misery.' So I owe a lot to him for that sort of advice. It may have been aggressive advice, but it taught me to look after myself.

VINCENT REID: In 1951 I went to Vernon Square Secondary Modern School, in King's Cross. I stayed there until I was fifteen. I was the only black child. I was very lonely and frightened, the whole thing was strange. They used to give you a third of a pint of milk. My first day in school, I was drinking this milk and some boy came up and said he was going to beat me up. I said, 'Why?' and he said, 'Well, you're a nigger.' I said, 'What difference does that make?' and he said, 'Well, you're a black bastard. And I don't like you.' I said, 'You don't know me. How can you say you don't like me when you don't know me?' He went on like that, so I kicked him down the stairs. Having done that and had one more fight that was it.

MICHAEL DE SOUZA: My school had very low expectations of black kids and I didn't have a great deal of expectation of the school. All I knew was that I was just using my brain to have the easiest life I could. I loved sport, and certain subjects I liked and certain I didn't like. I couldn't stand history: they were telling me about Kaiser Wilhelm and bloody Jethro Tull – what did that mean to me? I wasn't disruptive: they always put me down as 'quite bright but easily distracted'. Which I was. I wasn't one of those thickies who just come to school and they don't give a shit and the teachers don't care and they're there playing draughts – though they couldn't have been that thick, some of them were playing chess. There was a lack of caring by the teachers. I clashed with some of the teachers. The Indian teachers, the women teachers. I didn't think about it that deeply, I just knew the whole school was shit and they just didn't care. All you need is for someone to sit next to you and say, 'Are you all right?' and it makes a difference. But there was none of that.

SHREELA FLATHER: In 1968 I got a job teaching English as a foreign language in a boys' secondary modern school. The sort of school that everyone writes off. Everyone who went saw themself as a non-achiever and nobody there had done anything to alter that self-image. Which was when I came in contact with, if you like, the *real* immigrants. Sikhs and Muslims, young boys who would arrive at the age of fourteen, spend one year in an English school and then go off to start work. They would do all the cooking for the all-male households in which they lived. Nobody cared about their education, because everyone could get a job and what did it matter if you learnt a bit of this or that or didn't. So there was this problem of complete non-motivation. The headmaster told me at my interview that the remedial department was just for 'our children'. The whites. So the school didn't bother about these immigrant children at all. They sat at the back of the class looking at colour supplements. Nobody bothered to teach them anything. I don't know how it was elsewhere. In larger communities, who had arrived earlier, there was some effort to help. In Birmingham, places like that, there were quite a lot of educational initiatives. There was the notion that they must have language support, that they must be helped to get over the culture shock. The policy was to encourage assimilation at that stage, and this was what you were meant to do. So the initiatives were there, although what effect that had on the ground I do not know. But the main thing was the status of these children, and their self-perception, frightened me. I tried to give them some sense of pride and some basic English so they could at least read the road signs and fill out forms.

MIKE PHILLIPS: The worst thing that has happened to the black kids in this country is to be educated here. Most of the teachers that I knew have a fixed sense of the black kids that they teach which is thoroughly racist. Even given that what they are concerned about is multiracial education or whatever, they still think of it in terms of the child's capacity. If you are teaching music the thing to teach the black child is not the violin or the cello or the piano, the thing to teach the black child is how to play in the steel band. Why? Because that's *his music*. This is a totally racialist view. I am always struck by the way in which this notion of different kinds of knowledge is characterized in a racialist way. I read Dickens when I was a boy – there was nothing else to read. I am deeply grateful that I did. I am deeply grateful that I studied English literature, I regard Shakespeare, Donne, whoever, as part of my heritage as an English speaker. I am deeply irritated by the notion that anyone would present to my son an idea of himself which distances him from those things and says you've got to read African poetry just because you are black. A version of that begun to happen twenty years ago and one of the things that has happened with the concept of multiracial education is that it has become a way of presenting second-class theories of images and knowledges to immigrant children, designed more to keep them quiet than to educate them. So they're saying, 'Don't teach him the history of the United States, just tell him about the

236

American civil rights struggle.' So many of the things that these kids are having presented to them don't make any sense outside the context in which they originally take place. Since there is very little writing about black people in Britain, all these kids are being told about Africa or at a pinch the Caribbean or black America. None of which they quite understand or identify with. But they are constantly being told to identify themselves only in terms of their race.

VERNA WILKINS: In Surrey, where we live, obviously the teachers believe that if you're not white you can't be all that compos mentis. So my sons had a bit of trouble at primary school. I took the older one to school, dropped him off and there it was. About five weeks later I got a message from the teacher saying that so far he hadn't done anything. I asked what he was supposed to have done. 'Well', she said, 'we're doing phonics and he just walks away.' She had interpreted all his behaviour: the fact that he walked away from the group was him being anti-social, the fact that he didn't stay put in the classroom meant he was hyperactive. Now this was the same list that would appear in the tabloids to describe the 'typical' black child. Hyperactive, disruptive, short concentration span, the whole list, and she had them off *pat* and she fitted them on to him. She had these labels she could fit on to him and he was just labelled. One time he scratched all the skin off his nose in class, so now he's disturbed. He was just bored out of his skull. Eventually I went in and I took my husband with me: I said, 'OK, I wasn't educated in England, but perhaps you'd like to talk to my husband and explain how you've interpreted our son's behaviour. But by the way, I hope by now that you've found out that he can read.' So they did a reading test on him and he had a reading age of ten. He was only four and three quarters and he'd taught himself. They had no idea. The truth was that when he walked away from the class, his 'hyperactivity', he was trying to get to the reading section, the quiet corner. That sort of behaviour was frowned on. He didn't want to listen to phonics – c-a-t and that sort of thing. But he couldn't verbalize what was happening. He was reading *Janet and John* at school and reading *The Hobbit* at home. So we moved him out of that school.

MIKE PHILLIPS: School actually put me off work to an amazing degree. I was totally confused. My parents' notion of a good thing for me to do as an educated person would be to become a lawyer or a doctor or a minister of religion. Nobody at school expected anything of the kind and this made for a ridiculous disjunction between who I was at school and who I was at home. I didn't make any friends. To this day I wouldn't want to see any of the kids I knew at school. There were fights, but that was normal. Partially because I was black, partially because I did the work. The one complicated the other: I was black, I wasn't supposed to be good at work, I was supposed to be an athlete – which I wasn't. The other black guy in my class was a very good cricketer and he sang and people respected him for those things. Me they despised, because I couldn't do what I was supposed to.

WILF WALKER: I was here two days and then I was sent off to school in Shepherd's Bush. That was when I began to realize that something, not exactly a reputation, had preceded me. What it was was that on the television, just as it happened with the Ugandan Asians many years later, there was all this discussion of the problems a mass of immigrants were bringing to England. So all the kids in my class and in my school – I was the only black boy in the upper school – had an attitude towards me as one of these people who were 'flooding the country'. It was a negative attitude. I was one of those poor people who had come over here to steal decent white people's jobs, blah, blah. So there were a lot of fights, I called a lot of guys out.

SIMI BEDFORD: Of course racism did exist at school. We didn't call it racism, not at the age of six, but what we did know was that there were a lot of tensions. The mathematics mistress told me later that she thought of me as a little savage. If, when I first went into her drawing-room, they had put a baboon or a little chimpanzee down on her carpet it would have elicited pretty much the same response. I didn't make it any better, because I was given a piece of madeira cake, which I had never seen before in my life, we didn't eat cake, and I thought what the hell is this? How do I go about eating it? There were a whole load of crumbs all over the floor. So the assumption was that I was a savage. She definitely had a problem – she was awful to me and I instinctively resisted. I was very arrogant myself, because I thought I was bloody fantastic. When I was greeted like this, I simply responded by a Nigerian brand of aggression. I just thought, 'These people are mad.' Which meant I had a very difficult time. On the other hand people were telling me, 'You've got to be an ambassador for your country.' On the other hand there was what I called the Masai warrior syndrome: they either attributed absolutely base or absolutely noble things to you. Either way it was stereotyping: the noble savage or the savage savage – and neither was me.

* * *

MIKE PHILLIPS: My real problem was that I had been to a school in Guyana which was a very good school: it was competitive, people expected to go to university abroad. Then I came to a typical north London school. On the first day the first thing I did was when the teacher came into the room I stood up. We had always stood up when a teacher came into the room. Everybody started laughing and swearing at me: 'Fuckin' siddown!' Nobody, nobody had ever sworn at me in my life. All the mistakes I made in the first week or two were to do with being polite, with treating the school work as if it was a good thing to

238

do. Back home when the teacher asked a question you stuck your hand up if you knew the answer. Here they all sat there, swearing. I found the classroom culture very difficult to cope with, that was the major thing. I found the work very easy. I had read a lot, that had been normal and conventional in Guyana. Here the kids I was with hadn't read anything and you couldn't talk to them about books. The teachers themselves found me very strange. There was one teacher who would always come up to me with a grin and ask, 'What are you reading now, Phillips?' One day I told him *The Meditations of Marcus Aurelius*, which was what I had been reading, and he pissed himself laughing.

VINCENT REID: One time we were doing Shakespeare, for some unknown reason, and there was a bit of a soliloquy, Brutus in *Julius Caesar*, and he said, 'Who can interpret this?' and I put my hand up. He said, 'Well, yes?' I said, 'It's about ambition, he's trying to justify the murder of Caesar by arguing that Caesar is in fact betraying the Roman people, that he's no longer an emperor striving for the people, he's simply usurped power for selfish reasons,' and so on, this detailed explanation. I was never asked a question again.

SIMI BEDFORD: I was seen as an enormous challenge. The greatest challenge the school had ever seen. When I arrived I did speak English, but it was a mixture of pidgin and a very heavy accent, because I spoke servants' English. While all the girls were talking 'properly'. When the headmistress, Madame Dulac, was faced with me she could not believe it. Also I was not an attractive child. Nobody could manage my hair, so it was shaved – I looked like Frank Bruno. So by the time I was twelve I was this very large, jolly hockey-sticks number, the gym-slip, the whole bit, but black. I was a real chameleon figure: in order to survive I had to do everything best. So I was top of the class, in all the teams, I could do anything. I had to. Otherwise I would have been pulverized. You had to be better so people couldn't put you down. Nonetheless, even after I had come top in English language and literature at O level and was starting A levels, the English master sat us all down and told us, 'We're going to have to be very careful with Simi, because she has not had the advantage of our cultural heritage.'

TONY GIRARD: My daughter goes to a convent. Everything has been all right but recently a new teacher has turned up who seems to dislike black kids. Every time he asks a question, no matter how many of the black kids put their hands up with the answer, he will pick a white one. But the class is very friendly and they got together and decided that no white kid will put their hand up, but they'll let the black kids answer. Then they can see how he'll react. So he asks a question, all the black kids who knew the answer put up their hands. He looked around and saw all black hands in the air. So instead of picking one, he just told them the answer. How do you beat that?'

GULZAR KHAN: Our children are not getting a chance. All our children are channelled into dead-end subjects. Subjects that will not lead you to a job after your have finished school. They are not trained in subjects that will help them. So our children are becoming under-achievers. Education is the key to society and if your name is Khan that won't let you inside the door, however clever you are, without qualifications written down on paper.

VINCENT REID: The new education act is going to do further damage to black interests and black people. Once you come to local authority control, and given the secretary of state can set limits on expenditure on education, then all kinds of courses and opportunities are going to dry up and go. They won't be funded. Some of those courses will be 'access courses', which give people who haven't benefited from normal education a second chance, and meet their aspirations and help them to contribute to society. But they will not be feasible under the act. The people who will lose out are black, because by and large these courses are set for them. And even at school level you're going to get deprivation and disadvantage. Once the proposals are adopted and people have the ability of opting out, they will. After the middle classes have gone, then the upper working classes, what've you got left? What you have left is schools to which teachers won't come, even if you can recruit them, what you will have will be ghetto schools, schools that are all black. What you will have is yet more evidence that black people are failures, that they're idiots, they can't learn anything.

MIKE PHILLIPS: This is what happens to black kids: the first thing is you go to school. Now that's crucial. Where you live and where you come from doesn't matter. I can't negotiate that. In my family if there was a gutter near by then we came from it. Though now in the terms of the countries we live in, we are all fairly successful people. What mattered was the kind of education we got. The kind of notions about ourselves and our possibilities that we were imbued with. That was all. What happens now when black kids go to school is that all, or almost all, emerge from school semi-literate. These kids are probably better off than I was, they are almost certainly less subject to racial pressure than I was – there's more of them, they have more things to do, there's more self-images and all the rest. So one way or another the system creates them in the way that they are. I think it begins with multiracial education; it begins with the idea that they are not capable of what a 'normal' English child would be capable of. So you don't give them this or that do do, you don't encourage them to do this or that, you hope that they'll be good athletes or boxers or something. I pay someone to give my son extra maths lessons every week, and the reason I do that is because I cannot trust the teacher in his school to teach him maths. Because it is clear to me that the teacher in his school, a very nice liberal young man, also thinks that it is not the sort of thing that a black kid will be good at. I teach him English myself – literature and so on. It's clear to me that the teacher at the school isn't too bright, and apart from not being too bright (which doesn't matter for a teacher), he actually doesn't see an understanding of English language and literature as being relevant to the needs of black kids. If you leave a black kid to this school system he (not she so much because the girls do better because white people aren't so afraid of them) will be very very lucky if he emerges being able to read. So it all starts in the school system. What happens then is that the black kids create their own culture within the school system. A culture of *not learning*. They start off by knowing – because everything around them tells them so – that they are not going to make it. So they erect a culture that is based on not making it, which makes a virtue of not doing well.

SIMI BEDFORD: In 1958 I went to London University, to be interviewed to read English. I had had to write an essay called 'An author should not be a judge of his characters but a witness. Discuss.' I thought that the way to make myself stand out was to talk about novels that nobody else would. So I talked about Disraeli. The interview went very well, which I expected, because I was very arrogant, thought myself bloody marvellous. Then they asked me to read a paragraph, which was all about a factory. I had to tell them the meaning of three words: input, throughput and output. I thought they were completely potty, these little middle-class academics with their pipes and their tweed jackets, and I said, well these are clearly Americanisms which have crept into the English language. So they said, 'Yes, yes.' I said, 'Do you ask all the students this?' They said, 'Oh no. Only where English is not the mother tongue.' At which point I said, 'I'm not coming to your university.' I went to read law at Durham instead.

16 The Problem of Identity

'It's the severing of childhood that makes the difference for an immigrant.'

BENNY BUNSEE: All Third World people who have been heavily colonized, and particularly those who have always been a minority, have enormous problems of identity and culture. We have faced the domination of the West and of the white people and we don't want to be integrated into their culture. Western culture is alien to us, especially the individualism of western life. We like a more communal society. Even the rationalism that dominates European society, on the basis of which such ideas as legality and human rights have developed, doesn't in the end seem to be very appealing. We want to rediscover our own cultures and our own histories. To adapt them to the modern world and build the kind of society in which we can be free, respected and dignified.

YASMIN ALIBHAI: My identity is very much that of a British Asian, which is not the same as being an Indian born in India. I don't see culture as a static notion. I see it as a volatile, ever-changing, re-processing dynamic, and it has to be if it's going to survive. What is important to me is that certain values that are gained through being Asian in origin, are extremely valuable in this very cold world. So I don't care who my son marries, or if he prays or whatever, but what is important is the lessons that my mother taught us: how you think about yourself, that you don't think that the world owes you personal happiness, which is the central philosophy of life in the West. The question of individual fulfilment at the cost of anything: personal happiness becomes a kind of apple to which everybody is entitled. Our lives are not like that. At least fifty per cent of our happiness is defined by the family or the community. From the time you are a child you learn to sacrifice a part of your life. I admire those values. I don't want to lose them, because if you've got that belief it isn't that difficult to look after the old, it isn't that difficult to occasionally make decisions which hurt you but which hurt others less. I don't find this in Britain or in the West generally. The spinal fluid of the West remains based on this central principle: every individual has the right to go for personal happiness and personal fulfilment, and that's the most important thing. It's completely different in the East: you learn that you are important but not the most important thing in the world. The circle immediately around you, and all the circles beyond that are equally important if not more so.

ZERBANOO GIFFORD: I do have different thought patterns and I do have different values and I know that. The way that I write and think is very much

242

in stories and I don't think in English words and patterns. My basic language is English and I dream in English but I often go into certain words which are Gujerati and there's no translation. We spoke English at home but my parents also spoke Gujerati. I really regret not doing Gujerati O level, but who would have thought that in politics at this stage there would be so many East African Gujeratis and how important knowing their language would be. Though in the late '6os Gujerati wasn't available anyway. Instead people talked about 'Indian': 'Do you speak Indian, do you speak Hindu?' I used to wonder what they meant.

SHREERAM VIDYARTHI: My father had inculcated in me a strong sense of personal character and he had given me a sense of identity and sense of pride in being an Indian and a Hindu. Which neither made me feel hatred for the rest of humanity nor did it give me any sense of inferiority or of superiority between races. My father was always at me, always giving me some kind of sermon or another. He never allowed me any time to play on the street or abscond somewhere and see a movie. Perhaps that was why I liked running away. I don't know, but certainly I used to run away every time I got the chance.

BENNY BUNSEE: My education in South Africa aimed me towards a wester-nized society. When you are born in that kind of milieu you don't have an authentic identity. You don't have a South African identity, you don't have an African identity – because you're cut off from that culture and assumed to look down upon that culture: Africans are supposed to be savages without any history or achievements. India was something I was clinging to, in an attempt to assert my own individual identity.

CHRISTOPHER HOPE: The nature of South Africa means that all of us have been denied an identity. We all pretend to have one, but our real role until now has been to be either white or black. So I never had a feeling of having any roots at all. It was impossible to locate yourself in South Africa, because it was just a geographical convenience, not a real place – I still feel that. For those of us who grew up in the '4os and '5os, it wasn't a question of feeling homesick when you went away, because you felt homesick before you left. South Africa is not a country or an issue, it's a cauldron. That makes it difficult either to leave or to rejoin. If you come out of the Caribbean, however small the island, if you once lived in Pakistan or India, you know who you are. You never have that sense in South Africa. There, you're not sure who you are and sure as hell, you're not sure who the others are.

BENNY BUNSEE: I wanted to become a writer and the medium I had chosen to do this was through the English language. I never looked upon it as a colonial language, I just saw it as natural. I never asked myself, 'Why am I

243

speaking English, this is not my native language?' I always aspired to be a good writer and speaker of English, which is something you find in all colonial situations. So I was acquainting myself mainly with English literature, with western literature. And I was acquainting myself more and more with the western way of life, with western philosophy, with western ways of thinking. All of which was taking me away from what I would now term my black roots.

VU DUY TU: We are the Vietnamese; we are quite different to the other ethnic minorities. Due to our education, to our traditions, to our life. We live quietly. Sometimes the English ask me, why don't you demand your benefits, your rights, like the blacks do? But we don't. We accept the situation. We just think we are lucky to be received as refugees. That's more than enough for us.

PETER VO: As Vietnamese people we are very concerned about maintaining our culture, our traditions, our customs, our way of life as Vietnamese. Because that could help us to maintain something for our children. If we lose our roots, it would not be good for the future. Therefore we maintain our community. We try to organize meetings in which our people can communicate, can exchange ideas. As the Vietnamese people we are an ethnic group living in Britain and we have something to offer, something to give our host country. In order to do so we have set up classes and many children attend them. We have a grant from ILEA – £1,500 per year – and we have four tutors helping our children learn Vietnamese.

We celebrate our national festivals – New Year, mid-Autumn – and try to make sure that our children still know the traditions. We also want to encourage our children to learn Vietnamese, and to learn more about the culture. The children are very enthusiastic. We also have a Buddhist temple, since Buddhism is the major religion of the Vietnamese people. We have used our own money to build a pagoda in Lewisham. This is another way of keeping people together and maintaining our culture. Vietnam also had seven million Catholics, and we have a Catholic centre in Peckham. I'm also one of the founders of that centre. But we are certainly worried by the inevitable breaking away that comes in the second generation of immigrants. Our children adapted very quickly to the western life. Western life has affected Vietnamese families a great deal. And we are very concerned about this. At the same time as we have to maintain the culture, we also have to accept these new western influences. A number of Vietnamese families have started to live very much like westerners. Many live completely like British people. For example in Vietnamese society we do not accept living together before marriage. But in Britain it happens. So it happens for our people too. There is a degree of intermarriage, and if it works that is OK, but the ones I know have not succeeded. People have been unhappy, the cultures are still too different. But perhaps in a few more years, when the

Vietnamese have learned more about Britain, and the British have learned about the Vietnamese, then it could be good, it could work out. What matters is that both partners should feel happy.

CHRISTOPHER HOPE: The argument about holding on to one's culture, it's simply not the case. The moment that as a black African, a Nigerian, a Zulu, you adopt as your first language, and in some cases as your only language, English, you can forget about preserving that sense of yourself which is most precious. But most people are so busy keeping afloat that taking a stand for your culture, for your racial disposition, your religious beliefs, I don't think it's on.

SIMI BEDFORD: In 1959 I rediscovered Africa. I had to wait a year before going to university and my parents had bought a house in Wembley Park and a load of my Nigerian cousins were in England by now, studying, and I began to meet them all. We formed this whole circuit and my life then went from being totally English to being totally African. I was back in the fold. They were all like me, refugees from this English education system. Every Saturday, at different town halls, there would be a Nigerian dance. Fela Kuti would play Nigerian High Life music – which didn't interest the West Indians, so it was all West Africans. We spent a lot of time going to parties at the High Commissions. There were four, one for each area of the country. I went around with this group, mainly black or Asian. Suddenly you could give up trying to look like Sandra Dee or whoever. There was the Ronettes. Changed our lives. Suddenly black girls were seen as beautiful. You went from being this hideously ugly Frank Bruno figure to being Ronnie Spector. It was quite extraordinary. By the time I went to university in 1960 black was where it was at. All that soul music. Then here were all these fine art students at Durham University who were into Benin bronzes and African masks and tall thin women and suddenly here were these people saying, 'You are a great beauty.' I thought, 'This is all right then.'

BENNY BUNSEE: I would describe myself as an African now, because I am committed to the African struggle in terms of South Africa. To me the Africans are part of that Third World that has been massively oppressed. I have always sided with oppressed peoples: if the English were heavily oppressed tomorrow I would side with them. At the end of the day it's about liberation, about freedom. I can honestly say I don't care about colour, but I have to care about it because I have to confront the world in which I live today. I know what has happened to black people.

* * *

RONALD HARWOOD: Coming here and being born here are two totally different things. It's the severing of childhood that makes the difference for an immigrant. I've written a play – *Another Time* – about coming to England. It starts in '51 with a young Jewish pianist coming here. The second act is thirty-five years later, and he still doesn't belong, he still feels isolated. I think the idea of coming here is not make a new life, but to be somebody in a bigger arena. That ambition to *be* somebody. Though you mustn't fall into the Faustus trap and be somebody at any price. But that's part of one's drive, this need to be somebody.

WILF WALKER: In my teens I spent all my time with my Holland Park friends, white middle-class people. Now some of them are dead, some of them are junkies, some of them have gone away. I had met them through this Anglo-Indian kid in my class who didn't see himself as black, although his dad was Asian and they lived in a council flat. He befriended me. Another outsider. And he knew a guy who went to Holland Park school. I didn't understand how fucked up the English were, in terms of who is English and who isn't, and class and all that shit. It was a totally white scene. There was a big black scene in the Grove, but I wasn't part of it. Though I had known the Critchlows back in the West Indies, they lived opposite my family. I remember hanging around outside the Rio and not daring to go in, it was rough, though Frank knew me and Victor knew me and if I had gone in I would have been welcome. I was family, but I couldn't make the transition. I could never go into the Mangrove either: candlelight, all the cool dudes. I was just out of that. I was just a little black English boy, and not even that, just totally lost. I could have been something else, the options existed, but they led you to a seedier side of life: down the West End, in the clubs, doing drugs, chasing women, running women. The shebeens, the gambling houses – I know nothing about that stuff. So for me the choice was hang out with these little white boys, go to their little parties, which were very boring – everyone brings a bottle and you dance all night, and if you are lucky you pick up a chick and get your end away – and I never was lucky. This is before Michael X, before black power, and these little girls couldn't get it together with a black guy. I got these Ray Charles glasses. A lot of money. I went to the Swan, where everybody was all sitting around, the Holland Park sixth formers, Polly Toynbee, people like that. This guy sat on my shades, 'Oh, sorry Wilf . . .' – today I'd fucking punch him.

MIKE PHILLIPS: The difference between my generation and the young blacks today is that we didn't think of ourselves as being defined by our race. Those of us who were born and partly brought up in the Carribbean have a different attitude. In this country I am one of less than a dozen black academics. Now most white people and black people brought up here take that to mean that somehow it is not the kind of thing that black people are good at. You can argue about education, and discrimination and so on until you're blue in the face, but at the back of their minds what most people think is that to do that kind of thing a black person must be terrible exceptional. But I grew up in a country where all the teachers I knew were black, the police were black, the judges were black. You didn't have this sense of there being a place for black people that in some way doesn't include things like being an academic or a doctor or whatever. The middle-class jobs. But for the young black kids in England the identity of blackness is a working-class identity. All those notions about being working class are totally negative. Not being middle class is being ignorant, being aggressive, all the rest of it. That's what happened to the black population more than anything else. It's been fed a series of negative images about itself.

WILF WALKER: In '67 I had these two girlfriends, these twins, who gave me acid and pushed themselves at me and I got hung up on my trip on these two bitches. The end result of the acid was that I ended up in mental hospital. I went literally screaming into the night. I packed a symbolic bag, left my house and went to my parents. I couldn't sleep, I was getting more and more distraught. While I was in my parents' house I realized that their life had not changed, they were still doing exactly the same things: getting up at six-thirty in the morning and going to jobs that were giving them no satisfaction and nothing but a very, very miniscule paycheck at the end of the week. The quality of their lives became very much part of my psychosis, this scream for justice. Not just for my parents but for me and all my family. They were trying to tell me what to do, and I was trying to tell them how they were being exploited, and this meant a real conflict. So I had this breakdown. My parents finally called in a doctor, who gave me sleeping pills. Which for me was what triggered the breakdown. Something in those pills made me lose all contact with reality. I slept but I woke tired. In the end they dragged me off to a mental hospital, Shenley. When I got there I had this blonde, blue-eyed psychiatrist. She was scared of me, and I knew she was scared of me. She wrote a report on me saying that she couldn't come to grips with my psyche and she couldn't come to any conclusions as to what to do. I was so stupid, so inarticulate, so backward – she was saying that here was this human being who in effect was finished. But I had a job, and I still had somewhere to live, and if you have these things, you're sane. So I got out after about six weeks.

WITOLD STARECKI: The role of the immigrant is very difficult and very sensitive. To start with, we Poles see ourselves as part of Europe. Our whole culture, our way of perceiving the world belongs to the European tradition so in this respect we feel in no way inferior to the British. The British may see themselves as superior, but you won't find a Pole who thinks that British is better than Polish. No way. We don't have much but we have honour and pride. There is no inferiority complex whatsoever. There may be economic and political differences, envy of standards of living, or of political freedom but not in cultural terms. I believe that my work does contribute to this country. I pay tax, I don't commit crime. I create jobs by hiring British crews. So as long as I am putting in, as long as I am creating, I feel good. I don't feel a parasite.

CINDY BLAKE: I absolutely do think there is an immigrant experience which makes no difference whether you're upper-class American or born in some wretched village in Pakistan. Because what you're talking about is, among other things, having no history. So that you can't say to the person you're with, remember something we did together five years ago, or look at that building, that's where I used to live. You can't refer back and you're very cut off. I think that nobody takes in properly what a major upheaval it is to move countries, and that you don't yourself until it's too late . . . You don't realize what culture actually means. What it means to be able to refer to having seen *Mr Ed* on television, having the same jokes, having the same references. When you can't share those you feel somehow missing. I think that that's why it's very difficult to be an immigrant. So you haven't lived through the same experiences and even when they're supposed to be similar – the '60s for instance – they can actually be so different. All those points of references have moved and you're left without a grid to chart anything. And you're supposed to start from the beginning, but at any age after 0 it's very hard to start from the beginning and build up another grid, especially if it's a grid that you're not particularly fond of.

MOSES SPITZ: I believe that one is rooted to the country of birth, to the place where one has grown up and has had the most significant early experiences. For instance, when we returned back home for the first time, after being away for two years in Sweden or more recently when we went back – under Alfonsin – after eleven years of absence, I then realized how much I missed my town, La Plata. The charm of its broad straight street. The sweet fragrance in the air emanated from the lined-up lime trees. The noisy students coming and going, chatting loudly completely unaware of my tender feelings. Every stone in the street, every tree I climbed when I was a kid, even some of the potholes I could recognize would bring back memories of my childhood and more . . . These things can never be replaced.

SHARI PEACOCK: Losing your country, being an immigrant, is a bigger deal than love affairs. You've lost your past, you've made this cut between the present and the past, there isn't any more flow. So it's the severment of time

248

that's most important. Also there's the severment with the place that is where your family are. You've left people behind. England is central and eastern Europe is peripheral, you have the same division of centrality and periphery as you do with money. Poor people from villages up north coming to the big city, they feel a bit of a bastard for having left the other people behind. You always have this feeling, 'I escaped, and they're still there.' Even though you know that things aren't all wonderful and there are all manner of problems, you still feel, 'I got away.'

VINCENT REID: I don't have to run around with black people to know who I am. I can put myself into any given place in any given society. As far as a lot of white people are concerned this makes you arrogant. Because you don't touch the forelock to them that makes you a racist. You should be grateful for their company, you should be grateful for their wit and wisdom. I don't happen to think they have any. I associate with the middle classes too, I play bridge and so on. I'm a teacher. I love to teach people that black people are not as written and set out in the *Sun*.

MIKE PHILLIPS: The crucial thing to me is the sense in which the black community is a bastard offspring of England. What interests me now is the sense in which blacks and whites in England, and especially in London, are coming to share a difficult identity, an identity which is difficult and which has to be constantly negotiated. Neither side is quite aware of what they are doing, even while they are engaged in the process. Most black people have more relationships with white people than they do with black people. When you go to work you're not working only with black people; you might even be the only black person there. So this theme interests me: the sense in which we are negotiating our identity in this country, what the country is, what the nation is, what we all are, without being conscious of it. The other thing is about London, the way in which I belong to London because London is partly what I have made it. Maybe a tiny part, but still a part that me and my brothers and sisters and friends have made it. When I look at London now it's not an alien city any more, it's a city that we've partly reconstructed. When white people say derogatory things about London, the inner city problems and so on, what they're really talking about is the black community. And what I say is, 'Bugger their luck' – because we ain't going nowhere.

JAROSLAV BRADAC: I'm actually glad that I am not pigeonholeable. When I say hello I can't immediately be put in a pigeonhole – aha, he went to that school, so on and so forth – and therefore he is all right or he isn't. I puzzle people because I have a funny accent, I am strange, they can't really put me where they would like to for convenience sake straight away. They have to wait a little longer. What I am is a foreigner.

WITOLD STARECKI: It's good to be a foreigner: you don't fit anywhere. I have a different accent and I'm not going to hide it or to imitate a British accent. I don't have to be upper, middle or lower class. I can be an outsider, which is the best position, because I can travel across the whole social spectrum. I have been in grand houses and I've been in the gutter and it all interests me. I want to learn about England so in the future I can say something about it.

JAROSLAV BRADAC: At times, when I'm stopped on the street and get asked for a direction, and I'm talking to a total stranger, then I do feel marginally embarrassed that immediately I say what he or she has asked me to say, they will know that I am not the native. They will know that I am different. It's curious but it's the last thing that worries me. Even though this is a total stranger. If I had a choice, I wish that I didn't have my accent, for the simple reason that it makes me classifiable in a different sort of a box. And whatever they are, I dislike boxes. I live in middle-class surroundings, I have an English wife, we have English friends, I don't speak Czech that often. I know I wouldn't be able to live in rural England. London is cosmopolitan and that suits me. These people who set up Chinese takeaways in remote villages, they're so foreign they become part of the local colour, a funfair . . .

---

17 The Question of Assimilation

'The British never thought that others could come to their
island and make a home here.'

FIRDOS ALI: For a white person to expect someone with a different cultural background, a different religious background, to forgo all that paraphernalia and simply to become one of them, eating bacon, egg and chips every morning for breakfast and fish and chips on Fridays is simply not acceptable. The world was not created for white people, the world was never white, it never will be and it never has been. So how can they expect that everyone who walks in over here has to become English overnight. You cannot change the colour of your skin like you can change your shirt, therefore how can you change just like that? If they say, 'We have welcomed you to our country', I say fuck them! They needed us, they didn't welcome us. The West Indians were brought over here by the shipload. So the Asian and Afro-Caribbean communities ought to say, 'OK, you want us out, given us £20,000 each and we will go home. Borrow it from the IMF and give it to us.' I don't think that would happen – the world is too small now. Otherwise they'll have to open up concentration camps, and that wouldn't surprise me.

BODRUL ALOM: Some groups of Asians have progressed a long way towards becoming westernized. The Patels from East Africa are like that – they have the shops, they are seen as doing well, as becoming English. I don't think the Bangladeshis will do that. They have kept their original culture much more. They are farmers and peasants, rather than merchants. Bangladeshis, especially people from that part called Silyhet, are very religious. And because of their religious identity they would like to retain their cultural identity. It would be wrong to pretend that this can be made part of some multicultural cross-fertilization. If change does come, and it may come, it will only come gradually. This is not something that will happen instantly.

MUHAMMAD ALI: It's very difficult to say whether people want to integrate into the mainstream society or not. People who have tried to integrate have had such bitter experiences. When I was at school there were a few Asian kids who considered themselves as English, as white. What they said was that they considered English to be their mother tongue – although it wasn't – and they didn't really want to mix with other Asian or Muslim boys. They wanted to adopt the English culture completely and they did their best to do so. We called them 'natives' and we generally teased them. We all left school and went our own ways. Ten years later I met some of them and they had become completely different. At least two had grown beards, become very religious and were completely involved in the Asian community. I asked them why. They said that they had tried their best to mix with the white community, but they had given up. The English would never accept them, when it came to the crunch they would always be isolated. When it really came down to being accepted as part of English society, it was impossible, and they found a lot more security in their own community. This must stem from colour. It's not just the English attitude to foreigners. Apart from colour there was nothing about these boys that made them different from the English. That was the only difference. They had English accents, they ate English food, drank in the pub, made the same jokes. Everything was the same except the colour of their skin, so logically, by a process of elimination that had to be the cause of their rejection. They might have thrown away their Asian identity, but still they were excluded.

CHRISTOPHER HOPE: What makes things worse here is the problem with colour. The French and Portuguese in Africa fraternized on a basis which was unknown in the British empire. As a result, however great the gap between

251

conqueror and conquered, the conquered spoke the language of their conquerors and it was a reciprocal process – there was literal intermarriage and linguistic intermarriage. This was not the case with the British. It's no surprise to see a black Frenchman, but it is to see black Englishman – he appears in TV comedies, or is the subject of approving noises in liberal circles.

SHREERAM VIDYARTHI: The problem is that the British never thought that others could come to their island and make a home here. They thought that they had the god-given right to colonize whatever territory in the world they chose, but that others didn't have the same right. We have come in – by invitation – and we have asserted our right to be here. So that has provided a great cultural shock to the British. Culturally people from the Indian subcontinent are very open-minded. They'll absorb anything good that you have and still maintain their identity without causing any friction. But the British, every time somebody tells you to wear a different style of clothing, you feel threatened. That's how fragile your cultural identity is. The British might not accept this argument, but they are bloody well suffering from it. Even today the British go on holiday abroad and when they get there they talk about 'bloody foreigners'. This is something that will take centuries to wipe out. It won't happen overnight. The Second World War brought an invasion to this country. It was not a German invasion but it was an invasion nonetheless, because almost all the soldiers, especially the middle and upper ranks, who were Indians, when they were demobbed in north Africa or in the European theatre all chose to come to England. They had lived with English officers, they enjoyed the whisky, the balls in the officers' clubs, and they thought they would come here and perpetuate that luxury.

MUHAMMAD AYYAZ: Our parents fought and died for the British empire. When people say we should change, we say, look at the British. They went to India, and not a bit did they change. I would have expected to see Muslim English, Sikh English in India, but there weren't any. They lived apart, they never changed a bit. It was the Asian people, in their own country, who had to change. So now we are here, why should we change? I will only get self-respect if I live the way I want to live rather than living the way somebody else wants me to live. I don't believe that I can be fully accepted here. At the end of the day I am always Asian. Even if I became a Christian. I am Muslim first and everything else comes second. There are limits: Mrs Gandhi invaded the Golden Temple – look what the Sikhs did. Rushdie was the same for us. We are in exactly the same position. There are places that cannot be violated, barriers than cannot be torn down.

SHREERAM VIDYARTHI: If the English are surprised by the Muslim community, they should realize that they have never assimilated anywhere. Look at

India: Greeks went there and became natives, Mongolians went there and became natives, Chinese went and became natives, some of the African tribes must have emigrated to the plains of south India and become assimilated; the only community who has gone to India and not accepted Indiannness is the Muslims. The British, who had been the imperial power, should have known that this would happen, but imperial powers can never appreciate that what they have done to others might happen to them. They were teaching us 'lessons in democracy' – did they ever give us any credit for living in a democracy? Democracy was for home consumption; in India they were the imperial power. Your police are being trained to address the British citizen as 'sir', ours are trained to hit us on the head. Yet it was the same training school. But that is the hangover of the Raj; it would happen to any imperial power.

RAJINDER SINGH: If I had come over here many years ago, when I was still young, I would have said to my community here, if you have got to live over here you should be part and parcel of this society; you have to take their traditions, you have to go with them otherwise you will be cut off. People who are born and brought up in England, they must follow these traditions. When in Rome do as the Romans do. It is harder for me, because I came only very recently and because I have a language problem – I cannot always express myself, I cannot always understand what they are saying. So I find it hard to mix in. So at my age I feel I'm an old dog who can't learn any new tricks, although I am trying my best. Family conflicts are arising day by day because the older generation doesn't want to give up the old ways and the younger ones, who have been born and brought up here, want to join English society. The youngsters don't want to listen and there is a big generation gap.

RAJAN UDDIN JALAL: People fail to understand why someone wants to maintain a given culture. They fail to remember that when the British went to Bangladesh or Sri Lanka they did not give up their bloody culture, they maintained it, and I believe in people maintaining their culture because as human beings we all have our own culture. Some elements in every culture are good and some may be bad. I look forward to the day when we will all be able to take the best aspects of every culture, but I am completely opposed to this idea that Asian culture is inferior and that European culture is superior.

MANZOOR BAHADUR: They tell us here that we should assimilate, that we shouldn't be talking about segregation, that 'when in Rome do as the Romans do', but I say to those people, 'If that's what you want, why didn't you abide by those standards when you were in India? Why did you have your own separate Christian schools – which still exist in Pakistan – with their own rules?' The British wore their own dress, they ate their own food – what did they give up, what did they take from the Indian culture, a country they had lived in for a very very long time? Just money. So these people who talk about 'doing as the Romans do' are simply ignorant. We'd love to do that if we could see other communities doing the same, but you tell me a race that does. The eastern European communities came here and people say they have integrated, but they haven't. They've still got their own supplementary schools, they speak their own language whenever possible, they still try to stick to their own culture and customs. The biggest difference is that they don't stick out in a crowd, whereas we do. Our actions are noticed straight away. An eastern European person stood in the middle of a white crowd, even if they're doing something wrong, isn't that noticeable, but it's certainly noticeable if I go in that white crowd and don't conform to their norms – this is due to my different appearance.

SIMI BEDFORD: I stayed at my first school until I was twelve, then went to another one. My father came to see me and he had this terrible shock. He had seen me at the age of six, with my little round face, and when we met again I had shot up to the height I am today. So there is this enormous girl, talking like an upper-middle-class Englishwoman. There was this very dramatic moment. The headmistress told me that I had two visitors. So I went in, this big black girl, all gym-slip and jolly hockey-sticks, and there were these two black men. As she closed the door she rather dramatically said, 'Your father is here.' Then shut the door behind her. I looked and there were these two men and needless to say I had absolutely no idea. So I walked in and in my best accent said, 'How do you do. I'm Simi. Which one of you is my father?' Whereupon my poor father went, 'Aaaarrgggh'. I hadn't seen any of my family at all for six years and what they got back was something very different.

BENNY BUNSEE: I have to be honest and admit that Europe is very much a part of me. Whatever I may feel about it, I can no more deny the European in me than I can deny the Indian or the African in me. They are all parts of my world. But I don't want to become an integrated white person. I want to assert my black identity, I want to find the roots of that identity, the historical basis of that identity, the cultural basis of that identity and I want to meet the white person and European civilization as an equal on that basis. Not on the basis of rejecting the West and its people. There are a lot of things about it that I like. It's like that Martin Luther King line: 'I want to be the white man's brother, not his brother-in-law.' Europe is civilized, it has tradition, it has culture, it has history, it's produced great writers and philosophers and so on, it's made a contribution and however much it may have exploited the Third World it remains a civilized, cultured place.

CHRISTOPHER HOPE: I think immigrants do assimilate here, it just takes longer for some. A lot depends on whether you want to. Americans have always wanted to, and the country has made it easier for them to do that. So a slow process of adherence begins and the immigrants assimilate, but of course you do lose your own cultural connections, in the long term. But then the Scots and Welsh still ponder deeply on *their* national identity – one would have thought battles long since fought. A certain plurality, I think, is possible.

ANWAR BATI: Around the time I went to university I decided that I didn't feel the old pull for Pakistan. It didn't mean what it had done as a kid. I no longer necessarily supported Pakistan in cricket matches, which I had always done, India and Pakistan against England. I started supporting England, although this was probably because England seemed to have the weaker team. Unconsciously one decided that one was more English than anything else. Almost my entire cultural inheritance was English. My parents had never pushed anything else at me, somehow they had faith that at some stage I would magically be what they wanted me to be.

RAMESH VALA: According to my friends I'm more English than the English. A lot of that has developed through my profession and the people I see regularly through it. Clients often become friends. A lot of manners that the English expect, when I act that way to my Asian friends – writing thank you letters after dinner parties, things like that – they find it very English. So yes, in many ways I've become a lot more reserved, a lot more English. I don't accept that being accepted in England means sacrificing one's own culture. Because that implies a one-way movement, assimilation, giving up your own culture, which to me is non-acceptable. I think there is a terrific onus on my generation. We have to preserve what is good in our culture, the culture we brought from East Africa, or lose it. We have a wonderful culture and now that Asians are becoming more established here they are bringing people from India and teaching that culture to the next generation. I cannot accept the idea that only by assimilation will we become accepted, because even if we do assimilate we will always retain the colour scheme, so we'll always be different in that sense. The Jews have assimilated to an extent. Some change their names. And unless you know them and their background, an outsider would not immediately identify them as Jews. Whereas for us our names, let alone the colour, give us away.

* * *

SIMI BEDFORD: Some of the most racist people I have ever met have been Indians and Jews, and some of the least racist people I have met have also been Indians and Jews.

BENNY BUNSEE: The Jews originally faced the same sort of struggle as the Asians. They have made a notable contribution throughout European culture because they had to fight. They had to fight to become doctors, to become lawyers, to become accountants, to become anything, because every single door was closed to them. That's why they were so brilliant. What the natives took for granted, they had to struggle for: life was a constant struggle. So in that sense there is a parallel between the two communities. Anyway the Jews are a black race, a Semitic people, like the Arabs. They identify themselves with whites at the moment, but really they are a black race.

LEENA DHINGRA: When I was a teenager, most of my friends were Jewish. They were all born here, they grew up here, they were here. I didn't have any problems when I said, 'My God I've got to be back at 9.30 otherwise . . .' they all knew what family obligations were. We could all sympathize about our parents: 'What the hell does one do with them?' They were also going through some of these *terrible* things. There was one friend of a friend who had married a Chinese girl. They were both just finishing medical courses. His family had performed the death ceremony, the *shiva* for him. He was dead. We could all do shock horror at this, but we knew about things like that from our own experience. They understood how I felt, there was this outside, for them gentile, world.

ZERBANOO GIFFORD: I spoke to the League of Jewish Women. I told them that for me the luckiest people in the world were Jewish women. Whenever I have done things, it has happened through a Jewish woman. They've put my name forward, they've helped me in charities, whatever. And people who I didn't realize were Jewish women, especially in politics, often turned out to be. My husband says there must be some bond between the Zoroastrians and the Jews, as far back as Cyrus when they freed them from Babylon and gave them money to rebuild the temple. Zoroastrians are the only people the Jews don't run down in the Bible. I think that today's Jews, having already gone through the process of moving into this society, understand what we are going through. I think that's it. I think they can identify with us.

GULZAR KHAN: I respect what the Jews have done in this country. They have established themselves. They had money, they were a close-knit community, and that is how they survived. Above all, there is no difference in their colour. There was someone on the council, a Jewish man, who asked me, when we were discussing the situation of the ethnic minorities, 'Why do you keep throwing this thing on that we are discriminated against and that we are from the ethnic minority. I am from the ethnic minority.' I asked him, 'Let us, you and me, go outside and stand on the edge of that road. Somebody will pass and see that there is a black man and a white man standing there. Unless you put on your Jewish skullcap or in some other way identify yourself as being a Jew, nobody will say anything about it. All they will notice is the colour.' That is where racism comes in. The Jews suffered in the '30s and '40s but that time is past. I don't say that they didn't suffer, but they have gone through it and it is over. They have many MPs, some are even in the Cabinet, they have many influential, powerful people in their community. Of course it has taken the Jews maybe two hundred years and today people don't have the time to wait.

DESMOND GITTENS: Marrying a Jewish woman changed my whole life. It certainly introduced me to England in a different way. Previous to that I'd never had contact with Jewish people. I didn't really know the difference between them and any other white. If you had stood next to any other white person I wasn't going to be able to say this is a Jew, that's a Scot. Even if you'd said you were Jewish I would have presumed it meant some abstract thing. Living with Mandy brought about a huge consciousness of the history of this country and the history of Jewish people, although that's by no means the same thing. It certainly enlightened me on a number of things, how Jewish people look on Britain and how the British looked on Jews. But while we're all immigrants I do think it isn't so bad to be a Jew. Because of the high profile of colour. If you stood next to an Englishman I wouldn't be able to tell the difference. But even if I was born in Britain, even for ten generations, as long as my colour remained then when I stood next to you I would instantly be recognized as something different. Jews would tell me, 'You've got to try to be invisible,' and I'd say 'I can't.' It isn't my experience. Jews can shut their mouths, not mention anything about being Jewish, and things will be OK. But a black person can't do that. But I don't want to be invisible anyway. There are people who say, 'Stay cool, stay in the background, nobody will know the difference – ' But that's impossible for us. As a black you do have a worse experience in Britain as far as discrimination is concerned. And it's worse on both sides. It's worse when you get the liberal who wants so much not to discriminate that they go overboard with a type of patronizing attitude that is just as bad as if he says, 'Get out of here you black bastard, I don't want to deal with you.'

VINCENT REID: I think that Jews have a favoured position here. Lawson, Brittain, Joseph ... these people are part of the establishment. If I were a playwright and I were going to stereotype a Jew I would go back to the East End of the 1930s, to the sweatshops, the tenements that they lived in, and try to replicate the language, which would seem extremely odd. But that's stereotyping: they've moved out of that world, out of the working class into a favoured position. The Jew can choose to assimilate or not, but even if he doesn't in a way it doesn't matter. But the black man cannot assimilate. Assimilation is suggesting that if you give up certain parts of your identity, certain things about yourself, then you can become one of us. That notion does not extend to a black man.

GRETEL SALINGER: People have been very kind to me here. I haven't had one nasty experience. I have met wonderful, interesting people. I have so many stories to tell. People were very, very kind. Also I have never met any anti-Semitism here. Everyone knows that I am Jewish and I make no bones about it. On the contrary, it's the first thing I tell people. 'I want you to know that I'm Jewish. I say that every time. They respect me for it. So I have only very good experiences. I am very proud of it. People who are ashamed of being Jewish – I can't understand it. I get very angry about that. I think it is a marvellous thing to be Jewish. Of course there are some people who don't behave very well, and I am very angry with them. There have been bad times, everyone has bad times, but on the whole I have had nothing but kindness and friendship.

Through my charity work I have met a lot of refugees and a lot of English Jewish people. Compared with the Jews in Germany when I lived there, English Jews are much more aware of their Jewishness. Much more. And the community is much more compact, more together. I am chairman of the League of Jewish Women, and I'm the chairman of one of the Jewish Friendship Clubs based in Hallam Street synagogue. They meet every week for people over sixty. We play cards, bingo, hold raffles, give them tea, go on outings. I founded that friendship club personally, thirty-six years ago, and I still go every Wednesday. Most of them come originally from Russia or Poland. Very few were born here. They adore me. You cannot imagine the love I get from them. They ring me, they send me cards, they give me presents. And if I don't manage to come one Wednesday, they get worried: 'What's happened to you, where have you been, we've missed you.' The Jews in England are very generous. Here people give, you don't even have to ask. They give whatever you want.

* * *

LEENA DHINGRA: In many ways the Indians are the new Jews. The sort of feelings that the English feel towards the Jews they also feel towards the Indians. But the difference is, when it comes to the final crux, you're all Pakis for the bashing. It doesn't matter what you feel, whether you're anti-Muslim or pro-something else, you're all lumped together. Nobody says are you a Muslim or a Hindu, are you from East Africa or India?

MANZOOR BAHADUR: Britain has a history of finding scapegoats. It's been the Jews at one time, the Irish at another, and these days it's the turn of the black

258

community. There are obviously differences between the Jewish community and the black or Muslim community. The Jews have been accepted more readily – at least their colour is the same. So while they get racism, they haven't had that first experience of having the door slammed in their face simply because of colour. At least they've made an entry. In the same way when I worked on the shopfloor in the engineering industry, once I was in there, once people got to know me, their attitude towards me changed, they weren't as hostile, because this somehow made me different from the rest of my community. I was somehow more like them. In the same way the Jewish community managed to get that first foot in the door, whereas we had the door slammed before we got that chance. The Jews eat kosher meat, the equivalent to halal, but that's always been accepted; nobody made any noises about it, no Animal Rights protestors. But when the Muslim community asked the Bradford council to provide halal meat in the schools for Muslim children, all the racist groups protested. The Muslim community was saying – we're tax payers, rate payers, why should we subsidize everyone else to get what they want, but in turn not receive the services oppropriate to our needs – we have a right to demand things which are within the law of this country.

SHREELA FLATHER: The Jews are not that keen to align themselves with anybody else, either. They've made it, but they still don't feel sufficiently secure in their own position to support other minorities. There was a period when people were making moves to bring in the Jewish community to help the poorer Asians, but there was definitely a reluctance. I wrote an article for a local Jewish magazine and called it 'Immigrants of Yesterday and Today'; they changed the title to 'Look Who Has Come To Live Next Door'. My theme was that there were parallels between all immigrants, but the magazine was keen to stress that there were none. But that is common to all immigrants: Asians who have been successful don't want to be associated with those who are less successful. So we are not helping our own either, because of our own fear that rather than them being helped up, we will be dragged down. While I was mayor I also approached an organization of Catholic businessmen who basically take care of fellow-Catholics, and I told them that they were very inward-looking and that it wasn't so long ago when their community had been going through the most incredible troubles. I believed that they should have a fellow-feeling for later immigrants who are suffering now. There was an audible intake of breath – they seemed quite surprised that they should see themselves as a community that had suffered. It's so easy to forget, even after just one generation.

BRYAN GOULD: It seems to me that there is a great tension in Asian culture between the self-help business ethic, which is very Tory, and the family responsibility ethic, which I think is on the Left.

LEENA DHINGRA: In India everyone does their own thing. Everyone has their own little apartheid. We don't regard that as odd. It is not easy to draw the line between what is a Hindu and what is a Muslim. You get people in a Muslim profession who do all the Muslim rituals, holidays and so on, but who at home are Hindus and who will marry their daughters according to Hindu rites. And vice versa. At a certain level people would carry on with their own faith, and at another there is this total tolerance, and at another there is total apartheid, totally separate development. You have houses in which there are separate cooks. If your Hindu friend comes to a wedding he won't eat the food unless it's cooked by a Brahmin cook, so you have a Hindu kitchen to deal with your Hindu friends. In certain Hindu households a non-right person will come and that person will never feel any different but their mug will have been different, their cup will have been different, their plate will have been different and none of those will be touched by anybody else. Unless he really knows, he won't know. It might be the best mug, the best plate whatever, but it will always be kept separate.

VINCENT REID: The Asian culture in a way complements English racism. We're given this notion that Asians are a homogenous whole, which they are not. A Muslim can't marry a Sikh, a Sikh can't marry a Hindu, and within Hinduism you can't marry from caste to caste. What you have is a basically racist culture that fits in very well with inherent racism of the English culture. Therefore an Asian will, in a sense, know his place. And colour matters in Asia – the lighter skinned you are the better you are. No Asian will ever tell you that he thinks the white man is better than him, but culturally he does. Therefore he doesn't strike out. The only time an Asian will strike out is when a West Indian is standing there. Then he calls himself black. On his own he's brown. Asians who come from the West Indies are just West Indians: Asians who come from the subcontinent or Africa are treated with a great deal of suspicion by West Indians: not animosity, but a great deal of suspicion.

RAJINDER SINGH: If the West Indians have a bad reputation, especially their young people, they have themselves to blame to some extent. They have followed white society too much. They have been taken over by English culture. They don't want to work, just like English young people. Whereas Asians have their own culture. It is true that our youngsters are starting to become more and more British, but because of the influence of their families they are still not as English as the West Indians.

SHREERAM VIDYARTHI: It is true that the Asian community has not been well treated. But I take a positive view of that situation. We come in and in order to find our bearings we let you exploit us to some extent. Once we find our bearings, we float our own boats. We don't rely on you forever to look after us. Unfortunately the majority of Afro-Caribbeans come in search of jobs. Very rarely do they branch out in business and no matter what they are doing, whether in a job or in their own business, they tend to consume it the same evening like any European. They neither save for tomorrow nor plan for tomorrow. The Asian community is, broadly, like the Jews, whereas the Afro-Caribbeans are more like the Irish. We have a perception of futures, we have a plan for tomorrow. You could call it an extension of the karma theory which Hindus believe in: what you do today will have a corresponding result in some way tomorrow. If that is to be the case, you must be ready for it, you must make room for it and you must plan for it.

* * *

BENNY BUNSEE: The Jews haven't played the game, they have very definitely retained their cultural identity. Look at the Rastafarians and look at the Muslim community, and their demands for separate schools. They all want to maintain their cultural and national identity in the face of an aggressive, in some ways overpowering, dominating system that just wants to absorb them and make them lose their sense of self. The black struggle is now moving into a new phase, a kind of cultural resistance and that is what the whole Rushdie affair is about. What is called 'Islamic fundamentalism' is a cultural response of the Muslim nations to European domination. It's not simply anti-imperialist, or simply a demand for self-determination, it's also a cultural response. At one stage everyone did try to fall in with the English way. We did try to integrate, to assimilate, but we were rejected. We realized: they don't really want us, they look upon us as aliens, and when they do take us in, it's on their terms – you have to be like them. But then we say, why must we be like them, why must we live here only on their terms? We have our own value system, our own culture, our own history, we have our own countries. And if people then say, why don't you go back to these countries, we say, the situation in these countries, where there is oppression, takes place because of help from the imperialist West. Those oppressive regimes could not last for a single day without the backing of the West.

DAVILIA DAVID: I feel these days that I've become too assimilated, which I regret now. Though it's easier being this way. I've been taking stock of myself – the well-behaving Euro-Pommie type side as well as my Australian side, and wondering where I do live. I do live here, but I'd like to spend more time there, and then make a decision. Emotionally I live in Europe, but all kinds of things are happening in Australia, spiritual, psychological, sociological things. I sometimes wonder if I fit in here. I think I do. I don't find myself talking about 'the English'. I feel that I belong here. Though I still have an Australian passport, even if that's a nuisance when it comes to travelling in Europe because you still have to get a visa. But I want to hang on to my identity.

LEENA DHINGRA: Somehow you have to be discreet. Somehow you have to disappear. But the next step from that is that then you hit out at the community which you've come from. Somehow you get alienated from your own community. You get alienated from the who that you are. You end up denying them. There is this situation in which you might find yourself actively trying, say, to be anti-Jewish if you are a Jew. Or not so much anti-Jewish, but against some of the things which are terribly conspicuous. You will deny those. If you look at the success stories of those Asians who have made it, that's what they have always done. Whether it's *My Beautiful Laundrette*, whether it is Salman Rushdie, whether it is Tariq Ali, whether it is V. S. Naipaul. It's seen as a mark of your independent thought, of your critical faculties. And all these things come together. In the Raj the British never interfered with religion. They made it very very clear that (UK Raj accent) 'you mustn't interfere'. The so-called Mutiny had been all about religion, so that was carefully kept at bay and you cooled the tempers down. The English saw Indian religions as this element of the irrational. They made people go slightly mad and you tried to keep that irrational element down. What the British were doing was 'getting on with the job of ruling and keeping a good administration going and keeping the whole thing well-oiled' and staying nice and polite. So when it comes to something like the Rushdie affair, England can't understand it. It's incomprehensible. So to an extent somebody like Rushdie has been totally colonized in his mind. Even though he talks about the position of the immigrants and so on, he's fallen into this colonized position. He thinks and speaks just like an English public-schoolboy. Which he is.

SHREELA FLATHER: To acquire another culture, a second culture, you actually don't have to give anything up. It's like saying that people only have a limited capacity to absorb culture. I don't think that's true. I think people have an unlimited capacity to absorb culture, and people ought to see themselves as being enriched by experiencing two cultures rather than being diminished by joining another culture. Then there is this issue of religion. I think that if you feel very deeply about your religion you have to set up some way of supporting it outside education. I don't think that school is the vehicle for nurturing religion. It can teach you about religion, it can perhaps teach you the reason why societies need religion and the ethics of religion, but it shouldn't actually be there to nurture your beliefs.

MIKE PHILLIPS: My parents' generation would agree with people who criticize the second and third generations of Afro-Caribbeans as too idle, too English.

They are shocked and startled at what has become of the West Indian kids. It is to do with British society. West Indians are known to be very successful in the United States; you're a West Indian there and you are a very desirable person. The black chief of staff in the White House is a Jamaican immigrant – it wouldn't happen here. That's the point: anyone can go to the United States and become an American, but for us to become English in the same sense is a long hard struggle. British society is for people like us deeply corrupting and enfeebling. One of the things that has happened to people like me and the generations after me is coming to accept an identity imposed on us and, exactly like the English, coming to know our place.

MARIA VOROSKOI: Maybe England's problems stem partly from the fact that England was behaving in such a correct way and let people from the old empire in. This is a small country and there are too many people. Society has become too fragmented. All of a sudden the Welsh must be Welsh, the Scottish Scottish, the Irish Irish and so on. It's like the head of a family who suddenly finds that the house is too small for all those who want to live there. When I arrived in 1947 I saw many coloured people, and I said, 'How come?' They said, 'We need them: the British working class doesn't want to clean the streets or the hospitals, or drive the buses – so we need them.' So I replied, 'If a country doesn't want to clean its own streets, look after its own hospitals or drive its own buses, then we don't deserve streets and hospitals and buses.' Somehow, in every family, there are more and less intelligent people, some who could do much higher work, others who could do lesser work. This is not a matter of knowing one's place, simply of knowing oneself. If somebody says, 'I'm not happy, I'm not satisfied,' I say, 'That is not the purpose of the exercise. We are here in this world to make ourselves a tiny bit better and pass it on. That's all. If during this process we are happy, so much the better.'

MARY ROSE: If you go to another country, just as you have to learn to speak the language, you have to adapt yourself. But there are private things I do keep to myself. I still have my Christmas tree on December 24, as in Germany, but I don't expect anyone else to do that. My friends can share it with me, but I'm not about to force it on anyone else. So while I think Rushdie is a fool to have written his book, I also don't think it really matters. I'd like to see all religion out of schools. On Friday afternoons the teachers can have a holiday and all the children can go to the religious group of their choice. But I have always believed, and I said it fifteen years ago, that the trouble in this country will not come from the black community but from the Islamic people because of their religious leaders. Let them have single-sex schools if they must, but not all the wrapping up, all the religious dress.

MUHAMMAD AYYAZ: To understand the Rushdie book, you must have one basic thing, which is faith. I've read about half a page, and in that half page he attacks five or six people only, but those five or six people are considered to be so respectable that Muslims just cannot question them. Muslims will not question them. This is something which an outsider cannot understand. Secondly, to understand that half page you must be able to understand about sixty-five years of early Islamic history. The majority of Muslims haven't read it, that's true. But their resentment comes from their faith. Here is this person attacking their prophet, and there's nobody who can attack their prophet. My own resentment comes because I know what it is that he attacks. I have read Islamic history, I understand the character of those people who he attacks and tries to destroy completely. These are characters who to me are far, far more respectable than Rushdie tries to make them out. He tries to destroy them, I try to defend them.

TESS WICKHAM: Whatever the content of the book it's totally irrelevant to the issue. What matters is freedom of speech, but unfortunately that has become an issue that is no longer of prime concern to this government. What they want is restrictions, many of which are already in place. The problem about it is that it is very convenient for the Thatcher government. Muslims don't want to fit in, and they deny the premise upon which they are here: that of tolerance of other peoples, of freedom of speech and of freedom of the mind. Initially the government felt affronted – this was an attack on British integrity – but on reflection they all supposedly went off and read the book or had someone read it for them, and suddenly said, 'Well, he's not nice about England either,' and watered down their initial defence.

CHRISTOPHER HOPE: At first the government rose to defend Rushdie, on any basis. Then Geoffrey Howe shifted a bit, saying, while defending his right of expression, that Rushdie had been rather beastly about the Muslim faith. Had Solzhenitsyn come here, or some Jewish writer come out of Germany saying beastly things about Adolf Hitler, would the Prime Minister have stood up and said, 'We understand the offence given to the Chancellor and the National Socialists'? The Rushdie affair exposed all sorts of canting nonsense. This is not a multicultural country, it's a white country that looks, thinks and speaks alike, into which have come groups of people from Asia, Africa and the Caribbean who are more or less tolerated. All the rest is well-meaning nonsense.

GULZAR KHAN: There is this problem with *The Satanic Verses*. People say it is a fiction, that what he says is not reality, but that is not right. If I take your real name, and your mother's real name, and your father's real name and your sister's or wife's real name then that means that I am making a direct attack on you. That is not fiction. Being a Muslim himself, Rushdie knew exactly what he was doing. In my opinion he has done this book very cleverly for his personal financial gain, because he realized how reactionary the Muslim community will become in the face of what he has written.

MUHAMMAD AYYAZ: I was very surprised to not to get any reaction from the Jews over this book. There is a part where he mentions Abraham and says things about him that are not very nice. Now the respect which the Jews have for Abraham is the same as we have for him. So I am really surprised that no Jewish people came out against the book. But then we have a Muslim country like Saudi Arabia and they haven't attacked it either. So maybe it's political.

GRETEL SALINGER: I understand the Muslims, and I understand that they want to keep their religion, but they do it the wrong way. Not this Rushdie business, that's *terrible*. I don't know what one should do to help him. I don't particularly want to read his verses, but everyone has free speech and you can write what you want. It's nothing to do with Mr Khomeini, a horrible person.

GULZAR KHAN: What the Ayatollah did, the *fatwa*, with that I don't agree. One should not interfere with the law of another country. But the press and media did not look deeply at what he said. They just wrote that the Muslims were going to kill a British national. But that is not the case. The Quran says that a *fatwa* must be pronounced if someone acts as Rushdie has done. But to put a bounty on his head, that is not Islamic law. Then politics have come in. No one claims that a person who comes to England and kills Salman Rushdie is any less a murderer than anyone else would be under the law of this country. This is not a Muslim country and the *fatwa* cannot be carried out here.

SHARI PEACOCK: The whole Rushdie affair is a joke, an absolute joke on every side. Looking at the Iranian position, there is no doubt that nobody has read it. I'd stake my life on it. There's no way that the Ayatollah read it. So he's using it as a second war on Iraq. Another way of maintaining some sort of equilibrium, like Mrs Thatcher and the Falklands. Then you come to England and you get all these absolutely ludicrous articles in the *TLS* or the *Guardian*, people pontificating about Islam, perhaps we should this perhaps we should that . . . it's just a joke. Fundamentalism is just an evil, backward system used basically to keep the country down.

STEPHEN VIZINCZEY: What worries me about England is not so much the committed enemy, like the Muslim militants, who are saying, 'By Allah, this country should become a Muslim country!' but all the people who have no allegiance to anything. As a European writer I am very conscious of the fact that I am making references to English culture, to European culture, that I have a frame of reference that is totally alien to Muslims. But a culture helps people to get along because they have common reference points and to have a homogenous culture you have to have those common reference points. If you have a society without such points, if you cannot write a play in the knowledge that all the audience knows what you are talking about, then you cannot have culture, and you cannot even have politics. Instead you get MPs of both parties standing up in Parliament and saying that Rushdie's book should be banned – which is entirely contrary to everything this country is about, or this continent is about today. It's putting us back to the Middle Ages, and I'm very much against that.

MUHAMMAD AYYAZ: I do believe that Rushdie is not going to get away with it. Not that I am going to kill him myself. I simply believe that justice will be done. I have heard people say that the book is the result of a deliberate plot to discredit Islam, and I would argue against that. I look at myself and I see that there are many many faults in our community. I don't believe this is a plot. This is a man whose books had been read by Khomeini himself, and were translated into Persian. To say that he just said what he did without reading Rushdie's book – that's unbelievable. I don't know why Rushdie did it, but he has presented a completely false picture of the faith. I have heard that he was a Muslim himself and then he became a non-Muslim. So he has changed his identity and when some people do that, they simply go against the old identity. Personally I am quite hurt by all this and I don't know what to do about it. Certainly he has done something very very wrong, but we have to consider where we are. The basic principle of our religion is don't point at others, because then they will point at you. I don't start attacking Jesus, saying he did this, that, the other, because then a Christian can say the same about Muhammad. We have to respect others, and here in this country we have to respect the legal framework, even though that legal framework goes against us.

SHREELA FLATHER: If you are non-Muslim in an Islamic country you are not allowed to celebrate your festivals, let alone demand from the State that it should provide for your religion; you're not even allowed to practise your religion quietly by yourself. Since the Muslims know that, how are they not able to see that in England they are not in an Islamic state? In any case, if the State bends itself to the point at which it is going to be able to cater for the Muslims, almost to the point of being an Islamic state, what about the rest of us? We didn't come to England looking for an Islamic country, we don't want it to be anything other than what it is – a very free society. It is not a secular state, it is still a Christian country and it would be presumptuous of me, or any
266

religious group, to demand from it equal status. They wouldn't expect others to do it in an Islamic country, it wouldn't permit them to do it.

MUHAMMAD ALI: People are bitter now. What Rushdie has done is to alienate the community from the mainstream society much more than they were in the past. The Muslim community has started focusing on its grassroots much more than in the past. The Asian community is generally seen as weak by the white world. They are supposed to be very passive. I think it's true. But when it comes to religion, then they have very strong views. England is a secular country and I think one has got to believe in something to understand any religion.

BHAJAN SINGH CHADHA: If you can blaspheme Christianity, then why can't you blaspheme other religions. Or if you don't need blasphemy laws for the other religions, then you don't need them for Christianity. The English always see things from an English point of view, although the Muslims also don't make an effort, they're full of fundamentalist prejudice themselves. In Pakistan, if you are not Muslim, your witnesses will not be accepted in court.

* * *

SHREELA FLATHER: People may say do away with blasphemy law completely, but it is not for us to demand that. It is up to the State itself, a Christian State, to say, we have now decided that law is no longer relevant. What worries me is that through the response of the Muslim community there may develop an attitude to the Muslims that is equally negative. That they are all illogical, unreasonable, that they behave in a way that is not acceptable here. Twenty-five years ago the Muslims would not have behaved like this. This resurgence in their feelings about their religion has come about in the last two decades; it may be that in two more decades they will no longer feel this way. Who knows? You can't live in a society and refuse to make some concessions to the larger society around you. And if it's just a way of complaining, of saying that the Muslim community doesn't get a fair deal in Britain, then there are so many better ways of complaining. There is a lot of racism, a lot of feeling against people of different colour – so why not take those issues up, things that you could actually make a good case for.

STEPHEN VIZINCZEY: It's too late for me to start feeling British, but it is very important to feel European. I'm very pro-English, very pro-European. I'm very much on the side of those who want to keep England English, because I translate that as keeping England a European country. I would not have the right to emigrate to Teheran, because everything that Teheran stands for is inimical to me. I come from a nation – Hungary – which has been oppressed and enslaved by Muslims. So I look at this very differently from the English liberal, who looks at it with guilt. I had a right to come here, because I believe in everything that England stands for. That's a prerequisite for an immigrant. It would be presumptuous for me to go to Teheran and say, 'You become Europeans and worship Shakespeare.' That would be absurd. I believe in the glories of the homogenous culture. I don't object to anyone coming here who says, 'I want to be part of that society.' A little spice in a meal makes it better, a little of something strange can make it stronger – but you can have too much.

MANZOOR BAHADUR: Islam means submission to Allah, to peace, and Muslims are peaceful. Very rarely does the Muslim community get involved in violent activities or start demanding its rights in a forceful way. If the Muslim community is just allowed to get on with life, it's quite passive. We, the Muslims, are willing to play the passive role, as long as people don't go around upsetting us too often. The problem is that many British people think that England is the most tolerant country in the world and people genuinely believe it. They see themselves as having 'allowed' us to come here. They don't know the reasons why we really came – that most of us were invited to do the work that the white people would not do. But they portray it as charity: they've *allowed* us to come to this country, they've allowed us to take over their houses, they've *allowed* us to dilute the education system, they've *allowed* us to take white people's jobs. Those people who think like that don't realize how intolerant and ignorant they are.

TESS WICKHAM: Everyone who is here is here by virtue of a certain degree of tolerance. Whatever party you belong to, inherent in the fact of other races being in this country is the idea of tolerance. That is an absolute one hundred per cent premise on the basis of which I am here as much as any other immigrant. That is the way that Jews have lived side by side with the English, Chinese have lived side by side and so on. I would never want any immigrant – including myself – to integrate one hundred per cent but on the other hand I would never want them to deny the very basis upon which they live here and are accepted here. So I am absolutely against the Muslim attitude to Rushdie. This is very racist but I would like to chuck them out, chuck them all out. I would like to devise some kind of list of questions that they should answer to prove basically that they are free spirits. I haven't actually managed to think up so perfect a list, possibly only God could manage that, but I do think that there is an unbelievable arrogance, an unforgivable arrogance, implicit in the attitude of the Muslim community to Rushdie.

MANZOOR BAHADUR: Most members of the Muslim community in this country think that the Rushdie affair has given the white community an
268

opportunity finally to break us once and for all. Divide and rule. Either to make us become British, or at least to make sure we fall out amongst ourselves. They certainly want to encourage that faction who do want to take on British values, and people like that to question. 'What's happening to the community? What's all this fuss about?' because it's causing a white backlash, white youths coming into areas where a large number of the Asian community live and causing trouble, breaking windows, attacking people. By the time the police get there the white youths have gone. This in turn agitates the youngsters from the Muslim community and when they come on to the streets they are in trouble with the elders and sometimes with the police. And old guy from the community says he is concerned for his safety. He says; 'I can't look after myself. It only needs one white youth to give me a duffing over. Please, for goodness sake stop all this, because I'm defenceless.' So this is a situation that is really testing the Muslim community, should it back off from asking for its demand to ban *The Satanic Verses*, or should it continue the campaign.

RAMESH VALA: *The Satanic Verses* has set us back many many years. I say 'us', because all this rebounds on the entire Asian community. The ordinary English person makes no distinction, to him I'm simply a 'Paki', although in fact I'm a Hindu who came from India via East Africa and he couldn't recognize a true 'Paki' if he saw one. People certainly don't understand the various groups – Shias, Sunnis – within Islam. The thing is that when there's a march in Hyde Park and there's fighting, even if it was deliberately started by somebody from the National Front or some other Fascist party, the adverse publicity hurts the whole community. People start writing to the papers: 'What are these people doing in our country?'

MANZOOR BAHADUR: Here is a community which is saying, 'Hold on, you can't just forget religion. We do believe in God and our whole way of life is characterized by our religion.' We have a complete code of practice which governs how we conduct ourselves in our daily lives. To understand the hurt caused to the Muslims by *The Satanic Verses* you must be able to understand what the prophet Muhammad (Peace be upon him) brings to the Muslim community. Our whole way of life is one of modelling our life around the teachings of the prophet. His life, the things he taught, are what we try to copy as good Muslims. The people who spread Islam, his disciples, when they are ridiculed, when the Prophet himself is ridiculed, only a Muslim can fully understand the actual degree of insult and antagonism. That this has come from a person who was one of us is a further insult. That's even harder for us to accept. That someone of that same background has used the knowledge and experience he had gained to ridicule billions of people around the world. I really believe that Salman Rushdie has miscalculated the book's effect. I don't

269

think he felt that the Muslim community would react so strongly, because he's out of touch. Maybe he thought the odd person might say something, but they would be seen as an extremists, fundamentalists and no one would take any notice of them.

GULZAR KHAN: I am not a very strict religious person, but I am a religious person. I have made the Haj, the pilgrimage to Mecca: I pray five times a day; I try to be as honest as I can; I try to control those sins that I can control; I don't drink, my family don't drink. But that does not make me superior to anybody else. It is my own belief and it is my own feelings that one should have some sort of discipline and that discipline is the basis of one's culture of religion. If you abandon that, then you have no base to your life. You are like a chicken without a head: you don't know which is your own direction. These are our laws. If you practise a religion and you don't believe that the laws of that religion are right – why have you adopted it?

*　*　*

BENNY BUNSEE: When people like Salman Rushdie dismiss the Muslim religion, they don't understand just what spiritual yearning means to people in a world which is insecure, full of anxiety and will always remain so. As Hobbes said, 'nasty, brutish and short'. You can't overcome that. But as science has developed, and rationalism has begun to develop, the idealistic concepts have gone, and a vacuum has been created, and that's why the West still suffers from an enormous spiritual crisis, because it has abandoned its religious roots, other than on the most primitive level.

GULZAR KHAN: Britain ruled India for more than two hundred years. There were many other colonies too. They never integrated into any of them, they never agreed that their own culture should be dissolved by these countries in any way at all. They saw themselves as superior people, they saw their language as a superior language; other people must go to them, not the other way. I respect that if by acting in this way they are saying that they have a religion and it should not be changed. That is their point of view and prerogative. But why do they have to force their views on others? The Muslim community is not trying to do that, they simply want to teach their own children their own religion. After that they can make their own decision. For Muslims there is a book, the Quran, that has never been altered. The Bible has been. The Quran has never been changed in 1,400 years. From day one it has never been changed, the law has remained the same. Now the interpretation may have changed, there may be different meanings for the same words, and because of this there are different sects within the Islamic community. Sunnis, Shias,

270

Wahabis and so on. But none of them differ as to the authority of the Quran and of the Prophet.

MANZOOR BAHADUR: Muslims feel that society at large in this country is unsympathetic to the Muslim community. Particularly since the Rushdie affair, and revolution in Iran, but it's always been there. The difference is that the mask has come off now. People are now in a position where they are actually having to make a decision, even the white liberals, who are having to come off the fence. They're either going to one side or the other. It's becoming a little bit uncomfortable for them now. Muslims think that this country has deliberately characterized this whole Rushdie affair as censorship, but that isn't it. The reason why the white community don't understand what the fuss is about hinges on religion. Whether we like it or not this country is becoming a pluralist society where most people no longer bother about religion. People are not that concerned about practising religion and we are seeing the demise of the Christian faith here. This lack of affection for religion does not allow the society to understand what Muslims are arguing about. People are drifting away from worshipping God, they want to get away from this all-superior being that's created the earth, that's created us and everything we have, and it would be far more convenient for us all to discard it.

ZERBANOO GIFFORD: The Muslims who are complaining about Rushdie have little desire to be part of the larger British society. From their point of view they have felt unwelcome and therefore they have retreated into their own communities and found comfort in their own communities and in their own traditions. The British on the other hand have presumed that they would prefer to take on a British way of life, although I don't know why they have presumed that. I wouldn't presume anything if I was them. Maybe British society ought to look at itself and ask why are these people wanting to cling to their old ways, or just their ways. Do they find them better? That at least would be a positive way of looking at the situation and trying to discover just why these people choose to be like they are. It would be better for everybody if they actually took part in mainstream life. Maybe what is good in Islam they could impart to the communities here.

YASMIN ALIBHAI: Why should the Muslims assimilate? Because of my upbringing, because of my eastern values, I can understand the Bradford Muslims better than I can sometimes understand, at a deep level, my next-door neighbour. Socially I feel more comfortable with my neighbour than with the Mullahs, but the fundamentals of life, what is deeply important to me and what I would like to be very important to my son, still keep me more in common with them.

MICHAEL IGNATIEFF: I can connect emotionally to what an Asian family feels. I remember how bitterly my father talked about his experience of coming here in the early '20s. How totally closed this society felt to him. How angry and hurt and tearful he often was as a result of stupid English schoolboys calling him a Bolshie, taunting him with this word just because he was Russian, when in fact his father was nearly bloody shot by the Bolsheviks. It was a particularly obtuse thing to call someone. I don't want to trivialize or ignore the emotional hurt that you hear in these black and Asian immigrant families, but there's another story to tell, at least about the Muslims I saw when I went to Bradford. What you see is something very subtle. They are negotiating the terms of their engagement with this culture, but they're not negotiating it only on the terms of the majority culture. The kids are watching the same telly my kids watch, then they were going off to the Mosque, then they were coming back and watching a little more telly, or talking about Bradford City football club, then they were coming back and eating their meal not at a table but on the floor. There is this constant interweaving of these customs. I felt that the first generation were often desperately uncertain about the outcome of this marriage of the two, but then I couldn't help feeling that they were still so much more fortunate because they spoke English, that they were raised in what was still a former British colony, than were the Portuguese labourers I saw in Toronto who simply came from Mars in terms of the receiving cultures.

GULZAR KHAN: In the early years, the '50s and '60s, the Muslim community in Britain had the same sort of equal share and part in Britain as any other community. There were no problems. The only difference then was there were less mosques, there were less places of worship, less places for religious teaching and so on. There weren't any children. But when the numbers of children grew, that built up the need for religious education – you have to teach them your culture and your background.

RAMESH VALA: What's needed here is a two-way process – both sides have to make some degree of compromise, but it has to start with the ethnic minority. They have come into a situation where the majority is different and I think that the onus is on them to say, 'Hold on.' If they insist on stopping their daughters wearing swimming costumes at the pool, or stopping them from marrying outside the community and accepting arranged marriages, these are things that have no direct bearing on the British. These are customs, very strong customs, because you are dealing with people who come straight from villages in Pakistan to Bradford. They don't leave Bradford, except to go back to the airport to leave. They stay in their community, and the areas in which they live are totally Muslim. The mosque is near by, the schools are near by – now they're saying, 'Fine, we want to set up our own schools, as the Jewish community did before us.' If they do that they'll have to fund them themselves – they can't demand of the host community that it funds these separate schools. There has to be a compromise.

MUHAMMAD AYYAZ: During the Honeyford affair in Bradford he [Ray Honeyford] was invited to Downing Street. So Mrs Thatcher made the point: she invited *him*, not us. My friend said to me that Honeyford was right, that my children shouldn't be learning Urdu, they should be learning English history. I asked her why. She said, 'It is very, very important that they should do this. This is English history, this is England.' But I said, 'If my son goes back to Pakistan and he can't speak Urdu, surely he needs to be able to communicate, which is more important than learning English history. If he learns English history, he should learn Islamic history as well.' Of course if you are going to a school that is ninety per cent white, ten per cent Asian, then for me to demand that they all learn Urdu is ridiculous. But my children should be able to learn it: they will need it in their life, whether they stay here or leave, and in their religious education, where a lot of the material is in Urdu.

* * *

MUHAMMAD ALI: When I arrived there was no form of multiculturalism. The idea was to send Asian and black people away from their own areas for their education, so there would be more mixing. So each school was given a quota and you were fitted into that. There was no multiculturalism of any kind. I don't think myself that it's a good idea to have separate schools. I do think that there should be a way in which different communities can work together, as opposed to having exclusively Muslim or white or whatever schools. I do favour separate schools for women. From all I hear and all I read women tend to do a lot better in single-sex education. Certainly there should be a provision within the mainstream system for them to be educated in single-sex classes. This is an idea that is being considered in Bradford. Girls in our school, particularly Asian girls, didn't do very well because they were very shy, they would sit at the back, they would only mix with other Asian girls, Muslim girls.

ANWAR BATI: My parents employed someone to tutor me in Urdu, which was the Pakistani national language. He, although a very nice man, was not a particularly skilful teacher in that subject – he was actually a chemistry teacher – but my parents felt that he was a teacher and as such could do the job as well as anybody. But he wasn't a language teacher and one needed a language teacher. Urdu wasn't our family language anyway. We spoke a form of Punjabi that is spoken on the frontier only. Certain bits of vocabulary were similar, but on the whole it was a new language. So I didn't really work. I thought, 'Bugger this! I have to come home from work, from school and now I've got to do two

273

more hours.' So I didn't really learn a thing, which is not something I'm proud of. I wish I had learned it, I wish I'd realized what it might mean: if I had learned to read and write and speak Urdu fluently, my attitude to my own identity might be different. If I had that knowledge to augment my general awareness of my roots, I might have turned out a different person. But I wasn't to know that.

MANZOOR BAHADUR: What Muslims would like in this country is the opportunity of practising their faith, their culture, in a dignified way, in a way in which they are free to go around and to ask for things which are within the law and are rightfully theirs. They talk all about education being responsive to the needs of the community. If the Muslim community is telling the government that we would like separate schools for boys and girls, where is the difficulty in complying with that if it's what a community wants? Of course if you can afford to pay for a public school, that's seen as quite acceptable. But that's class. The 1988 Education Act offers the opportunity for minority ethnic communities to remove their children from Christian assemblies and religious education lessons. This will hopefully allow the children from the Muslim communities to receive a religious education which is in accordance with parental wishes. Some Muslims disagreed with multicultural education because it didn't offer purity of anything. For example, children attending state schools pick up the views there; then when they go to their religous schools in the evening they get a different type of education which causes confusion. Muslims want the schools to teach Islam to those kids that want it, to teach Christianity to those kids who want it, and in some ways the 1988 Education Act allows it and if it were implemented properly it might go a little way towards meeting our demands. But there's so much resistance from various people. If my daughter is taught Islam, if she is taught Urdu instead of Greek, Spanish or some other language, she won't have to go to supplementary school every evening.

SHREELA FLATHER: The whole idea of multicultural education didn't take off till the late '60s, early '70s – and wasn't it a disaster. I'm against separate education. I believe that you have to build a socially cohesive society and you can't build that if children are not educated together. If they are educated separately you can't bring them together later as adults and then assume that they will have some kind of feeling for each other and understanding for each other. On the other hand the law says that if you can do this, that or the other you can get a grant from the government to set up a separate religious school and until that law goes, the right remains. But I still deplore the development of separate education, I would like to see all separate religious education done away with, including Catholic and Jewish schools and indeed Church of England. But the Church of England is the State religion, although people forget that: in this country we are so free to do what we want that people forget that there is a State religion.

SHREERAM VIDYARTHI: I fear for the future of real multiracialism here, because what has been done quite deceitfully is to insert phrases like 'multicultural education' and 'multireligious education', and in the name of multiculturalism what has crept in so insidiously is separatism. So Muslims have Islamic schools in the Mosque, Sikhs have Sikh schools in the *gurdwaras*, though Hindus have never identified themselves as a separate entity from the rest of the human race. Even Catholics and Jews and Afro-Caribbeans are all starting their separate entities and they call that 'multicultural education'. What's multi about it? It's all isolationist, it's all cultural, educational ghettoism and it's all leading to apartheid by invitation rather than apartheid by imposition.

MARIA VOROSKOI: When the Jews came in they didn't immediately ask for big synagogues to be built, they didn't ask for Hebrew to be taught in the schools, they were working hard and keeping up their culture within their own community. They also contributed a great deal to the English culture. I cannot understand how it happens that all of a sudden people arrive, who were allowed to come to better their lives, and demand. I can't understand why the Muslims did come. If they are feeling so terribly disadvantaged, why do they stay? If you look at the map, at the huge Muslim territories, and consider the huge fortunes of the oil states, why don't they look after their own? Why do they have to fill blessed, marvellous England? The resources go to teaching a language which, if they really want to learn it, they can learn at home. Any Hungarian who wants to teach his or her child Hungarian can do it at home. What right do they have to make these demands? I can't understand it. It's an absolute mystery.

MANZOOR BAHADUR: When the black community asks for something, especially the Muslim community, we're seen as negative. Even if our demands are already quite legal. There are Catholic schools, Jewish schools, and they've been established over a long period of time, they haven't just sprung up yesterday – what then is the problem when the Muslim community asks for their schools? It's so daft. It just doesn't make sense. It appears as though double standards are being practised.

VINCENT REID: I don't think racially separate schools are the way. Culture is not to me the be all and end all of human development, whether that be seen in terms of ethics or morality. There are certain things in any culture that I find repugnant and disagreeable and unacceptable. So far as Islamic schools are concerned, I have a daughter. I wouldn't want her to be schooled in that kind of a tradition, to be second-rate and second-class. I wouldn't want her to be taught to walk ten yards behind her man. This theocratic approach to education is just reactionary.

GULZAR KHAN: What we are saying as far as separate education goes, let our children understand their religion first, then they can make their own decision as to whether they want to follow it. I would love to see that sort of education in proper, equal terms. The problem is that if we set up these schools, we might risk getting second-class education, of being put into a ghetto. People will check what school a person has been to and categorize them accordingly. And those who went to Muslim schools will be considered low-class. We might not get the best teachers working in these schools, only the leftovers.

STEPHEN VIZINCZEY: In the end people cannot change, and they shouldn't go where they cannot change. It's all right, say, to set up some kind of expatriate Little England in New York, because New York is a half European city anyway and the English belong there somehow. You can say, 'This is what the British imperialists did', but what they did was wrong and two wrongs won't make a right. There is a lot to be said for offending people's feelings and beliefs and if everybody thinks the way he wants to think and says what he wants to say, some bright ideas may come through. How can I write if I have to worry about whose feelings I offend? That's the essence of the whole thing. That's what this civilization is about. We are where we are and India and Pakistan are where they are because there you can't offend the feeling of caste, and that's why India is the mess it is.

PETER TATCHELL: One of the things I liked most about Britain when I came here was its multiracial and multicultural diversity. That's part of what makes this country such an interesting place to live. For myself, without forgetting my Australian origins and influences, I've chosen to adapt to life here and found it quite easy, having come from a similar culture. Though I remain critical of many aspects of British society, this is my adopted home and I wouldn't want to live anywhere else.

MUHAMMAD AYYAZ: People ask me, 'Why not integrate?' My answer to that is, what kind of integration? Is it for me to give up my beliefs and simply integrate into a society where there are certain laws that I have to accept, although I completely disagree with them, and with which, because I am not in a position to change them, I just have to go along? Things like abortion. That is what the majority community mean by integration. From us only. We go that way, they do not. If my religion suffers through doing integration, then I won't do it. The other thing is that even if we do integrate, and we do give up things

276

we believe in, then still we find that we are not accepted. The majority of what we see of white attitudes to the Muslims is what we see on the TV: the Imam [Khomeini] was doing this that or the other, the Palestinians are doing this that or the other, and in Bradford, the Muslims are calling for single-sex schools, but only for their own girls, or they want halal meat in schools or they will kill somebody who is walking up the road because they disagree with them. So it's all negative stuff coming from the majority community. We're still Asians. At the end of the day I say that I am an Asian, that I have a clear identity and I must make the most of that identity.

18 Feeling English

'I have these occasional, alarming moments of feeling estranged.'

MIKE PHILLIPS: The crucial issue in this country for both black and white people is what does it mean to be an English person? Am I English, having lived here since 1956? I was coming in from France the other day and I had forgotten to fill in a landing card – I still have a Guyanese passport. This girl in her twenties, working as an immigration officer, told me to fill it in. So I did. But it struck me that I had been living in this country considerably longer than she had been alive. And that goes for a number of my white colleagues, and the kids whom I am teaching. So I feel that they can't tell me what it means to be English. I've been English longer than they have. I feel English, my kind of English. I'm not an English person like Ken Livingstone or Prince Charles, I'm my own kind, the kind of English person who came here in 1956 and lived in bloody Islington and lived in London most of his life. With a different history and so on, but that's still what it means to be English too. That is the struggle, that is one of the things that *we* have to begin to understand. In the United States a black population like ours would be saying, 'We are Caribbean-Americans.' If we worked by the same logic here we would be saying, 'We are black English people, this is the kind of English people we are; as such we are part of this state and this state should reform its identity to allow for that.' In fact, what we do is this business of adopting or re-adopting Caribbean manners and dialects and music and so forth. Which seems to me a sort of cop-out, this never having had the confidence to make a claim on the identity of this nation.

ALLA WEAVER: You can't become English, ever. One never becomes English, but one likes them. I don't feel British. I don't know what that means. I like

England as a geographical entity. I like the way of life. I am sure that if I were in France I would have found all the good sides of France as well. Or Italy. I think I'm pretty adaptable. Things haven't been as forbidding as England was in the spring of '34. One is quite welcome, as long as you know that you're not one of us. As long as one knows one's place.

MARY ROSE: I lived here since 1948. I don't feel English or German. Not even in between. And it doesn't worry me at all. As somebody said, if Mary were at the North Pole the North Pole would just become 'at Mary's'. I have to watch myself to make sure I don't start taking over. I go to stay with friends and I have to remember, don't do anything without asking first, even the washing-up. It is very easy for me to put my stamp on things. Knowing this I try to avoid it.

TEDDY SCHWARZ: I'm purely driftwood on the shores of England, and I'm still here. I have no reason to be here particularly, but now I'm so integrated into English life. I do feel English in some ways – in my habits. Germans always say I'm now more English than German. I don't resent that, but it surprises me because I consider myself more German than English. In fact I'm not one nor the other.

SIR CLAUS MOSER: I was naturalized after the war and have had a varied career in the academic world, in banking, and in government since. Although I've lived for fifty-three out of sixty-six years here, yet I don't feel totally English. That may sound a mystery, but it's not really. It doesn't mean I feel insecure or without roots. In fact, I wouldn't live anywhere else. No day passes without gratitude to this wonderful country. But it is different from *feeling* totally English – which I think is only possible if one is!

CINDY BLAKE: Every year I feel more and more foreign and less and less English. I did want to be to absorbed, to become assimilated. But I feel more and more alien and I don't particularly like feeling alien. It doesn't turn me on. But if I go to America now and somebody speaks to me in the elevator, which they do in America, I jump. It's like aaaggghhh! But I miss that open feeling in America. I feel incredibly claustrophobic – it's the only word I can use. I feel less and less English and I buy my satellite dish and I watch CNN and I just glory in it. I'm insulating myself against the English to some extent. Though I don't know what it would be like if I went back. I think a lot of my feeling towards America has to do with the fact that it was my youth. So I feel if I went back to live there I could relive my youth instead of being old and boring the way I am here, married with responsibilities.

JOHN LAHR: I'm vaccinated against the deliriums of both cultures. I'm neither English in England nor quite American in America. I'm rooted in my community in Hampstead, with my family, my church. I'm a school governor. My wife started the community school here. We must know a hundred and fifty people within ten minutes, which is the kind of community we would never find in New York. So I am very rooted here. But psychologically it makes me feel free. When I go to the States I just don't buy into it, which is great. Coming from a background of being trained almost to overachieve, to not do that is like an alcoholic being able to sip a drink without going over the top. I consider myself an American living in England. An expatriate rather than an immigrant.

* * *

KATHY ACKER: I don't feel English, but I have become mid-Atlantic and I feel that if I lived here long enough I could become a Londoner. Friends tell me that I am already on the way. I love London, and I do understand the differences between London and the rest of the country. I could never become English. A Londoner is something else. That certain lifestyle, that way of life. The date book you have with appointments three weeks ahead, the way you form circles, the way you handle work, all that – it's urban life. I very rarely venture out of London, except for work. I love the countryside, but that's to go see the trees, not the people. If I go to the country it's as a city person: to sit in the woods and look at it.

SHARI PEACOCK: I'd say I was part of London, but not part of England. I would even say that particularly I'm part of north London. Which makes me very parochial. It's familiarity. There are certain parts of south London that I don't really like. It has to be said that despite all my complaints, I can't think of anywhere in Europe where I have felt more at ease.

WILF WALKER: I'm a Londoner. These streets are as much mine as anyone else's. I would hate ever to come back here and be a tourist. I want to leave, but I'll always be a Londoner. If I did leave, it would be to Tobago. I hate this thing where people come back, 'I used to live here, I used to have a place over there . . .' No way. I pay taxes. I've paid my fucking dues. There ain't nobody going to push me around out there. This is my country. I have the passport. I'm a Brit.

VINCENT REID: I belong, I have rights, and there's *nobody* going to take my rights away. You better believe it. I don't join things, I'm not a joiner. I belong. The National Front can't say to me: if you don't like it, then why don't you go

279

home. They can't say that. I've defended this country, I've got a medal for being in Malaya. I've helped to make this country what it is.

SHREERAM VIDYARTHI: I feel very British. I wouldn't swear by the Queen, and I wouldn't promise to be loyal to her personally, but if anything goes wrong or anyone attacks Britain in a way that would harm the national interest, yes, I would fight for it. I did swear an oath when I was made a citizen but that doesn't make me a patriot. Millions do it. After all, what Mrs Thatcher is doing to Britain, selling most of it to America, is hardly patriotic. So definitions of loyalty and patriotism might differ; but if I see anyone doing positive harm to the interests of Britain as a community I will fight to defend it. I don't need an oath for that, it is what comes naturally. I am not an alien, I am a part of this community; they might not like me, but that doesn't worry me one way or another: I am here and I am part of it.

GINA ADAMOU: I am a Greek person, I don't want to be English. I am Greek and I am proud of it, but I want to mix with this society and accept it and be today's person, not yesterday's person. That doesn't make you any less of a Greek. This is where I differ from my husband and from some of my family. I'm a today's person. I adjust to situation. With my children's lives, with changes in my life . . . I'm not scared of losing my identity, I'm a Greek person. Though I don't belong in Cyprus – I'm so different from traditional women there – and I'm not English. So really I'm somewhere in between. I love Cyprus, it's beautiful, but I don't feel I belong there. And obviously I'm not accepted as an English person here.

PETAR OBRATOVIC: I will never become a part of society in a political way here. I could never become highly politicized. I don't like any of the parties and I never know where I would fit, I really don't. I'm not a citizen, though I will ask for a passport in another four years. I shall get it, I think it would be useful. I can keep the Yugoslav one too. I shall always feel Yugoslav. If I gave up my Yugoslav character I feel I would be deprived of my originality, of the characteristics that make me valuable here. I could never see myself as increasing my value by becoming British. I would always rather be first-class Yugoslav than second-class British.

MUHAMMAD ALI: I don't feel English. If anything I feel good about having had the opportunity to have been born in Pakistan and to have lived there for fourteen years. I know that culture fairly well and I could fit in there if I returned. Yet I also know this country fairly well too. I was educated here, I went through the system, including university, and I've worked in the textile firms where my father worked, and I've worked in the voluntary sector and the

280

private sector. So I know the culture. I don't feel grateful. I struggled hard for what I have.

MUHAMMAD AYYAZ: Our parents think we should be grateful, that we are here, that we have jobs, that we can send money back home. I disagree. I say we have done a lot of work, we have given this country the best part of our lives, we are as British as anyone else, in any sense. We have contributed to the economy. Yet we haven't had a good deal in return. We tend to be forced into areas where the housing is not very good, the roads are not very good, you can see it – you don't have to go far. So we have not really received a fair exchange for what we have done. But we shall keep on contributing. Now people accuse us of being unemployed and of taking money from the state, but if an Asian is offered a job he will work. If you can't get a job you can't work.

MANZOOR BAHADUR: I've been here twenty-eight years now, it's a long time. I don't feel English, I don't feel Pakistani, I feel a Muslim. An individual with a religious identity, and the religious identity comes first. If it comes down to nationality I feel more English, I think in English. I dream in English. Having said that, I can switch in a split second from being English to being a Pakistani. I am contented with life here in England, but there are problems: the difficulty of achieving real equality, things like that. Becoming aware of the injustices in English society is pushing me more and more towards a stronger Pakistani identity. I think this is something common to a lot of people in my position.

ANWAR BATI: I see myself as precisely what I am: somebody of Pakistani/ Indian origin – I don't really recognize Partition – who happens to be culturally English, and that is exactly what I am. I feel almost completely English. Although there is the very strong knowledge that I am not. I don't feel alien, but I do feel an outsider. I know that I'm not English, and would never, as some people do, make any decision for instance to change my name and pass, say, as east European. In an argument I will always bring up the point that I am not English, if it is relevant to the argument. Just before the '79 election, I met a chap from the Conservative research department. I was saying that I wasn't going to vote Tory. I agreed on the whole with the policies Mrs Thatcher was putting forward, and on the whole I agreed with her immigration policy, but there had been a very callous speech on race relations she had made quite recently, and the end product of that would be that some poor sod in the East End was going to be beaten up. So I said that was why I wouldn't vote for her. He said, 'But Anwar, you must understand about immigrants . . .' and started telling me how they all stuck together, cheated the system, etc, etc. So I said, 'Excuse me, Adrian, I am one.' 'Ah,' he said, 'you're different.' I said, 'No, I'm

281

not, and if I saw somebody being beaten up in the East End I would pile in and help him.'

RAJAN UDDIN JALAL: I see myself as a British Bengali. I won't become British, but then nobody would want me to become British, including the British themselves. I'm British in the same way as a Scot: he sees himself as British, but he's Scottish first. You have to distinguish between race, culture and nationality very carefully. We were Pakistanis when we were under their umbrella, but our culture was distinct in that we were still Bengalis, whose history goes back thousands of years. Whatever happens I can't change my colour, I can't become an Englishman. Whatever happens to me I can't give up my eastern culture. I can go and live next door to Maggie Thatcher but I'll still be a Bengali. And my East End habits will come out now and then. So why be ashamed of it? I'm not.

ANWAR BATI: Obviously I'm not the same as a Bengali living in Brick Lane. I think that my experience is almost unique in this country. I don't know of any other Indians or Pakistanis who are like I am, in the sense of my attitudes. There are people who are quite successful and who still retain their Indian or Pakistani identity, whether or not they live there or visit or not. I move in reasonably smart circles, I speak with a posh accent – though that's no more than the accent I was brought up with. I've never suffered consciously from being a Pakistani – though maybe I have and just haven't realized it. Certainly it helps being quite light – if I'd been two shades darker things might have been very different. Likewise if I hadn't spoken with a posh accent and had I not been bright. I'm perfectly assimilated.

* * *

SIMI BEDFORD: I don't feel British at all. I know that I think British, a particular kind of British, that kind of bohemian, middle-class post-hippie British, but I don't feel British psychologically. I'm black and I'm Nigerian. I don't rule out the possibility of going back. There is certainly a qualitative difference between my children, who were born here, and me. They really are English. Black British, which is what they feel. They are middle-class but in school what matters is colour, not class. I'm pretty sure that if you asked them, 'What are you?' they'd say black first and British second.

VERNA WILKINS: When my boys were very young we went to the pictures and we were in the queue and my younger son had a comic. And this little white boy said could he borrow it. So my son lent it to him. As the queue started to move he asked for it back, but this boy said no. So the little one told his big brother who asked for it back again, then took it away without waiting for him to proffer it. So the little boy said, 'I don't like you. And look at your mother, she's black all over. Are you French or something?' So my son told him, 'I suppose this whole thing is a big mystery to you. Well I'm Welsh-Grenadan and any more from you and you're going to get a face full of pavement!' They were very young, but they just dismissed him. A lot of people see me as foreign still and assume therefore that I have a problem with English. I was in the supermarket and this checkout girl starts enunciating very clearly every word. Telling me how to use a credit card. And she's going on and on and I'm standing there looking at her and the queue is building up and she's explaining over and over things that I knew perfectly well. But I thought, no, I won't say anything, you carry on, you're obviously having a good time.

SUSAN WILSON: I wrote on my migration application that I was a Polynesian Celt, and I think that that about describes me. I'm not English and I accept that. One of my friends called me an over-emotional Celt and I thought that was quite good. I thought, 'Yeah.' My family is quite emotional and its very Celtic. I have no sense of being displaced, no feelings that I don't know where I am or whether I'm stuck half-way between here and New Zealand. As time goes by I feel more and more a New Zealander. I still make all those comparisons that you make if you're an immigrant. I still compare everything to what I knew. This after nearly twelve years. The fields, the countryside, the houses . . . not all the time, but certainly quite a bit. Light and landscapes, so many things.

CASH BHOGAL: I don't feel very English. Not a lot. Obviously you are influenced by the society in which you live, how you look at things, but deep down you can never say, 'I'm fifty per cent, I'm seventy per cent English.'

MICHAEL DE SOUZA: At one time I did feel English, and I felt proud to be English. I would never wave the Union Jack, but I felt proud that I was in England, because I liked the language very much and I felt like I belonged, because I'd been here for a long time. That didn't last so long – through my formative years, but it went. I've got a Trinidad passport and I want that. Even if I had to get a visa for every minute, I want that Trinidad passport. I never had an English one. But I don't need work permits and so on. I reside here, I was educated here, I'm a British subject.

MARCEL BERLINS: I started to feel British when I took on British nationality in '73 or '74, though there was no moment when I said to myself, 'Gosh, I'm English,' and over the past four-five years I've begun to feel more French again. That certainly has something to do with the present regime. I've now spent much longer in England than in any other country, but I still can't decide,

283

say, over a rugby match, whether to support England or France. Certainly to the French I'm very typically English. I don't regard myself as English, I don't regard myself as an insider. I'm totally comfortable here, and I suppose now more comfortable here than I would be in France – I'd have twenty years catching up to do in France. I go there for a few weeks at a time, but I've not lived there for twenty years. I do have a greater and greater emotional attachment to the south of France, the area where I spent my early childhood. But that doesn't make me feel French, just as I don't feel English. Certainly I have an emotional attachment to England, engendered perhaps by the fact I was so easily accepted here. It's given me a satisfying and full life. I'm therefore both grateful to it and loyal to it in many ways, which I hope is not tested in any dramatic way. I don't think I'd have gone to the Falklands for England, but neither would I have liked to have fought in Algeria for France.

LEENA DHINGRA: There is definitely a racial thing in England whereby you have a British passport which makes you British, but the racial thing doesn't allow you to be truly British. I feel quite comfortable and quite learned in the particular aspect of British culture that I have learned. The Quaker culture, which is already slightly off-beat, because it has a built-in tolerance. Though many aspects of the culture haven't come my way. The English culture that I have learnt is the England of the eccentrics and I have a lot of affection for it. It's one of the more positive sides of the English culture. But I haven't encountered the mainstream culture very much. It probably intimidates me – which it sets out to do. I have encountered the barriers it puts up. The class thing doesn't come into it that much because people, especially in those days when I was in the theatre, assumed that I came from an acceptable class background, whatever that was. It's difficult to say how the mainstream works, or the ways in which you withdraw yourself because you realize that it functions on a different wavelength, which denies you to an extent. Even if with the best will in the world it doesn't want to. Even to say things like how well integrated I am, or how beautifully I speak English and how I could help? Shouldn't I find some nice job helping 'them lot'? The wogs, who haven't quite made it? Very often, that comes up. In the end I belong to the world of the cranks. That's a class in itself. And we also form an international community.

CHRISTOPHER HOPE: I don't feel part of the mainstream, rather perched on its shoulder. One can probably apply to join. If you've come from the old colonies – Australia or South Africa – it's very difficult for the British to class you accurately. I think the immigrants of the last thirty years ought to be given a medal. The richer and wider the mix here the more comfortable I feel. That reflects back on South Africa, a place where people were very clearly structured and grouped. I developed a hatred for that early on and for what goes with it.

284

Here one has delicate culminations of hundreds of years of groupings, stabilities, structures and class arrangements, as compared with brutal framework of South Africa. But I still don't feel easy with the structure here, and sometimes feel I'd like to see it all come tumbling down. However, I do take a certain joy in seeing people from that elsewhere coming here.

BIANCA GORDON: I became a naturalized British subject after the war. I have a British passport but it is very difficult to say what 'feeling British' means. I was the child of Polish Jewish parents, born and educated in Berlin, and as an adolescent was uprooted. I started a new life in this country. Each period of my life has deeply influenced me. When I lecture abroad I might say, 'In England we do it this way.' I could not bring myself to say, 'We British do it this way.' My home is here and my friends are here. My home is the place where my late husband and I struck roots and turned a derelict garden into a beautiful one. There we reinstated the homes both of us lost suddenly in Nazi Germany. We both worked hard to continue our education and our studies. I entered the helping professions as many of those of us who came here as children did. I hope that some of us have been of service to Britain. I've worked hard in my own little corner. I've been involved in preventive psychological work in hospitals from the inception of the NHS. Work has been an important part of my life, which I have found fulfilling.

* * *

CARMEN CALLIL: Australians, they think I'm a Brit. I think I'm an Australian, through and through. I'm a exile. Without regretting it, I think I made a mistake coming here, cutting off my roots. They're section A of your life, and now section B is truncated, permanently. My work wouldn't have been as interesting out there, because of the year in which I was born. If I was born now, or fifteen years earlier than I was, I wouldn't leave. I was born at a bad time, just before the war. I've become too peculiar here, and that's wearing. It would be nice to be able to crack a joke, to be appallingly rude and not feel that everybody would have a nervous breakdown. A ruder culture might have suited me better. I never wanted to be British, I couldn't be British. I still have my Australian passport. I wouldn't become a citizen unless I was forced to, because I don't feel British.

ENNIO CAMISA: I always felt the same. I don't feel English. I haven't changed at all in sixty years. I like here the same as I like Italy. As a matter of fact I like it more here. When I go to Italy I don't like going to the city, living in the city. If I want to live in the city I've got a city here. If I went to live in the city there I'd be a stranger. I'd be Italian, speak Italian, but I'd be a stranger. If you live in the country in Italy it's all right in the summertime, but in the wintertime it's worse than here. I have no more family in Parma. My brother lives here. We're the only two in the family left. I've got my two nephews here. My sons look after the shops. One looks after the shop in Berwick Street and the other after the shop in Charlotte Street. Sometimes they change. They work together. They're very, very nice. But if you go to Italy in the wintertime, it's like going to Epping Forest, living in a small village, nobody in the village, you can go to the public house but you can't be in the public house all the time. You get annoyed with nothing all the time. If you want to keep yourself fit, you've got to do something, I'm not going to say, 'I'm retired, I'll not do anything.' That way you're finished.

DESMOND GITTENS: How British do I feel? I went to Paris on one of my early forays into Europe and hung out with black Parisians. They called me English. 'Hey Eeengleesh!' and I realized there and then that I couldn't escape England. I couldn't be French. Even though I stayed in Paris I would still be called English even by black people from the Caribbean. They think French, their desires, the way they do things, their culture is French. They see the English in me, not just the language, but what I wear, the songs I sing, the way I phrase things, the way I think. It's all 'Brittanique' and not 'à la France.' So yes, I do feel English. I do feel British in the sense that I use the language and the culture to communicate and live. But I don't feel English in a patriotic sense of waving our flag and so on. But especially in the face of non-English-speaking peoples I feel English. I have Moroccans who come to my office and they look up to me to correct them, their language, their behaviour, to help them fit into an English standard of living. Like most Caribbeans I've been inculcated with English. Not just the language, but English the thing. I've lived here many more years than I did in the Caribbean. I'm not half-way across the Atlantic, I'm here. I do want eventually to retire in the Caribbean, but that's nothing to do with the culture there, just the sun and the sand. And the anonymity. I won't be identified as a black man. That's a treasure, you're just another person walking down the street. There's nobody black in the Caribbean in that sense. Like you're not Jewish in Israel.

BIANCA GORDON: My parents were religious Zionists and in my youth I belonged to a Zionist youth movement – a very fine one, which made a deep impact on our lives, particularly during the Nazi period. When my husband and I went to Israel after the Six Day War we toured the Golan Heights. A friend, who knew the area well, showed us around. He was able to describe to us the military positions and to explain where the battles were fought. Pointing in a certain direction I asked, 'Is that ours?' and he said, 'Yes' or 'No' – I forget which. Suddenly I had a twinge, it wasn't a pain, but it was something. At this moment I realized that I had never before referred to a landscape as 'ours'.

Neither in Germany, which had beautiful places, nor in England, parts of which I love. I had never felt that a landscape might be 'mine' or 'ours'. I thought about this brief interchange. Neither I nor my Israeli friend considered my question as being out of turn. He had answered quite naturally.

RONALD HARWOOD: I do feel British, not South African, though I know it's still there. I can never really say that I'm English. I can't say that I'm an English writer. I write in English, but I'm British. I'm a citizen of the United Kingdom, that's how I feel. My assumptions are primarily British assumptions, I view the world politically from a British standpoint. I always felt that I'd found my home in Britain, that I really belonged here. I don't think I was ever excluded from any kind of establishment, any inner circle of any kind, through being a foreigner, an immigrant, an outsider. But in the last ten-fifteen years I've become aware that I don't actually belong. You might think that I have all the credentials of the upper middle class, or at least the middle class. Yet sometimes I sit and think how alien I am. My life's experience is deeply alien. Not opposed, just foreign. I have these occasional alarming moments of feeling estranged. It's to do with the journey one's travelled – it's to do with the past. Not with the present at all. It's not only to do with emigrating, perhaps its being Jewish, perhaps not being born here.

HANNAH KODICEK: I don't feel British at all. I used to want to be British because I just wanted to fade into the wallpaper as well as succeed. There was a side of me that couldn't bear going to the market to be asked, 'Oh, where are you from, love?' when all you've said is, 'Can I have a bag of potatoes.' But I never lost my accent and you stick out like a sore thumb, though you don't hear the accent and you think that you're like everybody else. It's a bit like when you're forty and lots of your friends are still twenty and you feel just like them but they don't think so.

IVAN KYNCL: I think I am part of the English theatre world. But I don't feel like a member of the greater society. That's why I haven't applied for citizenship, for a British passport. I don't feel that it would be right. It isn't so much that I have suffered from xenophobia – maybe once or twice because of my funny accent – and I don't feel deliberately excluded, but really I have chosen not to join. Though I may try harder to be a part of this society and do more for it than a lot of immigrants do who actually have British citizenship. I feel that I have the right to speak out against things I don't like here, politics or anything else, but at the same time I will never be English. So I sometimes disagree with people who have only been here a few years and are already asking for citizenship. But I can understand it: maybe when you are older you need some safe haven in an unsafe world. It doesn't matter if it's only a piece

287

of paper, but I don't need it on those terms. I still use an English travel document. At the same time I would like to live here for the rest of my life. Every time I go to Europe, I think that's nice, because in many ways the countries are similar to Czechoslovakia, but at the same time when I come back to England, I feel, OK now I am going home.

CUI QU: The main thing about having taken British citizenship is that were we still Chinese passport holders and we went back to visit, at any time they can keep us there. At any time. You cannot go out. If you are British you can go back. We need a visa to go now. Being British makes it much easier to travel around everywhere. But I feel a little lost between the two countries. I am always thinking about my family in China, my friends, what is happening whether it is good or bad. When I went back last year, really I didn't want to come back.

NGUYEN DUC PHUONG: I don't feel British and I don't want to. Everybody has their own culture. You do take on some of the new culture, like we did when the Americans came over, but why should we be English? I find it very strange when I meet someone who says that they feel British or feel American. Very strange. I've left Vietnam physically, but emotionally I am still there. I still remember every detail. I don't think that will change for the rest of my life. I'm not like, say, the Indians, whose children come here and start living the English way of life. I'm not like that and I don't expect to change.

VU DUY TU: No way do I feel I am English. Never. Even if we we wanted to we can't, and we don't want to. We want to keep our own traditions. We teach our children, bear this in mind: we are Vietnamese. We never, never can become English. For many, many reasons. We live in the UK, we have to study, we have to get a job, we will have our future here, but never forget you are Vietnamese.

PETER TATCHELL: Having a mother who taught elocution, and coming from the most anglicized part of Australia, my accent was never very strong. People tended to assume that I was Englsh, but had lived overseas for a while. So I rarely had to explain my Australian background. That's probably made it easier for me to see myself as being more English than I really am. Nevertheless, I suppose I do feel English to the extent that I feel comfortable living here and fairly well accepted.

MARIA VOROSKOI: I don't feel English or Hungarian, I just feel myself and there's no problem. The world is here, I have the sky over me and the soil under me, and there you are. There was a Hungarian soldier, Count Zichy,

288

who was also a poet. He wrote in one poem that he didn't mind where he would be buried, because there will be only the sky above and the soil beneath. It's the world.

YASMIN ALIBHAI: The English are so scared of diversity. People in my position can unlock three completely different world cultures: East African, Indian, and English. I think, God, what a gift to have three keys, when most people get maybe half a key, if that. So I see myself as quite internationalist now. I used to be quite scared of it, wondering where I really belonged, but now I see it as really exciting. I've always wanted respect, that's something I've always fought for, but I've never wanted to belong.

VICTOR WILD: By 1939 I felt absolutely English. I had been indoctrinated, brainwashed, whatever, and I felt that the English were right. It was quite obvious to me that there was no question about where justice was. I had a great sense of what was fair and what was not fair. I don't know whether I'd learned this at school in England or what. Though today I don't feel completely English. I can't totally feel at home. If I walk into a pub I still feel slightly as though I am not one of them. I don't always join conversations. I'm not a great pub-goer but when I do I tend to talk about the wrong things. It's supposed to be sport and women and motor-cars and I tend to talk about the wrong things.

19 Xenophobia: The White Man's Burden

'If they think foreigners are funny, well, I'll be a funny foreigner for the rest of my life.'

GINA ADAMOU: In Greek there is no word 'foreigner'. There is *xenos*, which means guest, so the English word 'xenophobia' actually means fear of guests, not foreigners. I have English friends. In every nationality you have the good and the bad, though I do think that the English are a little more racist than other people. For instance the Cypriot people make others feel welcome. We feel it is our duty to make them feel welcome. We like them to feel one of us. We would hate them to feel resented. That is our natural way with foreign people. I wouldn't even call them foreign, The problem is that some English people think that they are the best, that they are 'it'. They remember the old England, the colonial England.

NAIM ATALLAH: There is a paradox between British xenophobia and British tolerance. You have them opening their doors to Jewish immigrants at the turn of the century – now they're everywhere and they've revitalized this country. So there's that, but at the same time there is the dislike of foreigners. If an Englishman starts quarrrelling with you he'll inevitably say, 'Why don't you bloody foreigners go home!' You'd never hear that in America. Here we like only the rich foreigners, the aristocratic foreigner. And women like them more than men.

CINDY BLAKE: It's not so much what the British say as their assumptions. I went to see *Uncle Vanya* the other day and an English woman leaned over and said, 'Are you familiar with this play?' and I said no, I'm not, and she said, 'Of course not, you wouldn't have read any Chekhov,' and I thought, 'Wait a minute . . .' because I'm American I couldn't possibly have read any Chekhov. I felt like saying, 'Hey, yah, right, I thought this was Agatha Christie.' That's what you get. They assume you've never been to an opera, they assume you've never been to the theatre, that you've never read any books, they assume that your university education is the equivalent of their O levels . . . They look at your clothes first of all, and you've got to have everything. Especially the women. They look from head to toe and if you've got the shoes wrong or something they mark it. You can see their little heads going click, click, click. When I was first here we were shooting in Ireland. And I had on some bluejean jacket or something and one of the wives said to me, 'You know, Cindy, I did this with Simon last year and maybe you should do it with Bill this year. I just left a little picture of a Harrods fur coat on his desk and said, 'Wouldn't this be nice for Christmas?' and I got it.' And there she is in her fur jacket. I'm sitting there thinking, 'I don't believe this . . . But they felt sorry for me, they felt desperately sorry for me because I didn't know the ropes, I didn't know the tricks of what I was supposed to wear, the right shooting kit, all that stuff.

PETER TATCHELL: Apart from the Bermondsey byelection, I've never experienced any prejudice because I happen to be Australian – except during the cricket season. However, coming back to Britain from trips abroad on an Australian passport, I have experienced the general disdain of immigration staff for people from overseas. Once, one even had the impertinence to tell me it was time I went back to Australia. I've always been shocked by the depth of racism against black and Irish people in this so-called liberal society. I remember the appalling anti-Irish hysteria during the IRA bombing campaign in London in the 1970s and the National Front terror-tactics against the black community during the same period. What really sickened me, was how few public figures were prepared to speak out in defence of the Irish and black communities.

290

CINDY BLAKE: I would go to these dinner parties and there would be Irish people there and the Irish jokes told by English people, told as if they pretended this person wasn't there or that they weren't going to be annoyed, the assumptions they made. And the Jews and the blacks and the anti-American jokes. They'd say to me, 'I've been to America and there isn't a building over two hundred years old, isn't that depressing?' What do you do? At first I didn't say anything, then I decided that I'd get more and more American and I'd get more and more outrageous, just to get some kind of emotive answer. I said to one man I'd just seen *Pretty Baby* with Brooke Shields and I said, 'All girls should be prostitutes at age thirteen, I think that's great,' and the guy said, 'Oh really,' and moved on. 'How interesting,' he said. The big thing is to ask them how do they feel. They say, 'I've shot ten grouse; and you say, 'How do you *feel* about that.' It stumps them every time and they don't have a clue what to say. I used to play games with them, though they never realized. They wouldn't.

MIRANDA LOVETT: I was sitting next to someone at a dinner party in our own house and he said, 'I fired my secretary this week – I found out her father was a member of the Labour Party.' I thought this man was despicable! Which of course is the reaction that the English absolutely adore. They love goading the Americans, and they love goading them and goading them and when it's gone too far, they say, 'Christ, you guys can't take a joke.' What I've learned over the years is the way to handle situations like that is not to be goaded. So I don't get it any more. Which is part of getting older and living alongside it and understanding this humour, and the way they do things. Understanding the culture. But if the English can dish it out, they can't take it. I sat next to a guy at a dinner party, he was English but he worked for Guinness and he was based in Ireland, and he was quite funny, this dry cynical sense of humour, but my sister was there too and he was doing the goading number with her and I could see it happening and I could see her bubbling and I could see her reacting. But he was perfectly sweet and nice to me and at one point he turned to me and asked whether I had any children. So I said, 'It's very sad, I can't have children.' He went beet red and he was deeply embarrassed. Nor did I ever tell him the truth and say actually I had two kids. But I felt I was giving him back a little bit of his own medicine. And it shut him up.

CINDY BLAKE: I remember one man actually *kicked* me during dinner. About five times. He started in at the beginning of the dinner party, 'Oh you ex-colonists, the worst thing that ever happened to you was breaking away from Britain, you bunch of yobs . . .' this kind of thing. I thought, 'When is this guy going to let up?' He didn't. He went on and on. I didn't rise to it, and he literally kicked me. He was so angry that he was kicking me under the table. He wasn't being cute and playing footsie, it was *bash*! Yankee-bashing, that's what it was. He just hated America. The upper classes really hate America more than anyone else. They still resent America for not coming into World War II quickly enough. A lot of cracks about that on the TV still. And we're crass. A bunch of crass individuals.

MIRANDA LOVETT: They may not call me a dirty Paki, but they do call me a dirty Yank. Oh yes they do. They do it very jokingly, but I always say that if somebody makes a joke like that about something there is always a grain of truth. I'll be with people who will make anti-American remarks and then they'll apologize to me, but I can say to them with my hand on my heart, 'Don't worry, it doesn't matter.' When I first came here it would make my hackles rise, but now it's just water off a duck's back.

CARMEN CALILL: The English are more obsessed than any other nation with people who are not natives. I don't think they like foreigners much. And they can't work out why foreigners are successful here. Why can't they, the British, be as successful as we vulgarians?

CINDY BLAKE: People's attitudes towards Fergie are actually people's attitudes towards Americans. They are very similar. This brash, uncouth, big-mouthed woman who should know her place and doesn't. And that's how people see Americans. Pushy, uncultured people. And as it happens I agree with them and you can see what it is people don't like about Americans if that's what they see. She goes down in LA, they love it, but that's exactly what makes me shudder too. Whereas Princess Di is the perfect English princess. She doesn't open her mouth, she knows her place and she dresses well. What more can you ask?

JOHN LAHR: Attitudes to Americans haven't changed with the Americanization of England. They're still the clowns of capitalism. All I had to do was don my Bermudas for all of Worcester College to peer out of their windows, sniggering. There was a Texan who was going to be a pro footballer, huge guy, and they would look at him as if he was something washed up on the beach. Extraordinary. We were bright and interesting, but they didn't like our energy, or the colour of our language, the colour of our clothes. And what the English will never understand, because it's built into the landscape, is our optimism. In the '60s there was an influx of excitement, of money, and although the English did respond to it, they could never really psychologically embrace it, so that the culture became hopeful. With Americans, that hope is built into the expansiveness of the land, the richness of the culture. You live for expectation. Here, our friends seemed to take whatever was handed out to them. Not an American response. You go for it, you try, you aim for something. America is a culture of abundance. England, even in the upper echelons, is a culture of scarcity. So there are always limits. Limits of space, of cost and so on. Then the English linguistic milieu is irony, which is something Americans are not very good with. They're very good at hyperbole, inflation. It would never be possible for the one to embrace the other.

FATIMA IGRAMHIM: I used to think that England was the home of tolerance and fair play but I haven't really found it here. I don't think that the English are very tolerant, especially not to foreigners. They don't like them. They're full of prejudices, they're incredibly afraid of opening up to a foreigner. I've now changed my name for some business work. If I say I'm called 'Fatima' I can hear their voices getting unfriendly because of this Islamic name. So sometimes I call myself Sara, which is my second name, and use my husband's English surname. I don't use my maiden name, I have to spell that. So even if I have an accent, nobody knows what I am and where I come from. I don't like it that I have to explain myself, but people don't take care. They're very very impatient with foreigners if they can't speak English well. They don't try to speak clearly, they don't try to listen, they aren't interested in what they have to say unless they say it very quickly.

PETAR OBRATOVIC: I went to a market in the East End and the man said something in cockney and I didn't understand and he really became insulted. To the point when he was so abusive that my feeling was to hit him. Not that I would, but he was really really rude. I really can't understand why they have to be that rude. What's the point? But some people really hate anything foreign. In class terms it's the lower-middle-class, the cab driver attitude. Well-off financially but completely ignorant. *Daily Telegraph* readers. But that's the way they think, that's the way the system benefits them, why should they think otherwise?

TEDDY SCHWARZ: They don't understand what goes on in Europe, the English. Mrs Thatcher is typical. She hasn't grown with the growing European-ism. One can't expect it of her sort: the class of little shopkeepers that supported Hitler.

* * *

TESS WICKHAM: The English attitude to foreigners surely stems from the fact that it's much easier to deal with things by avoiding them. So why should you let in all these problems? Why should you tolerate all this fraying of the edges of the system that you've defined for yourself? England is an island, keeping foreigners out is very convenient. When it was powerful it was by managing people who were far away, people who put up no immediate threat. To have all the edges frayed, to have all one's security turned upside down – no wonder the English don't like foreigners, it's quite logical. But there was no way that you could avoid frayed edges, they are the direct result of history. You can't do what Enoch Powell wanted; the problem existed and there was no way you could deny it. But I can easily understand the xenophobia. This is a very defensive country: you don't have a public social life, instead you go from door to door. If you want to go anywhere you have to book, to plan. This clubbishness, this exclusiveness, I hate it. Keeping them out. That's what it's all about. Making sure that people know their place. It's all based on knowing just who you are and making sure you know it too – it's loathsome.

BRIGITTE NEWMAN: There is nothing in France towards England anything like the anti-French feelings you still encounter here. There is this difference in manners. It is very obvious to anyone who has lived in England for the past ten years that the English have not forgotten Joan of Arc, and wasn't it jolly that they burned her. Her name is dropped at every single dinner party I attend. As are Admiral Nelson and Wellington boots. Such things are inconceivable in France, where the French have definitely stuck to World War II and the British as allies. They would never be so childish as to start scoffing about Joan of Arc or whatever. I still get teased about my accent. In France, in any social background, if you came to dinner it would be inconceivable to make a remark on your accent. People would bend backwards to make you feel comfortable, and would compliment you on your excellent French even if you could only massacre four words.

EVA JIRICNA: People are conscious of your accent, they are conscious of the fact that you were not born here and they ask you different questions, but otherwise ... Of course it is a question of expectations. You have to assume that the fact that you have decided to live in a different country is your personal decision and why should you really burden everybody else? If you want to live somewhere else than where you were born you just have to accept that people are somewhat hesitant. But really I haven't experienced any great deal of suspicion or rejection. Yes, people do laugh at you when you say something very stupid and very funny so you have to laugh as well. If the English think foreigners are funny, well, I'll be a funny foreigner for the rest of my life.

PALOMA ZOZAYA: I was very surprised when I came to college, although now I am going through a very slow process of rebuilding my self-confidence. I knew that England had had a great empire, with colonies all over the world, but actually to see those colonial attitudes still alive within the young generation was very shocking. People used to laugh at my accent. I started off by talking freely in class, but after that I stopped because every time I opened my mouth people would giggle. In Mexico there might be the odd joke about an English person trying to speak Spanish, but the difference is that in Mexico we have learned to worship everything foreign. Perhaps Mexicans might laugh at the accent of another Latin American person, they would laugh at the Chilean accent or the Argentine accent, but they would not laugh in this patronizing way at an American or English accent, because that is the white person talking.

It's OK in England to be a Latin or any kind of foreigner, as long as that remains in the realm of being exotic. The emotional Latin. Basically fitting your stereotype and knowing your place. But outside that . . . I would never live out of London, or far away anyway. Because I go to the local shop in some little village and at first people are incredibly friendly. You walk through the door there's a big smile, but the moment you talk with an accent, the attitude changes.

PETAR OBRATOVIC: I was always shocked by how little the average person knew about anything that didn't relate to Britain or the Commonwealth. How little people knew about Yugoslavia, the differences between us and other Communist countries, the fact that we could travel and so on. They were always surprised that there was so little cultural difference between my upbringing and theirs. They would always ask the same questions and they would always be very cautious. Basically they were ignorant. 'Did you have difficulty getting out?' that was one of the biggest. 'How was it there, are the Russians there?' 'Where do you come from in Yugoslavia?' they always asked that, but then they don't ask anything about it. If I don't come from Dubrovnik they don't know.

BERNIE GRANT: There's no excuse for the English attitude to foreigners. They came to our countries, or our ex-countries, and they expected us to treat them with deference. Whenever the British go somewhere they set up the British club and so on, and everyone tolerates it. So when other people come here, the British should treat them a lot better than they do, but clearly they don't. It's all tied up with the empire, the Commonwealth. They're pretty bad. Even to this day I can't support the English cricket team. If it's England against Australia I'll always back the Australians. One Tory MP accused me of 'treachery' because I put down an early day motion congratulating the West Indian team on beating England when they were here a couple of years ago. How could I be a British MP and support these foreign teams? I said, 'I'm sorry, that's the way it goes.'

DESMOND GITTENS: English xenophobia comes from being an island. No doubt about it. We in the Caribbean experience and perhaps carry out similar discrimination. Not based on colour, but on people coming from a different island. I think's it's insular, you build up a sort of a self-protection about who are your friends, who you can trust. Not only that, Britain has had a terrible experience being an empire. They have grown up with a sense of superiority that doesn't really exist. It comes over time and time again. I have a boss like that and I have to tell him time and time again, 'Look, that sounds very colonial. You don't say that sort of thing to young people – it sounds patronizing, colonial, as if you think that we the English have the answers and you the blacks don't.' That's not true. And that persists, in government, in every area.

LEENA DHINGRA: Everyone has their view of India – and they all know very little about it. They know absolutely nothing. It amazes me how little everybody knows. If you are an Indian, or you go to India, you are very much aware of that relationship. Here they don't know a sausage about it. Haven't a clue. What they do know is messed up. Often it's romanticized: marvellous philosophy, whatever, *Jewel in the Crown*. When the film of *Gandhi* came out many people were really surprised to learn – and they didn't really believe it – that they had in India been thuggish and oppressive, repressive.

BALRAJ KHANNA: The English have a problem with all foreigners, but they have a unique problem with the people from the Indian sub-continent. This was essentially due to the problem of race, imperialistic attitudes which they might deny or even dislike, but which were still deeply ingrained. They were part and parcel of the construction of the British psyche. India had been the jewel in the crown; it had been the country which for the last two hundred years they had gone out to rule; they regarded it with a strange mixture of affection and contempt. But if you placed the two feelings in a balance, contempt far outweighed affection.

DAVILIA DAVID: People's attitude to Australians was slightly superior. The old convict, living the wrong way up, the usual stuff – all terrible clichés. The only thing that really upset me was the way people implied that I knew nothing. English people feel threatened by immigrants. They react adversely to our openness. I was warned to draw back, to keep myself covered and not say what I felt.

YASMIN ALIBHAI: I became very irritated by the way Africa was discussed. If you said you were from Uganda, the automatic response was, 'That's a terrible place. How nice it is for you to have reached this haven.' The way people would discuss the situation in Africa with no understanding of the mess that colonialism had left behind.

LEENA DHINGRA: I wrote an autobiographical essay once, and one of the things I said was that remarks like 'If you cut your hair, darling, you could easily pass off as Greek or whatever and no one would ever know' were meant to be taken as a compliment. That I spoke beautifully. But in spite of all that I was nearly, but not quite right. Or white. There was always a difference, which I felt, about being Indian in England and being Indian anywhere on the Continent. Here, people were never particularly interested. There's this feeling that British is here, and everything else is down there. So if everybody's trying to get up here, then you're not terribly interested in what all those other things are. A lot of people have that attitude. On the Continent this wasn't the case. Either you were seen as exotic, romantic, or you were just a person, an individual. The French see themselves as having a superior culture too, but in a different way to the English. In France the fact I spoke good French with a perfect accent would actually make them delighted. They felt it was marvellous. It would really thrill them. No one saw it as 'trying to pass'.

SIR CLAUS MOSER: England was much more welcoming to us Jewish refugees than any other country. That's in a way surprising, since the English are not always all that keen on foreigners. So it remains a historic mystery why at that time the English were so extraordinarily welcoming – with notable exceptions such as the medical profession. There were a number of high-ranking MPs – not Jews – such as Victor Cazalet who spoke out to urge that England must take these poor people in.

BIANCA GORDON: I went to school in Norwich. I was the only refugee at that school. Everyone was extremely kind: teachers did not normally fraternize with pupils, but they made an exception for me, because I had no family. I was invited one day to have tea at my history teacher's home. The discussion turned towards Germany. 'Is it true about the concentration camps?' I was asked. 'Yes it is.' 'Have you seen them?' 'No, they are not places you visit.' 'So how do you know?' 'Many men I know disappeared and were sent to such camps. My father was taken away.' She looked sad and was silent. After a few moments she asked, 'Bianca, why is it that for centuries people have hated the Jews?' I was at a loss for a reply. She was a historian, a kind and humane woman. Had I not felt startled by her question, I might have replied: 'Can you answer? Is that not your problem?'

I was invited to spend Easter Week 1939 with my headmistress, a formidable woman. She had a beautiful house in Sheringham, on the Norfolk coast. She could not have been kinder and more hospitable. She taught me how to knit, took me around to show me places. She shared her house with our art teacher. We were having lunch when the one o'clock news came on. Italy had marched into Albania. My reaction was the same as my parents' had been whenever the Nazis marched into yet another country and spread their empire: if only the free world would stop them! A heated discussion ensued between the two women and culminated in the art mistress saying, 'We should stop the Germans, we should go to war.' My headmistress was aghast. 'Go to war? Why?' 'Look what they are doing to the Jews,' said the art mistress. 'I'd rather sacrifice the Jews,' said my headmistress, 'for one English child.' I was stunned. I was her guest – her refugee child to whom she had extended much kindness both at school and now in her home. At that moment I wished that the earth could have opened and swallowed me up, or that someone would give me a ticket to return to my mother in Berlin. This experience, so soon after I had left Germany, gave me much food for thought.

GRETEL SALINGER: England is a racist country. I'm afraid that's true. I'm afraid so. They are insular. They got used to the Jews because we brought them a lot of good things from Germany. We brought them a lot of intelligence, we brought very good business people. On the whole I think we have been quite an asset for England. They got the best.

BRYAN GOULD: I did experience some xenophobia, very slightly. Anyone arriving with an accent has it pointed out. Ethnically I was of British stock, so my experience of discrimination, it's hardly right even to use the word, was utterly minimal compared with what other people experience, but nevertheless I got just the slightest inkling of prejudice. I was very easily patronized. New Zealanders are rather childlike in their social behaviour to others. They have an accent which reinforces that – it's designed to show that you're all mates together, a deliberately, self-consciously classless accent. It's an accent that depends on being slovenly in your speech. By virtue of slurring your words you're saying to people: the barriers are down. Here was I with all the advantages – Rhodes scholarship and so on, there's no better entrée into English society in many ways – but by virtue of being patronized a bit, I felt at times a tiny inkling of the meaning of a class-ridden society.

SUSAN WILSON: New Zealanders don't experience any of the xenophobia that, say, a European might find. It's got a lot to do with the war: there's still a residue of good will from the war. There's a bit of sensitivity. People used to ask, 'Are you Australian,' and I used to say, 'I'm not,' and they'd say, 'Oh good, I don't like Australians, they're awfully brash.' Though that's changed. People love Australians now. But New Zealanders can be relatively invisible, compared to Australians. I often think we are regarded as people who live in an English county which is a hell of a long way away but still very much part of England. Someone said to me, 'New Zealand – just turn right out of Dover and keep going.'

JAROSLAV BRADAC: I'd meet people, maybe the people who lived upstairs, and they'd say, 'Oh you come from there. Say something in Yugoslav,' and I'd

298

say, 'Well, it's not really "Yugoslav". . .' and I'd try to correct them. Then a week later I met two of them in a pub and while I had forgotten it had stuck in their mind, and they'd made a bit of a boob, so they actually told me, 'I'm sorry about all this, I didn't realize . . . We don't have much knowledge of Iron Curtain countries, they're all the same to us. We've been influenced by our propaganda, but surely it must have been the same for you? So just as we admit that we know very little about eastern Europe, you must know very little about some aspects of the western world.' I said, 'Possibly, what do you have in mind?' So he said, 'Let me give you a test. If I say "Australia", what do you say?' I couldn't believe it, what he was asking. So I said, 'What do you mean?' He said, 'Well, if I say Australia, what do you say to that?' It suddenly dawned on me that he was checking on me, whether I knew what and where Australia was. I was so absolutely shell-shocked. I said, 'What do mean, what are you asking me?' But he wouldn't give me an answer. Just, 'If I say Australia, what do you say?' I began to stutter . . . 'It's a continent in the Pacific and there's Melbourne and Sydney . . .' and suddenly they looked at each other with a kind of surprised look and said, 'He knows.'

* * *

TEDDY SCHWARZ: When I was in Dartford, I bought my tobacco from the shop next door and the shopkeeper and I had great times. But when the war came, the only good German was a dead German. As if I represented the might of the German army. Being a refugee in a small town was a relief, because of the class divisions. One day a Labour man asked me to become a member of the working men's club. So I did. Then another day, someone from the Conservative Club said: 'We heard about you coming here, we'd like you to become a member of our club.' I said I couldn't possibly, what with the feeling around, and besides, I was a member of the working men's club. 'Oh splendid, splendid, but you're always welcome, just use our club as you want.' So I went there too. I was sitting there one day, talking, and the licensee, Colonel White, came round: 'No politics in this bar.' The third time he said: 'As an officer and a gentleman, I request you to leave and not use my house again.' He couldn't have heard what we were talking about. I was furious. It was the beginning of hostility towards me which hadn't been there before. War had broken out by then, you see. You feel so isolated after that. If there was a knock at the door, I thought: they've come to lynch me. Then the chap from the Conservative Club came to see me again: 'This boycott, absolutely monstrous to treat you like that. My dear old chap, you must show yourself. I insist, you must come to the club.' I couldn't protest. He dragged me to the Conservative Club and there it was. 'For he's a jolly good fel-low', etc. Drinks all round. One man took out a postcard he'd had for years of the auxiliary cruiser *Emden*. 'Fine ship, fine crew.' Of course I was heartened by all that, but

299

it was all for the wrong reasons. They were not fêting me as a refugee, they were fêting Germany as a good enemy. I felt a bit uncomfortable.

TEDDY PEIRO: During the Falklands I couldn't watch TV without crying – the best of the youth on both sides dying stupidly. I felt sad that the two countries I love best were at war. When blood was shed I felt I would have to do something I didn't want to do: leave this country. I had put together a South American revue – very big and glamorous with gauchos, singers, flamenco dancers, etc, and we had big backing, with bookings in big arenas, heavy advance sales. Then two weeks later, there was only seventy-five pounds left in the kitty. Cancellations all over the place. People were ringing up the management: 'Why are you putting on an Argentinian show?' 'No, it's South American, not Argentinian.' 'Well, it has gauchos in it.' But that was right. You could not go on with it at a time like that.

NELLY SALAS: During the Malvinas war I had to go to the post office and send some letters to my family in Argentina. I was desperate to find out what was happening. The queue was very long and the clerk seemed to be asleep. But I didn't want to make a fuss, I hardly wanted to speak in case people heard my accent. So I put the letter on the counter, and asked him to register it. He asked me, 'Where is it going?' Son of a bitch, I thought. It said it on the letter. 'Argentina.' 'Where?' 'Argentina.' I had to repeat it louder and louder. Then the people behind me started saying, 'Well, it must be Argentina, look how stupid she is . . .' I paid, and I left, but then I really was very stupid, because I was so angry with them. I finished what I was doing, I took my change and I walked out. They were still talking and pointing, looking at me like a piece of rubbish. So I said, 'You know what. I tell you something. The Malvinas are Argentinian!' Then I rushed out. A lot of these feelings came from people reading the *Sun*. People read it and they believed what was written.

TEDDY PEIRO: I despise the gutter press. I was doing five weeks in Edinburgh with my son at the time the *Belgrano* was sunk, and then the *Sheffield* followed. On the programme it said that I came from Argentina. And the people were marvellous, the same reception as if nothing had happened. People came to the dressing-room to say how sorry they were this had happened, apologizing. The day the *Sheffield* was hit, I was sitting watching it at the theatre, with some of the band members, with tears pouring down my face. The musicians were watching the deaths of their own people, but when the news was over, one came and put his arm round me and said, 'If anybody bothers you, says anything to you, we'll break his neck.' How can you leave a country that treats you like that?

* * *

SHARI PEACOCK: There is this deeply underlying contempt for foreigners, because many of the English are so parochial. When you go out of London, visit little towns, those weird colourless English towns with their own shopping precinct and that's it, and the people all dressed in monotone colours, I get a glimpse of this essential parochialism. The people with whom I shared a flat in London were like this, essentially parochial people who themselves had only just arrived in the big city. I was different and they couldn't deal with it. We had a row one day and one of them told me, 'You're a savage from an uncivilized country and you may have managed to get away with behaving the way you do there, but here you won't manage.' That was really upsetting. I didn't understand that it was their limitations, I thought that I must be in some way inferior.

STEPHEN VIZINCZEY: I'm not accepted here, basically, as a writer. What moved me when I went back to Hungary is that people there felt better about themselves because of my success. I was a kind of role model and they felt that if I could do it, it was proof that they could do it. If you're an alien writer this doesn't work for you. I never felt I had that role in English. But that's the most a writer can do – and I wish that if I did something well then someone here would be more aware of his own possibilities through my success – not because of my success, but as a promise of his own success. I'm not part of the English literary mafia, though that's not by design. But I could never write for the *Observer*, for instance. I am a liberal person, and I don't know in what sense from my works I could be called a reactionary, but I have found that 'Little England' thing more evident amongst the Left than the Right, which is interesting. I don't think the Left has ever given me the chance it would have given me had I come from Pakistan. I was a refugee from the wrong country. Or perhaps I reminded them that Marxism doesn't work. Sometimes I do feel that I would have an easier time here if I'd been Indian or Pakistani.

RONALD HARWOOD: In 1983 I was invited to become Visitor in Theatre at Balliol, which I accepted with alacrity. The idea of going as a member of the SCR to Oxford, and to Balliol, was pretty terrific. It was just for one term but I had a wonderful time. I felt totally embraced by an establishment: there was no question of class, of Jewishness, just excellence. But then when I did a television series on the history of the theatre I came in for terrible stick, personal stick. Done subtly as the English always do, through pretending it was about the work. I'm not being paranoid, but it was really about my weight, my look, my affected diction and so on. It's to do with not being part of their image of what people should be like who appear on television. Impossible to analyse, but that treatment really alienated me, even though at the same time all this savagery was being heaped on me I had an Oscar nomination for *The Dresser*.

301

As a dramatist I've been praised to the skies and savaged in the gutter, but after that series the attacks were personal and it set going this chain, this feeling that one really isn't part of this society. I suppose secretly I do aspire to be part of it all. I don't know what form this being part would take, though. I can only think of it in the abstract. Though I now call myself an immigrant much more than I used to.

SIMI BEDFORD: Some of my best friends, as they say, are English, but I still have this impression that once one moves out of the circle one really knows, then wherever you go, whatever you say, they still have this idea that behind your head they can still see the tropic moon, the waving palms, and hear the beating of the tom-toms. So everything you say, they say, 'Oh,' in surprise, and its rather a question of ticking things off against these assumptions. In Newcastle when I had the kids and I was talking to people in my best English accent they'd say, 'Are you going to teach him English?'

LEENA DHINGRA: There was a man at Hyde Park corner and he turned to this Indian-looking man who was giving his talk and asked him, 'What are you, sir? Where are you from, sir?' the Indian replied, 'I am British.' And the Englishman turned round and said, 'Christ was born in a manger. Does that make him a sheep?'

CHRISTOPHER HOPE: The blacker and poorer you are the harder it is. And if you do start to get beyond that, along comes something like the Rushdie affair to put everything in perspective again. Immigration is a vital and volatile issue. People dislike, and with increasing intensity, aliens and foreigners, and even more so those who do not happen to be the same shade as themselves and have other customs. And that will continue.

---

20 Racism: Keep Britain White

'The worst thing is knowing that people have a clear picture of
you which is absolutely nothing to do with you.'

BRYAN GOULD: I firmly believe that there is not a single black person in Britain – using the term in its wider sense – who does not have a daily experience of discrimination. It must influence your outlook; you cannot live in a society if that is your experience without it colouring your views and attitudes enormously. I can probably count on the fingers of less than one hand the episodes I can recall of when I have felt that in any society I was discriminated against for any reason, but even on that level the sensation of that discrimination was very powerful. Now if that is what you have to encounter every day . . .

RAJAN UDDIN JALAL: The fear is there. The fear is something like this: you live in an area and you know that there are certain places you cannot go into. It is psychological. You feel the pressure, you know that certain places are hostile, and this feeling stays with you from the first day that you encounter racial violence or racial harassment. It never goes away. I travel widely throughout the country and still I know that there are places I will not go into. I know people do not want me there, do not like my presence. Which basically is because of the colour of my skin. It's a social problem: people feel insecure, they don't know what will happen and this is a problem for the whole community. Hostility and discrimination have grown because of the increased strength of the community – both numerically and otherwise.

VINCENT REID: The thing about racism in this country is that you can never put your finger on it and pin it down – it's very subtle. It comes in many guises, from the overt provocation that makes you react and people say, 'Hang on mate, it was only a joke. Don't be so thin-skinned.' This is somebody who's telling you a nigger joke. When you say, 'Why don't you fuck off and don't tell me that rubbish,' they tell you it's only a joke and *you're* put in the wrong. Then there's the more covert and discreet geeing-up. Which is very subtle, and therefore you can never have any concrete case to put forward to say that this is a simple incident of racism. When you examine it, what black people have to learn is how to think as a white man. White people don't have to think like me; their safety, their security isn't dependent on thinking like me. But mine is dependent on thinking like them. I have to think all the time. 'What would a white man think of this, this and this?' I've got to think that way because my very survival and security depend on it.

SIMI BEDFORD: Instinctively one knew that a lot of one's problems were to do with racism. The sort of racism one experienced in Thornton Heath was quite affectionate, that racism that people wouldn't put up with now because of the implications, but then it was, 'Do you live in houses in Africa?' – that sort of thing. They had really strange ideas, mainly based on Tarzan films, missionaries in cooking pots, that stuff. So I spent a lot of my time putting this right. You knew that this was nonsense, but racism didn't come into it yet. But by the time you were thirteen or so you knew that this was a very patronizing and ultimately wrong attitude. They were ignorant, rather than actually nasty, although later on we began to appreciate how it could fuck you up. And it did.

MIKE PHILLIPS: The worst thing is knowing that people have a clear picture of you which is absolutely nothing to do with you, simply because of your colour. That doesn't matter in itself. It's the sense that you come round the corner and somebody sees you and you can see that they're frightened. You are talking to somebody who can barely decipher two lines of print without moving their lips and you understand very clearly that they think they must be miles cleverer than you are just because they're white. Things like that make you feel humiliated. When I first started teaching there was a sense, not among the teaching staff who had appointed me, but among cleaners, porters, technicians, who had it absolutely clear in their minds that I was only on the staff through some kind of positive discrimination policy.

MUHAMMAD ALI: There was certainly racism at school: name-calling, fighting, white boys beating up Asian boys. I was beaten up at least twice myself. They gave you no reason, but they didn't like you because you were different. It was ignorance: some of these children had the notion that back home we were living in the jungle and climbing trees and so on. I used to explain that actually the way we lived was very sophisticated but they had this notion that we were completely backward and they didn't want to change it. There's no doubt that this was a result of the old empire. This kind of image was promoted deliberately. One of our teachers, an English teacher, told me that she was terrified of people who wore turbans, because when she was a little girl her parents used to frighten her, 'If you're naughty the man in the turban will come and snatch you away.' So she was terrified of Sikhs.

MICHAEL DE SOUZA: I began to come in contact with racism in school. You'd hear little snidey remarks. There was this rhyme: 'Pal meat for dogs, Kit-e-Kat for wogs'. Stupid little things, but terrible. But the people who said it didn't say it to me, because I was really volatile, I could have killed people easily when I was younger. So these young boys wouldn't say anything to me. Maybe older boys, teenagers would, but I didn't mix with them. I knew that I would kill someone, really. That's why a lot of young black kids were put in institutions. They couldn't cope with the language, they couldn't cope with people not understanding them and they were just exploding, they wouldn't hold back. I could hold back, and instead I exploded at home.

RAJAN UDDIN JALAL: In '73 I moved down to London with my father. We went to a council flat in Bow. There were only a few Bangladeshi families and you did feel very isolated. There were only two Bengali children at our school – myself and a friend. There was quite a bit of hostility. We were attacked on several occasions. The first time was outside the school: there were five or six of them, calling us 'Pakis', asking for money. Another time was when I went to

304

a funfair and I was beaten up, absolutely for no reason. The same name-calling, and so on. I didn't go to the police – the beatings were not so serious; anyway the reality of policing in this country is that they only arrive after the incident is over. And there are some things that the police cannot deal with. No one can live inside your mind and support you twenty-four hours a day.

* * *

GULZAR KHAN: One of my children, sixteen years old, was attacked in our own garden. Just because he was looking at the people who live across the road. They called the police. When the police came my wife was there, but they just ignored her, and asked my son, 'What have you been doing to those people across the road?' My son showed him where they had hit him. The policeman told him to look up, 'You are very immature, why can't you look me in the eye?' My son told him that he hadn't reported the attack himself because I, his father, was out, and I was a community leader with lots of contacts with the police. He wanted to wait till I came home. The policeman wanted to know why I knew the police. My son said, I don't know but he knows your chief inspector. The policeman said, 'I don't mind if your father is Chief Sitting Bull, I am the investigating officer round here.' When I came home I heard all about it and we went to the police station. The inspector knew me and apologized. He asked me to make a formal complaint but I would not. I told him, 'You would have to start defending your policeman.' He admitted the man was wrong, he took him off the case, but that makes no difference. I am a leader of the community, I have a number of positions, I am on six or eight different committees, I am well known to the judiciary, I know the chief constable, we talk on first-name terms, but whatever I am, I'm still a black Paki and still my children are treated the same. It doesn't make any difference at all. It doesn't make any difference.

BODRUL ALOM: I have too much evidence through my own experiences and those of the community not to believe that police are racist. A couple of years ago I was driving a brand new Sierra and this police car drew up next to me. He started abusing me: 'You Paki bastard!' all that kind of thing. When I asked him what the problem was, he just said, 'Mind your own business!' I didn't want to take it further because I knew if I argued he could have done anything. I just drove away quietly. I have been on a committee enquiring into racialism, chaired by Ian Mikardo, MP. It was looking into cases of police harassment of members of minority groups. There were only two blacks, I was one. The others were these professional idiots: police inspectors, housing inspectors, all whites. I would bring up these lists and when I asked the police what had been done, they gave no answer at all. They always tried to avoid addressing the problem.

GULZAR KHAN: If a black boy is running, maybe he's just running for a bus, the policeman will always say, 'He's done something, he's stolen something . . .' And they stop him. One young man, from Jamaica, had a new leather coat that his mother had bought him. The police stopped him, 'Come here, where you get the coat?' 'My mother bought it for me.' They put him in the car, put him in a cell for three hours. They bring him out, 'Now then son, let's have the truth.' By then he had found the receipt and that was what he showed them. They had to let him go. That is how things are. So when activists say to me we must be confrontational, what worries me is that we can never fight these institutions. We are only hurting ourselves. We must sit down and talk to them and try to explain our point of view – what we feel, why we feel it and find out why do you treat us like that. What is the difference? We are human, we have feelings, the colour of our skin cannot make that much difference.

MICHAEL DE SOUZA: I was waiting for this girl and I was stood up on the corner and he says to me, 'What are you doing here?' 'I'm waiting for my girlfriend.' 'Fucking hell, I never knew monkeys had girlfriends.' I said, 'We do, we do. We got monkey girlfriends.' He said, 'Cheeky bastard.' I was about fifteen, sixteen, and I was really shocked. It was the first time I'd ever had that kind of treatment.

WILF WALKER: I got busted. I spent a week in Brixton and when I came out my parents had packed my bags and told me they didn't want anything more to do with me. I moved out and went to live in the Grove. They were that kind of naïve West Indian parents who think that if your kid has got into trouble with the law, he must have done something wrong, not the police. Those old-fashioned parents who have children who are languishing in jail right now because they didn't believe that the system was racist and corrupt. They believed that what the white man said was right, so they didn't support their kids. I met people whose stories were just so disgusting, because they're nobody it doesn't matter. You read so many stories about young black people, the injustice they go through and the example they are made of. You never hear about them once they go inside.

CASH BHOGAL: You're more likely to be picked up if you are black than if you are white. And to bring a private prosecution, or to succeed in making a complaint against the police is extremely difficult. The police complaints board itself is run by police officers. We have made a few complaints but in the end it doesn't help. What you usually get is, 'We'll investigate the matter. There is lack of evidence. There are no criminal charges, but we will look into it and see whether a disciplinary action is involved.' That rarely happens. You ask for statements which have been taken: those are not available. So I usually tell our

306

clients that the chances of a successful complaint are very slim and I have to advise them not to try. If a client instructs us, despite that advice, to go ahead with a complaint, we obviously will do it, but my practical advice is that you have the right to complain at any level, but in practice it's not always successful. It is the same in court: there is no doubt that a black person, in the broadest sense of black, is more likely to be found guilty and to be imprisoned than a white person. So on those grounds one can certainly question whether the courts are fair. They appear to be fair, but that is not the case, especially in the criminal courts. This is not said without knowledge, but on the basis of published Home Office statistics.

WILF WALKER: I knew these people, they were importing grass from Africa to England, selling it for hash, which they sent to the States and then got mescalin, which was brought back to England in return. A heavy operation. I was just a ligger in this company. But when they got busted so did I and the bust was such that they decided that I was one of the ringleaders, which was absolute bullshit. But I was black and there was no real ringleader that they knew and they put me up for it. I waited two years on bail before the case came to court. It began to dawn on me that I was a black person and I had to do things from that perspective or I would never get over. It just hit me. And that's when I started to get militant, and that's when I started to become black in terms of my perspective on the world. So by the time I actually came to trial I had become the dangerous black man they wanted me to be. Trial by your peers – bullshit. They weren't my peers, they were just these comfortable white people. There were thirteen people busted, some of them had very respectable families, and I was the only black. They all got suspended sentences except me. The next morning the probation officers were coming round talking to all the white kids, but they all avoided me like the plague. I'll never forget it, as long as I live. Talk about justice. My first ever offence, at anything, and that judge gave me three years and they all got suspended sentences. He called me 'the African in the case'.

CASH BHOGAL: Black barristers don't always lose, and we get quite a number of people off, because at the end of the day the judge, whatever he may think, doesn't make the decision, the decision is left to the jury. The chances of success in a magistrates' court, where there is no jury, is nil, maybe five per cent acquittal for black defendants. Sometimes when a judge is too aggressive to the defence, the jury don't like it. Sometimes they'll come back with a unanimous verdict of not guilty just to annoy the judge.

* * *

TONY GIRARD: When I came to live here, in Camden, I had a dog. You have to take a dog out for exercise. I used to take him round the block last thing at

307

night. I lost count how many times I was stopped on the road by the police while I was walking him. One day I came home late, I couldn't take him out. It was pouring down. But I thought, I must take him out and I thought, I'll just go round the block. So I'm hurrying up, but he's taking his time. I look back to find how far behind me he is and the next thing I know there's this car draws up next to me. Four or five policemen inside it. One gets out, and starts asking me questions. More and more questions. I answered perfectly calmly. He still kept asking, and eventually another one came out of the car, pulled him aside, whispered something in his ear, and he turns back, 'Sorry. The person we're looking for doesn't have a dog.' I said, 'That's all right.' He went away. Of course if I'd have lost my temper, you know what would have happened.

A fortnight wouldn't pass without my being stopped in those days. Once I was stopped right outside, almost on my doorstep. Where do I live? 'Right there.' What's the number? I told him. What's my name? I told him. He was writing my name down and his mate was playing with my dog. 'Hello Rex,' he says. I hadn't told him the dog's name yet, but they already knew me so well. It happened that regularly.

The day I did lose my temper was one Sunday. A friend had moved in round the corner and he called me to ask for some help with his water system. I left with my tools, but half-way there I remembered something. I came back, opened the front door, left my bag on the steps and went downstairs. By the time I came back there were two policeman standing at the door. 'Can I help you?' I said. 'Whose bag is this?' 'Mine.' 'What's it doing there?' I explained what had happened. But they started questioning me – my name, things like that, totally irrelevant questions. Then my aunt, who was living in the basement, came upstairs. She wanted to know exactly when I'd be back, because she wanted to get lunch ready. I gave her a time and she went back downstairs. Then the policeman asked me my address. I showed him on the door. 'Can you prove to me that you live here?' That was when I exploded. The other one pulled him aside, said something, and they left. 'Thank God,' I said.

SIMI BEDFORD: The only people who ever treated my children in a racist manner were policemen. Three years of it. Endlessly being picked up and hassled. The second one was thirteen and I got this phone call at two in the morning to say that my son had been picked up in Putney High Street and he was carrying an offensive weapon. He'd been spending the night with some friends. I was laughing, I said, 'What are you talking about?' 'This is no laughing matter,' they said. So we dashed off to the police. They hadn't picked him up at two in the morning, but that was when they got round to calling us. When we got there we were not allowed to see him – and this radicalized my husband in a big way, because up till then he had always seen me as a bit paranoid – and when we finally did see him this child, who up till then had been a jolly, happy thirteen year old, was a nervous wreck. Nothing much horrid had ever happened to him until he met these policemen. They had threatened to beat him up, they had mug-shotted him, they had fingerprinted him. None of which was legal. By the time I saw him I couldn't believe this was my child. The guy was absolutely dreadful, he said things like, 'Of course these half-castes are criminal types, he'll be back . . .' all this. During all this the bloke was telling my husband, 'She your wife is she? I can understand a bit on the side, but marrying one of them!' Immediately I got home I called my friend Paul Boateng and eventually we got him off. They had just been picked up with a group of white friends and he was the only one they kept.

In the next three years he was arrested eleven times. We lived in a very grand road in Putney, there were no other black children, and none of the whites were ever arrested, just our sons. One time my older son was arrested on the doorstep, picking up a bottle of milk as he came in from an all-night party. The policeman said, 'Gotcha!' and he said, 'I live here,' and the guy would not believe him. By this stage they were so pissed off that they were deliberately harassing us, because every time anything happened I was causing a lot of fuss. The last time they picked him up on a tube train. They'd been to a party and after they'd gone the people at the party rang the police and said someone had stolen something. So they came onto the tube at South Kensington, grabbed him, the only black kid, and in the end all they could accuse him of was using a foreign language calculated to offend passers-by. He had apparently sworn in French. But it's certainly left its mark. They're very pissed off, though they're not bitter. It's like being a political prisoner.

MANZOOR BAHADUR: There is a trend amongst the black community to join the police, although there is still a lot of apprehension. I know one youngster who left social work to join the police force, but left after nine months. There was so much racism in the police force, he said, it was unbelievable. So he went back to social work. He couldn't stick it, though he'd been a special constable for a long time. I do think it would improve things if more black people joined the police, they would certainly bring about changes, but there are two problems that are perceived here. The feeling is that they get used by the white community: we get into the police force and we have to do the dirty on our own community. The other problem is this racism. Not just from the police, but from the community as a whole. There are always some examples of police being made targets by the hooligans, who say, 'Let's have a go, let's get in there', regardless of whether the copper is black or white. But if it's a black policeman the thrill is even greater.

TONY ROBINSON: My son has been in the Navy and the Royal Marines and in the police and he'll sit down and tell you about the things he has been

309

through, especially in the Navy and the Marines, because racism is high there. 'Don't care what they tell you,' he says, 'there is racism there.' He's in the police now, and there's racism there. I encouraged him to join the police. He rose to be a sergeant in the Marines, but as a black person he wasn't going to go any further. He had reached his limit. No way he will ever cross the border and get a commission. It wouldn't be allowed. In the police force I think he can do better. He can make the grade. There are very few blacks in our police force, maybe 23 in all out of 2,500 in the force. Not even one per cent. Some young people have tried to stick themselves in the police, but they still suffer lots of things. My son has been in the Navy and in the Marines and suffered the racism there, so when he comes across it in the police, he knows that he can deal with it better than a young lad who joins from off the street. He's been through it all.

*   *   *

SHREERAM VIDYARTHI: The British are suspicious of foreigners, indeed, but everyone is suspicious of foreigners. This is what I tell my compatriots in this country, that we all dwell in glass houses and that we shouldn't cast stones at each other. We all have got failings. The British are not a particularly racist or a particularly prejudiced community. All of us, Indians too, have their prejudices – caste prejudices, religious prejudices. How were we treating the Africans in Uganda or Kenya where we settled and made fortunes? I don't think we treated blacks any better than the English did. The Indians were imported into Africa by the British to build railways, work as Civil Servants and what have you. And when they went there as traders and made their fortunes, did they treat Africans any better than the English did? I don't think so. I had four black Kenyan journalists training alongside me in Bombay and my fellow Indian journalists were not treating them any better. So I continue to tell my compatriots, yes, if an Englishman shows any racist tendencies I would be happy to criticize him and tell him to his face, but it does not give me an automatic licence to presume that I am whiter than white. We all have our failings, we all have our prejudices. And if others have a few, OK, knock them on their heads for those prejudices, but don't knock them down as people, they're humans too.

FIRDOS ALI: Asians are racist. Particularly East African Asians. This is the majority, although there are a minority who are not. That carries over from the class system in East African countries: first the white people, then the Asians, then the others and fourth and last the Africans. Right at the bottom. Those attitudes, that sense of superiority on the sociological and economical ladder, has been carried on over here. Even though the black people they dislike are not Africans, but West Indians and quite different. As a result you will find

310

that the majority of the shops that get broken into or burnt down in riots are East African, or the Asians who get mugged tend to be from East Africa too. At the same time Afro-Caribbeans are also prejudiced towards Asians. They call them 'coolie-men'. Labourers. So there is a degree of tension between the two communities, which is being carefully fostered by the government, which keeps saying how well Asians do, how hard they work, all that. And they make sure that all the research about Afro-Caribbeans having problems in education and so on is well publicized. What people don't say is that the family atmosphere is quite different. The older generation of West Indians don't muck about; they establish their homes, they go out and do their work, come home and sit down with their families. But the western culture has fucked up the younger generation of West Indians so much. The gadgetry, things like that. But they are offered no work, no proper alternative to the streets. So that's where the trouble lies – it's a powder keg.

MICHAEL DE SOUZA: Everywhere is racist. I don't know a country that's more racist than Trinidad. That is so blatantly racist it's not real. If you're an Indian, a Syrian, or any sort of European, then everything's fine there. If you're black, there's worries. Especially if you're a cultural person, a roots man, it's just terrible. They are just blatantly racist. All the banks, the good jobs, they go to white people. The difference here is that really you're better off. Economically. And everywhere, if you're better off economically you can do what you like. Hate me if you want, but I've got my house, I've got my car, I can do what I want. But if you're in a situation where they hate you and you can't get no work, you can't educate yourself, you can't get an opportunity to aspire to anything, it's terrible.

* * *

YASMIN ALIBHAI: The worst kind of racism is obviously violent, people are beaten up, nobody can say that isn't racism. The other kind, where you are marginalized, is equally damaging because in the end it becomes a self-fulfilling prophecy. Then there's another very pernicious kind of racism which negates you – where you don't exist. That in a way is much more difficult than being bashed on your head. When you're bashed on the head you can fight it, but where is this negation, this invisibility, how do you fight it, how do you even address the issue? You have to watch yourself. I have to teach my son: I tell him when things go wrong in your life it could be because you were simply no good at what you were doing; it could also be because people didn't think you could do it because of who you are. Both those things could happen together. What you must never do is every time things go wrong is blame somebody else, you must constantly say, is there something about me that needs improving?

311

Don't ever say, however, that this problem of invisibility, of other people not seeing you doesn't exist.

JASWINDER AMAR: I think this is a racist country. About fifty per cent of the people are racist, they simply don't want to see you at all. But if you are determined you can fight against that, you can tell them, 'Hey, look, I'm working here, the same as you are. The only difference is our skin colour.'

BALRAJ KHANNA: The trauma of coming here was devastating. I was deeply disillusioned in England. I had been born during the Raj, but I had no knowledge of, no direct experience of it. My family was very affluent, landed gentry. But my father, my grandfather, both had great affection for Britain, both of them were educated here. They had great affection, although they also felt great angst and bitterness towards it. They both fought in India's struggle for independence. They did not go to jail, but they supported Congress and its leaders, they gave money and so forth. But having got rid of the British, having removed them from our system, we could appreciate what had been good. They had left behind a very rich legacy. So England to me was the beautiful, lovely country of equality; indeed the question of equality never entered one's scheme of thinking. It never occurred to one that there was a word called inequality, or injustice or oppression in the racial sense. England for me was the brave new world. That was my fantasy. I had always seen England as the home of freedom and democracy, that kind of thing. But what I found was notices in the shop windows in London saying, 'No blacks, no Indians.' But as far as my life was concerned there was this constant feeling of total alienation, this remarkably intense feeling. We were simply invisible to them, literally invisible.

BENNY BUNSEE: I thought the British were a nice people, a friendly people. Until I began looking for a job and looking for a room. Then I began meeting the racism. And that began to bring into myself something new: I began to start understanding my roots on a global level. I had left the parochialism of South African politics and what I had experienced there now had a global setting. I felt I had been born in South Africa, my parents had come from India, I had moved to England and I was rejected in all three continents. I asked myself, 'Where do I belong, what am I?' It took a long time to answer that question, but what happened was that I began to appreciate the way racism was a global phenomenon that black people face.

YASMIN ALIBHAI: I've done very well. To reach the upper echelons of journalism in a country like this is very hard. I edit the 'Race and Society' section of *New Statesman and Society*. It's hard to get there but I have and that's success, success against all odds and I am proud of it. But the subtle racism that I work with, which surrounds me even in the offices of the lefty *New Statesman*, it's still there. It's extraordinary that I'm the only non-white person on the entire staff of a magazine which prides itself on its politics.

There was this enormous party, for the launch of a new section for the yuppies, 'Artifacts'. All the editors were asked to invite all the trendy people they know. It hadn't occurred to anybody that there might be black trendy people. It hadn't occurred to ask me if I knew anyone from the black community. It's not that they made a specific policy to exclude them, but the assumption is that they don't exist. It's there all the time. It is racism and the nearer you get to those very competitive areas, where you're not meant to be, the more racism you get.

BODRUL ALOM: There are two forms of racism that we experience. One is overt, the other is institutionalized. And people living in this area are victims of both. Overt in being abused by a neighbour on the housing estates, other inhabitants who share this borough, who live in this borough, the traditional racism; poor housing given to Bangladeshis, places that are reserved for new immigrants. Things like that. But whenever an organization emerges that devotes itself to the grievances of the community, the council immediately condemns them. There have been some very strong Bangladeshi organizations, but they have had to be closed down – their funds have been withdrawn by the council. The CRE will give grants, but only on a borough-wide level, not locally. Which type of racism is worse, you cannot say. The one that one is facing at the time. Both are equally bad for us.

BERNIE GRANT: Once I started working in local government I found that the worst racism in this country is institutional. When I arrived there were still the signs on the windows – no blacks, no Irish, no dogs, no children. Then there was the Race Relations Act of 1964 which outlawed all that. But what I found was that the problem lay in this institutional racism, hidden policies which you found in housing, in education and so on. There would be a policy which said that to get a house you needed such and such connections with the borough. Then they would define 'connections' as having your family living there for three generations or whatever. It was moving the goalposts, and it meant that black families hadn't a hope of getting a house. Then there were many policies in education that discriminated against black people. It was easy enough to deal with overt racism: you could fight the people concerned and that would be the end of it. The institutionalized variety just kept going. So I became involved with a lot of anti-racist work: racism awareness training, all sorts of things like that.

* * *

MUHAMMAD AYYAZ: You are always going to get racism. You're walking across the road and somebody may say something, that is natural. I care. If I am not going to say anything to you, why should you say something to me? People shout 'Rushdie!' at you these days. My son comes home from school and tells me, 'We are Pakis.' I say, 'No, we are Pakistanis.'

MIKE PHILLIPS: If you're a secure human being, who cares what people shout out of cars? There are obstacles in the way of anybody in any situation. Our problem is not that there is racism outside, but that we have internalized racist assumptions. There is a lot of racism in the States but I don't think that West Indians are as depressed in the States as they are here. In many ways the English population is very depressed. We're certainly not West Indians any more. We are English. And one of the highly depressing things is the way that lots of us have become English in the sense that the black Liverpudlians were English when we arrived, and we have come closer to them, rather than the other way round. When we came we thought that what was wrong with them was that they were English. We thought, how on earth can they accept their position in a place like Liverpool and be proud of being Liverpudlians? I interviewed a man called Mekonnen, in Kenya, for the BBC, about his life here in the '30s and '40s. I eventually asked him, 'When you finally left England, did you feel any regrets?' He said, 'No! I shit the dust of that accursed place from my feet with joy. Liverpool, Manchester, what were they to me!' That generation did feel like that. If you couldn't get on in this place, and you could go to another place where you could get on, then you left. But we have become a very different black population. We've become limited by the circumstances in which we live. Those limitations are essentially racist limitations, though some English people will say, 'No. What you're talking about is class.'

PETAR OBRATOVIC: English racism is very strictly connected not with colour, but with class. I don't feel myself a great Marxist, but I was educated in Yugoslavia and the only approach I learnt was the dialectic approach, and I can't see things any different. Coloured people arrive in this country uneducated, on the poor side of the spectrum, outcasts, non-integrated; they are used in the same way that Yugoslav workers are used in Germany. And what you get at the end is quite a lot of unpleasant people, in the way that unhappy people, people who live on council estates and are going to steal my bike, who get me cross, are unhappy. I had to buy my own bike back on Portobello. It had been stolen and I saw it there, this old West Indian was selling it. In Yugoslavia we would have discussed the problem, but he was absolutely behaving like a bastard. I can understand that here is someone who is an outcast, who exists on the brink of society and who is always kept on the brink of society, and I

314

understand that in this country are a great number of people who are non-integrated, people who are not part of the society. And that I see as a problem of class.

VERNA WILKINS: I took my books to the local bookshop. He patronizes any local writer, and there aren't many of them. They get a window display, 'Local Author', and so on. So I took my books in and told him what I was doing and where I lived. This was only a couple of weeks after he had given his whole window over to a local woman who had written about her stay in Jamaica. I thought, 'Gosh, this is great,' there was this white woman's book all over the window, with the Jamaican scenery behind her and so on. So I took my books in and told him about them. Claude Gill and Dillons sell them so I dropped those names, Galt had had them. And he did not unfold his arms to talk to me, just kept them folded. Well this was an immediate barrier. But I said, 'Would you like to look at the books. I thought that since I am local' – and I said local about three times – 'you would consider displaying them.' He asked what the discounts were. So I suggested thirty-five per cent. Wouldn't look at it. So I said I'd up it depending on the order. But I suggested that first of all he should look at them. He looked at the covers, all my covers present black children, and said, 'Well, perhaps it's not our sort of book. I'm only here for a few minutes, I'll show them to my colleagues.' He went upstairs, he can't have been gone for more than two seconds, then came back and started saying, 'Well, it's not our sort of thing . . .' He was very apologetic. 'Have you thought of taking them to the inner cities?' Then I got the whole 'We in England don't like buying books, really.' He went on and on. He was obviously in a terrible mess. So I said, 'Look, save yourself all this heartache, I'll take them somewhere else.' I was very upset. And it struck me that if, as he said, my books were not 'for us', white England, then if these books with black children on the covers were not for 'them', conversely their books were not for 'us', black England. My children had been living, had been learning in this system with books that were not for them. How were they going to succeed in the system? If my books are not for you and yours not for me, how could these children learn in a system where the literature that underpinned the whole society, the whole educational system, how could they survive mentally in a situation where the literature was not for them?

ANWAR BATI: I lived with a girl at university who was half English and half American. Her father farmed a few thousand acres of Hampshire and her mother's great-great-grandfather had been twelfth president of the United States. Pretty grand on both sides. I went down to stay with her father. He picked me up at the station and said to me, 'My daughter tells me you're a socialist. What do you think of the budget?' Really trying to put me down all along the line, which was something I had never encountered. This man was outrageously unpleasant throughout the whole period I stayed there. But I couldn't be rude back: I was staying under his roof. He'd turn up to play tennis in lederhosen and tell me, 'Hitler was a good man, he liked animals.' 'The only good Jew I know is Keith Joseph. I was at Harrow with him. Don't like them otherwise.' I had to grin and bear it. He made no specific reference to me, not as such, but a couple of months later my girlfriend was staying with them for the weekend and rang me up in tears on the first day to tell me, 'My father has just asked me if my boyfriend is still slitting animals' throats?' She walked out. He was a great animal-lover and presumably didn't like halal or kosher slaughter. It made me feel very angry, but in the end I knew that there were all these loonies about. I was quite left-wing at that time so I saw it more as a class problem than as a racial one. The more crushing blow came when I went to stay with her in America. I had persuaded my father to give me the fare to see 'a chum in America' although I didn't say it was a girl. It was a lot of money. The night before I was due to leave she rang me up in tears at 3 a.m. and said, 'Talk to my mother,' who came on the phone. Her mother had already asked her daughter, did I *look* Pakistani, and had been assured that I didn't. She then told me, 'You have not introduced my daughter to your parents?' I said, 'No, why should I have done?' 'Don't you realize that coming out here constitutes an engagement?' I said, 'No, I didn't realize that. I was just coming for a holiday.' 'Well, I think it's better that you don't come.'

SIMI BEDFORD: There is a two-tier system about blackness. A lot of people even now have this idea that black people have no culture. They don't understand Africa, so we are assumed to be savages. As my father used to say, when the British go to China or Burma or wherever they see the people in their little hats and busy in their little fields, and they are doing things the British can relate to. But in Africa they see these Masai with lions' manes on their heads charging all over the place and they've got nothing to relate to at all, they just think it's very dangerous and label it as such. In India they built on the system that was already there, whereas in Africa they destroyed it. After that it was more convenient for everyone to say that there was nothing there. So that was what we were struggling with in Britain. Not that it's exclusively British. The Chinese have words for various countries. That for Germany is 'virtuous', America is 'beautiful', England is 'heroic' and the whole of Africa is 'bad'. Also people who refuse to accept the current ideology are known as 'black'.

CUI QU: The Chinese are very racially prejudiced. They don't like black people. There are no blacks in China. A few students from Africa, and they are hated. They don't like the Indian people either.

* * *

BENNY BUNSEE: It was only when I came to England and began to meet discrimination that I began to think, 'Bloody hell, just where do I belong?' The discrimination in South Africa had been very different. It was institutionalized there. Here, in Britain, you are in the midst of white people and it jabs you, you suddenly realize how powerless you are. You can get a group of white people who are nice to you for years, but you just have to get one person to jab you and that upsets you. Suddenly you're not sure what people are thinking, although they seem to have been nice for a long time. In South Africa you're totally isolated from whites. The only time you meet them is when you go on a bus, though in my time the buses were segregated. Or you'd pass them on the beach, on your way to your side of the beach, or you'd meet them at your workplace, but you would *never* otherwise have any kind of social intermingling. A very different kind of experience from the kind of racism you meet in Britain. Though you know it's there: you see their wealth and you see your poverty and it's there all the time. But it permeates your life in a very different kind of way.

CHRISTOPHER HOPE: I'd always thought the British were a pacific, easy-going, tolerant people, with a well-developed sense of humour. I discovered none of this to be true. I saw the British attitude towards coloured foreigners: I'd always imagined the South African situation was unique but it dawned on me both in France and England that a lot of people behaved in that way, but they didn't make a virtue out of it. They were as uncomfortable with blacks, with Chinese, with curious foreigners as white South Africans had ever been. More uncomfortable. When I was teaching, my students would say things about one white man being worth several blacks with an openness that no South African would ever have had. Because I was a white South African I was presumably expected to understand such sentiments. I felt their openness was because of the lack of experience of racial problems. All this made me feel rather homesick in a curious way. The French will freely admit to being racist, but you'd never expect such a forthright attitude here. In the mid '70s here immigration was the big thing and people just said, 'There are too many of them', the swamping bit and so on. Sentiments that would have gone down very well in the sort of places in South Africa that I'd come from. People here didn't seem to be aware of the implications of what they were saying.

BRYAN GOULD: I'm sure England is a racist country. But as is true of so many things that are English, it's subtler, not quite as brutal and overt as it is elsewhere. But it's very deeply ingrained and has a huge range of expressions. I think that to be black in Britain is quite a burden. The poorer you are and the blacker you are the harder time you are going to have.

DON ATYEO: You do become conscious as an immigrant of the benefits of being white very quickly. Standing in the queue at Heathrow with far less claim

317

in many ways to get into the country than lots of others, you'd be taken out of the queue by an immigration officer who'd send you through while they slowly processed all those jumbos from Kenya or wherever, with people all of whom had a British passport. But being an Australian, which means you're coming from a country which does have known racist views, every cabbie in the land opens up to you. 'Those fucking black bastards . . . I'd go to your country like a shot, no fucking nonsense with these niggers . . .' all that shit.

* * *

ZERBANOO GIFFORD: When I was standing in elections people would break into the car and tear the gears out; we used to have telephone calls threatening me; we had a break-in to the house one day in broad daylight. One day the windows had been broken and someone had left a death threat for me. Someone nearly pushed my car off the road one evening when I was coming home from a meeting. I've had police guards. So it's unnerving. You do need a lot of courage. At one stage I sat with my father and told him that I wondered whether what I was doing was right. I've got young children, I don't know whether it's responsible as a mother to carry on. He said, 'Nobody at all would hold anything against you if you did give up, they would quite understand. But having said that, if you do you will never be able to do anything in life because these people have cowed you. You're a fighter. Tell them to fuck off!' So when they phoned up the next time I said exactly that. I said, 'You're not going to stop me. Every newspaper in the country has my photograph. If you want to make a martyr out of me, please do. But I am determined to do what I am going to do and you will not stop me.' They used to be quite reasonable on the phone. Which really surprised me. The voices were quite reasonable. They weren't yobs. We never knew who was doing it. I would be speaking on the phone and somebody would come on to the line and start abusing both of us. British Telecom tried to track down who was making the calls. It was quite remarkable: whoever it was knew what I was up to. They would know when I was alone in the house. Once they thought I was by myself, presumably they'd seen someone leave, a nurse, quite an old lady, but she had come back through the back door. She had worked for the police and when the phone rang and she saw I was distressed, she picked up the phone. They said, 'We know you're alone, we know the lady has left.' They'd only speak to a woman's voice, never to my husband.

SHREELA FLATHER: I have had phone calls from people who told me what they thought of me. I've had hate mail, some of which could be quite upsetting. I don't mind political abuse, but emotional, racist stuff is much worse. In 1982, when I was on the CRE, we also had a very nasty racial attack by a group called the White Defence Force. It was a bad time and I was expecting something:

318

somebody threw a metal bar through our kitchen window. Our oak table is still dented. They daubed 'Wogs out!' and 'Race traitor lives here' – my white husband – on our gate. There was some very nasty literature going around. But my son and husband chased them off, although they left another big metal bar outside the front door. Presumably they intended to break our windows. I was just grateful that nobody was hurt. The police said to us, 'Don't tell anybody.' We replied that if people like us don't tell anybody who is going to? We had a little conference and decided to tell the quality papers, which we did. *The Times* did a very good piece. I was disappointed by the police. I always keep hoping that they won't behave in the way everyone says they do behave. One of them told me, 'It's only a prank.' We weren't too thrilled with that. Then they sent us somebody to stay with us over the next couple of weekends and I wondered whether I'd have preferred him inside or outside – he was a real thug. Having said that, I still have a lot of respect for the police. It's not a job I'd want to do. But the police have a lot to live up to, and we expect a lot from them.

ZERBANOO GIFFORD: My family has been subjected to racial attacks from a minority of very sick people and it has been most unpleasant and most distressing, especially when you have young children. I've stood up to be counted and they have not liked it. I don't have to become an MP, I don't have to become a councillor, I can stay in my house and mind my own business. I have a husband who is wonderful, I have lovely children and I don't have to be doing what I have chosen to do, but I do get up and I say what has to be said. I don't care what these people think. It is very important that the British public understand that racial attacks don't just happen to people in the East End of London. It happens across the board. I don't know who they are, I don't know where they come from, but they are vermin and they need to be exterminated. Anybody that threatens these extremists is likely to be attacked. But they are vermin and they are making people's lives unhappy. What is so distressing is that when it happens, everybody thinks that it is the British character. But the British character is not like this. I can't tell you all the people who wrote to me when I was attacked and said how ashamed they felt and what could they do, because this is not how they like to think that their country is, and that these people are getting away with this sort of extremism and they don't like to see that.

SIMI BEDFORD: Dealing with racism is like living with the bomb – it's there and you live with it. It is an absolute underlying fact of life. It becomes so much so that you notice it, but you can't let it get on top of you. Depending on the circumstances of your own life it is either more or less impinging, but certainly it's always there. It colours every single thing that I feel and think about. It's always there. There are times when you sit on a bus and someone very obviously pulls their skirt out of the way; you just cannot account for hostility in some situations, what the '60s called bad vibes.

TONY GIRARD: You can pass legislation, but you can't change people. Though the legislation of the '60s has worked. You may not like me but if I want a loaf of bread, you've got to sell it to me. That's all I'm paying for. As long as I get the bread. I don't care whether you like me or not. So that's something. But it doesn't alter individuals one bit. Racism in England is worse than in America. There at least it's in the open: you know who your enemies are, you know how to cope with it. Here you don't know and that is dangerous. People are very nice on the surface but that means nothing. It's British hypocrisy. If I know someone doesn't like me, fine, then I know you don't like me. Everybody has a right to like or dislike who they want. I'm the only black man who owns a house in this street, and it doesn't go down too well with some neighbours. Maybe they think I'll bring the property prices down.

MICHAEL IGNATIEFF: People are always making these fatuous parallels between the British race relations scene and the American one. I've never thought it's the same here. I'm not the slightest bit sentimental or romantic about what it's like being black in Britain, but it is different. I've always had this feeling that British post-imperial identities are in a mess. What's awful about the United States is that the society still believes in itself in this fervent, bug-eyed way. The cross you have to bear for failure in that society, for not buying the whole bloody dream in all its murderousness, is just terrible. Whereas British society, partly because it is in such a mess, partly because it doesn't work terribly well for lots of people beyond just blacks and Asians, and because it doesn't have all this striding, ranting jingoistic sense of itself, *pace* the Falklands (which I never believed was as jingoistic as people said), there's a place for me in this society, and there's a place for them in this society and that's partly because this society doesn't believe in itself in the same way that it did. And that's all to the good if you come into it. The culture of grandeur, and self-confidence and assurance left absolutely no place, not just to the working class, but to anybody who had different face or accent or skin. And all that has gone. Which means it is a different scene for people and it's all much more up for grabs and the old white-English-only crap won't work.

ZERBANOO GIFFORD: It's up to the Asians to stand up. In the '30s the Jews stood up and they had rallies and they stopped these people marching through the East End and everything else and we've got to stand up and say we're not accepting this kind of behaviour. We're in this country, we're taking part, we're contributing, we want to be recognized. We're not some kind of illegal immigrants. The only person who can do it is ourselves. We can't rely on other people. We've got to get up ourselves and look after ourselves. The Jewish community did it. They made money, they helped each other. When they were kept out of clubs they changed the situation – they founded their own clubs. They did it. They had the guts to do it. It took them generations. How many times did Rothschild have to stand before he got into Parliament? He didn't get in first time. There was prejudice but he kept standing and the Jewish community had money and used their money and realized that they could become something in this country. How many Jews are there in Parliament now? An extraordinary number. They are still a minority in this country but they've made a huge impact. Jews all laugh and say to me that they weren't so united, but in the end they were. They had a common purpose.

* * *

DESMOND GITTENS: How do you react to discrimination? How do you cope with it? Do you get angry, throw bottles, riot, or do you reason it out, do you try to educate the person who is being discriminatory? Everyone has to deal with their own situation as they find it. A black woman shopping in the market, touching a bit of tomato, the white seller saying, 'Don't touch me tomatoes.' She could interpret it that it's her black hand touching the tomato that gets him mad. It may well not be true, the man may just hate anyone touching the stall, but we have the option to wonder because of discrimination. There are a lot of cases where it really doesn't exist but its been implanted in the person who thinks they are being discriminated against. They expect discrimination and it happens.

RAJINDER SINGH: I don't think that the English character is racist. But because they were taught by their rulers that ruling an empire meant they must be superior to everyone else, now they are just big-headed, even though they have nothing. The economy is down every day, they can't compete with the people they beat in the last war – Germany, Japan – but they still think that Britian is best. Look at the way Thatcher supports South Africa. They are torturing black people there, but she supports it. It's in the blood now. It will take time for things to change. Not until we fight over here, when our kids fight over here then they will get their rights because then the government will not be able to deny them. There is so much discrimination. If you attempt to get into an educational institution, if you are white you will be welcome, if you are any other colour you won't be accepted, unless you show that you can beat them at what they do. And discrimination will remain for many years yet.

YASMIN ALIBHAI: How can you tell a nation that they had the right to go out and rape and plunder all over the world because those countries were full of appalling, stupid, barbaric people, and suddenly when they arrive on your shores you're supposed to forget that and pretend that it wasn't true. Being an immigrant to the country that once had this colonial relationship with you and your ancestors, it's like sending an abused child back home. It's a very odd relationship and it's bound to produce problems. The British do have this problem with foreigners of any colour – they're always seen as second-rate – but the position of people from the Third World is especially negative. Every country is wary of foreigners, but here it's a profound dislike, a profoundly horrible distaste which is then justified in all manner of ways. And because the British are so retentive, because they hold everything inside, you can't even clear the passages out.

VINCENT REID: My quarrel with white people is not that they made slaves of black people. It isn't that. White people were also slaves. My quarrel isn't with that physical brutality, although I think that aspects of it were exceptional. Even so, that is not really my quarrel. My quarrel is that we were excluded from the benefits of slavery. And were excluded in spite of the fact that we brought enormous skills to the development of capitalism in western society. What do white people know about tropical agriculture? Nothing. The people who did know must have been black. Although our bodies were enchained and we were undertaking this brutal labour, we were nevertheless contributing to the successful development of the enterprise. You might well say that it was an involuntary contribution, but a contribution nevertheless. Yet when you read about, for instance, the successful growing of crops they don't mention black people. It's as if these things happened by themselves. Black people were given no credit. In so far as economic benefits went, black people got nothing. Slavery also smashed Africa. It wasn't a rape, it was a catastrophe from which Africa has not yet recovered. But I'm not even complaining about that. What I am complaining about is that the enslavement of one people by another for the first time in human history was justified on the basis that the people that were enslaved were not humans. Greek slaves could be freed, so could Roman ones, but with black slavery, your progeny was a slave. And the white people believed that this was almost a god-given thing to do, to enslave black people.

MANZOOR BAHADUR: A lot of feelings towards black people came from the British empire. And that's still there in the British culture. It will take many years to go away. A classic example of the influence and the power of the British raj in India is that even today many people there think that it is good to speak English, that Urdu is a second-rate language, the laws are still based on the English law, it's good to be white. If you're dark skinned you are looked down upon. It's the result of generations of British rule in India; this drumming in of 'white is beautiful', of 'white culture is superior', has left a long-lasting impression.

322

SHREELA FLATHER: Not only do the British think that they are superior as people but they think that their culture is superior to other cultures. That's why the whole multicultural thing came a cropper. You can't teach a variety of cultures if you don't give them all equal status. If you are going to talk about somebody else's culture with the underlying belief that really it is not as good as ours but really we *ought* to learn a bit about it, it's worse than lip-service. You're actually denigrating that culture by giving it a lower status. It's also selective: you can use a careful selection of aspects of that culture to turn the whole thing upside down.

VINCENT REID: Arguments developed that attested to black inferiority in so many ways. All the kinds of contributions to human development and know-ledge that black people had made were expunged from human knowledge. I think the ultimate example of that is the notion that black people's concept of the divine, of God, of the origin of man and man's purposes was held up to ridicule, so much so that now all the concepts of the black god are associated with ridiculousness, like voodoo or obeah or juju. The very nature of those names denigrate the black man's spirituality and seek to justify the white man's civilization by substituting his morality, his ethics and so on. If you deny people their gods you deny them their humanity. That's why as a young man I admired the Jew. Regardless of the brutality that was meted out in Warsaw or Auschwitz, it isn't wrong to be a Jew. They're like everybody else, they make mistakes, they do terrible things, they do good things, but they have no need to apologize to anybody for this, for being a Jew. There's no reason to apologize to anybody for being black and yet if you look at the Christian Bible you have a story in the Song of Solomon where the Shulamite maiden, who is a black woman, says to Solomon, 'Look not upon me because I am black, I am black but comely.' Is that a racist statement? The Bible is full of that, yet blacks accept that, they accept that white people have redeemed them. If you accept that, then you must forever remain a mimic, an imitator, you can never be yourself and that means you're always going to be second-rate and second-class. In your position. Not in our own native wit or intelligence, but because somebody has inculcated that into you, you've had it done to you and you've done it well, like a trained fucking monkey.

RAJAN UDDIN JALAL: Even the worst of the white working class assume that they are better than any Asian or Bengali. That's rubbish. I have done plenty of jobs that most white people couldn't get. Yet the drunk lying in the gutter still sees himself as better than me, just because he is white. That's the superiority notion and it's wrong. It is false consciousness on behalf of working-class people. It's something that happens within our community when people start to do well. They find themselves confused about their own culture and start to reject it. I say, 'I will have friends, I will have allies, I will have everything to do with other communities – but if I give up my own identity, then none of them will respect me.' That is our experience. There are people in my culture who believe that the white man is superior – you can find them back in Dhaka, when Prince Charles comes they think he is so superior – but we have to overcome all that.

SIMI BEDFORD: England is racist, but it's also very class-ridden. So people meeting me are in a dilemma. A working-class person sees a black person and thinks that's one of them that we used to rule, but in my case nevertheless comes out with a voice that they associate with the oppressor, which gives them a big problem. Middle-class people when they see you come rushing over to patronize you and give you sixpence or whatever, then they find you speak in exactly the same way as they do, that you've had exactly the same education, they can become very aggressive. In fairness, my experiences were evenly divided between those whites who were absolutely appalling and those who were absolutely super.

SHREERAM VIDYARTHI: When I bought my house in Sittingbourne some upwardly mobile idiot bought the house opposite us. He changed his front door, put up an eight-foot-high timber fence round his property, and one day, quite casually while mowing my front lawn, I asked him why he was wrapping himself up in this way? He turned around and said quite seriously, 'To keep your sort out.' Now that is racism. If I had taken him to be typical of every English person, I would have declared you all morons. But I don't.

VINCENT REID: The image of the black man has changed. In the old days, the 'fifties, the racists said we were all out there raping white women. Now all they say is that we mug them.

MANZOOR BAHADUR: People who got to know me would say, 'Yo're all right, you're not like the other Pakis. You're different.' Patronizing, see. So I'd ask them, 'Tell me, for goodness' sake, how I'm different? I eat the same food, I'm of the same religion, the same colour, I speak the same language, how am I different to those people you're calling Pakis?' There wasn't any answer to that – they thought they were patting me on the back.

ZERBANOO GIFFORD: People get too concerned with whether they are called Asian or black, or whether they're called chair or chairman or chairwoman or whatever. People say to me that terminology is important, terminology is what changes people's attitudes, which it does, very slowly, but really at the end of the day what matters is how you treat an individual. What I have also found is
324

people telling me, 'Oh but you're not an Asian, you're so nice.' Or 'You speak such good English' or 'You're so different from them'. So I ask them, 'What makes me so different? Only because you know me. I'm no different. I'm an Asian, nothing else. I'm an Indian and I'm proud of it. If you like me, you'd like them, but you haven't taken the time to get to know them.' I never found it very easy to go to meetings and find myself the only Asian, you do feel slightly uncomfortable, that you're something of a token and people are expecting you to be different, but somebody's got to do it.

* * *

PETER VO: As soon as we came to live here in Bermondsey, on this very large council estate, we were attacked. My wife was stoned by them. During that first winter people used to throw snowballs at us in the street. Why? We had no idea. She was on the way to the market and someone stopped her and abused her, but she couldn't understand what they were saying. These things happened more to my wife than to me. Perhaps it's because I could speak English and explain myself, I don't know. Perhaps just because I am a man. My son had a very, very hard time at school because of the language problem. There were no special classes, anyway not enough. The other children were unpleasant. There was even fighting between the Vietnamese and the local people in Deptford. At first I was very very surprised and very unhappy and I did not think that in a country like this which is supposed to be so civilized that this would happen. But I appreciated that this kind of racist attack was not the policy of the British government. This kind of thing would happen anywhere. There are many people unemployed. I have to try and understand.

VU DUY TU: I was given a flat at Sydenham Hill. Unfortunately only twenty-four hours after I moved in we started to suffer harassment. Somebody used an air-gun to shoot through my door. They put National Front stickers on my door, they frightened my children, smashed my windows. I reported it the police. They checked it out and suggested that I move to another flat – 'We cannot guard your house permanently.' I said that I understood. I don't know what it was, I don't know why they did it. The police tried to explain to me that the National Front were only a minority in the UK, extreme nationalists. Not only anti-Vietnamese, but everyone not English. They hated us and the police couldn't stop them. But we had to stay for a year, waiting for somewhere else. There were a couple more incidents, but fortunately I had very good neighbours.

One day a young man, about twenty-five years old, tried to stop my son, who was only fourteen. My son came running home and knocked on the door, crying, 'Daddy, please save me, someone beat me!' I opened the door. I was so upset and so angry and there was this boy and I asked him 'Why? Why do you threaten my child?' He said, 'I want him to kneel down to lick my shoes. He has spat on my shoes.' I said, 'Mister, no way. I know my son very well. You are very tall, he's very small, very young. Never he dare spit on your shoes. Nor would I allow him to do what you request.' My neighbour heard it all. She opened her door and told him, 'Go away now. I know that family and I love that boy. Don't cause him trouble.' And he went away. But my son had to stay home for a week, he didn't dare go to school.

RAJAN UDDIN JALAL: The problem here is not the NF. They can be squashed by our communities without any outside help, within twenty-four hours. There can always be another battle of Cable Street. We are becoming the community guardians now. Of the whole community. I have been selected as a council candidate and I shan't, if I get elected, only be representing Bengalis, I shall be representing the people who support our manifesto, black and white. The entire community. This is important and this is typical of the sort of changes that are happening. The real problem is the racism we find in institutions, the respectable racism. The racism of papers like the *Sun*, the racism of Mrs Thatcher, the racism of the middle classes. Although the middle classes cannot ignore the realities, they don't have to live among us, as the white working classes do. And that is why we have to work on the white working classes and their racism. Racism is primarily a problem for the white community. They have got to tackle it. If they don't, then there will be unrest.

GINA ADAMOU: It's a class thing. The working-class English person hates foreigners and black people and all the ethnic minorities more than the more educated person does. They have more to fear in a way. They think we are taking their houses away and their jobs away – which is completely wrong.

MANZOOR BAHADUR: Our problems are similar to those experienced by disadvantaged whites, except they are worse. Yes, a lot of the racism comes from them. They've made us into their scapegoats, the people who've taken their jobs. It's a matter of divide and rule. The tabloid newspapers deliberately foster that belief and make people believe that, which keeps them away from the real issues.

ZERBANOO GIFFORD: The Prime Minister has attacked Labour councillors for allegedly threatening Tory councillors and said how appalling it is for anyone to be threatened in this way. I would have liked Mrs Thatcher to have got up and said how appalling it is that there are racial attacks against Asians or any other community in this country. But she has never once stood up and said that. At the end of the day leadership comes from the head. The only leader in the whole country that has ever got up at a party conference which can be seen by the whole nation, not just some little hole-in-the-corner gathering where they can say, 'No, I hate racial attacks too and if you boys support me and give me money and votes I'll see you all right', but really standing up and being counted, was David Steel, who did just that, and underlined the importance of the ethnic minority community. Most people are decent, but they're nervous, because all they hear is this sort of vileness from people like Terry Dicks. I was on a programme with Dicks and we were talking about a racial attack and he turned round to me and said, 'You encourage blacks to rape whites.' I told him that I found that deeply, deeply insulting. I spend my life trying to highlight these appalling acts against women, and how could he possibly say anything vile? All he said was, 'You don't understand, white women are raped every day.' These people are so forceful, so maniacal. The British media has the cheek to say that Enoch Powell, Dicks, whoever it is, is articulating the views of the British people. Politicians aren't there to 'articulate the views of the British people', they're there to lead the British people into a decent way of living, a better lifestyle, not to articulate base, vulgar attitudes.

FIRDOS ALI: Powell won't come and kick your arse himself. No, he'll make the fucking dockers or someone do that. The docker doesn't understand what the hell Powell is saying, it's all Latin and Greek, but he will titillate him to do the dirty work.

* * *

SIMI BEDFORD: To my shame the Notting Dale riots of 1958 simply didn't impinge. I was at school in Somerset. There was this great difference between Africans, like me, and West Indians. It was a mutual thing: West Indians by and large looked down on Africans. They had largely internalized all the negative propaganda about Africa. They genuinely believed that Africans were savages. They wanted to distance themselves as far as possible from all those negative images of Africa. You wanted to be pale-skinned, straight-haired, as American as possible. The Africans, in the crudest way, saw the West Indians as slaves, as fools – the ones who got caught. There was the class thing: Africans who come here are by and large middle class; the West Indians are workers. Which naturally divides you in British society. Once, when I was fourteen, I saw a whole load of West Indians in a church in Birmingham and I was shocked. I thought, 'My God, all these black people!' We never saw them in all these shires we were living in. I had no idea that there were black communities like that in England. I read about Notting Dale and I'm sure it touched me, but it was a foreign country, like things in South Africa.

VINCENT REID: My interpretation of the Notting Dale race riots is that the middle classes weren't sure just what this kind of immigration would mean.

Not just any immigration, but black people. All the ways in which black people were portrayed – brutal, savage – were not very nice. But they had a need to use their brute labour. They weren't certain what the reception of this black labour force would be. Because of this, even before one black immigrant set foot in this country, they prepared a white working-class backlash. So that if anything went wrong, they could wash their hands of it, like Pontius Pilate, and say, 'Well, it's down to working-class ignorance.' They prepared it all in terms of the ridiculous arguments that black people were 'coming to take your jobs'. But black people were doing jobs that white people didn't want. The hours and the pay and the conditions were not acceptable to white people. This was after the war, there was a Labour government in power, you had a supreme notion of progress, the belief that the mass of people in this country were better off in terms of education, housing, you name it. Nevertheless they prepared this notion that black people were going to rob them of this progress. This was done through the press, you only have to read something like the *South London Press* from about 1952 . . . you have arguments that 'black men were taking our jobs, and taking our white women', all kinds of things like that. I might be giving them more credit than is their due but I do think that they were deliberate, they worked it out in advance. They created a fall-back position.

By 1958 this racist rubbish had gathered into a storm. Moseley was saying, 'We are going to drive you back to the sea, drive you out of the country', and I think the authorities were happy to see that; it was evident by then that the black people who were here were not going to return to the poverty that they had escaped from. They were willing to stay and to fight. And the government was prepared to find out which way the storm was blowing and what the outcome would be, with this white backlash. Here was Moseley, a fascist who was interned during the war, with his headquarters in Princedale Road, leading this rabble. What were the police doing? What stopped the realization of middle-class fears, the race riots, was the judgment of Justice Salmon, when he gave four years to white boys for causing an affray. This judgment was crucial in stopping those bizarre attacks.

ZERBANOO GIFFORD: Britain has been quite remarkable in the way in which it has opened its shores to many people. I don't know other countries which would have been so magnanimous. What I see now is a number of very unpleasant politicians, leading politicians, who have decided to make the Asian community into scapegoats. I find that sickening. Look at people like Moseley, that's sickening. Their actions and words do have repercussions, great repercussions. Basically people are very decent, but there is a minority that is vile and it is up to everybody to get up and say that these people are vile and stamp their vileness down. What I don't like are politicians or anyone else who appeal continuously to the baser instincts. That is what is so sickening. That has

328

repercussions, every action, every word has repercussions. I can see that when somebody gets up and makes some silly statement the weak-minded actually react to it. You can see the unpleasantness and the racism happening. One could say that while the British are fine as a nation, the problem is with the people they choose to lead them. And the reason why we have the leaders we do is that most people don't want to go into politics and don't want to lead.

DESMOND GITTENS: There's very little you can do about discrimination. We as human beings have discriminatory processes that we need to have to survive. You have to be able to discriminate between a friend and an enemy. Whether he be black, white, green, yellow or blue. If I have enemies I discriminate against them, no matter what colour they are, if there is some reason. And although racist discrimination isn't against real enemies, I've had discussions with rampant racists who are prepared to talk about it and they say, 'Yes, you are a threat. You have no right here, you're discolouring the country. We see our country as a white country, with a white race and people who come here not of the same culture, not of the same colour, not of the same religion constitute a threat.'

WITOLD STARECKI: In my film on the British mystique is this true British eccentric. Not a nutcase, not mentally ill, but an extreme eccentric. I find him sincere, I find him very nice, interesting, the sort of person you dream of meeting when you do this sort of film. This guy, he's about sixty, he's white and he lives in Brixton, feels threatened by his local community. He is afraid of leaving his home. He has a whole philosophy to explain his position: he disagrees with all this openness to other cultures, he believes that the only way Britain can survive is to become more aware of its Britishness and to preserve the mentality, the tradition and so on – otherwise it will disappear. It's like in drama: a good drama is when both sides have rights, not when one side is right, the other is wrong. The people who live in his house were mugged, beaten or whatever and I believe that he is genuinely frightened.

VERNA WILKINS: I meet these white liberals whose sole aim in life is to help me and by Christ they get really angry when I can't be helped! There is a lot of good to be said for white liberals, but I have met people who seem to be obsessed with getting together and comparing notes on the negative images of black people they've managed to find in the media. They're supposed to be fighting racism in schools and in the press and in libraries and all they'd be doing was comparing notes: my nasty piece in the paper is nastier than your nasty piece in the paper which is nastier than ... Round and round it goes. I kept saying, 'Excuse me, we're here to fight something, not just to sit around gorging yourself on outrage.' But they needed to do it. This self-flagellation I

329

didn't need. My attitude is, are you going to come and do something or are you just going to talk? I could find racism just by opening my front door, but I'm not interested in looking. Let's just do something positive. Gradually we've weaned them off peeling the golliwogs from the jamjars. The fact is, don't just compare notes, do something. Then there's the problem when a black person tries to do something in this company and it doesn't work. But the white liberals can't come out and tell her it doesn't work. Because she's black they can't just say, 'You're wrong.' Her ideas were actually self-destructive and the whites would murder her for it, but they don't say that, instead they just say, 'It's fine, it's lovely.' It's very difficult, but I had to step in and say that was wrong, whoever was saying it.

BENNY BUNSEE: I became involved in anti-racism here, I was very active, very much a socialist. But one of the things that disturbed me at this time was the racialism of the white socialists. I began to have a lot of battles with the white Left. I found them terribly racist and slowly I am realizing that this great philosophy – socialism – is also racist. These people who were meant to be my political comrades were also betraying us. These people with whom we were supposed to be working to create a just, non-racialist world for all regardless of race, colour and creed, were equally racist. So I started to abandon European intepretations of socialism and Marxism. Which pushed me more and more into this vision of the world as a straight dichotomy: black and white. Which is where I remain today. To me European socialists have failed, European humanists have failed, European progressives of all kinds have failed – and they have all participated in our exploitation and our oppression. They might have things like Live Aid, but that frankly is an insult. Black people don't want that kind of thing. We don't want that kind of aid – we just want them to get off our backs. The first step to create truly independent countries is to get rid of every type of foreign, white domination and interference. We must rewrite the history of the world, and remove it from the white, European viewpoint.

VINCENT REID: W. E. B. Dubois said that the major problem of the twentieth century is the problem of race. I'd want to tell him if he were still alive that he was wrong: the major problem of the twenty-first century will also be race. We have a cultural perception of people that is hierarchical. And that hierarchy is not merely cultural but based on colour as well. If England is a dance to which the immigrant has to learn the steps, the black people are not allowed on the floor.

21 Politics: Taking a Stand

'At the end of the day the people who fight will win. The people who fight will gain.'

DESMOND GITTENS: In 1968 I set up a restaurant in Portobello Road – Backayard. There were three of us involved. There was Darcus Howe, Rhodan Gordon and myself, who were friends. We realized that we needed a place where we can hang out, we needed a place where we can have discussions. Not only that but this Black Power thing was really taking off. Darcus got involved with Vanessa Redgrave. There was already a West Indian restaurant on the site of Backayard, the Las Palmas, owned by a chap from Jamaica who we called Son, and his wife Annie. They were selling up to go to the States and they wanted £9,000 for the lease. Vanessa Redgrave offered to give this money to us to buy the lease. Vanessa got the money somehow. $22,000 in cash. Darcus put the whole lot in his back pocket and I said, 'Look man, we've got to stick by what we planned, don't go off and have a binge with it.' Anyway we managed to get the lease and set up the Backayard.

MICHAEL DE SOUZA: I wouldn't eat there, I found it intimidating, I didn't know what it was. It was all right if you were a black intellectual but how many black intellectuals were there? People I was going to school with had joined this thing called UBIO (United Black Immigrants Overseas) and some of them became really extreme. They don't like white people, they don't like this, they don't like that. But I've never been an extremist and those things didn't appeal to me. My brother went through the Black Panthers and all that. Little Afro – he didn't have that much hair – big black fist on his chest, he was a brother, he was this and that. But not me.

DESMOND GITTENS: We had Backayard restaurant on the ground floor, and we had a little boutique and right above we had a little office so that Darcus could give advice to people. We called it the Black People's Information Centre. There were a lot of people who had come over here who were illiterate. We gave a lot of advice on employment, housing and, initially, racial discrimination. From your landlord, or in a shop, and most of all industrial, where people got fired without compensation, things like that.

LEENA DHINGRA: I didn't become a member of the Black United and Freedom Party, things like that, but I did join a group and we debated the black identity, defining it as a political identity, mobilizing and talking to people.

331

The black identity really was a way of coming together in a political way. It was a way of identifying with all those who were experiencing the same things for the same reason – colour. There is a fragmentation – you're West Indian, you're Indian, whatever – but basically our reality here is that we are all black. Therefore don't split yourself up from certain other people because they are your brothers in their oppression and the way that they are exploited. One of our people had been sent off to check out some new group. We asked him what was the composition. He said, 'Well, the usual – blacks and Jews.' And that's how it was at that time. These little groups who weren't quite within the social mainstream, looking at things from an ideological viewpoint.

SIMI BEDFORD: My sisters and I all rebelled in different ways. I did it by going the bohemian route, rejecting money and materialism and politics and looking for the high moral purity of literature, self-fulfilment and so on. My sister believed that one needed strictly political solutions for change. I felt that by marrying a white man, by having half-caste children, by going into places where blacks couldn't previously go, this also changed things, although in a different way. A lot of the black gains of the '60s have been completely eroded, but the people I've met, my children's white grandparents, people like that, they've had to give up their prejudices if they had them. A lot of people who say quite happily that they'll vote for black sections, say, are not so good at actually living next door to a black person. I have an adopted daughter. Now this was not for a moment done for altruistic reasons. I had two sons and I desperately wanted a daughter. This is a while ago now, she's eighteen, but I fought all sorts of little battles. It's one thing to sit around saying yes, we should have a law that gives black children to black families, but it's another thing actually to do it, actually to adopt a child and have it. It's a different level of commitment. Political people tend to look down on those who don't march but just do things, but I'm all for the prosaic details of just doing things rather than all the shouting and marching. I am very concerned about certain things – South Africa for instance – but I also know that there is a limit to what I can do. Petitions and so on are fine, but in the end you are here and they are there.

BERNIE GRANT: We had a row with the university over South Africa in 1969. They were sending student engineers out to South Africa and Zambia for work experience during the summer vacation. But they were sending white students only; black students weren't allowed. South Africa certainly wouldn't permit black students in any kind of managerial position. I argued that if black students couldn't go, then nor should whites. This caused a row and I dropped out: I didn't go to classes and I didn't sit my exams. I came back to London for the holidays though I still intended to go back in October, to finish my course and go back to Guyana. That summer I took a holiday job as an international operator for the Post Office. While I was there I helped organize a strike and when I was about to go back to Edinburgh to continue my work, a delegation from the union asked me to stay and continue the struggle. I said, 'What? I'm going back to my career,' but they pleaded and eventually I said, 'OK.' So I stayed and spent the next ten years organizing the union. I had joined the Socialist Labour League in 1971 and stayed until 1974. In 1975, I joined the mainstream Labour Party, at the time when Reg Prentice was deselected and there were all these young guys who were taking the Labour Party to court for everything. I joined them, to help bolster up the Left. Through this I got involved in all sorts of anti-Fascist work, fighting the National Front and so on.

* * *

ZERBANOO GIFFORD: I got into local politics for the Liberals. I fought an election in a safe Tory seat, which I had been told was unwinnable, and I split it and was elected on a twenty-five per cent swing as the first Asian in the whole area. The next year I was asked by the party to put my name forward as candidate for Hertsmere. I doubled the Alliance vote and came second to Cecil Parkinson. Then the Sara Keays thing blew and I got a lot of publicity from that and I was also endorsed as the candidate in case of a subsequent by-election. This was quite an honour because in those days the party was always asking people to stand down so Shirley Williams or Roy Jenkins could get back into Parliament. It was quite something. I visited India again and met Mrs Gandhi, then when I came back I was made chair of the Liberal Party's community relations panel. I took part in their commission on women; I wrote the paper on women and the law and then in 1986 David Steel asked me to chair the party commission looking into the whole area of ethnic minorities in this country. In the 1987 general election I fought but lost Harrow East. In some ways I'm not even sure how much I would like to be an MP. When ethnic MPs get to Parliament many of them are stifled.

SHREELA FLATHER: When I came to Maidenhead as an Indian woman, I wasn't anybody. I rang people up, they'd say, who are you? When I arrived in '68 I talked. I talked and talked and talked. I used the boys I taught to help set up a club for Asian women and their toddlers, to teach them English, get them out of the house, help with their problems. I set up a summer school, I set up a boys' club, I tried to set up a girls' club. It was all voluntary, a desire to do something useful. I used to go visiting people two evenings every week. The first thing I would do is pick up the brown envelopes from their mantelpieces which they had dumped there because they were scared to open them. They couldn't read them themselves. It was a classic example of British voluntary work, though I didn't know it at the time. So my entry in politics, especially Tory politics, was the classic British way: you work in your community, you

333

become a local person who is useful, you become a JP – which I did in 1971 – and you follow that with local politics. In 1976 I was invited to stand for the council here by the Conservatives in my local ward. It was a bold step for them. I was elected and found that I was the first woman from any ethnic minority to become a councillor in the whole of the UK. I've moved into international politics, in the EC, because I knew that I didn't have a chance of getting selected as a Tory MP in Britain. I didn't think the constituency parties were ready to select anyone from a minority. You can get selected for a non-winnable seat, but I don't really fancy that.

ANWAR BATI: My brother, who has qualified as a barrister, although he works as a senior executive at BP, has ideas of becoming a Conservative MP. At one time he was thinking of taking a job at the head of some type of race relations unit, and I told him, 'Don't do it. Take that job and you'll be shoved into some unwinnable wog constituency and you'll never get away. Those are the terms in which they'll think of you. You've got to get in as a straight candidate on your own terms.'

MANZOOR BAHADUR: Even a Third World country like Pakistan has reserved ten per cent of seats in parliament for ethnic minorities – can you imagine that down at Westminster? We don't want to have quotas, and there aren't any, but in the end even quotas would be better than the position we are in at the moment. We influence nothing, unless we are in a position of power. Black people may get selected to stand for Parliament, but mainly for non-safe seats. But even in safe seats there is prejudice. An Asian candidate can stand in a safe seat and suddenly it's lost.

PETER TATCHELL: When I joined the Labour Party in Bermondsey it was a right-wing dominated and moribund organization. Labour had been in power virtually unopposed for over fifty years. The party was run like a dynasty by a handful of interrelated families who didn't want new members, whom they regarded as interlopers and intruders. The community was incredibly parochial. So if you weren't born and bred there, you were seen as an outsider. At one extreme, some people said that if you weren't born in Bermondsey you didn't have the right to live in the area, let alone have any say in how the community was run. Despite these prejudices, a mixture of new younger Labour members like myself, and disaffected old-time left-wingers, started organizing to democratize the local party. We doubled the membership and took up issues of concern to the local community. These changes were tremendously popular. Nobody seemed to mind the fact that I wasn't locally 'born and bred' (though because I had little trace of an accent, many were unaware that I was born in Australia).

334

In November 1981, I was selected as the Labour candiate for Bermondsey. By this time, I had become generally accepted as a local person. I was chosen as the candidate because I lived in the area, knew its problems and had a proven track-record as a local campaigner. However, the right-wing of the party still resented me. To them, I was an outsider and always would be. More important, I had played a significant role in displacing them from power. They started a whispering campaign against me: I was an Australian, so what did I know about Bermondsey? They tried to discredit me as a foreigner, left-wing extremist, draft-dodger and homosexual.

These smears became public in December 1981 when the then leader of the Labour Party, Michael Foot, ordered me to be banned as a Labour candidate. His justification was that I had written an article in a left-wing magazine which called for extra-parliamentry protests to challenge the Conservative government's political and moral right to rule. I had argued that many Tory policies were in violation of their election manifesto promises and were opposed by a majority of the electorate. Other policies were undermining people's fundamental social rights and civil liberties. In my opinion, non-violent civil disobedience was therefore a legitimate way of resisting an unaccountable government. In Australia, these ideas would have been quite unexceptional and I wrote the offending article partly influenced by my experience in Australia in organizing civil disobedience against the Vietnam War. In Britain, however, these views were outside the parameters of legitimate political debate. The press immediately seized on the fact that I was an Australian (as if it was a crime or a sin of the worst order) and attacked me remorselessly as an outsider who was attempting to impose alien ideas and values. In fact, all I was doing was restating the long-standing radical tradition of the Chartists and the Suffragettes, which I had learnt about when I was reading British history at school in Australia.

* * *

BERNIE GRANT: I found myself in the House of Commons in much the same way as I had become a councillor. It wasn't a great personal ambition. I had been asked before, but I'd said no, no, I'm not interested. I was approached in 1985 by a group of comrades who asked me whether I'd like to stand in Tottenham, which is a multiracial constituency and we'd been hammering away at this idea of multiracialism, and the need to get black representation in all areas of government. People felt there should be an MP who reflected the change in Tottenham. So this time I said, 'Fair enough, I'll have a go.' And I won.

I see the House of Commons as giving me an opportunity to make the odd speech, get a little media coverage for black causes, and most important of all, when there are issues that come up, we are able for the first time to put forward a black point of view from within Parliament. That is important in terms of image for the black community. I don't know whether I'm a good role model myself, but the fact that black people can become MPs does get some esteem.

SHREELA FLATHER: I am a conformist and I think you'll only beat the system from within the system. There is too much pessimism in the black community: they do keep their heads below the parapet and it's time they settled into the mainstream institutions. There are more blacks in those institutions today, but they seem to play the role of saying, 'This is a bad institution', and that doesn't necessarily help. What you have to do is make sure that the institutions look after everyone's interests. Individuals, not institutions, effect change and there is a lot that individuals can do, which they don't always realize. I may be talking from a position of strength now, but even if I had been a poor uneducated person and therefore operating within a different social stratum, I would still have joined my trade union. Whatever your level of involvement in the mainstream may be, educated or uneducated, rich or poor, you must be in there. That is my message.

BODRUL ALOM: The only way for the immigrant community as a whole to change things is for it to become part of the power structure in England. I am a Labour Party member. We have been fighting for the last eight years to nominate a black person to our constituency, Tower Hamlets, the only place in the whole country which could return a Bengali person to Parliament. I'm not absolutely in favour of black sections but there has to be a section within our party which can address the needs of ethnic people who have come to live in this country.

BENNY BUNSEE: Blacks don't want to be integrated any more; they want to assert themselves. The call for black sections reflects that dimension in black politics today and it's something that white people have to understand. Their approach has always been – whether in the name of humanism or socialism or liberal values – one of integration: come and join us, become one of us, and then you'll be accepted. But we've moved past that stage. It's naïve. Black and white have to relate, but they must relate on the basis of a genuine policy. Not a dominating/dominated relationship.

RAJAN UDDIN JALAL: The party must accommodate black sections. Blacks and Asians in this country feel isolated, they feel that they are not a part of the political process, and they feel that they can only naturally belong to the Labour Party, and if the Labour Party doesn't have the common sense to allow these black sections, then they will be making a blunderous mistake. The mainstream who oppose black sections and talk about 'marginalizing' the community, forget

336

that we have not started from an equal footing here. If we had started from an equal footing, there would be no need for black sections. But because we have not started from that equal footing it is necessary for us to mobilize and equalize; after that there will be no need for black sections. When no matter which party is running the government at least six or seven of the Cabinet will be black or Asian, just as under Mrs Thatcher they have been Jewish, then we won't need that kind of separate forum. Now we do need it – for our sake and for the sake of the party too. The black section will have very little influence over policy-making, it will be just a single voice, nothing in the face of the whole system, but it is a focal point, a platform from which issues can be raised.

SHREELA FLATHER: I wouldn't want black sections; I don't believe in these separate groupings – I think it's very dangerous. I don't want to be part of a protected species, because that is the end of life. You have to fight your way into the mainstream, although you must have some encouragement and you must have people looking to see whether there are any good people coming out of your group and then encouraging them into various positions. Labour has done extremely well out of the immigrants. They paid lip-service to their needs and they got their support in the beginning. But they didn't repay this support and now they're reaping the whirlwind because they didn't manage to get anyone elected until the candidates threatened to set up black sections.

ZERBANOO GIFFORD: People do use the Asian community. For money and votes, simple as that. They like to tell them, 'We're supporting you, we're fighting for you, so vote for us.' They must think we're all nincompoops. The majority do still vote Labour, but a growing minority, perhaps fifteen per cent are starting to vote Tory, mainly in north London.

SHREELA FLATHER: People say, why would an immigrant become a Conservative? All of my upbringing, all of my attitudes are Conservative. A lot of the Asians who vote socialist, if you actually discuss politics with them you'll discover that they are not really socialists. India is supposed to be a socialist state, but you'd be very hard-pressed to find a real socialist there. That's not the way they think. I don't think people really assume that every immigrant will vote Labour any more. They are rather more canny.

MUHAMMAD AYYAZ: Basically we are Conservatives. We believe in the things that Conservatives believe: you must have your own home, you must have a car, this that and the other. The majority of the community may vote Labour, but the fact is that none of the parties are going to do anything for the Asians.

SHREELA FLATHER: The black community is beginning to realize that the Labour Party promises a lot more but delivers a lot less. The Conservatives don't promise anything, and they don't deliver a great deal, but they don't deliver much less than Labour. After all, racism among the working class, who are supposed to vote Labour, is much greater than from any other class. The only local estate on which I was scared to canvass was supposedly made up of solid Labour voters. Though there are elements within the Tories which are very racist too.

GINA ADAMOU: Margaret Thatcher has been very clever. She appears to be for family, for morals, high morals, which Asians like, and she scares the daylights out of them with the gay issue in schools, things like that. The media make anything like that horrible and evil, and the Tories capitalize on it.

* * *

YASMIN ALIBHAI: Immigrants vote Tory on the grounds of money, as simple as that. East African Asians, certainly, are such apolitical animals. The only way they could survive in East Africa was to shut their eyes and ears to everything else but the shop. As long as you keep going on that track you're all right and your family is all right. Getting involved in politics is like discussing religion – it gets you into trouble. They've brought the same attitudes here. They didn't learn from our experiences in Uganda. That blindness, that ostrich mentality which they expect will save them here is simply not going to work. Mrs Thatcher actually performed the opening ceremony of the Mosque in South Kensington. Yet the community is so entrepreneurial that they could see no contradiction between a woman like Mrs Thatcher and a place of worship.

FIRDOS ALI: Margaret Thatcher is the most obscene person I have ever seen in my life. The Asians who love her are mostly the East Africans. Rich people, commercial people. But even some shopowners around Southall will vote Tory. My friend's eleven-year-old son asked me, 'Uncle, who do you think are good for us. Tories or Labour?' I said, 'Neither of them at the moment.' He said, 'Why?' I told him neither was any use from my point of view. 'No,' he said, 'I think Tories are good. They're good for business people.' His father must have been talking like that. And of course he's right.

GINA ADAMOU: I'm afraid to say that when the Cypriot community does get on and does make some money they become Tory voters. People from my background, for God's sake! Tory voters! I found it incredible. They have their rights to be what they want but I don't understand it. Because you become rich, because you have money, that doesn't mean you become a Tory. Foreigners who have made money here have this attitude: if we've made it, why can't you? They look upon the unemployed, the old, the young, people without money, as if they've failed. The Cypriot community claim they look after their

338

poor, but it's not happening. They drive their Mercedes and they look down on everyone else.

ZERBANOO GIFFORD: They feel that they've truly arrived; they feel that they can shake hands and meet ministers and name-drop and have their photograph taken and somehow through all this they will feel accepted. I've had so many tell me, 'Well, if you were a Tory you'd have a safe seat and so on,' and I tell them, 'But I'm not a Tory.' I don't want a safe seat thank you very much, I want to do what I think is right and proper. I'm a fighter. I'm not really interested in having my photograph shaking hands with ministers. The sad thing is that the ministers themselves don't have a very high opinion of these sort of people. That is the irony of the situation.

RAMESH VALA: The Asians who used to give enormous donations to the Tory funds, the sort of people who paid £28,000 for a bottle of Scotch signed by Mrs Thatcher, have given up. These people, who are seen as having sold out, people who join the Tories and go on radio to defend immigration policies, were only doing it because they were hoping to become Tory MPs. Then they were sent to strong Labour seats and virtually lost their deposit. So they become very disillusioned and many have left the party. Speak to Tory Central Office, to the people who are supposed to liaise between the party and these Asians – all of whom are hoping for OBEs, CBEs, some kind of award – and they despise them. Yet it's hard to explain to them that it's in the Tory Party they they'll really come up against the snobbery, the discrimination. They have only themselves to blame. The wrong calibre of people tend to get accepted by the Tories. These public Tory Asians are often people who are not particularly articulate, who don't speak when it matters, and are people who are really despised by their own community too. They are not seen as Asian leaders. They have no real ability to communicate any view, Asian or otherwise. Which for the community is absolutely disastrous. I have the simplistic view that one reason the best Asians don't go into politics is that there is no money in it. If there was they'd all be in it. But our people do have to get into politics, because that is where decisions are made. If the people who should represent the community are to emerge, the Asian community must promote them, perhaps even fund them. Otherwise it will be very difficult to attract the right people.

SHREELA FLATHER: Young Asians and blacks see people like me as having sold out in every possible way. But we all have a different way of working. I believe that I can only work the way I do – which is from within the system, which lets me into places where nobody else is. I know that I don't compromise on important issues, and I don't feel the need to. I'm never frightened of any situation. I don't remember in the whole of my political career ever being too

339

frightened to say exactly what I want to say, knowing at the same time that I would be the only one to do so. If you want to achieve something in a political situation, other than just getting the satisfaction of saying your piece, then you must bide your time, you must see when you can carry the majority with you; nothing can be done by yourself. Sometimes you succeed, sometimes you don't. When you know you absolutely can't win them over, then you can say your piece as emotionally as you want, because there's nothing else you can do. Sometimes you do win some ground and that's fabulous, to think that you have moved something just that little bit.

* * *

ZERBANOO GIFFORD: People have a right, Asians or anyone else, to belong to every political party or no political party or whatever they want to do. You have no right to deny them this. I remember in 1983 I was attacked in a meeting and told that I should stand for Labour, not the Liberals, because the Labour Party had given India independence. So I said, 'I'm sorry. I think you've got history wrong. Nobody *gave* India independence. Many fought and died in prisons to *take* independence. Get your history straight.' People like to think that in some weird way you're obliged to other people. They forget that we look at history from our point of view. I was talking to someone who talked about India's 'first war of independence' and it turned out to be what I had been brought up here to call the Indian Mutiny. It depends on how you look at things.

BERNIE GRANT: Until 1978, when I became a councillor, my relation to politics was primarily as a union official rather than a black activist. This had begun to change in 1977 when we formed the Anti-Nazi League to fight the National Front, who had won a few local elections. I was heavily involved in that. We forced the Fascists off the streets. Once we'd defeated them, because they started losing their electoral support, we had to do something else. I started holding meetings and talking to black activists in Tottenham, the area where I lived. We wanted to carry on using the impetus that had been gained during the anti-racist campaign. The aim was to take things one step further – from attacking overt racism to dealing with institutionalized racism in the councils and among policy-makers. People then told me, 'You should become a councillor', so that was what I did. My speciality was tackling institutionalized racism. I got involved in housing, education, dealing with the whole gamut of policies as they effected individual black people. I took up cases, started fighting for equal opportunities policies, started for a head count, so we could know exactly what councillors had done for black people.

RAJAN UDDIN JALAL: At the same time as the Bangladeshi community was starting to get involved in politics, racial violence was increasing in the East

End. The NF was fielding a number of candidates in the local elections; its local headquarters was in Shoreditch; it was selling its newspapers in Brick Lane, which was becoming an increasingly Bangladeshi area. People like me who were politically involved became very active in the anti-racist struggle. We did have some support from the Left, but some of them misunderstood our movement. They didn't understand that ours was a community movement, which could not be SWP-fied instantly. But we did get solid support from the Anti-Nazi League and some Labour activists. I had no interest in party politics in those days, although in 1978 I did join the party. But this was a time when a Bengali would apply for membership and nobody would write back: their forms had apparently been 'lost'. We weren't really wanted, only by a few active individuals who tried to involve us off their own backs. This is a bad tradition that has prevailed in the Labour Party for a long time. Partly it's the same, traditional East End racism that was experienced by the Jews before us. Sadly those who have themselves historically fought against racism are now forgetting their own past too. This is regrettable. Racism is a divisive tactic. I live in Wapping where I know blacks and whites, neither of whom can afford to buy any of the new houses that are going up. But there is this escapist attitude in the white community: we had it bad in the '30s, why should they have it any better? But the economic situation has changed so much, the welfare state means that no one should have to go back to living as they did in the '30s. People can't see that. The end product is that this attitude lets down everyone in the community, black and white. At the end of the day the people who fight will win. The people who fight will gain. In Tower Hamlets it is the Bengalis who are very determined and who are fighting, fighting back. They are achieving and they will win. And if our comrades, our neighbours, are not with us, then this escapist attitude will just leave them behind. We are racing for survival and in this race if the rest of the working-class community does not race with us, then they will be left behind. The only people who will benefit from this escapist attitude are the ones who want to divide us.

22 Black Self-images

'Perhaps you need "Little Black Sambo"? You need him, you have him, I don't.'

FIRDOS ALI: There are a million television sets owned by the minorities, the black people, the Asians, the Cypriots, the Irish, but all they are given is programmes like *Shalom Salaam*. Stereotypes: the only levels they can think

341

about. They can't deal with anything that might be a positive image. The BBC makes sure that people only see minorities as problems, not people who live normal lives. They cannot be seen as normal. Which is typical of the BBC. Channel 4 is moving in a different direction and there is hope there. It has *The Bandung File*, which the BBC would never have allowed. The BBC did have some Asian programmes in Urdu, Hindi and Bengali, but they scrubbed them and replaced them with *Network East*, a shitty programme. Which seems to say that we can only produce mediocre presenters, mediocre producers, mediocre researchers; the technicians are all white.

MANZOOR BAHADUR: Our children feel more confident if their community identity is being portrayed in a positive way in the schools. That their religion is important, and their language is important and that message gets across to all the other children in that school. At the moment they feel isolated, different, but they should be made proud of their own identity, to feel comfortable within it. I was going round one school with a colleague, and the whole class contained Asian children and we started to speak to the kids in Punjabi and we were having a good conversation. The teacher, who had been out, suddenly walked in and immediately the kids just switched to English, the Punjabi just stopped immediately, because those children felt shy.

ZERBANOO GIFFORD: It is so important to recognize that there are large numbers of people in this country who speak Hindi, who speak Urdu. These are the countries of the future: Asia and the Far East. And here is a population who can already speak these languages. Britain is a trading nation and surely it is important for a trading nation not just to speak English, but to speak every language so that when you go and trade you understand what is happening. Here is a core of people who have these talents – why aren't they used? It is as important today to speak Urdu or Mandarin as it is to speak French or German. If you explain things like that, if you talk sanely, in marketing terms, they understand you, but when you scream and shout about rights and so on people become defensive. In the same way it is more enjoyable for people to read books of African myths or fairy stories than it is to read about *Little Black Sambo*. Why not bring up children with the best instead of rubbish?

VERNA WILKINS: I write children's books with a heavy educational bias, and I present positive images of black and minority groups. I go into schools now and talk to black kids and white. Those black kids, at three, are tremendously bright and alive and they produce a lot of work. Then something happens. They're categorized, they're stereotyped, they're squashed. That's what I believe. People expect black children to fulfil a low norm. People expect *me* to fulfil a low norm. I've written all the books myself, I run my own publishing company,

342

I have them printed, I sell them, I do everything and it's all done to a very high quality. So I show them to people and they say, 'Who's doing this?' 'I am.' And they say, 'Yes, but who is doing it *really*?' As one said to me, 'This is too good to be true.' The thing is my books look too good to be 'ethnic'. Because 'ethnic' has become synonymous with tat. Forget it: I'm a peacock, I'd rather be invisible than be included negatively. Do we have to jump straight from exclusion into tat without any middle way? But this is about knowing one's place. Accepting one's image. You have to release people from this.

MICHAEL DE SOUZA: I started growing my locks about nine years ago. That was a major turning point. I was working as a lathe-turner and miller. I used to work with the these white people and we got on all right but I began to get aware. The Rasta thing was giving me a real heavy message, talking about sufferation, real suffering, about freeing yourself from oppression – anyone, anyone that oppresses you, vanquish them, that's it. Your parents, your workmates, the government, anyone. They shouldn't stop you from being free and being a man, and that appealed to me. The physical appearance is not particularly important to me. Rastas grew their hair just to be anti-social. Where it originated, in Jamaica, the accepted thing was to have nice straight European hair, and look as light as possible. So the further you got away from that, the nearer you were to the gutter. The darker you were was worries. I really liked that aspect: the anti-social appearance but the total social awareness. I found it interesting, and I found it frightening: I found it difficult to commit myself and locks up. I thought if I do something like that it's got to be forever. I was about nineteen and forever was a long time. So I stayed away from it until later on, after a few ups and downs, I told myself, 'Right. I really am a black man in this country, so let me really find myself.' So I went back to Rasta. At work all these people would see me combing my hair in the mirror: ''Ere, Michael, wot you doin' that for? What you combin' your 'air for? It don't move.' I told them, 'It's mine. I'll comb it.' Then I decided to locks up now and I decided that I was going to leave the job, and for three weeks I didn't comb my hair. So it was ''Ere, what you done to your hair? Why don't you comb it?' 'What, I thought you said I didn't need to comb it.' But I left it and they couldn't deal with it. Then I started working as a play leader in Acklam Road. When I went back to see them at the factory they still didn't like it and they told me, 'You're different, you're not that kind of person . . .' I said, 'What're you talking about? I'm me and I've always been me, whatever my physical appearance is like. All it really means is that you've never understood me and you've never known what was going on.' Which was when I knew that it was very important for me to take on a positive black image. What they were trying to do was say, 'You're one of us, not one of them' and it's meant to be sweet, the nicest thing they can say.

343

BERNIE GRANT: Unless you actually take a stand against these things, unless you actually expose them for what they are and for the effect they have on black kids, unless you are able to do that and explain it properly, then you would have to accept the conclusion that black people are more stupid than white people. Which I certainly don't accept. I don't think that things like 'Baa Baa Black Sheep' are really important, though the papers take them up and talk about 'loony Left' because they're the most ridiculous thing they can find. But by and large I do support the people who say that nursery rhymes should reflect the society that everyone lives in. Rather than banning 'Baa Baa Black Sheep' I would look instead for more positive poems that deal with the situation as it is. Then people will say, 'Well, we don't need "Baa Baa Black Sheep" because it's not relevant.' Certainly things like *Little Black Sambo* and some Enid Blyton stories, I'd ban them tomorrow. No problem.

ZERBANOO GIFFORD: The political campaign for multicultural teachings was done indelicately. The intent was so good, but it all went wrong. The media said these people were forcing it on the great British public and there was an outcry. 'The loony Left'. The great British electorate have to be taken along gently, they have to be stroked. They hate to feel that they are being forced into anything. It could have been done much more cleverly. They could have taken the whole nation with them. In the end this stuff *is* offensive. *Little Black Sambo* is a racist tale. His mother is Mumbo Jumbo and so on. They have this piccaninny hairstyle. There's lots of it, *Dr Doolittle*, so on. If a child keeps seeing blacks portrayed in these stereotyped ways, ringlets, bones through their noses, so on, it doesn't do much for their self-esteem. People do react to the way in which they are treated and if you treat somebody as if they are remarkable and wonderful they behave as if they are remarkable and wonderful, but if you treat them as if they've just come out of the jungle with a bone through their nose, their self-esteem isn't going to go up very high. I just don't think it is necessary to have this kind of literature. You don't need to ban anything, just put through a policy that ensures that local libraries start buying sensible books. And the others will just fade away; they'll be no more than historical documents which people read in universities.

VERNA WILKINS: There is a kneejerk reaction to positive imaging. The tabloids automatically condemn it. I don't know why. Perhaps you need *Little Black Sambo*? I just throw it back. If you need him, you have him. I don't. I don't deal with race as such in the books. I just have black children carrying on ordinary lives, but, as opposed to the traditional material, the black children have a deliberately high profile. To bring up the balance which is missing elsewhere. They're highly educational, concentrating on all the mechanisms for early reading. With all the physical extension to the actual reading process.

344

I took on board a lot of the criticisms white teachers have about black children and built them in to my system. I worked backwards from the national curriculum, backwards from the list of criticisms. The positive images are there as a subliminal reinforcement and it works. It is fantastic.

WILF WALKER: When I started my company Black Productions I started doing posters of positive black images; because my biggest hangup had always been that you don't see any positive black images. You buy *The Times*, the *Observer*, any newspaper, and every day you go through and you don't see a positive black image. It's always the piccaninny, some primitive people featured next to the models, the fine asses, the fine bitches, it's always on that level. You go down the underground station and there are all these posters: if you see one black image, it's only that big.

VERNA WILKINS: Omission is bad for black children. They don't see images of themselves reflected anywhere. Even on nappy bags. You wouldn't think that black kids wore nappies in England. You get these images right from birth, before you're even properly conscious. The early books are the same. My kids had nothing that reflected a positive image of themselves. The children don't question this, but that's because what they're learning is not to be included. They're being conditioned through these omissions. However ambitious you are, however able you are, these things mean that you are systematically excluded. My own total ability to counter this exclusion comes from my early upbringing and the fact that I was brought up to be confident. Although I too had to learn from books which pushed white images, because we were colonized and because you learn from books. Yet in a way I've exorcized all that, I know what it is.

* * *

MICHAEL DE SOUZA: The disadvantage of black people really is that they speak English. If you have another language, it's different. We speak the language, but it's not understood. And there is this slave mentality and we have to shake off the chains. You've got to shake off the chains and don't believe that you're a house nigger, you're a man or a woman and that's that. What people have to do is be realistic. Don't just go into areas that black people go into, go into areas that you want to go into. I don't know how much success that will bring, but things can be done. People with skills and talents can cross over. I've crossed over a lot of cultural boundaries. Whether it's English upper class or black working class. The majority of black people weren't even considered as working class. We came below the working class.

VERNA WILKINS: My work is very well received in the black community. I talk to young parents, carers, librarians and so on and they are very interested. I talk about the way forward. I don't go back over the history, I'm not about to reinvent the wheel. I just say, 'We have a problem and we are going to deal with it in this way.' Racism is a problem that the black community has to deal with, but it's not a problem you have created. You have to learn how to deal with it and find out how to go forward. I see the way forward as accepting the struggle and getting on with it, and getting on with your life and enhancing your own existence. My books give young people positive images of themselves at the earliest age. So at an early age they can already identify with the whole process of a rich, fulfilled adult life. So if they read the tabloids they don't accept what they say, or that they're going to end up like these stereotypes. I counter that. These images are not elitist, they're just about feeling good about yourself. It's up to them to take that to the next stage in their own lives. What I'm fighting for is balance. Not superiority or inferiority, just balance. I know black kids who are tremendously able, yet that ability is diverted into destructiveness simply through frustration.

MICHAEL DE SOUZA: You have to be positive in every aspect of your life. Whatever you want to do, don't put any boundaries on yourself. Don't say I'm not doing it because white people do it, I'm not doing it because Indian people do it, do what you want. The world is here for us to do what we want, without limitations of colour or anything. I'm not going to apply for a job as some big blond actor, but that won't stop me going for some job in a film, and not just because I look like this, a part which has me standing on a corner selling drugs. Some black guy, Dutch, approached me on Portobello. They were shooting a video for some silly group. So this guy approach me, with another idiot from the Grove, 'Hey Rasta, come, come. You wanna be in this thing, this video?' I said, 'How do you mean, do I want to be in this video?' I'm just watching. 'We want you to do something.' So I say, 'If you want me to do something, you have to chat to me about money. Tell me what's going on.' So we sorted that out. What they wanted me to do was to stand on the corner and offer them weed and they turn their back. I said, 'No, I'm not having that image.' This other guy, who I knew, tried to persuade me. I said, 'Look, I don't know how you check yourself, but I'm very positive and I'm fed up of black people selling themselves in this negative way, really, literally selling themselves. I don't care how much they want to give me.' Just because you're a certain colour that shouldn't control your brain. To white society if that means that someone with locks has to be seen as selling weed on the street corner, that's fine.

WILF WALKER: You don't hear about the blacks like myself who are coming through. What happens is this: the only blacks who get into positions are those who have been to college and get the bullshit degree. The blacks who do well, who get qualifications, who go to college, people say, 'OK you're hip, you know

346

the score, now go off and free your people.' The majority of the kids, their experience has been closer to mine, rather than to these so-called intellectual blacks. There is a black race industry, there is all that money there and it's supposed to be helping young black people. If they really want to help, then they have to help people like me. If someone like myself can actually get over, that will inspire all those other black kids who are suffering the same kind of injustices that I have suffered, to inspire them to try and do something rather than try to burn the fucker down. Which is what they're going to do if they can't see none of their kind getting through. What the community needs is not just me, but twenty-five, fifty people who can do it like me. People who haven't just read about it but have got it in their gut. Those kind of people have got to be there in the front line. There are some people, the old '60s activists, and they've done well, got into television, whatever, but they're all very fat and they're out of touch. They were never really exposed. I never ever hear about a black person who has been in jail or been in a mental hospital and has come out and has made something of himself. Yet there are – there must be! It's not just the people who went to university who turn out to be good people, who can make something and be substantial. All the kids who don't get to college feel cowed by it. It isn't class. It's race. There are loads and loads of white working-class heroes who white working-class kids can relate to. Historically and currently. Whereas in terms of black people here and now there are no examples of black people going up against the system and winning. Until we start to have that coming through the kids will continue to disrupt and be disruptive and be the mass of people in the mental hospitals and the prisons. Because it's hard for your brain when you turn on the television and all you see are these fucking black jokers and you don't see anyone you can really relate to; everybody you see is trying to be white. I believe that I have something to contribute. But I, who some people might say has got somewhere, I'm nowhere. I get all these calls from people low down who see me as a high-profile black who can help them – in reality I've got nowhere and I can't help them. It's very frustrating. You get a profile, but then everyone's scared to give you any power.

MIKE PHILLIPS: For West Indians the process of corruption, of cultural assimilation that Indians and Pakistanis fear has already happened. I'd be more worried about my kid in some ways if he were not mixed race. He has a very firm sense of his own identity as a mixed race person. When I was young they would say of mixed marriages, 'These things never work. Think about the children.' Well, there ain't nothing wrong about the children! The fact that they don't necessarily get inducted into the sort of reggae/violence culture of front-line Brixton is a damned good thing. That is the thing that corrupts black kids, this image of themselves. Not all, but some. And there is a great sense of aggression among these kids, and most of it is either undirected or misdirected.

347

For someone like me the point of expressing your anger by being at the bottom of the ladder and going to prison is difficult to understand, and I don't believe for one moment that the culture that these kids are engaged in is really to do with anger or with revolutionary rejection or any crap like that. Most of those kids are in a box; they don't know very much, they haven't been taught very much, they're doing what they can to defend their identity as individuals. They're hanging out with their mates in the same way as I would have done when I was their age. The big issue for them is finding something to do that will allow them to express themselves as individuals. I do not believe in that notion of the heroic 'culture of anger'. It's crap. I've never known one black kid that *wanted* to be that way. That was something that happened.

I used to run a hostel in Notting Hill for homeless kids. One of the guys who went to prison for seven years, for armed robbery, came to see me a few months ago. He'd just written a book about his experiences. He told me, 'The only reason I got into trouble, the only reason I spent seven years in prison, is because at the time nobody ever told me I could do what I wanted to do. I really thought that was what I *had* to do.'

WILF WALKER: The bulk of black youth are in the resistance movement and they're being caught and dragged off to one form of institution or another, daily, and with no way of seeing how they can come out of it and be anything else and make their experience work for them in a positive way, which is what I have done with mine. They just come out more angry, they accept the stereotype, the definitions of white society. I've served three years in prison, they tell me I'm a criminal, but I still don't know how to pick a lock or pick a pocket or steal a candy bar. So fuck them! I'm not a criminal! That's their definition and I've never accepted it. But the majority of these kids, they begin to accept the definition of themselves as whatever the cop tells the judge they did, and eventually they start being that. Until they can start using black people who have experienced the harshness of the system and who have survived it by dealing with it, the situation won't change, because putting college kids in positions where they've got to advise these youth is not going to work. You need to get people with hard, street experience, who can demonstrate that and give the youth their experience. College is not everything. There are a lot of black kids who have not got to college and who will never get to college who still have a lot of potential. There are thousands of people out there who couldn't pass an exam to save their lives, but still have talent. When they have the qualifications they have problems getting jobs, so if you can't prove that you have the qualifications just to get on the first rung of the ladder, then it's impossible.

23 Pictured by the Press

'Papers tend to cater for their clients. So if so many people buy the *Sun* it shows that a lot of people do want to see that kind of journalism.'

SUSAN WILSON: My father and my uncle coming here shed light on lots of things. My father trotted around to the newsagents the first morning he was here and went into the newsagent and said, 'Tell me the name of the paper that most of the population buys.' He felt that if that's what all the British people buy it must be good. So he was handed the *Sun*. He looked at the newsagent and said, 'No, this can't be right. Surely this can't be right?' 'Oh yes it is.' 'Well show me the second favorite.' They gave him the *Mirror*. He came home and he was really amazed. He said, 'How can this be? How can they read it?'

FIRDOS ALI: The *Sun*. Who owns it? Murdoch. The descendant of a nation of convicts – what would you expect. I can't take him seriously. That guy is an outrageous pirate. If a person like him can manipulate a whole nation, and the *Sun* has an amazing effect on the way people think in this country, then good luck to that nation. You get what you deserve. If a working-class person votes Tory, what has he got to conserve except his misery? What else? Yet they do.

BERNIE GRANT: When you get targeted by the media, you just take it in your stride. When the Broadwater Farm riot occurred I had a hell of a lot of hassles, apart from the doorstepping the media were doing. All sorts of threats – death threats, threats of violence. I couldn't travel on public transport. The few times I tried it people would threaten to beat me up. I don't go into pubs any more.

There's no doubt that the reaction would not have been so vitriolic if I'd have been white. Absolutely. It was very clear: I was the baddie of the year for the Tory Party conference of 1985. In 1984 it was Arthur Scargill, but it was not the same thing. In 1985 someone got up at that conference and said, 'This man should be deported.' Now I'm a British citizen just like Scargill, but nobody would get up and say Scargill should be deported. So there was the extra racism element, over and above the normal abuse. I've talked to Ken Livingstone and other people that have been attacked but none of them have ever had the level of treatment I did. It's very much through the advent of papers like the *Sun*. What happens is that the *Sun* runs a headline 'Barmy Bernie'. So somebody cuts it out and sends it to me with some obscene message or something. Or they cut my picture out of the *Daily Mail* – another

349

paper that was pretty bad – and they'd draw a noose around my neck and send that to me. So it's as if these papers and the racists are working hand-in-glove.

MICHAEL DE SOUZA: The unfortunate thing about the *Sun* is that it is the most popular newspaper in England and it puts out the most powerful shit message and all you can do is just talk to people and try to get them not to read the damn stupidness. You have to educate people.

PETER TATCHELL: Throughout the Bermondsey byelection campaign in 1983, the press would nearly always prefix my name with the description, 'the Australian-born extreme left-winger'. It was as if my birthplace and politics were synonymous. Sometimes, the tabloid papers made being an Australian seem like a grotesque personality defect which rendered me unfit to hold public office. For much of the media, I was a dangerous foreigner, coming from a far-away culture and bearing an alien political philosophy. For others, I was an ignorant immigrant who couldn't possibly know about Britain or understand the problems of Bermondsey (though by this time I had lived in Britain nearly all my adult life).

The popular press also pilloried me as a draft-dodger, coward and traitor who refused to defend Australia against communism. My lack of patriotism was proof, they implied, that I was unable and unfit to stand up for the interests of the people of Bermondsey. With this level of vilification, it was hardly surprising that the byelection was fought in an atmosphere of intense hatred and violence. There were slogans painted in every street: 'Tatchell is a communist poof', 'Tatchell is a nigger-lover' and 'Tatchell get back to Russia' (the latter slogan showing either little awareness of geography or the misplaced notion that Australia is some far-flung outpost of the Soviet gulag). The death threats, abusive phone calls and hate mail would frequently combine the themes of homophobic prejudice, rabid anti-communism, racism and xenophobia. As one letter put it, 'You filthy communist queer, why don't you take all those damn niggers and get back to kangaroo land where you came from.'

BODRUL ALOM: In 1978, I think July 16, about 10,000 Bangladeshis gathered at Hyde Park Corner to protest the racism of the National Front, but only one or two newspapers even bothered to cover it. Most of them didn't say a word, which means that they do not recognize the existence of this community in Britain.

MANZOOR BAHADUR: A large majority of the Muslim community feels that the problem with facing a hostile press as we do is that we had made peaceful protests [about *The Satanic Verses*] long before Khomeini came on the scene but nobody was listening. It was too comfortable, we were doing everything

350

within the law and we still are – we can't be held accountable for the odd situation that gets out of control, especially through all sorts of frustrations and the provocations we receive. People who went on a demonstration in London said the police were deliberately provocative to them so they could make sure that there would be no more marches like this in the future. It wasn't 20,000 people on that demonstration, there were many, many more. People felt that the police did not want to give the true figure. This demonstration saw the Muslim community come out in mass numbers to show solidarity for perhaps the last time on the streets of London. What happened when Ayatollah Khomeini made his statement about *The Satanic Verses* was that it gave the press the chance to demolish the Muslim community by creating a barbarian image of the community. It's had a go at us before: on community education, on arranged marriages, halal meat, the way we treat women. Always with white eyes. They don't accept that our culture, our religion is as good as anyone's. Who is to say that our culture is inferior to anyone else's. We get portrayed as this extremist society, lying there ready to pounce on the mainstream society and force it to accept our ideas.

MIKE PHILLIPS: When I first came here there was no point in reading any newspaper, because you'd feel sick and disgusted and offended, because they were all so totally racist, and so insulting and humiliating in the things they said about you. The local press was the worst, but they were all pretty bad. That was the image we had, but we didn't believe it.

ZERBANOO GIFFORD: During the last election one of the local papers published a letter telling me to go home. So I called the editor and said that this wasn't exactly the normal wear and tear of political debate. It's one thing publishing letters critical of my policies or whatever – 'Mrs Gifford's gone to America because she's so ignorant they've got to train her up', I don't mind that – but this kind of public racism . . . Especially from a 'Mr Smith' in a road that isn't listed in the electoral register. He replied that whether or not the man existed was irrelevant, but the point is 'that is what people feel and "Mr Smith", whoever he is, is articulating their feelings'. I told him that I found that unbelievable: 'You wouldn't publish a letter suggesting that the Jews be exterminated, although people have those feelings.' He admitted that he wouldn't. Which I told him was because of the Jewish lobby. I said, 'I'm telling you that if you publish any more letters like that there will be trouble. This is not politics. This is just incitement to racial hatred.' But there was no retraction, not even personal.

The national media were very different. They dealt with the racial issue very well and I'm very grateful. In fact it took me two elections before I'd go public about the attacks I'd suffered, and then it only happened by accident. Some

351

journalist rang up one day when I was particularly upset and I blurted it all out. I hadn't told anyone before. When I first stood for local government the NF boys put leaflets round the council estates saying they shouldn't vote for a non-English person. The press contacted me then but I said, 'No comment'. I felt that any story would just publicize the racists. I wanted to starve them of publicity, to deny them credibility. But when I did go public it was because I felt on this occasion the time was right. It was time that people should realize that these sort of attacks weren't just happening to Asians in Brick Lane, that it happened to people like myself who lived in Harrow in a lovely house, were married to Englishmen, who were in every way trying very hard to take part in British life, and trying to contribute to British society.

MANZOOR BAHADUR: A local journalist on the *Telegraph and Argus*, wrote a piece about the Muslim community. He gives an example of this guy who's supposed to have just come back from Pakistan, and the guy asks, 'What's the fuss about? Everything's so good here, so peaceful?' From this guy's remarks, the journalist concludes that meeting this guy has assured him that somebody sensible is still around from the Muslim community. And he goes on to say that the Muslim community claims that race relations have never been good in Bradford and fighting for their religious rights is far more important, whatever the effect. So he says, 'Thanks very much for all that we have done for you.' Bradford has given, he says, the Muslim community has taken. And he gives this list of examples.

When you get that sort of crap being published in our own local press it really does hurt. But what have we been *given*? I have a third of my salary taken every month, I pay rates. Do we not contribute to the city's economy, is he saying that the whole of the Muslim community, fifteen per cent of the city's population, are scroungers? You've given us nothing. These things are rights, not hand-outs, the Muslim community has paid through the rates and taxes for these benefits. There are degrees of being a Muslim. There's a difference between those who practise and those who don't, but the media classifies them together, and the non-practising Muslims are referred to as the sensible and moderate Muslims, while the religious Muslims are labelled militants, fundamentalists and extremists. So the non-practising Muslims, who might as well be atheists, are the ones people listen to, they're the ones that are used as a model of 'good sense' Muslims.

24 The Black Community

'The larger black community is a political idea, but individually
we all have different fights, different struggles, different issues.'

BENNY BUNSEE: 'Black' has a very particular meaning to me. In contra-
distinction to the oppression that white people have visited upon us for
centuries, black is my association with all those countries that have a similar
colonial history to which I as an individual and my people in general were
subjected. In other words, what is known as the Third World. The people who
have been plundered, decimated, murdered, killed, suffered genocide; whole
continents and countries have been taken away from us. So everyone that has
suffered like that I call black, in contra-distinction to the white ethos that has
been imposed upon them.

MICHAEL DE SOUZA: When people talk about the 'black community', I ask
them where it is? I don't know. The really heavy black community is in South
Africa. If people really want to talk about the black community, then that is
South Africa. Because those black people are suffering every single day and
their suffering is solely because they're black. They're not the only ones
suffering in the world. I'm not saying that, but if we are talking about specific
black issues, then they are the real black community. You can't claim that here.

MUHAMMAD ALI: I do see the black community as embracing people of all
colours except white. The reason for that is quite simple: I don't look at black
as a colour. If you say that, then I'm not black, because my skin is brownish.
Look at India or Pakistan, there's a very wide variety of skin colours. Some are
even whiter than you, some much darker than me. So blackness is not a colour.
It's a term that you use to describe the similar experiences that people face in
this society.

SHREELA FLATHER: In America they are much more sensible than we are.
They have names for each different group, they don't try to bracket everyone
as 'black'. What you have here is one homogeneous group – which is white –
and all the other divided little groups. If all the blacks got together and voted
tactically we would be able to influence the choice of government, but when
would everyone get together? In Slough, for instance, there is a twenty-two per
cent minority community, and that's a group that can sway an election. If you
did that in all the areas where you have large minority groups it could have a
real effect.

RAMESH VALA: There is a big debate: should Asians be part of the larger 'black community'? On the whole people have chosen to isolate the West Indians: Brixton, it's a black problem. At first everyone was lumped together – 'the immigrant community' – then after the St Pauls' riots in Bristol the press said that we must differentiate between the Asians and the West Indians. Then there were problems in Southall and people realized that this was an Asian problem too. Not all the Asians are as religious as the Muslims in Bradford and those who are outside that world and who have become successful professionals and business people will become part of the majority community. They might not be fully accepted, but they will also turn against the extremists, and they too will be saying, 'Hold on, what are these people doing in our country? This black problem must be tackled – they can't go around flouting the law.'

RAJAN UDDIN JALAL: I don't see the black and Asian community as one united monolith, though politically I do talk in terms of the black and Asian community. Because what you do not do is create a situation where one community is seen as advancing at the cost of the other. In terms of the movement for anti-racism we must not have a situation where one community advances at the expense of the other. I want to make sure that the Vietnamese refugees who have settled in this area are treated no less well than are immigrants from Bangladesh. Bengalis have the political focus now, but that should not get them preferential treatment. The communities who are advancing have a duty to ensure that as they go forward, the less successful communities are carried forward with them.

RAMESH VALA: The successful Asians will turn against the Bangladeshis. They are the poorest, the least educated, they face the worst problems in this country. They haven't made any real attempt to change, to come to terms with Britain. Go to Whitechapel, nothing has changed: they stand around, they don't speak the language, they spit in the streets, whatever. These things offend a lot of Asians as well as British. If you go to the successful assimilated Asians and talk about racist attacks in Brick Lane, a lot of them can't associate with it. They see them as a different group of people, 'nothing to do with us'. It's these successful Asians who join the majority community, who will look at the situation in Bradford or Brick Lane and say, 'Hold on. We cannot have this.' But if these people can be accepted by the white establishment they must not forget the rest of the Asian community, and instead use their position to do things for the benefit of that community.

MANZOOR BAHADUR: The larger black community is a political idea, but individually we all have different struggles, different issues concerning us. The

354

one issue that unites us is racism, but as a Muslim there are certainly things that I want that a Sikh might not want or a Hindu might not want. But we are still going to support each other in the larger issues. We all have different objectives to achieve. They cannot be achieved by individual communities but collectively we have a stronger voice. The Muslim community has over twenty-five years' reputation in this country as being a very tolerant community in comparison with some of the other minority ethnic communities who might not have tolerated some of the things that we have. Bradford is unique in the percentage of Asians who live here and there has been a lot of mutual good will. Policies are made to please the community, but those policies are never implemented. It's things like that which are behind the current situation. People are saying, 'OK, enough is enough, let's stop playing these games.'

DESMOND GITTENS: There is some truth in the idea that the Muslims are encouraged to assimilate and choose not to, and the West Indians would like to assimilate but are rejected. We are what you might call a mongrel people. We're supposed to be Africans but we don't have an African culture *per se*. We're not Nigerians or Yoruba. We are either French or English. If you went to Martinique and met a black Martiniquan he would tell you that he was French. He would be almost more French than the French. St Lucia, Dominica, Martinique, Guadeloupe and Haiti – they're all really French. Though the St Lucians and the Dominicans have the twin thing, because they were first settled by the French and then by the British. So you get the patois. On the British islands you get a British West Indian culture and that's what you see here. People who come over, go to church, love the Queen.

BERNIE GRANT: We have tried to adopt the Jewish model. We have to look after our own. What we are saying is that we are no longer depending on the majority population of white people, because of their past record. Of course if people come along and make offers, we'll accept it, but we are also looking to doing things for ourselves.

MARY DENYS: West Indian people can succeed here. You've got to fight, you've got to use the system. I've told my children: go to college, use the system, you can beat them with their own tools. But they wouldn't do that. If I could afford it now I would go to college. People would say, what do you want to do that for? I want to do it for my satisfaction. I want to show that I could do something and that I could achieve something. Quite a few of the young are achieving a lot. They haven't given up.

RAMESH VALA: The blacks, the Afro-Caribbeans suffer in terms of both communities, who are telling them that they are totally different, that they have

355

to abide by the laws, that their culture offends everything that the British like. Though there is this paradox that the British working class have far more respect for the West Indians than for the Asians. They see the Asians as soft, whereas the West Indian seems to share a culture – sports, things like that. They find it easier to make friends with West Indians. The West Indians here don't have as strong a culture here as do the Asians. Also they are Christian whereas Asians are not.

---

25 Staying On

'Why do people stay if conditions are so bad? Why did we fight against colonialism? Why did we fight for independence?'

GINA ADAMOU: My parents decided to go back to Cyprus four years ago. My mother is happy. She had a hard life here and worked so many hours. But my father can't settle there and he can't stay here, so he's on an airplane most of the time. Two months here, two months there. A lot of people are like that. After you've lived here for a while England has a certain grip. He's sixty-four. He's not retired yet. But he loves London like me. I'm a Londoner. I belong more to London than to any other place. It's my home. I've lived in towns all my life. I never had any fear of London. There was no fear that it was big or frightening. I always loved it.

LEENA DHINGRA: We did always intend to go back, there was no doubt about that, and once we did try to go back. But it was as if independent India was rushing on in its own way and somehow we'd got left behind. I did go back, with my European husband, and we planned to stay and we did everything to stay. I had actually sent all my luggage, although we hadn't sold up here completely . . . But we did go back. Then there were a few other things . . . fate conspired. One was that my daughter was blind so I was a bit apprehensive as to where to be and there were a lot of problems of that kind. We'd been there from '68. By '74/75 there were a lot of problems of that kind. We'd come back to London and she was born here, then we went back in '73. Then I came back for a short while in '74, intending it to be a short while, but six months later the Emergency was declared and we got letters saying, 'Don't come. It's too dangerous, the place is mad.' But the idea of going back is always there. I keep hoping and wishing that I can go back.

ANWAR BATI: I visited Pakistan in 1977, the last time I've been. The worst thing was that when I was trying to buy something in the market in Karachi they all thought that I was foreign, that I was European. My manner and the fact that I didn't speak the language. Which made me feel acutely embarrassed. I thought: I come from here, yet I can't even speak the language and yet I make my living writing and being very articulate in the English language. Yet I had to stumble, I had to speak in the wrong accent, even to make myself slightly understood in Pakistan amongst people to whom I am supposed to be kin. The only time I felt comfortable on that trip was when I returned to the town in which I was born on the north-west frontier, where people, including my relations, live in the same way as they have always lived for hundreds of years. I felt at home there: I could speak the language, and there was none of the pretence that you found in Karachi, that this was a proper city, almost a European city. In proper cities things work. What happens is that you see it as a failed imitation of a European city and I had my critical English hat on; I thought, isn't it hot, isn't it sweaty, aren't there a lot of insects about, and I despised myself for thinking it. I arrived at Karachi airport and there was this soldier in full combat dress with a great big Lee-Enfield rifle with a bayonet stuck in it. I just thought anywhere else in the world there'd be security guards with a shoulder holster or whatever, and here was this soldier with his gun and I burst into tears. Then there were all these relations who had never met me before but loved me because I was my mother's son and that was also a great emotional jolt. I could respond to it on the emotional level, but it was a feeling from which I had to distance myself on an intellectual level. Otherwise it would complicate my life too much. I wouldn't want to live in Pakistan, I wouldn't be able to do the things I want to do. Nearly all the parents of the children I used to play with as a child have gone back. They made some money here, they intended to go back, and they actually did it. Much of it was their belief that modern Britain would corrupt their children, especially their daughters; otherwise they might have stayed.

MUHAMMAD AYYAZ: I always think about leaving. I have never really settled here. My passport may be English but I have never felt English. I came here when I was fifteen or sixteen and my loyalty to Pakistan just won't go away. I also believe that my children won't have a proper chance if they stay here. My main concerns are for them. There are two worries: one is that if I allow them to stay here and be educated and if I am unlucky and they move away from me I will be left with nothing. My children are the thing I want to hold on to. The majority of my family members are still at home. My mother is there and I would like to spend some time with her. For religious reasons – I have to respect her, which I do, but I have to help her too and if I am here the only help I can offer her is finance, but I cannot offer the physical help that she needs. At the moment I am forced to stay here because I have tried to get a job back home, but I can't (because of my age), and because there are family

357

members here who depend on me. But if I am going to be here for a few years, then I shall take my children home every couple of years so at least they know about our culture. It is expensive and it means I shall have to suffer, but it is a suffering I have decided I shall have to make.

MANZOOR BAHADUR: There is a fairly strong feeling about going back to Pakistan among the youngsters who are leaving school and finding that things aren't all that rosy in terms of getting employment. The parents, if they can afford it, are taking them back to Pakistan, to visit their relatives, to give them a taste of the country over there. What they're seeing there is that when they get on a bus they're just the same as everyone else, that nobody's staring, nobody's looking down on you. It's such a different environment and they become attracted to it. They find that society there is very welcoming. So when they come back here and they can't find any of that, they are starting to think about going back. If I could afford it I would not hesitate to go and see how things work out in Pakistan. If they didn't work out I could always come back here, but I'd like to give it a try. When I did go back in 1987, after thirteen years, I felt at once that I couldn't live in a village. It's too remote. But there are big cities and I honestly felt that there I could slot in without much difficulty.

MUHAMMAD ALI: I would go home, if I could be sure of finding a reasonable standard of living and a reasonable job. My children are young enough for me still to take them back without affecting their education. It's a developing country with a lot of opportunities. I do go back quite regularly. In fact I went back for two years to work there before I got married. I worked for a pharmaceutical company and found it a very good experience. I didn't feel inferior in any way. Everybody was the same. It was a good feeling.

GULZAR KHAN: You want my gut feeling: I wish I were back in Pakistan today. It has all been disappointing. If I speak from my heart, I cannot honestly feel safe walking anywhere in the evenings in the centre of the city in which I live without being molested, without being insulted. So how can you stay and live in a society where you are treated in that way? I wish there could be some way in which we could feel at ease here. I am British, my children are British, but I am not accepted as British in this society. I am still a 'Paki'. I am still a black man. That's life, that's reality, and that is what you feel every day and that is what hurts you. You are a human being, you live in this society, you contributed to this society – I have contributed more than many people who were born here in the seventeen years I have been here. I have never taken anything from the state, though I have paid every tax, every due. But still I am not considered an

358

equal in this country. I cannot live here and happily and openly say, 'Yes we are the same.'

* * *

MIKE PHILLIPS: I stay because I'm stubborn. I felt that I had put so much into this country that I was going to get something back. I always thought that I was going to conquer London and that I was going to conquer Britain no matter who stood in my way. It's partly to do with the sense that life is a struggle anyway and partly with a kind of sense that, as they used to put it in the States: 'They used to call me "nigger"; now they have to call me "Mister Nigger".' I kind of feel like that. That's the way I personally reclaim my identity, that's the way I make up for the offences and humiliations I had when I first came to this country, with the sense that I am not in that position any more.

RAJAN UDDIN JALAL: Why do people stay when they say conditions are so bad? Well, why did we fight against colonialism? Why did we fight for independence? Why did we fight against the military rule of Pakistan? You don't give up. You fight. And that is equally true here. On a personal level I have grown up in this country and there is no going back. Nobody will have me in Bangladesh. I can't do many jobs there. My life is here, my peer group is here, my political activity is here, my work is here, everything is here. Also, for people like me who are politicized to a certain extent, we don't give up. You have got to fight for your existence.

MANZOOR BAHADUR: I want to stay in England, to win in England. It would be interesting and a challenge to try life in Pakistan, to set up my own business and see if I could succeed once and for all without the problems of racism, but I don't want to desert this sinking ship. People in my position who are able to express their concerns, able to express their needs, we owe it to the community to stay. The more we contribute to the development of our own community, the more we are contributing to the welfare of this country: I don't think we can see ourselves as something separate. We retain our own community identity but we are still part of the larger community. We have our own colour, our own culture, language and religion, but we all contribute our bit to the larger world. We want to compromise, but that involves asking for our rights, and when we do that, sometimes the people who have the power to grant them are not willing to do so.

BENNY BUNSEE: I definitely wouldn't come now. I very definitely want to get out now. I have no roots here, and on that level Britain has failed me. It's very disappointing. Here is a comparatively rich country that has everything yet basically has nothing – people are basically miserable and unhappy. I would like to go to a Third World country, perhaps Zimbabwe. The problem in the Third World however is this paradox: whatever you can say about Britain, you still have a relative amount of freedom and democracy to do certain things that you can't do in Third World counties because there they really kill you on the spot. These regimes are brutal and oppressive – you couldn't go putting out leaflets in the streets there: they pick you up, throw you in jail, and you'd rot. It's as simple as that. But I can't live in a country when I don't feel that the totality of that country is mine. The totality of Britain is not mine – its institutions, its history are not mine. It is alien, I am totally cut off from it. The culture, the history and so on is not mine and can never be mine and I can never belong here.

CARMEN CALLIL: I never intended to go back at all, but when I started to go back in '72 I liked it so much. It was incredibly good to go back to, because it was home. I've been back every eighteen months since, but never for long enough. But now I couldn't go back to stay, too much time has gone by, even though I'm perceived here as not being British. I think I'll die here. All my old Australian mafia has moved back but if I did leave it would more likely be France, it's nearer.

GERTRUD HARTWIG: I have been back to Germany once, very briefly. It was like a foreign country. It was in connection with my husband's job and he took me along once when he had to visit Germany. It was strange. You didn't find anyone you knew in any of the places where you had lived. In 1988 I had to go to a sanatorium in Germany, I couldn't find the right treatment here in England. I stayed there for a couple of weeks. There was no anti-Semitism. You were accepted and I must say that the atmosphere was good, but whether I would like to live there again, I have my doubts.

* * *

PETAR OBRATOVIC: I didn't know I was going to stay. Consciously I did not know. I had applied for my course, and that was to last for four years. They accepted me for an introductory period, and said they would assess me later and see how it went. I had money in the bank, I knew I could survive for a year. I had met some people who were shooting a film in Yugoslavia and they offered me a free flat in Maida Vale for the first four months I was here. Then I spent the next ten months with a colleague who offered me a room in his house. So I spent the first period of my life really having a lot of help from the people here. But as far as I knew I would eventually go home. Then I was accepted for a major course, for three more years, and I realized that I don't want to go back. I wanted to stay for a bit longer. I didn't think whether I

360

wanted to stay for ever. I didn't know quite how much longer I wanted to stay, but I knew that I wanted to stay for a few years more after my training. At this point it became clear that my first wife would not want to come here, and it was increasingly clear through my therapy that I didn't want to stay with her. At the same time I met my second wife.

SHREELA FLATHER: I didn't intend to stay here for ever when I arrived. I wanted to have my education and then go back. But when I married an Englishman that changed. Being uprooted from Lahore during Partition had made such a difference. My home had gone, my roots had been destroyed – I had been desperately miserable when we couldn't go back. So once you've gone through that trauma, the idea of home, of staying in one place for ever, is no longer that important. Once you've made one forced emigration, then you tend to feel, what does it matter where you live, if you are no longer allowed to live where your roots were. I shall certainly stay here. When I visit India I feel very happy, but I don't feel I could live there. If I had to leave England then America would be much easier to live in now than India.

PALOMA ZOZAYA: I am always talking about going back, and I visit, with my husband, quite a bit. Mexico has been changing a lot. The last time I was there I was frightened, although Mexican people were frightened too. Mexico City is becoming a very violent, a very dangerous city, which was not how I grew up. I'm not used to that, but then nor are Mexican adults. But after a few months in Mexico I start to feel very happy about having the possibility of coming back to England, and then after I've been back here for a while I started seeing all the bad things about living here and I want to go back to Mexico again.

NAIM ATALLAH: If I went back to live in Palestine, I would probably feel very strange. I've been here since I was eighteen. It's such a different life there – I'd be like a fish out of water. Basically, England is my home now.

ENNIO CAMISA: I always like the British. That's why I stay. I always get on very well with the British people. In fact it changed my mind about going back. I go back to Italy for holidays, but I wouldn't want to live there for good. Now I have my family here, my sons here. I knew I was going to stay here for the rest of my life right at the beginning.

SUSAN WILSON: The moment I realized that I wasn't going back was in 1978 when I married my husband. Then I knew I was going to stay for a long time. I had a lot of qualms about it. I was homesick for the landscape, not for anything as much as that. I really need to see proper open countryside. I still need to see mountains, to see open landscape. I need that, I feel terribly cramped sometimes.

MIRANDA LOVETT: I got very homesick in the early days. I'm very close to my family, I have four sisters whom I adore, I'm very close to my mother; I missed New York, I missed America, I missed English muffins, I missed Pampers when my kids were babies when they didn't have Pampers here – I'd go to north London to buy Pampers at £7 a box when you get Peaudouce at the corner store for £1.50. I did ridiculous things. My sister came over when I had my second child and brought ten packets of Thomas's English muffins.

CHRISTOPHER HOPE: I constantly feel homesick. I don't know if all immigrants feel this – unless they've been forced into immigration. For me it's a kind of bereavement. The problem is that there's nobody to bury. I'm allowed to return and do so roughly every two years, but that doesn't improve matters. Going home doesn't bring me closer to home than leaving it. I have increasingly strong feelings of not being European, but African. I think many people who leave their own country and make a place for themselves elsewhere do attempt to some degree to fit in, and don't hark back too much if they're sensible. In my case, I write books about the place, or aspects of it, so it's more difficult to sponge the memories from one's mind. In time your emotional attachment to your homeland does return. But the opposite sometimes occurs. But whether you settle or not, what happens is that you drag behind you this great cavalcade of memories and emotions.

ESTHER IZUNDU: I still feel African, more African then anything else. I'm quite pleased at how far we've come, but I'm disappointed at the way things are going back home, because I would like to go back. It would affect my children too much though. We have Nigerian passports, but we've been invited to take up British citizenship. We're still considering that. Of course my children have British passports, they were born here. I do dream of home a lot. I think of the people back home, the country, then come to and realize I'm walking along a British street. I've been home quite a few times, the last time in 1986. But most of our friends are here.

*　*　*

VU DUY TU: Sometimes I ask myself where I am now, what am I doing, and I miss my country very, very much. I want to go back. We want to go back, but it's not possible now. Perhaps one day there will be no more Communist regime. But after seven years living in their prison and in their system I can't believe how so many western politicians believe that Communism will change. Never. Things may be changing in China or in Russia, but those are changes in those societies. Vietnam will not become a western society ever. It's very different even to other Communist regimes. We were born under a free regime, and we cannot adapt to Communism. If we had been born under that regime, maybe we would have been happy, but unfortunately we were not and we cannot accept it.

PETER VO: Throughout the history of Vietnam, however bad things have become, there has never been this exodus of people from the country. Not until now. In 1945, when there was a big famine and one million people starved to death, still nobody left the country. During the war between France and Vietnam, nobody left the country. People have only left since the Communist regime came to power. We had no choice. We escaped that regime by any means possible. We just saw that it was too awful, that it was something that we could not accept. Therefore in exile everybody hopes that if the situation changed, we could return. Everyone hopes that one day we could return. Things do change. Czechoslovakia is changing, Hungary is changing, Yugoslavia, even Russia. So our Communist regime cannot deny the people freedom for ever. Look at China: people stood up and fought for their freedom even if they were crushed and massacred. People know what freedom is and they want it. If they rise up once, they will rise up again. I do hope that one day things will change and one day, perhaps, I will be able to go home. One day hopefully I shall see it again, see the people again, my old house, the places I lived and visited. The cafés, the other places I liked in Saigon. I would like one day to sit in my favourite café, in the same seat, and look at the country where I was born and where I come from. That would be wonderful. But in the meantime I shall make the best of England, and contribute to England as well as I can.

NIEN-LUN YEH: We are quite settled here. We have British citizenship. We were the first ever couple from mainland China to get citizenship by naturalization. There have been mainland immigrants but they got their citizenship by marriage. They took a short cut. We hope to start travelling again with our British passports. But we miss China and our parents very much. We want to go back often, to look after them now they have become older. Meanwhile we want to make the fullest use of our present status to see as much as possible of the world. Maybe, as the Chinese saying has it, the falling tree will return to the roots.

JOHN LAHR: I haven't left America. I like going back. I like seeing my friends, I keep up with them all there. I have discovered a much wider America. Pockets that I like much more than the East Coast. I find a lot of dignity in fundamentalist America. I'm forty-seven now, and my son is thirteen, and I find I like going back to the States and going to baseball games, eating hotdogs,

Oreo cookies and egg creams. I like the look of the fire-escapes, the green and red tops of the buildings in New York, I like Chinatown. I go back every other year to teach for three weeks in Colorado, and we've been to various parts of America over the years – in a sense as a way of finding out if there is a part of America I could live in. Never found it. Nothing is sophisticated enough for my taste – what I mean is that it doesn't turn me on. Every place outside of New York is too parochial, there's not enough happening, it's too isolated, too bland, too violent. Though no doubt living in Berkshire, for instance, would have the same effect.

TESS WICKHAM: There never came a time when I said, 'OK I'm going to stay'. I still haven't. I've lived here, I have two children who are leaving home, I've been here for twenty-five years but I've never thought, I'm here. Ever. Quite often people ask me why I am here and I find it quite difficult to answer. I normally come out with a diatribe of loathing, and other people have to remind me of the things that originally I quite liked.

KATHY ACKER: I don't regret coming. I do get homesick – I can't imagine anyone leaving their country and not feeling homesick. Whether I'd want to live here for the rest of my life I don't know. That depends on so many personal factors. And I do go back all the time. I don't see myself as an immigrant. I see myself as an exile if anything. When I left it was because I wanted to leave the United States, not because I specifically wanted to come to England. I wanted to get out of New York. I didn't even think in terms of countries. I was considering cities. I might have considered Paris, but in the end it's down to the language. I write, I have work in London.

* * *

NELLY SALAS: I often dream about Argentina, about being with my friends again. I have had a dream about being back in the house I lived in when I was very young. I am adult, although the house is still just as it was when I was a child. Sometimes I dream I am flying. I have a chair, and a little joystick that I control. Once I dreamt that I went to Chile. I flew over the sea, which was beautiful, the sun was shining on the sea, and I went to see the family of my best friend in England, who looked after me when I arrived. I talked to them, her aunts and all her people. Then I said, 'It's going to be dark now, I must go back,' and I get back into my chair and fly away. When I woke up I felt very happy, as if something really nice had happened to me. Which it had done, because that dream is beautiful. My dreams are always linked to the past or the future, never the present. Years and years ago, in Argentina, I used to dream about gardens, beautiful, beautiful gardens, incredible flowers, everything. My friends made fun of me, they told me I was dreaming in technicolor. Indeed, I had never seen such gardens in Argentina. But when I came here, I saw gardens like that. And it was more than twenty years later. In another dream back in Argentina I was driving a black taxi – in Argentina they don't exist, there are no cars like that – and suddenly I was in the countryside and the car took off and started to fly. It was beautiful countryside. Twenty years later I went to Spain in a plane, and I looked down, and there was the same countryside.

DAVILIA DAVID: I used to have this dream every time I thought of going back: I'd be walking down a street back home, saying hello to everyone, a general feeling of delight to be back, then having a great black hole open up inside when I realized that I'd never be able to get back to Europe. I'd burnt my bridges. The first time was when my sister went back, eighteen months after we had arrived together.

HANNAH KODICEK: I have two sorts of dreams. In one I find myself in Prague incognito. Nobody can recognize me and it's quite fun, because nobody knows that I understand everything that they are saying. But it's also quite frightening because I am thinking, 'What am I doing here? How will I get home?' and home means England. The other sort is returning to Prague and the city looks very surreal. In no way is it the Prague that I remember. When I wake up I try to decipher which was the dream Prague and which the one I knew in reality and I can't really work out the details of the streets that I used to know and which were part of my life. But it matters.

ANNE-MARIE WOLPE: I do have some nightmares. I dream that Harold's gone back and I don't know why he's gone back but I do know that he'll be arrested. That's the only dream I've had about South Africa, never anything else. It does recur, but not often. One of my children has a recurrent nightmare of faceless police who are enormous.

NIEN-LUN YEH: All my dreams are about China. Never about England. We went to Denmark, to stay with friends in Copenhagen and then travel around the countryside. Every night I would dream about China. About my youth, about what I suffered during the Cultural Revolution. During the day my reality is so different, yet whenever I dream it is about China. They are always very sad dreams. So every night in Denmark these are my dreams, but when I open my eyes, there I am in Scandinavia. These dreams make me miss China. Even though that period of my life was very hard, it is still a very significant time.

NGUYEN DUC PHUONG: I miss Vietnam a lot. The first two years I was here I had a nightmare. I was back in my country. Then I'd be woken up by the

365

security forces. Then I would really wake up and I'd go to the window and see the usual road in front of my house and so on, and I'd go and wake up my wife to show her my happiness. That went on for the first two years.

SHARI PEACOCK: I dream often about my parents. I dream in Bulgarian or Iranian. My recurrent dream is that I am coming back home to my flat in London and my home has been invaded. Either there is somebody already in, or I can't get in. I'm trying to close all the doors and somebody's trying to get in. Very often there are a whole lot of people who are already here and I can't get rid of them. Basically in my dream there's this constant closing of doors of keeping people out. You think you've moved away, but somehow like getting old and remembering more things about your childhood, you come back.

* * *

DAVILIA DAVID: The last time I went back it was for the longest time I'd spent there since leaving. I loved it. Part of me still very much belongs there, but the other part belongs here in Europe and I'm a bit torn. It was my career that kept me here, and if I had gone back, it would still have kept me away from my family, in Sydney or Melbourne rather than in Perth. Though after twenty-nine years in Britain I might give Australia a try. If I can get some work. People are so approachable there. I'd call up a casting person and actually get to speak to them. Here you're lucky if you get through to the secretary. I think I'm starting to get sentimental about the incredible beauty of Australia, the smells and the memories – it's all very much in my blood. The elemental qualities in me belong in Australia. Though I don't fit in when I go back. They see me as English. The negative reaction I felt for my country cousins over here when I arrived is what I feel now for the loud Australians back home. They're different from me, an oddity, distasteful. When my marriage collapsed I nearly went home, but I didn't. It would have been going back as a failure, and I had to go back as a 'somebody'. I don't regret coming. I go back home to my old small town when I visit and I see how bitter and narrow all the people I grew up with have become. Meeting old school friends is uncomfortable. They're all so provincial.

MARY DENYS: I do like England. There are pros and cons. Going back home is a difficult decision. I don't particularly want to leave England – I like England, though it has its pros and cons – but people say to me, 'You're a pensioner, you should go back home.' But to go back you need a home to go to. I haven't got that. Even though I could get one. But I like something that I have worked for, something I have done for myself. I like to be independent. I don't want to depend on someone who one day can turn round and say, 'You have to leave here now.' I am sixty-one and people of my age are all over the

366

world. I've got children down there, I've got grandchildren down there, but everybody expects you to be giving all the time. You have to be giving, giving, giving, and then when what you have has gone, then you are left alone. The few friends I have here, I know that if I call them they will come. I have other children here and grandchildren here and even if they don't come all the time, they are here. I don't see any future for me in St Lucia. If I go back I shall have to work, and at my age, to go home and work again, I won't do that.

TONY GIRARD: I arrived in October 1960 and in February 1961 I wrote my mum: I'm coming back. No one ever intended to stay for ever. The idea was to come here, get a job, get some money, go home. I don't think there were many of us who left home with the intention of staying here permanently. But after I wrote she wrote back saying, 'What are you coming back for?' and I knew I had to stay. Try and bear it and see what I could do. I did go back in '67 to see her but by then I was established. What happened was that I went from strength to strength as a plumber, then I became a deputy foreman. But I'd always talk about when I was going home. One day, one day . . . Then one day our team leader told me, 'Look, Tony, ever since I've known you you're talking about going home. Let's face it – you're here to stay.' I didn't agree with him at the time, but it was the start of realizing that I had a long way to go here before I'd be able to go home. Yet it was always at the back of my mind. In fact right up to the early '70s, whatever I used to buy, it was with the thought, 'That will do nicely back home . . .' I wasn't alone. Lots of West Indians thought on the same lines. I remember a Jamaican friend, she bought a fridge, and she was worried: would it work back home? I was the same. Only a very small percentage actually do go back. Very few. Would I go back? That's a question not many West Indians can answer, especially when they've been here as long as I have. You're trapped. You're afraid. To go home is to start all over again. Going home when I retire, that is at the back of my mind, and there are people who do go. But really, how many of us will make it back? I'm lucky, I own my house and if anything happened I could sell it and buy somewhere in St Lucia. But that's all I've got. The majority don't have anything. To go home – what for? Too old to get a job, can't get a pension over there. So maybe you stay here until you qualify for a pension and then go home, that may help. But most of my friends are here. So . . .

MANDY MERCK: I feel trapped. I feel I came to a place that no longer exists. Sometimes I get the heebie-jeebies about it. What I've got here which is irreplaceable is a fantastic group of friends. They are now my family in some sense. I now like going back home, and go more than I used to. My father's getting on, there are good reasons to be going back. I actively seek my parents out for holidays, going for trips with my mother, etc. I've been back three times

367

this year. We're all meeting in Oregon for a fortnight soon, and I'm really looking forward to it. But my peer group – the people here are my friends. A lot of them are Australians, Canadians, but I don't feel I live in an expat community, nor would I want to. There's no point in living here if you don't have strong relationships with British people.

NIEN-LUN YEH: I don't feel English. I've become very different to people in China of course. I could always read some English, but there I had to think in Chinese first and then translate it. Now I can think in English. Of course I haven't lost my Chinese identity – I shall never lose it. But when we go back we feel very uncomfortable in many ways. Gradually we are losing touch. We can understand what is going on there very easily, but to lead that kind of life again – that would be very difficult. When I go back to China I still feel that there is my home; when I return to England, I feel this is my home. I don't feel trapped in between in any way. I feel I have two homes and I am ground in both.

DESMOND GITTENS: Initially I always expected to go back. Once I get a few pounds together, buy myself a nice house and a car and whatnot. But it didn't work out like that. I bought a farm in the Caribbean in 1970. I went out and almost killed myself because I knew nothing about farming. It was just one of those dreams that you get when you're sat in Hampstead or Notting Hill somewhere dreaming about the world. And the money's there and you buy a farm and then you realize that you can't do farming. So I came back. So I still travel to the Caribbean often but I've decided that Britain is my home. I've got children here. I've got my place in the Caribbean, my place in the sun and I see it as a retirement place. I'll go out there, have my place by the beach and if I need medical care come here for it and that's how I see it.

SHREERAM VIDYARTHI: I wouldn't think of leaving England under any circumstances now. I have my home here, I have put down roots here, I know no other home. The question of going back to India doesn't arise. I have never thought, 'After I retire I'll go back to India and have a good time on the UK pension.' That has never occurred to me. I speak the language, I think in local terms, I experience things that happen around me and I plan on a local plane. I invest my money here, I earn my money here, I profit from here, I lose here, I go sleepless here and I sleep well here. There is no reason for moving anywhere. If things go bad here – can't things go bad there? I would rather be here than anywhere else. This is a part of my being now. What goes on, it doesn't worry me. People talk a lot about the British weather, it doesn't worry me one bit. I lived in Bombay for seven years and there it rains perpetually. I have a small property in France now. I do hope to go there and live. The

368

surroundings are tranquil, plenty of land, of open spaces. I want to sit back, relax and write and read. That is my greatest joy.

* * *

SUSAN WILSON: Quite a few of the New Zealanders talk about going home one day to live on their pensions. A lot of my friends did go back and that was painful. They all seemed to pack up and leave about five years ago and I did start feeling that I was going to be the only one left. I seemed to be saying perpetual goodbyes and that was very difficult. In some ways I've been lucky: my husband has a son, who was four when we met, and because of him we could never shift back and forth to New Zealand like some of my friends have done, which I think is very traumatic. Crazy. So they never settle properly anywhere. I do go back about once every four years but because of my relationship I felt I had to stay here. And that was actually a great advantage because I had to get going with my work and make things happen here. I do know people who are in a peculiar state of mind. You live two years here, two years there, two years somewhere else – it's not very good, I wouldn't like to do it. But I won't be buried here. I want to have my ashes scattered in the Tagus River in Spain, near Toledo, thrown off the Tagus bridge.

CINDY BLAKE: I don't want to be buried in this country. I have a big thing about that. I want to be buried in Boston. I would be really angry if I were buried in this country: I've put it in my will. I don't know where my hatred actually springs from, I wish I knew. But it is profound and I wish I knew because I don't like feeling this way. I think it's partly because this country puts me on the defensive so much and because they make me feel less of a person for some reason.

YASMIN ALIBHAI: If I came from a country where I could go back to I would do just what the racists say: go back to where I came from. But East African Asians can't go back. Britain and I have a bond now, like it or not. Most of my friends went to America or Canada, but I deliberately came here because at the time England seemed to have the values that I really admired. Especially the welfare state. Ironically this is where I feel at home; the only place I've felt at home in all my life is London. I really feel that I belong to London in a way that I have never felt I belonged anywhere else in my life. I miss it when I go away and I'm not tempted by other places.

* * *

MICHAEL DE SOUZA: Home is still really Trinidad. I have a great advantage over kids who were born now or even in the '70s. I'm fully aware of two cultures. I've been through the whole system in both countries and I'm aware

369

of the schooling here and the schooling there, and the life there and the life here too. It's much harder if you're born here and you still get treated badly. That's hard. At least I could tell people, 'I'm going home.' Though when I'm there, England is home. So I'm stuck in the middle. You're taken from the place where you were born, your first home and you miss it. You grow up here, you have your life, and in reality this becomes home. But spiritually and emotionally it's very difficult to accept it as home. Then when you go over there, back to where you come from, that's very difficult and it can't be home. You don't fit in there. No one knows you, you're just a stranger. Apart from anything else you're an adult now. So there are a lot of difficulties, but in one respect I'd prefer to be there. It's a black society. It's a wonderful experience to get on a bus and know that people won't stare at you just because you're black. Which they still do here. They stare at me there because of my hair, but that's fine.

FERDIE ERASMUS: I went back for three weeks for Christmas. Although it was great to see the family, I was homesick after a week – I wanted to be back here. This is my home. I love it here. You make friends with anyone, talk to anyone, do anything you like.

MICHAEL IGNATIEFF: I can go down the streets of Toronto blindfold. I'm there a lot of the time. My family is there, my earliest memories are there, I'm terribly attached to it. I don't feel haunted by the question of home. My home is this house, my wife and my children. I think a lot about home, and what I think is that expatriation and exile and emigration are now much more the norm than the rule. We now live in a world where everybody has a bunch of homes, negotiates their homes, constitutes their homes instead of inherits them, creates them rather than is born into them, and that's going to continue, to increase. I think that's the best thing in the modern world, where races are intermarrying, where we all live in a variety of cultures not just in our own tight world close to our old parish pump. All that stuff I am a real believer in. It also creates identity problems on a very large scale, but I think that a lot of the expatriate friends I have rejoice in the freedom that you get in having a couple of homes and negotiating the terms of your engagement to each. So I negotiate the terms of my engagement to London and the terms of that engagement change. They're not metaphysical or abstract, they're very much tied to a particular culture, the culture of the media, these institutions that work. They work now and they might not work in the future, in which case I would have to renegotiate. I think I did come here originally obeying the Judy Garland injunction to 'play the Palace' but as I cruise into middle age I don't think that. I could have had an equally interesting life in Canada, but it would have been different.

SHARI PEACOCK: Where is home? I have pondered that so much. Because you've carved out your life yourself, home becomes very very small. So home is this room, or home is my knowledge of English, the language. Most important, home has become the language. So if I go up north to visit a friend whose parents are very working class I don't have the solace of the language. I feel totally naked and totally vulnerable and a complete foreigner. As to roots, I don't even know what the word means. I left Bulgaria, my parents left Iran, their parents left Russia. It's like asking the child of a film star, 'What would it be like to be a normal child?' They don't know and nor do I. I hear black people talking a hell of a lot on Radio 4 about 'roots', but I just do not know what they mean. It's one of those words where the penny hasn't dropped. I just don't understand it. Maybe it works in reverse. If I leave this country and, say, visit my parents for two weeks, I'm really terrified about coming back. It's the primitive fear that you won't be let in, you've forgotten the language, nobody knows you and you'll have to start all over again.

NELLY SALAS: When I wonder where is my home, I feel like I am in the air: I am not in Argentina, I am not in England. I am in the middle. For me to go back, now it would be impossible. The first thing is because my family is still very, very poor. If I did go back I would have to live with my family and that would mean problems for them. I don't know whether I would find any work there, but I don't have any money of my own. So why would I go back? I must live here. I know many people, many people know me, I can do things for the Latin American community here and there. All the things I do here now make me feel more of a human being, and that makes me happy. That's not England, not any country, it's what I do with my own life, which is to help others.

RAJINDER SINGH: I am somewhere between England and India. My family is over there and a whole lot of my interest lies with them, not over here. If my family came over here, it might be entirely different. When I talk about home, I am still thinking of India. I wanted to settle over here, but if my family cannot come, I cannot settle. So I may well go back and settle in India. I cannot leave my son alone. How long I stay here all depends on my job.

STEPHEN VIZINCZEY: Where do I consider home? Well, I know I'm Hungarian. I'm a European. I cannot make sense of myself any other way. I'm not home in the same sense that I would have been home had I never moved from Hungary. Canada has ten years of my youth and many friends and some family. An English friend described me as a true internationalist. I'm happy everywhere. In the end my real home is the English language and the British Isles is the closest I can come to that home.

ANNE-MARIE WOLPE: I don't know where home is. If I hear black music, if I hear the anthems sung, I can weep, so on that level South Africa is my home. But obviously I can't go back unless some massive change takes place, or pardons are given out. Friends of mine have been murdered there. Harold missed being in the room when Ruth First was blown apart because he happened to have a bad cold that day. He's Joe Slovo's best friend and vice versa ever since they were at university. But I don't know where home is. Home is in France, we holiday there. Home may be where your children are, but my children don't feel that this is home. A number of our friends are British, a number are not, and a number, while British academics, have their origins elsewhere. That's weird: because for many years I thought I was totally integrated into British society and then I realized that actually I am not.

PALOMA ZOZAYA: I still see Mexico as home, although in the end I'm probably somewhere over the Atlantic. A friend of mine told me, and I experience it every day, that once you start travelling you just don't belong anywhere. Another friend told me, 'The more I'm here, the more I settle into the English way of life, the more my roots dig into the Latin American soil.' This beautiful image of a tree stretching across the Atlantic with your branches stretching out to England, but your roots going deeper and deeper into Mexico. I think this is double-edged though: if you live here, and especially if you never go back to Latin America, you tend to lose your perspective, your sense of what is really going on in Mexico. You stick to what was going on when you left, and things have changed. What England has given me is freedom. In Mexico I couldn't be doing all the marvellous plays – about Mexico – that I do here. Being here gives me freedom at a personal level that I could not have achieved there. But being here is in some ways not having any past.

PETER VO: After eight years, I feel that England is my home. In a way I do feel English. The first thing is that I must accept the situation. I must accept what I have. And the best way for me to feel better is to accept the situation as it is at the present time. Because by accepting, one is half-way to making a success of one's life. You have to get over believing that this isn't really home, get over thinking all the time that soon you will go back. At the beginning of being in Britain sometimes I would wake up and think this is not my home. I think of Vietnam, in my dreams I had nightmares – what is happening. I dream a lot of the camps and other hardships I went through, I dream of being recaptured, of being tortured. Sometimes I just dream of being back in Saigon. It was very hard to cope with my memories when I arrived here. It made me very very unhappy. But now, after eight years, I only rarely have those nightmares.

FIRDOS ALI: If they say to me, 'If you don't like it, why don't you go?' I say they can fuck off! I'm staying. I confine myself to my world. I'm not bothering

372

you – you don't bother me. Whether they dislike us or like us, that's not the problem. I am far away from home, so this is my home now, in so far as it is my house. They say the Englishman's home is his castle, but that's not quite what I mean. If my neighbour is good to me, then I shall be good to him; if he's nasty to me, I will ignore him. If he sends his dog to shit in my front yard, I'll poison his fucking dog. If they say, 'Fuck off', I'll say, 'Wait a minute: I've paid my taxes. I've worked, I've sweated here, I came as a young man, a boy almost, I gave you the best part of my life, are you so fucking ungrateful?' They say I should be grateful? I say fuck that. Grateful for what? We kept their economy running. We have generated income for them. Suppose you are running a record shop selling Indian and Pakistani records. You pay VAT. Where does that go: to the Treasury and the Treasury uses it to manufacture weapons. Anybody who has come to this country has come to boost the economy of this country. Nobody is sitting around like a parasite unless the state creates the situation where they have no choice. And now the state is making sure that that happens. Yet Thatcher has been elected three times. These people who can barely sign their name, barely write a literate line, they've elected her. If they can do that, what is the future of this country?

PO-YEE WONG: When I came here, I didn't think about racism, coming from a different culture or background. I was in medicine, working for humanity, and everybody who came to see me, I saw as a human being I wanted to help back to health. I experienced racism when I tried to advance, they tried to put me down because I wasn't English. Although you accept others, they may not always accept you. So you need your own background to fall back on for comfort, etc. But you must also be open, because we live in a multicultural society. With the English the main attitude is still, 'If you don't like it here, why don't you go home?' They ignore the fact that some foreigners are now second generation, were born here. And home is where you are born.

NAIM ATALLAH: I believe in the old Arabic proverb – one who denies his roots has no roots at all. My roots are part of my life that I cannot forget. I cannot forget the land, the happy days I spent with my grandmother in her little house in Nazareth. That too is part of my life. When my father died I took my family to Nazareth and I showed them that house. I came into Quartet Books in 1976 and since then I have tried to redress the political balance by highlighting the Palestinian people. Every time I see the Palestinians being bashed I feel great sadness. I could have been in one of those camps had my circumstances been different.

I came to this country out of choice. At this time in my life I could go and live somewhere else, but I've chosen to stay here. I must be very attached to the country, that I call myself British. This is home. I have nothing in Palestine now. I travel a lot. To me home is where my friends are. My mother lives in Toronto. I have a sister in Washington. There is a Palestinian community here and I feel very sympathetic towards it, but I'm so involved in my work that I don't have any spare time. My hobby is my work. I do my bit for the Palestinian cause by highlighting their plight, helping wherever I can, but I don't belong to any Palestinian group.

PETER TATCHELL: I only intended to stay in Britain for a couple of years, until the Vietnam War was over. However, I quickly settled into life here: setting up home, getting a job, completing my education at evening classes, falling in love, and immersing myself in the political struggle for lesbian and gay liberation. It was very easy for a temporary stay to become permanent.

Now, I regard Britain as my adopted home. I've no intention of going back to Australia, except for visits.

Because Britain is the country where I now live, what happens here affects me personally. So obviously I care very much about the state of the country and I'd like to contribute something towards making it a better place for me and for others. That's why I'm involved in politics. What I admire about Britain is not the State with its feudal rituals and bloody history of Empire. It's the democratic and humanitarian ideals of ordinary British people embodied in their struggles for things like the right to vote, the Welfare State, and the fight against Nazism.

* * *

NISSIM ELIJAH: I would never go back to India. Israel is the next choice. But definitely not India. I've given up my Indian citizenship. I don't want to go to a place where I'm not wanted. I feel British, always did, even in India. The Crown was something to be looked up to, the form of government as something worthwhile – and it is. OK, I've been messed around here, but you can't help that. I'm not the only one. It's as much my fault, although my circumstances were difficult. But I should have looked for a better job.

CINDY BLAKE: I don't regret the move, because anything that's difficult is worthwhile. What I have to do is learn how to live with it better than I have done. That's why I'm disappointed in myself that I haven't. That whatever this anger is that I have towards the British – why I haven't figured that one out. When I've worked that through then I will have learnt something and it will be worth it, because it has to mean something. I can't still have such strong feelings after ten years here without there being something at stake. It's a big thing in my head and I don't know why it has become such a major factor. Why it upsets me so much. Whether I've met the best people or the worst, whatever element it is that I've met, there's something in this country that just irritates the shit out of me, and until I figure out why, I'll feel really stupid, and I will feel like a dumb, ugly American until I figure out what it is that irritates me so much.

BRYAN GOULD: After I had spent two years at Oxford I wasn't sure what to do: to stay on or to go back to New Zealand. I resolved this partly by applying to the Foreign Office. I had been offered a job by the New Zealand External Affairs department but I thought if I take that I'll be back in the New Zealand environs, and I'll never get back to Britain. On the other hand if I stay here, I can always nip back to New Zealand if that's what I want to do. So I enquired as to whether the Foreign Office would accept me, as a New Zealander. They said they didn't see any problem, why didn't I apply? So I did and went through this curious entrance procedure and came top in my year. I thought that this was a good pointer for the future – things would be OK. But I thought that if I ran into the slightest expression of any prejudice, or any indication that there might be a limit of how far I could go, I won't do it. But that never happened; no one ever asked me why as a New Zealander I wanted to join the British Foreign Office. They just assumed it to be the most natural thing in the world.

EVA JIRICNA: England is my home, it definitely is. I don't really think about going back to Prague. I feel no temptation to go back. Anyway I can't go back. I haven't applied for an emigrant passport, because if I did so I would have to have to ask the government for a pardon and I don't feel that I have done anything wrong, although I have been sentenced to three years' imprisonment in my absence. I don't actually know what for, they haven't sent me a copy of the sentence. But they informed my mother that I have been sentenced to three years' imprisonment in my absence. I think they just said 'political reasons'. They didn't give her any details. I resist that in principle – I really think that it's wrong to ask for a pardon for something that you haven't done. Of course I don't know what I would do if somebody in my family were seriously ill – under those circumstances people do behave completely differently. When my father was dying in 1972 it was really very, very awful. The fact that we couldn't go to see him and he couldn't come to see us. That was extremely difficult.

IVAN KYNCL: I would never go back. I want to stay here. The first reason is that it is easier to be a foreigner in a foreign country than it is to be a foreigner in your own country. I think that were I to go back to Czechoslovakia I would be a foreigner for ever, because I already think differently, completely differently from the day I came here. Also because I think that the people there all the time will know: 'Yes, he was in the West, he is different.' I still have lots of friends there and I like them but I know that if I were to talk to them today there are a lot of things on which we would disagree, especially about the West.

375

Mainly because it isn't as good as they think. Of course in some ways it is better, that's why I am here, but it isn't perfect either.

MOSES SPITZ: In the end we are foreigners and will be foreigners now wherever we go, including Argentina. Even if we went back. It is fine to go back as a tourist, things are wonderful and the experience of warmth, hospitality and friendliness leave no doubt that one is welcomed. But if we were to go back to live there, then I think it is all different. Life has gone on without us for much too long, people have changed, the place has changed somehow. I would like to go back. My most common expression is 'I do not want to die in England'. And I believe that quite strongly, although for one reason it would be easier to die here because here you can get cremated without any trouble, whereas over there the whole business is extremely difficult.

KAREL KYNCL: I would go back if I could, but I am not sure whether I would be prepared to live there for the rest of my life. I love the country. I am still very much connected with it. I am interested in its fate, but I would not be sure whether I would be strong enough. On the other hand, one of the nightmares that I have is that I left it because I thought it is unbearable, and hundreds and thousands of people who I know and I am very fond of are still there. It's a sort of inferiority complex this situation provokes. Almost like survivor guilt. This is not such a rare feeling. There was a time when I was in jail and by some strange luck I wasn't to be interrogated for two months, while friends were interrogated every week. I began to feel, may I have done something wrong?

NGUYEN DUC PHUONG: I very much hope that we will go home one day. I don't know whether things will change that much but I hope so. We can't expect that the Communists will just die automatically, it doesn't happen like that. I just hope that the economic situation will force them to modify the system. We don't expect them suddenly to give up Communism and change to capitalism. But I would like to go back and contribute to my country. But I don't really think that I could go back and work with the Communists as they are now. I have lived with them for three years and I know. Even when I was at secondary school and I saw the Berlin Wall I knew something was wrong. I would think: If East Germany is so civilized, why do people want to escape? Something must be wrong. Which is also why I don't hesitate when I have to join the armed forces. We just want to get rid of the Communists. We want freedom in the South, nothing else. My friends said they didn't care whether it was Communism or capitalism, but I did.

WITOLD STARECKI: I chose to stay on for various reasons. I lost some of the belief in what I had been doing in Poland. Polish cinema was functioning only in connection with the political situation. For me there was absolutely no hope or reason to stay: personal reasons, artistic, so on. I needed to extend and grow. There is another dangerous symptom that comes from fighting too long in that sort of world: after a while you become the mirror image of what you are fighting, you don't relax, you lose perspective. There is a very interesting paradox: when I came here and at last I could make films with harder subjects – whether on Poland or something else – I was no longer interested. I began getting interested in music, in comedy, things I would never have considered in Poland, where I was fixed on things that had to be fought and had to be conquered. Certainly as far as personal artistic development is concerned, emigrating was the most important thing I ever did.

SHREERAM VIDYARTHI: Throughout the period of living here on a visitor's visa I was still planning to leave after six months when it expired. I had no desire to stay. I wasn't going to take the family. I wanted to go to Scandinavia, get a job, get a home, then when I was ready I would call them over. But time passed, I lingered on, I overstayed my visa and meanwhile I had started working freelance for the BBC, the World Service. That was very attractive, I was a journalist again, I was back in my own waters and I could swim there quite well. The work fascinated me and I wanted to carry it on. So I overstayed and carried on for a couple of years. Nobody noticed. They were looking for illegal immigrants but not too strenuously.

RAJINDER SINGH: People don't come here to get rich now. They don't come here to earn money to send home. India is a prosperous country now. But people do stay. They have children here who become part of English culture and they wouldn't like it if they had to go back to India. So we have to make up our minds: we have to stay here and if we do stay here then we have our rights, and we have to fight for them. The young people have very little interest in life in India. They tell their parents, 'You want to go back, go back, we are not interested.' But if you say that, then you have to fight for your rights in England. The problem for the older people who were brought up in India is that they have migrated here, they have worked here and now they have kids and the kids don't want to go back. But mentally those older people are not satisfied here, they want to spend their last years in India, but if their children won't come with them, they have no alternative but to stay in England.

BHAJAN SINGH CHADHA: I've had to make an effort, but in the end I'm satisfied. Especially after what I have seen happen in Kenya. Our family proper is still in Kenya, but I would still rather be here. I've been back once or twice: it's not bad, but I still prefer here. I imagine I'll die in England. I wouldn't say England has been bad, it's been not bad. When you compare it to so many other countries, they're still worse. People expect a lot. There are many good points about the British, for all that I've had bad experiences, but in spite of all that, they're still quite tolerant. I've seen the way Hindus treat people, how Muslims treat people. The English are not so bad. I was in India at one time and I asked for some water from this Hindu. He gave me this jug and I drank some water. There was a riot, they beat me up. I was a Sikh and I had drunk from a Hindu jug – I should have drunk from my hands. If you look at India, at Pakistan, the British come out as quite tolerant. We complain a lot about the British, but things aren't that good elsewhere. We all expect a lot, and we should all compare it with elsewhere. If I had to start again tomorrow and given a choice of all the European countries to live in, I would still choose England.

DON ATYEO: In the end England has been good to me. The weather's shit, and the weather determines a lot of the bad things in the English psyche. When it's sunny there is not a nicer place to be. The English countryside when it is sunny, the people are forthcoming and so on, it's just a wonderful place to be, but they're a miserable cold fucking race a lot of the time. It is a haven for people, refugee or anyone, because you do still feel this is a centre. There are three places you can make it big – Los Angeles, New York and London. The rest is fairly in thrall. As big cities go London is one of the most civilized, unaggressive places.

I'm not going back to Australia. I might leave England to retire somewhere but I won't actually go back. I realized that the balance had tipped and that I was staying here when I realized that I had no friends left over there and that all my friends were over here and it's as simple as that. You can live without the weather. If you've had twenty years of Australia with its hot sunny climate you can manage another twenty years without it. There are lots of other benefits to living in England. It is the best place, it really is for all its faults – corrupt cops, racism, the class system which is crippling, the two-party system swinging from one extreme to the other – but you feel safe here and these are a race of people who actually do the decent thing more often that not. If you're not on the sharp point of one of these things in English life, then this is a good country to live in. In the end, this place is not as bad as the rest of the world, which is what everyone here, even the real critics, know deep down. When you look at crack cities in New York or the problems all over the world. *Faut de mieux*. Nowhere is that good, and here is better than most. You have a sense of security. You know the government isn't going to fall in some terrible revolution. I've been in too many countries which really are unstable, even in the structure of the buildings. These are jerry-built countries and this patently isn't one of them.

SHARI PEACOCK: When you arrive you do want to become part of the country, but as time passes it becomes less important. I think it's a mixture both of

378

becoming more British and of not caring to what extent you do become British. When I go to America I have this feeling that I have to conquer this country all over again, which a tourist wouldn't feel. I hate that feeling, of being a foreigner again. So when I first came to England I did everything I could to get rid of my foreign-ness. I went out of my way to cut off, to amputate every Iranian connection. I changed my name, which nobody could pronounce. My real name was a wilderness. I was so eager to be accepted, there was this deep visceral longing rather than a mental thing. So even now I have never really resented anything about the English, because I needed them. I need them more than they need me. If you come from America, or France or even India, it may be different: the place where you have come from has its own importance, its own value. But if you come from Iran or Bulgaria, the idea of going back is inconceivable. So you have to accommodate. Maybe I haven't lived in enough countries, because I'm always hearing the English complaining about England, but to me it's not a bad place.

MICHAEL IGNATIEFF: I sometimes feel like I'm sitting on the dock, drinking a few too many planter's punches; you hail a fishing smack, 'Row me out!' and off you go, the liner slips away over the horizon. Sometimes I feel that I should have got on the boat a long time ago, but it's late and I've had a few too many drinks, I've forgotten my passport, I've run out of money, I'm here. I don't think I have entirely decided to stay. Which is crucial to the expatriate's mentality. It's crucial even to the immigrant mentality. One of the enormous advantages of expatriation is that you always have a way out. I feel tremendously implicated in this country in every kind of way, but in the back of my mind there is always this feeling that if it gets too tough here, if things turn nasty, then I'll go. This society has now lived for twenty years with a kind of armageddon scenario, the shorthand for which is 'when the oil runs out'. This tremendous anxiety does dominate hearts and minds, the other shorthand being 'when a deficit in manufacturing trade becomes unmanageable' leading to a collaspe of the exchange rate, leading to massive and completely unmanageable degrees of unemployment, leading to Christ knows what. That's been a scenario in this country's emotional landscape for a very long time. It is possible that we're out the other side: that what we call the armageddon scenario is basically the nightmare that any vulnerable middle-sized economy faces as it makes the transition from an old manufacturing base to a post-modern, post-industrial, service-based economy. But it's a very dicey transition and some societies make it and some don't. You have this nightmare, you wake up in the early hours sweating and thinking, 'What if it doesn't make it?' That might be the situation in which I would have to go home.

MOSES SPITZ: Next door we had Italian neighbours. Always dreaming of going back home. And all the time we knew them they were saving up for their tickets

379

so that they could eventually leave Argentina and go home to Italy. But every time they reached the amount they had needed, the ticket price had gone up. They never could go back. I think they died still saving.

26 Thatcher's Britain

'If someone had given Thatcher a charter to wreck the country, she couldn't have done a better job.'

CHRISTOPHER HOPE: People talk so much about change here, but what is really surprising is how little has changed, how obstinate the country's institutions are, and the class divisions within the country, and the quite remarkable sense of self which the upper middle classes do have, in the professions, in their clubs, villages, pubs, and their separate residential areas. It's just astonishing that so much should have apparently changed in order to remain so much the same. When you do come up against it – and London is not the place to do it, because London is so cosmopolitan – but out of London, into Britain proper the assumptions upon which the Army, the monarchy and the constitutional arrangements are founded seem to be remarkably intact.

IVAN KYNCL: I think English society has changed a lot during the eight-and-a-half years I have been here. From my point of view the changes are for worse and worse. It's not just Thatcher – though I don't agree with her, and I don't agree with Kinnock either – but I believe that if somebody is in power too long then that power doesn't just change that person, it changes the whole society. I would love to see a Labour government tomorrow, but I would also like to see the Tories two years later. Why not? What matters is change. Otherwise you start to get a totalitarian system developing. I recognize it happening already.

KATHY ACKER: The thing that I most regret is how the country has changed since Thatcher's second term began. That's what has made things really uncomfortable. It's incredible that very soon the majority of people will have known no life without her in power. So I do think, 'What am I doing in this country dominated by this appalling woman?' The codes, OK, I was a naïve American and I learnt that yes, codes are different and I really have to learn how to be in this culture. I've been nothing but glad that I had that opportunity. After all, difficulties don't mean you regret them. But I do regret that a lot of the reasons which made me leave America are suddenly starting to happen here. I feel, 'God, I ran away and now it's followed me over here.' At times I think, 'Well maybe I should just get out.' But you can't keep running away every time governments change.

I don't think I would have come here now. Certainly not. Sometimes I get really paranoid about what's going to happen here, about how bad it'll get. The rise of censorship and the erosion of freedom of speech. Then I think, 'No it can't, it really can't, that's just paranoia.' Sometimes I wonder, 'Is this the end of the Weimar republic? Should I be packing my bags before the Nazis take over?' There are many similarities. People were saying, 'Things are a bit bad, but at least the economy is OK' – the same thing they say here.

TESS WICKHAM: I wouldn't come and live here now. The current situation has made me so livid that I've almost daily been saying that I am leaving. Various laws are being passed that essentially erode freedom. It all gives me the creeps. I can eat, which not everyone can, but I am horrified every day by the changes in the country. It stifles me and frightens me, just like I was stifled when I left Holland. But the world is getting smaller and smaller and in the end one just ends up being here, like it or not – where the hell do you go? You can go and stick your head in the sand somewhere but . . . There isn't much you can do to avoid the issues you come up against here, they're everywhere else. Unless you set off for the moon, you have to retreat into yourself. I've certainly retreated into myself, and that sometimes makes me wonder, why in that case am I not, say, in Italy, where it is more comfortable? In the end it doesn't make much difference any more. I wouldn't still be here if it wasn't for the fact that all sorts of specific things – mainly professional – are binding me. I loathe what that old crow has done to this country. All she wants to do is bring everything down, to make everyone lower middle class like her so she can understand how they all operate.

MANDY MERCK: If someone had given Thatcher a charter to wreck the country, she couldn't have done a better job. I hate the way the country's turned out. You don't feel safe anywhere – breathing the air, eating the food, drinking the water, safe in your job, safe in your future. Who would have imagined it when I came in '69? I thought it was all going to get better, I thought more people would be able to go to university – fewer can now. There's a brain drain of left-wing intellectuals to America. They can't do research and teach the way they would like to be able to do here. They have to go round raising money for the Scotch Tape Memorial professorship or something. It's driving them all out. I can see a time when my peer group will be gone. Then I'll go. If I lose those friends, I'm gone.

MARCEL BERLINS: When I came in the late '60s people were trying things out, taking risks. Sometimes it was awful, but it was much more exciting, and I

381

found the atmosphere and the people in London far more helpful, less petty than France. Things were more open in English society and the barriers against an outsider like me were not put up. Now there's less tolerance, less willingness to accept those who don't conform, more rigidity in their views about people, more suspicion. For the first time since I left, I've started to think France is a nicer country to live in than Britain, or certainly London. Had I come over now, I would have a different time, would find it more difficult to come in and establish myself. But the last few years have changed people for the worse – attitudes are not as pleasant as they used to be. I don't think they approach the Parisian brusqueness and desire to mislead, but in shops, in service industries, there is an attitude which I'm sure was not present when I first came. I don't think it's that I've got older. I think objectively attitudes are different. I'm not saying Thatcher is responsible for it, but it has come to fruition in the last few years.

KATHY ACKER: Sometimes I think the English are just the sweetest, nicest people who will absolutely never finally stand for Thatcher if they just realized what was going on. Except that they do stand for her. I can't believe all that is going to go. Thatcher is just an American, just horrendous. It's like her attitude to the intellectual world, to education – she'd just like to get rid of it. But she has this charisma and the funny thing is that she doesn't know her place. She's about the only thing that has made a dent in the class system here and that makes it very confusing. That's the basis of her support.

JOHN LAHR: Europeans talk about how exciting New York is, how much energy Americans have. What they see as energy I see as panic. That energy is people in a free market economy terrified of getting a heart attack and being wiped out, terrified they're not going to make the college fees, terrified about their second home. Part of the reason I was more aware of life over here was the sense of the security of the culture, a sense that basic human needs – for health, for education – were not a privilege, but a right. Therefore you could relax in life. I don't mean not work hard, but you could slow down. That was in every way healthy. What's happened in the last decade is that Mrs Thatcher has been injecting this culture with large doses of that same insecurity and envy, intended, as it is in America, to agitate the populace, to make them work harder, to make them want more, to seek prestige, to be seen as better. Which makes me very sad. If you instil envy you get anxiety, which must culminate in violence and unhappiness. It's meant to stimulate unhappiness, to get people to buy.

CINDY BLAKE: The English have become more Americanized while I've been here, but they've taken all the wrong things – those City people with their

382

telephones and their BMWs. Thatcher has changed things to an extent – money does get you more, she has broken down certain class things, but the problem still remains: the pie that she's trying to share out is simply not big enough. There's not enough here: all these newspapers and there's just not enough to write about, there's not enough that *happens*, there aren't enough stars to interview. You read the same things – because not enough happens here. And there's not enough money to go round. In America there might be the chance that a guy starting his business under a Prince Charles scheme can do something with it but there's very little chance here. What they should start doing is shipping people out again, like in the nineteenth century. I'd ship out anyone endemically English and keep all the foreigners.

DESMOND GITTENS: I wouldn't come here now. No way. I wouldn't have chosen to come here. Not with all the information I've collected and collated. Not with what I understand now. I would have probably opted for America or Canada. But now that I am here I wouldn't choose any other place. I wouldn't leave now. I've learnt too much here.

BRIGITTE NEWMAN: The biggest change I have found in ten years of being here is the change in the food. Not just the immigrants and their corner stores – if it was just the immigrants then the Sloanes would not have taken on rocket, because suddenly what you served at a dinner party became important, though I don't know why. I actually think that it was the big food chains who wanted to make more money and realized that if they kept on selling bad lamb and jellies this wouldn't happen, but if they made it a fad to eat imported rare herbs this would work. Ten years ago you could go into a good greengrocer and ask for shallots and they would ask what they were. It's a class thing too. English foodies are *much* worse than any French foodie.

ENNIO CAMISA: When I came back to Soho it had changed. It was empty. Newport Buildings had been bombed. A lot of people had been interned. A lot of people lost their lives when Newport Buildings were bombed, in the blitz. Then, when it was empty, all the Chinese started coming in. Before the war Gerrard Street had shops: a baker, the post office, all kinds of shops, Italian shops, mixed. A barber's shop, a music shop, a French shop selling coffee. Now it's all Chinese. The Chinese people started coming in during the '50s. There used to be two or three Italian restaurants: Bologna Restaurant, Isola Bella. Then after 1960 they start to buy up, buy up. Greek Street used to be the same, full of shops. Now it's all offices. Same in Frith Street. Wardour Street, there's always been films. It hasn't changed much. There were gangsters, but they came up from the East End. People who came around in the evening to see what they could do. There were girls on the streets, plenty.

383

Too many. Gerrard Street used to be full up. Everywhere. Soho Square the same. Poland Street. Even on the corner here (Berwick Street and Rupert Street). Now there's a lot of shops empty again. Nobody is opening – the rents are too high. We've been in this shop since 1944. We bought the freehold, thank God. That's why I'm still working!

* * *

GRETEL SALINGER: England is no longer the England which I loved. The violence is very bad now, and child abuse – all the things that I would never have believed would be possible in England. People were so kind and animal-loving . . . and now they are *terrible*. I am very very upset about what is going on here. I think a lot of it has resulted from the way things have changed after the war. And please forgive me, I should not say this, but I believe it is the foreigners who have come to England. Not Jewish ones. I am not a racist. On the contrary I am very pro racial equality, but really I think we have taken too many in. Not just the Asians but the West Indians too. The problem is that they should not have been let in. Now their children cannot get jobs. In fairness they started off by needing them. I love the West Indians, I go to Jamaica every year for several months and I have six god-children in Jamaica, and they are wonderful people. But they are different people in Jamaica to here. They are much better people there. Here they all so *naughty*. Very, very badly behaved. They do have a hard time here, but even so they should not behave as they do. I have spoken to people I know in Jamaica and asked them to use their authority to see that people in England behave themselves better. Though I do accept that it goes both ways. I am sure that the police treat young blacks badly too.

ANNE-MARIE WOLPE: Over the years I've come to dislike the British more and more. That I find quite disturbing; London had had a magic about it for me, and I do think it's a most fascinating city, though I have not participated to any extent in the riches which it has to offer, but I cannot deal with the hypocrisy of the British. There is a way in which you assume that you talk the language, but you don't. There is a way in which you are open and people are not. There is a way in which you touch somebody and they shrink. There is great uptightness in this country, an enormous uptightness. I have found over the last couple of years an increasing tension and anger and frustration and aggression, which mainly seems to come out on the roads. The aggression is very covert, but it comes out in the most extraordinary situations. I would tie this in with Thatcher; prior to Thatcher England was not nearly as aggressive and was a much easier country. The politics of Thatcher have had a marked and devastating effect on the promotion of individualism and the 'stuff you' philosophy.

384

PETER TATCHELL: The England I found in 1971 had a much stronger sense of community and social solidarity, which I greatly valued. Sadly, a lot of this has been destroyed by the Thatcherite enterprise culture of the 1980s, with its me-first and grab-it philosophy. Britain is no longer such a liberal society either. Many of the liberties and freedoms that I admired have been dangerously eroded and the Welfare State is now only a shadow of what it once was.

HANNAH KODICEK: I'd definitely come here if I had to make the move again today. Whenever I get cross about the things that I see as being not quite right here, I sit with myself and say, 'Right, where am I going to emigrate to now?' and inevitably every time I get back to living here. There really is no other place. There is still more freedom here, still more democracy and still civilized human beings in the best of senses, if one forgets the lager louts and the yuppies and the rest of materialistic Britain that one doesn't like.

MARIA VOROSKOI: What has happened is that the essence of England has become watered down, by the vast number of people. The largest group here now are the *nouveaux riches*, the middle class. They see themselves as deprived of this that and the other and expect that the government should provide them with everything. The vast number of people want to be spoon-fed, they do not wish to bring up their own children, they no longer know how to bring up children, they no longer understand standards of honesty and decency. They talk about needing more modern prisons – no, what we need is more mothers staying at home and bringing up their children properly. Feminism has been the greatest tragedy. It absolutely makes me boil. When I grew up people were taught properly, they were disciplined and they knew their duty to their family. They looked after their old. Now mothers are never at home, but people still crave a mother and the government has taken her place. The government has to look after the old, to pay for hospitals, to lock people up (but not too long), there should be prisons (but the prisons should not be too harsh). For heaven's sake, even the churches have absolutely forgotten that their first duty to the world is to teach people morals. Now they are more interested in politics. Turn on the radio and there are clergymen talking about politics. People expect too much: their own houses, continental holidays, everything. And it all has to come from the government, but who, financially, is the government? It is all of us, the taxpayers. I'm not disappointed in England, but I am very sad about what I see. Today we live at the lowest common denominator, whereas it used always to be the other way around.

NELLY SALAS: What has happened here is that England has become a Latin American country too. Another Third World country. For the workers things have become worse and worse, they've lost the protection they used to have.

The law no longer acts for them. Open your eyes, read the paper, read the news – you'll find it. This is not the country I found when I came here in 1977. When we came here I remember one day in the street we saw a television set and a refrigerator and because nobody was at home, they just left it in the street – and nobody would touch it. So we thought in this country the workers must be very honest – they have money, they have work. Nowadays people will beat you up to steal £5. When we lived in Leamington somebody went into a house and stole some money and it was in the local paper for the next three weeks. It was big news – things like that didn't happen. Now it's different.

---

27 The Generation Gap

'I taught them right from wrong, let them choose everything else themselves.'

YASMIN ALIBHAI: When my son was born I couldn't stop crying. We'd really wanted him, but I couldn't stop crying. It was as if everything had come to a head. I looked at this child and I didn't know what he was going to grow up to be, and I was aware now of how awful England could be and how he would be more seduced than I was to want to be part of this community which would never accept him, and yet I had to teach him that he would be accepted otherwise he would grow up screwed up and paranoid. On top of this was the feeling that something was already getting lost from my past, from my culture, from my people. We were being drained of our culture and this next generation was going to be even more drained. I used to have the most profoundly disturbing thoughts: we were here to stay, there was a second generation and everything was going to be bloody awful.

RAJINDER SINGH: We are always worrying about our children. We don't enjoy ourselves without thinking about them. We have our culture, we work hard to make money and we try to pass it on to the next generation, but this is not always the best way of doing things. One of the good things about the British is that they say, 'Look after yourself first. If you are not fit, if you don't enjoy yourself, then what's the use of that hard work, what's the use of that money?' At the same time we spoil our children. Whereas English kids are more independent and more competitive. Though because of this materialistic time people have no time to give their children parental love. The man and his wife are out working and the kids are looked after by some kind of caretaker, and they do not get proper affection from their parents. The next thing is that the

386

children have no respect for the parents. The parents are down in the pub enjoying themselves and the kids are locked up at home. To me, if you don't pay them any attention, why should they bother about you?

FIRDOS ALI: There is a difference between the Asian and the West Indian community when it comes to the young. The Asians are very protective towards their families. My next-door neighbour, for example, an Asian couple, they have a little girl. The grandmother comes to see the girl, the wife's four brothers come to see her. Their car had an accident, the brothers turned up, set it right. West Indians don't do that, the English don't do that. But the Asian community helps each other. Just as the Jewish community does. I don't see assimilation. They don't want it, and they won't want it: they have the example of the way the English family is breaking down. Not even among the more successful commercial families: brother still helps brother, sister helps sister. I knew a family, six sisters, six brothers, the mother is not feeling well. They gather every evening to see her – nobody is ignoring her. One has an exam next week, she still makes sure she goes every night for an hour or two. I know a lady, about thirty. She got married. She had a job as a linguist which she gave up to look after her son. In the morning her father, who has his own business, comes round for an hour and a half to look after the boy while she cleans the house. Then he goes. Every word the little boy utters is in a diary. Midday she washes him, puts him to sleep. Two o'clock she wakes him up, gives him his food, takes him out for a walk. Her husband comes home at six, he plays with him. Their world is that little boy. The world of that little boy is his family. You don't get that attention in English families.

RAJINDER SINGH: There are certain very good traditions within the Asian community. We have love and respect for each other. Not everybody carries it out, but we are taught from the beginning that we have our close relations and we must have some give and take. Here it is simply 'mind your own business'. That is not something we find in our society. My niece respects me not just because I live with her, nor because I am older than her. In my turn I also give her love. She listens to me and I love her and I try to look after her interests so that she should be happy in her life. And I think that this is something that the white society should learn from us. In the same way we are learning from them that we must live a more independent life. So there must be give and take. If they don't want to learn anything from us and we don't want to learn anything from them, it is a pity.

LEENA DHINGRA: We try to go to India with my daughter but how much is it her native culture? After all, how native is it to me? We go there because I love the country and it's a part of her heritage and she certainly has an Indian grandma and lots of Indian cousins and an Indian name and I suppose because my husband and I are separated and she's with me, she sees that part of her. She doesn't sense any kind of rejection on her part from the mainstream. I'm not worried about her losing our culture. She goes to a very English school, but it's very civilized. It's not offbeat like mine was, but it's part of the '80s style – very tolerant, whatever. She goes to the local church and sings in the choir and sits through the service on Sundays. The only thing I would worry about is if for some reason or another she found herself in a situation where she needed to put down or dismiss or deny her Indian-ness. But she doesn't. When she has encountered certain kinds of attitudes and she has felt the need to play her Indian-ness down, she hasn't felt that what she is denying is not up to some mark, but that the other people lacked imagination. So she just takes a low profile.

PO-YEE WONG: The first generation survives better in a new country if their own culture is a very strong one. For the second generation it's different. No matter how strong the ethnic background is in the parents, they can't force it into their children. You can't bring children up with a predominantly Chinese identity – you're so much enveloped in the English system and language. So my children are more English than Chinese. I don't worry about them losing the Chinese traditions. I taught them right from wrong, let them choose everything else themselves.

NIEN-LUN YEH: I don't think our son will have much of a Chinese identity. I hope that when he has grown up I can send him back to stay a couple of years in the Chinese countryside in the way I did. Though he might not be so keen. The young generation in this country are just so spoiled. They just don't know what human hardship is. My niece, who has been here for ten months, she is a teenager, and she is almost entirely westernized already. My teenage was an entirely different life. Politically, whatever. My experiences were so hard but now I so appreciate them. Compared with the teenage life here. Chinese youngsters today also adore the West. So when they come here they find it very easy to identify. They lost their own identity. They see it as so colourful, although I don't think it's very attractive. Maybe that's just because I'm older now. But in the end children do what they want. You cannot control them here. Which is bad, very bad. I don't see whether there will be a future for this country if the next generation behaves like that. They are badly spoiled. They know no hardships, they are always unsatisfied.

CHRISTOPHER HOPE: Your children share none of your feelings about the place you were born. So you don't have the same hinterland as your kids. My kids think of South Africa as a rather mad and violent relative that I keep in a cupboard in the back of my mind, which occasionally breaks out and behaves badly, begins assaulting people – and they give me rather pitying looks. There's nothing to be done about that. But the roots they put down anchor you too.

NGUYEN DUC PHUONG: I made this display [of scenes from the Vietnam war] because I want to create something, to show my children some aspects of the war. The first layer shows a battle from the Tet offensive of 1968 when the Communists attacked the cities. That was a pivotal period and our war effort began to fail from then on. There are American soldiers and Viet Cong, although I can't buy models of them, I had to paint them myself. They have rubber sandals. It's not a real battle but it's to show my children. There's some people and some hardware. The second layer is a battle in the Central Highlands. A Communist tank and some US helicopters and so on. The rest is a military airport in our country. Various types of airplanes and so on. The children are eleven and ten but they aren't much interested. Not much. I show them films and they ask funny questions: 'You show us these films and your side seems very good, many soldiers, why were you defeated?' I can't explain, I say, 'You don't know. Defeat or victory does not depend on the number of soldiers. It depends on help. If I give you money now, but in the future I don't give you money, you have nothing.' But I can't explain more because they are too young. My wife has taught them some Vietnamese culture, told them some stories, but it seems to me that they were not interested. They like the stories, but they don't care about the way the Vietnamese people live. They don't understand. If we ever do go home, we might buy a single ticket for my wife and me, but we'll buy a return ticket for them.

VU DUY TU: My children are quite grown-up, the youngest is now nineteen. Their lives were formed in Vietnam but they've been born again here. They've become different. They learn English very quickly, they speak it, not perfectly, but nearly perfect. They will have new lives here, so they may not understand or remember anything about Vietnam. That's our worry. A worry for the whole community. That's just for the next generation. What happens to the generation after that, I don't know. They may think they are English. Our community wants as long as possible to give our children the Vietnamese culture, to let them know our traditions. How long they can keep that up I don't know, but we all try out best. Maybe when they grow up they may think they're English, but if at any time they think back, they'll find out that they came from somewhere else. But if they don't pay any attention to the past, if they just keep working to survive, just thinking of money, they may forget their culture.

NGUYEN DUC PHUONG: I am afraid that my children will grow up English. Of course. Because I still hope that one day I shall return to my country and it is very difficult for the Vietnamese who speak English there. If one day we do go back, what would happen to my children? If you showed you understood English, or sometimes put a few English words into your speech, the people didn't like you. It was the same with using French. So I ask my children to talk Vietnamese to me and my wife. They do, but when they talk together they talk in English. Or they mix the two languages. The older generation mixed French with Vietnamese, the younger generation mixed English, like my children, but my generation, we try to use Vietnamese properly. My wife and I talk Vietnamese to each other. Even my teachers at university suggested that I speak English to my children – they said it had worked for the refugees from Hungary in 1956 – and they suggested that I should do that too, but I don't think so.

* * *

GINA ADAMOU: I don't know whether I'm unique but I have very high standards for education. I feel that my sisters and I were all intelligent girls and we missed out. We all owe it to ourselves if nothing else to help our children to do it. Although of my sisters two of them have still done what my parents did. They have put their kids in their own shops to work. A very small percentage of my community wanted to educate their children. Even now it hasn't changed that much. My own children are an exception. The percentage of British-born Cypriots who go to college is still very very small. Very few go on to degree standard. It's not that they are not expected to do well, it's that many people still have my parents' mentality. Children should stay in the house, in the family. Many of my Cypriot neighbours still have that mentality. A girl can do a year or two secretarial course, then she can work as a secretary and then she'll find a husband. The boys will try to learn some kind of trade.

BHAJAN SINGH CHADHA: I have two daughters. One is thirty-one, she's married now. The other is twenty-nine, she makes films. She's not married, although I should have got her married, even if it meant sacrificing her career. I wouldn't do that. I didn't want to be repressive. I didn't bring them up in a traditional Sikh or Indian way. I should have bred them very strictly, as strictly as a dog: they should be in purdah, have arranged marriages, all that. I didn't want any of that, and I didn't care what my relatives or my community might think. I wanted them to be fully educated and to choose their own way, and I did that. They both did very well. It's a reasonably exceptional attitude for my community, even now. If I mix in the community the first thing they say is, 'Look, he still hasn't got both his daughters married.' But I shut my ears, I go my own way. My father had to go to India, he had to leave my brothers to run his business in Kenya, and all because of the tradition that said he had to get proper husbands, proper marriages for my sisters. I looked at that and I thought, I wouldn't do that. I have no sons, only daughters, and daughters are considered as lower than sons in our community. Only good enough to marry off. I didn't have any sons, so I was just as ambitious for my daughters.

SHREERAM VIDYARTHI: I have two sons and a daughter and they are more English than Englishmen could ever be. The eldest is twenty, the younger is sixteen and my daughter is thirteen. The eldest wants to be an actor, the others are still at school. I feel optimistic about their future in the sense that yes, they are not in danger. The fact that they are not white just doesn't occur to me. I have never paid much attention to the fact that I am brown and you are white and the other one is yellow and the other one is black. That just doesn't affect my pysche. Once one of my children came home and said that the boys at school had been calling him 'Yorkie', presumably because of the chocolate. My daughter used to be called 'Malibu' because of her brown skin. When they came home and complained, I just told them: 'Don't they call the boy "Ginger" because of his ginger hair, how is that different from what they call you?'

VICTOR WILD: My son was interviewed on Radio 4 recently and he surprised me when he said that he saw himself as half-immigrant and said that immigrant families find it very important to win approval, and to be recognized and approved of. In a sense that sets us apart from people that have their roots totally in the country. I was surprised that he felt like that.

GINA ADAMOU: My children don't see themselves as English. British, yes, but not English. I don't think they feel that they are accepted as English. They were born here and it's their country but at the same time they know they don't belong one hundred per cent. They have experienced racism and they are very much aware that even though they were born here they have Greek parents and they are not entirely English. *They* may feel English but they are not accepted as such. I don't want them to become totally assimilated, I don't want them to lose their culture altogether. It's obvious that they are a part of this country and I want them to be a part of this country. I don't want them to go back, but at the same time I don't want them to forget where they came from. I want them to hold some of that, their background. I want them to know their culture and be proud of it. And to take part in English culture and to mix the two. It would be sad if they were so Anglo-Saxon that they lose their own identity. But the English won't let them do that anyway.

MIRANDA LOVETT: Our kids will not be stereotyped, will not be taken over by the institutions that they're going into. I'm pretty convinced of that. I have a lot of faith in our kids. I think that the kids who are stereotyped have always been stereotyped. Three weeks every summer I take my kids to America. We go to the places that I went when I was growing up – the same beach club, we see

391

the kids of the people I grew up with. I feel very strongly that when my kids are sixteen they'll work in the summer, preferably in America. You hardly see that here. They go holiday with their parents, to Scotland to the South of France, wherever. But when I was sixteen I worked at Lily Pulitzer in South Hampton. OK, it was a very WASP-y job, but I still worked. I still had to get up and go to work, I still got my pay cheque at the end of the week, it was an experience. It's important to have that responsibility when you're young.

ZERBANOO GIFFORD: Our children are brought up primarily in the prevailing culture, but I've also taught them the Zoroastrian prayers and I've taught them the Zoroastrian mythology. People always ask how you bring your children up, but you don't bring them up, children bring themselves up in the sense that they are part of the household and part of our lives and they obviously take half of their character from my family and they are half Norman and half Zoroastrian, and they can't help themselves. We have an open house which is very Indian, and throughout their lives people have appeared and come to stay and they don't see it as funny.

ANNE-MARIE WOLPE: Living here is very difficult for them. They haven't grown up in a conventional British home. It's more like a hotel, where people come and go and come and go. They feel uneasy. The youngest was nine months was he was brought here, he's twenty-six now, he's the most British and he feels more comfortable in America. He's in financial management. A Thatcher job, yes, but he's always said that he disapproves of his father's politics, they've buggered up our lives. My eldest is thirty-three, she's a psychiatric social worker in London. The second one is in film production. The children have to work out a number of problems. You go and see the film *A World Apart* and it's there. The problems of children of political parents are enormous. Living under threat, conscious of that, nervous of that. Somewhere in South Africa, they're saying, 'It doesn't matter where he goes, one day we'll get that fucking bastard!' and maybe one day they will come for him.

SIMI BEDFORD: My children have had problems of their own. My eldest son is going to be a barrister, but it's hard to get into pupilage. He wants to do commercial law, but the received wisdom is that black barristers do criminal law – there's a load of black criminals and they have to be defended. I say, fine, get in there, break the stereotypes. But we have nine rejections plonking through the letter box and here you come up against the feeling, how important is it that he's black?

TONY GIRARD: Some black kids do give up too easily, but that doesn't mean all black kids give up. The white people who say that, they should realize that

392

people are people. Just because they're black why should they have to put more in than the white kids? Though it's true – they have to be ten times better just to get the same chances. Some people can take that and some can't. Why do people kill themselves, things like that? People are people and just because they're black doesn't mean their resistance to problems should be so much better. Some people give in quicker than others, it just depends on the person.

MIKE PHILLIPS: My father and his generation had no sense of limitations whatsoever. They might be working on the railway or the buses or whatever but they'd be dreaming of being millionaires. These days the young people actually have far more real opportunities, but we don't have the same dreams. The most active people in the second and third generations tend to want what the group of English around whom they've grown up want, the white working class, which is never anything much. You can have in the same family two children with completely different attitudes. One has stayed in the Caribbean, the other had lived here. I saw a friend of mine in Grenada. His wife's sister had a boy who was brought up in Streatham and who got into trouble in London. They sent him back to keep him out of trouble. His cousin, whose family he lived with in Grenada, was in the sixth form at school, was just about to leave to go to Harvard. That boy's sister was doing well at school. The older members of the family were very respectable. But this boy was roaming around doing nothing, except stealing cars. The school wanted to get rid of him. Had he been brought up in Grenada he too would have been working, going to college, but he had been brought up in London. He had this sense of himself which was to do with being a delinquent, a deprived, under-privileged person. Even though it was clear that his family in Grenada was nothing like that, he still fulfilled that role. They couldn't cope, and they sent him back to London. He didn't want the things he was supposed to want as a good West Indian boy.

TONY GIRARD: Black kids haven't been corrupted by white culture. Don't be ridiculous! In one way I don't envy the Asian kids at all. That whole society: it's next to slavery the way they treat their women and so on. But I think that had I stayed there my elder son would have done better. There would have been less pressure and more opportunities.

DESMOND GITTENS: I do not feel at all optimistic about the future of young West Indians. They've never been made to feel at home here. From the nursery onwards. They've met discrimination, this insidious, mind-boggling discrimination. Much, much more than I did. They were unprotected. I came here as a young man. I had my personality already formed and set up. If you send a baby, a three-year-old, to a nursery where it starts meeting discrimination and starts being to feel less than others there's no comparison for that baby to make. It can't say, 'Well I am being discriminated against.' It grows up with a lack of consciousness of itself. This was something that you saw in the ESN days, when there was a label on black children: educationally subnormal. When you are a part of a minority, if something affects your community it affects you totally, so if some black children are labelled ESN it affects everyone, whether they're your children or not. We are a small minority, we are not a huge community. A lot of people in London think London is lovely, it's all black, but that isn't so. Maybe there's one million coloured people, and that includes people from the subcontinent. Compared to the white population it's nothing. In America you have twenty million blacks and they can sustain many different kinds of communities. You've got black millionaires, pilots, generals, everything. So a young black lad in New York, bad as it is, can still look up and say, 'I can achieve that.'

VINCENT REID: Given the covert racism in this society, the increasing criminalization of young black people, the way in which educational psychologists are constantly talking about young black people as ineducable, backward, slow – put them in the sin-bin, the special schools – it bodes ill for us as a country. I don't think that the young black people are going to accept it. We already have evidence of that: Brixton, St Paul's, Toxteth. Even in Southall the Asian kids won't accept it. Unless we're prepared to practise some kind of genocide, the alternative must be to improve. But I see no signs of improvement.

VERNA WILKINS: I'm worried about my children. I'm worried that institutional racism might stop them achieving their full potential. That would be a tragedy. But they are very aware and not negatively aware. The younger one said to me once, 'Mum, we've had more racism in our lives than you've ever had. I have had more racism pushed on me in and out of school than you have ever had.' And that's true. But he's learnt to deal with it, because it's a problem other people have which they see fit to inflict on him. It hurts the perpetrator as much as it does the victim. If you have to hurt somebody to feel good you have a problem! You may not see it at the time, but you have to be a pretty twisted human being if that's what makes you feel good. Parents must be active, they must deal with it, talk about it. I'm always saying to parents, white or black: how are your children reading your action or your inaction about racism?

TONY ROBINSON: The children of today and the children of tomorrow, they will see racialism in a different way. I have a son and he meets racism, but to him, within himself, when you say, 'Blackie', he just laughs, because you don't know what you're talking about. As far as he is concerned, he's born in England, England is his home, he is an English person. So he looks at things

394

differently from the way a child who is born in Jamaica did. He says, 'I am black', right away he identifies himself with the black community. If you're born here and educated here, they have a different vision from my generation. They have every right. But the point is that they don't get them.

GULZAR KHAN: Now we have many youngsters who were born here, and their white counterparts who have come through the same education system but are less clever than they are, and are underachieving, they are still getting better jobs, getting a better life. And when that happens our young people are going to look at British society and turn against it. People always said that Asians are much more respectable citizens, much more law-abiding. That is changing. Our youngsters are saying, 'We are called "chicken" and we are not going to take it any longer.' They are getting it from both sides. They are getting it from the white youngsters and from the Afro-Caribbean youngsters. The Afro-Caribbeans say, 'You say you are black, why don't you stand with us? Why do you always say, "Yes sir, no sir, three bags full sir"?' Our advice to them is still not to fight, not to confront; if they get beaten up, we accuse them: 'You got beaten up – what did you do wrong for someone to do that?'

CASH BHOGAL: First-generation immigrants do have to swallow a lot, but their children feel they have every right to stand up and express their views on any matter they choose. The first generation didn't feel that. Certainly in the riot the young people were more violent, while the older people were more peaceful. The second generation were just outraged that violence occurred. I see myself in between the two groups.

MARY ROSE: I feel optimistic about the immigrant children. The ones who are disadvantaged, to use that awful word, are the Bangladeshis, who are suppressed a lot by their own people. If the teachers, in particular the schools inspectors, do not make sure that these kids go to schools and don't sit in some sweatshop sewing, which means you have to support them financially, these kids will cause a lot of trouble. In the first place they will fight each other for religious reasons.

ZERBANOO GIFFORD: The most remarkable of the young Asians now come from the Bangladeshi community. They get rather pissed off with this stereotype of their community being disadvantaged, because they've been brought up very well. They don't feel downtrodden, quite the opposite. This is a whole generation who are very articulate and very confident. They're not going to take any shit from anybody. They're past that.

GULZAR KHAN: First-generation immigrants have to swallow a lot and we swallowed a hell of a lot. The young people today don't realize that and that is why now we are getting complaints from both sides. We suffered that racism when we came, and now our youngsters think that we are keeping them behind, or that we actually colluded in the system. We say that confrontation, fighting, throwing stones is not the way to get the situation improved, but we should use negotiation and consultation, to work through talking, but they don't agree with that.

SIMI BEDFORD: The gains that were made on the racial front in the '60s can't be completely eroded. If nothing else it is now not considered acceptable to be overtly racist, but I do think that any future gains are going to have to be made by the black people themselves. It will have to be more like America. People like my children who were born here and consider themselves to be English, rightly or not, will not have the attitude that we, the first generation had, which was never mind, we're going to be going home in a while anyway. I can put up with things that they will not accept.

---

28 Into the Future

'People will keep on living here. To suggest that if they don't
like it they will simply go away is asking too much.'

BHAJAN SINGH CHADHA: I think the younger generation can be much more optimistic than we were. They can see greater prospects. I think that both immigrant and British cultures have got to move on somewhere. We will have to sacrifice more than the British; in the end this is England. What we resent is that they did not do the same thing in India. They came as masters and that was how they behaved and that was how the colonial system encouraged them to behave. It was the same wherever they went.

MUHAMMAD ALI: I have three children: one is four, one three and one three months. I see the future for them as being no different. If anything they will have more disadvantages than probably I had. Their expectations will rise considerably. Our parents arrived here with no expectations. They weren't bothered about racism and they accepted it in all its forms. We, the children they brought, are less tolerant, but people who were born here and brought up here in the same educational system and gained the same qualifications as white people, they will expect a lot more. But they won't get it. Which means that they will be more frustrated. The fear I have for the next generation is that having gained a good education, and the highest qualifications, when it comes

396

to using those qualifications to get employment, to play an active role in the mainstream, they will not get it. Whether it will bring the riots back I don't know, but there will certainly be a good deal of bitterness. One can see the next generation following the same pattern as the second-generation West Indians have done. Asians are still relative newcomers, their teenagers are only now growing up, and they haven't yet had the opportunity to face the wider world and to compete for resources, employment, whatever.

BODRUL ALOM: We've been swallowing abuse for thirty years now, but how long are we supposed to do that? We are a peace-loving people, and we wish to continue in peace. But if we continue being made into victims, then we can certainly fight back.

RAMESH VALA: We have the same problem here in some ways as we did in East Africa. We considered ourselves as an island, we didn't want anybody else and we lost out. This attitude has to break up and in the next generation I think it will. They go to school together, play together, these are children who were born here. The Asians believe very firmly in education and the private schools are full of Asian children. Asian parents believe very much that it's worth sacrificing their lives to improve the situation of their children. When these children grow up they'll have the old names, but the accent will have gone, and they will be more likely to intermarry, mix in with the white society, bring them home – because even now when you have English friends you don't really socialize that much or mix that freely.

This assimilation isn't happening for West Indians. Even if they work hard, and have better qualifications than a white person, they still don't get the job. Which makes them very rebellious; they feel, 'Hold on, I was born in this country, I grew up in the same way . . .' I don't blame them. Now I think that what has happened to the young West Indians over the last decade is beginning to happen to the Asians in the Midlands. They came out of their school and find they can't get jobs. If Britain hits another recession they will feel the same pinch: 'Hold on, why have I been left out?' But at that stage the Asian answer seems to be to opt out – either to leave, or more likely to start off their own business or go to another Asian and see if they can help. He's not automatically going to riot, but if the Sikhs in Southall and the Muslims of Bradford and Leicester stand up and demand their rights then there could be some problems.

MUHAMMAD AYYAZ: People will keep on living here. To suggest that if they don't like it they will simply go away is asking too much. Many people have nothing to go back to. I don't believe that the multicultural and multiethnic thing will happen ever. We would like to see it but I do not see it happening. What I would like to see is just people left alone to live their own lives. I don't want to see immigration become a political issue, with the Labour and Conservative parties fighting wars: 'We did this for immigration, we did that . . .' Yet every five years it gets dragged up and all that happens is that race relations suffer and the community that has settled suffers. Everybody respects Enoch Powell as a politician. Every Asian I know respects him: his principles never change, even if they are the wrong principles. Why does he have to bring up immigration every five years? The Rushdie affair is even more damaging. There are social problems I do not like, but they do not affect me and I have no need to change them. The main thing is that we must be able to get jobs. Then we will feel more at home.

CASH BHOGAL: The concentration of Asians or blacks is no longer as dense as it was. People are spreading out. They get better jobs, move away from the ghetto into better areas. Even Southall. Southall was basically concentrated to one side of the railway, gradually it has spread out, moving on to Harrow, Greenford and so on. There's no longer that very tightly knit community. If anybody is being exploited these days as far as housing and conditions go it is probably the Bengali community in the East End, who are the latest Asian arrivals. The conditions there are extremely bad, and there seem to be more incidents of racial violence there than in Southall, which has defended itself in the past, and by doing that become stronger, whereas the Bengali community is still very vulnerable. They are also much poorer and they have far greater difficulties in adjusting to the English language. We have had Bengalis in England for fifteen–twenty years who still cannot read or write English. They stay in the community and they can go through the entire day without needing to speak a word. You're more likely to be racially abused if you haven't made some effort to adjust to England in your own self. One must make such an effort, there must be an element of compromise. But while the Asian and black community have always been prepared to compromise, the English community have not.

MANZOOR BAHADUR: I have two scenarios: one is that we become completely passive and become submerged into the host community, and become completely assimilated. That would be all too comfortable, though the white community might not let us do it anyway. But if it happened it would be easier, we wouldn't worry about the kids losing their cultural identity, their religious identity and so on. The other scenario is a bleak one: that my kids, when they grow up, will be the lost children of the next generation. Nobody will give them the opportunity of realizing their full potential and when that happens frustration will set in, then the generation after theirs will be wondering what the hell I was all about. Why was I here? And maybe that's when England will finally have its revolution of black people demanding equal opportunities.

398

CASH BHOGAL: The time has passed when the Asian community was passive, where they took everything that was dished out to them. The climate changed when people started standing up to prejudice and objecting to the way in which they were being treated. In 1979 and 1982 there were riots in Southall. The main one was in 1979 after the London borough of Ealing had allowed the National Front to have, in the heart of the biggest Asian community in the United Kingdom, their meeting in the town hall. Objections were made but they weren't heeded. That was one of the main events, a turning point for the Asian and other immigrant communities, who decided to stand up and protest strongly and physically and violently. Not only the young, the second generation, but the whole community.

BENNY BUNSEE: I don't see much future for black people in this country. We're not wanted here and the authorities will apply all kinds of pressures to get us out, in one way or another. I just see this great struggle ahead. Blacks are fighting back very hard, but white people have to fight back too and hopefully they can fight back together.

MARY DENYS: England hasn't done a lot for me. But while there's life there's hope. I don't know what will happen in the next year or two. I think things are going to be terrible for the young people, the children. They will have to fight, fight, fight, very, very, very hard. These Indians are seeing to it that their children go far. With this woman [Thatcher] doing all her mischief, closing the doors in everybody's face, what's going to happen?

SHREELA FLATHER: I don't think that there will be any more riots. They were an enormous statement at the time, and nobody expected them and they shook the country, shook the nation. Willie Whitelaw did something fantastic, which was to set up the Scarman enquiry. It didn't have a long-term effect, it wasn't acted on, so it wasn't successful on that score, but nothing ever is. But that's what happens, not only in race issues. Nonetheless, whether Scarman was acted on in its totality or not, it has permeated thinking, people did actually sit up and take notice. That is important. In the end you can't have a riot every time you want something. There is a notion among some blacks: because we are deprived let's have a riot. That's not going to work. First of all the police are unbelievably better at it, there is no way there is ever going to be urban disorder of that kind again. In the second place the nation isn't going to respond to it in the same way. And the third thing is that the government isn't going to respond to it the way it did. So the riot as a weapon of protest is no longer useful. The riot has also been brought into disrepute by all the things that are attendant on it: the burning, the looting, the breaking up of Asian shops.

BERNIE GRANT: In a funny way what Thatcher has done is forced people to look after themselves, and really for some of the black youngsters who have come from the ghetto and have had to struggle, it has made them tough, psychologically tough. So in any kind of dog-eat-dog situation they are going to look after themselves. Whilst I don't subscribe to that philosophy myself, I'm optimistic for them: they will be able to handle themselves in the current situation and in any future situation.

* * *

MICHAEL DE SOUZA: I tell the youth educate themselves. Common sense is the first thing. What you don't know, ask. What you know, express. It's as simple as that. But these kids don't get help. What they have to do is backtrack and accept the fact that even though they're born here they're still not English. I've been here for a very, very long time, and there was one time when I had a real cockney accent, I was around with English boys and that's how you develop. But quite consciously I stopped being lazy and started taking my time and talking clearly. I'm not a cockney and I don't like it. But when I did talk like that they still asked, 'Where were you born, what country you come from?' and once they're telling me that I know that even if my beard grows long and white down to my feet, still they'll never accept me. So go back to your roots, stop the argument, because they won't understand and there's no point in trying to make them. Leave them at stage one and you go and deal with more intelligent people at stage two. Because really you're talking about progress, the progress to do what you want to do, not what someone wants you to do. In the end it's deluding yourself to say that just because you were born here you're English. It's common sense really. Nobody does anything for you. Nobody is doing anything for anybody. White people who were born here are living down in Cardboard City, and you should just count yourself lucky you're not there with them. You've got no god-given right to anything. You've got civil liberties and so on, food, clothes and shelter, but who realistically is giving you your clothes? The government should provide a roof for most people but they don't. The government should provide food but they don't. It's the same everywhere. You've got to look and see how really powerless you are, and the only power you've got is the power within yourself and the power to develop your mind and get into a position where you can help the people that *you* want to help. You can't just sit there and say, 'Oh, poor me,' or you will be poor you. This whole feeling of 'poor me' is a factor that holds a lot of people back. It's difficult when you're young, when you're fifteen, it is difficult. So there's no guidance from the old to the young. I hate to see young boys and old men down Ladbroke Grove all doing the same shit. Both selling, hash or whatever. There's nothing positive there: if all you can show someone is that you can sell weed, that's a disgrace. But in the end I'm optimistic. I've equipped myself

400

with a number of skills and that's what you can do. If more black people took an interest in things, like the ones who are writing sensible things, talking about sensible issues, they'd be better off and know that things are not just for blacks or just for whites. They're not. We've been affected through slavery very very badly, but before that what were we doing? Just sitting down eating mangoes? We weren't. You've got to have a community, you've got to produce things. We could do all that because we did it before slavery. So now slavery's gone why do people think, 'Well, all I want is a big stereo and video and all I want to do is watch bloody Joan Collins?'

SHREELA FLATHER: I am hopeful about the young, certainly the Asian young; I'm hopeful about many of the black young, but I'm worried about unrealistic expectations and the notion that society will suddenly stop being racist. This expectation is being created among some of the young blacks, but this society will never stop being racist; what we have to do is try to minimize the effects of it. You can't make people not be this or that. These elements exist in any society. The black young don't behave like the English.

What worries me is that there is a fabric to a society and the body, the main body will only move a certain amount – it is not going to move completely into your camp. It will make concessions, but you can only persuade it to make them. The notion that everyone has to have power – well, five per cent of the people will never have power. As an individual, anyone may hope to get power, or at least a position of influence, but minority groups, the five per cent, are not going to get it, they are not going to be in ascendance over the mainstream ninety-five per cent.

SHARI PEACOCK: I do feel this profound compassion for anyone who has come from these Third World countries. Anyone who has been manipulated and exploited by western colonialism. The whole history of the Third World has been made by that system. So I think anyone from those countries who arrives here has every right to do so. I also believe that it's because of this that countries like Britain, which were once prosperous, will become Third World countries themselves. The Indians and Pakistanis who have been allowed in because of the colonial past, will gradually take more and more important positions here and good luck to them. You can see so many changes already. Just the way the colour of Londoners has altered. Even in the fifteen years I've been here. Look at New York, that's the shape of things to come. At least London has changed, although I'm not sure how much the rest of England has. I think Third World immigrants are an excellent thing for England. It broadens everyone's horizons. I think half-caste children are just the best thing. It's great. This racial mix is one of the best things about living in London.

Maybe people do get afraid of all the clichés about blacks, the raw power and so on, but it's a good thing. It's like travelling, it also broadens the mind.

RAJAN UDDIN JALAL: The hostility towards foreigners that you find in Britain is because of the colonial past, the imperial past, the last vestige of this belief and this conditioning. But I am very positive about things and I do not see this as an everlasting phenomenon because interracial marriages are taking place, people are beginning to know each other better, and I think this battle, instigated by the respectable racists, is the last one of this sort that will have to be fought. At the end of the day very few white liberals really count. At the end of the day it doesn't matter who is the sympathetic social worker, the liberal councillor – at the end of the day I'm living with Joe Bloggs next door and that is where we have to create our understanding. There are liberals who can help, but largely it is a job that has to be done within our communities.

MIKE PHILLIPS: The role of the black community is changing and part of what is changing it is that so much of the black population is actually mixed race. Nobody talks about it. Neither black nor white people. My own son is mixed race. For the black population this is the most crucial and interesting thing in terms of our identity. This business of confidence: one of the things that happens is that we talk continually about our identity in terms of external things: the Third World, the Caribbean, Africa, so on. It's grotesque that of all these people most of them do have mixed-race children. This gets ignored but it is actually becoming crucial in any discussion of the black community. It is no accident that out of the four black MPs, one, Paul Boateng, is mixed race, and he represents a very substantial part of the black community.

VERNA WILKINS: What people still see as bred-in-the-bone British attitudes to foreigners, blacks and everyone else, will go with the new generation. Things will change because the black community must make sure that we get into positions of authority, that we are on the panels of selection for jobs. Immigrants of every nationality need to come up and get fully involved in society. We have to find ourselves in positions of power and not take a back seat. Be jurors, be magistrates, get on the governing boards of schools – we're quite able to to it. Empower yourself, you have it in your power to change things. I have changed things and I will continue to change things, in a small way. But you only need a small group of people to make the big changes.

ZERBANOO GIFFORD: All first-generation immigrants have got something. Like my parents, they were the ones with the true guts. Second and third generations become more comfortable, they do lose that sort of grit that the first generation have to have. The first generation have to compromise a great deal. The second generation – and in many ways I am slightly both – are born here. They're British, they won't take the humiliations. Their parents were the immigrants, they're not.

RAJAN UDDIN JALAL: The future in England is of a multiracial country. It is already happening and short of repatriating people forcibly – which I don't think will happen – there is nothing that can be done to stop it. I think that there will be problems. I accept that the first generation of Afro-Caribbeans came with positive attitudes and now their children, who have been denied their chance, are hugely alienated. But there is a great deal of dynamism. People want to do things. Economically, politically and socially. I also feel that the first Afro-Caribbeans didn't have the muscle that we have. We have four MPs, they had no one. Next time round there will be more. These are advancements that are of symbolic importance, they mobilize people in the direction of wanting to do things. At the end of the day I live here, it is my home, and as our community expands, our young people are going to grow up and they are going to take control of things in this community, which is their community. The people who are now preaching repatriation and everything else are a people who are still living in the past and don't want to face up to reality. There is no point in carrying on with racial hatred; there is much more point in showing that Britain is able to compete within the European community in terms of economic and social development. The country should be using all its available potential, and not scapegoating certain communities on account of their race. There is a service sector in Britain that needs more and more trained people, and given the fact that the birthrate in the Asian community is so high, I think that the main source of those people will be the Afro-Caribbean and Asian communities. That's reality – and the country had better prepare for this, rather than incite racial hatred.

29 Multicultural Britain?

'The development of this country as a multicultural institution
does not depend on the English any more.'

BERNIE GRANT: In some areas multiracial Britain is already a reality. In Tottenham, for instance, there's no problem. My kids, who are half white, and their friends run around in a group with every single nationality there. Haringey is like that and I think that it became like that because we took the very conscious decision that we were going to get it like that. It didn't just happen overnight. But now you don't get racial attacks, harassment, anything like that. Thirty per cent of the community is black, but we've managed to create a situation where the races can exist very harmoniously. Which has been done without anyone sacrificing their own identity. On the contrary, it has been done by us encouraging the differences. I think the problems start when you come against this nonsense about integration, which means that you have to drop all your customs and traditions and so on, and adopt the majority culture.

CASH BHOGAL: I can't see a multicultural Britain coming. I think the hierarchy of British society is so strong that it's really extremely difficult to penetrate the positions of power or to influence the decision-making process. There are token judges, one or two, a handful of magistrates, but largely they remain tokens. There are a few MPs but I don't see that changing a great deal.

BHAJAN SINGH CHADHA: In another generation England will become a more multicultural society. All this racialism is inherited. The next generation won't know the same things. People will be considered as people. There will always be extremists but when the colonialism has been forgotten then things will change. But people in the minority communities, people in the first generations, mustn't expect too much, they must learn to be tolerant themselves. Nobody can get one hundred per cent what they want. I've learned that from my religion, and life teaches you that as well. You always have to pay a price. If you think you can get everything without paying a price, you are heading for a shock.

BENNY BUNSEE: There is a tremendous amount of vitality within the immigrant community. The immigrant community can help the British get out of their parochialism, of their insularity. They can assist them to understand the black world, assist them in de-colonizing themselves, de-imperializing themselves, and possibly to create in this country a genuine kind of multiracial society where the values of all the communities can be seen as of equal value. We need an education system that underlines those new attitudes. We don't have it yet. The education system is not just British-dominated but it is very much English-dominated. Britain is a multiracial country, but this is not manifested in today's society.

FERDIE ERASMUS: This country is England only in name and people, those who own it are foreigners. They're pumping millions into Britain. There'll always be an England, but not a 'great' Britain any more. A strong government is like a strong company, you invest in it. Maggie has a strong government, so those with a few billion to spend, spend it here. If the government becomes less strong and Australia or America takes off, all the money will come out of

Britain and be ploughed in there. So all this money is coming in, we're all building, but it will come to an end. El Jappo and Mr Arab don't want to live here though. England is wonderful. You go to Birmingham – it's like the middle of Harare. Go to Brixton – like the middle of Barbados. Go to Harrow – like the middle of Peking. I find it difficult to find an English station on the radio. But it's still a wonderful country, and the English are wonderful, they do stick together.

DON ATYEO: I don't see England becoming a multicultural country. No way. Not in a hundred years. It's not a get-rich-quick place like Australia is. You hear these people in Hong Kong. They don't want to stay here, just get here to escape the Chinese and then move on. So there won't be this influx of a minority which will be large enough to change the complexion of the society. They don't want to come here – what are they going to do? Become butcher's apprentices in London? These are people who can add up in their heads faster than a computer. England is just going to potter along much as ever. I don't see the Muslims as such a threat, I don't see them ever growing to be anything but a minority and a painfully small one.

SHREELA FLATHER: What I see is a change in the mainstream British culture. There are no two ways about it: the mainstream culture has already undergone a tremendous change. People travel further, they use new words, they talk about music and art and culture of other countries in a way they did not before, on a much more general level; they've changed the way they eat, the way they dress. The British, especially the young who go to school together and mix completely naturally, have got used to other nationalities. That to me is the most encouraging sign. You very rarely see blacks and whites together in America; you may see them doing business, but you don't see total, unconscious socializing in the way that you do here. The social attitude surveys among the young are very encouraging. Not among the old, who don't seem to be showing any improvement in these attitudes, but the young are very different. So what we have to talk about is not other cultures, but the fact the British culture now encompasses a wide variety of culture. We should appreciate this and also not be frightened of it.

ANWAR BATI: I do think that mass immigration from another country, of people who have a completely different culture, cannot in the end be good for this country, in the sense, perhaps the trivial sense, of how one lot of people feel about their neighbours. When I put this to other Pakistanis they don't necessarily agree with me. I'm quite tough on race issues, when I'm wearing my English hat. After all if one is living in England as some sort of an Englishman one is living here because it's England, and not because you want it to be part of the Punjab or whatever. Of course the criticism I get is that I am trying to be more English than the English, that in some way I have 'sold the Pakistani community out' but in fact I am what I am. No more.

TONY GIRARD: I can't really believe that England will come to terms with its immigrant community. Things will get better but wherever you go you get racism. This doesn't only go for England, it goes for the West Indies too. When I left home St Lucia was one of the most docile, the most friendly islands. Now, when I visit, there are some people who have become hostile to white people. In my day that would never have happened. Everybody was welcome, any stranger, and who could be more obvious a stranger than a white person. But now the world is a little smaller. If bad things happen here the news gets home a lot faster. I hope there won't be any more riots. It's up to the government to do something about the situation. But if they let things go on the way they are . . .

BRYAN GOULD: Britain could become a multicultural society, although it will take a long time, a long, slow progress. But that's not a reason for not engaging with it. I was for some years the joint chair of an all-party working group on education for the eradication of racial prejudice in Britain. The idea of that was not to counter discrimination by whites against blacks in multiracial inner city constituencies, but to ensure that the school curriculum in deepest Wiltshire or wherever didn't reinforce racial stereotypes. I do think that that sort of effort is vital. The notion that foreigners are funny is in its own way perfectly natural coming from an island people. I saw much more intense expressions of it when I was in China ten years ago.

MIKE PHILLIPS: This country has got to become truly multiracial in the next generation or so. It's got to happen. Either the racial English will turn on us and throw us out, or this will become a multiracial country. There are no two ways, it's not something you can stop. It isn't yet a multiracial country, because the sign of a multiracial country is when different groups negotiate rights on equal terms. This is still a white country with black people in it. But there ain't nothing that can stop it becoming a multiracial country.

RAJINDER SINGH: The English will let us in to their culture. What else can they do? The people who have migrated over here are not going back. Idi Amin may have thrown out the Asians from his country, but I don't think that the British will throw out kids who were born over here. So if they can't turn them out, they will have to accommodate them and if they do that they will have to learn something from them. So in the long run everyone will have to get together to solve this problem. How long that will be, I cannot say. Probably a very long time.

RAJAN UDDIN JALAL: There is no going back. Alis will not go back, Alis are here to stay, Alis made Britain their home and the latest generation of Alis are growing up here – and they are not going back.

MICHAEL IGNATIEFF: I don't think that the development of this country as a multicultural institution depends on the English any more. I think it depends on the fate of the white peoples of the world. Will the great Russians finally accept that the Asian citizens of the Soviet Union are equal? Will the French white shopkeeper accept that the Mahgrebian streetsweeper is part of his society? Will the Wall Street lawyer hurrying up the subway steps accept that the black man who sells him the *New York Daily News* is a fellow-citizen? Will the Canadian businessman getting out of his Pontiac accept that the native Canadian drinking whiskey from a brown paper bag is a fellow-citizen and an equal human being? This is the great story of the twentieth century. There isn't really another more important story. What makes me hopeful is that nobody is that stupid, that blind to what has happened historically. Nobody believes that old imperium of white domination that goes back four or five centuries in our imperial past can be reconstituted. For a host of reasons, some of which have to do fundamentally with the fact that we're hung by the petard of our own rhetoric. We're hung by the contradiction between what we do, which is imperial, dominating, often racist, and which is what we say, which is that we're brothers. We taught it to them in colonial schools in the nineteenth century, we're teaching it to them in our schools now, and they will hang us with it if we don't deliver, and good luck to them.

A Note on Immigration Law

1. Aliens Acts
The first Aliens Act, of 1905, was passed to control the influx into Britain of Jews fleeing the pogroms of Russia and central Europe. Further legislation – the Aliens Restriction Act (1914), the Aliens Restriction (Amendment) Act (1914) – reflected the anti-German feelings generated by World War I. The refugee population fluctuated between and after the wars, but it remained controlled, by the Aliens Order, published every year from 1920 to 1953.

2. Commonwealth and Immigrants Acts
The arrival of the Commonwealth immigrants during the 1950s and 1960s led to the passing of four acts between 1962 and 1988. Although this immigration had been deliberately encouraged by government recruitment, public concern about its effects led to political control. The Commonwealth and Immigrants Act (1962) attempted to regulate the flow of workers into the country. This had little effect – since the market was the true controller of labour demand – and in fact reversed what had begun to appear as a slackening off in immigration when many potential immigrants, still uncertain whether to leave home or not, now rushed to beat the ban. Post-1962 the act worked more successfully, limiting any further arrivals, and screening attempts by dependants of earlier settlers to make the trip.

The Commonwealth Immigrants Act (1968) was a direct response to the arrival of East African Asians, whose numbers were beginning to mount as newly independent African countries promoted their own nationals, whether in business or bureaucracy, at the Asians' expense. The main provision of the act was to state that a British passport-holder no longer had automatic rights of entry to the UK: it was necessary to have either a parent or grandparent born here. Both acts, plus the 1965 White Paper on Immigration from the Commonwealth, were incorporated in the Immigration Act (1971). Abandoning the old distinction between 'aliens' and Commonwealth citizens, this focused on the distinction between patrials (those persons born, adopted, naturalized or registered in the UK, or born either of a parent or grandparent with UK citizenship) and non-patrials (those lacking in such credentials). Patrials had the right to enter and settle; non-patrials had to apply for permission. Even were they accepted, they had to work at a specific job in a specific place for an initial period of twelve months maximum.

The Immigration Act of 1988 is in essence a set of fine-tuned amendments to its predecessor, designed primarily as a way of streamlining the process whereby those who flout the immigration rules can be dealt with. Its most important provisions work to short-circuit the formerly lengthy review given to the cases of those who were considered ineligible to stay in the UK, notably those who continued to work in breach of their conditions of stay. The process of deportation, which formerly went through the Home Office, and took up to fourteen days, with the opportunity of appeal, can now, under the rules of 'supervised departure', be initiated on the spot by any immigration officer of the rank of inspector or above. Those who have been in the UK for less than seven years no longer have the right to appeal through the courts, and must return to their country of origin before attempting to overturn the deportation order.

3. Nationality Acts
Nationality acts, determining who is a British citizen, and who an alien, have been passed since 1914. They include the British Nationality and Status of Aliens Act (1914), the British Nationality Act (1948), the British Nationality Act (1964), the British Nationality Act (Number 2) (1964), and the British Nationality Act (1981). Like its predecessor of 1914 the 1948 act classified all Commonwealth citizens as British citizens, with the automatic right to settle in the UK. Although this included a notional thousand million people, the act was not challenged until members of the 'New Commonwealth' began asserting their rights. The Commonwealth and Immigration Act (1962) and the Immigration Act (1971) (see above) both redefined what was meant by a 'British citizen' and the Nationality Act (1981) underlined the changes, particularly those set out in the 1971 legislation.

4. Race Relations laws
Immigration controls spring from public concern; that the flow of immigrants has been checked has not stemmed the less palatable side of that concern: out and out racism. In an attempt to modify, if not actually remove the effects of racism, a number of Race Relations Acts have been passed, outlawing racial discrimination. All, to some extent, balanced controls that were put in place at approximately the same time. Thus the Race Relations Act of 1965 paralleled the restrictive White Paper of that year; the Act of 1968, instituting the Community Relations Commission (CRC), was actually part of the immigration law of the same year, and the 1976 Race Relations Act, in which the CRC was amalgamated with the Race Relations Board to form the Commission for Racial Equality (CRE), can be paired with the 1971 Immigration Act.

Interviewees

KATHY ACKER was born in New York City in 1947. After publishing widely in America she moved to England to pursue her career as a successful novelist and poet. Her best-known book is *Blood and Guts in High School Plus Two*.

GINA ADAMOU was born in Nicosia, Cyprus, in 1946. She came to England, to join her parents in 1961. After an arranged marriage, she qualified as a hairdresser. She has three children. A Labour Party member since 1972, she remains active in local politics. She lives in north London.

FIRDOS ALI was born in Kashmir in 1942. He came to England, as a student, in 1967, joining in much of the student activism of the time. He combines a job with Brent Council with regular work for Channel 4 TV, as an expert in Indian film and music. He lives in Southall.

MUHAMMAD ALI was born in Pakistan in 1955. He arrived in Bradford, where his father has already settled, in 1969. He works in the Bradford branch of Fullemploy, an organization which is committed to enabling black people to play a better role in economic life of the UK.

YASMIN ALIBHAI was born in Kampala, Uganda, in 1949. She came to England in 1972 to study as a post-graduate student at Oxford, and stayed on after Idi Amin expelled Uganda's Asian community. Since then she has worked as a journalist, most recently for the *New Statesman and Society*.

BODRUL ALOM was born in Bangladesh in 1955 and followed his father to England in 1967. A member of the Brick Lane community in London's East End, he intends to stand as Labour candidate in local elections.

JASWINDER AMAR was born in India in 1952. After an arranged marriage she joined her husband in Leamington Spa in 1984. When that marriage collapsed she moved to London, qualifying as a British Telecom engineer. She lives with her uncle (Rajinder Singh) in Ilford.

NAIM ATALLAH was born in Haifa, Palestine, in 1931. An engineering student in England when the state of Israel was founded in 1948, he decided to stay, taking a series of labouring jobs. A move to banking laid the foundations of financial success and he is best-known as the publisher of Quartet Books.

DON ATYEO was born in Colac, Australia, in 1950. Following a national tradition he migrated, via the hippie trail, to Earls Court in 1971, working first at a burger bar and then in London's 'underground press'. After a successful career as a writer and magazine editor he moved to satellite television in 1990.

MUHAMMAD AYYAZ was born on the north-west frontier of Pakistan in 1954. He arrived in Bradford in 1969, joining his father, who had come in 1961. An active member of Bradford's Muslim community, he continues to live and work in the town.

MANZOOR BAHADUR was born in the Campbellpur district of Pakistan in 1951, the son of a sailor who emigrated to England in 1953. He arrived in Bradford in 1961 and in 1967 began seventeen years of work in engineering, rising to management level, before he left to involve himself in full-time community work in 1983.

ANWAR BATI was born in Pakistan in 1953 but spent only a year there before his father, whose business was based in London, brought him to England. After university he began a career as a journalist and television researcher, working widely in both media. He lives in west London.

SIMI BEDFORD was born in Lagos, Nigeria, in 1941, into one of the country's leading families. Sent to an English boarding school in 1948, she grew up here, married and had children. Since university she has worked mainly in television. She lives in Wandsworth, south London.

MARCEL BERLINS was born in Marseilles, France, in 1942 and brought up in South Africa, to where his family moved after the war. He arrived in England, via France, in 1967 and graduated to writing law reports for *The Times*, in time becoming the paper's legal correspondent. He lives in north London.

CASH BHOGAL was born in the Punjab, India, in 1956 and arrived in England in 1962, joining his father in Birmingham. Qualified as a barrister, he lives in London and works for Southall Rights, an organization dedicated to providing legal advice for the local community.

CINDY BLAKE was born 'a brahmin' in Boston, Massachusetts, in 1952, and after working for the Carter administration came to England in 1978, to marry

411

her English fiancé. She worked as a journalist before turning to novels, the first of which appeared earlier this year.

JAROSLAV BRADAC was born in Prague in 1945 and studied as an art student. He worked as an illustrator until the Russian invasion of 1968 when he decided to leave Czechoslovakia and move to England. An increasingly successful artist, he lives with his English wife in west London.

BENNY BUNSEE was born in Durban, South Africa, 'about fifty years ago', into a poor Indian family. Largely self-educated and highly politically motivated he moved to England, starting work as a journalist in 1962. When this ended he involved himself heavily in anti-racist politics, and later led two major strikes in the Midlands, campaigning to improve the lot of black workers.

CARMEN CALLIL was born in Melbourne, Australia, in 1938, to a Lebanese family. After university she left Australia for ever, arriving in England in 1962. After working in Marks & Spencers she moved into publishing. Currently head of Chatto and Windus, she founded, in 1973, the first popular feminist imprint, Virago.

ENNIO CAMISA was born in Tornolo, near Parma, Italy, in 1906. He came to England to join the family delicatessen in 1920. Other than a period of internment during the war he has spent seventy years introducing the English to the delights of Italian food.

BHAJAN SINGH CHADHA was born in Nairobi, Kenya, in 1932. The gradual Africanization of the country meant less work for Asians and in 1958 he moved to England, working at the Post Office until 1966 when he set up his own shop. He is still a shopkeeper, living in Walthamstow.

DAVILIA DAVID was born in Perth, western Australia, in 1938 and came to England in 1960, to pursue a career in the theatre. She has mixed acting with a variety of odd jobs and has featured on television promoting her own variety of pickles. She lives in Hertfordshire.

MARY DENYS was born in St Lucia in 1928. After working as a schoolteacher (from the age of thirteen) she came to England in 1961. She has worked in a number of jobs, as well as spending some time on the Westminster Community Relations Council. Now retired, she lives in west London, in the same street to which she first came.

MICHAEL DE SOUZA was born in Trinidad in 1954. He arrived in England in 1960, joining his parents in north Kensington. Since school he has worked in

412

youth clubs, as a sports counsellor, and teaches football and swimming. He lives in west London.

LEENA DHINGRA was born in Simla, India, in 1942. After a cosmopolitan upbringing – her father worked for UNESCO – and a partially English education, she settled here in 1958. After drama school she turned to writing. Her first novel appeared in 1988. She lives in Hampstead with her daughter and mother.

NISSIM ELIJAH was born in Bombay, India, in 1916, into the Indian Jewish community known as the Ben Israels. After working as a Civil Servant until 1962, he found life in India was no longer appealing and duly moved to England where, once more, he joined the Civil Service. He has now retired and lives in north London.

FERDIE ERASMUS was born in what was then Rhodesia in 1951 and grew up all over southern Africa, following his father, a construction engineer. Qualified in South Africa as a quantity surveyor he rose quickly to a senior position before leaving for England in 1986. He continued to work in construction, combining building with property development.

SHREELA FLATHER was born in Lahore (then still India) in 1934 into a very wealthy family. She came to England in 1952 to read law at University College, London. In 1976 she became the first Asian woman councillor (Conservative) and subsequently Lady Mayoress of Maidenhead. In 1990 she became England's first ever Asian life peeress.

ZERBANOO GIFFORD was born in Calcutta, India, in 1950. In 1953 her parents moved to London, where they ran a hotel, and she joined them a year later. An active member of the Liberal Party (now SLP), she continues to be involved in national and community politics. She lives with her family in Harrow.

ANTONIUS 'TONY' GIRARD was born in St Lucia in 1937. After moving to England in 1960 he began work as a plumber with St Pancras Council. He is still working as plumber, now for Lambeth Council, and lives in Islington with his family.

DESMOND GITTENS was born in 1938 in Port of Spain, Trinidad. After working as a seaman he emigrated to England in 1960 and began working as a coal miner near Manchester. After Army service, he opened the Backayard restaurant in Notting Hill. He is currently employed by Kensington & Chelsea Council, as a careers adviser for the ethnic minorities.

BIANCA GORDON was born in Berlin in the 1920s and was among the 9,000-odd Jewish children who in 1938 were selected to come to England via the *Kindertransport*, special trains permitted to leave Germany by the Nazis. During her life in England she has worked as a psychoanalyst, specializing in the problems of the young.

BRYAN GOULD was born in North Island, New Zealand, in 1939. He came to Oxford on a Rhodes Scholarship and subsequently joined the Foreign Office. He emerged in the 1987 election as the architect of Labour's revived image, and is currently the party's trade and industry spokesman.

BERNIE GRANT was born in Georgetown, Guyana, in 1944. He came to England in 1963 to join his mother and take A levels. He went to Heriot-Watt university but his increasing involvement in left-wing politics curtailed his course. He left in 1969, since when he was been an increasing visible political figure. Elected a councillor in 1978, he entered the House of Commons in 1987.

GERTRUD HARTWIG was born in Hamburg in 1906. Faced with the worsening situation in Germany she and her husband sailed for India in 1939. They spent the war there, during which time she contracted polio. They moved to England in 1949. Today she lives in Croydon, working with her son, a solicitor.

RONALD HARWOOD was born in Cape Town in 1934. He came to England in 1951, and studied acting at RADA. In 1952 he became the dresser for Sir Donald Wolfit, an experience that formed the basis of his internationally successful play *The Dresser*. He lives in Chelsea and continues to write for the stage, television and film.

CHRISTOPHER HOPE was born in Pretoria, South Africa, in 1944. An increasingly politicized situation, in which he found it less and less possible to write, led to his emigration to England in 1974. A spell of teaching ended when he began devoting himself full-time to his novels, the latest of which, *My Chocolate Redeemer*, appeared in 1989. He lives in north London with his family.

MICHAEL IGNATIEFF was born in Toronto, Canada, in 1947. His first stay in England was in the mid-'fifties, with his father, a diplomat, and he returned in 1979, as a fellow of King's College, Cambridge. Since then he has worked as

414

an academic and in the English media. He lives in north London with his (English) wife and family.

FATIMA IGRAMHIM was born in Frankfurt, West Germany, in 1954, daughter of a Tajik father and a German mother. After working as a journalist in Munich and New York she came to England in 1985, joining her husband, whom she had met in America. She continues to work as a writer and they live in north London.

ESTHER IZUNDU was born in Lagos, Nigeria, in 1955. She came to Britain in 1978 when her husband began studying at Strathclyde University. They moved down to London, where they now live, in 1987 and are both working in local government.

RAJAN UDDIN JALAL was born in 1959 in Bangladesh and emigrated to England in 1972, joining his family in Birmingham. A year later he moved down to east London, where he remains, working within the Bangladeshi community of Brick Lane and aiming to make a mark in Labour politics.

EVA JIRICNA was born in Zlin, Czechoslovakia, in 1939. She qualified as an architect and began work, until in 1968 she chose to escape the Russian invasion and move to England. Here she has made a successful career, notably as the designer of the chain of Joseph shops.

GULZAR KHAN was born in Kashmir in 1933. After military service and work for the Customs, he moved to England in 1962, starting work for British Rail in Nottingham. Since then he has opened his own shops, established himself as a landlord, and remains a major figure in the local Muslim community.

BALRAJ KHANNA was born in India in 1940. He came to England in 1962 to read English at Oxford but instead devoted himself to a burgeoning career as a painter. He has continued to paint ever since, winning a growing reputation, and lives in west London with his French wife and their family.

HANNAH KODICEK was born in Prague, Czechoslovakia, in 1947. She trained as a pianist and in 1968 was about to enter film school when the Russians invaded. She and her husband left at once, taking refuge in England. Here she has worked widely as an actress, and lives in south London with her son.

IVAN KYNCL was born in Prague in 1953. He worked as a photographer and in 1974 was arrested, as part of the campaign against his father Karel. From

1977 he was the unofficial photographer for the dissident Charter 77 group, finally moving to England in 1980. Today he works as a theatrical photographer and lives with his wife in south London.

KAREL KYNCL was born in Czechoslovakia in 1927. He was the country's leading radio journalist, 'the Czech Robin Day', until the Russian invasion of 1968, after which he was banned from any state employment. Despite illness and arrests he refused to leave until 1983, when he joined his son Ivan in London. He currently works for the magazine *Index on Censorship*.

JOHN LAHR was born in New York City in 1943. After studying at Oxford he returned home to write the best-selling biography of his father Bert, the 'Cowardly Lion' in *The Wizard of Oz*. He moved to England in 1971, fleeing the pressure of youthful fame, and has remained here. His biography of Joe Orton appeared in 1978. He lives with his son in north London.

MIRANDA LOVETT was born in New York City in 1951. After a conventionally upper-class childhood she came to England in 1974 to join her English husband and has lived here ever since. They have two children and live in South London.

MANDY MERCK was born in Mobilene, Missouri, in 1947. She arrived in England in 1969, to read English at Oxford. Since then she has worked as a journalist – *Time Out*, *City Limits* and Channel 4 – and as an active campaigner for gay and women's rights.

SIR CLAUS MOSER was born in Berlin in 1922. In 1936 his father, a Jewish banker, brought the family to England. During his wartime internment Sir Claus first encountered the science of statistics, the basis of his professional life. He has held many notable positions, and is currently Master of Wadham College, Oxford.

BRIGITTE NEWMAN was born in Le Mans, France, in 1953. She was nineteen when she starred as Edith Piaf in a film of the singer's life and followed this with a TV series. She moved permanently to England in 1979, joining her English husband and working with him in his career as a photographer.

BENTHE NORHEIM was born in Norway, in 1960. An art student, she came to England in 1983 to study at the Royal Academy. She has stayed here ever since, working as a sculptor and living in west London with her baby daughter.

PETAR OBRATOVIC was born in Belgrade, Yugoslavia, in 1952. He qualified as a doctor, then moved into psychotherapy. A chance for further training

416

brought him to England in 1984 and his meeting his wife here meant that he chose to stay. He continues to practise as a therapist, and lives in west London.

SHARI PEACOCK was born in Sofia, Bulgaria, the daughter of exiled Iranian communist parents, in 1957. She moved to England in 1975, to study at the Architectural Association and at St Martin's School of Art. She dropped architecture in favour of drawing and works as a magazine illustrator and journalist. She lives in north London.

TEDDY PEIRO was born in San Juan province, Argentina, around 1930. His show business career began a decade later and with his brother he became an internationally celebrated variety star, playing several Royal Variety Perform-ances. He moved to England in the 'sixties. Intimately involved with the Latin American community, he lives with his wife in Wembley.

MIKE PHILLIPS was born in Georgetown, Guyana, in 1941. He arrived in England, where his father had already settled, in 1956. His parents left for America in 1966 but he has stayed, teaching at a London polytechnic and developing a growing reputation as a novelist.

NGUYEN DUC PHUONG was born in Can Tho province, then South Vietnam, in 1950. A naval officer at the time of the North Vietnamese victory of 1975, he was 're-educated' in a jungle prison for two years. In 1980 he navigated a boatload of refugees out to the sea-lanes where they were rescued by a British ship. He arrived here that year. Qualified as a an engineer, he lives with his family in Milton Keynes.

CUI QU was born in northern China in 1953 and brought up in Beijing. The daughter of a party official who became a famous novelist, she enjoyed a privileged childhood. In 1980 she followed her husband (Nien-Lun Yeh) to London. Although qualified as a paediatrician, she has been unable to pursue her chosen career.

VINCENT REID was born in Jamaica in 1935. In 1948, aged thirteen, he was the youngest passenger on the *Empire Windrush*, the first ship to bring Caribbean immigrants to England. A spell in the RAF was followed by immersion in '60s Notting Hill before he began working in market research. Today he teaches black history at a polytechnic and lives with his family in west London.

TONY ROBINSON was born in Jamaica in 1921 and arrived in England in 1957. He went straight to Nottingham and began a career working on the buses. At the time of his interview he was the Sheriff of Nottingham.

417

MARY ROSE was born in Leipzig, Germany, in 1918. A nursery-school teacher in 1939, she spent the war in her home country before, in 1945, meeting her English husband-to-be. They moved to London in 1948. She continued to teach for many years and is a prominent figure in her community's (Notting Hill) affairs.

NELLY SALAS was born in Argentina in 1932. Politically active, she was forced to flee to England in 1977, at the height of the 'dirty war'. She works extensively with the exile community here, and runs Mafalda, the Latin American nursery. She lives in north London.

GRETEL SALINGER was born in Frankfurt, Germany, in 1895. Like many other supposedly assimilated Jews she and her husband were forced to flee, escaping to England in 1938. An indefatigable worker for the war effort, she has remained deeply involved with a variety of charitable institutions, and is still a leading figure in the Jewish community.

TEDDY SCHWARZ was born in Sotterbach, Germany, in 1918. The protégé, at university, of a radical professor, he escaped the Nazi purges of the left by moving first to Paris and then to England, where he arrived in 1936. During the war he published a widely-read refugee magazine, and since then has worked as a freelance photographer. He lives in west London.

RAJINDER SINGH was born in Tanganyika (now Tanzania) in 1932. Although most of his family made the move to England, he waited until 1984 to join them, hoping in vain to bring his son with him. His wife has since returned. He works for London Transport and lives with his niece (Jaswinder Amar) in Ilford.

LYDIA AND MOSES SPITZ Lydia Spitz was born in Buenos Aires, Argentina, in 1937, to Russian-Jewish immigrant parents. Her husband Moses was born in a Jewish settlement in the Argentine countryside, also to immigrants. Mr Spitz taught chemistry at the University of La Plata; his wife headed the psychiatric department at a large hospital. Political pressure forced them to emigrate in 1975. Since then Mr Spitz has been able to continue work, although his wife has had to abandon her professional life. They live in Kingsbury, north London.

WITOLD STARECKI was born in Bytom, Poland, in 1947. After film school he began making films, few of which were passed by the state censors. In 1983 he won a scholarship to study the film musical in London, and after making a brief return to Poland, moved to England for good. He works as a freelance film director and lives in Acton with his family.

PETER TATCHELL was born in Melbourne, Australia, in 1952. He was a leading political activist, both in the anti-Vietnam movement and in gay rights until in 1971 he moved to England. Here he continued in politics, standing as the much-vilified Labour candidate in the notorious Bermondsey byelection of 1982. He still lives in Bermondsey and remains a committed politician.

VU DUY TU was born in Haiduong City, north Vietnam, in 1933. A career officer, he was a member of the ARVN from 1954 to 1975, after which he spent nearly seven years being 're-educated'. He managed to obtain permission to leave in 1984 and moved to England, where his sister-in-law had lived since 1962. Qualified as a community worker, he works for the Vietnamese community in Hackney.

RAMESH VALA was born in Nairobi, Kenya, in 1953. He came to England in 1973, to read law at the London School of Economics. Since then he has pursued a successful career as a solicitor, combining it with an active role in the Asian community. He lives in Rickmansworth, Hertfordshire.

SHREERAM VIDYARTHI was born in the Punjab, India, in 1938. He worked as an English teacher, then as a journalist until, in 1967, he came to England, intending to further his education. When that scheme collapsed, he spent three years wandering in Europe before returning to England and settling here, at first illegally. He now works freelance for the BBC, runs 'Books from India' in Bloomsbury and lives with his family in Sittingbourne.

STEPHEN VIZINCZEY was born in Budapest, Hungary, in 1933. A successful young writer, he moved to Canada after the uprising of 1956 and in 1967 gained international celebrity with his book *In Praise of Older Women*. He still writes prolifically and has homes in both London and Toronto.

PETER VO was born in Phangh Hoa province, central Vietnam. He fled south after the partition of Vietnam in 1954 and qualified later as a teacher of English. An adviser to the US Army during the war years, he spent thirty-one months in a variety of 're-education' camps after the war. In 1980 he was able to join a group of 'boat people' and escape. He works for the Department of Education and lives in Peckham, where he is one of his community's leading figures.

MARIA VOROSKOI was born in a small town in Hungary in 1912. A member of a cultured, Anglophile family, she left Hungary after the war, moving to England in 1947. Here she worked as a photographer and met her husband. She lives in Berkshire.

WILF WALKER was born in Trinidad in 1945. He arrived in England in 1960, in time to immerse himself in the whole swinging London, alternative culture world of the 1960s. Today he lives in west London and runs one of the few black music promotion companies, arranging the fortunes of a number of artistes.

ALLA WEAVER was born in Odessa, Russia, in 1915. After the revolution her family moved first to Vienna and then to Berlin. In 1934 she was sent to London, to study art under Anthony Blunt at the Courtauld. Her parents moved again, to Paris, in 1939, but were unable to escape the German invasion. She married an Englishman and today lives in Stockwell, south London.

TESS WICKHAM was born in Zurich in 1945, and brought up in Holland by her Dutch parents. She came to London in 1964, to read anthropology at the London School of Economics. After meeting her husband, an architect, she decided to stay and today works with him in his practice. They live in Paddington.

VICTOR WILD was born in Switzerland in 1923. In 1936 he was sent to England for his education and, other than a brief spell at the start of the war, has lived here ever since. He is owner of a chain of Yorkshire teashops, 'Betty's of Harrogate', which was founded by his uncle, also an immigrant, in 1919.

VERNA WILKINS was born in Grenada in the 1940s and with her husband came to England, to study nursing, aged eighteen. Her husband died suddenly and she considered returning home but in time remarried, to an Englishman. Today she lives in Surrey and runs Tamarisk Books, a company devoted to creating school textbooks which promote positive black images.

SUSAN WILSON was born in Dunedin, New Zealand, in 1951. She came to England via Peru in 1976, intending to work as a nurse, but loathed the English hospital hierarchies. She married in 1978 and abandoned thoughts of returning home. Today she works as a painter and lives with her family in north Kensington.

ANNE-MARIE WOLPE was born in Johannesburg, South Africa, in 1938. Her husband Harold was one of the lawyers involved in the anti-ANC Rivonia arrests of 1963 and when he managed to escape, she followed him soon afterwards. After a difficult start, they both found jobs as university teachers and remain involved in teaching. They live in Muswell Hill, north London.

PO-YEE WONG was born in the republic of China and came to England in 1970 to study nursing. She left the state sector after six years and has established herself as an independent herbalist and acupuncturist.

NIEN-LUN YEH was born in the republic of China in 1950, the son of a novelist and academic who had been an intimate of England's Bloomsbury group. After surviving the cultural revolution he moved to England during the liberal period of 1980 to further his studies. He worked for a while in electronics but recently set himself up as a translator. He lives with his wife, Cui Qu, and their son.

MIGUEL ZAMBRANO was born in Chile in 1946. He worked as a journalist until the fall of Allende in 1973, when his socialist views began to bring him unpleasant attention. After spells in jail, he left reluctantly, in 1975, followed by his wife and children. They live in south London and he works as a correspondent for a number of South American papers.

PALOMA ZOZAYA was born in Mexico City in 1955. She trained as an actress and in 1980 came to London to study stage management. Her marriage, to an Englishman, ended thoughts of going home, and she has stayed here, living in Hammersmith and working in the theatre, ever since.

Inevitably in a book of this nature, with the massive cutting that its preparation involved, there are those who were interviewed but whose contribution failed to survive the editorial scissors. To all of those who gave so generously of their time, I offer my sincere thanks: Hans Bakker, Vanessa Beresford, Baldev Daliwal, Nina Fishman, Hoshang Jungalwallah, Michel Knipe, Anja Krauze, Victor Lownes, Michael McKnight, Judy Martin, Patricia Miller, Leszek Nowicki, Franta Provaznik, Ian Rich, Silva Rubashova, Ludvik Rys.